Close Encounters

Third Edition

To our daughters—Gabrielle, Kristiana, Kirsten, Leila, and Rania.
Our relationships with them bring us great joy.

Close
Third Edition
Encounters
Communication in Relationships

Laura K. Guerrero
Arizona State University

Peter A. Andersen
San Diego State University

Walid A. Afifi
University of California, Santa Barbara

Los Angeles | London | New Delhi
Singapore | Washington DC

For information:

SAGE Publications, Inc.
2455 Teller Road
Thousand Oaks, California 91320
E-mail: order@sagepub.com

SAGE Publications India Pvt. Ltd.
B 1/I 1 Mohan Cooperative Industrial Area
Mathura Road, New Delhi 110 044
India

SAGE Publications Ltd.
1 Oliver's Yard
55 City Road
London EC1Y 1SP
United Kingdom

SAGE Publications Asia-Pacific Pte. Ltd.
33 Pekin Street #02-01
Far East Square
Singapore 048763

Printed in the United States of America

Library of Congress Cataloging-in-Publication Data

Guerrero, Laura K.
Close encounters : communication in relationships / Laura K. Guerrero, Peter A. Andersen, Walid A. Afifi. — 3rd ed.
   p. cm.
Includes bibliographical references and index.
ISBN 978-1-4129-7737-1 (pbk.)
 1. Interpersonal communication. I. Andersen, Peter A. II. Afifi, Walid A. III. Title.

BF637.C45G83 2011
153.6—dc22   2010033453

This book is printed on acid-free paper.

10 11 12 13 14 10 9 8 7 6 5 4 3 2 1

Executive Editor:	Diane McDaniel
Editorial Assistant:	Nathan Davidson
Production Editor:	Eric Garner
Copy Editor:	Gretchen Treadwell
Typesetter:	C&M Digitals (P) Ltd.
Proofreader:	Theresa Kay
Indexers:	Peter A. Andersen, Jean Casalegno
Cover Designer:	Glenn Vogel
Marketing Manager:	Helen Salmon
Permissions Editor:	Karen Ehrmann

BRIEF CONTENTS

DETAILED CONTENTS

PREFACE

We are pleased and privileged to release the third edition of *Close Encounters.* We wrote the first edition of this book in response to the increasing number of upper-division courses on relational communication and advanced interpersonal communication being taught at colleges and universities across the country. Since then, more courses in relational communication are being offered, and research on close relationships has continued to flourish. Indeed, it was challenging to incorporate all of the new research on relational communication into this edition, and because of space limitations we could not include everything we wanted to include. Nonetheless, we believe that this edition contains an appropriate mix of current and classic research related to communication in relationships.

Our goal in writing *Close Encounters* continues to be to produce an informative yet readable textbook that will help students understand their relationships better and be more critical consumers of information about relationships. This book is research based. We strive to present concepts and theories in more depth than the average textbook on interpersonal communication while writing in an accessible style. For us, writing this textbook is a rewarding experience; it lets us reach beyond the pages of scholarly journals to share information with students who are eager to learn more about relationships.

APPROACH

The book takes a relational approach to the study of interpersonal communication by focusing on issues that are central to describing and understanding close relationships, particularly between romantic partners, friends, and family members. One of the most exciting trends in the field of personal relationships is the transdisciplinary nature of research and theory. Scholars from fields such as communication, family studies, psychology, and sociology, among other disciplines, have all made important contributions to scholarly knowledge about relationships. This book reflects the interdisciplinary nature of the field of personal relationships while focusing strongly on interpersonal communication.

ORGANIZATION

In line with our relational approach, this book is organized loosely around relationship trajectories. We use the term *trajectory* loosely because all relationships are different, with no two following exactly the same path. Nonetheless, from a developmental perspective, it is helpful to think of how relationships progress from initial meetings toward farewells. Of course, interesting and important communication occurs throughout the course of a relationship. For example, conflict can be studied in terms of a couple's first big fight, the mundane disagreements that people have on a fairly regular basis, the conflicts that enhance relational functioning, or the argument that ultimately marks the destruction of a relationship. Thus, even though this book is organized somewhat chronologically, we believe that relationships do not always unfold in a linear fashion and that many types of events, such as having conflict, communicating love, and managing uncertainty, occur at various stages during the course of a relationship.

FEATURES IN THIS EDITION

For this edition, we retained the features that have made *Close Encounters* successful while adding additional research. As in the last edition, all the chapters start with a scenario that features fictional characters dealing with communication issues, and each chapter ends with a section called "Summary and Application." These chapter endings tie back to the scenarios at the beginning of each chapter so that students can see how the information they learned can be applied to a specific situation. Throughout each chapter, we refer to the opening scenarios at various times to provide examples of how the concepts we discuss relate to real-life situations. With the exception of Chapter 1, all chapters include at least one "Put Yourself to the Test" box, including two boxes on uncertainty and attachment that are new to this edition. Our students have told us that they find these boxes very helpful in identifying their communication style as well as some of the characteristics of their relationships. Some instructors incorporate these self-tests into their course assignments. For example, students may complete some of these tests and then write self-reflection papers about their own communication style.

Some chapters have undergone significant changes and reorganization. For example, the chapter that formerly focused on intimacy is now organized around the broader concept of closeness. The uncertainty chapter has been reorganized around new concepts and principles that have emerged related to this topic. The introductory chapter now includes new principles related to both interpersonal and relational communication. In addition, the first half of the chapter on relationship termination is organized around an updated list of the reasons why people divorce. Baxter's (1990) relational dialectics theory and Duck's (1982) theory of relational dissolution have both been updated to reflect recent revisions to those theories. New research has also been added to each chapter, including sections on generational differences related to identity, chemical attraction, communication skills related to friendship formation, invisible support, communication variables related to Lee's (1977, 1988) love styles, antisocial maintenance behaviors, common couple violence, intimate terrorism, and Gottman, Gottman, and DeClaire's (2006) advice regarding how communication can help prevent divorce, among other research. This edition also includes more research related to the use of computer-mediated communication in relationships, such as Facebook. Cultural similarities and differences are also highlighted more in many of the chapters. For instance, the chapters on attraction, uncertainty, love, equity, and privacy management all include boxes discussing aspects of culture.

FEATURES

In addition to the features already discussed, *Close Encounters* is designed to appeal to students and professors alike based on the following features:

Current, interdisciplinary research: The research in *Close Encounters* reflects the interdisciplinary nature of the study of personal relationships and draws from across the social science disciplines while maintaining a focus on communication. This edition has been carefully updated to include recent cutting-edge research on interpersonal communication.

High-interest topics: Intriguing subjects, such as long-distance relationships, cross-sex friendships, flirting, sexual interaction, cohabitation, and the "dark side" of relational communication are explored in depth.

"Put Yourself to the Test" boxes: These exercises, found throughout the book, assess various aspects of students' own relationships and communication styles.

Highlights: These boxes take a closer look at issues in relational research and challenge students to think critically about research and popular concepts.

Discussion questions: These questions, found at the end of each chapter, can help students prepare for class or they can be used as springboards for classroom discussion. Some instructors also have students write position papers in response to some of the discussion questions.

Instructor's manual: The new instructor's manual includes chapter outlines, class activities, suggestions for film and TV clips that can be used during class, test bank questions, and PowerPoint slides. The manual is available online.

ANCILLARIES

Additional ancillary materials further support and enhance the learning goals of the third edition of *Close Encounters: Communication in Relationships.* These ancillary materials include the following:

Student Study Site

www.sagepub.com/guerrero3e

The new open-access student study site provides additional resources to build on students' understanding of the book content and extend their learning beyond the classroom. Students will have access to the following features for each chapter:

- **E-Flashcards** reinforce student understanding and learning of key terms and concepts that are outlined in the book.
- A "**Learning From SAGE Journal Articles**" feature provides access to recent, relevant full-text articles from SAGE's leading research journals. Each article supports and expands on the concepts presented in the chapter. Discussion questions are also provided to focus and guide student interpretation.
- **Surveys and assessments** from the book that can be printed for easy accessibility and use.

Instructor Teaching Site

www.sagepub.com/guerrero3e

The updated instructor teaching site provides one integrated source for all instructor materials, including the following key components for each chapter:

- The updated **test bank** in Microsoft Word offers multiple choice questions and answers for each chapter of the book to help instructors assess students' progress and understanding.
- **PowerPoint presentations** designed to assist with lecture and review, highlighting essential content, features, and artwork from the book.
- **Sample syllabi**—for semester, quarter, and online classes—provide suggested models for instructors to use when creating the syllabi for their courses.

- **Activities** provide lively and stimulating ideas for use in and out of class to reinforce active learning.
- A "**Learning From SAGE Journal Articles**" feature provides access to recent, relevant full-text articles from SAGE's leading research journals. Each article supports and expands on the concepts presented in the chapter. Discussion questions are also provided to focus and guide student interpretation. This resource is also featured on the student study site.
- **Discussion questions** from the book that can be printed for easy accessibility and use.

ACKNOWLEDGMENTS

Writing a textbook is an exciting challenge as well as a daunting task. As we worked on this edition of *Close Encounters,* our dens were cluttered with articles and our families had to listen to the click-click-click of our computer keyboards even more than usual. The support of our families and colleagues was critical in helping us complete this project and we owe them our sincere gratitude. We are especially indebted to our partners—Vico, Janis, and Tammy, who provided not only social support but also examples and feedback.

We would also like to thank the many people who helped during the writing and editing process. We are especially grateful to our editor, Todd Armstrong, who stepped in to publish a second edition and has been enthusiastic and supportive regarding this latest edition as well. Thanks are also due to his assistants, Nathan Davidson and Aja Baker, who guided us through many aspects of the publication process, and to our copy editor, Gretchen Treadwell, and production editor, Eric Garner. We would also like to acknowledge Holly Allen, our editor for the first edition. A conversation between Laura and Holly back in 1998 started the *Close Encounters* ball rolling.

Many of our colleagues across the discipline also deserve a word of praise. We have received formal and informal feedback from many valued colleagues throughout the years, including (but not limited to) Katherine Adams, Jess Alberts, Buy Bachman, Dawn Braithwaite, Erin Bryant, Brant Burleson, Daniel Canary, John Caughlin, Scott Christopher, Victoria DeFrancisco, Kathryn Dindia, Steve Duck, Norah Dunbar, Jen Eden, Renee Edwards, Lisa Farinelli, Cara Fisher, Kory Floyd, Michael Hecht, Susanne Jones, Leanne Knobloch, Pamela Lannutti, Jennifer Marmo, Tara McManus, Sandra Metts, Claude Miller, Paul Mongeau, Larry Nadler, Sylvia Niehuis, Donna Pawlowski, Sue Pendall, Sandra Petronio, Pam Secklin, Adam Smith, Denise Solomon, Brian Spitzberg, Susan Sprecher, Laura Stafford, Glen Stamp, Claire Sullivan, Paul Turman, Alice Veksler, Richard West, Christina Yoshimura, and Stephen Yoshimura. A special thanks goes to Judee Burgoon (Laura's and Walid's PhD adviser and an exceptional role model) who suggested that we use the term *close encounters* as part of the title.

Finally, we would like to thank all the students we have had in our classes over the years. We use some of their examples in this book, and we have incorporated their feedback into this third edition. Just as important, lively dialogue with students has helped sustain our enthusiasm for teaching courses on interpersonal communication and relationships. We hope this book contributes to spirited discussions about relationships in your classrooms as well.

—L.K.G.

—P.A.A.

—W.A.A.

1

Conceptualizing Relational Communication

Definitions and Principles

People accomplish a lot by communicating with others. For example, take these three situations: Jake is having trouble with his statistics homework, which is due tomorrow. His friend and roommate, Dave, is a whiz at math, so Jake tries to persuade Dave to stay home (rather than go to a party) and help him. Meanwhile, Su-Lin recently arrived in the United States as an international student and feels a lot of uncertainty about the university and student life. However, after joining a couple of student clubs and getting to know some of her classmates, she starts to feel more comfortable in her new surroundings. Kristi's husband moves out of the house and tells her he wants a divorce. Rather than sitting at home alone, moping around and feeling sorry for herself, Kristi drives over to her parents' house where she receives comfort and support from her mother.

Personal relationships are central to being human. McAdams (1988) suggested that "through personal relationships, we may find our most profound experiences of security and anxiety, power and impotence, unity and separateness" (p. 7). People are born into relationships and live their lives in webs of friendships, family networks, romances, marriages, and work relationships. In fact, research shows that when people talk, the most common topics are relationship problems, sex, family, and romantic (or potential romantic) partners (Haas & Sherman, 1982). The capacity to

form relationships is innate and biological—a part of the genetic inheritance that has enabled the human race to survive over time. Humans have less potential for survival, creativity, and innovation as individuals than they do in relationships. Personal relationship experts have begun to unlock the mysteries of these universal human experiences, to assist people with problematic relationships, and to help people achieve greater satisfaction in their close encounters.

As Jake, Su-Lin, and Kristi illustrate, communication plays a central role in relationships. When we need help, comfort, or reassurance, communication is the tool that helps us accomplish our goals. Relationships cannot exist unless two people communicate with each other. "Bad" communication is often blamed for problems in relationships, whereas "good" communication is often credited with preserving relationships. In this introductory chapter, we take a close look at what constitutes both communication and relationships. First, however, we provide a brief history of the field of personal relationships. Then we define and discuss three important terms that are central to this book: relationships, interpersonal communication, and relational communication. The chapter ends with principles of interpersonal and relational communication.

THE FIELD OF PERSONAL RELATIONSHIPS: A BRIEF HISTORY

People have been curious about their relationships for thousands of years, but the formal study of personal relationships is a fairly recent phenomenon. Today we take the study of personal relationships for granted, but a few decades ago, the scholarly investigation of relationships was considered unscientific and a waste of resources. In 1975, Senator William Proxmire of Wisconsin publicly criticized two of the finest and earliest relationship researchers, Ellen Berscheid and Elaine Hatfield (formerly Elaine Walster), for their research on love. Proxmire gave the "golden fleece award" for wasteful government spending to the National Science Foundation for supporting Berscheid and Walster's research on love with an $84,000 grant. The senator's objections to "squandering" money on love research were twofold: (1) Scientists could never understand the mystery of love, and (2) even if they did, he didn't want to hear it and was confident that no one else did either (E. Hatfield, personal communication, August 20, 1999). Of course, like many Americans, Proxmire had problematic relationships of his own and had just been divorced at the time he gave his "award." Months of harassing phone calls and even death threats to Berscheid and Walster followed (E. Hatfield, personal communication, August 20, 1999). Even Elaine Hatfield's mother's

bishop, whose name is changed in the letter below, got into the act.

Dear faithful in Christ:

This week, the *Chicago Tribune* announced that the National Science Foundation will unravel the most sacred mysteries of love and life. Soon they will be in a position to dictate to the whole world. If "Science" were not such a sacred cow, we would all laugh at such ponderous nonsense. Who has granted these "scientists" the ability to see into men's minds and hearts? Are their "findings" going to eliminate pride, selfishness, jealousy, suffering, and war? Sex research. Birth control. "Swinging." This is not the face of America. . . .

Rev. Richard S. Moody
Bishop, Diocese of Chicago (Hatfield & Rapson, 2000)

Within decades, most people, including priests and politicians, came to realize that close relationships are as important to study as earthquakes or nutrition, especially since having good relationships is associated with better mental and physical health (Ryff, Singer, Wing, & Dienberg Love, 2001; Taylor et al., 2006; Willittis, Benzeval, & Stansfeld, 2004). People now find social scientific knowledge compatible with personal political and religious beliefs. In fact, some churches conduct premarital workshops and marriage encounters based on relationship research. Bookstores and newsstands are crammed with books and magazines that focus on every aspect of relationships, providing advice (of variable quality) on topics such as "How to Deal With His Ex" (Nanus, 2005), "Who Not to Marry" (McKinnell, 2006), and how to "Catch Her Eye" (Beland, 2005), as well as offering "Five Sex Tips . . . What Can Lesbians and Gay Men Teach Each Other About Great Sex?" (Westenhoefer & Mapa, 2006) and "Six Secret Ways to Turn Her On" (Miller, 2004), just to name some of the advice in the popular press. One critical function of scientific research on relationships is to provide a check-and-balance system for the popular advice given in the media. Critical consumers can compare the scientific literature to the popular, often inaccurate, advice in magazines, best-selling books, and television shows. Box 1.1 presents one such comparison.

BOX 1.1 Highlights

The Importance of Being a Critical Consumer: Comparing John Gottman to John Gray

People are bombarded with advice about relationships from best-selling books, magazine articles, and talk shows. How accurate is this advice? The answer is, it depends. Sometimes the advice given in the media is consistent with social scientific research; other times it is not. In a *Psychology Today* article, Marano (1997) put John Gray to the test by comparing his credentials and conclusions to those of John Gottman. John Gray is the author of the number-one best seller in nonfiction, *Men Are From Mars, and Women Are From Venus*. John Gottman is one of the premier social psychologists in the study of personal relationships. So how did Gray stack up to Gottman? Here is what *Psychology Today* reported after researching and interviewing both men.

	John Gray	John Gottman
Education	PhD through correspondence school	PhD from the University of Illinois
Licensing	Driver's license	Licensed psychologist
Number of journal articles	None	109
Number of couples formally studied	None	760
The cardinal rule of relationships	Men and women are different.	What people think they do in relationships and what they actually do are very different.
Defining statement	"Before 1950, men were men and women were women."	"It's the everyday mindless moments that are the basis of romance in marriage."
What makes marriage work?	Heeding gender stereotypes	Making mental maps of each other's world
What makes marriage fail?	Gender differences in communication style	Gender stereotypes and reactions to stress
What they say about each other	"John who?"	"I envy his financial success."

SOURCE: Hara E. Marano—Gottman and Gray: *A Tale Of Two Relationship Gurus* © Copyright 2010. www.Psychologytoday.com.

Several major tributaries have contributed to the steady stream of scholarly research on personal relationships. The early pioneers in the field could not have envisioned the vast amount of research on relationships that exists in several disciplines today. The young field of personal relationships has always been transdisciplinary, although it sometimes took years for scholars from different disciplines to discover one another's work. Duck (1988) commented that the field of personal relationships is unusual because it is truly interdisciplinary and has the power to impact people's everyday lives. Scholars from disciplines such as communication, social psychology, child development, family studies, sociology, and anthropology are all in the business of studying human relationships. In particular, research in interpersonal communication, social psychology, and other disciplines has contributed to the establishment and evolution of the field of personal relationships.

Contributions of Interpersonal Communication Research

The earliest research in this area dates back to the 1950s, but interpersonal communication research began in earnest in the 1960s and 1970s (Andersen, 1982). Previously, communication scholars were preoccupied mainly with public speeches, political rhetoric, and mass communication. In the 1960s, scholars realized that most communication takes place in small groups and dyads consisting of close friends, family members, and romantic partners (Miller, 1976). The study of interpersonal communication thus began to focus on how people communicate in dyads and small groups. The first books on interpersonal communication emerged soon thereafter (see McCroskey, Larson, & Knapp, 1971).

Scholars also realized that interpersonal communication differs based upon the type of relationship people share. Miller and Steinberg (1975) proposed that the defining characteristics of interpersonal relationships are that they are unique, irreplaceable, and require understanding of the partner's psychological makeup. By contrast, noninterpersonal or "role" relationships, like those with store clerks or tech help-line staff, possess few unique qualities, are replaceable, and are relatively impersonal. These shifts in communication scholarship reflected broader societal changes. The youth movement of the 1960s represented a rebellion against a society thought to be impersonal and manipulative. Sensitivity training, encounter groups, and other personal growth movements of the 1960s and 1970s turned people's attention inward to the dyad and to close relationships.

The evolution of interpersonal communication as a primary emphasis in the communication discipline was an outcome of the recognition that relationships are the primary locus for communication. Scholars also realized that relationships are an inherently communicative phenomenon. It is difficult to imagine how human relationships might exist in the absence of communication. As Miller (1976) stated: "Understanding the interpersonal communication process demands an understanding of the symbiotic relationship between communication and relational development: communication influences relational development, and in turn (or simultaneously) relational development influences the nature of the communication between parties to the relationship" (p. 15). By the 1980s, interpersonal and relational communication research had become increasingly sophisticated and theoretically driven (Andersen, 1982).

Contributions of Social Psychology

Early research in social psychology also laid the groundwork for the scientific investigation of interpersonal relationships, with much of this work focused on social development and personality. From the late 1950s through the mid-1970s, however, social psychologists increasingly began studying interaction patterns related to group and dyadic processes (for some of the major early works, see Altman & Taylor, 1973; Berscheid & Walster, 1969; Heider, 1958; Thibaut & Kelley, 1959). This movement was not limited to social psychologists in the United States; in Great Britain, Argyle and his associates spent several decades studying aspects of relationships (see Argyle & Dean, 1965; Argyle & Henderson, 1985).

During this time, several highly influential books were published. For example, Thibaut and Kelley's (1959) *The Social Psychology of Groups* eventually led to an explosion of research on social exchange processes in groups and dyads, bringing issues such as rewards (the positive outcomes people get from relationships) and reciprocity (the way one person's behavior leads to similar behavior in another) to the forefront. Berscheid and Walster's (1969) *Interpersonal Attraction* also had a major impact on both interpersonal communication research and the study of dyadic behavior in social psychology. This book focused on emerging relationships between strangers, as did much of the early research in social psychology (see Altman & Taylor, 1973). A short time later, however, relational research began to focus on love, and the study of close relationships began to flourish (see Berscheid & Walster, 1974; Rubin, 1970, 1973). Finally, Altman and Taylor's (1973) *Social Penetration: The Development of Interpersonal Relationships,* which examined the role of self-disclosure in relationships, helped generate research in communication, relationship development, and relationship disengagement.

The prestigious *Journal of Personality and Social Psychology* also included a section on "Interpersonal Processes"; this journal still publishes some of the best research on relationships. However, until the mid-1980s there were no journals devoted entirely to the study of relationships. In fact, the first professional conference devoted entirely to interpersonal relationships was held in the 1980s, again indicating the youthfulness of the field of personal relationships compared to other academic disciplines (see Kelley, 1986). This conference, which was organized primarily by social psychologists, laid the roots for the creation of two organizations that focused exclusively on personal relationships: the International Network on Personal Relationships (INPR), which was established by Steve Duck, and the International Society for the Study of Personal Relationships (ISSPR), founded by Robin Gilmour and Steve Duck. In 1984, the INPR established the first journal dedicated solely to the study of personal relationships, the prestigious *Journal of Social and Personal Relationships.* A decade later the ISSPR launched a second journal, called *Personal Relationships.* Now these two scholarly societies have merged into one professional association, the International Association for Relationship Research (IARR).

Roots in Other Disciplines

Disciplines such as family studies, sociology, developmental and child psychology, clinical psychology, humanistic psychology, and anthropology have also made important contributions to the field of personal relationships. One study reported that approximately 37% of the research on personal relationships comes from social psychologists, another 37% from communication scholars, and much of the rest from sociologists and family studies scholars (Hoobler, 1999). Sociologists' relationship research often focuses on issues such as cultural values, class, religion, secularization, divorce, marriage, gender equality, political attitudes, and generational differences, with an eye toward determining how relationships are embedded within the larger society. Family studies scholars examine relationships from a different lens, looking more at the internal dynamics of relationships between family members, either as a family system or as an interpersonal dyad within the broader family structure (e.g., parent-child or spousal relationships). Family scholars also examine developmental issues, such as determining how relationships within one's family of origin influence later relationships in adulthood.

Personal relationship research draws from these different disciplines, so a level of richness and diversity that is often absent in other fields characterizes the field of personal relationships. It is precisely because scholars in the various disciplines— communication, social psychology, sociology, family studies, and so on—have different theoretical and methodological approaches that the field of personal relationships has been so vital and is evolving so quickly (Duck, 1988). Although this book draws upon knowledge from various fields, the primary focus is on communication in close relationships, with three terms central to this book: **relationships**, **interpersonal communication**, and **relational communication** (see Box 1.2 for definitions).

BOX 1.2 Highlights

Definitions of Key Terms

Role relationship: Two people who share some degree of behavioral interdependence, although people in such relationships are usually interchangeable and are not psychologically or behaviorally unique. One person in a role relationship can easily replace another.

Interpersonal relationship: Two people who share repeated interactions over time, can influence one another, and have unique interaction patterns.

Close relationship: Two people in an interpersonal relationship characterized by enduring bonds, emotional attachment, personal need fulfillment, and irreplaceability.

Interpersonal communication: The exchange of nonverbal and verbal messages between two people, regardless of the relationship they share.

Relational communication: A subset of interpersonal communication focused on the expression and interpretation of messages within close relationships. Relational communication includes the gamut of interactions from vital relational messages to mundane everyday interactions.

RELATIONSHIPS

Think about all the different people with whom you interact in a given day. Do you have relationships with all of them or only some of them? With how many of these people do you have close or personal relationships? Defining the term *relationship* can be tricky. When do we cross the line from interacting with someone to having a relationship? And when do we move from having a casual or functional relationship to having a close relationship?

General Types of Relationships

Take a moment to think of all the different relationships you have. Now imagine a piece of paper with a circle representing you in the middle of the page. If you draw additional circles that represent each of the people with whom you have relationships, where would you place those circles in comparison to yourself? You would likely place some individuals nearer to yourself than others based on the closeness

you share with each person. How many people would be really close to you and how many would be near the margins of the paper? Would anyone's circle overlap with yours? Research suggests that among the many relationships most of us have with friends, coworkers, family members, romantic partners, and others, only a select few of those relationships become really close. Most of these relationships stay at an interpersonal level, and others may never really progress beyond a role relationship.

Role Relationships

According to many relationship scholars, the basic ingredient for having a relationship is that two individuals share some degree of **behavioral interdependence** (Berscheid & Peplau, 1983). This means that one person's behavior somehow affects the other person's behavior, and vice versa. Based on this definition, we have relationships with a variety of people, including the salesclerk who helps us make a purchase, the waiter who takes our orders and serves us dinner, and the boss whom we rarely see but on whom we depend for leadership and a paycheck. These basic role "relationships" are not true interpersonal relationships. Rather, role relationships are functional or casual, and often are temporary; also, people in such relationships are usually interchangeable and not unique. An interpersonal or close relationship with someone requires more than simple behavioral interdependence.

Interpersonal Relationships

In addition to basic behavioral independence, interpersonal relationships require that two individuals influence each other in meaningful ways. This type of **mutual influence** goes beyond basic tasks such as exchanging money to get coffee at Starbucks or thanking your hygienist after she cleans your teeth. In interpersonal relationships, influence extends beyond mundane tasks to activities that create connection at a social or emotional level rather than a task level. For example, while helping Jake with his statistics homework, Dave might offer words of encouragement to boost his confidence. After the homework is finished, they may start talking about a political issue, and in doing so affect one another's thinking. Knowing that Dave dreads public speaking, Jake may later reciprocate by offering to listen to a speech that Dave is preparing. These tasks take extensive time and effort and include providing emotional support and engaging in self-disclosure rather than just getting something done. Thus, these activities imply that Dave and Jake have moved beyond a simple role relationship.

Interpersonal relationships also have **repeated interaction** over time. Because they interact with one another frequently, Jake has the time and opportunity to reciprocate by helping Dave, which can strengthen their friendship further. Interactions that are limited in length or frequency rarely develop into interpersonal relationships. Finally, interpersonal relationships are characterized by **unique interaction patterns**. This means that the way Jake communicates with Dave will be different in some ways from how he communicates with other friends. They have a unique relational history, including shared experiences, inside jokes, and knowledge of private information, which shapes how they communicate with each other.

Close Relationships

Close relationships have all the features of interpersonal relationships plus three more: **emotional attachment**, **need fulfillment**, and **irreplaceability.** In a close relationship we feel emotionally connected; the relationship is the basis of why we feel happy or sad, proud or disappointed. Similarly, close relational partners fulfill critical interpersonal needs, such as the need to belong to a social group, to feel loved and appreciated, or to care for and nurture someone. When a relationship is irreplaceable, the other person has a special place in our thoughts and emotions, as well as in our social network. For example, you may only have one "first love" and one "best friend," and there may be one person in particular whom you reach out to in times of crisis.

It is important to recognize that distinctions between these three types of relationships are often blurred. Our close relationships contain some of the same features as interpersonal and role relationships. For instance, Kristi's close relationship with her mother is partially defined by her role as a daughter. Behavioral interdependence also characterizes all relationships, but as people move from role to interpersonal to close relationships, interdependence becomes more enduring and diverse (Berscheid & Peplau, 1983). Diverse means that partners are interdependent in many ways, such as needing each other for emotional support, striving to reach shared goals, and influencing each other's beliefs and attitudes. In role relationships, such as those we have with salesclerks or waiters, behavioral interdependence is temporary and is defined by the situation. Need fulfillment is also part of all three relationship types, but the needs that our closest relationships fulfill are more central and personal than the needs other relationships fulfill.

Need Fulfillment in Close Relationships

Researchers suggest that a plethora of human needs are satisfied in close personal relationships, with the three most central interpersonal needs being affection, inclusion, and control (Schutz, 1958). In the scenario at the beginning of this chapter, each person used communication to fulfill one of these needs. Kristi went to her mother for affection and social support. Su-Lin joined student clubs and talked with classmates to satisfy inclusion needs. Finally, Jake tried to exert behavioral control by persuading Dave to stay home and help him with his statistics homework.

Affection

Throughout life, our need for affection is satisfied through our ability to love other people and through having other people love us (Schutz, 1958). Neglected infants who are never touched suffer from "failure-to-thrive syndrome" and even risk death (Andersen, 2008; Montagu, 1971/1978). Adults who regularly give and receive affection report more psychological and physical health, as well as better relationships (Floyd, 2006). Affectionate communication is a resource that strengthens relationships and makes people feel better about themselves and others. Affection, according to Schutz (1958), occurs in dyads. Inclusion and control, by contrast, can occur either "between pairs of people or between one person and a group of persons" (p. 23). Affection forms the basis for our most powerful and closest relationships (see Chapter 6).

Social Inclusion

Feeling part of a group is another crucial need (Schutz, 1958). It is through primary group relationships that basic needs such as safety and survival are satisfied. As Ruesch (1951) observed: "In the fold of the family, clan or group or in the widest sense of the world, the herd, he [or she] feels secure. Reliance on other members of the group increases his [or her] chance for survival in a troubled world" (p. 36). Humans evolved as members of hunting and gathering bands of one hundred to two hundred people (Donald, 1991). This may explain why belonging to groups—from youth groups to corporations, from sports teams to service clubs, from street gangs to fraternities and sororities—is so important to most people. In any case, Schutz (1958) suggested that feeling included is a crucial part of social development that enables us to have successful interactions and associations with other people. A lack of social interaction and inclusion can contribute to loneliness and low self-esteem (Segrin, 1998).

Behavioral Control

The third basic interpersonal need revolves around the desire to feel in control of one's life (Schutz, 1958). People in successful interpersonal relationships share control (Scott & Powers, 1978), including making decisions together involving work, money, sex, children, and household chores. Indeed, a whole body of research suggests that partners who share tasks and resources in a fair manner are more satisfied with their relationships (see Chapters 9 and 10). By contrast, partners who believe they lack control or who are denied free choice may deliberately sabotage their relationships, defy rules, and engage in other destructive behavior. For example, if you have a friend who always shows up late, you might retaliate by leaving before he or she arrives. Prohibition of a relationship by parents sometimes increases the attractiveness of the relationship. According to Cialdini (1988), this effect is based on the idea that scarce objects or people are most attractive. This explains why advertisers offer "limited time offers" and sales "while the supply lasts" and why people who are "hard to get" are more attractive than people who are "easy to get"—except, of course, if they are easy for us to get but hard for others to get.

Relationship Categories

Another way to think about relationships is to categorize them based on type. We do this every day; in our ordinary talk we refer to some relationships as "friendships," others as "romances" or "marriages." We introduce someone as our "best friend," "brother-in-law," "wife," and so forth. These categorizations, although simple, help people understand the relationships we share.

Relationships come in all shapes and sizes. When college students think about what constitutes a close relationship, they typically think about dating or romantic relationships. However, as the categories just listed suggest, we live in a network of relationships that includes family members, lovers, acquaintances, coworkers, employers, and so forth. We also have "blended" relationships, such as having a sibling who is also your best friend. Some relationships fit into neat categories such as boyfriend, coworker, wife, or student, but others fit into overlapping categories. As Wilmot (1995) put it, "Relational types are not necessarily mutually exclusive—their boundaries are often fuzzy" (p. 28). Moreover, relationships often move from one category to another as when a coworker becomes a friend, a friend becomes a dating partner, or a fraternity brother becomes an employee. In these "fuzzy" relationships people can be uncertain about how to behave appropriately, especially if they use different relational definitions.

Another way to categorize relationships is based on how typical or "mainstream" they are. When most people think about a romantic relationship, they think of a man and a woman. When asked to imagine a pair of best friends, most people picture two men or two women as opposed to cross-sex friends. Even in an age where nontraditional families are increasingly common, most people envision the typical family as a mom and a dad with a couple of children. Yet romantic relationships, friendships, and families vary immensely, and diversity is increasing. Researchers have acknowledged this diversity by focusing on a variety of relationship types, including gay, lesbian, and bisexual relationships (Huston & Schwartz, 1995; Kurdek, 1991); polygamy (Altman & Ginat, 1996); cohabitation between unmarried individuals (Cunningham & Antil, 1995); single-parent families, stepfamilies, orphans, and interracial couples (Gaines, 1995; Williams & Andersen, 1998); cross-generational and Internet relationships (Lea & Spears, 1995); long-distance relationships (Rohlfing, 1995); and cross-sex friendships (see Chapter 9).

Despite advances, romantic relationship research on gay men and lesbians lags far behind research on heterosexual romantic relationships, although this gap is not as large as it once was. Peplau and Spalding (2000) reported that, of 312 articles published in the *Journal of Social and Personal Relationships* from 1980 to 1993, only 3 examined any aspect of sexual orientation. Similarly, Wood and Duck (1995) noted that most research has focused on the relationships of young, white, middle-class heterosexuals. To determine if the situation has improved, we conducted a search of articles published in the *Journal of Social and Personal Relationships* and *Personal Relationships* from 2000 to 2009, using the keywords *gay, lesbian, homosexual, bisexual,*

and *sexual orientation*. This search produced 21 articles that focused on these issues, which is a significant improvement compared to the 1980s and early 1990s. Nonetheless, these articles still represent a small portion of the research available on romantic relationships.

In this book, we make an effort to include research about various types of understudied relationships. However, because this book is based on existing research, the majority of the discussion necessarily revolves around heterosexual romantic relationships. We also discuss research related to friendships and family relationships, albeit less often. So, as you read this book, keep in mind that so-called traditional models of relationships do not apply to all relationships. Nonetheless, many types of relationships have elements in common: connection and conflict, joy and grief, meetings and departures. Indeed, the more scholars study less common relationships, the more they conclude that all relationships are patches of the same quilt.

Of course, there are important differences sprinkled in with the similarities. Relationships are as unique as the different combinations of patchwork that create a quilt, and individuals in certain types of relationships do encounter particular difficulties that can affect communication processes. For example, Huston and Schwartz (1995), in their research on gay men and lesbians, stated: "The relationships formed by lesbians and gay men are in many ways very similar to heterosexual ones; in other ways distinct factors influence relationship formation and survival" (p. 120). Gay and lesbian couples, as well as interracial couples, often have to deal with societal prejudices and pressures with which opposite-sex and same-culture couples do not have to cope.

Characteristics Distinguishing Different Relationship Types

Relationships vary on many characteristics or dimensions. For example, some relationships are more satisfying or committed than others, and some families are traditional whereas others have more liberal values. When it comes to putting relationships into categories, such as friend, romantic partner, or family member, at least five characteristics are relevant—how voluntary the relationship is, the degree to which people are genetically related, whether the relationship is sexual or platonic, whether the relationship is romantic, and the sex or gender of the partners.

Voluntary Versus Involuntary

Relationships can be voluntary or involuntary. People make a conscious choice to be involved in some relationships but they enter other relationships without volition. For instance, children cannot choose their family; rather, they are born or adopted into relationships with parents, siblings, aunts and uncles, grandparents, and other relatives. People also have little choice in choosing steprelations and in-laws; these relationships often emerge based on other people's choices (e.g., your father or brother gets married).

By contrast, people usually choose their friends. In most Western cultures, people also choose their romantic partners, whereas in some other cultures spouses are selected through arranged marriages, thus making them less voluntary. In many ways, voluntary relationships develop differently than involuntary relationships. When developing friendships and other involuntary relationships, we often use communication to determine whether or not we want to be in the relationship in the first place. If the conversation flows, similarities are uncovered, and trust develops, then a friendship emerges. With family relationships, the relationship is there regardless of the type of communication we share, although communication will have an enormous impact on the quality of that relationship.

Genetically Related Versus Nonrelated

The degree to which two people are genetically related also defines the type of relationship they share. Unless someone has an identical twin, people share the most genes (around 50%) with their biological parents and siblings, followed by their biological grandparents, aunts, uncles, nieces, and nephews (around 25%), and their biological first cousins (at around 12.5%). Some researchers

have suggested that people communicate somewhat differently depending on how genetically related they are. For example, some studies have shown that people are more likely to give affectionate communication to relatives than nonrelatives, beyond what is predicted by relational closeness (Floyd, 2006; see also Chapter 6). To some extent, the degree of genetic relatedness is also associated with how voluntary or involuntary a relationship is. For instance, even if you do not get along with your cousin, your cousin is your cousin for life, making the relationship involuntary. Genetic relatedness also differentiates biological children from adopted children or stepchildren and helps researchers better understand the dynamics of blended families such as those that include stepsiblings.

Sexual Versus Platonic

Relationships are also characterized by their sexual versus platonic nature. Typically friendships and relationships with family members are platonic, which means they do not include sexual involvement. Dating and marital relationships, by contrast, are usually marked by sexual activity. Of course, friendships can also include sexual activity, as is the case with "friends-with-benefits" relationships, which are defined in terms of having repeated sexual interaction with someone who is considered a friend but not a romantic partner (Hughes, Morrison, & Asada, 2005). Sexual activity is an important component of many relationships, but it is helpful to remember that platonic relationships can be just as close and satisfying as sexual relationships. Indeed, many people rank their relationships with their children, parents, siblings, and best friends as especially close and satisfying (Argyle & Furnham, 1983).

Romantic Versus Nonromantic

As the case of friends with benefits illustrates, there is an important distinction between having a sexual relationship and having a romantic relationship. Friends with benefits have sex but not romance. So what does it mean to be in a romantic relationship? Mongeau, Serewicz, Henningsen, and

Davis (2006) noted that both romantic relationships and friendships can contain sexual activity and high levels of emotional involvement. The difference is in how the partners mutually define the relationship. Generally, romantic relationships are viewed as being a couple, which may include the possibility of marriage in the future (if they are not already married), as well as sexual exclusivity.

The distinction between emotional closeness and sexual intimacy is reflected in how various relationships develop. Guerrero and Mongeau (2008) suggested that there are three general trajectories or pathways toward developing a romantic relationship. The "traditional" trajectory is acquaintanceship to romantic relationship. Here two people meet, are physically attracted to one another, start dating, form an emotional attachment, and become a romantic couple. In this case, the sexual and emotional aspects of the relationship tend to develop together. Other times, people follow a trajectory that moves from platonic relationship to romantic relationship. These individuals develop emotional closeness first as friends and later add sexual intimacy, which often lead them to redefine their relationship as romantic. The third trajectory moves from being friends with benefits to having a romantic relationship. In this trajectory, sexual activity and emotional closeness are usually present in the friends-with-benefits relationship. Thus, these aspects of the relationship are not what changes when the relationship turns romantic. Instead, it is the definition of the relationship that changes. (Although this trajectory does occur, most friends-with-benefits relationships do not turn into romances.)

Male Versus Female or Masculine Versus Feminine

Some scholars label sex or gender as a component defining types of relationships (Wood, 1996). Sex refers to an individual's biological makeup as male or female, whereas gender refers to how masculine, feminine, or androgynous a person is; androgynous individuals possess both feminine and masculine traits (Bem, 1974). Sex is biologically determined, whereas gender is socially and culturally constructed. Sex helps define family relationships into categories such as father-son or father-daughter, or romantic relationships into categories such as lesbian, gay, or heterosexual. Most research on friendship makes these distinctions by comparing male friendships to female friendships, or same-sex friendships to cross-sex friendships (see Chapter 9). Other research focuses on gender by looking at how masculine, feminine, or androgynous individuals are. For example, a romantic couple consisting of a feminine person and a masculine person functions differently than a romantic couple consisting of two androgynous individuals. In this book, we use the term *sex* to refer to biology (male versus female) and the term *gender* to refer to culturally constructed images of men and women as masculine or feminine.

PRINCIPLES OF INTERPERSONAL COMMUNICATION

Now that we have defined various relationship types, we turn to a discussion of the kinds of communication that occur in those relationships. The terms **interpersonal communication** and **relational communication** describe the process whereby people exchange messages in different types of relationships. The goal of message exchange is to cocreate meaning, although as we shall see shortly, not all message exchanges are effective and miscommunication occurs frequently. A broader concept than relational communication, interpersonal communication refers to the exchange of messages, verbal and nonverbal, between two people, regardless of the relationship they share. These people could be strangers, acquaintances, coworkers, political candidate and voter, teacher and student, superior and subordinate, friends, or lovers, to name just a few relationship types. Thus, interpersonal communication includes the exchange of messages in all sorts of relationships, ranging from functional to casual to close. Relational communication, by contrast, is narrower in that it typically focuses on messages exchanged in close, or potentially close, relationships, such as those between good friends, romantic partners, and family members. In this section we focus on six specific principles related to interpersonal communication.

Verbal and Nonverbal Messages

The first principle is that *interpersonal communication consists of nonverbal and verbal messages.* Although much of our communication consists of verbal messages, nonverbal communication is at least as important as verbal communication (Andersen, 2008). In fact, some studies suggest that 60 to 65% of the meaning in most interactions comes from nonverbal behavior. In addition, when emotional messages are exchanged, even more of the meaning may be gleaned from nonverbal behaviors (see Burgoon, Guerrero, & Floyd, 2010). Words are not always to be trusted. For example, someone can say "I love you" and not really mean it. But the person who spends time with you, gazes into your eyes, touches you lovingly, tunes into your moods, interprets your body language, synchronizes with your behavior, and uses a loving tone of voice sends a much stronger message. Nonverbal actions often do speak louder than words. As Eliza Dolittle sings in *My Fair Lady*:

> Don't talk to me, show me. When we sit together in the middle of the night, don't talk at all just hold me tight. Anyone who's ever been in love can tell you that this is not time for a chat.

Nonverbal communication includes a wide variety of behaviors. In fact, nonverbal behavior is particularly powerful because people can send messages using numerous nonverbal behaviors all at once. For example, Kristi's lip might tremble while she wipes a tear from her cheek, gazes downward, slumps back in her chair, and lets out a sigh. These actions prompt Kristi's mom to reach over and hug her. Similarly, in the photo on this page, several nonverbal cues are being emitted simultaneously. Nonverbal behaviors such as these have been studied with the context of relationships and

SOURCE: ©iStockphoto.com/477434sean.

What nonverbal cues do you see in this photo and what messages do they send?

have been classified into the following categories (Burgoon et al., 2010):

- *Kinesics:* facial expressions, body and eye movements, including posture, gestures, walking style, smiling, and pupil dilation, among other kinesic cues
- *Vocalics:* silence and the way words are pronounced, including vocal pitch, loudness, accent, tone, and speed, as well as vocalizations such as crying and sighing
- *Proxemics:* the use of space, including conversational distances and territory
- *Haptics:* the use of touch, ranging from affectionate to violent touch
- *Appearance and adornment:* physical attributes such as height, weight, and attractiveness, as well as adornments such as clothing, perfume, and tattoos
- *Artifacts and environmental cues*: the use of objects, such as using candles and soft music to set a romantic mood, and how the environment affects interaction through cues such as furniture arrangement and the size of a room
- *Chronemic cues:* the use of time, such as showing up for a date early or late or waiting a long or short time for someone

Which of these categories of nonverbal behavior are represented in the photo of the man and woman sitting back-to-back? The kinesic and haptic cues should be easy to pick out. Some environmental cues may also provide contextual information. What about the way they are sitting in relation to each other? Sitting back-to-back may convey a lack of intimacy, but in this case, the man and woman are sitting in similar positions with their backs touching each other. They are smiling, with the man looking back toward the woman—both indicators of closeness and affection. The boxes behind them suggest they may be moving, with nowhere to sit to rest except on the floor. From these cues, one might guess these individuals are a young romantic couple (perhaps in their 20s), that they live together, and that they get along well. This guess may be right or wrong—the point is that we infer a lot about people based on their nonverbal behavior.

Interpersonal communication also consists of many forms of verbal behavior, including verbal content and self-disclosure. Self-disclosure, a vital form of interpersonal communication, is used to reveal personal information to others (see Chapter 5). The use of formal or informal language, nicknames, and present or future tense are also examples of verbal behavior that affects interpersonal interactions. For example, when dating partners first talk about sharing a future, such communication is likely to reflect a shift toward a more committed relationship.

Communication as Inevitable

The second principle is that *one cannot not communicate in interpersonal settings*. In one of the important early works on communication, Watzlawick, Beavin, and Jackson (1967) stated: "Activity or inactivity, words or silence, all have message value: they influence others and these others, in turn, cannot not respond to these communications and thus are themselves communicating" (p. 49). Unless two people simply do not notice each other, some communication is inevitable. Even if someone does not intend to send a message, something that person says or does is often interpreted as meaningful by the other person. This does not mean, however, that everything people do is communication. For communication to occur, a person has to send a message intentionally or a receiver has to perceive and assign meaning to a behavior. For example, if you are blinking while interacting, your friend is unlikely to attach any meaning to such an ordinary, involuntary behavior. Similarly, not all body movements are communication since many go unnoticed. But some movements you make and most words you say will be received and interpreted by others, making it impossible not to communicate at some level (Andersen, 1991).

To illustrate, recall the last time you sat next to a stranger—perhaps at the mall, at the movies, or on a bus. What did you notice about the person? Did you check to see if the person looked friendly or notice the stranger's appearance? Did the person look older or younger than you? If you can answer any of these questions, Andersen (1991) argued that communication took place because you perceived and interpreted the stranger's behavior. In our relationships, our partners interpret much of what we do as meaningful. For example, a smile might be perceived as heartfelt or condescending, while a neutral facial expression might be perceived as reflecting boredom or anger. Even silence can communicate a message. For instance, if a close friend stops calling you and fails to return your messages, you will likely suspect that something is wrong. You could attribute your friend's lack of communication to a variety of causes, including being ill, depressed, or mad. In any case, the way you interpret your friend's silence will probably lead you to communicate in particular ways that will further influence the exchange of messages between you and your friend.

Interpersonal Communication Goals

The third principle is that *people use interpersonal communication to fulfill goals.* This does not mean that all communication is strategic. As discussed earlier, people often send spontaneous messages that are interpreted by others as meaningful. In addition, much of our communication is relatively mindless and routine (Burgoon & Langer, 1995; Langer, 1989). However, interpersonal communication likely developed as a way to help people meet their everyday goals. Communication helps people make good impressions, connect with others on a social level, and get things done. Even mundane communication, such as saying hi to acquaintances when passing by them on campus, fulfills goals related to being civil and polite. Although communication fulfills numerous specific goals, many of those goals fall under one of three overarching categories—self-presentational, relational, or instrumental (Canary & Cody, 1994).

Self-presentational goals relate to the image we convey. Andersen (2008) claimed that the most common objective of persuasion is selling ourselves. Other scholars contend that people resemble actors on a stage, presenting themselves in the most favorable light (see Chapter 2). Indeed, a central set of communication principles suggests we are only as attractive, credible, competent, or honest as others think we are. Objective personal qualities have little to do with our image, especially when we first meet people. From an interpersonal standpoint we are what people think we are. Predictably, people spend a lot of time trying to look and act just right

for that big date or that important interview. For example, before attending her first student club meeting, Su-Lin might purposely dress like a student from the United States so that she will fit in.

Relational goals have to do with how we communicate feelings about others, including the type of relationships we desire. Canary and Cody (1994) maintained that "nothing brings us more joy than our personal relationships. We spend significant amounts of time, energy and emotion in the pursuit of quality relationships" (p. 6). At every stage in a relationship, we have goals and plans for the future of that relationship. For example, you might want to meet that attractive student in your class, impress your date, avoid the person who won't leave you alone, or spend time with your sister whom you haven't seen all year. Canary and Cody (1994) described three primary sets of relational goals. The first is activity based and involves doing things with someone, such as attending a party or going skiing. The second is relationship based and involves wanting to initiate, escalate, maintain, or deescalate a relationship. The third is advice based and involves giving advice to peers and parents.

Instrumental goals are task oriented. For example, making money, getting good grades, buying a car, getting a ride to school, and completing a homework assignment are all instrumental goals. People often facilitate attainment of instrumental goals by asking for advice or assistance from a friend, getting permission from a parent or boss, eliciting support from a friend, or influencing someone's attitudes or behaviors (Canary & Cody, 1994). Achieving relational goals involves *giving* advice to others; achieving instrumental goals involves *seeking* advice and assistance to meet one's own task-related goals. Thus, in the scenario involving Kristi and her mother, Kristi may reach instrumental goals related to coping with a divorce by asking her mom for advice. Of course, having a goal and reaching a goal are two separate issues. Goals are most likely to be reached when communication is effective.

Effectiveness and Shared Meaning

The fourth principle is that *interpersonal communication varies in effectiveness, with the most effective messages leading to shared meaning between a sender and a receiver.* When one person sends an intentional message, understanding occurs when the receiver attaches approximately the same meaning to the message as did the sender. Of course, such perfectly effective communication may never occur since people typically attach somewhat different meanings to the same messages. It is impossible to get inside people's heads and to think their thoughts and feel their emotions. Thus, it is difficult to truly and completely understand "where someone is coming from." Nonetheless, communication is most effective when the sender and receiver attach very similar meanings to a behavior. Less effective (or less accurate) communication occurs when sender and receiver attach different meanings to a behavior.

Guerrero and Floyd (2006) provided a way to think about how different types of messages are more or less effective. In their model (see Figure 1.1), communication necessitates that a sender encodes a message or a receiver decodes a message. Therefore, behaviors falling in the box labeled **unattended behavior** do not qualify as communication. The exchanges in the other boxes are all relevant to interpersonal communication, but the most effective form of communication, **successful communication**, occurs when a sender's message is interpreted correctly by a receiver. For example, Jake may ask Dave to stay home and help him with his statistics homework, and Dave may understand what Jake wants him to do.

Other exchanges are less effective. **Miscommunication** occurs when someone sends an intentional message that is misinterpreted by the receiver. For example, you might teasingly say "I hate you" to someone who takes your message literally. **Attempted communication** occurs when someone sends an intentional message that the receiver fails to receive. For example, you might hint that you want to leave a boring party, but your partner fails to get the message and keeps on partying. **Misinterpretation** occurs when someone unintentionally sends a message that is misconstrued by the receiver. You may be scowling because you are in a bad mood after a trying day at work, but your roommate misinterprets your facial expression as showing anger toward her or him. Finally, **accidental communication** occurs when someone does not mean to send a message, but the receiver observes the behavior and interprets it correctly. For example, you might try to hide your joy at acing an exam while a classmate who studied harder than you did poorly, but your classmate sees your nonverbal reaction and correctly assumes you did well. Although such communication is an authentic representation of your feelings, your emotional expression would be ineffective because it communicated a message you did not intend (or want) to send. All of these forms of communication can thus impact the communication process and people's relationships. Certainly, effectiveness is important to high-quality communication, but it is not an attribute of all interpersonal communication.

Content Versus Relational Information

Another factor influencing whether communication is effective is the extent to which partners

	Behavior Not Interpreted	Behavior Interpreted Inaccurately	Behavior Interpreted Accurately
Behavior Sent With Intention	Attempted communication	Miscommunication	Successful communication
Behavior Sent Without Intention	Unattended behavior	Misinterpretation	Accidental communication

Figure 1.1 Types of Communication and Behavior

have the same relational interpretations of messages. This leads into a fifth principle of interpersonal communication, namely, that *every message contains both content and relational information.* Bateson (1951) observed that messages, whether verbal or nonverbal, send more than literal information; they also tell people something about their relationship: "Every courtesy term between persons, every inflection of the voice denoting respect or contempt, condescension or dependency, is a statement about the relationship between two persons" (p. 213). Building on Bateson's work, Watzlawick and colleagues (1967) discussed two levels of communication. The **content level** of a message conveys information at a literal level, whereas the **relational level** provides a context for interpreting the message of a relationship. Both the type of relationship people share and the nonverbal behaviors people use influence the relational level of a message.

The content or literal level of the message, however, should be the same for most people within a given situation. For example, a simple statement, such as "Hand me your book," contains both a content (namely, the request to hand over the book) and a relational message or messages. The relational message depends on whether the request is delivered in a harsh, polite, sarcastic, bored, or warm vocal tone. It also depends on the communicator's facial expressions, posture, gestures, use of touch, attire, eye contact, and a host of other nonverbal behaviors. Finally, the context or situation can affect how the relational information in a message is interpreted. Thus, a message can have multiple meanings at the relational level.

Another example may be helpful. Suppose that late on Friday afternoon your romantic partner calls and asks, "So what are we doing tonight?" At the content level, this seems to be a fairly simple question. But at the relational level, this question could be interpreted a variety of ways. You might think, "It sure is nice to know that we always do something together on Friday nights, even if we don't plan it in advance." Alternatively, you might think that your partner takes you for granted and assumes that you have nothing better to do than wait around for her or him to call before you make plans. Or, if you had argued with your partner the day before, you might think that this is his or her way of making up. Yet

another possibility is that you might think your partner always leaves it up to you to decide what to do. Based on which relational information you get from the message, you are likely to react in very different ways.

Symmetry in Communication

Finally, *interpersonal communication can be symmetrical or asymmetrical.* This principle of communication, from Watzlawick and fellow researchers (1967), emphasizes the dyadic nature of communication. That is, communication unfolds through a series of messages and countermessages that contribute to the meaning people attach to a given interaction. Symmetrical communication occurs when people exchange similar relational information or similar messages. For instance, a dominant message may be met with another dominant message. (Jake says, "Help me with my homework" and Dave responds, "Do it yourself!") Or, an affectionate message may be met with another affectionate message. (Kristi's mother says, "I love you," and Kristi says, "I love you too.") Nonverbal messages can also be symmetrical, as when someone smiles at you and you smile back, or when your date gazes at you lovingly and you touch her or him gently on the arm.

Asymmetrical communication occurs when people exchange different kinds of information. One type of asymmetry arises when people exchange messages that are opposite in meaning. For example, a dominant message such as, "I need you to help me with my homework now!" might be met with a submissive message such as "Okay, I'll cancel my plans and help you." Or, Kristi's declaration of love to her soon-to-be ex-husband might be met with a guilt-ridden silence and shuffling of feet, after which he says something like, "I'm so sorry that I don't love you anymore." Another type of asymmetry occurs when one person uses more of a certain behavior than another person. For instance, imagine that Su-Lin is from an Asian culture where people generally touch less than do people from the United States. During a social gathering, a new friend of Su-Lin's might casually touch her arm five times, whereas Su-Lin might only initiate touch once. Although there is some symmetry because both Su-Lin and her new friend engage in some touch, the difference in the amount of touch each person initiates constitutes a source of asymmetry. As these examples suggest, the verbal and nonverbal messages that two people send and receive work together to create a unique pattern of communication that reflects their relationship.

PRINCIPLES OF RELATIONAL COMMUNICATION

As mentioned previously, relational communication is a subset of interpersonal communication that focuses on messages exchanged within relationships that are, were, or have the potential to become close. Thus, all of the principles of interpersonal communication apply to communication in relationships. Relational communication includes the entire range of communicative behaviors, from vital relational messages to mundane everyday interaction. Relational communication reflects the nature of a relationship at a particular time. Communication constitutes and defines relationships. In other words, communication is the substance of close relationships. Communication is dynamic. Change and contradictions are constant in relationships. Five principles of relational communication are consistent with these ideas.

Relationships Emerge Across Ongoing Interactions

Relationships form not from thin air, but across repeated interactions (Wilmot, 1995). Cappella (1998) argued that "experience and common sense tell us that relationships are formed, maintained and dissolved in interactions with partners. At the same time interactions reflect the kind of relationship that exists between the partners" (p. 325). According to Wilmot (1995), "Relational definitions emerge from recurring episodic enactments" (p. 25). In part, relationships represent collections of all the communication episodes in which two partners have engaged over time, and each episode adds new information about the relationship. In new relationships, each episode may add considerably to the definition of the relationship. Even in well-developed relationships, critical turning points such as a declaration of love, a heated argument, or an anniversary can alter the course of the relationship. The bottom line is that without communication, there is no relationship.

Relationships Contextualize Messages

In various relationships, messages have different meanings (Wilmot, 1995). For example, a frown from your partner has a different meaning than a frown from a stranger; a touch from your mom does not mean the same thing as a touch from your date; disclosure from a coworker communicates something different than disclosure from a good friend. In Wilmot's (1995) words, "Relationship definitions 'frame' or contextualize communication behavior" (p. 27). Thus, the context and relationship are critical to understanding the message. According to Andersen (1989), "It has become axiomatic that no human action can be successfully interpreted outside of its context. The term 'out of context' has become synonymous with meaningless or misleading" (p. 27). This principle reflects the idea that every message contains both a content and a relational meaning.

Communication Sends a Variety of Relational Messages

People send a variety of messages to one another about their relationships. After reviewing the literature from a range of disciplines, Burgoon and Hale (1984, 1987) outlined seven types of relational messages that people communicate to one another: (1) dominance/submission, (2) level of intimacy, (3) degree of similarity, (4) task-social orientation, (5) formality/informality, (6) degree of social composure, and (7) level of emotional arousal and activation. These messages, which have been referred to as the **fundamental relational themes** of communication, all reflect the nature of a relationship at a given point in time. Of these seven dimensions, dominance/submission and intimacy are the two main themes that characterize relationships (Burgoon et al., 1996). See Box 1.3 for further information on each of these seven themes.

BOX 1.3 Highlights

Seven Fundamental Themes of Relational Communication

1. *Dominance/submission:* Dominance is often defined as the actual degree to which a person influences someone, and submission as the actual degree to which a person gives up influence and yields to the wishes of someone else. Dominance is communicated verbally and nonverbally a variety of ways (see Chapter 12).

2. *Level of intimacy:* Intimacy is a multidimensional construct related to the degree to which people communicate affection, inclusion, trust, depth, and involvement. Intimacy is conveyed in a variety of ways, including through self-disclosure and nonverbal displays of affection and immediacy (see Chapters 5 and 6).

3. *Degree of similarity:* Similarity is achieved through a wide array of verbal cues, such as expressing similar opinions and values, agreeing with each other, reciprocating self-disclosure, and communicating empathy and understanding. Nonverbal cues such as adopting the same posture, laughing together, dressing alike, and picking up someone's accent also communicate similarity.

4. *Task-social orientations:* This message reflects how much people are focused on tasks versus having fun and socializing. People are generally rated as more task oriented when they seem sincere, reasonable, and more interested in completing the task at hand than participating in off-the-topic conversation.

5. *Formality/informality:* When an interaction is formal, people maintain their distance, and the overall tone of the interaction is serious. They are also more likely to feel and look nervous. By contrast, less distance and a more casual approach, including feeling and looking more relaxed, characterize informal interactions.

6. *Degree of social composure:* Social composure relates to the level of calmness and confidence people show in a given interaction. When people are socially composed, they appear sure of themselves. Social composure is conveyed through verbal cues such as making strong, convincing arguments and saying the appropriate words at the right time, as well as nonverbal behaviors such as direct eye contact and fluent speech.

7. *Emotional arousal and activation:* This message theme refers to the degree to which an interaction is emotionally charged. It addresses the types of emotion a person experiences and expresses, as well as how much arousal the person feels. Emotional states such as distress, anger, and sadness can sometimes impede communication, whereas emotions such as happiness, excitement, and interest can lead to more effective interpersonal communication.

The seven message themes are important within all types of interpersonal interaction, but especially in close relationships. In role relationships, relational messages stay fairly constant, with people generally following prescribed rules and scripts. For instance, in manager-employee relationships, a certain level of formality, friendliness, dominance, and task orientation usually prevails across most interactions. By contrast, in close relationships, the range and impact of relational messages typically is much greater. For example, a romantic couple might be hostile during an argument and then intimate when making up; a parent might act with an unusual level of formality and dominance during a serious talk with a child; or friends might have a hard time switching gears and moving from a conversation to a task. Such messages can have a powerful impact on how relational partners view each other and their relationship.

Relational Communication Is Dynamic

Relationships constantly change, as does relational communication. Successful relational partners—whether they are family members, friends, or lovers—learn how to adjust their communication to meet the challenges and changes that they face. For example, a parent's communication style often becomes less authoritative as a child gets older, friends learn to interact with new people in each other's social networks, and spouses may need to find new ways to show affection to each other when they are preoccupied with their children and careers. Long-distance relationships provide a great example of the dynamic nature of relational communication. Partners in long-distance relationships sometimes idealize each other, in part because they are always on their best behavior when they spend time together. When the relationship becomes proximal, however, their communication may not always be as positive, leading many couples to break up (Stafford & Merolla, 2007).

Dialectic theory also highlights the dynamic nature of relational communication by emphasizing contradictions in messages (see Chapter 9). For example, a person might say, "I can't wait to see you tomorrow night even though it's been good to get away from each other for a while." This seemingly contradictory message ("I want to be with you sometimes but not others") reflects the changing nature of the relationship. Therefore, rather than thinking of relationships as hitting a plateau or becoming completely stable, it is better to conceptualize stability as a relative concept. In other words, relationships can be committed and they can include a lot of routine communication, but they are still ever-changing entities.

Relational Communication Follows Both Linear and Nonlinear Patterns

Considerable research has examined how relationships develop over time. In fact, early research on interpersonal communication focused much more on how people begin and end relationships than on how they maintain relationships once they have developed. Some researchers believe that communication follows a linear trajectory (see Chapter 5 for more detail). This means that communication is characterized by increasing self-disclosure and nonverbal affection as a relationship gets closer. Think of this like a diagonal line going upward, with the line representing the degree of closeness that is communicated as a relationship moves from being casual to close. If the relationship is ending, the linear approach would predict that there would be a similar line going downward, meaning that closeness is communicated less and less as the relationship deescalates.

Other researchers believe that relational communication follows a nonlinear trajectory characterized by ups and downs and contradictions (see Figure 1.2 and the turning point approach discussed in Chapter 5). For example, you might show increasing levels of affection to a new romantic partner until you get into your first big fight. When the fight is over, affection might increase again to a new and even higher level. And sometimes, your communication may be affectionate and distant at the same time, as would be the case if you say, "I like you a lot, but I need some time with my friends this weekend." These types of events would not coalesce to create a nice smooth linear pattern; instead, displays of closeness would spike upward and downward at different times depending on what was being communicated.

Most relationships include communication that reflects both linear and nonlinear patterns of development. Take Su-Lin as an example. Figure 1.2 depicts the trajectory that her relationship with a new roommate might take over the first 12 months of their emerging friendship. Notice that the relationship starts out rather low in terms of self-disclosure and affection but that this type of communication increases as they get to know one another, which is

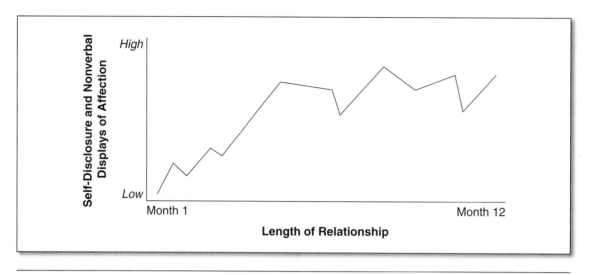

Figure 1.2   Possible Trajectory of a New Relationship

consistent with the linear approach. However, rather than consistently displaying more positive communication with each other, there are times when Su-Lin and her new roommate communicate relatively high and low levels of self-disclosure and affection. One relatively low point may occur during final exam week when they are both studying so hard that they don't talk as much to each other. A high point may occur when they have mutual friends over to their dorm room. Looking at the overall pattern of Su-Lin's relationship with her new roommate, it is clear that self-disclosure and affection have increased somewhat linearly, although there is also some nonlinearity (or up-and-down patterns) embedded within the trajectory.

Of course, relationships do not always follow the pattern depicted for Su-Lin and her roommate. Some relationships take more linear or nonlinear paths than others, but it is difficult to conceive of a relationship where all the progress is linear, or where the relationship is all peaks and valleys with no stability. Beyond self-disclosure and affection, other types of communication also follow patterns. Conflict behaviors, and any of the messages falling under the relational themes discussed previously (intimacy, formality, dominance, and so forth), can also be communicated in linear or nonlinear patterns during various points of a relationship's development. The point is that every relationship has a unique trajectory that reflects the dynamic nature of the communication that occurs between two people.

SUMMARY AND APPLICATION

This chapter introduced you to the field of personal relationships and provided information on key concepts that will be discussed throughout this book. After reading this chapter, you should have a better appreciation for the complexity of your relationships and the communication that occurs within

them. Communication does not occur in a vacuum. Rather, communication is shaped by contextual and relational factors, and communication both reflects and influences the nature of a given relationship. In the scenarios that opened this chapter, Jake's communication with Dave reflects his expectation that a good friend should help him in a time of need. Su-Lin's communication is shaped by the context of being in a new cultural environment, and Kristi's communication is embedded within a social network that includes her husband and her family.

Communication is essential for accomplishing personal and relational goals, as well as for fulfilling the basic human needs of affection, inclusion, and control. Only through communication can Jake persuade Dave to help him, and only through communication can Dave give Jake the knowledge that he needs to do well on his statistics assignment. It is through communication that Su-Lin will learn about and adapt to the U.S. culture, and it is through communication that her new friends will learn more about her and her culture. The scenario involving Kristi also highlights how communication reflects people's goals and needs—Kristi's husband used communication to inform her that he wanted a divorce; in turn Kristi searched for comfort by communicating with her mother. While the importance of communication in these scenarios and in everyday life may be obvious to you, it is amazing to think about how much we rely on communication every day in so many ways.

This book is designed to help you better understand how communication functions within your close relationships. We do not provide a blueprint or list of "rules" for how to communicate effectively in relationships. Instead, we summarize research related to significant relational communication topics in the hope that you will be able to apply the concepts and theories we discuss to your own life. As this chapter has shown, being able to communicate effectively is a key to good relationships, and having good relationships is a key to a happy life.

DISCUSSION QUESTIONS

1. What qualities distinguish your close relationships from your casual relationships?

2. In this chapter, we defined interpersonal communication as the exchange of nonverbal and verbal messages between two people, regardless of their relationship. Do you agree or disagree with this definition of interpersonal communication? What types of behavior should not count as communication?

3. As illustrated by the comparison of John Gottman and John Gray, there is a lot of popular press material on relationships that does not necessarily correspond with what academic researchers have found. Why do you think the public is so fascinated with popular books, talk shows, and magazine articles on relationships? What type of role, if any, do you think relationship researchers should play in this process?

STUDENT STUDY SITE

Visit the study site at **www.sagepub.com/guerrero3e** for e-flashcards, survey and assessments from the chapter, and SAGE journal articles.

2

Communicating Identity

The Social Self

Cindy has a page on Facebook with over 250 people on her friend list. Several of her favorite quotes are on her page, with her personal motto "carpe diem" prominently under her name. She also posted some quotes in Italian since she is proud of her ethnic background and feels a connection to her relatives who live in Rome. Her page also indicates her current relationship status, which is updated continuously. During a tough stretch with her boyfriend, her status changed to "single," which caused nearly everyone she knows to "Facebook" her. Cindy has posted over 300 pictures; most are of her partying with her friends and sorority sisters or performing in a local dance company. A few are from her trips to Italy. She also has tons of messages on her message board, or "wall," with some friends wishing her happy birthday, others making inside jokes, and yet others reminiscing about the previous night or just saying hi.

What does Cindy's Facebook page say about her? It lets others know whether she is dating or not (though the information she posts may or may not be true), gives others a sense of how popular she is (from the number of "friends" on her list), gives strangers a glimpse of who she is, and provides a peek into her personal and social life. Whether her presentation of herself is effective or not probably depends on who views her page. Cindy's page certainly speaks to her friends in important ways; through her pictures and wall, she can identify herself as a good friend to certain people. Her page communicates to classmates and potential friends; her Facebook profile can help shape their impression of her before they really get to know her. But what if potential employers, professors, or her parents look at her page? Putting our identity out there for everyone to see raises questions about appropriateness, audience analysis, and privacy. Unlike everyday interactions, social networking sites are less nimble in creating multiple identities.

Of course, the Internet is but one venue people use to present and manage their identities to others. Identity management occurs in face-to-face interaction, on the telephone, in text messages, and even in letters and gifts. Research on identity management, which has focused most often on face-to-face contexts, offers a glimpse into how people develop and maintain their perceptions of self. Identity management is particularly important at the beginning of relationships when people try to make a good initial impression, but it is even important in well-developed relationships.

In this chapter, we examine how people use communication to manage their identities in social interaction. First, we briefly discuss the development of personal identities and the role that relationships play in their development. Second, we discuss general principles of identity management, such as whether trying to make a good impression is deceptive and manipulative or is simply a natural, often unconscious process. Finally, we review literature on three perspectives on identity management, including Goffman's (1959) dramaturgical perspective, Brown and Levinson's (1987) politeness theory, and research on facework.

THE DEVELOPMENT OF PERSONAL IDENTITY

Sociologists, anthropologists, psychologists, family researchers, and communication scholars, among others, have studied how personal identities affect us throughout life. In the present era, identity is increasingly important. Today people are concerned about many aspects of their identity: popularity, education, relational partners, cars, homes, income, bodies, facial attractiveness, clothing styles, sororities, occupations, health, mental well-being, and happiness. The list is a long one. But identity is more than just a personal experience; it is inherently social, communicative, and relational. Our identity is inextricably interwoven with the messages—verbal and nonverbal—we send about ourselves and how other people respond to them.

Defining Identity

We define **identity** as the person we think we are and communicate to others. More specifically, it is the personal "theory of self that is formed and maintained through actual or imagined interpersonal agreement about what self is like" (Schlenker, 1985, p. 67).

Identity is the sense of self or the "I"; this has been a central topic in psychology and other disciplines over the years (Brown, 1965; Deikman, 1973). Identity is the self, the face, the ego, the image we present to others in everyday life. Recent research suggests that identity is composed of self-esteem, continuity, distinctiveness, and meaning (Vignoles, Regalia, Manzi, Golledge, & Scabini, 2006).

Human Nature and Identity

Human beings are conscious creatures who can reflect on who they are and how they fit into the greater social fabric. Indeed, a universal quality of all human beings regardless of culture is a sense of self as being distinct from others (Brown, 1991). Thus, a sense of identity is a genetic legacy of our species that becomes increasing focused as we develop. Of course, our identities are largely shaped by culture and communication, but our essence as humans includes an individual identity.

Communication and Identity

In large part, our identity is formed in interactions with other people. No force is as powerful in shaping identify as the feedback we get from other people and the self-image we form from observing ourselves behave and interact. In short, "A person's identity is forged, expressed, maintained, and modified in the crucible of social life, as its contents undergo the continual process of actual or imagined observation, judgment, and reaction by audiences (oneself and other)" (Schlenker, 1985, p. 68). The way we see ourselves is shaped by our interactions with other people, the image we seek to project, our anticipated interactions, and the way they respond to and judge us. But how do we come to think of ourselves?

Social identity theory provides an explanation for how our identities are developed and how we maintain our self-view. Identity does not develop in a vacuum. It unavoidably links to our membership in social groups as broad as our ethnic, sexual, or religious affiliation or as narrow as small cliques—for example, Italian American, bisexual, Catholic, alumnus of West High School, a resident of the

Bronx, a softball player, and a member of "the big four" (a group of childhood friends). Based on Cindy's Facebook page, for instance, you would probably associate her with at least two key groups— her sorority and her dance company. A key principle of social identity theory is that membership is characterized by in-group behaviors that signal membership and define someone as being a part of a group or as an outsider (see Hogg & Abrams, 1988) and accordingly, promote differential behavior toward that person. Group members may dress a certain way, get similar tattoos, talk with an accent, use particular gestures, play the same sports, or have conversational routines that identify themselves as belonging to the group. In order to maintain positive views of ourselves, we often think of "our" groups as better than other groups. It is common to think that our way of doing things is the best, what we wear looks the best, what we say is the smartest, our view of the world is most reasonable, our perspective on a conflict is a sensible one, our values are most connected to God, our beliefs are correct, and so forth.

Several factors influence the impact a group has on our identity, including how central the group is to our self-view (see Oakes, 1987). So, for example, an ethnic group association may be important for someone like Cindy, who has visited relatives in Rome, but unimportant to those who have little connection to their ethnic roots. Several studies have also shown that minority groups are especially likely to identify with their ethnic backgrounds. African Americans or Latinos, for example, see their ethnicity as more central to their identity than do Caucasians (see Jackson, 1999). In fact, people in minority groups are typically more aware of their membership in that group than are majority members. Why is that? Everyday events remind them of their minority status. Think about this: How many black mannequins have you seen in clothing stores? Even if you visit stores in an African American neighborhood, the answer is likely to be "none." Because clothes look different on dark skin than on white skin, African Americans have to imagine how that piece of clothing would look on them.

Think about the examples in your exams and textbooks: How many of them describe the lives of

individuals with a homosexual orientation? Probably very few. Despite our efforts to be inclusive of all sexual orientations in this book, research on gay relationships is not abundant, so gay or lesbian students cannot always relate to examples of heterosexual relationships. In all these cases, group identity is more salient to minority group members because the lives of minority group members are surrounded by reminders that they don't "fit" into the majority group's way of thinking or doing.

To clarify how identities and personal identities are merged, Hecht (1993) introduced the **communication theory of identity**. He argued that identity construction can be viewed through four "frames of identity" or "lenses" (see also Hecht, Collier, & Ribeau, 1993; Hecht, Warren, Jung, & Krieger, 2004). First, identity is viewed through a **personal** frame. In this sense, identity is an image we construct within ourselves: We perceive ourselves to posses certain characteristics and not others. Second, identity can be viewed through an **enactment of communication frame**. Identities develop through communication with others; not all communication messages are designed to create our identity, but identity is a part of all messages. Third, identity can be viewed through a **relationship frame** developed through communication over time that defines ourselves in terms of relationships with other people. For example, your identity might be shaped by the kind of friend, romantic partner, and son or daughter you are. Moreover, you might act and feel differently about yourself depending on whether you are with your best friend, a first date, your spouse, or your parents. Finally, identity can be viewed through a **communal frame**. Identities are partly a function of the groups to which we belong and they often are constrained by our cultural or group identities, and these identities teach us rules regarding the "right" way to behave. These rules become so ingrained that they necessarily affect our identities. "Indeed culture is so basic, learned at such a tender age, and so taken-for-granted that it is often confused with human nature itself" (Andersen, 2000, p. 258). Something as deep as ethnicity or culture cannot be easily manipulated.

These four frames work together to affect identity development (Hecht, 1993). Recent research has discovered identity gaps both between conflicting frames of identity such as personal and relational frames (Jung & Hecht, 2004) and between different roles within a given frame, such as between a wife and a granddaughter (Kam & Hecht, 2009). All couples routinely deal with identity issues, but interracial or intercultural couples often face special challenges (Williams & Andersen, 1998). They must each deal with who they are as individuals, for example, as a white man and an African American woman (personal frame). They must also deal with how they present themselves to others (enactment frame), what it means to be an interracial couple (relationship frame), and how to best blend their different cultural backgrounds (communal frame). Scholars are increasingly aware of these identity-related challenges in interracial or interethnic relationships. Studies have shown that the difficulties they face may include differences in language, conflict styles, communication preferences, and sexual scripts, as well as pressure from family and friends to dissolve the relationship (see Gaines & Liu, 2000; Williams & Andersen, 1998). In the past, most U.S. states banned interracial marriages, with Alabama most recently removing that law in 2000 (Hartill, 2001). As a result of ethnic norms and of the societal pressures confronting them, U.S. Census data show that interethnic couples in the United States are more likely than same-ethnicity couples to get divorced (Bramlett & Mosher, 2002). On the other hand, most research finds very few differences in the quality of inter- and intraracial couples and emphasizes that the differences within an interracial couple, if managed, may help the bond grow between partners in such relationships (Troy, Lewis-Smith, & Laurenceau, 2006).

Cultural and Ethnic Identity

As the prior discussion indicates, culture and ethnicity are central to our core views of ourselves. Most people, but especially people from minority groups, have some sense of ethnic identity, for example, African Americans, Asian Americans, or Latin Americans. Some identities relate to a specific country such as Mexican Americans, Swedish Americans, Chinese Americans, Italian Americans, or Filipino Americans. Groups sometimes identify

with the concept of race or color and describe themselves as black, brown, or white (Orbe & Drummond, 2009). "Whiteness," of course, does not literally exist and is a cultural construction of many groups who have tended to be more or less privileged in American society (Lipsitz, 2006); it is also really only a function of how far one's ancestors lived away from the equator, as lighter skin was necessary in northern Europe for greater vitamin D absorption (Jablonsky & Chaplin, 2000). But since most voluntary immigrants to the United States during its first two hundred years were "white," it became part of the identity of many Americans and even a term used by the Census Bureau, despite the fact that most "white people" choose American as their primary identity (Orbe & Drummond, 2009). A more accurate term is *European American*, but most European Americans use the terms *white* or *Caucasian*, if they have any racial identity at all (Martin, Krizek, Nakayama, & Bradford, 1996).

Terms are complex and there is almost always controversy over the correct term: Hispanic versus Latina(o) versus Latin American; or black versus Afro-American versus African American (Orbe & Drummond, 2009). The safest and most sensitive move in communication is to use the term that people themselves use in establishing their identity. As the United States has become more diverse, people increasingly have become multicultural and identify with two or more groups. Even the U.S. Census Bureau has begun to permit designation of multiple racial categories on the census form.

The Image: Creating an Identity

We are known by our image. Few people know the real us, but they know us by the image we project. Few of us get to peek behind the curtain and learn if the image we see is the real deal. From a communication perspective, images constitute reality, a concept not lost on advertisers, sports figures, celebrities, and even the general public. Today many people employ makeup, nose jobs, workouts, plastic surgery, cars, and homes to enhance their physical image. And, in our busy and web-based world, we often do not get to learn much more about people than what they look like, what they wear, and what they drive.

Sports figures such as quarterback Peyton Manning, forward Lebron James, and shortstop Derek Jeter have become idols who exceed their prodigious athletic accomplishments. They have turned themselves into icons that transcend reality. Their pictures are on television, magazines, in airports, and on the Internet. They rise above their human status into symbols of success and credibility, so long as they can avoid scandal, slumps, or debilitating injuries that shatter the façade they and their agents have created. Our political leaders are no different. As Andersen (2004) stated:

> Neither President Bill Clinton nor President George Bush ever saw military combat, but as commanders in chief they frequently appeared with troops in flight jackets and military uniforms. An image of a president supporting the troops, saluting the flag, or dressed in a military uniform communicates patriotism and exudes leadership. (pp. 255–256)

These images trigger involuntary reactions in people, often called *heuristics* or what Cialdini (1984) calls our "heart of hearts," automatic processes that circumvent criticism and analysis.

"Talkin' 'Bout Your Generation": Millennial Identity in the Twenteens

College students today are mostly *millennials*, sometimes also called *generation Y* (because they followed generation X) or *echo boomers* (because they are the sons and daughters of baby boomers—people born in the late '40s and '50s). Research suggests that since the mid-20th century, people have become increasingly preoccupied with their identities. In fact, America in the 1960s and 1970s became so preoccupied with image and artifice that Herzog (1974) wrote *The B.S. Factor: The Theory and Technique of Faking It in America*, and so self-absorbed that Lasch (1979) wrote *The Culture of Narcissism: American Life in an Age of Diminishing Expectations*. Both books were echoed in the media with Jackson Browne singing: "It's who you look like, not who you are" in his 1978 song, "The Load Out," and a dozen years later with Andre Agassi's series of Cannon Rebel camera commercials themed, "Image is everything," displaying a buffed body and long hair for the public. Recently, Agassi (2009) revealed that his hair was indeed all image; he was going bald his and his long hair was a wig. The popular culture had thus discovered what communication researchers already knew: *Perceptions are reality.* If you can manipulate other peoples' perceptions, you can seem credible, cool, attractive, rich, whatever—even if you're not.

To help illustrate that anything worth doing is worth overdoing, research shows that the current generation of millennials, who are in their late teens or 20s, are more self-absorbed, self-centered, confident, entitled, and narcissistic than even their parents (Twenge, 2006; Twenge & Campbell, 2009). In *Generation Me,* Twenge (2006) makes the case that millennials are more hedonistic, image conscious, sexually active, and unlike their parents were in the '60s and '70s, the millennials take these qualities for granted. She argues that they are the most entitled generation and yet the most miserable generation, presenting good over-time data to make the case.

In *The Narcissism Epidemic: Living in the Age of Entitlement,* Twenge and Campbell (2009) show data documenting a 30-year trend of increasing narcissism, hedonism, and entitlement. She makes the case that MySpace and Facebook perfectly match the needs of the millennial generation by working as a feedback loop to both satisfy and amplify these narcissistic qualities. While a lot of Web 2.0 interaction is beneficial—linking up friends, staying in touch, posting photos—the dark side is the excessive attention seeking, including profanity, nudity, manipulated images, building large friends' collections to boost egos, and seeking endless popularity. In *Generation MySpace,* Kelsey (2007) summarizes four principles that young people soak up from Web 2.0, which are paraphrased as follows:

- *Entertainment rules!* Life is about video games and social networking.
- *If you've got it, flaunt it.* Modesty is uncool; privacy is lame; and sexuality, materialism, and attractiveness are the paths to success.
- *Happiness is a glamorous adult.* Fame is the ultimate goal, or at least looking like a rock or screen star is imperative.
- *Happiness is about consumption.* Materialism and sex are the ultimate goals in adulthood.

This is not to diminish the positives of the millennial generation; they are tech savvy, can access information like no other generation, and are connected to their peers like no other group; street crime is down, and they are ready for the information age. Nonetheless, as Twenge (2009) maintains, MySpace, Facebook, and YouTube are burgeoning and online narcissists dream with manipulated images, easy access to new images, and a culture based on beauty, partying, and materialism. Like Cindy, who we introduced at the beginning of the chapter, life is all about her and she has "friended" 250 people and posted hundreds of pictures to prove it. Research also suggests that style has become so important in youth culture, that while "style failure" can have major social costs, the constant updating of designer clothes is also extracting huge economic costs on this generation of young people (Croghan, Griffin, Hunter, & Phoenix, 2006).

Like generations, age groups and life stages are important aspects of a person's identity. Each stage of life carries with it a new identity that one can accept or resist. Small children often state insistently, "I'm a big boy (girl)!" *Teens, young adults, adults, people of middle age,* and *senior citizens* are terms commonly used to designate membership of self or other in a particular group. Likewise, our relationship to others establishes our comparative identities; for example, grandparent-grandchild is an important but relative part of our interpersonal identity (Kam & Hecht, 2009; Williams & Nussbaum, 2001). The fact that we may be an adult, a woman, a lawyer, a wife, and a granddaughter may create discrepant roles that sometimes produce dissatisfying identities and identity gaps (Kam & Hecht, 2009). Identity gaps can catch us between roles that are disconcerting and disorienting.

Identity, Perception, and Self-Esteem

Our identities help us understand ourselves in relation to the world in which we live. Self-esteem and identity are part of a person's **theory of self**, or **vision of self**. Self-esteem refers to how positively or negatively we view ourselves. People with high self-esteem generally view their traits and behaviors in a positive light, while people with low self-esteem

mostly see their traits as negative. Identity defines who we are and what we are like (see Schlenker, 1985; Vignoles et al., 2006) by specifying the characteristics that define us (African American, student, smart, heterosexual, attractive, introvert) and comparing ourselves to others (smarter than John, not as smart as Haley). Unlike self-esteem, however, one's identity is not only evaluative; it is basically a perception of oneself as a person. For example, both Cindy and her friend Lindsay may see themselves as partiers who like to have fun. However, Cindy may think that partying is a cool aspect of her personality, while Lindsay may be depressed because she realizes that partying is interfering with her success in school yet she can't seem to stop going out every night. Thus, while partying is a part of each of their identities, it could contribute to high self-esteem for Cindy and to low self-esteem for Lindsay. The focus of this chapter is on identity and identity management rather than self-esteem, despite their influences on one another.

Expanding Identity

One theory in particular seems especially well suited to explain the benefits of relationships. Specifically, A. Aron and E. N. Aron's (1986, 1996) **self-expansion theory** helps explain how identity influences the development of close relationships after first impressions are made. Self-expansion theory is framed around three primary predictions. First, people seek to expand the self, to be more than they are. Studies completed by E. N. Aron and A. Aron (1996) have shown that a fundamental human desire is to broaden our experiences and extend our identities. We do not seem satisfied with a static sense of self. Instead, we seek to develop our sense of self as part of our physical, cognitive, and emotional development. For example, if you are good at oil painting, you might try other kinds of art, such as ceramics or watercolors. If you like reading or television, you may search for new types of books or shows you have not seen previously.

Second, one reason people enter into relationships is the opportunity to expand their identities. An excellent way to expand the self is by becoming close to someone who contributes to our identity development by exposing us to new experiences. Aron, Aron, and Smollan (1992) found that the more partners defined their relationship as a meshing of both identities, the closer they were likely to be. Figure 2.1 shows the inclusion-of-others-in-self scale that these authors have used in their studies. Research consistently finds that an expansion of self through inclusion of others characterizes close relationships. In a recent study where couples were randomly called over a week's time, the more activating and expanding a couple's activities were at the time of the call, the greater the relational satisfaction and quality (Graham, 2008), suggesting that the effects of self-expansion are continuously being experienced. Finally, relationship interventions designed to mindfully seek new and exciting possibilities with one's partner can dramatically improve relationships (Carson, Carson, Gil, & Baucom, 2007).

Rather than having two completely separate identities, people in close relationships tend to merge identities, allowing each partner's identity to expand through new experiences. In a novel test of this prediction, Aron, Paris, and Aron (1995) over a 10-week period asked students to list as many self-descriptive words or phrases that came to mind in response to the question, "Who are you today?" and answered questions about whether they had fallen in love during the task. Consistent with the theory's prediction, those who reported falling in love during the task showed a marked increase in the number of self-definitions they could list, an indication that their identity had expanded. Likewise, consistent with the theory, a breakup of a self-expansive relationship leads to a significant contraction of one's working self-concept and a detrimental impact to one's own identity (Lewandowski, Aron, Bassis, & Kunak, 2006).

Self-expansion theory does not suggest that in strong relationships partners are completely intertwined. The theory emphasizes the importance of self in relationships. Losing one's sense of self or one's individual identity in favor of a relational identity is not what the theory would predict as a "healthy" relationship outcome. Instead, the theory predicts that close relationships are those in which both individuals have strong self-identities that can grow from the new experiences that each partner's identity brings.

Third, a relationship's success depends on the ability of the relationship to expand the partners' experiences and sense of self. A common phenomenon in many relationships is stagnation; that is, over time, the relationship gets bogged down by routine, which decreases satisfaction for both partners. Self-expansion theory offers an interesting explanation and remedy for this common problem. Specifically, A. Aron and E. N. Aron (1986, 1996) argued that relationships stag-

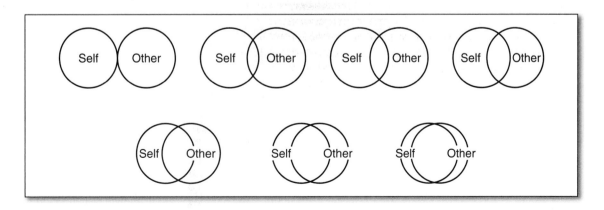

Figure 2.1 The Inclusion-of-Others-in-Self Scale: Which Drawing Best Describes Your Relationship?

SOURCE: Copyright © American Psychological Association.

nate when they stop serving a self-expansion function. The remedy for stagnation is for partners to continuously help one another find new and exciting experiences that can be incorporated in their experiences. Research suggests that infidelity is often associated with insufficient self-expansion with one's primary partner, so need fulfillment and self-expansion is pursued in an alternate relationship (Lewandowski & Ackerman, 2006). Self-expansion theory also has been fruitful in understanding people's connections to their communities, neighborhoods, and to their social networks (Mashek, Cannady, & Tangney, 2007). This theory, to our knowledge, has not been applied to interracial relationships, though its premises seem especially well suited for the identity-expansion opportunities found there.

Of course, ethnicity is but one aspect of identity that challenges relational partners. Sexual identities hold an important position in individuals' sense of self in relationships. Think about how we manage public displays of our sexuality or sexual orientation. These expressions, including how we initiate relationships with prospective partners, whether we hold hands in public, or if we are comfortable with intimate displays of public affection, are public messages about our relational identity. Such displays are more benign for heterosexual couples since that sexual orientation is more normative. The decisions to initiate a relationship, hold hands, or display public intimacy are far more significant identity issues for gay or lesbian couples.

The double trouble of identity in interracial, gay couples was studied by Steinbugler (2005) who interviewed eight black-white couples, four of which were heterosexual, two were gay, and two were lesbian. Her results offer a fascinating glimpse into the ways in which people manage these diverse identities. One of her participants (a 28-year-old black, gay male dating a white male) reflected on the couple's behavior this way:

> We have a lot of PDA [public displays of affection] but not overt, not loud PDA. It's very quiet. For example . . . we'll walk and one of us will rub the other on the back. Or if we hold hands it's sort of brief, very brief. (p. 435)

He continued by noting that he felt more comfortable with these expressions when he knows "for a fact that there are other gay people around." His words emphasize the public nature of our identities and suggest that his sexual orientation occupies a more central position in his construction of self than his ethnicity, at least in the context of his public interactions with his boyfriend.

PRINCIPLES OF IDENTITY MANAGEMENT

Identity affects how we perceive ourselves, how others perceive us, how we behave, and how we evaluate our behavior and relationships. Six principles provide a summary of this research.

Identity and Hierarchical Structure

The first principle is that *our identities provide us with a hierarchical structure of who we are.* Although we define ourselves in myriad ways, our identity helps organize these various facets into a hierarchical structure that fluctuates according to context (Schlenker, 1985). Our identity includes our relationships (boyfriend, friend, son); roles (student, basketball player, law clerk); goals (live in Europe, get a job helping others); personal qualities (friendly, honest); accomplishments (3.5 GPA, organization president); group or cultural membership (sorority member, Asian); and appearance (moderately attractive, wears Abercrombie clothes). These facets of our identity vary in the degree to which they centrally define who we are. The more central they are to our definition of self, the more stable they are across our lifetime and prominent when we present ourselves to others during interaction. Think back to Cindy and her Facebook page. Although its content gives visitors a good sense of Cindy's identity structure, Cindy is probably only displaying part of her identity when she edits that page. Thus, people who frequent her page might have biased impressions about Cindy. For example, they might think that Cindy cares for her friends more than her family, when actually the reverse is true.

Identity and the Looking-Glass Self

The second principle is that *the feedback we receive from others helps shape our identities.* Charles Horton Cooley (1922) first developed the notion of the looking-glass self, a metaphor that described his belief that identity is shaped by feedback from others. He argued that social audiences provide us with an image of ourselves like the one we see when we look into a mirror. The way people treat us is reflected in the way we see ourselves. For example, think of how you came to believe that you were smart enough to pursue a college degree. Your identity as an intelligent person was cultivated through interactions with parents, teachers, or peers. Perhaps a specific teacher in high school said you were smart enough to go to college, or your parents gave you positive feedback and encouragement, or a friend kept complimenting you on your ability to learn quickly. Regardless of the source, one or more of these people likely helped develop that aspect of your identity. Many parts of our identities are similarly formed through our interactions with significant others.

Identity and the Interpretation of Feedback

The third principle is that *our identities help us interpret feedback from others.* Just as people's feedback affects our identities, our identities affect how we perceive others' feedback (Schlenker, 1980). For example, people like Cindy who see themselves as extroverts react differently than those who define themselves as introverts when someone says to them, "You're awfully quiet today." The emotions they experience and perceptions of what the statement means, as well as what it says about the sender of the message—and the intent—are

SOURCE: © Karen Struthers./Istockphoto.com.

The concept of the looking-glass self specifies that our identities are shaped by how others see us. Do you think the image you have of yourself matches what others see?

influenced by their identity as an introvert or extrovert, to say nothing of other aspects of their theory of self.

Research also suggests that we are likely to interpret feedback from others as consistent with our identity (Swann, 1983; Swann & Read, 1981). For example, people who consider themselves attractive may interpret someone's negative comment about their appearance as an expression of envy rather than a true reflection of their attractiveness. An unattractive person may interpret that statement as consistent with a negative self-image. Moreover, we are generally more likely to remember information that is consistent with our identity and to discount information that is inconsistent (Kahneman, Slovic, & Tvesky, 1982). However, some research suggests that this tendency applies only to those aspects of our identity that are central to our definition of self and for which we have strongly held beliefs (Stangor & Ruble, 1989). For less central aspects of self, inconsistent information is more easily assimilated. For example, a 21-year-old who is still adopting an identity as someone who enjoys drinking on weekends, may struggle mightily when a friend says that she thinks people who drink are irresponsible. This feedback may influence his identity development and his relationship with her. However, if the negative feedback comes after drinking has become a stable aspect of the person's identity, it is less likely to affect his identity, though quite likely to affect his relationship with her.

Identity, Expectations, and Behavior

The fourth principle specifies that *identity incorporates expectations and guides behavior.* The central characteristics that we see ourselves possessing create social expectations for our behavior (Schlenker, 1985) and self-fulfilling prophecies (Merton, 1948). These expectations strongly influence how we act (Bandura, 1986). As such, our identity carries with it expectations for how people with that identity typically behave. To live up to that identity means to behave in a certain manner. For example, if a person's identity includes being a good student, the individual must behave in ways that reflect that characteristic or the identity will not

be maintained. Such individuals are likely to study harder and to attend classes more regularly than those who see themselves as average or poor students. If a person's identity includes being an excellent athlete, the individual's daily workouts become central to that identity. Notice that these behaviors set up a self-fulfilling prophecy because people who study and attend class more are likely to get better grades and people who work out more are better athletes. A **self-fulfilling prophecy** occurs when an expectation exists that something will happen, and a person behaves in a way (often unconsciously) that actually makes it more likely that the anticipated event will occur. In any case, the maintenance of our identity requires us to behave in an identity-consistent manner.

Identity and Self-Evaluation

The fifth principle is that *identity influences our evaluations of self.* The expectations and behavioral guidelines connected to identity provide people with comparison points against which to judge their performance (Schlenker, 1985; Vignoles et al., 2006). As a result, our identity influences our evaluation of how well or poorly we performed. For example, good students are likely to get upset if they receive a C on an exam or a paper, whereas those who see themselves as poor students might be delighted to receive a C. Interestingly, self-esteem and identity may be most closely connected through this expectation-evaluation link. Unrealistically flattering self-definitions lead to expectations of self that are unlikely to be met, which leads to a string of perceived failures. As a result, self-esteem can suffer.

Identity and Goal Achievement

The sixth principle is that *identity influences the likelihood of goal achievement.* Achieving goals is facilitated by the presence of qualities that are consistent with that particular goal. Thus, people who see themselves as good students are likely to get better grades because they see studying and attending class as important behaviors to help maintain their identities. The same type of process influences goal achievement in our relationships. For example, the likelihood that Bill will achieve his goal of dating Jeff depends on the extent to which Bill believes he possesses characteristics desired by or appealing to Jeff. If an important aspect of Bill's identity is his sensitivity and Jeff prefers to date a partner who is macho, Bill may feel he has little hope of attracting Jeff. Self-fulfilling prophecies also relate to goal achievement. For instance, if Cindy believes that she can become a dancer on Broadway, she is likely to have confidence, be more motivated, and perhaps work harder, all of which will make it easier to achieve her goal.

Identity and Relationships

The final principle is that *our identities influence what social relationships we choose to pursue and maintain.* Robinson and Smith-Lovin (1992) found that people prefer interactions with individuals who provide identity-consistent feedback, even if such feedback is emotionally hurtful. In short, those who define themselves in negative terms, such as unintelligent, unconsciously seek partners who confirm that negative identity. Why is this the case? People distrust feedback inconsistent with what they believe, so they perceive those who offer contrary feedback as dishonest (Swann, Griffin, Predmore, & Gaines, 1987). The consequences of this tendency are serious, especially for abused women, who may unconsciously find themselves attracted to individuals with the same characteristics as those who abused them in the past.

Identity-consistent behavior may be particularly important in established relationships. Swann, De La Ronde, and Hixon (1994) investigated whether our preference for "authentic" feedback (feedback consistent with our identity) or "positive" feedback (feedback that is more favorable than our view of self) changes across relationship stages. They asked partners in dating relationships and marriages about their self-identity, their partner's assessment of their identity, and the level of relationship intimacy. Their results showed that a shift occurs between dating relationships and marriages. Although intimacy was highest in dating relationships when a partner's feedback to the individual was more positive than the individual's self-image, the most intimate marriages were those

in which "authenticity" prevailed—that is, in which the partner's view of the individual matched the individual's own view of self. It seems that we want others to view us through rose-colored glasses while dating but that successful marriages are those in which the partners view each other more authentically.

In sum, how we view ourselves plays a critical role in what interactions we select, what relationships we pursue, and how these interactions and relationship develop. Thus far, however, we have not addressed how we communicate our identity to others, how we manage to maintain our identity despite threats to its validity, and what social rules are in place to help us navigate the pitfalls of identity management. The next section focuses on communication and how identity management influences our behavior across a variety of situations.

COMMUNICATING IDENTITY TO OTHERS

> *Antonio: I hold the world but as the world, Gratiano; A stage where every man must play a part, And mine a sad one.*
>
> *Gratiano: Let me play the fool. . . .*
>
> —William Shakespeare, *The Merchant of Venice,* Act I, Scene I

Shakespeare's writing popularized the notion that "all the world's a stage" upon which we are merely actors. Scholars have also widely embraced this concept when describing the process of identity management (see Tracy, 1990). To better understand how people use communication to present themselves in a positive light, research and theory relates to three general perspectives: (1) self-presentation, (2) Goffman's (1959, 1967, 1971) dramaturgical approach (the approach most closely aligned with Shakespeare's famous reference to people as actors on a stage), and (3) Brown and Levinson's (1987) politeness theory, including preventive and corrective facework. In general, our efforts at **self-presentation** reflect the things we do to portray a particular image of self to others (e.g., I'm a rebel, I'm smart, I'm helpless, I'm creative), while the latter two approaches involve activities more generally ingrained as part of everyday interaction (e.g., politeness, image maintenance, image repair). Obviously, these perspectives share more similarities than differences since they all deal with ways in which our behavior manages identity needs.

General Issues in Self-Presentation

On any given day, chances are that you present an image of yourself to others; you try to portray a certain impression of yourself to your boss, your parents, your teacher, or your romantic partner. Doing so requires managing your behavior to hide or minimize potential faults while maximizing strengths. Here is where Cindy's Facebook page is especially relevant. The image she presents to her friends (i.e., partier) is likely quite different from the image she wants displayed to prospective employers when she interviews for jobs. In fact, Cindy may be worried or embarrassed to learn that someone who was considering hiring her looked her up on the web. Some people wonder if impression management is hypocritical, manipulative, and deceptive; reflects communication competence; or simply represents the way people unconsciously present themselves to others. Summarized as follows is what research has to say about these questions.

Is self-presentation
hypocritical, manipulative, or deceptive?

When discussing self-presentation in class, we typically find that a majority of students think, at first, that self-presentation is the height of hypocrisy, evidence of insecurity, tantamount to being phony, or downright deceptive. Many students are uncomfortable with the notion that we are chameleon-like in our behavior, changing according to the audience and situation. Are we not trying to deceive people into thinking we are something or someone we are not? The answer is sometimes but not usually. Most instances of self-presentation are merely a matter of highlighting certain *aspects* of ourselves for different audiences. We may possess

elements of intelligence, sociability, respect, crassness, career orientation, and laziness in our identity, but we segregate these elements when communicating to various audiences. This segregation is not usually deceptive because those characteristics are all real aspects of ourselves. For example, Cindy may display her social side to her friends and her serious side to teachers and employers. Her family might see both these sides of Cindy's personality.

Of course, people do fabricate identities. Indeed, the news is full of people leading double lives, faking their resumes, or posing as someone or something they are not in Internet chat rooms. Computer mediated communication provides increased opportunity to fabricate our identity. Research has shown that such fabrications have various intentions (Caspi & Gorsky, 2006; Toma, Hancock, & Ellison, 2008; Utz, 2005). Younger, more frequent users, who are computer competent, are more likely to engage in online deception (Caspi & Gorsky, 2006). Attractiveness deception is a ubiquitous form of online identity enhancement, and usually fairly small to its degree (Toma et al., 2008), yet common on Facebook and MySpace. Gender switching is associated with role exploration but is also sometimes used by sexual predators. Some people try to conceal their online identity, which is usually motivated by concern over privacy in the online world (Caspi & Gorsky, 2006; Utz, 2005).

All of us employ less extreme examples of identity manipulation. Have you ever pretended you understood someone, hidden your anger or sorrow from others and "put on a happy face," feigned interest in a boring conversation, or acted as if you liked someone you actually disliked? These are called **display rules** (Andersen, 2008) and are part of face maintenance. Recently, communication researchers have begun to investigate the consequences of a similar construct, termed **emotional labor**, where people must display a certain attitude or set of emotions at work (Tracy, 2005; Tracy & Trethewey, 2005). We act these ways for a variety of reasons, but all involve a belief in the importance of self-presentation. We may not want people to know that we are angry or sad because we want to maintain our composure, we may have an occupation requiring a certain demeanor, we may not show boredom because that would be disrespectful, and we may not express our dislike because that would disrupt group dynamics.

Attempts to manage impressions in the hope of advancing a desirable image of ourselves can sometimes backfire. First, it is stressful to display an inauthentic identity or emotion (Tracy, 2005). Also, a key element of a successful performance is that it is perceived as sincere (Goffman, 1959) and as a true reflection of one's personality. Cases in which individuals are caught lying in order to manage their identity actually damage their identity. Research has shown that when deception is detected it produces detrimental personal and relational consequences (Buller & Burgoon, 1994; O'Hair & Cody, 1994; see also Chapter 13). Indeed, honesty is an important impression that we want to foster in others because it goes to the core of our identity. Being perceived as inauthentic will likely put in doubt the sincerity of all other positive qualities that we have successfully portrayed and that accurately reflect who we are.

Exaggerating the truth or putting too much effort into self-presentation can produce negative outcomes as well. For example, research on narcissism (self-focusing behavior) has shown that boastful individuals are rated as less socially attractive and less liked than less self-promoting people (Vangelisti, Knapp, & Daly, 1990). Behaviors meant to bolster one's image in the eye of an audience can fail if the person is perceived as selfish or insincere. Schlenker (1980, 1984, 1985) discussed a dilemma that people often face of having to choose between presenting the best possible image of self and presenting a plausible or realistic image. Jones and Wortman (1973) used an example of a first date to show how such dilemmas affect our behavioral choices. When people on a first date describe their positive qualities and accomplishments, they can come across as conceited and unattractive. But, if they neglect to mention these qualities and accomplishments, they may be perceived as closed or uninvolved. This is also the case in online dating. One study found that online daters had to maintain a balance between impression management and authenticity (Ellison, Heino, & Gibb, 2006) by attempting to present a real but ideal self. The ideal self-presentation strikes a balance between positivity and plausibility.

How is self-presentation related to communication competence?

According to researchers who study communication competence, people who are socially skilled have a knack for engaging in behavior that is both polite and situationally appropriate (Spitzberg & Cupach, 1988). Competent communicators also usually have more successful lives and relationships. For example, you would probably not have many friends if you acted as formally with them as you would during a job interview. Similarly, you would probably not be hired if you acted like you do at a party, when meeting a prospective employer. Among friends we act relaxed, discuss social activities, get a little crazy, and often trade stories about humorous events. We want to display a persona that contributes to the group's fun and is a good, interesting person. During the job interview, we want to emphasize very different aspects of ourselves—as a reliable colleague, a smart person, and someone who can contribute to the company's development. If we switch gears this way, does this mean that we are phonies? No. It means we understand that we must fulfill different roles for different audiences, just as they do for us. Role flexibility can help us be more effective communicators, as long as we are not manipulating others for nefarious purposes.

Even among friends we may display various aspects of ourselves. We are more likely to present an overly favorable impression of ourselves to strangers than to friends. We assume that strangers do not know much about us, so the importance of disclosing favorable information about ourselves is relatively high. By contrast, our friends probably already know of our accomplishments, so pointing them out again would likely be perceived as conceited, thus backfiring; also, close friends can recognize realistic from unrealistic stories, while strangers may be unable to make such a distinction. Tice, Butler, Muraven, and Stillwell (1995) conducted five studies that compared the differences in people's self-presentations to friends and to strangers. They concluded that "people habitually use different self-presentation strategies with different audiences, relying on favorable self-enhancement with strangers but shifting toward modesty when among friends" (Tice et al., 1995, p. 1120). Indeed, one of the charms of very close friends is that we can present the most authentic self.

Several studies show that we vary the impression that we want to project based on the relationship or situation. For example, Daly, Hoggs, Sacks, Smith, and Zimring (1983) observed restroom behavior of men and women in restaurants and bars. They recorded the amount of time that people spent preening (adjusting their clothes, straightening their hair, looking in the mirror) and recorded the relationship with the person with whom they attended the establishment. Not surprisingly, they found that those who spent the most time managing their appearance were in the newest relationships. Research on **affinity-seeking behavior**, actions designed to attract others, discovered numerous impression management activities that we do early in relationships to increase our partner's attraction to us (Daly & Kreiser, 1994). These include attending to how we look, appearing interested in what the person has to say, emphasizing similarities, and portraying an image as a "fun" person. In sum, the way people present themselves to others is flexible and dynamic, with people managing their behavior differently depending on the relationships and the audience so as to maximize positive impressions and social competence.

To what extent is self-presentation a deliberate, conscious activity?

Self-presentation is so commonplace that it often becomes routine, habitual behavior that is encoded unconsciously. DePaulo (1992) offered several examples of habitual impression management behavior, including postural etiquette that girls learn as they are growing up and the ritualistic smiles given by the first runner-up at beauty pageants. Other examples include the ritualistic exchange of "thank you" and "you're welcome," table manners, classroom etiquette, and the myriad taken-for-granted politeness strategies. These behaviors were probably enacted deliberately and consciously at one time but

have since become habitual, automatic aspects of interaction.

At times, however, even habitual behaviors become more deliberate. When we especially want to make a good impression or expect difficulty in achieving our desired impression, our self-presentations are more planned and controlled (Leary & Kowalski, 1990; Schlenker, 1985). For example, when you first meet the parents of your girl- or boyfriend, you will probably be more aware than usual of your posture, politeness, and other normally habitual impression management behaviors. Your deliberateness in enacting these behaviors may be further heightened if your partner's parents do not approve of the relationship or you expect resistance from them. In sum, in certain circumstances, we are deliberate and conscious using impression management tactics—for example, on first dates, at the dean's office, or in an interview—but most of our self-presentational strategies are relatively habitual and performed unconsciously.

Even "autonomous" people, who claim not to care about what others think of them, tend to manage their identities in ways that make them more socially competent, providing further evidence that self-presentation is often an unconscious, habitual process. Schlenker and Weigold (1990) compared "autonomous" individuals with individuals who place significant weight on others' attitudes. If self-presentational concerns are irrelevant to autonomous individuals, we would expect their reported attitudes to be unaffected by audiences. Instead, Schlenker and Weigold found that both autonomous and more socially driven people change their attitudes to maintain a certain image of themselves; only the kind of image differs. Autonomous individuals changed their attitudes "if expressing their actual beliefs would have jeopardized their appearance of independence" while socially driven individuals did so "in order to conform to the expectations of their partner" (p. 826). Thus, even those who claim not to care about societal attitudes seem to be motivated by self-presentational concerns. Indeed, research shows that those who are insensitive to audience characteristics and self-presentation needs are less successful relationally and professionally than those who are sensitive to these issues (Schlenker, 1980). This suggests that there are social incentives for all people to adapt their behavior based on the audience.

"Life Is a Stage": The Dramaturgical Perspective

In his classic book, *The Presentation of Self in Everyday Life,* Goffman (1959) advanced a revolutionary way of thinking about identity management— the **dramaturgical perspective.** Borrowing from Shakespeare, Goffman used the metaphor of theater to describe our everyday interactions. Specifically, Goffman maintained that we constantly enact performances geared for particular audiences, with the purpose of advancing a beneficial image of ourselves. In other words, we are concerned about appearances and work to ensure that others view us favorably.

The evidence for this view is strong. Several studies have shown that some sexually active individuals refrain from using condoms because they are afraid such an action may imply that they (or their partners) are "uncommitted" or "diseased" (Lear, 1997). Holtgraves (1988) argued that gambling enthusiasts pursue their wagering habits partly because they wish to portray themselves as spontaneous, adventurous, and unconcerned about losing money. Snow and Anderson's (1987) year-long observational study revealed that even homeless people present themselves to their communities in ways that help restore their dignity. For instance, a 24-year-old male who had been homeless for two weeks told them:

> I'm not like the other guys who hang out at the "Sally" [Salvation Army]. If you want to know about street people, I can tell you about them; but you can't really learn about street people from studying me, because I'm different. (p. 1349)

This man clearly made an effort to distance himself verbally from what he considered to be an undesirable identity: being homeless. In fact, distancing was the most common form of self-presentation these authors found among the homeless.

Since Goffman's early work, scholars have outlined certain conditions under which impression management becomes especially important to us

(Schlenker, Britt, & Pennington, 1996). Although researchers still consider impression management to be something that is always salient to us, the following three conditions seem to make it especially important.

Condition 1: The behavior reflects highly valued, core aspects of the self.

We are more concerned about the success of our impression management when we try to portray an image that is at the core of our identity than less central aspects of ourselves. Our identities are tied to the distinctiveness of ourselves as the person that we assert to establish as our unique identity (Vignoles et al., 2006). For example, Cindy sees herself as fun loving and particularly outgoing but only moderately career oriented, so she is likely to portray herself as more social than professional. Situations such as planning a party or college reunion are likely to call forth a particularly strong need for Cindy to present her distinct self and exhibit a social rather than professional image.

Condition 2: Successful performance is tied to vital positive or negative consequences.

If your success in a cherished relationship depends on your ability to convince your partner of your commitment, the importance of impression management efforts heightens. You might send your partner flowers, give gifts, and say "I love you" more often as ways to show you are a devoted, committed partner. In a similar vein, if you are told that your raise at work depends on being a team player, you may devote more attention to that aspect of your identity. Consistent with this notion, studies have shown that we are especially motivated to be perceived in a positive light when interacting with attractive or valued others (see Jellison & Oliver, 1983; Schlenker, 1984). In one study, participants were less likely to ask for help on a task from attractive opposite-sex strangers than from unattractive opposite-sex strangers, presumably because of their desire to be perceived as competent to attractive others (Alain, 1985).

Condition 3: The behavior reflects directly on valued rules of conduct.

We all consider certain rules of conduct to be especially important. For example, some people strongly believe that engaging in conflict in a public setting is inappropriate (Jones & Gallois, 1989). These people are careful not to engage in public conflict because violating that norm would be threatening to the public identity they wish to portray. Similarly, some people believe that public displays of affection are inappropriate. If a friend shows too much public affection to such people, they might become embarrassed and unaffectionate to avoid appearing inappropriate. When important relational rules such as these are violated frequently, it not only is very face threatening but often leads to relationship deterioration (Argyle & Henderson, 1984; Metts, 1994).

These three factors are prominent in close relationships, especially in early stages, when partners try to make positive first impressions (Swann et al., 1994). In early relational stages, people typically display central aspects of themselves to their partners (condition 1); success in these displays can make the difference between attracting or repelling a friend or romantic partner (condition 2); and ground rules are often set as to what rules of conduct will be most highly valued (condition 3). For these and other reasons highlighted throughout, studying identity and identity management is critical to understanding the success and failure of relationships.

To the extent that the three conditions outlined here are salient, people will engage in impression management. Consistent with his dramaturgical perspective, Goffman (1959) referred to social behavior designed to manage impressions and influence others as a performance. An actor gives a performance in front of a set of observers, or an audience, and in a particular location, which Goffman referred to as the stage.

Front Versus Back Stage

As in any theatrical venue, there are two stage locations: front and back. The front stage is where our performances are enacted, where our behaviors are observed by an audience, and where impression management is particularly important. Conversely, the back stage is where we can let our guard down and do not have to think about staying in character. According to Goffman (1959) the back stage is "where the performer can reliably expect that no member of the audience will intrude" (p. 113). In the backstage and surrounding area, which Goffman referred to as **wings**, we often find materials and individuals who assist us in giving a successful performance. For example, cologne or perfume, a hairbrush, and a mirror are backstage materials that we use to improve our appearance, thereby increasing the potential success of our self-presentational performance on a first date. We might also ask friends to help us in improving our appearance or to give us information about the person whom we are about to date. In fact, a primary way that we gain information about someone is by consulting other people (see Baxter & Wilmot, 1984; Berger, 1987). The information is used to improve our impression-management strategies. Answers to questions such as "Is he dating anyone right now?" and "Does she like sports?" can help reduce uncertainty and give people an idea of how to manage their impressions (see Chapter 4). For example, if you learn that someone you want to date is interested in sports, you might portray yourself as a sports enthusiast and invite that person to a college sporting event. If you learn that the person dislikes sports, you will probably take a different approach.

Tedeschi (1986) made a distinction similar to front and back stages by comparing public versus private behavior, with public behavior being subject to observation and private behavior being free from such scrutiny. Indeed, several studies have shown that we often behave differently in public than in private (see Baumeister, 1986). Can you think of something that you typically do only in the back stage? Singing is a common example of a backstage behavior. Many people are too embarrassed to sing in front of others (in the front stage) but, when pressed, admit to singing in the shower or in their cars (which are both backstage regions). In a similar vein, hygienic activity, despite its universality, is reserved for backstage regions. Relationships also determine if we are front or back stage. For example, unless you have a good singing voice, you would probably not sing in front of strangers, but you might sing with your best friend or romantic partner. When people are with their closest friends or intimate partners, behaviors that typically are reserved for the back stage are moved to the front stage. You might not swear in public but do so with your closest friends. Our close friends and family members are back stage, so they get a more authentic and unrehearsed version of us. Again, we are reminded of Cindy's Facebook pages. The pictures that are posted (some by her, and others of her by others without her consent) are often things done in backstage settings (with friends, at home, and so forth), but are presented on front stage and viewed by whoever visits the page. This mixing of back and front stages on webpages is dangerous for identity management but hasn't been adequately studied.

Role, Audience, and Context

Whether behaviors occur in the front or back stage depends on the role enacted, the audience being targeted, and the context in which the activities are performed. For example, you might feel free to sing in front of strangers at a karaoke bar in another city but not in a bar that you hang out in regularly in your own town. Similarly, some teenagers manage their use of swearing with parents or other adults to display proper and respectful identity. With their friends, by contrast, they might want to convey a carefree, rebellious, and "cool" identity that is bolstered by swearing. The only viable criterion on which performance success is judged is whether it successfully advances the image that the performer desires to advance for a particular audience (Baumeister, 1982; Leary, 1995; Schlenker, 1980). When a performance threatens the image that one wants to convey to a certain audience, it is reserved for the back stage. Thus, in the swearing example, the teenagers would consider swearing a backstage activity when interacting with their parents, but a front-stage activity when interacting with peers. Thinking back to Cindy's Facebook page, we see a problem concerning identity management. The page is a clear identity message, but she has little control over what audiences access it or what gets posted, so identities are merged, to Cindy's detriment.

This discussion of stage-appropriate behavior highlights the relative difficulty of defining what constitutes a "back" stage. "Public" and "private" may capture part of what is meant by such a distinction, in that "front" stage is the area to which a particular audience in question has access, and the "back" stage is that area to which the audience has little access. Thus, parents may be unaware that their teenage son or daughter swears with his or her peers because they have little or no access to that part of their child's communication network and performance.

Finally, it is important to note the audience's role in the impression-management process. When self-presentation is successful, the audience and "actor" interact to help each other validate and maintain their identities. After all, we can work hard to establish a certain identity, but it depends on the audience to accept or reject our self-presentation. In fact, Goffman (1967) argued that the validation of another person's identity is a "condition of interaction" (p. 12). In other words, we expect other people to accept the identities we show them and to help us save face when we accidentally display an undesired image. We have all been in situations where we inadvertently said or did something embarrassing, and the last thing we wanted was for someone to emphasize the error or laugh at our mistake. In fact, Goffman (1967) called people who can watch another's "face" being damaged without feeling sorrow, hurt, or vicarious embarrassment "heartless" human beings. Moreover, research shows that people who fail to help others save face are often disliked and shunned (see Cupach & Metts, 1994; Schlenker, 1980). Most people know how it feels to be made fun of after an embarrassing event, so instead of laughing, they try to relieve the distress that the embarrassed person is feeling. This leads to the next theory of impression management, politeness theory.

Politeness Theory

As an extension of Goffman's work, Brown and Levinson (1987) developed **politeness theory**, which focuses on the specific ways that people manage and save face using communication. A large portion of their theorizing was a distinction they made between positive and negative face.

Positive Versus Negative Face

Positive face is the favorable image that people portray to others and hope to have validated by others. It essentially reflects our desire to be liked by others. By contrast, **negative face** reflects our desire to "be free from imposition and restraint and to have control over [our] own territory, possessions, time, space, and resources" (Metts & Grohskopf, 2003, p. 361). Put another way, our positive face is the "best face" we put forward so that others like us, while our negative face is the part of us that wants to do what we want to do or say, without concern about what others would like us to do or say.

Politeness theory revolves around four general assumptions (see Brown & Levinson, 1987; Metts & Grohskopf, 2003). First, the theory rests on the assumption that threats to positive and negative face are an inherent part of social interaction. People have to deal with a constant struggle between wanting to do what they want (which satisfies their negative face needs) and wanting to do what makes them look good to others (which satisfies their positive face needs). On some occasions, the same action can satisfy both aspects of face. For example, suppose your best friend asks you to help prepare food for a party he or she is giving. You might agree to help your friend, which supports your positive face needs because it makes you look good. But if you happen to love cooking, your negative face needs also would be satisfied because you are doing exactly what you wanted to do. However, it is much more likely that a behavior will fall somewhere between the two face needs or that supporting one face need may threaten the other. For example, you may agree to help a friend move despite your desire to relax at home. In this case, if you attend to your negative face needs by staying home, you would come across as a poor friend and threaten your positive face needs. Central to politeness theory is that positive and negative face needs are managed in every interaction. If you need to go, at what point do

you end a conversation and how do you do it? In what tone of voice do you talk to your parents despite your desire to express displeasure? How do you respond to someone's question about what you're "doing this weekend?" in a way that is friendly but doesn't commit yourself to do something you don't want to do? These examples illustrate that every interaction involves communication decisions that have implications for both positive and negative face.

Second is the assumption that people's positive and negative faces can be either validated or threatened by interaction. Identity is validated when a person's behavior and the receiver's response to that behavior support the image the individual is trying to advance. For example, you may validate your identity as a caring partner by taking your significant other for an unexpected dinner date after he or she had a long week at work. In return, your partner may validate your identity as a caring partner by saying how nice surprises like special dinners are appreciated. In this example, both you and your partner have done things to validate *your* positive face.

A study by Albas and Albas (1988) examined how students validated their positive faces following receipt of a good exam grade. The researchers identified several strategies that "acers" (as they labeled them) used to reveal their grade to others as a way to bolster their positive faces without directly bragging. These strategies included "repressed bubbling" (nonverbal signals of elation), "accidental revelation" (leaving the test facing upward, with the grade in full display), and "question-answer chain" (asking other students how they did, which sets the stage for them to reciprocate with a similar question). In these ways, students who performed well on the test could "publish" that fact to others, thereby supporting their identity as an intelligent person and good student. However, if the person appears to be bragging or fishing for a compliment, these strategies could backfire. Although they would be validating their identity as an intelligent person, such strategies could threaten their identity as a nice, modest person.

When a person's behavior is at variance with the identity desired to convey, a face-threatening situation occurs. **Face-threatening acts** (FTAs) are behaviors that detract from an individual's identity by threatening either their positive or negative face desires (Brown & Levinson, 1987). For example, forgetting a dinner date with your significant other is a self-inflicted threat to your positive face—your identity as a caring partner. Your partner may further contribute to this face threat by publicly chiding you for getting stood up at the restaurant. Of course, not all behaviors are equally face threatening. Certain behaviors cause people to lose more face and lead to more negative personal and relational consequences than others.

The third assumption on which politeness theory is based is that both members of an interaction are typically motivated to avoid threatening either their own or the interaction partner's face needs. Given our desire to avoid face threats, we generally try to avoid making others look bad (i.e., threatening our positive face) and respect others who refrain from making us look bad. So, interactions are typically dances where both partners understand the social expectations that help them maintain each other's face needs. Cindy might understand that it is important to respect Lindsay's time and space and not point out her flaws, and she might also expect Lindsay to do the same for her. Of course, you may know some people who enjoy violating social expectations and embarrassing others. How would politeness theory researchers respond to that? They would offer two explanations: First, those people who are also often shunned, socially reprimanded, or disliked by most other people (e.g., seen as bullies, jerks, and so forth) have little to lose and feel as though they can enhance their status by putting down other people. Second, all threats to face are not equally bad; some are seen as much less severe than others. In fact, this issue forms the basis for the fourth assumption underlying politeness theory: the severity of FTAs depends on several factors.

Research suggests that at least six factors affect the degree to which an FTA is perceived to be severe. The first three factors, identified by Schlenker and his colleagues (Schlenker, Britt, Pennington, Murphy, & Doherty, 1994; Schlenker & Weigold, 1992), focus on behaviors that threaten a person's own face. The remaining three factors, from Brown and Levinson's (1987) politeness theory,

focus on behaviors that threaten either one's own or one's partner's face.

1. *The more important the rule that is violated, the more severe the FTA.* For example, forgetting your relational partner's birthday will be a greater rule violation than forgetting to call your partner to say you will be late coming home from work.

2. *The more harm the behavior produces, the more severe the FTA.* If you trip and lose your balance, you may feel some loss of face, but if you trip, fall to the ground, and tear your outfit, the loss of face will be much greater. Similarly, if you get caught telling a lie about something that has serious implications for your relationship, the loss of face will be greater than if you get caught telling a "little white lie."

3. *The more the actor is directly responsible for the behavior, the more severe the FTA.* If a store clerk refuses to accept your credit card because the expiration date is past, it is much less face threatening than if the clerk phones in your card number and is asked to confiscate your card and cut it up because you are late on your payments.

4. *The more of an imposition the behavior is, the more severe the FTA.* For example, you would be more concerned about your negative face if someone asked you to help move furniture to a new house (a major imposition on your time) than if someone asked you to write down their new phone number (which is hardly an imposition).

5. *The more power the receiver has over the sender, the more severe the FTA.* If you make a silly comment that your boss could misconstrue as an insult, you will probably be more worried than if you make the same silly comment in front of a friend. With your boss, you are more likely to worry about appearing incompetent.

6. *The larger the social distance between sender and receiver, the more severe the FTA.* For example, you will probably worry less about threatening the face of your best friend than that of an acquaintance, presumably because the foundation of the friendship is more solid and less susceptible to harm from face threats.

Although research has generally supported the validity of these factors, some research has shown that the sixth factor, which relates to the social distance between receiver and sender, may not always be true. Work by Holtgraves and Yang (1990, 1992) suggests that in many cases, instead of being *less* concerned about threatening the identity of those close to us, we are actually *more* concerned about doing so. Often we are particularly concerned about making a good impression and getting along well with a new acquaintance; other times we are more concerned with protecting our close relationships from harm. The point here is that identity-management concerns become more salient as the consequences of impression-management failure increase.

Facework Strategies

Given the importance of facework in people's everyday lives, it should come as no surprise that people use a variety of intricate strategies to manage face needs during interaction. In fact, most, if not all, interactions inherently include examples of facework that help people maintain or repair, or that strategically threaten, their own faces or those of others. Even a simple request ("Since we live so far apart, would you mind meeting at a restaurant that is somewhere halfway between us?") are phrased in a way that respects the positive and negative face needs of the other person. This fact becomes clear if you think of other ways that these requests may be phrased ("I don't want to drive that far. You have to meet me halfway").

Given the many ways that concerns for facework influence our interactions, Brown and Levinson (1987) offered five options that individuals have when considering an FTA. The strategies differ in the degree of balance achieved between the goals of accomplishing a face-threatening task and managing face concerns (see Figure 2.2).

The **bald on-record strategy** is characterized by primary attention to task and little or no attention to helping the partner save face. It is the most efficient strategy but also the most face threatening. Brown and Levinson (1987) offered the examples of a mother telling her child to "Come home right now!" or someone in need of assistance telling a bystander to "Lend me a hand here!" Bald on-record strategies are typically used when maximum task efficiency is important or where there is a large difference in power or status between actors.

The **positive politeness strategy** is intended to address the receiver's positive face while still accomplishing the task. It includes explicit recognition of the receiver's value and the receiver's contributions to the process, and couches the FTA (often a request) as something that does not threaten the identity of the receiver. For example, complimenting someone on attire, haircut, or performance is an example of positive politeness that might precede a

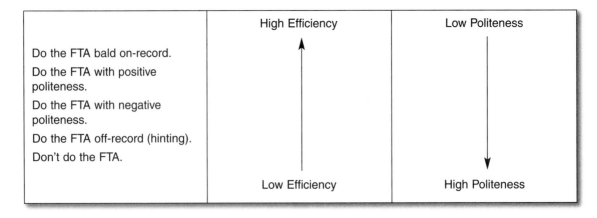

Figure 2.2 Options for Dealing With Face-Threatening Acts

SOURCE: Document courtesy of Dr. Sandra Metts, Professor of Communication, Illinois State University.

request. Similarly, if you want a friend to help you write a resume and cover letter, you might say, "You are such a good writer. Would you help me edit this?"

The **negative politeness strategy** is intended to address the receiver's negative face while still accomplishing the task. The key is that receivers not feel coerced into complying, but instead feel that they are performing the act of their own volition. Often, negative politeness also involves deference on the part of the sender to ensure not being perceived as coercive. For example, you might say to a friend, "I suppose there wouldn't be any chance of your being able to lend me your car for a few minutes, would there?" Brown and Levinson (1987) noted that requests phrased this way clearly emphasize the freedom of the receiver to decline.

The **going off-record strategy** is characterized by primary attention to face and little attention to task. It is an inefficient strategy for accomplishing tasks, but given the importance of face, it may serve the participants well and so is often used. Examples include hinting, using an indirect nonverbal expression, or masking a request as a joke. For instance, if you want your partner to take you on a vacation, you might make comments such as "I've always wanted to go on a Caribbean cruise" or "It would be great to get away and go somewhere tropical."

Finally, people can **decide not to engage in the FTA**. Brown and Levinson (1987) noted that individuals often choose to forgo face-threatening tasks completely in favor of preserving face. For example, even if you are upset because your roommate's partner always spends the night at your apartment, you might decide to say nothing for fear of embarrassing or angering your roommate (particularly if you do not want your roommate to move out). According to Brown and Levinson (1987), people perform a cost-benefit analysis when deciding what type of strategy to use. Bald on-record strategies are the most efficient but also the most damaging to face, and as such may be most damaging to the relationship. However, by going off-record, people run a much greater risk that the receiver will not recognize the request or will simply ignore it.

Metts (1992) applied this logic to the predicament of breaking up with a romantic partner. The act of breaking up is face threatening in many ways.

For example, suppose Cindy tells her current boyfriend, Alex, that she wants to end their relationship but Alex does not want to break up. This act threatens Alex's negative face because he is being forced to do something he does not want to do. Alex's positive face also is threatened because Cindy's request suggests that he is no longer a desirable relational partner. Cindy's positive face may also be threatened if she worries that Alex (and perhaps other people) will see her as selfish, egotistical, or uncaring. Her negative face could also be threatened; she may change her relationship status on her Facebook, but feels it would be premature to do so without talking things over with Alex. According to Metts (1992), Cindy is likely to use different strategies depending how face threatening she thinks the breakup will be for both herself and Alex. If she thinks the breakup will be highly distressing, she is likely to use an on-record-with-politeness strategy. Conversely, if Cindy thinks the breakup will cause little distress, she is likely to use an off-record strategy (e.g., avoiding the person) or a bald on-record strategy (e.g., blunt statements about wanting to break up).

Preventive and Corrective Facework

Certainly people often are task driven, and perform FTAs, with little attention to the consequences of threatening their own or another person's face. But people are more likely to avoid face threats or attempt to repair a damaged face. Research on preventive and corrective facework highlights other ways that concerns for face affect our interactions (Cupach & Metts, 1994).

Preventive facework is characterized by efforts to avoid or minimize potential face threat. Preventive strategies seek to prevent future damage by framing the message in friendlier, softer terms. Studies have identified types of preventive facework in daily interaction. **Disclaimers** are the most common form of preventive facework. Hewitt and Stokes (1975) outlined five general disclaimers that individuals use before saying or doing something that is face threatening: (1) hedging ("I may be way off here, but . . ."); (2) credentialing ("I'm your father, so I'll be straight with you"); (3) sin license

("Well, since we're all disclosing embarrassing situations . . ."); (4) cognitive disclaimer ("I know you're going to think I've lost it, but . . ."); and (5) appeal for suspended judgment ("Hear me out before jumping to conclusions").

Other researchers have included the notion of **verbal self-handicapping** as a method of preventive facework (Higgins & Berglas, 1990); that is, people will sometimes offer an excuse that serves to minimize the face threat of a potentially poor performance. For example, prior to an important dance competition, Cindy may inform her team captain of a knee injury she has suffered. This strategic precompetition disclosure serves two functions. If Cindy dances her routines well, she bolsters her identity as a "tough" professional who can perform with pain. But if she performs poorly, she has a built-in excuse for her subpar performance. Unfortunately, research shows that these self-handicapping tactics often become self-fulfilling prophecies because they offer the individual a reason *not* to do as well as possible. In sum, the various disclaimers all serve to soften the potential face threat that might result from impending action, and essentially ask the audience to consider that act within the perspective of the context.

Corrective facework is characterized by efforts to *repair* an identity already damaged by something that was said or done. Like preventive facework, corrective facework may be performed by the person whose face was threatened, or by others who are assisting in the protection or repair of the person's face.

Of course, preventive and corrective facework are part of a cycle or sequence, as illustrated in Figure 2.3 Both constantly occur in the course of communication and are interactively achieved in everyday communication.

Embarrassing moments are good examples of situations that often lead to corrective facework because they undermine a person's positive self-image. As Cupach and Metts (1994) argued, people become embarrassed when they are perceived to have acted incompetently, that is, when behavior is judged to be "inappropriate, ineffective, or foolish" (p. 18).

In a comprehensive review of embarrassment research, Miller (1996) outlined 10 types of embarrassing behaviors that typically threaten one's face. The two most common causes of embarrassment were "physical pratfalls or inept performance" and

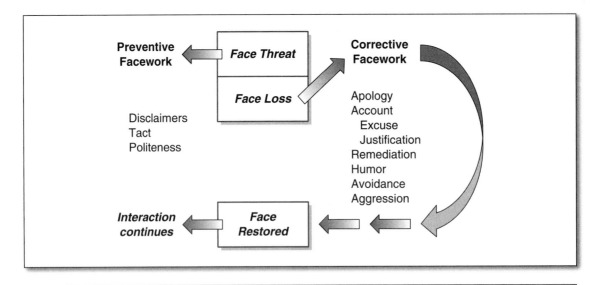

Figure 2.3   Face Threat/Loss Sequence

SOURCE: Document courtesy of Dr. Sandra Metts, Professor of Communication, Illinois State University.

"cognitive errors." The former category includes instances in which people appear unnecessarily awkward or incompetent—for example, missing a pole on which you intended to lean, falling over after leaning back too far in a chair, and catching your hair on fire as you light the grill. The latter category includes mistakes in judgment (trying every key before realizing you are at the wrong door), forgetfulness (forgetting your phone number or people's names), lack of attention or "temporary stupidity" (saying something that gives away a secret you are trying to keep for others), or clumsy answers. One of the best sources for examples of clumsy answers is Petra and Petra's 1993 book *The 775 Stupidest Things Ever Said.* One example of clumsy answers in this book is a response that then vice president of the United States George Herbert Walker Bush gave at a campaign rally: "For 7 1/2 years I've worked alongside President Reagan. We've had triumphs. Made some mistakes. We've had sex . . . uh . . . setbacks."

People typically use corrective facework in response to embarrassing situations such as these, as well as to other situations involving FTAs. You can take the test in Box 2.1 to determine which types of corrective facework you are most likely to use in a particular situation. There are six general corrective strategies for repairing a damaged face (Cupach & Metts, 1994; Schlenker & Weigold, 1992):

1. *Avoidance:* The common thread underlying avoidance behaviors is the goal of distancing oneself or one's partner from the act. Often, distancing occurs when individuals pretend that the act never happened or otherwise ignore its occurrence. For example, continuing to walk down the aisle after knocking over a display in a grocery store and glossing over an obvious Freudian slip are instances of avoidance. The hope is that the audience may pay less attention to the act if the actor avoids reference to it.

2. *Humor:* When the consequences of the FTA are relatively small, people often resort to humor as a way to deal with the threat. By using humor after an FTA, people show poise and come across as competent communicators, thereby repairing their damaged faces. Sometimes it is best to laugh at yourself so others will laugh with you, not at you.

3. *Apologies:* Apologies are "admissions of responsibility and regret for undesirable events" (Schlenker & Weigold, 1992, p. 162). In that sense, they may help repair some of the damage to face by emphasizing the actor's nature as a moral individual who intends to take responsibility for the action. Unlike avoidance, where actors deny responsibility, apologies tie the incident directly to the actor and, as such, may further threaten face—especially if the apology is deemed insincere.

4. *Accounts:* Accounts, or attempts to explain the FTA, come in the form of excuses or justifications. Excuses are explanations that minimize personal responsibility of the actor for the actions. For example, if you engage in a silly fraternity or sorority prank that causes you to lose face, you might excuse your behavior by saying that your friends pressured you into action or that you had consumed too much alcohol. With justifications, actors do not try to distance themselves from the act, but instead "reframe an event by downplaying its negative implications" (Cupach & Metts, 1994, p. 10). Arguing that your behavior at the fraternity or sorority party was "not that big of a deal" or that the prank did not really hurt anyone are examples of justifications for FTAs.

5. *Physical remediation:* This strategy involves attempts to repair physical damage. For example, you might quickly clean up a coffee spill on the table, or you might zip up your pants once you recognize that your fly is open. Relational partners, especially if sympathetic, often engage in physical remediation as well. For example, if you see a food smudge on your partner's chin, you might wipe it off before other people see it.

6. *Aggression:* In some cases, individuals feel the need to repair their damaged face by using physical force. For example, people sometimes start a physical altercation in response to a put-down or personal attack. In fact, research shows that dating violence often follows a perception of face threats (for a review of violence research, see Gelles & Cornell, 1990). People may also become aggressive when they are embarrassed or violate a norm. For example, if you accidentally bump into someone while walking through a crowded shopping mall, you might angrily say, "Watch where you're going."

BOX 2.1 Put Yourself to the Test

How Do You Attempt to Repair Face?

Imagine yourself in the following situation. You are assigned to work in a group of four students to complete a class project. A number of personal issues interfere with your ability to get things done as quickly and effectively as you usually do, and you fall behind the rest of the group. Midway through the semester, one of the other group members puts you on the spot by saying, "You haven't been doing your share, so I'm afraid that if we give you something important to do you won't get it done on time or you won't do it well." How would you respond to this face-threatening comment? Answer the questions using the following scale: 1 = you would be very unlikely to react that way, and 7=you would be very likely to react that way.

	Very Unlikely						Very Likely
1. I would ignore it.	1	2	3	4	5	6	7
2. I would apologize.	1	2	3	4	5	6	7
3. I would explain why I hadn't been able to do my fair share.	1	2	3	4	5	6	7
4. I would say something sarcastic or rude to the person who made the comment.	1	2	3	4	5	6	7
5. I would promise to do more than my fair share in the future.	1	2	3	4	5	6	7
6. I would laugh it off and say that I've always been a procrastinator.	1	2	3	4	5	6	7
7. I would change the subject.	1	2	3	4	5	6	7
8. I would admit that I had not done my fair share.	1	2	3	4	5	6	7
9. I would tell everyone why I wasn't able to put forth my best effort.	1	2	3	4	5	6	7
10. I would say something to put down the person who made the comment.	1	2	3	4	5	6	7
11. I would take on a task no one else wanted to do to make up it to everyone.	1	2	3	4	5	6	7
12. I would make fun of myself and my lack of time management.	1	2	3	4	5	6	7

To obtain your results, add your scores for the following items:

Avoidance: Items 1 + 7 = _____

Apology: Items 2 + 8 = _____

Account: Items 3 + 9 = _____

Aggression: Items 4 + 10 = _____

Remediation: Items 5 + 11 = _____

Humor: Items 6 + 12 = _____

Higher scores indicate a stronger likelihood of using a particular type of corrective facework in this type of situation. How might your use of corrective facework differ on the basis of the situation or the relationship you share with the people around you?

Of course, several of these strategies may be combined in efforts to repair a damaged face. For example, after spilling coffee on the boss's desk, you might say you are sorry (apology), explain that you were distracted by the boss's stimulating presentation (account), and then clean up the mess (physical remediation). Indeed, the more face threatening the act, the more energy will be expended in multiple repair attempts.

In other situations people are more likely to ignore face threats or to respond with humor. This is especially likely when FTAs are expected. For instance, embarrassing and face-threatening actions are more expected and accepted at wedding and baby showers. Common activities at baby showers include having people guess how big the mom-to-be's stomach is or what she weighs; at wedding showers, the bride-to-be often receives revealing lingerie. Braithwaite (1995) observed behavior at coed wedding and baby showers to investigate the tactics people used to embarrass others and what tactics people used to respond to face threats. She found that wedding and baby showers are contexts where embarrassment is expected, so these actions are not as face threatening as in other contexts. Yet the dance between embarrassment-producing face threats and face-repairing responses was still evident. Other situations, such as "roasting" someone at a retirement party, may require this same delicate dance.

SUMMARY AND APPLICATION

Our desire to present particular images of ourselves shapes our social interactions and influences our relationships. In this chapter, we outlined the factors that influence identity and the ways in which we communicate this identity to others during initial encounters and in established relationships. A person's identity is based on a complex theory of self that incorporates expectations, self-fulfilling prophecies, and feedback from others. People project a certain identity to the world, and that identity is either accepted or rejected by the audience, causing the identity to be either reinforced or modified. In this chapter we also emphasized the ways in which other people help us maintain our public identities.

It is important to note, however, that this chapter covered only a small portion of the literature on identity and impression management. Research looking at psychological processes such as self-esteem and self-concept are also relevant to identity and impression management. In this chapter, our focus was on identity management in social and personal relationships. Other researchers have studied self-presentation within different contexts, such as first impressions during employment interviews or self-presentation strategies used by teachers in classrooms. The information posted on Cindy's Facebook functions for both established and new relationships—the page serves to maintain relationships with friends who can click and see all Cindy's pictures in which they are featured; the page also serves as an introduction for new friends, acquaintances, and classmates who don't yet know Cindy very well.

Interpersonal communication researchers have also studied identity and impression formation within the attraction process. People are attracted to those who convey a positive self-identity while appearing to be modest and approachable. Physical appearance, which plays a key role in impression management, is also one of several bases for attraction in close relationships (see Chapter 3). Cindy's Facebook page reflects some of the characteristics that people find attractive, including sociability and popularity. The pictures she and others have posted also show viewers what she and her friends look like, and also give viewers an idea of what kinds of activities she and her friends enjoy. The people viewing Cindy's Facebook pages will perceive her differently depending on how they evaluate the identity she has portrayed. Some people might have a positive impression of Cindy as a popular person, a talented dancer, bilingual, and one who visits exotic places such as Rome. Other people, however, may perceive Cindy as a superficial, narcissistic person, more concerned about her large social network than developing high-quality close relationships. Viewers' perceptions would be influenced by their own identities and the characteristics they value in themselves and others. If Cindy learns that some people she cares about have a negative impression of her when they view her Facebook pages, she might change her postings.

Finally, identity can be expanded and protected within close relationships. Self-expansion theory suggests that relationships provide a venue for one's broadening identity and growing as a person. Facework is also important to project one's own desired image and to protect the positive and negative faces of a relational partner. Indeed, an awareness of the importance of face can go a long way toward helping people understand the development and deterioration of relationships.

DISCUSSION QUESTIONS

1. What personal characteristics are most central to your theory of self?

2. In this chapter, we discussed some ethical issues related to identity management. Under what circumstances do you think that techniques used to manage one's positive identity are unethical or deceptive?

3. Think about one of your most embarrassing moments. Did you do any facework? If so, what identity-management techniques did you employ? Did people around you help you save face? If so, how?

STUDENT STUDY SITE

Visit the study site at **www.sagepub.com/guerrero3e** for e-flashcards, survey and assessments from the chapter, and SAGE journal articles.

3

Drawing People Together

Forces of Social Attraction

Julie is frustrated with her dating life. Even though she considers herself smart and pretty, she always seems to be the single one among her friends and she is tired of feeling like the third wheel all the time. It seems so easy for her friends to find long-term boyfriends, while she seems to struggle. When she does find a boyfriend, the relationship never lasts very long. At first Julie thought her last boyfriend, Steven, was perfect for her. Steven was extremely good looking and his personality was exactly the opposite of her shy self. He loved to socialize and was flirtatious and fun. Eventually, however, Julie got tired of trying to keep up with his fast-paced social life and she became jealous of the women he hung out with even though Steven swore they were only friends. When they broke up, Julie wondered why she had been so attracted to him in the first place. She also wondered if she was attracted to the wrong type of men. After all, her friends often had good relationships with men whom she didn't find particularly attractive.

Attraction is a force that draws people together. It can occur as quickly as a flash of lightning or develop slowly over time. Sometimes a surge of arousal accompanies attraction, with a pounding heart and sweaty palms. Other times a warm, cozy, comfortable feeling accompanies attraction. Of course, attraction is not always mutual; people are often attracted to individuals who are not attracted to them.

The reasons people are attracted to some individuals and not others are complex and dynamic, and frequently attraction is hard to explain. Julie's concerns about being able to find the right person are understandable; she wonders why she always seems to be attracted to the wrong person. She also wonders why her friends are attracted to certain people whom she finds unappealing. After Julie and Steven break up, she realizes that the qualities that attracted her to him were not enough to sustain their relationship. After an experience such as Julie's, people sometimes tell themselves that they will never again be attracted to a certain type of person, only to later find themselves dating the same type of person.

Although attraction is complex, and the characteristics that attract people to others vary widely, there are fundamental reasons attraction develops. Social scientists have devoted considerable energy to determining the causes of social attraction. In this chapter, we review some of the research in this area. Specifically, we focus on how the personal attributes of two individuals work separately and together to affect attraction. We also look at the role that context and the environment play in the attraction process. This chapter provides insight into the many factors that influence whom you are attracted to and why people are or are not attracted to you.

DEFINING ATTRACTION

There are many types of attraction. We can be attracted to someone physically, sexually, intellectually, or relationally. We also might be attracted to someone who can help us accomplish goals. Sometimes we are even attracted to people who are "bad" for us, which is a tendency called *fatal attraction*. In this section, we examine differences among these forms of attraction.

The Big Three: Physical, Social, and Task Attraction

Usually people are attracted to someone based on their physical appearance, their sociability, or their ability to complete tasks (McCroskey & McCain, 1974). **Physical attraction** results when we are drawn to people's look, whether it is someone's body, eyes, hair, attire, or other aspects of a person's appearance. **Social attraction** reflects the feeling that we would like to "hang out" and be friends with someone. When people are socially attractive, we also usually think that they would fit in well with our circle of friends and our family. Finally, **task attraction** refers to our desire to work with someone to fulfill instrumental goals, such as completing a project or making a presentation. For example, think of people with whom you would like to work on a group project; they are probably smart, hard working, fair, and friendly. Box 3.1 lists some of the test items used to measure these three types of attraction.

BOX 3.1 Put Yourself to the Test

What Types of People Attract You Most?

To see what types of people attract you, try rating your closest friends and current or recent romantic partners using this scale. Think about the qualities that attracted you to them when you first met, and rate them accordingly by circling the appropriate number. Perhaps you are more attracted to people based on their ability to help with tasks, their sociability, or their physical appearance, or perhaps all of these types of attraction are important to you. You might also notice that different forms of attraction were present when you first met your close friends versus your romantic partners. Use the following scale to make your ratings:

1 = strongly disagree and 7 = strongly agree.

Task Attraction	Disagree						Agree
1. If I wanted to get things done, I thought I could probably depend on her/him.	1	2	3	4	5	6	7
2. I had confidence in her/his ability to get the job done.	1	2	3	4	5	6	7
3. I thought I would enjoy working with her/him on a task.	1	2	3	4	5	6	7

Task Attraction	Disagree						Agree
4. I thought this person would be an asset in any task situation.	1	2	3	4	5	6	7
5. I thought this person would take her/his work seriously.	1	2	3	4	5	6	7
Social Attraction	1	2	3	4	5	6	7
1. I thought she/he could be a friend of mine.	1	2	3	4	5	6	7
2. I wanted to have a friendly chat with her/him.	1	2	3	4	5	6	7
3. I thought she/he would be easy to get along with.	1	2	3	4	5	6	7
4. I thought she/he would be pleasant to be with.	1	2	3	4	5	6	7
5. I thought I could become close friends with her/him.	1	2	3	4	5	6	7
Physical Attraction	1	2	3	4	5	6	7
1. This person struck me as handsome or pretty.	1	2	3	4	5	6	7
2. I found her/him attractive physically.	1	2	3	4	5	6	7
3. This person looked appealing.	1	2	3	4	5	6	7
4. I thought she/he was good looking.	1	2	3	4	5	6	7
5. I thought she/he had an attractive face.	1	2	3	4	5	6	7

SOURCE: Adapted from McCroskey and Richmond's revised version of the Interpersonal Attraction scale. In Tardy, C. H. (ed.), *A Handbook for the Study of Human Communication Methods and Instruments for Observing, Measuring, and Assessing Communication Process.* Copyright © 1988. Reproduced with permission of Greenwood Publishing Group, Inc., Westport, CT.

Obviously these types of attraction are related. In fact, both task and physical attraction can contribute to more general perceptions of social attraction. For example, if you meet someone who is physically attractive, you might decide that this person is also charming and intelligent, and thus socially attractive. This tendency to perceive physically attractive people as more sociable is part of the **halo effect**, which is discussed later in this chapter. You also might be socially attracted to certain people, such as roommates and coworkers, because you find them task attractive. This is likely if you are the type of person who attends carefully to tasks and takes your work seriously.

Despite the similarities, these types of attraction are distinguishable. For example, the person you would like to be part of your group project may not always be the first person you would ask to a party.

Engineers and accountants often get a "bad rap" for fitting that stereotypic mold of people who are respected for their knowledge but can be dull socially. In a similar vein, if you had a choice of partners for an important project, you would rarely use someone's physical appearance as the main criterion for selection. So, despite some overlap between these types of attraction, there are also definite differences.

Sexual Attraction

In many cases, physical attraction leads to sexual attraction. (In Chapter 8, we review literature related to sexual attitudes and behaviors, which includes the notion of sexual attraction.) **Sexual attraction** reflects the desire to engage in sexual activity with someone and typically is accompanied by feelings of sexual arousal in the presence of the person. Although people can be sexually attracted to those they find socially attractive, social attraction is not necessarily accompanied by sexual thoughts. For example, your attraction to others as friends (part of what defines social attraction) is often a platonic feeling that does not include a sexual component. Even if we think of attraction to a potential dating partner, the qualities that attract us sexually may not be the same qualities that attract us socially. Reyes and colleagues (1999) found that physical attractiveness relates more closely to sexual attraction than social attractiveness. As this study suggests, physical and sexual attraction often occur together in romantic relationships. In other relationships, however, physical and sexual attraction may be unrelated. For instance, you might initially be physically attracted to someone because the person dresses well and is about the same age. But this does not necessarily mean that you desire sex with this person.

Relational Attraction

Another type of attraction, **relational attraction**, refers to the desire to have an intimate relationship with a person. Some scholars maintain that there are differences between initial feelings of social attraction and well-thought-out feelings of relational attraction, although relational attraction can be thought of as a subset of social attraction. Initially, for example, you might feel social attraction to someone and think you would like to get to know this person better. However, for other reasons you may think the person would not make a good long-term relational partner. Some women might be socially attracted to Steven, for instance, because he is outgoing, physically attractive, and fun to be around, but they might also think that Steven would be too flirtatious and fickle to be a serious boyfriend.

A study by Johnson, Afifi, and Duck (1994) found support for this difference between initial social attraction and long-term relational attraction. Specifically, in their study on attraction to partners after a first date (with the dates set up through a dating service), Johnson and associates distinguished between instant or "flashbulb attraction" and "expected relational course." Flashbulb attraction occurred when people felt a surge of immediate interest. Expected relational course was measured by asking participants to assess the potential for a future relationship with their date. Johnson and colleagues (1994) found that people who experienced flashbulb attraction did not always want to have a long-term relationship with someone.

Chemical Attraction

Since the 1990s, new technology has allowed researchers to begin to unlock some of the mysteries of **chemical attraction**, which focuses on the physiological and neurological aspects of the attraction process. As a result, we now know a lot more about physiological and neurological aspects of attraction than we ever have before. While there is still a lot we do not yet know, what researchers *have* found out on these fronts is eye-opening.

One of the most potent attraction hormones seems to be oxytocin (OT). OT is a chemical released naturally in our bodies that has earned the name "the hormone of love" and the "connection chemical" because of its effects on the attraction process (Kuchinskas, 2009). Specifically, the release of OT creates a warm afterglow, tinting our subsequent experiences with rose-colored glasses. Studies of high-OT mothers soon after birth showed that they were more likely than low-OT mothers to gaze at the baby's face, use baby talk, touch the child affectionately, and frequently check on the baby (Feldman, Weller, Zagoory-Sharon, & Levine, 2007). To further illustrate the effect of OT, Guastella, Mitchell, and Dadds (2008) nasally injected some participants with a burst of OT and then showed them images of several faces. Participants who received the OT "gazed longer and fixated more frequently" at the eye region of the faces (p. 4). Other studies have shown that OT increases our trust in others, makes us better able to read the emotional states of our interaction partners, and increases the likelihood of social approach (for review, see Guastella et al., 2008; Marazziti, Consoli,

Silvestri, & Dell'Osso, 2009). No wonder OT gives a boost to the attraction process. It is also no surprise that drug companies are devoting considerable energy to developing a drug that mimics the effects of naturally produced OT.

Studies of brain activity are also enlightening and suggest that particular regions of the brain are activated during the attraction process. For instance, Fisher, Aron, and Brown (2005) recruited college students who reported being "intensely in love" and used functional magnetic resonance imaging to capture their brain activity as they looked at a picture of their partner. Results showed how the body influences the attraction process by providing a burst of activity to parts of the brain rich in dopamine, the primary pleasure chemical in the human system. That led the researchers to suggest the presence of an "attraction mechanism [that has] evolved to enable individuals to focus their mating energy on specific others" (p. 58). Bartels and Zeki (2004), using a similar procedure but this time with mothers looking at pictures of their children, found that feelings of love not only activate reward centers of the brain but also deactivate parts of the brain that are associated with critical judgments and negative emotions. In sum, researchers are increasingly concluding that the attraction process and related emotions are facilitated or hindered by the release of chemicals in the brain. Once released, those chemicals may have a lot more to do with whom we are attracted to and what we do with that attraction than previously believed. Chemical attraction may well relate to many of the other types of attraction we have discussed, including relational and sexual attraction.

Fatal Attraction

Regardless of whether we are initially attracted to individuals because of their winning personality, their ability to help us accomplish goals, or their good looks, we could eventually discover that the very qualities we once found attractive are not as desirable as first thought. Felmlee (1995, 1998) studied this phenomenon by conducting a number of studies on **fatal attraction**, which she defined as occurring when the very qualities that draw us to

someone eventually contribute to relational breakup. That is, certain qualities may seem attractive initially but spell danger ahead. Felmlee asked people to think of the last romantic relationship they were in that ended and then to describe both what initially attracted them to the person and what ultimately led to the breakup.

Felmlee's analysis of the answers led her to some interesting conclusions. First, differences were consistently the most common type of fatal attraction. In other words, being attracted to someone because the person is one's "opposite" might be exciting in the short term, but this novelty is likely to wear thin over time as it did for Julie in her relationship with Steven. Except for the sexes, opposites do not attract in the long run. Second, initially attractive qualities such as being fun, exciting, or easygoing can also contribute to breakups, especially if someone has these qualities to an extreme. For example, if you are attracted to someone primarily because of the person's sense of humor, that attraction could turn to dislike if you realize that your partner can never be serious. Similarly, Steven's attractive, outgoing, flirtatious nature became distressing to Julie when she saw him socializing with other women and when she preferred to stay at home rather than go out.

Being attracted to a narcissistic person also appears to be a common type of fatal attraction. **Narcissism** is a personality trait that involves a "pervasive pattern of grandiosity, self-focus, and self-importance" (Back, Schmukle, & Egloff, 2010, p. 132). Studies have shown that people are initially attracted to narcissists (Back et al., 2010; Morf & Rhodewalt, 2001; Paulhus, 1998). They appear extroverted, self-confident, charming, agreeable, and competent. They are also "entertaining to watch" (Young & Pinksy, 2006, p. 470). However, as people get to know narcissists, they tend to become less attracted to them. One study even showed that the very characteristics that make narcissists most attractive when people first meet were the same characteristics that were most damaging in the long run (Back et al., 2010). Behaviors that were initially seen as showing confidence and motivation were later viewed as exploitative and self-absorbed.

A FRAMEWORK FOR UNDERSTANDING ATTRACTION

Unfortunately, few scholars have examined the subtle differences between forms of attraction to ascertain which types are most strongly associated with our relational decisions. Instead, most scholars define social attraction broadly as "a motivational state in which an individual is predisposed to think, feel, and usually behave in a positive manner toward another person" (Simpson & Harris, 1994, p. 47). This definition embraces many motivations for thinking, feeling, and behaving positively toward someone. For instance, such motivation could stem from wanting to work with someone, wanting to be someone's friend, wanting to be someone's lover, or thinking that someone is physically attractive. However, when most relationship researchers measure attraction, they focus on social or physical attraction. Thus, most of the research reported in this chapter is most relevant to these two forms of attraction.

In the rest of this chapter, we attempt to answer the question, What attracts us to others? As you will see, the answer to this question is complex. Indeed, researchers have found that many factors influence attraction. To organize these factors, we will use a framework first presented by Kelley and colleagues in 1983. Our application of this framework to the attraction process is depicted in Figure 3.1. Kelley argued that four general factors influence how we behave during interactions:

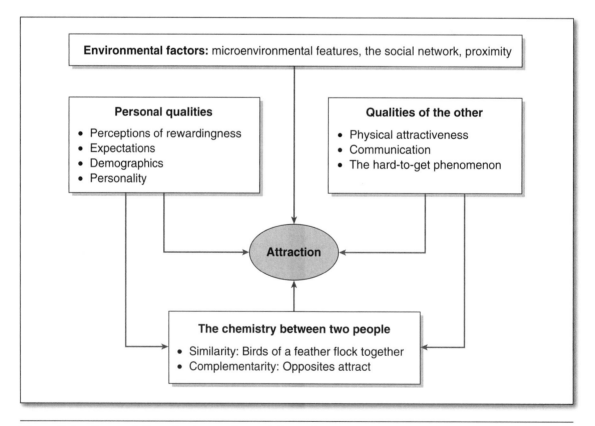

Figure 3.1   Factors Influencing Interaction and Attraction

1. Personal qualities and preferences that *we* bring to the interaction, including our personality, interpersonal needs, expectations, self-esteem, physical appearance, and level of communication skill, among other qualities

2. Personal qualities that *the other person* brings to the interaction, including personality, needs, expectations, self-esteem, physical appearance, and level of communication skills, among other qualities

3. Qualities that reflect the chemistry or synergy between two people, including similarities and differences between relational partners across a range of characteristics, and that emerge only when the two people are together

4. Features of the physical environment or context in which the interaction takes place, called *environmental variables*, including details of the location in which the interaction takes place (e.g., size, temperature, furniture, public versus private setting, etc.) and feedback from friends and family

These factors have been shown to relate to how interactions develop (see Kelley et al., 1983) and to whom people become attracted. Although not envisioned by early relational scholars, recent technologies have allowed researchers to examine the physiological and neurological aspects of attraction, with interesting results. The proceeding section reviews research relevant to each factor.

PERSONAL VARIABLES RELATED TO ATTRACTION

What personal preferences, personality traits, and perceptions do we possess that might influence our attraction to others? The considerable research that has focused on this question suggests that our evaluations of a person's reward value, our expectations about a person's behavior, and a number of demographic and personality variables all impact how attractive we find people.

Perceptions of Reward Value

When people enter relationships, they hope to obtain benefits or rewards, such as companionship, affection, sex, fun, and sometimes even financial resources. Therefore, one of the most powerful influences on our attraction to others is our perception of their reward value, which relates to our interpersonal needs and preferences. In fact, ideas from interdependence theory (see Chapter 10) serve as a foundation for research on attraction. According to this theory, we are attracted to others when we think they offer more rewards than costs. Thus, if someone seems to have a host of positive, rewarding qualities (e.g., a good sense of humor, good looks, a positive outlook, and a willingness to sacrifice for others) and only a few negative, costly qualities (e.g., being late all the time or being too possessive), attraction should be high. Furthermore, individuals will be perceived as especially attractive if they have more rewards to offer than other people.

Although many of these rewards can also be considered qualities possessed by the other person (e.g., the other person's physical attractiveness) or are associated with the chemistry between two people (e.g., similarity in beliefs and attitudes), it is people's own perception of these rewards that are relevant; if a person is perceived as rewarding or attractive to someone, the person is in fact rewarding or attractive. Because these perceptions are our own and may have no basis in objective reality, they reflect our personal preferences and biases. Anything that impacts our perception of the rewards that others can offer plays a role in determining to whom we are attracted. Additionally, what qualifies as "rewarding" varies from one individual to another. For example, in the scenario that opened this chapter, Julie may find that the qualities she sees initially rewarding in a prospective partner (e.g., he has a large social network) are actually something that may be harmful for long-term dating success (e.g., he spends all of his time with his friends). So, one key for Julie is the qualities that she finds attractive and whether those jive with good attributes for long-term mates.

Expectations

People's perceptions of reward value are influenced by our behavioral expectations. Numerous studies have shown that people's expectations of others play a large role in the attraction process (see Afifi & Burgoon, 2000). This process operates in two ways. First, people's expectations determine what they notice as being unusual or usual, which influences their attraction to others. When people act in unusual ways, others take notice (Burgoon & Hale, 1988). In general, if the unexpected behavior is perceived as rewarding, attraction should increase. By contrast, if the unexpected behavior is perceived as unrewarding, attraction is likely to decrease (Afifi & Burgoon, 2000). For instance, if Julie expects Tim to lend her his class notes and he refuses, her attraction for him will likely decrease. In the same vein, people are attracted to those who positively violate their expectations. Thus, if Tim not only offers to lend Julie his notes but also tells her she can call him at home with questions, her expectations may be exceeded, and her attraction for him is likely to increase. So, something that Julie should also consider is her expectations of potential dating partners and how those impact her attraction to others.

Second, people's expectations have a way of becoming reality, regardless of the other person's actual behavior, and in so doing influence to whom people are attracted. This suggests that our expectations of other people lead us to treat them in ways that make it more likely that they will confirm our expectations. For example, if Julie thinks Philip is a friendly, considerate person, she is likely to treat him with respect, which, in turn, will make Philip more likely to treat Julie in a friendly, considerate manner. This also suggests that we tend to perceive people as acting in ways that fulfill our expectations, regardless of their actual behaviors. The extensive research on self-fulfilling prophecies supports these ideas. In one study, new teachers were told that certain students were "smart" and that other students were "less smart" (see Rosenthal & Jacobson, 1968). Although the two groups of students actually were no different from each other, by the end of the semester, the teachers' expectations about the students' intelligence translated into different grades and even IQ scores for the two groups. The students whom the teachers expected to be smart received better grades and had higher IQs than the students

saddled with lower teacher expectations despite the initial similarity in ability and intelligence between the two groups.

This important study was followed by a series of studies that investigated why the teachers' expectations resulted in different grades and performance. At least two explanations have been given. First, teachers treated student comments and essays differently. Specifically, when supposedly poor students gave good answers, teachers focused on superficial aspects of their answers and attributed the smart-sounding parts of the responses to luck. By contrast, when supposedly smart students gave poor answers, teachers tended to look for something positive in their responses. For example, if a student labeled as smart commented that a political candidate won a debate because the candidate "was nicer," the teacher might interpret the student's answer to mean that viewers put too much weight on style compared to substance.

Second, the teachers' expectations led them to treat the two groups differently, which eventually influenced the actual quality of the students' work and their performance. Teachers gave mostly positive feedback to the supposedly bright students and mostly negative feedback to the supposedly poor students. Eventually, the students in the "poor group" simply stopped trying, while those in the "bright group" were encouraged to try harder (Rubovits & Maher, 1973).

After these studies on teacher-student interaction were published, numerous other studies showed a similar pattern across a range of contexts, including courtrooms, job interviews, and athletic fields. Expectancy effects have also been found in research on attraction. For example, Snyder, Tanke, and Berscheid (1977) tested the impact of men's perceptions of women's physical attractiveness on the women's behavior. The researchers found that, when interacting with men who found them physically attractive, women behaved in a more sociable, likable, and friendly manner than when interacting with men who found them unattractive. Thus, subtle interpersonal cues of men's expectations had the power to actually influence the women's behavior.

Research on beliefs about future interactions provides another example of how expectations influence attraction. When people expect to see someone again, they are more likely to find that person attractive, regardless of the individual's behavior, than if they do not have expectations of future interaction (Kellermann & Reynolds, 1990). The expectation of future interaction motivates people to look for positive qualities in someone so that they will look forward to future interactions rather than dread them, and increases the chances that people will find the individual attractive. Conversely, when people interact with someone whom they do not foresee meeting again, they have little reason to search for positive qualities. In fact, doing so may be depressing given that they may not have the opportunity to get to know the person better in future interactions. Indeed, people are sometimes motivated to find negative qualities in individuals whom they do not expect to see again, thereby minimizing any attraction.

Demographic Characteristics

As we have seen, perceptions and expectations have a direct effect on whom people find attractive. Sex, age, and other demographic variables also affect attraction, although the effects of such variables appear to be somewhat weaker than those connected to expectations. The demographic characteristic that has received the most attention in the attraction literature is sex.

Sex Differences

One of the most frequently asked questions is whether men and women differ in what qualities they find attractive. The popular belief is that men are primarily attracted by looks whereas women are more often attracted by personality, but is this belief supported by research findings? In fact, the majority of studies show that men are attracted to others based on physical appearance more than are women (also see Chapter 7). For example, Feingold (1991) reviewed results from seven studies conducted in the 1970s and 1980s and concluded that "men valued physical attractiveness more than did women, and that women valued similarity more than did men" (p. 357). Similarly, Sprecher (1998a) found

that men rated physical attractiveness as a more important reason for attraction than did women, while women rated personality as a more important reason for attraction than did men.

One explanation for these sex differences, and others like them (see Hamida, Mineka, & Bailey, 1998), stems from social evolutionary theory (also see Chapters 7 and 10). Social evolutionary theorists argue that sex differences in attraction are consistent with our evolution as a species. A central idea in social evolutionary theory is that humans, like all mammalian species, are driven by a desire to advance the species. Because only the strong survive, people are attracted to those whom they consider to be the "strongest" (see Buss, 1994; Schmitt, 2008). Because men and women fulfill different roles in the evolutionary chain, they look for different qualities in their mating partners. Specifically, theorists argue that women "are looking for men who are willing to commit and who can provide security for them and their offspring" (Pines, 1998, p. 148), whereas men are simply looking for the most attractive (and most potentially fertile) women available.

Social evolutionary theories suggest that these specialized sex roles evolved over thousands of years and are responsible for many of the sex differences observed today. According to this view, women are attracted to older men with more resources, whereas men typically are drawn to younger women in their reproductive prime (Buss, 1994). Also, men are more easily influenced by physical appearance, while women attend more closely to personality, resources, and compatibility.

However, sex differences in attraction are not always as clear-cut as these studies suggest. In fact, sex differences between men and women may be exaggerated in studies in which the researchers rely on data from questionnaires. In these studies, respondents rate the extent to which physical appearance is an important part of their attraction to others. Women appear to be more hesitant than men to report that physical attraction is an important part of their selection process. Indeed, when researchers use a different measure to test whether both men and women are more attracted to physically appealing others, they find that men and women are both influenced by physical attraction. Sprecher (1989) conducted a study in which men and women were given a wide range of information about someone of the opposite sex. Of all the information provided, that which was related to the person's physical attractiveness was found to be the most important determinant of attraction for both men and women. However, when Sprecher later asked participants how much the person's physical attractiveness influenced their attraction, men were more willing than women to acknowledge its effect. In sum, as is typical in much of the research that we will discuss in this book, sex differences in social attraction may be overstated. Men and women seem more similar than different in terms of what they find attractive in others.

Gender Differences

Rather than studying sex differences, several scholars argue that we need to think of everyone as varying on a continuum of masculine-feminine qualities labeled as "gender orientation" or "sex-role orientation" (Archer, 1989; Bem, 1974). For instance, you may know men whose beliefs and behaviors are relatively feminine and women whose beliefs and behaviors are relatively masculine. Many men and women display a mix of feminine and masculine behaviors and beliefs, and are classified as **androgynous** (Bem, 1974). Clearly, socialization affects much behavior. Thus, men who grow up in an environment that encourages emotional expression and that values personal qualities are not expected to behave similarly to or be attracted to the same types of partners as men who grow up in an environment in which emotional expression is discouraged or masculinity is defined by inattention to relationships. The same can be said for women. Mayback and Gold (1994) found that women who agree with "traditional" female roles are more attracted to aggressive, "macho" men than are women whose attitudes toward female roles are more unconventional. Thinking about differences between people based on their location on a masculine-feminine continuum, rather than based simply on their biological sex, may be the better way to understand differences and similarities between people.

Sexual Orientation and Age

Two other important demographic characteristics that have received little attention from scholars are sexual orientation and age. The few studies that have examined the impact of these variables suggest that they do not have much effect on the qualities that people seek in their mates. For example, gay men are attracted to many of the same qualities that heterosexual men and women are (Boyden, Carroll, & Maier, 1984). In a similar vein, scholars studying aging have found that people show remarkable consistency in whom they find attractive, regardless of age. In fact, people seem to find essentially the same qualities attractive whether they are in their preteen or teen years or in their 70s or 80s (Aboud & Mendelson, 1998; Webb, Delaney, & Young, 1989). In sum, although these studies did not find differences in attraction due to sexual orientation or age, given the small number of studies, it seems premature to dismiss the possibility that differences exist.

Personality

Many aspects of personality are important in relationships. Our personalities influence the types of partners to which we are the most attracted and are the most compatible. Numerous facets of our personalities impact the attraction process. We examine four of these: attachment style, relationship beliefs, self-esteem, and narcissism.

Attachment Style

A substantial amount of research has investigated how attachment style functions within relationships (see Chapter 7; see also Creasey & Jarvis, 2008, for discussion of attachment theory and attraction). **Attachment styles** reflect how people view themselves and their relationships with others. These views are represented by four attachment styles (Bartholomew, 1990): (1) Secure individuals are comfortable both alone and in relationships; (2) dismissive individuals prefer to be alone and are unmotivated to develop and maintain relationships; (3) fearful avoidant individuals fear intimacy and lack self-confidence; and (4) preoccupied individuals want intimacy and fear being alone.

Attachment style influences to whom we are attracted. For example, Bartholomew (1990) argued that one way people maintain their attachment styles is through the unconscious process of selectively choosing interaction partners who confirm their sense of self and others. This may explain why people who are treated badly as children are attracted to romantic partners who also treat them badly. In a related vein, Sperling and Borgaro (1995) found that preoccupied individuals are more attracted to people who provide a hint of positive feedback than are securely attached persons. Apparently, because preoccupied individuals strongly desire to be in relationships, they grab onto any potential opportunity suggested by someone giving them a compliment. Secure individuals, by contrast, are not so quick to jump at the potential opportunity; other factors influence their relationship choices. So, an important piece of the attraction puzzle with which Julie is struggling resides in her attachment style and related relational behavior.

Relationship Beliefs

Knee (1998) examined how relationship beliefs impact attraction. Two dimensions underlie people's beliefs about the nature of relationships: destiny beliefs and growth beliefs. **Destiny beliefs** are based on the idea that first impressions of others are fixed and enduring, and that people cannot change. **Growth beliefs** are based on the belief that impressions of others evolve over time, and that people and relationships grow when faced with challenges.

Not surprisingly, studies have found that the process of attraction is quite different for people based on which type of these types of beliefs they hold (for review, see Knee & Bush, 2008). Those who hold strong destiny beliefs are quick to discount someone whom they see as less than an ideal partner. Conversely, they strongly pursue those with whom they have a "perfect" first encounter. They believe that some people are destined to meet (e.g., "soul mates"), rely heavily on their "gut" instinct to make that assessment, and are only attracted to those for whom they have that sense of destined connection. In contrast, those who hold growth beliefs believe that relationships

are always a work in progress and that they require regular work. As a result, "imperfections" in others are not a "deal breaker" when it comes to attraction.

Self-Esteem

Several studies have shown that how people feel about themselves strongly influences whom they find attractive. For example, Joshi and Rai (1987) found that people's self-esteem directly relates to their level of attraction to others. That is, those who have high self-esteem consistently find others more attractive than those whose self-esteem is low.

Self-esteem can operate in even more subtle ways. In two studies, Hoyle, Insko, and Moniz (1992) assessed students' self-esteem, asked students to complete a bogus test on intelligence, and then provided them with either positive or negative feedback about their performance. After this feedback, the students talked briefly with another person and completed a survey about their attraction to the interaction partner. The students with low self-esteem were more attracted to the other after being told good news about their performance on the "intelligence test," compared to being told bad news about their performance. In other words, good news made them more attracted to others, perhaps because they associated the person with a rewarding situation, or perhaps because they were simply in better moods, felt confident, and were more receptive to their interaction partner's positive qualities.

People with high self-esteem showed the exact opposite pattern in Hoyle and fellow researchers' (1992) study; that is, they were more attracted to others after hearing bad news about their performance on the intelligence test than they were after hearing good news. Why would that be? One explanation is that people with high self-esteem recognize the need to boost their self-image after receiving bad news, and one way to do so is to view others as attractive and to interact with them. In that case, the most likely time that people with high self-esteem are likely to be attracted to others is after experiencing a failure (e.g., doing poorly on an exam).

Narcissism

Recall that narcissism is defined in terms of having an exaggerated sense of self-importance and a focus on oneself at the expense of others. Campbell (1999) conducted five studies to determine how individuals' degree of narcissism affects their attraction to others. He found big differences between the qualities that are attractive to narcissists and to non-narcissists. Most noticeably, narcissists are attracted to others who admire them, while non-narcissists are drawn to others who exhibit caring qualities. Other studies have found similar results, showing that narcissists are more focused on the short-term rewards they get from relationships, and therefore look for someone who provides them with immediate admiration rather than long-term mutual liking (Emmons, 1989; Mofr & Rhodewalt, 2001).

Despite their illusions of self-importance, research suggests that some narcissists have relatively low self-esteem and seek self-esteem boosts. In fact, in Campbell's (1999) study, narcissistic were partly drawn to admiring others because of their own need to improve their self-esteem. Narcissists may also protect their self-esteem by downplaying situations where they are rejected. In one study (Rhodewalt & Eddings, 2002), highly narcissistic men were especially likely to elaborate on positive aspects of their dating history if they had been rejected by a potential dating partner, perhaps as a defense mechanism that protected them from feeling badly after being rejected.

OTHER PEOPLE'S QUALITIES

So far, our discussion has focused on personal perceptions and predispositions people have when evaluating others' attractiveness. Of course, other people's qualities increase one's likelihood of being attracted to them. As noted earlier, one view of attraction boils down to a perception that someone can offer us more rewards than costs relative to other potential partners. Thus, the key question becomes: What qualities do people find especially rewarding? People seem to prefer those who are physically attractive and communicatively competent.

Moreover, people who are perceived to be in high demand and moderately "hard to get" are also highly valued. In this section, we discuss these variables, starting with the quality that has received the most attention—physical attractiveness.

Physical Attractiveness

Studies have consistently shown that physical attractiveness is one of the top two predictors of social attraction (Dion, 1986; Huston & Levinger, 1978). For example, Sprecher (1989) found that the more physically attractive the other person was, the more attracted participants were to the person. Similarly, Johnson and colleagues' (1994) research on first dates among dating club members showed that, more than any other quality, people's physical attractiveness determined whether their dates found them socially attractive. These findings may not be surprising, but the more interesting question may be what specific "looks" we find attractive.

The answer to that question is too complex to be fully addressed here and in some ways is culturally determined (see Box 3.2), but several studies have yielded some insights. One feature that has been shown to strongly influence women's attraction to men is height. In fact, studies have found that women tend to find very short men unattractive as potential mates even when the researcher assigns them a whole host of other rewarding qualities, such as a positive personality, intelligence, and high earning potential (Jackson & Ervin, 1992; Pierce, 1996). Tall women also seem to be at an advantage, but less than their male counterparts (Hensley, 1994). Across many different cultures, when men are being evaluated, a strong jawline, broad shoulders, and a hip-to-waist ratio or slightly less than one (i.e., a waist just slightly smaller than the hips) contribute to judgments of physical attractiveness. For women, a soft jawline and an hourglass figure (i.e., a waist significantly smaller than the chest and hips) is preferred (Buss, 1989, 1994; Singh, 1995). Both men and women also value physical fitness and an athletic build in their dating partners. Overweight people, particularly in the United States, are not considered attractive.

BOX 3.2 Highlights

**When Beauty Is in the Eye of Some Beholders: Attributes
of Beauty That Vary Based on Culture and Individual Preferences**

Coloring: People have different preferences for eye, hair, and skin color. Often these preferences vary on the basis of what is perceived as scarce in a particular culture or coculture (e.g., dark skin and hair is more prized in places where light hair and skin is common and vice versa). In the United States, women have a slight preference toward men with darker coloring, whereas men have a slight preference toward women with lighter coloring.

Weight: Preferences regarding weight vary by culture, especially for women. In most industrialized countries, such as the United States, thinness is prized because it indicates that a person has the resources needed to eat healthy foods and stay in shape. However, in other places, such as the Ivory Coast, plumpness is prized because it is associated with wealth and having enough to eat. Importantly, the .70 waist-to-hip ratio can characterize women regardless of whether they are thin or heavy.

Height: Although the preference for tall men has been found in many cultures, there are differences in how much this attribute is valued. Preferences related to women's height vary quite a bit as a function of culture and personal preference. In general, men prefer women who are shorter than they are, whereas women prefer men who are taller than they are. Thus, a person's own height influences who that person finds attractive.

SOURCE: Information compiled from Guerrero and Floyd (2006).

Perhaps preoccupation with looks seems unfair and people should be judged by their inner character rather than their outward appearance. This may be true, but the research suggests that, fair or not, people use outward appearances to make judgments about people's inner character. Specifically, research has shown that people often associate good looks with a wide range of other positive qualities. This tendency, often called the **halo effect** or the what-is-beautiful-is-good stereotype, leads people to believe that physically attractive individuals are more likely to succeed, and are more sociable, popular, intelligent, and competent than their less attractive counterparts (Dion, 1986; Dion, Berscheid, & Walster, 1972; Hatfield & Sprecher, 1986b). The halo effect means that people are drawn to attractive individuals because most people are looking for someone who offers the "complete package." Because looks

are a shortcut for other positive traits, physically attractive people receive more positive attention from others throughout life (Dion, 1972), often develop more positive self-esteem (Nell & Ashton, 1996), and may actually develop some of the skills people assume they have (Chaiken, 1979).

The halo effect helps explain why good looks are so important in the attraction process. Social evolutionary theorists offer a complementary explanation for why physical attractiveness matters. Specifically, they argue that people's attraction to particular physical traits is due to the genetic drive to mate with the fittest person possible (Buss, 1994). To that end, physically attractive individuals should be socially attractive to the greatest number of people because they are essentially the most highly evolved physical specimens in our species and so are highly prized. Physical fitness, especially body shape and size, is also an outward sign of health and fertility. Thus, although cultural standards for beauty vary, social evolutionary theorists predict that some preferences cut across cultures (see Box 3.3). For example, physical attributes related to health and fertility, such as a clear complexion and a physically fit body, have been found to be valued by most cultures around the globe (Buss, 1994). In fact, Buss's now-classic 1989 study showed remarkable consistency across 37 cultures in what they found to be physically attractive. Langlois, Kalakanis, Rubenstein, Larson, Hallam, and Smoot's (2000) summary of 130 samples found the same. Specifically, we seem to be unconsciously drawn to features such as body and facial symmetry, body proportionality, and particular waist-to-hip ratios, among many other attributes (for review, see Guerrero & Floyd, 2006).

BOX 3.3 Highlights

When Beauty Is in the Eye of All Beholders: Universal Attributes of Beauty

Body and facial symmetry: When two sides of a face or body mirror each other, a person is rated as more physically attractive.

Body proportionality and the golden ratio: The ratio of ϕ (Phi), or 1 to 1.618, is an index of attractiveness (e.g., bodies are rated as more proportional if the distance from the navel to the bottom of the feet is 1.618 times the distance from the navel to the top of the head; faces are rated as more proportional if the width of the lips is 1.618 times the width of the nose, among other comparisons).

Waist-to-hip ratio: For women, the ideal ratio is .70 (the waist is 70% the size of the hips). For men the ideal ratio is about 1.0 (hips and waist about the same size).

Koinophilia: Faces are rated as more attractive when they have "average" features, with studies showing that a computer composite of multiple faces is perceived as more attractive than any single face.

Facial neoteny and maturity: Faces are rated as more attractive when they are characterized by a combination of babylike and mature features that represent youth and sexuality (e.g., a woman with large eyes, full lips, and high cheekbones or a man with large eyes, a small nose, and strong jawline).

SOURCE: Summarized from Guerrero and Floyd (2006).

Judgments of beauty, however, are not always objective. For example, people involved in romantic relationships tend to see members of the opposite sex as less physically attractive, perhaps as a way of maintaining their current relationship (Simpson, Gangestad, & Lerma, 1990). Research testing **interaction appearance theory** has also demonstrated that people perceive others as more physically attractive if they have warm, positive interactions with them (Albada, Knapp, & Theune, 2002). Thus, in some cases, relationships and interaction can lead people to revise their initial impressions of people or to regard their relational partners as more physically attractive than an objective observer would judge them to be.

Finally, people may be drawn to physically attractive individuals because they hope to gain rewards through association. For instance, think about when you are with your most attractive friends; perhaps you have more opportunities to meet people and feel more attractive yourself. Research suggests that, whether intentional or not, people benefit by interacting with more attractive others. Sigall and Landy (1973), for example, found that people were rated as more attractive when they were with comparatively more attractive individuals than when they were not. The idea here is that some of the attention that physically attractive people get spills over to their friends through what is called the **assimilation effect.**

In sum, most people are attracted to good-looking persons, but what other qualities do we find attractive in potential partners or friends? Is physical appearance all that matters? The answer is a resounding no. People notice those who are physically attractive and are more likely to initiate communication with attractive people, but that does not guarantee that highly attractive people will continue to be valued after initial attraction fades. In fact, they can be at a disadvantage in trying to live up to the high expectations imposed by the halo effect. For example, Hatfield (1984) wrote about a beautiful woman who was insecure because she worried that men would be disappointed if they saw her for what she really was, rather than what they dreamed a beautiful woman should be. Physical appearance only goes so far, and there are other significant qualities that make people attractive.

Interpersonal Communication Skills

Are we so drawn to physically attractive people that their interpersonal communication skills do not matter initially? For years, scholars ignored the role of interpersonal communication in favor of studying the impact of other variables on our attraction. Sunnafrank (1991, 1992) was among the first scholars to study how communication influences attraction. In the mid-1980s, he began a series of studies that added what was, until then, a novel element to studies of attraction—he actually had participants interact with the person they were rating on attraction. Most previous studies had only shown participants a picture or given them information about

some fictitious character. Sunnafrank argued that, unless people communicated, experiments would not be representative of the real qualities that people consider when evaluating the attractiveness of others. In fact, he suggested that many of the factors that scholars had found to predict attraction, such as similarity and physical attractiveness, might not matter as much once people started talking to one another. Instead, he claimed, people would be influenced by another's communication style and behavior to determine how attracted they were to each other.

Many studies have supported Sunnafrank's contention. Reyes and fellow researchers (1999) had students view a still picture of an actor and asked them to answer several survey questions, including questions about their attraction to the actor. Then the students watched an interaction in which an opposite-sex actor was either nice or acted like a jerk and answered the questions again. The power of communication was evident. Although physical attractiveness was a primary quality that drew people to the actor prior to watching the interaction, the actor's behavior during the interaction, whether positive or negative, became a primary determinant of their attraction to the actor afterwards; physical attractiveness hardly mattered. Thus, communication plays a key role in determining to whom we are attracted. But what specific communication styles do we find appealing? Some studies provide important clues as to the connection between communication and attraction.

One communication quality that seems to emerge relatively consistently in studies of attraction is warmth. A generally positive attitude and a show of concern for others typically communicates warmth (Folkes & Sears, 1977); nonverbally, such behaviors as smiling, making eye contact, and showing interest in the other person also communicate warmth (Andersen, 1985; Andersen & Guerrero, 1998a; Friedmann, Riggio, & Casella, 1988). In fact, Sprecher (1998a) conducted three studies, all of which revealed that warmth and kindness were rated as the two qualities of the interaction partner that were most responsible for the participant's attraction to the partner.

Sociability and competence are two other communication qualities that been have shown to influence attraction (Krueger & Caspi, 1993). Here, sociability refers to one's ability to communicate easily among a group of people. People who are extroverted and expressive are perceived as highly sociable. Competence is determined by one's level of composure and knowledge. People are often evaluated as competent when they communicate without showing signs of nervousness and seem knowledgeable, although when people go out of their way to seem knowledgeable they are often rated as unattractive (Vangelisti et al., 1990).

In contrast to these "softer" qualities of warmth—sociability and competence—some people are drawn to potentially "darker" qualities. For example, several studies have shown that women in particular are attracted to men who show a certain degree of assertiveness or power. This is consistent with social evolutionary theory in that women should be attracted to behavioral expressions of dominance in men because it reflects a reproductive advantage. In other words, women should be subconsciously attracted to the strongest and fittest men, who will produce the best offspring. To test this idea, Sadalla, Kenrick, and Vershure (1987) created perceptions of dominance by having male actors take seats close to the subjects. The "nondominant" actors sat up straight and chatted quietly among themselves; the "dominant" actors sat in a very relaxed posture and showed a lack of interest in the women while talking loudly, quickly, and clearly. They found that the women were most attracted to the men who showed these signs of dominance.

Does this mean that women prefer dominant men to nice men? Jensen-Campbell, Graziano, and West (1995) attempted to address the question of whether "nice guys really finish last." They argued that from an evolutionary perspective, women should also value altruism in men because they want partners who make sacrifices and invest considerable resources in the relationship. This is exactly what they found. First, women were attracted to altruistic men (men who were willing to do something boring so that the woman did not have to) much more than to nonaltruistic men (men who jumped at the opportunity to do something fun and left the boring task to the woman). The study was

consistent with the research showing that people are attracted to individuals who are warm and caring. However, men who were altruistic but otherwise unassertive and weak were not very attractive. Men who were assertive or dominant and nonaltruistic were not attractive to the women either. Instead, women found the combination of assertiveness or dominance and altruism most appealing. Thus, strong but altruistic men may be perceived as most attractive.

Interestingly, the same results did not emerge with regard to men's attraction to women. That is, men's levels of attraction were unaffected by a woman's level of dominance but the men were much more attracted to altruistic women. So, again, the importance of communicating care in interactions shines through; nice men, and women, do not necessarily have to finish last.

Finally, the timing of positive versus negative behavior seems to influence attraction. Several studies have identified what has been called the **loss-gain effect** (Afifi & Burgoon, 2000; Aronson & Linder, 1965; Sharma & Kaur, 1996). This effect reflects what happens to attraction when a person's behavior moves from positive to negative or from negative to positive. For example, if someone seems very nice to you early in the interaction, but then begins to act like a jerk, would you be more attracted to that person than if the person was a jerk from the start? Studies suggest that you would not. In fact, people are more attracted to individuals who are consistently negative than to people who initially behave positively and then switch to negative behavior. People who start out being nice get our hopes up, so the letdown we experience when we discover that they are not nice makes it worse than if they had acted badly from the start. Of course, people are most attracted to those who are pleasant throughout an interaction.

The "Hard-to-Get" Phenomenon

In some situations, the person who acts somewhat hard to get is perceived as attractive. For example, Roberson and Wright (1994) put males in a situation in which they had to try to convince a female stranger (who was actually working for the experimenters) to be their coworker on a project. The men were told that the woman either would be easy to convince, might be difficult to convince, or would be impossible to convince. Results showed that the men rated the woman whom they were told would be moderately difficult to convince as most attractive. The authors concluded that playing hard to get has its benefits but that it can backfire if the person is seen as unattainable.

These findings were consistent with prior research by Wright and colleagues. Wright, Toi, and Brehm (1984) were interested in whether the amount of energy that people put into pursuing someone relates to how much people like the individual they are pursuing. In this study, Wright and colleagues told male participants that they could work with a female actor on a project if they could memorize a certain number of sentence combinations in two minutes. Participants were assigned to memorize either two (the easy condition), five (the moderately difficult condition), or eight (the very difficult condition) combinations. Before the researchers had the men try to memorize these combinations, they asked them to rate the actor. Remarkably, given that the task was all that differed, the men who were about to try memorizing five combinations rated the actor as more attractive than the men in either the easy or the very difficult condition.

Similarly, Wright and Contrada (1986) found that people rated members of the opposite sex as most attractive when they were portrayed as moderately selective rather than as very selective or nonselective. Why is that? Apparently, we are more attracted to individuals who present a bit of a challenge than to those whom we perceive to be too easily attainable or completely unattainable. One reason for this may be that, in our effort to shoot for the best possible "catch," we think that we are not shooting high enough if we are attracted to those who are not at least somewhat of a challenge. Consistent with this reasoning, research has shown that we are most likely to be attracted to hard-to-get people if they are easy for us to attract but difficult for others to attract (Walster, Walster, Piliavin, & Schmidt, 1973). One explanation is that when a person is hard for others to get but easy for you to get,

people view you in a more positive light. In other words, people will likely perceive that you must have outstanding personal qualities if you were able to obtain such a high-quality partner. Another explanation is that scarcer resources, including people, are more valuable.

In sum, in addition to individuals' own personal qualities, many qualities of other people increase or decrease feelings of attraction. However, unique qualities emerge when two people interact with each other. These factors, which we call the *chemistry* or *synergy* between people, also affect attraction.

INTERPERSONAL CHEMISTRY BETWEEN PEOPLE

When two people interact, the synergy of their interaction creates a certain chemistry that determines their mutual interpersonal attraction. One of the strongest and most important aspects of interpersonal chemistry is the degree to which people are similar to one another. This conclusion is far from new. As early as 1870, Sir Francis Galton, the cousin of Charles Darwin and a scientist best known for his research on intelligence and heredity, concluded that spouses usually are similar on several characteristics. Over the next century, many studies showed that friends and spouses tend to be similar on everything from attitudes and beliefs to height and visual acuity (Byrne, 1992). These studies all reached the same conclusion: The more similar others are to us, the more we will be attracted to them.

Similarity: "Birds of a Feather Flock Together"

Do similar individuals really tend to hang out together as this saying suggests? Think about your friends and dating partners. Do most of them have a lot in common with you? Maybe you like to do the same things, think the same way, or have similar personalities. Or perhaps you come from similar backgrounds. This preference for similarity has been shown to hold true across a whole host of personal qualities, including demographic characteristics such as race, cultural background, educational level, socioeconomic status, and religion, among other demographic characteristics (Hill, Rubin, & Peplau,

1976; Kandel, 1978). However, similarity has been studied most extensively in the context of similarity among attitudes.

Attitudinal Similarity

When people are similar in their attitudes, beliefs, and values, they are said to share attitudinal similarity. People can have perceived similarity (thinking that they are similar to the other person) or actual similarity (actually being similar to the other person), or both. Two people may think they share attitudes and beliefs but later find out that they have very different likes and dislikes. The importance of this distinction quickly became evident to researchers. In one of the first extensive studies of attitudinal similarity, Newcomb (1961) found important differences between actual and perceived similarity. Newcomb gave a group of male undergraduates room and board in exchange for their participation in a study on friendships. The participants were randomly assigned roommates and were given surveys throughout the school year. The results showed that roommates liked one another more when they were similar. Interestingly, at the beginning of the year, perceived similarity and actual similarity did not match. New roommates were often oblivious to the actual level of similarity they shared, so they relied heavily on their perceptions of similarity to determine liking. As the year went on, however, the actual degree of similarity between roommates gradually became evident. By the end of the year, those who were actually dissimilar did not like one another, even though their initial perceptions of similarity had led them to like one another at first. This distinction between actual and perceived similarity has continued to play an important role in studies of attraction.

Recently, Morry (2005) reminded us that both actual and perceived similarity have important relational implications. She studied the attraction similarity in ongoing same-sex friendships. Like other researchers, she found similarity to be important, but also showed that the happier people were in their friendships, the more similar they reported their friends to be. Importantly, she was able to show that the attraction came *before* the bias toward perceptions

of similarity in her study. In other words, we tend to see people to whom we're attracted as being more similar to us than they really are. Relatedly, we see people we dislike as being less similar. This finding does not discount the importance of actual similarity, but it underscores that we also have biases that make us feel more similar or different than we actually are to others.

At about the same time of Newcomb's now famous experiment, Byrne (1961, 1971) began to research the impact of attitudinal similarity attraction, which has contributed greatly to our understanding of the relationship between similarity and attraction. One of his main methods for testing the effect of similarity on attraction was what he labeled the "bogus stranger" method. Byrne would first ask participants a series of questions assessing their likes and dislikes. He would then take the questionnaire to a different room and create answers on another, similar questionnaire that ranged from being almost identical to the participants' answers to very different from the participants' answers. Next he took the "bogus" survey back to the participants, told them that the survey belonged to a participant who had already taken part in the study, asked them to read it over, and then rate the extent to which they would be attracted to this "bogus stranger." Byrne and his colleagues repeatedly found that participants were more attracted to bogus strangers who were similar to them (Byrne, 1997).

Not surprisingly, the real-life applicability of this method has been challenged, with some scholars arguing that this similarity effect disappears when two people communicate with each other (Sunnafrank, 1991). Nonetheless, the remarkable consistency of the finding that people are attracted to attitudinally similar individuals is hard to dispute. Thus, the question becomes centered upon what it is that makes attitudinal similarity so important.

According to Byrne's (1971) **reinforcement model**, we are attracted to similar others because they reinforce our view of the world as the correct perspective. People do not like it when others challenge the correctness of their own attitudes and values. The best way to avoid such a challenge is to interact with individuals who think the same way. For example, imagine disagreeing about everything with your friends or dating partner; that would get tiresome rather quickly, so you probably avoid people with whom you think that may happen. By contrast, when two people are similar, they usually have more in common to talk about and like to do the same things, which makes interaction enjoyable. Similarities make people's lives much easier, as well as make people feel that their way is the "right" way since others share their views. The disadvantage, of course, is that people fail to grow very much if all their friends are just like them.

Similarity in Communication Skills

People also have a preference for similarity in communication style. Burleson (1998) examined why people are attracted to others who have similar levels of communication skills and are happier with similarly skilled individuals than with those who are not similarly skilled. What intrigued Burleson was not that very good communicators are attracted to other good communicators, but that poor communicators are also drawn to other poor communicators. Why might people with limited communication skills be attracted to others who are similarly limited? Burleson (1998) advanced four possible explanations:

1. *The differential importance explanation*: Communication may not be a very frequent or important activity for those with low communication skill. As a result, low-skill people may not care if their partner is unskilled. In other words, since low-skill people do not engage in communication very often, they may not be looking for a high-skill partner. Other factors affecting attraction may be more important to them.

2. *The "ignorance is bliss" explanation*: Low-skill individuals are not aware that some people communicate better than they do. Because they have relationships with similar others, most of their interactions have been with people with relatively low social skills. As a result, they are happy with the way their low-skill partner communicates.

3. *The "sour grapes" explanation*: People who have poor communication skills are painfully aware of their shortcomings in the social arena. Although they might like to have partners with

better skills than they have, they perceive highly skilled communicators to be hopelessly out of their reach. As a result, they settle for partners with lower social skills, figuring these partners are as good as they can get, while downgrading more skilled people.

4. *The skill-as-culture explanation*: What some people consider to be poor communication, others might actually see as effective communication. Thus, individuals who are defined as low-skill communicators by researchers may be enacting communication behaviors that they and their partners consider to be quite competent. For example, some people might perceive low levels of expressiveness as indicative of incompetence, but an inexpressive dyad might feel most comfortable keeping their emotions hidden.

Similarity in Physical Attractiveness

A final form of similarity extensively studied for its impact on attraction is similarity in physical attractiveness. Have you ever noticed, for instance, how people who are dating tend to be similar in terms of physical attractiveness? In fact, people take notice when one member of a romantic couple is much better looking than the other, as is evidenced by the popularity of the MTV show, *Is She Really Going Out With Him?* Fair or not, the automatic assumption is that the less attractive partner must have other exceptional qualities (e.g., a great personality, wealth, or high social standing) that led the more attractive partner to choose this person over better-looking alternatives.

Our tendency to be attracted to people who are similar to us in physical attractiveness has been called the **matching hypothesis** (Berscheid, Dion, Walster, & Walster, 1971). This does not mean that people search for partners who look similar to themselves in terms of physical features, for example, brown-eyed people looking for brown-eyed partners, or people with high cheek bones and fair skin looking for partners who have similar bone structure and skin color. Instead, the matching hypothesis predicts that people look for partners who have roughly the same level of overall physical attractiveness as themselves. Thus, even though Julie is a petite, fair-skinned, green-eyed blonde and Steven is a tall, dark-skinned, brown-eyed brunet, because they are both good looking they fit the matching hypothesis. By contrast, if you think you are fairly good looking but not stunningly beautiful or devastatingly handsome, the matching hypothesis predicts that you will look for a partner who is somewhat above average but not extraordinarily attractive. Interestingly, the matching hypothesis has been shown to hold true across a wide variety of relationship types, from friendships to marriages, and cultures (Feingold, 1988).

However, this matching hypothesis appears to be in stark contrast to the research on physical attractiveness. Those studies found that people are most attracted to individuals who are very physically attractive. By contrast, research on the matching hypothesis suggests that people are most attracted to individuals who are similar to them in physical attractiveness. In other words, less attractive people should be attracted to other similarly less

attractive people rather than to the best looking ones. These seemingly inconsistent findings lead to two questions: (1) Which of these hypotheses is right? and (2) Why would less attractive people be attracted to other less attractive individuals as opposed to more attractive ones?

The answer to both of these questions depends on people's sense of what is ideal and realistic. Ideally, people want to date others who are more attractive than they are, but realistically recognize that physically attractive individuals are likely to have many options and are somewhat selective about whom they date. Recall the research on the hard-to-get phenomenon. These studies showed that people are attracted to individuals who are somewhat hard to get but tend to shy away from individuals who are too selective because they do not want to waste their effort on people they see as too selective, choosy, or conceited. Thus, people may label someone who is much better looking

What assumptions do people make about couples who do not fit the matching hypothesis? Are these assumptions fair or unfair?

than themselves as conceited and instead select a dating partner who is similar to themselves in terms of physical attractiveness. In short, the matching hypothesis is based on the idea that people want to maximize the attractiveness of their partner by choosing someone who is at least as attractive as themselves while minimizing their chances for rejection by choosing someone who is attainable. Based on this reasoning, both the beautiful-is-good and matching hypotheses appear to have some basis in truth.

Similarity in Names and Birth Dates

Recent evidence suggests that our affinity for similar others may go to absurd lengths. Using the notion of **implicit egotism**, several scholars have shown that we are attracted to others based on similarity on the most arbitrary things. These scholars argue that even similarity in first or last names, in the size of earlobes, or in the date of birth, among other subtle similarities, activate liking for others because these characteristics are subconsciously associated with liking for ourselves (e.g., our names, our earlobe lengths, our birth dates). If this sounds crazy, it is worth pointing out that several studies have observed this trend. For example, Jones, Pelham, Carvallo, and Mirenberg (2004) summarized seven studies they performed that systematically tested this implicit egotism effect. In the end, their studies showed that people were more attracted to others whose arbitrary experimental code assigned by the researchers shared similarities with their birth dates or were subliminally connected to their names. Moreover, their investigation of marriage records showed that people are disproportionately likely to marry someone whose first or last name shares at least some similarity to their own (e.g., their first or last name starts with the same letter), even after accounting for ethnic similarities in names. More research is necessary to determine the extent to which implicit egotism plays a role in the attraction process. In particular, implicit egotism would probably be most relevant when a person has high self-esteem, but this possibility has not yet been tested. Also, researchers need to see if similarities in things such

as names and birth dates are more or less important than similarities in other areas, such as physical appearance.

Complementarity: Sometimes Opposites Attract

Although the research discussed thus far shows that there is a strong similarity effect when it comes to attraction and liking, this does not mean that people are always similar on every valued characteristic. Sometimes relational partners or good friends also complement one another in some areas. For example, Julie and her best friend, Brittany, might both be intelligent, have the same major in college, and enjoy winter sports such as ice skating and skiing, but Julie might be the better student while Brittany might be the better athlete. Instead of envying each other's skills, they may be proud of each other's special talents and Julie may benefit from Brittany's contribution to their tennis team, while Brittany benefits from Julie's help in studying for an exam. They also might be completely different in some ways. For instance, Julie might be shy and reserved, carefully thinking before talking, while Brittany is extroverted and impulsive. Likewise, these qualities could complement one another; that is, Julie might appreciate having Brittany around to help her make new friends, while Brittany might appreciate it when Julie tells her to think before acting on certain impulses.

As this example suggests, the old saying that "opposites attract" can have some basis in truth. However, **complementarity** seems to be a much better predictor of attraction and liking when it is linked to behavior or resources, and not attitudes and values (Strong et al., 1988). When it comes to people's core attitudes and beliefs, similarity seems to be much more important than complementarity. Additionally, as noted previously, sometimes people are initially attracted to someone who is completely unlike them, only to discover that those "opposite" characteristics eventually drive them crazy. This happened in Julie's relationship with Steven who was too much an extrovert and player for Julie. As Felmlee (1998) suggested in her work on fatal attraction, "Be careful what you wish for," because sometimes you might get it and then regret it (p. 235).

Similarity and Complementarity in Initial Versus Committed Relationships

The vast majority of studies on the similarity-attraction link have looked at the advantages or disadvantages of similarity during the initial stages of a relationship's development. However, we know less about the role that similarity plays beyond that stage. Amodio and Showers (2005) examined this issue more closely by having undergraduate students who were in an exclusive dating relationship for at least three months complete two surveys, one year apart. Their results suggest a very important role for commitment in our understanding of the way that similarity operates in ongoing relationships. Specifically, the benefit of similarity for liking and attraction seems to hold primarily for high-commitment couples. Those who reported being highly committed to their relationship benefited from their attribute similarity over time. However, those who reported having low relationship commitment were actually harmed by that similarity.

Amodio and Showers speculated that dissimilarity may actually be exciting for dating partners whom we don't see as long-term mates. In essence, you can experience new things with this person, while knowing that this person is not someone whom you will be with forever. In contrast, being dissimilar to someone with whom you see yourself in a relationship with for a long time is likely to gnaw at you, eroding that liking over time.

So, which characteristic is more attractive—similarity or complementarity? The answer may depend on the goals you have for a relationship with the person. If you hope for, or are in, a highly committed relationship with your partner, then similarity seems to be a key ingredient to success. But if instead you are looking for a somewhat casual relationship experience without considerable commitment, then dissimilarity or complementarity may, in fact, be more what you should look for. Just keep in mind that those differences may come back to haunt you if your relationship goals change. For example,

Julie may like the excitement of having an outgoing and physically attractive boyfriend like Steven, but if she is interested in pursuing a long-term committed relationship, she may be well advised to look for someone who is more similar to her.

In sum, several studies have shown that similarities in attitudes, likes and dislikes, and physical attractiveness are related to attraction and liking. Some complementary features may also be related to attraction, especially when there is complementarity in behavior (e.g., a shy person paired with an outgoing person) or resources (e.g., a wealthy person paired with a beautiful person). The best relationships may be characterized by both similarity and complementarity, with similarity in important attitudes and values sustaining commitment, and complementarity sustaining excitement. The final influence on people's attraction to others is environmental features.

ENVIRONMENTAL FEATURES RELATED TO ATTRACTION

How does the environment or context influence people's attraction to others? The ways the environment can affect attraction and liking may be surprising—environmental features, social networks, and proximity are all contextual elements that are associated with attraction.

Microenvironmental Features

Research suggests that the environment has subtle effects on attraction and liking (see Andersen, 2008). For example, research on room features and their effects has shown that room temperature (Griffit, 1970), the presence of music (May & Hamilton, 1980), and even such seemingly irrelevant characteristics as the size of the room, the presence of high ceilings, the linear perspective of the room, the type of couch material, the color of the walls and ceilings, and the lighting may influence whether people are attracted to one another (Andersen, 2008; Burgoon et al., 2010). For example, environments that encourage interaction by providing a cozy atmosphere can promote attraction.

Similarly, low lighting and soft colors may make certain people look particularly attractive, while brighter lighting and bolder colors may cause other people to look appealing. Environments that put people face-to-face in close proximity also enhance attraction (Andersen, 2008).

Byrne and Clore (1970; see also Clore & Byrne, 1974) have also explained the environmental effects on attraction using the **reinforcement affect model**, according to which certain types of environments are more likely to make people feel good. For example, an intimate setting with comfortable chairs and couches, soft wall colors, low lighting, and soft music relaxes people. These environmentally induced positive emotions get transferred to the interactants in that environment. In other words, people unconsciously associate the feelings they experience in a particular environment with the individuals who are part of that environment.

Other studies have shown that under some circumstances, the emotions people experience due to the environment can also be related to attraction. Dutton and Aron (1974) conducted an unusual experiment to test the impact of environmental cues on attraction. They had male participants cross either a stable or a relatively unstable bridge. To make matters worse, the stable bridge was low-lying while the unstable bridge spanned a steep ravine. After crossing the bridges, the participants were met by either a male or female research assistant and told to write a brief story, which was later coded for sexual imagery. The participants also were given the assistant's phone number and invited to call her or him at home if they wanted more information. Amazingly, the researchers found that the men who crossed the unstable bridge and met the female assistant included more sexual images in their stories and were more likely to call the assistant at home. Apparently their misattributed fear and arousal increased their attraction to the female assistant.

It may seem odd that a negative emotion such as fear can lead to attraction. Why does this happen? Zillman (1978), an emotions theorist, identified the presence of a process called **excitation transfer**. What sometimes happens, Zillman argued, is that people mistake the cause of their emotional arousal.

This is especially likely to happen when people experience arousal in response to two different sources in close proximity to each other. In those cases, people mix the two states of arousal together and attribute excitement to the second stimulus. In the Dutton and Aron study, participants experienced high arousal or anxiety after walking over an unstable bridge and then immediately experienced emotional arousal when they met the female research assistant. In doing so, they may have unconsciously and mistakenly attributed their rapid heartbeats and other signs of intense emotional arousal to the presence of the female assistant, leading them to believe that they were more attracted to her than they objectively might have been. Although this may sound far-fetched (and scholars have challenged the validity of excitation transfer; see Riordan & Tedeschi, 1983), other studies have confirmed this finding (White, Fishbein, & Rutstein, 1981). Apparently, in some cases, people who share scary experiences are more likely to be attracted to each other due to excitation transfer. A recent hit television show might have offered some evidence for this phenomenon. Midway through Season 14 of the hit ABC show *The Bachelor*, Jake (the bachelor) and one of his dates (Vienna) went bungee jumping together off a very high bridge, despite both being deathly afraid of heights. At the end of the jump, as they dangled at the end of the cord, they had their first kiss. Maybe it should have been predictable at that point, given research on the excitation transfer, that Jake proposed to Vienna at the end of the show. However, the notion of excitation transfer and its association with love does not predict relationship longevity: Jake and Vienna broke up soon after the show.

Social Networks

Another factor that impacts attraction is one's social network, including family and friends. For example, have you noticed that what you find attractive in others is often similar to what your friends find attractive? If so, you are not alone. In fact, hundreds of studies have shown that people's attitudes and intentions are strongly influenced by the attitudes of their friends and family (Sheppard, Hartwick, & Warshaw, 1988). Many scholars argue that the attitudes of members of our social circle, known as **subjective norms**, are the strongest predictor of our own attitudes and intentions. Given that attraction represents an attitude toward other people, the feedback we receive from friends and family certainly plays an important role in whom we find attractive.

In most cases, approval by one's social network promotes attraction and liking. For example, if you meet someone you would like to date, and your friends all tell you how wonderful the person is, you are likely to feel even more positively toward this potential dating partner. However, the reverse can also occur. Perhaps you find someone attractive, but after your friends question what you see in the person and discourage you from pursuing a relationship, your attraction decreases. There is one notable exception to this phenomenon, however. Some research has supported the **"Romeo and Juliet" effect**, which predicts that parental interference can strengthen attraction between two people. Specifically, Driscoll, Davis, and Lipetz (1972) found that partners in dating couples reported more love for each other when their parents disapproved of their relationship. Driscoll and fellow researchers retested their hypothesis 10 months later using the same couples and found the same results, with parental interference still positively related to the amount of love couples reported.

There are at least four viable explanations for the Romeo and Juliet effect. First, rebellious young couples may exert their power by defying their parents and becoming romantically involved with their forbidden partner. These feelings of power and excitement may be attributed to their relationship, much as the excitation transfer process suggests. Second, some writers believe that autonomy is so important to young adults that every day is an independence day and differences with parent is a sign of their emerging maturity and independence. Third, as discussed earlier, people may be attracted to individuals who are somewhat challenging or hard to get yet attainable. Finally, if their love is especially strong, the partners can endure disapproval from the social network. Two people who are less in love might be quick to break up when parents and friends disapprove, making it unlikely

that they would be together long enough to be in a research study.

Keep in mind that the Romeo and Juliet effect does not always hold true. In Chapter 15, we report that some couples may break up due to disapproval from parents and friends. Similarly, in Chapter 9, we report that involvement in each other's social network helps keep relational partners close. Sometimes interference from others draws people closer together, but other times such interference tears them apart.

Proximity

Of all the environmental features that impact attraction, proximity has received the most research attention. This is not surprising. Proximity gives people the opportunity to meet and be attracted to one another. Have you ever thought that the perfect friend or romantic partner was somewhere out there but that you would never find her or him? If so, you were worried that lack of proximity would prevent you from meeting someone to whom you would be attracted.

Several studies have confirmed that proximity is extremely important in attraction and relationship development. The earliest set of studies was conducted by Festinger, who found that the location of college students' apartments affected who became friends (see Festinger, Schachter, & Back, 1950). Students who lived close to one another were much more likely to become friends than were students who lived in the same building but farther apart. Similarly, Newcomb's (1961) famous dormitory roommates study demonstrated a strong proximity effect during the second year, even though proximity did not affect attraction during the first year. Newcomb's findings were especially intriguing because they suggested that proximity can outweigh similarity as a basis for attraction. Specifically, Newcomb paired half of the male undergraduates with similar others and the other half with dissimilar others (unbeknownst to the participants). Regardless of whether they were similar or dissimilar, the students were more likely to be friends with their roommates than with other dormitory residents.

The tendency for people to develop romantic relationships and friendships with individuals they meet in the workplace has also been attributed primarily to proximity. Indeed, 75% of the organizational members Dillard and Witteman (1985) surveyed could identify at least one workplace romance involving themselves or someone they knew. This statistic is not surprising given the amount of time most people spend in the workplace. As Westhoff (1985) put it, "Corporate romance is as inevitable as earthquakes in California" (p. 21). Similarly, a *New York Post* article began with the declaration that the workplace is "the best dating service" around ("The Best," 1988, p. 14). Other times, work associates become close friends (Bridge & Baxter, 1992). Proximity is a major contributor to the development of these friendships, as is similarity and shared tasks (Sias & Cahill, 1998; Sias, Smith, & Avdeyera, 1999).

In sum, the effects of proximity are all around us. We are more likely to be friends with our neighbor than with someone who lives a few miles away, and we are more likely to marry someone we meet at work or school than someone we meet in a bar. This is because we have more opportunities to interact with and become attracted to people whom we see on a frequent basis.

SUMMARY AND APPLICATION

Many factors help determine your attraction to friends and romantic partners. Although knowledge of these factors does not guarantee that we will be attracted to the "right people," it helps us better understand why we are attracted to certain people and not others. Awareness of the ways that we stereotype people based on factors such as physical appearance is also important so that we might consider a more complete package of attributes when deciding whether to pursue a relationship with someone.

So what advice does the literature on attraction offer for individuals like Julie who are having trouble finding the right person? First, as the research on fatal attraction suggests, it is important to understand what is attractive over the long haul, rather than being lured by "flashbulb attraction." If we are attracted to someone only because the person is opposite to us in some characteristics, research suggests that the attraction may not be lasting. People like Julie may find themselves in the same types of doomed relationships over and over again because they subconsciously choose partners based on initially attractive qualities that become fatal attractions, rather than the more stable factors of social or relational attraction. Recognizing what qualities lead to fatal attraction in our relationships is the first step in breaking this cycle.

Second, it is important to recognize our own biases and preferences as well as common stereotypes such as the "what is beautiful is good" hypothesis.

For example, Julie may be attracted to especially good-looking men because she perceives them to have an array of positive attributes that they may or may not actually possess. When she discovers their negative attributes, she is likely to be disappointed. If she was less focused on physical appearance, she might find someone with whom she is more compatible on a social and relational level. Julie might also benefit from taking stock of what she would find rewarding in a long-term relationship. She might decide that qualities such as being able to spend quiet time together would be more rewarding to her than having a partner who likes to socialize all the time.

Third, it is important to remember that similarity and complementarity are important factors in the attraction process. Similarity in key characteristics that are important to us, such as family values or life philosophies, is a critical part of the recipe for relational success. Indeed, social attraction is only a starting point. After two people who are attracted to each other become initially acquainted, they usually have a long way to go before they develop a truly intimate relationship. Having core similarities will help sustain commitment over the long term. Complementarity can also be beneficial, especially when different abilities help partners get tasks done and different personality traits help sustain novelty. The key might be for differences to be helpful or exciting rather than distracting or distressing. In Julie and Steven's relationship, their personality differences in sociability were initially appealing but soon become distressing. Thus, this is an area where Julie might want to look for similarity rather than complementarity.

Finally, it is good to know that chemicals released in our body that take us on a ride, for better or for worse, shape part of the process of attraction. Understanding the ways in which oxytocin and dopamine, among other chemicals, shape our reaction to others is important to increasing our awareness that who we become attracted to may be less in our control than we once thought. After all, we all vary in the basic levels of these chemicals in our body. Moreover, situations and contexts having little to do with the attraction process also change the speed with which these hormones are released.

There is no magical way to determine if someone to whom we are attracted will be a true friend or a long-term romantic partner. There is also no magical formula regarding what to look for in a potential mate. However, the research presented in this chapter summarizes what we know about why we are more attracted to some people than others. Attraction can occur as quickly as a flash of lightning, or it can develop slowly over time. Either way, attraction often provides the initial stepping stone into new relationships that may become your closest encounters.

DISCUSSION QUESTIONS

1. Think about five people in your social network. What initially attracted you to these people? Do all of the qualities you thought of fit into the framework discussed in this chapter, or are there factors you would add to the model?

2. In this chapter, we discussed an abundance of research on similarly as a force affecting attraction. Less research has been conducted on complementarity. Based on your own experiences, which old adage do you think is truer: Do birds of a feather flock together, or do opposites attract?

3. This chapter also discussed the importance of proximity in the attraction process. In long-distance relationships proximity is missing, which has led people to debate whether "absence makes the heart grow fonder" or "out of sight means out of mind." Based on your experiences, which of these sayings is truer?

STUDENT STUDY SITE

Visit the study site at **www.sagepub.com/guerrero3e** for e-flashcards, survey and assessments from the chapter, and SAGE journal articles.

4

Making Sense of Our World

Managing Uncertainty

Vish sat excitedly waiting for Serena to arrive for their Friday night date. He had spent all day cleaning his apartment and preparing dinner for her. This was going to be a special night that would draw Serena closer to him. She was supposed to arrive at 6:00, but 6:00 came and went and no Serena; 6:30, no Serena. This was odd; she had always been on time in the past. He called her cell but there was no answer. At 7:30, still no Serena. By 8:00, Vish realized that she wouldn't be coming. He was really down. What was going on? Was Serena okay? Was this her way of ending the relationship before it became more intimate? Why would she do this to him? He went to bed feeling angry and confused, and was surprised when Serena called in the morning. She sounded like nothing was wrong. "Hi Vish," she said. "What's up? Did you do something fun last night?" Now Vish was even more confused. "What?" he responded, with his frustration clear in his voice. "We had plans last night and you blew me off, so, no, I didn't have fun last night." Serena sounded genuinely surprised. "What do you mean?" she asked. "Our plans were for tonight, not last night!" Vish scanned his mind for any way he could have gotten the night wrong. Was she just trying to make something up to explain her absence last night? Or was it really just a misunderstanding?

This type of scenario may have happened to you. There are times in all relationships when expectations are violated and people experience uncertainty. For example, Vish expected Serena to show up on time (or at least not too late) for their date. When she violated this expectation, he experienced uncertainty about her and their relationship.

Communication researchers have examined how both uncertainty and expectancy violations affect perceptions and behavior. In fact, this area of research has increased dramatically in the past 20 years. No fewer than 10 research programs have been developed during that time to better understand uncertainty (see Afifi & Afifi, 2009, for review).

In this chapter, we examine how uncertainty functions within both budding and well-established relationships. After defining uncertainty, we explore the answers to three central questions that researchers have asked about uncertainty: (1) How motivated are people to reduce or manage uncertainty? (2) What strategies do people use to manage uncertainty? (3) Does having more information always reduce uncertainty? The chapter ends with a discussion of two models of uncertainty in relationships—the turbulence model and a model of relational uncertainty.

DEFINING UNCERTAINTY

Uncertainty has been studied in almost every discipline involving the investigation of human interaction. As a result, we know that our experience of the world is inextricably linked to our level of uncertainty. When we receive information that reduces uncertainty, we are more confident that we understand ourselves, other people, and the world around us. In most cases, the more information we have about someone, the more we feel we know that person. A lack of information, or information that violates expectations, often increases uncertainty. Given this book's focus on close relationships, our examination of uncertainty relates to relationships, but it is also important to realize that uncertainty extends well beyond our relationships with others. For example, job loss creates uncertainty about a wide range of issues, people who become refugees from wars or natural disasters face uncertainty about nearly every aspect of their lives, and so on. These uncertainties have impacts across all phases of our lives, including relationships.

Berger and Calabrese (1975), the first communication scholars to study uncertainty in interpersonal contexts, defined **uncertainty** as the inability to predict or explain someone's attitudes or behaviors. More broadly, Brashers (2001, p. 478) argued that uncertainty occurs when people "feel insecure in their own state of knowledge or the state of knowledge in general [about a topic.]" For example,

part of Vish's uncertainty might stem from feeling that he doesn't understand women or relationships despite his many experiences with them. Thus, we define **high uncertainty** as feeling unsure or insecure about the ability to predict or explain someone's attitudes and behaviors. **Low uncertainty** is felt when people feel confident in their ability to predict and explain someone's behavior, often because they believe they know someone well. Notice that *being confident and secure* about one's explanations and predictions is the key feature in these definitions.

So far, our definition of uncertainty has focused on uncertainty about a partner. People also experience uncertainty about themselves and their relationships. Knobloch and Solomon have found that uncertainty in relational contexts revolves around three primary questions (for review, see Knobloch, 2009; Knobloch & Solomon, 1999, 2002, 2005). First, questions can pertain to **self-uncertainty** or people's own feelings about how involved they want to be in the relationship. For example, after Serena failed to show up, Vish may question how much he really likes her. Second, people experience **partner uncertainty**, and feel uncertain about their partner's feelings and intentions, including whether their partner reciprocates their feelings (Knobloch & Solomon, 1999). Finally, people can experience **relationship uncertainty**, which involves having questions about the state of a relationship. In particular, Knobloch and Solomon (1999) noted that people often experience uncertainty about relationship definitions (Are we casually dating or is the relationship more serious?); the future of the relationship (Is this relationship likely to last? Will we eventually marry?); the types of behaviors that are acceptable versus unacceptable with a relationship (Vish may have initially wondered how tolerant he should be with Serena's tardiness); and other behavioral norms (Are we sexually exclusive? How much of our free time should we spend together versus apart?). See Box 4.1 for questions to reveal how much uncertainty you perceive to exist in one of your relationships.

BOX 4.1 Put Yourself to the Test

The Relational Uncertainty Scale

Respond to the following questions by using the following scale: 1 = completely or almost completely certain, 2 = mostly certain, 3 = slightly more certain than uncertain, 4 = slightly more uncertain than certain, 5 = mostly uncertain, and 6 = completely or almost completely uncertain.

Think about a specific relationship. How certain are you about:

Self

1. How committed you are to the relationship?   _____

2. How you feel about the relationship?   _____

3. How much you are romantically interested in your partner?   _____

4. Your view of this relationship?   _____

5. Whether or not you want this relationship to last?   _____

6. Your goals for the future of the relationship?   _____

                                                          Subdimension total _____

Partner

7. How committed your partner is to the relationship?   _____

8. How your partner feels about the relationship?   _____

9. How much your partner is romantically interested in you?   _____

10. Your partner's view of this relationship?   _____

11. Whether or not your partner wants this relationship to last?   _____

12. Your partner's goals for the future of the relationship?   _____

                                                          Subdimension total _____

Relationship

13. What you can or cannot say to each other in this relationship?   _____

14. The norms for this relationship?   _____

15. Whether or not you and your partner feel the same way about each other?   _____

(Continued)

(Continued)

16. The current status of this relationship? _____

17. The definition of this relationship? _____

18. How you and your partner would describe this relationship? _____

19. Whether or not you and your partner will stay together? _____

20. The future of the relationship? _____

Subdimension total _____

Add up your scores for each dimension. The maximum score for the self-dimension and the maximum score for the partner dimension is 36, and the minimum scores are 6. The maximum score for the relationship dimension is 46 and the minimum score is 8. The higher your score is, the more relational uncertainty you have. (You might want to reanswer these questions later in the semester to see if your certainty level changes.)

SOURCE: This is a sampling of the items that make up the relational uncertainty scale (Knobloch & Solomon, 1999).

In sum, we experience uncertainty about countless issues throughout our days. In this chapter, though, we will focus on uncertainty as it occurs within relationship contexts. Berger and Calabrese's (1975) **uncertainty reduction theory** (URT) was the first communication theory to focus on uncertainty and the one that has been commonly applied to understand uncertainty within relational contexts. Importantly, the theory focused on understanding what happens during initial interactions (i.e., the first time two people meet). Berger and Calabrese maintained that the driving force in initial encounters is obtaining information about the other person to get to know the person better and, ultimately, to reduce uncertainty. Numerous studies have been conducted to test and modify the original theory (Berger, 1979, 1988, 1993; Berger & Douglas, 1981; Berger & Kellermann, 1983). Although the original theory offered 7 general predictions and 21 more specific predictions, we will focus on three general questions that have shaped research in this area since uncertainty reduction theory's introduction: (1) Are people always motivated to reduce uncertainty? (2) How do people manage uncertainty? (3) Does information always

decrease uncertainty? In each case, a brief discussion of the position taken by uncertainty reduction theory is provided, followed by more recent research findings.

Motivation for Reducing Uncertainty

One of the primary principles underlying uncertainty reduction theory is that *people generally dislike uncertainty, and are therefore motivated to reduce it.* Berger and Calabrese (1975) argued that our reason for behaving the way we do during initial interactions with strangers is simple: We want to get to know them better. Not only do we *want* to get to know them, we *have* to get to know them better so that we can reduce uncertainty and create order in our world. In other words, we dislike situations in which we are not sure about the outcome and do our best to create a more predictable environment.

There is a good bit of evidence that supports this desire to create more predictable environments. From an evolutionary perspective, it makes sense (see Afifi, 2009; Inglis, 2000). Imagine if our ancestors weren't motivated to reduce their uncertainty about where to gather food or who was a friend versus foe.

Our species would not have lasted long were we not motivated, at a basic level, to reduce uncertainty about some things. It should not be surprising, then, that a lot of research has shown uncertainty to associate with anxiety. In fact, brain-imaging studies have shown uncertainty to activate similar regions of the brain as we see when we experience anxiety. Relationship studies have also shown uncertainty about a partner to link to dissatisfaction. For example, Parks and Adelman (1983) found that high levels of uncertainty had a negative impact on relationships. They asked students who were currently in romantic relationships for an average of a year and a half about their attraction to and uncertainty about their partner, among other variables. They then contacted these students three months later and asked them similar questions. Their results confirmed the predicted negative link between uncertainty with attraction and satisfaction in relationships. In fact, the respondents who reported being uncertain about their partners on the first questionnaire were more likely to have ended their relationship than were the respondents who had initially felt relatively low uncertainty. However, researchers have challenged the notions that people are always motivated to reduce uncertainty and that uncertainty is always undesirable.

Predicted Outcomes as Motivation for Communication

An alternative to uncertainty reduction theory, called **predicted outcome value theory** (Sunnafrank, 1986, 1990), is based on the idea that people are not driven by a need to reduce uncertainty in all cases. Instead, whether we seek more information depends on whether outcome values are positive or negative. In this theory, **outcome values** relate to people's predictions about how rewarding or unrewarding future interactions with a particular person would be. People are judged as having a **high outcome value** when they are perceived to be more rewarding than other potential partners. For example, when Vish first met Serena he might have perceived her to be more self-confident and physically attractive than other women he could date. This perception of Serena's high outcome value would lead Vish to ask her out. When people have a **low outcome value**, they are perceived to be less rewarding than other potential partners. Suppose that when Vish first

approached Serena she seemed cold and arrogant. Obviously, if Vish had perceived Serena this way, he would have had little desire to reduce uncertainty with her, he would have been much less likely to ask her out, and he would have likely looked for a more rewarding partner.

According to Sunnafrank's theory, we initially reduce uncertainty as a way to find out how we feel about a person or an interaction. After that, the positive or negative outcome value, *not* the level of uncertainty, becomes the driving force behind whether we try to seek further information. Thus, when someone reveals negative information to us during an initial encounter, we are likely to predict negative outcome values and to cut off communication with that person. Put another way, when outcome values are positive, we will be motivated to reduce uncertainty; when outcome values are negative, we won't. For example, think back to the scenario with Vish and Serena. Vish's belief that Serena stood him up could dramatically affect his perception of how rewarding it would be to interact with Serena in the future. If Vish reduced uncertainty by concluding that a future relationship with Serena would be filled with late arrivals, forgotten dates, anxiety, and frustration, his desire to continue reducing uncertainty about her would be low.

Research has supported the idea that predicted outcome values are an important predictor of communication in initial encounters. In one study, students engaged in brief first conversations with another student at the beginning of the semester (Sunnafrank & Ramirez, 2004). The level of outcome value the students associated with their conversational partner after these brief, early interactions predicted later communication and relationship development. Specifically, when a student evaluated the conversational partner as having high reward value, he or she was much more likely to develop a relationship with the partner over the course of the semester.

People's Preferences for Certainty or Uncertainty

Social psychologists have suggested that, instead of always being motivated to seek information, as uncertainty reduction theory originally suggested, the motivation to reduce uncertainty varies from person to person. This construct is variously called *need for closure* (Kruglanski, 1990), *tolerance for uncertainty* (Kellermann & Reynolds, 1990), *uncertainty orientation* (Sorrentino & Short, 1986), *tolerance for ambiguity* (Martin & Westie, 1959), and *coping style* (Miller, 1987). Regardless of the label, these scholars essentially propose the same thing: Some people have a high need to reduce uncertainty and are especially uncomfortable with it, while others are less bothered by uncertainty and less concerned with predictability and certainty. Box 4.2 contains a scale to measure your own need for closure in relationships.

BOX 4.2 Put Yourself to the Test

How Much Need for Closure Do You Have?

To determine your need for closure in relationships, mark the extent to which you agree or disagree with each of these statements using the following scale:

1 = strongly disagree and 6 = strongly agree.

	Disagree					Agree
1. I don't like situations that are uncertain. (A)	1	2	3	4	5	6
*2. I like to have friends who are unpredictable. (P)	1	2	3	4	5	6
3. When dining out, I like to go places where I have been before so that I know what to expect. (P)	1	2	3	4	5	6
4. I feel uncomfortable when I don't understand why an event occurred in my life. (A)	1	2	3	4	5	6
5. I don't like to go into a situation without knowing what I can expect from it. (P)	1	2	3	4	5	6
6. When I am confused about an important issue, I feel very upset. (A)	1	2	3	4	5	6
*7. I think it is fun to change my plans at the last minute. (P)	1	2	3	4	5	6
*8. I enjoy the uncertainty of going into a new situation without knowing what might happen. (P)	1	2	3	4	5	6
9. In most social conflicts, I can easily see which side is right and which is wrong. (A)	1	2	3	4	5	6
10. I don't like to be with people who are capable of unexpected actions. (P)	1	2	3	4	5	6
11. I prefer to socialize with familiar friends because I know what to expect from them. (P)	1	2	3	4	5	6
12. I like to know what people are thinking at all times. (A)	1	2	3	4	5	6

		Disagree					Agree
13. I dislike it when a person's statement could mean many different things. (A)		1	2	3	4	5	6
14. It's annoying to listen to people who cannot seem to make up their minds. (A)		1	2	3	4	5	6
15. I feel uncomfortable when someone's meaning or intention is unclear to me. (A)		1	2	3	4	5	6
16. I'd rather know bad news than stay in a state of uncertainty. (A)		1	2	3	4	5	6
17. I dislike unpredictable situations. (P)		1	2	3	4	5	6

Add together the scores for the questions that are *not* asterisked. Then subtract the scores for the questions that are asterisked. The maximum score is 81, and the minimum score is –4. The closer you are to 81, the stronger your need for closure. The questions marked with a (P) measure your preference for predictability, whereas the items marked with an (A) measure your discomfort with ambiguity.

SOURCE: Copyright © American Psychological Association. Used with permission.

People with high need for closure generally show a "seize and freeze" pattern—they "seize" by grabbing onto the first piece of information that reduces their uncertainty and then "freeze" by hanging on to the closure that the information brings (Dechesne & Kruglanski, 2009). In contrast, people with an uncertainty orientation (or low need for closure) tend to engage in more exploration. In fact, they enjoy the opportunity to broaden their knowledge by seeking information regardless of whether it increases or decreases uncertainty (e.g., Sorrentino & Short, 1986). Not surprisingly, uncertainty-oriented individuals generally fare better than certainty-oriented ones in any situation of elevated uncertainty (Sorrentino, Short, & Raynor, 1984). The dating scene is full of uncertainty (What should I say? What does he mean? Does she like me? When should I call? Where should we go on the next date? When should I make my move?). As a result, if you are a certainty-oriented person, you probably hesitate to initiate relationships with people and fare relatively poorly on first dates. But you also may be more satisfied in relationships than are uncertainty-oriented people. Certainty-oriented people have been shown to possess higher levels of trust for their partners (Sorrentino, Holmes, Hanna, & Sharp, 1995). Uncertainty-oriented people adjust their predictions about their partners with every new bit of information, which magnifies any inconsistency in the partner's behavior and hinders the achievement of complete trust in the partner. On the other hand, certainty-oriented people are not as concerned with every piece of information about the partner (they would rather ignore information that increases uncertainty, for example), so they find it easier to develop confidence in their partner.

So, who is better off in relationships—someone who can ignore inconsistent information, thus maintaining trust in a partner, or someone who is always trying to figure out the partner? Neither type of orientation seems to have a clear advantage. Because of their information vigilance, uncertainty-oriented people are more likely to detect changes in their partner's moods and to react accordingly. Their awareness of inconsistencies also means that they will likely discover deceptions earlier by their partner than will certainty-oriented people. Yet, certainty-oriented people may have smoother, more stable relationships because of their relative disinterest in focusing on every piece of information about their partners.

Preference for Uncertainty Over Certainty

Another perspective that departs from the traditional view that uncertainty is always associated with negative emotions comes from findings that people sometimes prefer uncertainty over its reduction. Health scholars, for example, have shown that people sometimes prefer uncertainty to knowledge (Mischel, 1981, 1988, 1990). Specifically, when reducing uncertainty might mean eliminating hope for recovery (e.g., by discovering that a disease is unmanageable or fatal), uncertainty is cherished because it keeps hope alive. Indeed, Brashers and his colleagues (Brashers, 2001; Hogan & Brashers, 2009), in articulating **uncertainty management theory**, have argued that "uncertainty is not inherently good or inherently bad, but something that is managed" (Hogan & Brashers, p. 48). More specifically, they note that uncertainty can produce positive emotions (e.g., when not knowing is better than knowing that harm is inevitable) or neutral emotions (e.g., when it doesn't matter whether one knows or doesn't know more about an issue). Uncertainty only produces negative emotions, such as anxiety, when not having information is perceived as harmful.

Indeed, there is considerable evidence supporting Brashers's logic. Take people's sexual behavior, for example. Despite the fact that hundreds of thousands of college students are at high risk of contracting a sexually transmitted infection (STI), only a very small percentage ever get tested for such infections. One of the reasons people give for not getting tested is that they would rather not know if they have an STI. For these people, the uncertainty is preferable to the potential knowledge that they have a stigmatized disease that may change, or even shorten, their life. This attitude is especially worrisome given that many STIs are quite treatable, especially if diagnosed early. Research shows a similar pattern in tests for breast cancer and colon cancer. Only a very small percentage of the population most at risk for these types of cancer actually get regular checkups, again despite the fact that with early detection, the consequences in many cases are relatively benign.

Similarly, research suggests that we sometimes prefer to keep a level of uncertainty in our relationships, especially if reducing uncertainty could reveal negative information or lead to negative relational consequences. For example, studies on "taboo topics"

that people avoid discussing in relationships show that the future of the relationship is one of the most avoided topics among romantic partners (Baxter & Wilmot, 1985). Studies have shown that even couples who have been together for many years sometimes avoid seeking information and reducing uncertainty. For example, one study included long-term dating couples in which one of the partners would be graduating from college in a few months (Afifi & Burgoon, 1998). Many of these couples avoided having the "dreaded discussion" about their future. Perhaps many were worried about their future together and feared that the relationship might change after graduation. In this case, uncertainty might be perceived as a better alternative than finding out that the relationship could be at risk.

Studies on cross-sex friendships also suggest that uncertainty is sometimes accepted and even preferred in ongoing relationships. Some cross-sex friendships are full of uncertainty and ambiguity regarding issues such as whether romantic potential exists (O'Meara, 1989). In these cross-sex friendships "sensitive" topics—especially about the relationship—are typically avoided at all costs (Afifi & Burgoon, 1998; Baxter & Wilmot, 1985). In fact, the current and future status of the relationship is often the most commonly avoided topic in cross-sex friendships. Guerrero and Chavez (2005) found that individuals were especially likely to avoid discussing the status of the relationship when they were romantically attracted to their cross-sex friend but feared that the friend did not reciprocate their feelings. Thus, people sometimes prefer uncertainty when they fear that information seeking might confirm their worst fears, such as that the relationship does not have a future.

When Too Much Certainty Is Undesirable

More evidence that uncertainty may be preferable to certainty comes from research on relationship stagnation. Specifically, people might prefer some uncertainty to keep their relationships unpredictable and exciting. According to this line of reasoning, knowing someone too well can become boring or unstimulating. Relationships that stagnate are usually characterized by a lack of uncertainty, as well as lack of growth. Being able to predict everything that someone is going to do or say is not necessarily a good thing, and some uncertainty may help keep the relationship exciting (Livingstone, 1980). One of the reasons that many heterosexual individuals enjoy cross-sex friendships is that there is often a sense of uncertainty or mystery about where the relationship is going. However, that sense of mystery and excitement may eventually fade if the friendship turns romantic. Similarly, some people thrive on roller coaster–type relationships that are hot one day and cold the next. For these individuals, uncertainty keeps the relationship challenging and exciting. Even in more stable relationships it is important to keep things from becoming too predictable.

The importance of both stability and excitement is also captured in **dialectics theory** (Baxter, 1990, 2010; Baxter & Montgomery, 1996; see also Chapter 9). According to this theory, people have opposing interpersonal needs. For example, people want to be close and connected to others, but they also want to be independent. People want to tell others about themselves, but they also want to keep some information private. Similarly, scholars adopting the dialectical perspective believe that people want both certainty (predictability) and uncertainty (novelty) in their relationships. Too much certainty or uncertainty can erode a relationship over time. Indeed, there is considerable evidence to support

this claim. We don't like to be in situations in which we know everything about our partner, to hear the same stories again and again, or go through the same intimacy routines, because it produces boredom. But we also don't like situations in which we can't predict what our partner is going to do from day to day, because that produces stress. Instead, we want a bit of both ends of this dialectic. As a result, people often swing back and forth between wanting more excitement and novelty, and wanting more stability and predictability, in their relationships.

Variations in Motivation to Reduce Uncertainty

The **theory of motivated information management** (TMIM) (Afifi & Morse, 2009; Afifi & Weiner, 2004) starts with the idea that people prefer uncertainty in some situations and certainty in others. The theory recognizes that individuals are only motivated to manage their uncertainty levels when they perceive a discrepancy between the level of uncertainty they have about an important issue and the level of uncertainty they want. In other words, someone may be uncertain about an issue, but be comfortable with that state, in which case this person would not deliberately engage in information management. Consistent with predicted outcome value theory, among other theories, TMIM proposes, though, that people who feel a discrepancy

SOURCE: (left) ©iStockphoto.com/kaiser sosa67; (right) ©iStockphoto.com/hidesy

In some cases, uncertainty can make us miserable; in other cases, uncertainty is exciting and gives us more choices.

between actual and desired uncertainty rely on an "evaluation phase" to decide whether to reduce the discrepancy. Their decision depends on (1) **outcome expectancy**, which refers to whether the outcome of the information search is expected to be positive or negative; and (2) **efficiency assessments**, which focus on whether people feel they are able to gather the information for which they are searching and then cope with it. These two conditions will then determine whether people seek information directly, seek information indirectly, avoid information (either actively or passively), or reassess their level

of uncertainty. TMIM also explicitly notes the role of the information provider in this exchange, arguing that the provider goes through a similar process of information management in trying to decide what information to give and how to give it (see Figure 4.1).

Several studies have successfully tested TMIM (for review, see Afifi, 2009; Fowler & Afifi, in press). Specifically, the theory has accurately predicted whether people seek sexual health information from their partners, whether teenagers talk to their divorced or nondivorced parents about the

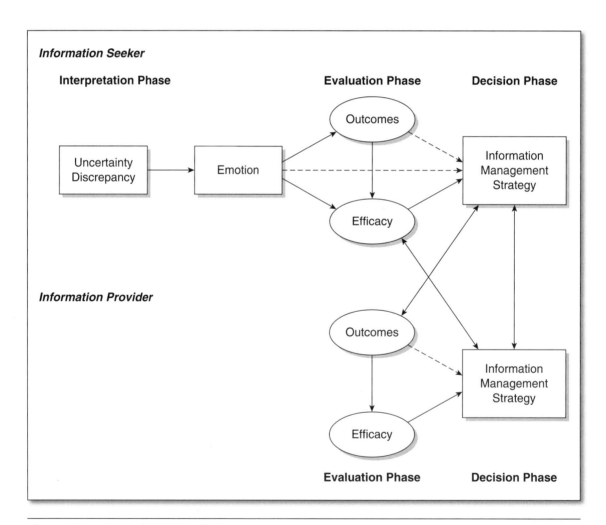

Figure 4.1 Model of TMIM Predictions

parents' relationship, and whether adult children talk to their elderly parents about eldercare preferences, among other issues. In all these cases, two patterns were found. First, there were some people (albeit a minority) who wanted more uncertainty, not less, or were satisfied with elevated levels of uncertainty. Second, those who wanted to reduce uncertainty generally did so only when their expectations and efficacy assessments encouraged the search for information.

In a somewhat similar vein, Ickes and colleagues (Ickes, Dugosh, Simpson, & Wilson, 2003) found that people differ on their **motivation to acquire relationship-threatening information** (MARTI). Consistent with the studies discussed, and others showing that knowing partners' relationally threatening thoughts and feelings creates personal and relational stress (see Simpson, Ickes, & Grich, 1999), Ickes and colleagues (2003) summarized four studies that demonstrated that people differed in the degree to which they sought relationally threatening information and whether such differences impacted their relational experiences. People consistently varied in their motivation to seek relationally threatening information and that difference affected their level of partner trust and the degree of manipulative surveillance behaviors in which they engaged. This impact was especially noticeable in troubled relationships (i.e., those rated as not particularly close). Their results showed that people with high MARTI scores (i.e., those especially motivated to acquire relationally threatening information) who were in emotionally distant relationships were 30% more likely to have broken up five months later than those in similarly emotionally distant relationships but with low MARTI scores. In other words, people who are inclined to seek relationship-threatening information are more likely to have shorter relationships than those who are not so inclined. Indeed, Afifi, Dillow, and Morse's (2004) application of the TMIM framework to close relationships showed a similar impact of information seeking about negative events on relationship commitment. These research efforts are important because they focus on tendencies to seek relationally threatening information, something about which not enough is known.

MANAGING UNCERTAINTY

At this point, it should be clear that the motivation to reduce uncertainty is complicated and not as simple as once believed. But what do people do when they *are* interested in reducing uncertainty? Researchers have answered this question by examining how people reduce uncertainty in both initial interactions and established relationships.

Three General Strategies for Reducing Uncertainty

In the original uncertainty reduction theory, Berger and his colleagues (for review, see Berger, 1988) identified three general ways people go about reducing uncertainty in initial encounters. These have been the cornerstone of work on uncertainty management ever since.

Passive Strategies

People who rely on nonintrusive observation of individuals are using passive strategies (Berger, 1979, 1987) that involve behaviors such as looking at someone sitting alone to see if a friend or date comes along, observing how a person interacts with others, or paying attention to the kinds of clothes a person wears. For example, on the basis of observation, you might make assumptions about someone's age, relational status (Is the person physically close to someone else? Does the person wear a ring?), and personality, among many other characteristics.

Passive observations are most likely to be effective and informative when they are conducted in an informal setting, such as a party, rather than in a formal setting, such as a classroom or business office (Berger & Douglas, 1981). Moreover, people usually make more accurate judgments when watching someone interact with others than when sitting alone. Most people's behavior is constrained in formal settings because behavioral rules in these situations are fairly strict. For example, it is unusual to see people behave inappropriately in a fancy restaurant or during a business meeting. By contrast, people act in unique, personal ways at an informal party because the "rules" are less rigid. When people are relaxed and interacting in an informal setting, their natural selves typically emerge. Therefore, it is more informative, and consequently much more uncertainty reducing, to observe someone in an informal, as opposed to a formal, setting. When passive observation strategies become compulsive, stalking or relational intrusion is the result (see Chapter 13).

Active Strategies

Often our strategies for uncertainty reduction are more active. Berger and Calabrese (1975) identified two forms of active uncertainty reduction strategy. One type involves purposefully manipulating the social environment in a certain way and then observing how someone reacts to this manipulation. The information seeker may not be part of the manipulated situation, although the seeker sets the situation up. These tactics are like mini-experiments conducted with the intent of seeking information about the target person. For example, a student in one of our classes used an active strategy on her boyfriend by typing a letter phrased as if it had come from another female admirer of her boyfriend. The letter included a request that they meet at a certain place and time, and was signed "your secret admirer." She then placed this letter on the windshield of her boyfriend's car. She had two goals in mind when she did this: (1) she wanted to see if her boyfriend would tell her that he received such a letter, and (2) she wanted to check whether he would show up at the location in search of this fictitious person. (As a follow-up, he did not tell her about the letter, but he also never showed up to meet the fictitious person.)

Several other of our students have admitted to using similar active uncertainty reduction strategies with their dating partners (e.g., flirting with someone else to see how their partner reacts) or leaving their relational partner alone with an attractive roommate. Serena could also have been using a form of this strategy if she intentionally decided to stand Vish up to see how he would react, thereby reducing her uncertainty about his personality and his commitment. This type of information-seeking strategy is useful because it can help reduce uncertainty without the need to rely on more direct methods. Of course, such manipulative attempts could backfire in the long run, making the person look paranoid or communicating distrust to the partner.

The second type of active uncertainty reduction strategy involves asking third parties (friends, family members) about the person in question. We often ask friends if they have heard anything about a particular person of interest or ask for help interpreting something that person did. In fact, one study found that 30% of the information we have about someone comes from asking others (Hewes, Graham, Doelger, & Pavitt, 1985). For example, before starting to see Serena, Vish may have asked Serena's friends whether she was seeing anyone, whether she ever mentioned any interest in him, or whether she'd consider going out with him.

Interactive Strategies

The third general type of uncertainty reduction strategy is interactive (Berger, 1979, 1987). Interactive strategies involve direct contact between the information seeker and the target. Common interactive strategies include asking questions, encouraging disclosure, and relaxing the target. We are especially likely to ask such questions the first time we meet someone. In studies of behavior during initial interactions, researchers have found that the frequency of question asking drops over time, coinciding with decreases in our level of uncertainty (Douglas, 1990; Kellermann, 1995).

It is important to note, though, that the questions being asked in initial interactions are usually very general. Research suggests that we hesitate to ask questions about intimate issues until we have a close relationship with the person and even then may avoid asking direct questions (Bell & Buerkel-Rothfuss, 1990). Studies have also shown that people sometimes disclose information about themselves with the specific hope that their disclosure will encourage the other person to do the same (Berger, 1979). However, we use disclosure as an uncertainty reduction strategy only after we reach a certain level of comfort in being able to predict the other person's attitudes and behaviors and enough trust to disclose ourselves. This comfort level typically is reached through the general questions that are so common during initial interactions. Finally, people sometimes try to relax the target so that the person feels comfortable revealing information. While people sometimes offer drugs or alcohol to achieve this effect, examples of less manipulative strategies include creating a comfortable environment that is conducive to talking, smiling a lot, deep massage, or acting interested to get the other person talking (Berger, 1979).

As these examples suggest, interactive strategies are not limited to verbal communication. We often reduce our uncertainty about someone through nonverbal cues (Kellerman & Berger, 1984). For instance, if you smile at and make eye contact with someone across a room, and the person motions you to come over, a clear message has been sent and received. That one motioning gesture provides considerable information and uncertainty reduction. Vish communicated much of his feelings to Serena just through his voice—angry intonation and abruptness, both nonverbal components. In fact, nonverbal behaviors can be the primary method of communicating our thoughts and feelings about other people and our relationships with them (Andersen, 2008; Burgoon, Guerrero, & Floyd, 2010). For example, research on sexual behavior (see Chapter 8) has shown that the primary way we go about discovering whether a partner is interested in escalating the level of sexual activity—that is, reducing our uncertainty about the person's sexual desires—is through nonverbal cues. So, although much of the research on interactive uncertainty reduction methods has focused on verbal strategies, we also often rely on nonverbal cues for information.

Of course, people use multiple uncertainty reduction strategies during a single interaction. Let's imagine that Vish did this when he first met Serena. Suppose he spotted Serena in a bar. After observing her for a minute, Vish thought she was probably a fellow college student, seemed very outgoing, and did not have other males around her (passive strategy), so he sent over a drink in hopes of receiving positive feedback to his gesture (active strategy using manipulation of the environment). The waiter brought Serena the drink and pointed over to Vish. Serena took the drink, glanced at Vish, and appeared to smile slightly. When the waiter walked back past Vish's table, Vish asked him if she said anything (active strategy using a third party). The waiter said that she didn't but that she looked pleased. Now that Vish had reduced his initial uncertainty somewhat, he felt confident enough to take the next step, so he approached Serena and started engaging in conversation with her (interactive strategy).

Secret Tests

On the heels of Berger and colleagues' work on uncertainty reduction strategies during initial interactions, relational scholars examined things that people do to reduce uncertainty in close relationships. Baxter and Wilmot (1985) labeled some of those uncertainty reduction strategies as "secret tests." According to their research, there are seven general strategies that people can use to reduce their uncertainty about their partner's commitment to the relationship:

1. *Asking-third-party tests:* This strategy relies on feedback from social network members. This test is virtually identical to one of the active strategies described earlier. For example, a week after the "date that never was," Serena might ask Vish's best friend if he is still mad at her.

2. *Directness tests:* This strategy involves talking about the issue with the partner, and includes strategies such as asking questions and discussing things that feel uncertain. This test is similar to the interactive strategies described earlier. Here Serena would go directly to Vish and ask him if he is still angry with her. Unlike the other secret tests listed here, this strategy involves direct communication.

3. *Triangle tests:* This strategy is intended to test the partner's commitment to the relationship by creating three-person triangles. Fidelity checks (e.g., seeing if the partner responds to a fictitious "secret admirer" note) and jealousy tests (e.g., flirting with someone else to see how the partner responds) are two examples of triangle tests.

4. *Separation tests:* This strategy relies on creating physical distance between relational partners. The two primary methods are having a long period of physical separation (e.g., seeing if the relationship can survive a summer of not seeing each other) and ceasing contact for an extended period of time to see how long it takes for a partner to call.

5. *Endurance tests*: This strategy increases the costs or reduces the rewards for the other person in the relationship. One such test, known as "testing limits," involves seeing how much the partner will endure. For instance, someone might dress down, become argumentative, start arriving late for dates,

or fail to call at a designated time to see if the partner stays committed despite these irritations. Another test, known as "self putdowns," involves putting one's self down to see if the partner responds by offering positive feedback. For example, Chan may say that he feels overweight in the hope that Hong will try to convince him that he looks great, thus indicating her support for him.

6. *Public presentation tests:* This strategy involves watching for the other person's reaction to the use of certain relational labels or actions. It is most commonly used in the early stages of a relationship. It is typified by the first public presentation of a partner as "boyfriend" or "girlfriend" (whereas before, the partner may have been introduced only as a "friend"), or by holding hands on a date, then observing the partner's reaction. Public presentation tests that might occur later in the relationship include asking someone to wear a ring or a sports or letter jacket, or asking someone to spend the holidays with one's family.

7. *Indirect suggestion tests:* This strategy involves using hinting or joking to bring up a topic without taking direct responsibility. The partner's response then provides insight into feelings about the relationship. For example, Allison might joke about moving in with Peter to check his reaction to the issue. Although Allison may have been truly thinking about moving in, the fact that she said it as a joke gives her an "out" that allows her to save face if Peter rejects the idea. Or Allison could say, "I wonder what color our kids' eyes will be" and then observes Peter's reaction. These tactics allow Allison to seek information about Peter's attitudes toward cohabiting with her or his interest in marriage.

These categories of secret tests were derived from interviews with college students who were asked to discuss information acquisition strategies that they used in one of three relationship types: (1) a platonic opposite-sex friendship, (2) an opposite-sex friendship with romantic potential, or (3) a romantic relationship. Beyond identifying these secret tests, Baxter and Wilmot's (1985) study revealed an important point about behavior in relationships—namely, the vast majority of uncertainty reduction strategies in relationships are indirect. The image of relationships as completely open and of partners as totally direct was refuted by this study. In fact, only 22% of the students who reported on a romantic relationship listed direct strategies as a tactic they used to reduce their uncertainty. By contrast, 34% said they used triangle tests and 33% reported using endurance tests in their romantic relationships. Especially interesting is the extent to which indirectness was used in friendships with romantic potential. Consistent with research showing these relationships to be ambiguous and uncertain (O'Meara, 1989), the students who were reporting on a relationship with romantic potential were more likely than those reporting on the other relationship types to mention separation tests and indirect suggestion tests as information-seeking strategies. Perhaps this is because relationships with romantic potential are still developing and are more prone to uncertainty than are stable friendships or romantic relationships.

Other researchers have shown that people are also more likely to use indirect secret tests in the early stages of dating relationships, when using direct information-seeking strategies may be riskier than these strategies are later in the relationship (Bell & Buerkel-Rothfuss, 1990). For example, Emmers and Canary (1996) found that when romantic couples wanted to repair their relationship after encountering an uncertainty-increasing event such as deception or infidelity, they used direct or interactive strategies more often than passive or active strategies.

People use a variety of direct strategies in response to uncertainty-increasing events in established relationships (Bachman & Guerrero, 2006a; Emmers & Canary, 1996; Knobloch & Solomon, 2003). Sometimes people use relationship talk or integrative communication, such as questioning the partner or discussing the state of the relationship. Other times people try to maintain the relationship through closeness or being romantic. Some people engage in conflict or distributive communication, such as arguing or making accusations. People also use indirect strategies, such as avoidance (not talking about the issue or doing nothing about it), distancing (pulling away from the partner), or loyalty (passively waiting for the issue to be resolved).

People are more likely to use direct and positive strategies, such as integrative communication and displays of closeness or romance, when they are in an intimate relationship. Specifically, a study by Knobloch (2005) examined the strategies people used in response to uncertainty-increasing events in close relationships. Her results showed that our reactions are influenced by the existing level of relational intimacy and by our emotional responses to the event. When people reported high levels of intimacy, they were more likely to use positive and closeness-enhancing strategies and to refrain from using distancing behaviors. In contrast, anger and sadness were associated with harmful and avoidant responses, respectively.

These findings also raise interesting questions. For example, we know that the people who are closest to us have the greatest capacity to affect us emotionally. We also know that uncertainty-increasing events in close relationships are often negative in nature. So what happens when a partner with whom we feel a lot of intimacy (which seems to encourage closeness-enhancing responses to uncertainty-increasing events) does something that saddens or angers us (which encourages distancing responses)?

Research that has looked at how people respond to events such as deception, infidelity, and other forms of betrayal provides preliminary answers to this question. This research suggests that people are most likely to respond positively under the following four conditions: (1) the relationship was previously satisfying, (2) the partner was previously considered to be rewarding, (3) the event produced low levels of uncertainty, and (4) the event did not represent a highly negative violation of expectancies (Bachman & Guerrero, 2006a; Guerrero & Bachman, 2008; see also Chapter 13). This suggests that people in highly intimate and satisfying relationships are more likely to use positive strategies to deal with uncertainty. However, even in satisfying relationships, if the event is regarded as especially negative and produces lots of uncertainty, people often respond with destructive communication or distancing.

Of course, this begs the question explored in the next section: Does information always reduce uncertainty?

DOES MORE INFORMATION ALWAYS REDUCE UNCERTAINTY?

According to uncertainty reduction theory, the more bits of information we have about someone, the more we "know" the person, the better we should be able to predict that person's attitudes and behaviors. Thus, as communication increases, uncertainty about the person with whom we are interacting should decrease. We should be more certain about someone after spending 20 minutes with that person than after spending 5 minutes because we will have had four times as much time to seek information about the individual.

Several studies have confirmed that uncertainty is related to the number of questions people ask and the amount of time they spend interacting. Douglas (1990) put unacquainted college students in same-sex pairs and asked them to interact for 2 minutes, 4 minutes, or 6 minutes. After the interactions, the participants completed a measure of confidence in their ability to predict the other person's behavior and attitudes. The uncertainty levels of those who interacted for 6 minutes was much lower than the levels of those who interacted for just 2 minutes. Douglas also found that the students who asked more questions were more confident, suggesting that the amount of communication (in terms of responses to questions) was related to decreases in uncertainty. Other researchers extended the interaction time to a maximum of 16 minutes and obtained relatively similar results for the first 6 minutes but did not find that uncertainty decreased significantly from the 8th to the 16th minute of interaction (Redmond & Virchota, 1994). Apparently, people gather information rather quickly during initial interactions and then stick with their initial impressions.

Behaviors That Increase Uncertainty

Research since URT, though, has challenged the argument that information always reduces uncertainty. In fact, we now know quite a few examples of cases where information increases uncertainty. Some of the earliest work in this area came from Planalp and Honeycutt's research on uncertainty-increasing events. Planalp and Honeycutt (1985) conducted a study to determine when people in established relationships experienced uncertainty. Specifically, they asked students whether they could recall a time when they learned something surprising about a friend, spouse, or dating partner that made them question the relationship. Ninety percent of the respondents in this study were able to recall such an instance, thus strongly supporting the claim that certain behaviors increase, rather than decrease, uncertainty, even in developed relationships. The researchers then categorized the responses into six uncertainty-increasing behaviors:

1. *Competing relationships:* These included the discovery that a friend or dating partner wanted to spend time with someone else.

2. *Unexplained loss of contact or closeness:* This occurred when communication or intimacy decreased for no particular reason.

3. *Sexual behavior:* This included discovering that a friend or dating partner engaged in sexual behavior with another person.

4. *Deception:* This involved discovering that friends or dating partners had lied, fabricated information, or been misleading.

5. *Change in personality or value:* This occurred when people realized that their friends or dating partners were different from what they used to be.

6. *Betraying confidences:* These included instances in which people's friends or dating partners disclosed private information to others about them without their consent.

For all six types of behavior, the participants felt less able to predict their friend's or dating partner's attitudes and behaviors following these events than they had before these events took place. In other words, they felt as if they "knew them less" following the behavior than they did prior to it. Studies confirm the high incidence of such uncertainty-increasing behaviors in close relationships. For example, one study found that 80% of marriages included uncertainty-increasing events (Turner, 1990).

The method that Planalp and Honeycutt (1985) used is worth noting. They asked participants to think about something "surprising." In fact, earlier, Berger had argued that unexpected (or surprising) behaviors increase uncertainty, and this study seems to support his claim. When people do something

unexpected, we are sometimes *less* able to predict their attitudes and behaviors. For example, Vish's uncertainty about Serena increased after his night alone waiting for her. If they had actually agreed to get together the next day, then Serena's uncertainty about Vish also likely increased because she may be surprised by his absentmindedness and his anger.

These sorts of examples led Berger (1993) to claim that unexpected behaviors always lead to increases in uncertainty. But let's examine that claim. Think about behaviors that fit in any of the six uncertainty-increasing categories. It is easy to see how they might increase uncertainty, but might they not also *reduce* uncertainty in some cases? Couldn't these behaviors sometimes make us feel as if we now know how the person *really* is? To illustrate, suppose a friend lied to you about his past. The fact that he lied about such an important issue may tell you a lot about the kind of person he is. Discovering that lie may not increase your uncertainty, but actually reduce it. Similarly, Serena might think that she now knows the *real* Vish after she hears him react the way he did on the phone. These counterexamples leave us with the question of whether all surprising events increase uncertainty or whether some actually reduce uncertainty. This question has been addressed by research on expectation violations in close relationships.

Unexpected Behaviors and Uncertainty

How do people react when they encounter unexpected behavior? Burgoon attempted to answer this question by developing and testing **expectancy violations theory** (Burgoon, 1978; Burgoon & Hale, 1988; Burgoon, Stern, & Dillman, 1995). In its earliest form, the theory focused on how people react to violations of personal space. Later, however, the theory was extended to encompass all types of behavioral violations.

People build expectancies largely through interaction with others. These expectations can be either predictive or prescriptive. **Predictive expectancies** tell people what to expect in a given situation based on what normally occurs in that particular context or relationship (Burgoon et al., 1995). For example, based on Serena's past promptness, Vish would have been surprised had she been even 10 minutes late. His expectations for "on-time arrival" are very different for other people he knows, though—people who are consistently 30 minutes late, for example. Predictive expectancies are generally based on the norms or routines that typically occur within a given context or relationship. **Prescriptive expectancies**, by contrast, tell people what to expect based on general rules of appropriateness (Burgoon et al., 1995). So, cultural norms would have led Vish to expect a call from Serena before the date had she known that she wasn't going to be able to make it.

According to expectancy violations theory, three factors affect expectancies: communicator characteristics, relational characteristics, and context. **Communicator characteristics** refer to individual differences, including age, sex, ethnic background, and personality traits. For instance, you might expect an elderly woman to be more polite than an adolescent boy, or you might expect your extroverted friend to be outgoing at a party and your introverted friend to be quiet and reserved. **Relational characteristics** refer to factors such as how close we are to someone, what type of relationship we share (platonic, romantic,

business), and what types of experiences we have shared together. Hearing "I love you" from a romantic partner might be an expected behavior, but hearing the same words from a casual acquaintance might be highly unexpected. Similarly, certain types of intimate touch are usually expected in romantic relationships but not in platonic ones. Finally, **context** includes both the social situation and cultural influences. Clearly there are different behavioral expectations depending on the situation. For example, if you are in church attending a funeral, you expect people to act differently than if you were at the same church attending a wedding. Behavioral expectations may also shift depending on whether you are at work or out for a night on the town with friends. Similarly, expectations differ based on culture (see Box 4.3 for a discussion of the impact of cultural differences on uncertainty). For example, you might expect someone to greet you by kissing your face three times on alternating cheeks if you are in parts of Europe, but not if you are in the United States.

BOX 4.3 Highlights

Culture and Uncertainty

Gudykunst and his colleagues have argued that elevated uncertainty is one reason that many people feel less attracted to members of other cultures (see, for example, Gudykunst & Nishida, 1984). According to this perspective, people feel more uncertain and anxious around interaction partners from other cultures simply because of uncertainty about their cultural norms and customs. This uncertainty could prevent the development of intercultural relationships.

However, when uncertainty is reduced, people from different cultures are often attracted to one another. Gudykunst (1988, 1989), in his theory of **intergroup uncertainty reduction**, described several conditions that make it more likely that uncertainty will be reduced in intercultural interactions. First, he argued that people who identify strongly with their own group identity feel more confident about interaction with someone from a different social or cultural group. Second, when people perceive members of another culture favorably, they are likely to look forward to interacting with them. These two factors combine to create a communication climate that makes information exchange and uncertainty reduction easier. For example, imagine visiting Brazil for the first time. If you are confident about your own cultural identity and are looking forward to communicating with Brazilians, you are likely to be comfortable and open during interactions, which will likely lead to uncertainty reduction and increased liking. By contrast, if you are unsure about your role as a person in a foreign country and you dread interacting with people who speak a different language, you are likely to avoid interaction and to remain uncertain and anxious.

What happens when expectancies are violated? For example, maybe your platonic friend says "I love you" and touches you in an overly intimate fashion, or maybe you expect to be greeted affectionately by a European friend but the friend offers only a stiff handshake. According to expectancy violations theory, your response will be contingent on at least two factors: (1) the positive or negative interpretation of the behavior and (2) the rewardingness of the partner.

The Positive or Negative Interpretation of the Behavior

When unexpected events occur, people often experience heightened arousal, leading them to search for an explanation (Burgoon & Hale, 1988). To do this, people pay close attention to their partner and the situation so that they can ascertain the meaning of the unexpected behavior and interpret it as positive or negative. As part of this process, the unexpected behavior is compared to the expected behavior. When the unexpected behavior is perceived to be more satisfying than the expected behavior, a positive violation has occurred. For example, if Serena had shown up on Friday night she may have been positively surprised by the care Vish took in cleaning his apartment and preparing her dinner since he normally does not go to such trouble. By contrast, when the unexpected behavior is perceived to be less positive than the expected behavior, a negative violation has occurred (for review, see Afifi & Metts, 1998). So, if Vish ends up telling Serena to forget about getting together over the weekend, Serena might be surprised because she expected Vish to be reasonable and understand that the mix-up was a simple mistake.

Expectancy violations can have positive or negative consequences for relationships. When positive violations occur, people are likely to be happier and more satisfied with their relationships. When negative violations occur, however, people might become angry and dissatisfied with their relationships (Burgoon et al., 1995; Levitt, 1991; Levitt, Coffman, Guacci-Franco, & Loveless, 1994). It is not surprising that Vish became frustrated when Serena violated his expectations by failing to show up.

The Rewardingness of the Partner

Sometimes people cannot determine the valence of a behavior simply by comparing the unexpected behavior to what they originally expected. This is because some behaviors are ambiguous; they can be positive in some circumstances and negative in others, depending on who enacts them. For example, imagine that you are working on a class project with several classmates. Because they are always together, you assume that two of the classmates, Terry and Alex, are a couple. However, Terry approaches you after the group meeting, smiles warmly, touches your arm, and asks you out on a date. You are surprised and ask, "Aren't you with Alex?" Terry replies, "Oh no, Alex and I are just really good friends."

How might you respond to Terry's unexpected behavior? The smile, touch, and request are not inherently positive or negative. Instead, the interpretation of these unexpected behaviors depends on how rewarding you perceive Terry to be. If you see Terry as attractive, charming, and intelligent, you likely will see the expectancy violation as positive and reciprocate by accepting the date. If, however, you see Terry as a deceitful person who is going behind Alex's back, you probably will see the expectancy violation as negative and refuse the date. In this case, it is not the behavior per se that is positive or negative; instead, it is the combination of the behavior and the rewardingness of the partner.

Interestingly, research on expectancy violations theory has shown that nonrewarding communicators are evaluated the most highly if they stay within the norms and avoid violating expectations (Burgoon & Hale, 1988). For example, suppose you have to work on a project with a coworker whom you dislike. The two of you do not talk to each other much, but so far you have tried to keep your relationship civil. If the coworker suddenly starts asking you to go to lunch with her and telling you her life's story, you will probably evaluate her even more negatively because you will see her as pushy and overbearing. Similarly, if the coworker starts pointedly ignoring you and makes sarcastic remarks while you are speaking, you will likely evaluate her even more negatively as a mean, rude person. Notice that whether the expectancy violation involves behaviors that are more friendly or less friendly, you might still perceive the coworker negatively. This is because people tend to interpret unexpected behavior as consistent with their initial impressions of someone. To produce a more positive result, the coworker would be better off remaining civil and gradually becoming less distant. Such behavior would confirm your expectations and perhaps lay a foundation for a better relationship.

With rewarding communicators, however, expectancy violations theory suggests that positive expectancy violations actually produce better outcomes than expectancy-confirming behaviors (Burgoon & Hale, 1988; Burgoon et al., 1995). When positive violations occur, people feel "bright emotions" such as joy excitement, and relief. When expectancies are confirmed, people also feel bright emotions, but they are less intense. Finally, when negative violations occur, people feel "dark emotions," such as sadness, anger, and disappointment (see also Levitt, 1991).

Unexpected Events in Relationships

To extend Planalp and Honeycutt's (1985) work on uncertainty-increasing events, with attention paid to their elicitation of "surprising events," Afifi and Metts (1998) used an expectancy violations lens. They asked people in friendships and romantic relationships to think about the last time their friend or partner did or said something unexpected. They emphasized that the unexpected event could be either positive or negative. Participants reported on events that had occurred, on average, five days earlier, suggesting that unexpected behaviors happen often in relationships. Some of the behaviors reported were relatively mundane, and others were quite serious. The outcome was a list of nine general categories of expectancy violations that commonly occur in relationships:

1. *Criticism or accusation:* Actions that are critical of the person or that accuse the person of some type of offense.

2. *Relationship escalation:* Actions that confirm or intensify the commitment of the person to the relationship, such as saying "I love you" or giving expensive gifts.

3. *Relationship de-escalation:* Actions that imply a desire to decrease the intimacy level in the relationship, such as reducing communication and spending more time apart.

4. *Uncharacteristic relational behavior:* Actions that are not consistent with the way the person defines the relationship, such as members of cross-sex friendships asking their supposedly platonic friend for a sexual relationship.

5. *Uncharacteristic social behavior:* Actions that do not have relational implications but that simply are not expected from that person in that context, such as a mild-mannered person raising her or his voice during an argument with a salesperson.

6. *Transgressions:* Actions that are violations of taken-for-granted rules of relationships, such as having an affair, being disloyal, sharing private information with other people, and being deceitful.

7. *Acts of devotion:* Actions that imply that the person really views the partner and the relationship as being special, such as going "above and beyond the call of duty" to help that individual through a difficult time.

8. *Acts of disregard:* Actions that imply that the person considers the partner and the relationship as unimportant, such as showing up late or being inconsiderate.

9. *Gestures of inclusion:* Actions that show an unexpected desire to include the partner in the person's activities or life, such as disclosing something very personal or extending an invitation to spend the holidays with someone's family.

Importantly, unlike earlier work that equated unexpected relationship behavior as negative and uncertainty increasing, these reported violations differed tremendously in the extent to which they were seen as positive or negative and the extent to which they increased or decreased uncertainty. Many expectancy violations reduced uncertainty by providing important information about one's partner.

This angle to the study of expectation violations in close relationships has been applied to several specific situations. For example, Afifi and Faulkner's (2000) study of sexual contact with otherwise platonic opposite-sex friends showed that participants generally rated those experiences as unexpected and that their impact depended on whether the event was seen as positive or negative and whether it increased or decreased uncertainty. Friends were most likely to perceive that their relationships were damaged when the sexual contact increased uncertainty and was evaluated negatively. Guerrero and Bachman (2010) investigated how people reacted to a dating partner's transgression (e.g., sexual infidelity or lying about something important). If the transgression created uncertainty, people were likely to forgive the partner with conditions, if they forgave the partner at all. In other words, they might say something like, "I'll forgive you, but only if you promise not to do anything like that in the future." In Guerrero and Bachman's study, uncertainty was unrelated to retaliatory responses. Instead, people were more likely to retaliate if the transgression was considered a particularly negative expectancy violation.

MODELS OF UNCERTAINTY IN RELATIONSHIPS

Much of the research related to the three general questions that have guided work on uncertainty in interpersonal interactions has been applied to relational contexts. Two relatively new models have recently emerged to better describe how uncertainty functions within the context of developing and established relationships: the model of relational turbulence (Solomon & Knobloch, 2001, 2004) and the model of relational uncertainty (for review, see Knobloch & Satterlee, 2009).

The Model of Relational Turbulence

Solomon and her colleagues introduced the **model of relational turbulence** that revolves around the idea that the transition from casual dating to commitment is a "turbulent" period in relationship development (Knobloch & Donovan-Kicken, 2006; Solomon & Knobloch, 2001, 2004; Theiss & Solomon, 2006). The model emphasizes that turbulence comes from partners' efforts to renegotiate their level of interdependence (see Chapter 10) and is a function of two primary factors: uncertainty associated with the question of whether or not to increase commitment (e.g., Is this "the" person?) and irritations from partners who come in the way of the person's goals.

One implication of the model is that, as opposed to earlier approaches suggesting that uncertainty gradually decreases across relationship stages, Solomon and her colleagues argued that relational uncertainty peaks in the middle stages of relationships. Relational doubts are highest when couples are deciding whether to escalate their casual relationship into a more committed relationship. It is also important to note, however, that different types of uncertainty may characterize various stages of a relationship. Uncertainty about another person's general beliefs, attitudes, and behavior may dominate initial encounters, whereas uncertainty about the relationship and the partner's feelings and intentions may dominate the transition from a casual to more committed relationship. The relational turbulence model focuses on the latter.

So far, some studies have shown the predicted upturn in uncertainty during the middle stage of relationships, but others have revealed that uncertainty gradually decreased as relationships develop, much like the original uncertainty reduction theory would predict (for review, see Knobloch, 2007a, 2007b). For example, the longer that you are with your partner, the less uncertainty you have about her or him. The findings for irritations across relational stages have been more consistent, with the middle stages of a relationship marked by increased irritation as predicted by the model of relational turbulence. Across studies, increased uncertainty was shown to accompany increased irritation. The inconsistency in these findings might suggest that some couples experience relatively smooth transitions from casual to committed relationships, without the irritations, whereas others experience considerable turbulence and accompanying irritations and uncertainty.

While the specific prediction about increasing uncertainty across relationship stages has not always panned out, the model has been a very useful tool for understanding highly important individual events within relationships, and relationship events more generally. For example, Theiss, Knobloch, Checton, and Magsamen-Conrad (2009) asked dating couples to report on their relationships once a week for six weeks. During that time, they asked the couples to report on uncertainty about their relationship and partner, the extent to which the partner made it difficult for them to achieve their goals (i.e., partner interference), along with hurtful things that their partner did or said and their impact on the relationship. Their analyses showed that the degree of uncertainty in the relationship and the extent to which the partner interfered with their goals predicted the hurtfulness of the event and the relational deterioration that resulted. In another study, Steuber and Solomon (2008) coded online messages posted by people managing their infertility diagnoses. Altogether, they found 438 messages from husbands or wives going through the difficulties of infertility. Both relational uncertainty and partner interference were evident in the messages. For instance, one person described her experience of relational uncertainty this way: "Once he [her husband] found out the problem was not him (my right tube was blocked) he told me that he shouldn't have to go to any appointments with me because 'it's your problem not mine'! . . . I don't understand why he is being like this, normally . . . he's very loving and supportive" (p. 842). Another participant described the unique aspects of partner interference, and related relational difficulties, that infertility treatments

sometimes bring onto a marriage: "But last night [her husband] came home with a cold and did not feel like performing his part. Yeah on the most important night of the month. I lost it and just started crying and all the stress that was building up just came out. It was pretty bad" (p. 844). The uncertainty and relational difficulties that come with turbulence-producing episodes are evident from these people's words and bring light to the challenges that couples sometimes face.

A Model of Relational Uncertainty

The model of relational uncertainty builds on the definition of uncertainty provided in the original uncertainty reduction theory by including all three forms of uncertainty discussed earlier in this chapter: self, partner, and relationship (Knobloch & Solomon, 1999, 2002). Within the model, Knobloch outlines the relationship process that surrounds relational uncertainty (see Figure 4.2) (Knobloch, 2007b; Knobloch & Satterlee, 2009). The first part of the process is the identification of aspects that influence relational uncertainty, labeled as **foundations**. The second part is the consequences that relational uncertainty has for the individuals within the relationship and the relationship itself, labeled as **outcomes**.

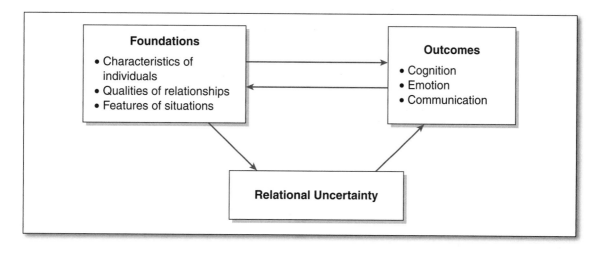

Figure 4.2   Model of Relational Uncertainty

SOURCE: Knobloch, L. K., & Satterlee, K. L. (2009).

Foundations include characteristics of individuals, relationships, and situations (Knobloch, 2007b). Under **individual characteristics**, Knobloch summarizes the work on personality differences in managing uncertainty (e.g., differences on need for closure, as discussed earlier, along with other personality differences). **Relational qualities** that have been shown to impact relational uncertainty include the degree of face-to-face exchanges and intimacy. For example, studies have shown that people in long-distance relationships who do not see each other frequently experience more relational uncertainty than those who do. Moreover, work on the relational turbulence model shows how intimacy levels impact relational uncertainty. Finally, the situation in which people find themselves has been shown to strongly impact their experience of relational uncertainty. Knobloch focuses on the expectation violations research discussed earlier—different types of unexpected behaviors have been shown to differ in their impact on uncertainty.

The next issue that the model of relational uncertainty tackles is identifying the consequences of relational uncertainty in terms of cognitive, emotional, and communicative outcomes (Knobloch 2007b; Knobloch & Satterlee, 2009). **Cognitive outcomes** of relational uncertainty include heightened awareness of partner characteristics and filtered perceptions of the partner's behavior. Specifically, studies have shown that people who

have relational uncertainty are especially sensitive to noticing partner faults and tend to view their partner's behavior through darker lenses. Relational uncertainty also has **emotional outcomes**. In particular, people who are relationally uncertain tend to show more emotional volatility, and often experience more negative emotions in relationships than do those who have little relational uncertainty. Finally, although findings on this front are somewhat mixed, **communicative outcomes** associated with uncertainty include less willingness to be direct about relationship concerns, more hesitation in the language used when talking to partners about relationally relevant issues, and more avoidance of sensitive topics. It is likely that the reasons for heightened relational uncertainty (e.g., has the level of relational uncertainty been high for a long time or is there a specific event that caused a temporary spike in relational uncertainty) make a big difference in how the uncertainty impacts communication directness, but what *is* clear is that the way people talk to their partner is strongly influenced by their levels of relational uncertainty.

By summarizing the various factors that both impact relational uncertainty and are affected by it, the model of relational uncertainty provides a useful window into the importance of uncertainty in relationships. In the end, the ongoing role that uncertainty plays in people's relationship lives is hard to overlook.

SUMMARY AND APPLICATION

Uncertainty plays an important role in the way people relate to one another. Taking a closer look at the case of Vish and Serena can reveal several common features of uncertainty's impact. For starters, unexpected behaviors, such as Serena not showing up for the date, often produce uncertainty. So, people who are in situations like Vish's should recognize that their feelings of uncertainty are natural.

In addition, people use a variety of strategies to try to reduce uncertainty. They might passively observe others, manipulate the social environment,

question third parties, or interact directly with the person. In established relationships people also report using a variety of "secret tests" to help them determine how committed their partners are to the relationship. People in established relationships also have a number of direct strategies at their disposal, including asking questions, showing closeness or being romantic, and engaging in distributive communication or conflict. The strategies that Vish uses may, in part, be dependent on the type of relationship he shares with Serena. If, previous to Friday night, Vish had characterized his relationship with Serena as close and satisfying, he would be more likely to use direct and positive strategies to reduce uncertainty than distancing or avoidant strategies. Of course, the degree of relational uncertainty will also impact the situation. Work on relational uncertainty shows that Vish's heightened uncertainty after Serena failed to show up might make him focus on her negative qualities.

The stage of the relationship may also matter. The model of relational turbulence suggests that couples are especially likely to experience uncertainty and irritations during the transition from a casual to a committed relationship. Given that Vish had planned the date with the hope of bringing Serena closer to him, their relationship may be at this transition point, which could intensify the frustration and uncertainty that either Serena or Vish is experiencing. If Vish and Serena had a long-standing committed relationship, Vish might have more readily accepted her explanation of a misunderstanding about the day of the date.

The scenario between Vish and Serena illustrates another important point about uncertainty. For Vish and Serena, there is a danger that the uncertainty they are both experiencing could seep into the fabric of their relationship and their feelings for one another. After their Saturday morning conversation, Vish may still not be convinced that Serena is telling him the truth about mixing up the night for the date. At the very least, this might lead Vish to question if he completely trusts Serena. For her part, Serena might be frustrated that Vish does not believe her and incredulous because he got the dates mixed up. As a result, Serena might reduce her uncertainty by reevaluating Vish as an unreasonable, forgetful, and paranoid person, thereby decreasing her attraction toward him.

Expectancy violations can also produce uncertainty. This is certainly what occurred for Serena and Vish. The more they perceive one another to be rewarding, the more likely they are to put their negative feelings aside and try to get closer. As the situation between Vish and Serena illustrates, uncertainty-increasing events can be critical points in relationships. How partners cope with uncertainty, including whether or not they are motivated to manage uncertainty, affects the future course of the relationship. Hopefully the research in this chapter provides a clearer picture of why these experiences occur and how best to deal with them.

DISCUSSION QUESTIONS

1. According to uncertainty reduction theory, people are driven by the need to reduce uncertainty during initial encounters. Do you agree with this idea? Are there certain circumstances that make uncertainty reduction an especially salient goal?

2. Think about the last few times someone violated your expectations, either positively or negatively. Does expectancy violations theory help explain how you reacted to these expectancy violations? Why or why not?

3. Think about a relationship in which you felt uncertainty about your own levels of commitment. How did that uncertainty impact your behavior? Did it influence what you did or did not discuss with the other person?

STUDENT STUDY SITE

Visit the study site at **www.sagepub.com/guerrero3e** for e-flashcards, survey and assessments from the chapter, and SAGE journal articles.

5

Getting Closer

Initiating and Intensifying Relationships

When Anne and Connor meet at a Sierra Club meeting, they discover they have a lot in common. They both have degrees in biology, love animals, and enjoy outdoor activities. Anne is a caretaker at the local zoo, and Connor teaches science at a middle school. For the first two months, their relationship goes smoothly. They have long talks on the phone and spend considerable time together. They subsequently decide to make their relationship exclusive, and Connor assumes that Anne will want to spend Thanksgiving with him. When she says she'd rather be with her family, Connor becomes hurt and distant. After a week of silence, Connor calls Anne and apologizes. They resume their relationship and, a month later, Connor tells Anne he loves her and hopes to someday marry her. She responds that she feels the same way. Six months later, Anne suggests they move in together. Connor, however, hesitates. He worries that living together before marriage could cause them to take their relationship for granted. He has seen too many of his friends move in with their girlfriends and then break up six months later. Anne responds by saying that his friends are good examples of why two people should live together before marriage— to find out if they are indeed compatible.

The process of starting and developing relationships has been the subject of plays, poems, and movies, as well as scholarly research. Researchers have tried to unlock the mysteries of how people can best use communication to help them get closer to one another and why some people are better at developing close relationships than others. In Anne and Connor's case, getting to know one another was easy. However, Connor has valid concerns about whether they should live together or not.

If you were in Connor's place, would you have similar concerns? What possible paths might their relationship take next?

In this chapter, we discuss several perspectives on the paths that relationships take as partners get to know one another and develop close relationships. First, we examine the skills and strategies that people use to form and develop relationships, followed by an in-depth look at the concept of self-disclosure. Many researchers believe that self-disclosure, which involves sharing personal information with another person, is a key foundation for relationship development. Next, we discuss Knapp's coming-together stages of relationship development, as well as specific stages that occur in the development of romantic relationships. The chapter ends with a focus on relational turning points, which are events associated with changes in a relationship.

HOW PEOPLE FORM AND DEVELOP NEW RELATIONSHIPS

Relationships do not just develop out of thin air. People must develop and nurture them. Some people are shy or worry about rejection, making it more difficult for them to establish new relationships. Other people are overzealous about forming new relationships, using too much self-disclosure or being overly pushy—and, as a result, scaring potential new friends or romantic partners away. Given these complexities, there are essential communication skills and strategies that can help people form and develop new relationships.

Communication Skills

Some people are more skilled at forming and developing relationships than are others. Buhrmester, Furman, Wittenberg, and Reis (1988) identified five types of communication skills that help people build relationships with new friends and romantic partners: (1) relationship initiation, (2) self-disclosure, (3) emotional support, (4) negative assertion, and (5) conflict management skills. To see how skilled you are in these five areas, take the test in Box 5.1.

BOX 5.1 Put Yourself to the Test

Interpersonal Skills Related to Forming and Developing Relationships

People have different ways of communicating. For the following items, rank how well you feel you can perform each type of communication, being as honest as possible. Answer the questions using the following scale: 1 = you are poor at the behavior described and would avoid doing it if possible, and 5 = you are extremely good at the behavior and would be comfortable in that situation.

	Poor at this				Good at this
1. Asking or suggesting to someone new that you get together and do something.	1	2	3	4	5
2. Telling someone you don't like a certain way he/she has been treating you.	1	2	3	4	5
3. Helping someone work through his /her thoughts and feelings about a major life decision.	1	2	3	4	5
4. Being able to admit you might be wrong when a disagreement begins to build into a serious fight.	1	2	3	4	5
5. Confiding in a new friend and letting him/her see your softer, more sensitive side.	1	2	3	4	5
6. Being able to put resentful feelings aside during a fight.	1	2	3	4	5

	Poor at this				Good at this
7. Finding and suggesting things to do with new people you find interesting.	1	2	3	4	5
8. Turning down an unreasonable request.	1	2	3	4	5
9. Saying no when someone asks you to do something you don't want to do.	1	2	3	4	5
10. When having a conflict with someone, really listening to his or her complaints and not trying to "read" his/her mind.	1	2	3	4	5
11. Being an interesting and enjoyable person when first getting to know people.	1	2	3	4	5
12. Standing up for your rights when someone is neglecting you or being inconsiderate.	1	2	3	4	5
13. Letting a new companion get to know the "real you."	1	2	3	4	5
14. Introducing yourself to someone you might like to get to know.	1	2	3	4	5
15. Letting down your protective outer shell and trusting others.	1	2	3	4	5
16. Being a good and sensitive listener for someone who is upset	1	2	3	4	5
17. Refraining from saying things that might cause a disagreement to build into a big fight.	1	2	3	4	5
18. Telling others things that secretly make you feel anxious or afraid.	1	2	3	4	5
19. Being able to do and say things to support another person when She/he is feeling down.	1	2	3	4	5
20. Presenting a good first impression to people with whom you might like to become friends.	1	2	3	4	5
21. Telling someone that she/he has done something that hurt your feelings.	1	2	3	4	5
22. Being able to show emphatic concern even when the other person's concern is uninteresting to you.	1	2	3	4	5
23. When angry, being able to accept that the other person has a valid point of view even if you don't agree with that view.	1	2	3	4	5
24. Knowing how to move a conversation beyond superficial talk to really get to know each other.	1	2	3	4	5
25. Being able to give advice in ways that are well received.	1	2	3	4	5

(Continued)

(Continued)

Add up the following items for your score on each skill.

Relationship initiation skills: Items 1 + 7 + 11 + 14 + 20 = _____

Negative assertion skills: Items 2 + 8 + 9 + 12 + 21 = _____

Self-disclosure skills: Items 5 + 13 + 15 + 18 + 24 = _____

Emotional support skills: Items 3 + 16 + 19 + 22 + 25 = _____

Conflict management skills: Items 4 + 6 + 10 + 17 + 23 = _____

Higher scores mean that you possess more of a particular skill. The highest possible score for a given skill is 35; the lowest possible score is 7.

Skill in Relationship Initiation

Skill in initiating relationships is critical if people are going to get to know one another. People who are skilled in relationship initiation know how to approach others and make good first impressions. They feel comfortable introducing themselves and striking up conversations with people they do not know. They are also effective in issuing invitations and making suggestions for things to do with new friends. The ability to initiate relationships appears to be a critically important skill for forming new friendships. Two studies that have looked at first-year students during the first few weeks of their college experience suggest even further benefits from having these skills (McEwan & Guerrero, 2010; Shaver, Furman, & Buhrmester, 1985). In these studies, the students who were more skilled at initiating relationships and issuing invitations reported being better adjusted to college life and building more rewarding social networks at their new university.

Skill in Self-Disclosure

Self-disclosure involves revealing personal information about oneself to others. As discussed in more detail later in this chapter, people who are skilled at self-disclosure gradually increase the depth of their disclosure so that it becomes more personal. They know how to self-disclose in an appropriate manner that allows them to get to know others without scaring them off. For instance, if Connor had approached Anne when he first met her, immediately told her that he thought she was beautiful, and then launched into a rant about his frustrations with the lack of progress on environmental issues, Anne would likely have viewed Connor's self-disclosure as premature and inappropriate. Instead, Connor started out by introducing himself and sharing impersonal information. As they got to know one another, both Anne and Connor felt comfortable sharing more personal information with one another. People who possess self-disclosure skills tend to be well liked (Fehr, 2008). They also perceive themselves to have more friends with whom to hang out and socialize (McEwan & Guerrero, 2010), which suggests that they build stronger social networks than those who have less skill in self-disclosure.

Skill in the Provision of Emotional Support

Being able to provide others with emotional support is another key skill related to the formation, as well as the continuation, of close relationships (see Chapter 6). This skill involves being able to listen empathetically to people's problems and concerns, as well as being able to offer advice that is well received by others. Effective emotional support also entails being warm and responsive to others rather than trying to tell people what to do. Indeed, Fehr (2008) described responsiveness as a major determinant of whether or not people form relationships with others. According to Fehr, **responsiveness** is a communication style that shows care, concern, and liking. People are attracted to others who have this type of warm, other-centered communication style. In addition to being perceived as more responsive, individuals who are skilled in emotional support tend to develop friendship networks that are rich in personal resources, such as having friends whom one trusts and can turn to for help in times of trouble (McEwan & Guerrero, 2010).

Skill in Negative Assertion

As relationships develop, people begin to reveal negative aspects of their personalities more often. Sometimes there is also a struggle for control or power within a relationship. Buhrmester and colleagues (1988) suggest that skill in negative assertion helps people to navigate these potentially problematic situations while "saving face." Recall from Chapter 2 that one part of saving face involves being perceived as able to make one's own decisions without being controlled by another person. Skill in negative assertion helps people accomplish this. Negative assertions include being able to say no to a friend's request, stand up for one's rights within a relationship, and tell a partner when feelings are hurt. If these types of negative assertions are stated in a constructive rather than a critical manner, they can help people avoid problems with their relationships. In McEwan and Guerrero's (2010) study on first-year students forming new friendships, students who reported being skilled in negative assertion were more likely to have joined groups or clubs to make friends. Thus, skills in negative assertion may help people navigate group settings and form friendships.

Skill in Conflict Management

As discussed in detail in Chapter 14, skill in conflict management is vital in both established and developing relationships. During the initial stages of relationship development, people are usually on their best behavior and refrain from engaging in conflict. However, as relationships get closer, people feel freer to disclose negative information and assert differing opinions, which makes conflict more likely. According to Buhrmester and associates (1988), people who are skilled in conflict management are better able to listen to their partner, understand their partner's perspective (even if they disagree with it), and refrain from communicating hostile feelings during conflicts. As for skill in negative assertion, McEwan and Guerrero (2010) found that the students who reported being skilled in conflict management were more likely to have joined groups as a way of forming new friendships.

Friendship Formation Strategies

People who possess these communication skills are more likely to use a variety of strategies to form new relationships with others (McEwan & Guerrero, 2010). According to Fehr (2008), proximity is one of the most important factors determining whether or not people initiate communication and form relationships with each other. Being in the same class, working in the same department, or living in the same neighborhood all make it more likely that people will meet and greet one another. Although proximity often happens by chance, people sometimes make choices that influence with whom they have the opportunity to interact. For example, Anne's decision to attend a Sierra Club meeting gave her the opportunity to meet a lot of new people who shared her commitment to protecting the environment, including, of course, Connor. Thus, group involvement is a specific strategy that people use to form new friendships.

People also use online social networking to meet new people. As Fehr (2008) noted, "computer-mediated communication has opened up a world of new possibilities for friendship formation in the absence of physical proximity" (p. 38). People can use social networking sites such as Twitter and Facebook to connect with people whom they do not know. Such sites offer options such as suggesting new friends for others and joining fan clubs or charitable organizations, all of which expand people's social networks in ways that were impossible for previous generations. Indeed, two of the top reasons for joining online communities are to make friends and receive social support (Ridings & Gefen, 2004).

Introductions and invitations are two other strategies that people use in an attempt to form new relationships. Introductions involve approaching someone and, typically, exchanging names and other fairly superficial information. Sometimes introductions occur within the context of opening lines. Invitations involve asking someone to attend formal or informal events. Some studies suggest that issuing invitations is the most helpful strategy people can use to form a satisfying and rewarding friendship network (McEwan & Guerrero, 2010).

Another set of strategies focus on communication that makes a positive impression on others. These include enhancing one's appearance, displaying similarity, being accepting and responsive, and self-disclosing personal information at appropriate levels (Fehr, 2008; McEwan & Guerrero, 2010). The last of these strategies—self-disclosure—is particularly significant to initiating and intensifying relationships.

Self-Disclosure

Communication is the primary vehicle for developing relationships and creating feelings of connection and closeness. In fact, much of the research on relationship development has examined how self-disclosure helps people move from being strangers to being close friends or lovers. As noted previously, **self-disclosure** occurs when people reveal something about themselves to others. Some self-disclosure, such as talking about where you grew up or what your major is, is fairly impersonal; other self-disclosure, such as talking about your future hopes and childhood insecurities, is much more intimate. As relationships develop, increases in personal self-disclosure typically characterize communication.

Dimensions of Self-Disclosure

One of the first theoretical explorations of self-disclosure was developed by Altman and Taylor (1973). According to **social penetration theory**, self-disclosure usually increases gradually as people develop their relationships. Self-disclosure can be conceptualized in terms of six dimensions: depth, breadth, frequency, duration, valence, and veracity (Altman & Taylor, 1973; Gilbert, 1976; Tolstedt & Stokes, 1984; Wheeless & Grotz, 1976).

Depth and Breadth

According to social penetration theory, the dimensions that are most central to the process of relationship development are depth and breadth. **Depth** refers to how personal or deep the communication is, whereas **breadth** captures how many topics a person feels free to discuss. As relationships develop, they tend to increase in breadth and then depth. In fact, according to social penetration theory, it is helpful to visualize the process of self-disclosure during relationship development as the slow unpeeling of an onion, as Figure 5.1 illustrates. An onion has a rather thin and flimsy outer layer, but as you peel through the various layers, they get harder, with the core of the onion very tightly bound. Similarly, Altman and Taylor (1973) suggested that there are three basic layers of self-disclosure: (1) a superficial layer that is easy to penetrate; (2) a social or personal layer that is easy for most friends, family members, and lovers to penetrate; and (3) a very intimate layer, or core, that is seldom revealed, and then only to people who are completely trusted.

At the superficial layer, people reveal commonplace facts about themselves that are not threatening in any way. For example, telling someone your name, major, hometown, zodiac sign, and favorite color are benign self-disclosures. At the social or personal level, people typically reveal more about their likes and dislikes, and hopes and fears, but they still keep their deepest hopes and fears a secret. For example, you might tell most of your friends that you'd like to marry a certain kind of person, that you had an unhappy childhood, or that you are worried about getting a job when you graduate from college. But you might not tell them all the intimate details related to these topics. At the core, people share all the personal details that make them who they are. Within the core are people's most secret, intimate

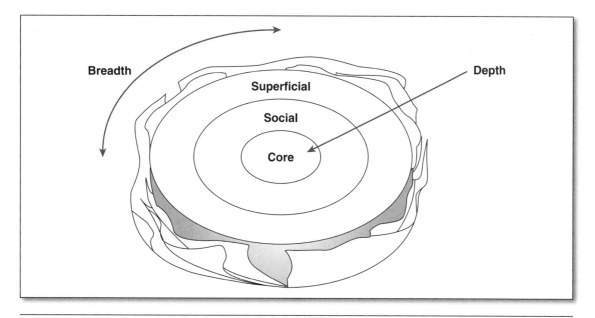

Figure 5.1   Depth and Breadth of Self-Disclosure

NOTE: Depth increases as people disclose about more intimate topics, while breadth increases as people talk about a wider range of topics. Different topics can be thought of as occupying different "wedges" of the onion.

feelings. For example, you might disclose negative childhood experiences that you would normally prefer not to think about, and you might confess all of your fears and insecurities about succeeding in your chosen profession. You might also reveal intimate, positive feelings about people by telling them how much they mean to you and how lost you would be without them.

Frequency and Duration

The next two dimensions focus on **frequency** (how often people self-disclose) and **duration** (how long people self-disclose). Various types of encounters can be characterized differently based on these dimensions. For example, when you have to work on a class project with someone you don't know well, you might need to get together with this person frequently in order to complete the class assignment. Although your self-disclosure with this person would probably be described as low in depth and breadth, it would likely be high in frequency—at least until you

complete the project. Of course, if you began to develop a close relationship with your classmate, the depth and breadth of your self-disclosure would probably increase, so that you'd be talking about more varied and more personal topics in addition to discussing the assignment. This example illustrates an important point: Frequent self-disclosure can lead to liking and relationship development.

It is possible for people to have self-disclosures of limited frequency but long duration. A common example of this is the "stranger on the plane" (or train) phenomenon. When you sit down next to someone on a plane, you might chat with the person for the entire duration of the flight. You might even disclose intimate details about your life to your seatmate, figuring that you probably won't see this person again, so you are not really making yourself vulnerable. Thus, it is the limited frequency of the interaction that allows you to confidently engage in self-disclosure that is high in both depth and duration. In other cases, you might have frequent self-disclosure with someone, but it usually is short in duration. For example, you might talk with a coworker every day, but only for limited amounts of time during a coffee break. One study showed that the duration of face-to-face interaction is more strongly related to closeness in friendships than is the frequency of interaction (Emmers-Sommer, 2004). This same study showed that friendships regarded as especially close and intimate tend to be characterized by high levels of in-depth communication. Thus, friends do not need frequent contact to stay close as long as they periodically have long, in-depth conversations.

Valence and Veracity

The final two dimensions relate to the specific content revealed by the self-disclosure. **Valence** refers to the positive or negative "charge" of the self-disclosure. For example, if you disclose your dreams, your warm feelings for someone, or your happiest childhood memories, the self-disclosure has a positive valence. By contrast, if you disclose your fears, your hostile feelings for someone, or your unhappiest childhood memories, the self-disclosure has a negative valence. Valence is a crucial dimension of self-disclosure because it helps determine how people feel about one another. Think about friends who call you all the time to complain about their lives. Their self-disclosure might be full of breadth and depth, but instead of feeling closer to your friend, you might end up feeling depressed and want to avoid such conversations in the future.

Similarly, some research has shown that couples show an increase in depth of self-disclosure when they are continually arguing or when their relationship is in decline (Tolstedt & Stokes, 1984). The types of comments they typically make, however, are negatively valenced ("I wish I'd never met you," "Why don't you ever listen to me?" "You make me feel unimportant"). Thus, high depth alone does not tell the whole story. Depth and valence work together to create the emotional climate of a self-disclosure. Of course, some negatively valenced self-disclosure can draw people closer. For example, when two individuals feel comfortable enough to reveal their deepest fears, worst failures, and most embarrassing moments, they probably have developed a particularly close relationship.

The key is to limit the number of negatively valenced disclosures relative to the number of more positively valenced disclosures.

Veracity refers to how honest or deceptive self-disclosure is. True self-disclosure is honest in that it reveals something real about oneself to others. However, there are times when people give false or misleading information to others that passes as self-disclosure. For example, when people like others they sometimes exaggerate their positive personal qualities to try to make a positive first impression. When first meeting an attractive woman, men often exaggerate about how successful they are, perhaps by describing their job as more high-powered than it actually is (Rowatt, Cunningham, & Druen, 1998, 1999). Women, in contrast, sometimes try to exaggerate or hide certain aspects of their appearance through the use of clothing or make-up. Good examples of exaggeration during the acquaintanceship process can also be found on the Internet, where people can post the best picture of themselves, add a couple inches to their height, or describe their background in overly glowing terms on their profiles. Of course, information that looks like self-disclosure but is actually deceptive can backfire, leading to lower levels of trust that hinder relationship development (Wheeless & Grotz, 1976, 1977; see also Chapter 13). Honest self-disclosure is the only real path for developing closeness.

Risks Associated With Self-Disclosure

Despite its benefits, disclosing personal information is risky. When we tell other people our innermost thoughts and feelings, we become vulnerable and open ourselves up to criticism. Scholars have used a dialectical perspective to explain the costs and benefits of self-disclosure (Baxter & Montgomery, 1996; Petronio, 2000, 2002; Rosenfeld, 2000). According to this perspective, people have strong needs for both openness and secrecy. As Rosenfeld (2000) put it:

> I want to be open because I want to share myself with others and get the benefits of such communication, such as receiving social support, the opportunity to think out loud, and the chance to get something off my chest. I do not want to be open because I might

be ridiculed, rejected, or abandoned. Open or closed; let others in or keep others out? Every interaction has the potential for raising the tension of holding both desires simultaneously. It is not that one desire "wins" and the other "loses." Rather, they exist simultaneously. Interpersonal life consists of the tension between these opposites. (p. 4)

Consistent with the dialectical perspective, scholars have delineated several risks associated with self-disclosure. Some of the most common reasons people avoid intimate self-disclosure include (1) fear of exposure or rejection, (2) fear of retaliation or angry responses, (3) fear of loss of control, and (4) fear of losing one's individuality (Hatfield, 1984; Petronio, 2002).

Fear of Exposure or Rejection

Sometimes people worry that too much self-disclosure will expose their negative qualities and cause others to think badly of them, like them less, and even reject or abandon them. As Hatfield (1984) put it, "One reason, then, that all of us are afraid of intimacy, is that those we care most about are bound to discover all that is wrong with us—to discover that we possess taboo feelings . . . have done things of which we are deeply ashamed" (p. 210). Hatfield gave an excellent example of how revealing one's real self can lead to rejection and abandonment when she told the story of one of her former graduate students. This young European woman was beautiful, intelligent, and charming; in fact, many men fell madly in love with her. Of course, she was not perfect—she had insecurities and self-doubts, just as we all do. But she put on a bright, charming facade in order to fit the perfect image that people had of her. The problem was that whenever she got close enough to a man to admit her insecurities, she fell off the pedestal that he had put her on. It was impossible to meet the high expectations of these men. When her perfect image was shattered, they lost interest and abandoned her.

Fear of Retaliation or Angry Attacks

People also worry that their partners might become angry or use what they disclose against

them. For example, you might worry that your relational partner will retaliate or withdraw from the relationship if you confess to a one-night stand, admit telling a lie, or recount happy experiences you had with a former relational partner. One of our students once told us that he was secretly in love with his brother's fiancé. The two brothers had always had a very close but competitive relationship and he worried that disclosing his feelings could lead to anger, suspicion, and even confrontation. He also worried that his brother's fiancé would end up hurt, confused, and maybe angry. In other cases, people use the intimate information we share with them as ammunition against us. For example, if you tell your best friend that you sometimes only pretend to pay attention to people, your friend might later accuse you of being selfish and of not really listening when he or she is disclosing personal problems.

Fear of Loss of Control

People also worry that if they engage in too much self-disclosure, they will lose control of their thoughts and feelings or the thoughts and feelings of others. For example, Connor fell in love with Anne after only a couple weeks, but he did not tell her he loved her then because he knew he might scare her away. Similarly, Anne might be afraid that if she starts talking to Connor about the reasons that their relationship might not work, she will break down and cry. People may also fear losing control of information, especially if they think that the person to whom they disclose to might share the information with others (Petronio, 2002; Phillips & Metzger, 1976). Additionally, people may worry that if they disclose personal weaknesses to their partner, they will lose their ability to influence the partner (Petronio, 1991).

Fear of Losing Individuality

Some people fear losing their personal identity and being engulfed by the relationship. According to Hatfield (1984), one of the "most primitive fears of intimacy" is that we could "literally disappear" if we become too engulfed in a relationship (p. 212). Consistent with the dialectical perspective, this fear represents the push and pull that many people feel between the competing forces of wanting to be closely connected to others and wanting to be independent and self-sufficient. The idea here is that if we tell people too much about ourselves, we risk losing our uniqueness and mysteriousness. Moreover, if we maintain high levels of self-disclosure, we may come to a point where there is nothing left to share. In this case, we may feel that we are part of a group or dyad, rather than a unique individual with some private, secret thoughts and feelings. We may even feel a need to "escape" from our relational partner in order to find privacy and assert our independence.

Self-Disclosure and Liking

Because self-disclosure comes with considerable risk yet also draws people together, the act of self-disclosure conveys both trust and closeness. Thus, according to social penetration theory, self-disclosure typically increases gradually as people get to know, like, and trust one another. If people do not develop trust or liking, self-disclosure will not progress very far, and the relationship will stagnate or terminate.

Many studies have examined the relationship between self-disclosure and liking. In a statistical review of 94 studies, Collins and Miller (1994) tested the **disclosure-liking hypothesis**, which predicts that, when a sender discloses to a receiver, the receiver will like the sender more. Collins and Miller's statistical review supported the disclosure-liking hypothesis, although this relationship appears to be stronger among acquaintances than strangers.

Collins and Miller's statistical review also supported the **liking-disclosure hypothesis**, which predicts that people will disclose more to receivers they like. Thus, you are more likely to disclose to close relational partners and to people to whom you are attracted than to people you dislike.

In some cases, however, high levels of self-disclosure are not related to liking. Derlega, Metts, Petronio, and Margulis (1993) suggested that there are three reasons for this. First, when self-disclosure violates normative expectations, it will not lead to liking. Sometimes people disclose too much information too quickly, or disclose negative information that leads others to dislike them (Bochner, 1984; Parks, 1982). As Derlega and colleagues observed, "Highly personal, negative disclosure given too soon inhibits liking unless some strong initial attraction already exists" (p. 31). Second, self-disclosure is a better predictor of liking when receivers think that the sender only discloses information to certain special people. If senders are perceived to disclose information indiscriminately, the self-disclosure may be seen as less valuable, and liking may not result. Third, "disclosure will not lead to liking if it is responded to in a negative manner" (Derlega et al., 1993, p. 32). If a sender discloses sensitive information and the receiver dismisses the information or responds in an unkind or critical manner, both sender and receiver are likely to feel negatively about the interaction and about each other. Usually, however, receivers match the intimacy level of a sender's self-disclosure. Box 5.2 gives examples of the relationship between self-disclosure and liking.

BOX 5.2 Highlights

Examples of Relationships Between Liking and Disclosure

The Disclosure-Liking Hypothesis: Disclosure Leads to Liking

Hannah and Emily pair up to work on a school project. Although they have had a few classes together, they don't know each other well. However, one evening, after working on their project, they start talking about personal issues. Hannah tells Emily about her long-distance relationship with her boyfriend and confesses to really missing him. Emily tells Hannah about her three-year-old son and confesses that it is difficult to concentrate on school when she is so busy as a single mom. The two women feel a new sense of connection to each other.

The Liking-Disclosure Hypothesis: Liking Leads to Disclosure

Patrick really likes his new neighbor, Spencer, who seems friendly, funny, and easygoing. Once in a while when they run into each other before work, Spencer tells Patrick a joke and makes him laugh. One day, Patrick wins a prestigious award at work. He doesn't talk about the award much at work because he does not want to appear boastful or conceited. But when he comes home after work, he sees Spencer out mowing his lawn. Spencer waves, and Patrick strides over to tell him the good news. Spencer shuts off the lawn mower, and the two men start to talk.

Too Much Disclosure Too Early Can Lead to Disliking

Madison and Joel are on a first date. They go out to dinner at a fancy restaurant and engage in chitchat. About halfway through dinner, Joel starts telling Madison his life story. He starts by telling her about how he was an unpopular kid in elementary school. Then he talks about how his dog died when he was 10 years old. He is just starting to get into the adolescent years when the waiter arrives to see if they want dessert. Madison says she is full and asks the waiter to bring the check, hoping that she can get out of the restaurant before Joel starts talking about his first sexual experiences.

Indiscriminant Disclosure Is Less Likely to Lead to Liking

Travis and Angela meet at a company party. Angela tells Travis about her dreams and career aspirations. She tells him, "I wouldn't tell just anyone this, but my secret ambition is to be a rock star. I know it is silly and probably will never happen, but it would be so much fun to turn on the radio and hear myself singing." Later she says, "Don't tell anyone, but I might be leaving the firm to concentrate on a possible music career." Travis feels honored that Angela told him these things until he runs into a coworker who says, "Hey, I saw you talking to that woman who wants to be a rock star. She's been saying she's going to quit for the last year. I doubt she ever will." Suddenly, Travis doesn't feel special anymore.

Negative Responses to Disclosure Reduce Liking

Amy's sister has been dating Diego for several months. Amy is very close to her sister and would like to get to know Diego better. One day, at a family picnic, Amy approaches Diego and says hello. She asks him how he has been. He says, "Fine," and looks away from Amy and out at the lake. Undaunted, Amy continues the conversation: "My sister tells me that you just got a big promotion at work. What will you be doing?" "More of the same," he says, still looking at the lake. Amy tells him about her job, but he doesn't seem interested. Eventually, Amy gives up and walks away, wondering what her sister could possibly see in him.

Reciprocity of Self-Disclosure

For relationships to flourish in the initial stages, self-disclosure must be reciprocated. Extensive research has focused on the reciprocity or matching of self-disclosure, starting with Jourard's (1959, 1964) pioneering work on patterns of self-disclosure. Jourard believed that reciprocal self-disclosure, which he termed the **dyadic effect**, is the vehicle by which people build close relationships (see also Altman & Taylor, 1973; Gouldner, 1960). Reciprocal self-disclosure occurs when a person reveals information and the partner responds by offering information that is at a similar level of intimacy. For example, if Connor tells Anne about his career ambition to get his PhD and teach biology at a university, Anne might respond by telling Connor that she wishes she could go back to school and train to be a veterinarian. Jourard's work suggests that self-disclosure usually begets more self-disclosure. In other words, people are likely to respond to high levels of self-disclosure by revealing similarly personal information. Of course, there are exceptions to this rule. For example, you might not want to continue a conversation with someone because you don't want to "lead the person on," or you might decide that the other person's level of self-disclosure is inappropriate and makes you uncomfortable. In these cases, you are less likely to reciprocate self-disclosure.

Nonetheless, research suggests that people typically feel a natural pull toward matching the level of intimacy and intensity present in their conversational partner's self-disclosure. In a statistical review of 67 studies involving 5,173 participants, Dindia and Allen (1992) concluded that the evidence overwhelmingly supports the tendency for people to reciprocate self-disclosure. Studies have shown that people typically match the intimacy level of their conversational partner's self-disclosure regardless of the context (face-to-face versus via telephone or the Internet), the type of relationship (strangers versus intimates), or the amount of liking or disliking (Derlega, Harris, & Chaikin, 1973; Dindia et al., 1997; Henderson & Gilding, 2004; Hosman & Tardy, 1980; Janofsky, 1971; Levinger & Senn, 1967). Research also suggests that individuals who violate the norm of reciprocity are perceived as cold, incompetent, unfriendly, and untrustworthy (Bradac, Hosman, & Tardy, 1978; Chaikin & Derlega, 1974).

Sometimes, however, reciprocity is delayed. This pattern is common in long-term, close relationships where people have ample opportunity to reciprocate in the future. For example, a husband might disclose his social anxieties to his wife, who simply listens patiently. Subsequently, the wife might reciprocate by sharing some of her deepest fears while the husband assumes the listening role. In initial encounters between people, future interaction is often uncertain so immediate reciprocity is more important.

Not surprisingly, research has also shown that partners who believe they reciprocate one another's self-disclosure tend to be more satisfied with their relationships, particularly when the self-disclosure is positively valenced (Chelune, Rosenfeld, & Waring, 1985; Rosenfeld & Welsh, 1985). Studies have found that spouses are usually dissatisfied with their relationships when there is a large discrepancy between the amount of personal information they share with their partner and the amount of personal information they receive from their partner (Davidson, Balswick, & Halverson, 1983; Hansen & Schuldt, 1984). Similarly, Afifi, Guerrero, and Egland (1994) found that perceived reciprocity of self-disclosure was the main predictor of relational closeness for male friends. These studies showed that self-disclosure is important not only in building relationships but also in maintaining them.

STAGES OF RELATIONSHIP DEVELOPMENT

Not surprisingly, self-disclosure, like other patterns of communication, changes as a relationship progresses. Indeed, much of the research on relationship development focuses on the stages that help define people's relationships (Mongeau & Henningsen, 2008). There are several popular stage theories of relationship development. In social penetration theory, Altman and Taylor (1973) described four stages that people go through as they get closer—orientation, exploratory exchange, affective exchange, and stable exchange—with each stage containing more depth and breadth of self-disclosure. Knapp expanded these to five stages—initiating, experimenting, intensifying, integrating, and bonding—and included other communicative behaviors beyond self-disclosure (see Knapp & Vangelisti, 2005).

Knapp and Vangelisti's five stages—initiating, experimenting, intensifying, integrating, and bonding—provide a useful means to organize the research related to the various stages that couples and friends go through as they move from being strangers to close relational partners. Knapp visualized these stages as a staircase leading upward, with each step or stage representing an increase in intimacy (Knapp & Vangelisti, 2005). Knapp also visualized stages of relational disengagement as a descending staircase, with each stage characterized by more avoidance and separation, as discussed in Chapter 15.

The Initiating Stage

Most stage theories include a beginning stage that focuses on the first time people meet or the first several encounters, particularly if each meeting is short in duration. This first stage is called the **orientation stage** in social penetration theory and the **initiating stage** in Knapp and Vangelisti's model. In social penetration theory, the orientation stage involves exchanging information that is low in both depth and breadth. By staying at the superficial level of the self-disclosure "onion" (see Figure 5.1), strangers and new acquaintances avoid making themselves vulnerable. In Knapp and Vangelisti's (2005) model, the initiating stage involves greeting each other and exchanging bits of information, such as one's name, occupation, or major. The valence of the disclosure is usually positive during this stage, with participants trying to make a good impression by following rules of social politeness.

A greeting or question followed by a reply is typical of this stage (Knapp & Vangelisti, 2005), which sometimes evolves into a back-and-forth exchange of superficial information that helps people reduce uncertainty about each other. For example, when Connor first met Anne he said, "Hi, I haven't seen you at our meetings before. Is this your first time coming?" Anne responded, "Yeah. Have you been coming for long?" Connor said he'd been to a couple of other meetings, but was also fairly new. Then they exchanged names and continued talking about rather superficial topics, such as what happens at the Sierra Club, until the meeting was called to order. This short conversation helped Connor and Anne reduce uncertainty and set a foundation for future interactions (see Chapter 4). In some cases, however, people never progress beyond this stage. Think of people with whom you work or take classes. You may recognize some of these people but not spend time taking to them. When you see these casual acquaintances, you likely exchange a quick greeting and reply ("Hi, how are you?" "Fine, thanks"), but nothing more, which indicates that you have not moved past the initiating stage.

Initial interactions play a key role in determining whether people like Anne and Connor develop their relationship further. Indeed, some researchers have argued that people determine their feelings for one another very quickly during initial encounters (Berg & Clark, 1986). They then communicate differently based on whether they like the person or not. According to predicted outcome value theory, during initial encounters people make decisions about how rewarding they expect a relationship to be (see Chapter 4). These initial impressions can have lasting effects on how a relationship develops. In one study,

undergraduates were paired with a stranger of the same sex to talk for between 3 and 10 minutes on the first day of class (Sunnafrank & Ramirez, 2004). After this initial interaction, students recorded their perceptions of how rewarding it would be for them to become involved in a relationship with the person they just met. When students were then surveyed again later in the semester, they were much more likely to report developing a relationship with someone they initially perceived as rewarding. They were also more likely to have sat near them during class, communicated with them frequently, and felt high levels of social attraction and liking. This study demonstrated that the first few minutes of initial encounters have a strong influence on if, and how, relationships develop.

The Experimenting Stage

Regardless of how people first meet, if their relationship is to progress they need to move beyond the exchange of superficial information. Yet as discussed earlier, revealing personal information to others is risky and can make people feel vulnerable. Therefore, people usually take small steps when disclosing information and deciding whether or not to pursue a closer relationship. The stage that encapsulates this process of discovery and learning about each other has been termed the **exploratory affective exchange stage** (Altman & Taylor, 1973) or the **experimenting stage** (Knapp & Vangelisti, 2005).

In terms of self-disclosure, this stage is characterized by increasing breadth and frequency but relatively low depth (Altman & Taylor, 1973). In other words, people in this stage will explore potential topics by increasing breadth first but disclose in depth only if they feel comfortable with each other. **Small talk** is defined as communication that is high in breadth but low in depth. According to Knapp and Vangelisti (2005), small talk is the key to understanding this stage of relationship development. Small talk allows people to fulfill a number of goals simultaneously, including discovering common interests, seeing if it would be worthwhile to pursue a closer relationship, reducing uncertainty in a safe manner that does not make them vulnerable, and allowing them to maintain a sense of connection with other people without putting themselves at much risk for hurt or rejection.

Small talk also lays the foundation for more personal disclosure. For instance, when Anne and Connor first talked, they touched on a variety of topics, ranging from the Sierra Club to sports, then politics, and finally to adventures with family and friends. However, they did not delve too deeply into any of these topics. Anne explained that she has a particularly close relationship with one of her sisters but not the other, but she did not reveal any of her innermost feelings about either sister. Connor told Anne that she was lucky to have sisters since he was an only child, but he did not elaborate on why he wished he had siblings. Despite its relatively superficial content, this conversation gave both Anne and Connor important information about one another. They learned that they had a lot in common, which made them feel comfortable with each other so that their subsequent conversations started to include more and more personal information. Thus, once partners have discovered enough about one another, they begin to trust each other and to disclose in more depth. The valence of disclosure, however, tends to remain more positive than negative in this stage because people are still trying to maintain positive impressions as they get to know one another (Guerrero & Andersen, 2000).

Of course, in some cases, people at this stage decide that they have little in common and should either remain casual friends or terminate the relationship. Indeed, most of people's interpersonal relationships stay at this stage—or at least do not venture far beyond it. Think about all the acquaintances and casual friends you have. Chances are that your conversations with them are composed mainly of small talk rather than more intimate disclosures.

The Intensifying Stage

With a select few individuals, people emerge from the experimenting stage feeling a special sense of connection and trust. They move from wanting to get to know the person better to wanting the relationship with that person to be close. But how do people move relationships from casual to close? According to social penetration theory, people increase the depth of their self-disclosure and start exchanging information on an emotional level (Altman & Taylor, 1973). The valence and duration of self-disclosure also may change at this point in what Altman and Taylor call the **affective exchange stage**. Rather than sticking mostly to positive self-disclosure, people in this stage feel freer to engage in negative self-disclosure. In some ways the "honeymoon period" has ended, and people no longer feel the need to be on their best behavior. The beginning of this stage is usually marked by long, in-depth conversations as partners strive to intensify their relationship and show affection and trust to each other. However, as the relationship stabilizes, the need for long conversations diminishes because partners already know a considerable amount about each other. One study showed that although people disclose more intimate thoughts and feelings to their spouses than to strangers, they disclose more self-descriptive information (such as basic facts about themselves) to strangers (Dindia, Fitzpatrick, & Kenny, 1997). This suggests that people's self-disclosure changes from an emphasis on self-description to an emphasis on sharing intimate thoughts and feelings as a relationship gets closer.

Besides in-depth disclosure, other types of communication common in this stage include displaying affectionate nonverbal communication to each other (see Chapter 6), using nicknames or forms of endearment, saying "we" instead of "I" ("We should go down to Mexico sometime"), and making statements that reflect positive regard and commitment, such as saying "I love you" or "You are my very best friend." Declarations such as these usually first occur in the intensifying stage and then continue into the next two stages as people integrate and bond.

Work by Tolhuizen (1989) gives further insight into how people intensify their relationships. In his research, Tolhuizen found 15 different intensification strategies; Box 5.3 lists these strategies. The three most common strategies are increased contact, relationship negotiation (which involves talking about the relationship), and social support and assistance (which involves asking someone for advice or comfort). Nearly 40% of the people Tolhuizen surveyed described increased contact as an important intensification strategy, while 29% and 26% mentioned relationship negotiation and social support/assistance, respectively. Thus, these three strategies appear to be fairly common ways of intensifying various relationships. The other strategies listed in Box 5.3 appear to play more minor roles in the intensification process, but they still represent important means by which people escalate their relationships.

BOX 5.3 Highlights

Tolhuizen's Strategies for Intensifying Relationships

1. *Increased contact* includes seeing or calling the person more often (39.2%).

2. *Relationship negotiation* includes openly discussing the state of the relationship and the feelings the partners have for one another (29.1%).

3. *Social support and assistance* involves asking people for support, advice, and comfort (26.1%).

4. *Increased rewards* include doing favors and making sacrifices for one another, such as helping someone move or helping with household tasks (17.6%).

5. *Direct definitional bid* involves asking the partner to make a definite commitment, such as seeing each other exclusively, moving in together, or getting married (16.1%).

6. *Tokens of affection* include sending flowers, cards, and gifts, as well as exchanging rings (16.1%).

7. *Personalized communication* includes using idiomatic communication, such as special nicknames and inside jokes, as well as listening empathically (15.1%).

8. *Verbal expressions of affection* include uttering declarations such as "I love you" and "I hope we are always this close" (14.1%).

9. *Suggestive actions* include flirting, trying to get someone jealous, and playing "hard to get" (13.1%).

10. *Nonverbal expressions of affection* include gazing at the partner lovingly, touching the partner, and smiling (12.1%).

11. *Social enmeshment* involves getting to know and spending more time with the partner's family and friends, sometimes through activities such as spending a holiday together (11.6%).

12. *Acceptance of definition bid* involves redefining the relationship through actions such as saying "yes" when the partner asks for more commitment, or agreeing to date exclusively, move in together, or get married (9.5%).

13. *Personal appearance* involves changing one's physical appearance to please the partner by engaging in behaviors such as trying to lose weight, changing one's hairstyle, or dressing particularly well (9.5%).

14. *Sexual intimacy* involves engaging in increasingly intimate behavior, often including sexual relations (8%).

15. *Behavioral adaptation* involves changing one's behavior to please the partner, perhaps by trying to secure a better job or to criticize the partner less and compliment the partner more (7.5%).

NOTE: The percentages in this table represent the percentage of people in a study by Tolhuizen who described or reported using each strategy. Because people were allowed to describe as many strategies as they deemed relevant, the percentages add up to more than 100%.

The Integrating Stage

By the time two people reach the **integrating stage**, they have already become close. Now they are ready to show that closeness to others by presenting themselves as a "dyad" or "couple." This type of presentation is not limited to romantic couples; friends often present themselves as a unified team as well. The key here is that the two people have developed a relational identity; they see themselves as part of a dyad with some aspects of their personalities and experiences overlapping (Knapp & Vangelisti, 2005). Once coupling has occurred, people outside the relationship see the partners as two halves of a whole. It is easy to see when this has occurred. For example, imagine that Connor attends a party alone and several people stop and ask him, "Where's Anne?" This indicates that people in Connor's social network regard Anne and Connor as a couple; they expect to see the two of them together. Connor and Anne may also start to receive joint invitations to parties or combined Christmas gifts, which shows that other people see them as a committed couple.

Other types of changes occur within the dyad in this stage. Close friends or romantic partners may be able to complete each other's sentences, and their tastes, attitudes, and opinions may merge. For example, in the classic movie *When Harry Met Sally,* the last scene shows Harry and Sally discussing their wedding. Sally describes their wedding cake, including the rich chocolate sauce that they had "on the side." Harry concludes the description by noting it is important to have the sauce on the side, because not everyone likes the same amount of sauce on their cake. This is an example of coupling since Sally, not Harry, was originally the person who insisted on ordering the sauce on the side. Other signs of coupling include wearing similar clothing, opening a joint bank account, designating a favorite tune as "our song," and merging social networks.

Although self-disclosure is likely to be very high in both the intensifying and integrating stages, it may fall short of complete disclosure. In social penetration theory, the final stage of relationship development is the **stable exchange stage**, in which people disclose openly about everything. Achieving a true state of stable exchange is very difficult. Even in our closest relationships, we keep some secrets from our partners (Vangelisti, 1994a). Baxter and Wilmot (1984) found that 91% of the partners in romantic couples said that there was at least one topic that they never discussed with their relational partner. Common taboo topics included the state of the relationship, past relationships, and sexual experiences. Although stable exchange may seem like a worthy goal, it is probably an unrealistic one. Partners in many couples exchange information on a regular basis, but very few actually share 100% of their thoughts and feelings.

In any case, complete self-disclosure is probably not the best prescription for a happy relationship. Later in this book we emphasize that many people have strong needs for privacy and autonomy (see Chapter 12). As Hatfield suggested, too much self-disclosure may rob us of our sense of privacy and make us feel overly dependent on others. In addition, it can be nice to keep some mystery in our relationships. This is not to say that people should purposely hide important information from their close relational partners. They should, however, feel that they have the right to control private information and to keep certain innermost thoughts and feelings undisclosed (Petronio, 2002). This helps explain why a stable rate of exchange is difficult to achieve—even in relationships that are exceptionally close.

The Bonding Stage

In the final stage of Knapp's model, the **bonding stage**, partners find a way to declare their commitment publicly to each other, usually through the institutionalization of the relationship. Perhaps the most obvious way of institutionalizing a romantic relationship is through marriage. Getting married shows commitment, and also makes it harder to leave the relationship. Most people cannot simply walk away from a marriage. There are possessions to divide, perhaps children to provide for, and a socially shared history that is hard to leave behind. Marriage can also be thought of a social ritual, in that two people come together before family and

SOURCE: (left) AP Photo/Gus Ruelas; (right) AP Photo/Jacquelyn Martin.

In the United States, people have strong opinions regarding whether or not same-sex couples should be allowed to reach the bonding stage through marriage. What do you think?

friends to declare their love for each other. Such a public declaration cements their bond even further. Importantly, in states that do not allow gay and lesbian couples to marry, these couples often still have public commitment ceremonies uniting them as life partners in front of friends and family. These ceremonies underscore how important public commitment is to most couples.

Other types of relationships also reach the bonding stage, although the institutionalization of these relationships is more difficult. Friends and family members, however, can make public, enduring commitments to one another in various ways. For instance, if you get married, the people you choose to stand up as your bridesmaids or groomsmen will be an important part of this critical life event, and they will hold that place in your memory forever. By choosing them, you are telling your social network that these people have a special place in your life. Similarly, if you have a child and choose

godparents, these individuals will be part of an important social ritual that publicly lets others know you value and trust them. Some friendship rituals, such as becoming blood brothers or getting matching tattoos, are also ways to show a permanent bond.

The Ordering and Timing of Stages

Before leaving our discussion of Knapp and Vangelisti's (2005) stages, it is important to note that people do not always move through these stages in an orderly manner. Knapp has argued that his five stages outline the typical pattern of relational development for many couples but that variations frequently take place (Knapp & Vangelisti, 2005). Couples, or friends, might go though the stages in a different order, or they might skip some stages entirely. For example, some romantic couples fall in love at first sight and quickly get married. Other couples skip stages or move too quickly through them; they might later go back and engage in communication appropriate for earlier stages. Picture a couple who meet and soon get married. Their friends and family might be surprised at the news of their marriage, and the newlyweds may need to work on merging their social networks and gaining acceptance as a couple. In this case, the processes that typically occur during the integrating stage would be occurring after the bonding stage.

FIRST DATES AND COHABITATION

The stages proposed by Knapp and Vangelisti (2005) can apply to a variety of voluntary relationships, including those between good friends and romantic partners. Those who move from being acquaintances to best friends are likely to pass through all of the stages in Knapp's model, as are romantic partners who move from a first date to marriage. Yet, there are differences in how friendships and romantic relationships develop. In some ways, initiating a dating relationship is more complex than initiating a friendship, and some romantic partners perceive cohabitation as a stage that occurs between serious dating and marriage. Thus, research on first dates and cohabitation provides a useful context for understanding the stages that occur as romantic relationships unfold.

First Dates

First dates provide a starting point for many romantic relationships. Whether the individuals are strangers on a blind date, acquaintances who are physically attracted to one another, or friends who have decided to explore romantic potential in their relationship, first dates mark the possibility of embarking on a new romantic adventure. The research on first dates has focused on several issues, including date initiation and the goals and expectations people have for first dates.

Initiating First Dates

The social norms that govern how men and women get acquainted have changed throughout history. Mongeau, Hale, Johnson, and Hillis (1993) noted that at the end of the 19th century, courtship involved men "calling" on women at their homes. The "call" often involved the woman inviting the man over for dinner or tea in the presence of her family. Around the beginning of the 20th century, dating started to replace calling. Dating involved two people going somewhere outside of the home together, often to have dinner out and go to a concert, play, or social event. This shift from calling to dating also entailed a change in who initiated the get-acquainted process. With calling, women largely controlled the situation—they could invite the man over and decide what food and home entertainment they would provide. With dating, men usually controlled the situation—they asked the woman out, provided transportation, and paid for the date.

Although it is now much more acceptable for women to ask men out than it was in the early to mid-20th century, the standard dating script still puts the man in the initiating position. When college students are asked to describe the typical request for a first date, they report that the man usually asks the woman. They also describe dates in heterosexual relationships as following a fairly predictable sequence (Honeycutt & Cantrill, 2001; Laner & Ventrone, 2000): The man asks the woman out. If she agrees, he plans the date and picks her up at her place of residence. She greets him and introduces him to her family or roommates. They engage in small talk and depart. During the date, they engage in more small talk as they try to get to know each other. The man takes the woman home; they thank each other, kiss, and in some cases, the man suggests that he will call or that they should get together again soon. The man then departs.

Even though this scenario is still regarded as the typical first date script, dates such as these are starting to be replaced by group activities, where potential partners meet amid interaction between groups of friends and then break off into dyads. In addition, although men still tend to initiate dates more than women, date initiation by women is fairly commonplace. In one of the first studies to examine this issue, 87% of men reported that they had been asked out by a woman at least once (Kelley, Pilchowicz, & Byrne, 1981). The men in this study reported having positive responses to date initiation by women even though the relationships that these initiations started were often short-lived. A later study by Mongeau and his colleagues (1993) found that 90% of men reported that they had been asked out on a date by a woman, and 83% of men had been asked out on a *first* date by a woman. These results suggest that women might feel freer to ask men on dates once a relationship has developed. Importantly, Mongeau and his colleagues also reported that almost all the men accepted dates initiated by women.

Because women-initiated first dates break the stereotypical dating script, researchers have investigated how women who initiate dates are perceived. Studies suggest that women who initiate dates are seen as more open, liberal, active, and extroverted, but less attractive than women who wait to be asked by the man (Mongeau & Carey, 1996; Mongeau et al., 1993). Some studies also show that men are likely to have higher sexual expectations for dates that are initiated by women, even though these expectations are not likely to be met (Mongeau & Johnson, 1995; Muehlenhard & Scardino, 1985). In other words, men might expect there to be more sexual activity on dates initiated by women, perhaps because the woman is perceived to be more liberal, open, and attracted to the man, but in actuality, dates initiated by women tend to be characterized by the same or less sexual activity than dates initiated by men.

Expectations and Goals on First Dates

Expectations related to sexual activity represent only one of several types of goals that people have on first dates. The goals people have vary based on the type of relationship people had prior to the first date and who initiated the date. The goals people have for first dates include having fun, reducing uncertainty, investigating romantic potential, developing friendship, and engaging in sexual activity (Mongeau, Serewicz, & Therrien, 2004). **Having fun** and reducing uncertainty are the most common goals. Having fun simply equates to wanting to have a good time and enjoy oneself. **Reducing uncertainty about the partner** refers to wanting to find out more about the person, including her or his attitudes, goals, and interests. The goals of investigating romantic potential and developing friendship are also fairly common on first dates.

Investigating romantic potential involves trying to determine if there are romantic feelings or chemistry between two people. **Developing friendship,** in contrast, focuses on trying to determine if two people have enough in common to be friends and do things together, or if two people should strengthen an already existing friendship. Finally, **engaging in sexual activity**, such as kissing and having sex, was the least commonly reported of these five goals. Notice that many of the goals people have for first dates represent ways of learning more about each other and determining the type of relationship they might share—goals that are consistent with the experimenting stage.

These goals influence the communication that occurs on first dates. When people have similar goals, the goals of both individuals are more likely to be fulfilled, leading to a "good" date. Take Connor and Anne as an example. Imagine that as they embark on their first date together they both believe that they have already established closeness at a friendship level. Their priority, then, is to determine if there is sexual chemistry and the potential for a romantic relationship. On their first date, they show affection to one another, share personal stories, and spend considerable time kissing, which helps them both decide that the relationship does indeed have romantic and sexual potential. On the other hand, imagine that Anne is still uncertain about Connor as a person and potential friend, whereas Connor's goal is to determine romantic potential and to engage in sexual activity. In this case, the different goals that Anne and Connor have could put them at cross-purposes, with both being frustrated that they could not reach their individual goals. As Mongeau and associates (2004) put it, "What constitutes a 'good' or 'bad' date, then, depends on the compatibility of partners' goals" (p. 143).

The goals that people have also depend on the type of relationship they share prior to the first date. Some people enter the first date as strangers or acquaintances, whereas others are already good friends. Strangers and acquaintances are more likely to have the goals of reducing uncertainty about the person and developing a friendship than are friends. By contrast, friends are more likely to have the goals of investigating romantic potential and engaging in sexual activity than are strangers or acquaintances (Mongeau et al., 2004). Friends are also more likely to expect high levels of intimacy and affection on first dates (Morr & Mongeau, 2004). The goal of having fun appears to be salient regardless of the type of relationship. These findings comport with ideas from social penetration theory and uncertainty reduction theory (see Chapter 4).

When people do not know one another well, their primary goal is to seek information. During the early stages of a relationship, people often exchange superficial information as part of the getting-acquainted process. However, once people have developed a friendship and exchanged in-depth information with one another, their goal on a first date may be to focus on other forms of intimacy that are undeveloped, such as sexual intimacy. Having fun is important on first dates because it reflects the valence dimension of self-disclosure—people tend to like and build relationships with those with whom they enjoy interacting. Similarly, people are more likely to develop close relationships with people whom they regard as rewarding (Sunnafrank & Ramirez, 2004).

Finally, some research has examined sex differences in goals and expectations related to sexual activity on first dates. This research suggests that men generally expect and desire more sexual activity on first dates than do women (Mongeau & Carey, 1996; Mongeau et al., 2004). However, the differences in sexual expectations for men versus women are not very large. College-age men tend to expect heavy kissing, whereas college-age women tend to expect light kissing (Mongeau & Johnson, 1995; Morr & Mongeau, 2004).

Cohabitation

Cohabitation, or living together without being married, comprises a special stage in some romantic relationships. Although cohabiting clearly suggests that a couple has intensified their relationship and engaged in integration, they have not bonded publicly in the same ways married couples have. For some couples, cohabitation is viewed as a stage between integrating and bonding, whereas for other couples cohabitation is perceived as the final relationship

stage. Some couples argue that the legal binds of marriage are not necessary. For those couples, cohabitation may be viewed as a better alternative than traditional forms of bonding, such as marriage.

Couples cohabit for a many reasons, ranging from convenience and financial advantages to love and the desire to be together. Some people live together rather than get married because they fear commitment or want to retain their autonomy, but most couples initially view cohabitation as another stage or transitional period that occurs between dating and marriage, or as a sort of "trial marriage." This is how Anne seems to regard cohabitation. One study showed that 90% of cohabiting couples expected to get married someday to their current partner or to someone else (Cunningham & Antill, 1994). Many of these couples see cohabitation as an "optional stage in the courtship sequence that may or may not end in marriage" (Cunningham & Antill, p. 78). Yet studies suggest that less than half of cohabiting partners end up getting married to each other (Blumstein & Schwartz, 1983; Brown, 2000; Bumpass & Sweet, 1989).

Much of the research on cohabitation has focused on determining whether cohabitation is beneficial or harmful to long-term relationships. To answer this question, researchers have compared couples who married without cohabiting first to couples who cohabited before getting married. Researchers have also compared cohabiting couples who marry to those who do not. These studies have focused on a number of issues, including relationship stability, relational quality, and communication patterns.

Relationship Stability

In general, marital relationships are more stable than cohabiting relationships. Some scholars have argued that cohabitation represents a looser bond than marriage because cohabitation involves more autonomy, less commitment, and fewer social and legal barriers to dissolution than does marriage (Schoen & Owens, 1992; Thorton, Axinn, & Teachman, 1995). For instance, a cohabiting couple is less likely to share property than a marital couple, and cohabiting couples can break up without having to file any legal paperwork. The **selection effect** provides another explanation for the instability found in some cohabiting relationships (Lillard, Brien, & Waite, 1995). According to the selection effect, people who choose to cohabit rather than marry have certain preexisting personal characteristics and attitudes that make it less likely that their relationships will last. These attitudes include greater acceptance of divorce and premarital sex, stronger needs for autonomy, and more negative feelings about marriage (Cunningham & Antill, 1994; Lillard et al., 1995; Rindfuss & VandenHeuvel, 1990). Cohabiting couples who plan to get married are more likely to stay together than those who have no concrete plans for marrying. However, couples who cohabit before marriage are more likely to get divorced than couples who move directly to marriage (Bennett, Blanc, & Bloom, 1988; Brown, 2000; Bumpass & Sweet, 1989).

Relational Quality

Given that cohabiting couples are more likely to break up than married couples, cohabiting couples might be expected to report less relational satisfaction than married couples. Yet, the research on this issue is mixed. Some studies have shown that married couples who do not live together prior to marriage are more satisfied with their relationships than cohabiting couples or couples who transition from cohabitation to marriage (DeMaris, 1984; DeMaris & Leslie, 1984; Nock, 1995; Stafford, Kline, & Rankin, 2004). Other studies show no difference (Yelsma, 1986). Brown and Booth (1996) found that cohabitors who planned to get married were just as satisfied with their relationships as married couples, whereas cohabitors who did not plan to marry were less satisfied.

Importantly, time in the relationship may be a much better predictor of relational satisfaction than whether a couple lived together before marriage. Satisfaction levels appear to decrease over time in marriages regardless of whether couples cohabited or not (Stafford et al., 2004; Yelsma, 1986). This same pattern has been found in relationships between cohabiting gay and lesbian couples. In one study, satisfaction dropped during the first year that gay and lesbian couples lived together, but then rebounded again after they had lived together 11 years or longer (Kurdek, 1989). Couples who move directly toward

marriage may still be in the honeymoon phase of their relationships. Those who cohabited before marriage may have already moved beyond the honeymoon stage. Thus, some of the differences that researchers have found may be due more to time in the relationship than whether a couple had cohabited (Stafford et al., 2004).

Communication Patterns

Time may also be a better predictor of communication patterns than whether a couple cohabited or not. Stafford and her colleagues (2004) compared three types of couples at two points in time over a five-year period: cohabiting couples who had not married, transitioned couples who had moved from cohabiting to marriage, and married couples. Across all three types of couples, people reported less satisfaction, less sexual interaction, more conflict, and more heated arguing over time. There were also some small differences in communication among the three types of couples. Cohabiting couples reported the most conflict, followed by transitioned couples. Married couples reported the least conflict. Cohabiting couples were also more likely to report violent behavior, such as hitting or throwing something, than either transitioned or married couples.

Other studies have found similar results. Brownridge and Halli (2000) reported that couples who lived together before marriage were 54% more likely to engage in violent behavior than couples who did not live together prior to marriage. Another study showed that cohabiting couples have more conflict than married couples (Nock, 1995). However, these differences may be strongest when the comparison is between married couples and cohabiting couples who do not plan to marry. Cohabiting couples who plan to marry do not differ from married couples in terms of conflict or violence (Brown & Booth, 1996).

Together, these studies suggest that cohabiting relationships are most likely to be characterized by satisfaction and high-quality communication when the couple plans to marry. Couples who cohabit because they fear commitment, want high levels of autonomy, or have negative attitudes toward marriage are less likely to be satisfied and more likely to use destructive communication. Communication is also an important ingredient in the recipe for whether a cohabiting relationship will be successful. Cohabiting relationships characterized by positive interaction and low levels of destructive conflict tend to be as stable and satisfying as many marriages (Brown, 2000).

THE TURNING-POINT APPROACH

First dates and cohabitation are two of many turning points that can occur in relationships. A **turning point** is "any event or occurrence that is associated with change in a relationship" (Baxter & Bullis, 1986, p. 469). Turning points are also major relational events. Interestingly, most of the scenes in romantic movies and novels consist of significant relational events or turning points, because turning points help tell the story of relational change. Rather than focusing on more mundane day-to-day events, the **turning-point approach** emphasizes events that stand out in people's minds as having the strongest impact on their relationships. Couples share stories about turning points with their social networks (such as "how we met"), and turning points are often remembered through celebrations and mementos,

such as anniversaries and pictures (Baxter & Pittman, 2001). This is not to say that mundane events are unimportant. Indeed, mundane events shape the way people see their relationships even if such events sometimes go unnoticed and unappreciated. These mundane events can be thought of as part of the regular road upon which a relationship travels. Turning points, by contrast, are the detours relationships sometimes take.

The turning-point approach is very different from stage approaches to relationship development and disengagement even though turning points can mark entry into a new stage. Social penetration theory, for example, suggests that relationships develop fairly smoothly and gradually as people's communication becomes more personal. By contrast, according to the turning-point approach, relationships can follow a choppier path, with both positive and negative events affecting their course. To determine the path that relationships take, scholars ask people to identify the events that changed their relationships. They can then create a map, which is referred to as a **turning point analysis** (Baxter & Bullis, 1986; Bullis, Clark, & Sline, 1993). As shown in Figure 5.2, these maps do not usually depict a smooth, gradual increase in commitment or closeness. Instead, this approach reveals a rockier road that includes all of

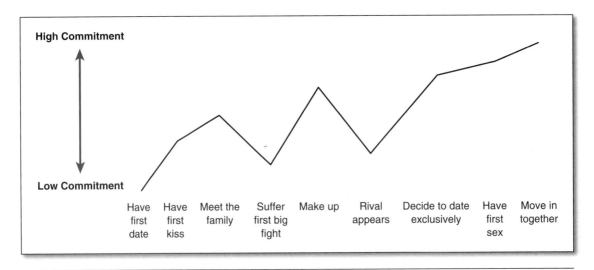

Figure 5.2 A Sample Turning Point Analysis

the many important ups and downs that influence the growth—and in some cases, the demise—of close relationships.

Research suggests that both the turning-point approach and stage approaches have merit; some relationships follow a linear, gradual pattern of developing intimacy; other relationships are characterized by periods of extreme growth or decline, or by a random pattern of highs and lows. For example, Johnson and her colleagues examined friendship development and deterioration (Johnson, Wittenberg, Villagran, Mazur, & Villagran, 2003; Johnson et al., 2004). They found that between 40% and 50% of friendships fit the linear pattern—closeness increased gradually as friends developed their relationships and decreased gradually in friendships that ended. The other 50% to 60% of friendships developed and deteriorated nonlinearly.

Various types of turning points are related to closeness and commitment in romantic relationships, family relationships, and friendships (Baxter, 1986; Baxter, Braithwaite, & Nicholson, 1999; Bullis, Clark, & Sline, 1993; Golish, 2000; Johnson et al., 2003, 2004). Some of the most common turning points that have been identified in the literature are discussed in the following sections.

Communication-Based Turning Points

Although most turning points include some level of communication, the act of communication itself constitutes a turning point in some cases. For example, **get-to-know time** includes initial interactions and focuses on the quantity rather than quality of communication and time spent together. First meetings and first dates typify this turning point (Bullis et al., 1998). By contrast, **quality communication** focuses on special times when two people have high-quality interactions, such as an especially long and intimate conversation. Both forms of communication are often integral to the story of romantic relationships. For instance, people often ask how a couple met. Connor might reply that "we met at a Sierra Club meeting and hit it off right away." Anne might tell people, "I knew we had something special on our first date when we sat under the stars together under a blanket and talked for hours." Communicative events can also be turning points in family relationships. In a study on turning points in relationships between adult children and their parents, communication issues such as finally talking about something important or feeling listened to were identified as turning points that increased closeness (Golish, 2000). Friends also identify self-disclosure about feelings and discovery of positive personality traits as turning points that help develop closeness (Johnson et al., 2004).

Activities and Special Occasions

Other turning points involve engaging in activity and spending quality time with others. For romantic partners, occasions such as meeting the family and going on trips together are common turning points (Bullis et al., 1998). For family members, this turning point includes vacations, engaging in special activities together, holiday rituals, and special occasions such as graduations. A study on blended families showed that quality time together is strongly related to bonding (Baxter et al., 1999). Blended families occur when two previously separate families merge together into one family, as is often the case when divorced or widowed parents remarry. In the study by Baxter and her colleagues, turning points related to holidays and special events made people feel like the blended family was "more of a family" about two-thirds of the time. Turning points involving activity, such as going on vacation together, were related to feeling more like a family 100% of the time. Similarly, turning points that involve engaging in special activities together are related to closeness in friendships. In fact, Johnson and fellow researchers (2003) found that activity sharing was the most common turning point identified in friendships.

Events Related to Passion and Romance

Some turning points mark particular junctures in the development of one's relationship based on the level of passion or romance that is present. **Passionate events** include the first kiss, the first time a couple exchanges the words "I love you," the first sexual encounter, and other passionate phenomena such as falling in love at first sight (Bullis et al., 1998).

According to Metts (2004), the order that passionate-event turning points occur affects relationship development; people were more likely to escalate their relationships and feel positively about one another when saying "I love you" preceded having sex. **Romantic relationship transitions** refer to the "point or period in time when a relationship changes from being either platonic or nonexistent to being romantic" (Mongeau, Serewicz, Henningsen, & Davis, 2006, p. 338). Some passionate events, such as love at first sight, qualify as romantic relationship transitions. Other romantic relationship transitions include when friends or acquaintances turn their previously platonic relationships romantic.

Events Related to Commitment and Exclusivity

While some passionate events, such as saying "I love you," may imply some level of commitment, other turning points more directly reflect how committed two people are to each other and their relationship. **Exclusivity** occurs when people decide to date only each other and drop all other rivals. Somewhat related to exclusivity (or the lack thereof) is the turning point of **external competition**, which occurs when a person feels threatened by a third party or an activity that is taking up a lot of the partner's time. Sometimes an ex-spouse or former girlfriend or boyfriend reemerges; other times a new rival starts to compete for the partner's affections; still other times responsibilities related to work, school, or childcare, or time spent with friends interferes with the relationship. External competition can reinforce or threaten partners' levels of commitment toward one another. Finally, romantic couples can show **serious commitment** by events such as moving in together or getting married.

Changes in Families and Social Networks

While marriage can change the structure of a couple's relationship, other turning points often involve changes in a family's structure. For blended families, **change in the household configuration** marks a primary turning point (Baxter et al., 1999). Children may have to deal with a new stepparent, parents with new stepchildren, and children with new stepsiblings. Contrary to the storyline in shows such as *The Brady Bunch,* the transition from one's family of origin to a blended family is often fraught with problems and confusion. **New family members** also constitute a turning point in other types of relationships. For example, a new baby changes the dynamics of a family for both the parents and any siblings. In Golish's (2000) study of adult children's relationships with their parents, some people said that a new baby brought them closer together. For example, a father and son may feel more emotionally connected when the son has his first baby and the father, as a consequence, has his first grandchild. Other times, sibling rivalry or jealousy may occur when a new baby becomes part of the family. In friendships, **interference from a romantic partner** can sometimes cause conflict and decreased closeness between friends (Johnson et al., 2004). As a case in point, imagine that Anne's best friend starts to feel increasingly left out and neglected as Anne spends more and more time with Connor.

Proximity and Distance

Another set of turning points deals with physical separation and reunion. In Bullis and colleagues' (1998) study of romantic partners, physical separation was reported when people were apart, often involuntarily, due to vacations, business trips, and school breaks. Reunions occurred when the period of physical separation was over and the couple was together again. Adult children also report that physical distance is an important turning point in their relationship with their parents (Golish, 2000). Specifically, when children move out of the house, they sometimes feel that their relationship with their parents improves because the parent now perceives them as an adult. So far, the turning points under this category focus on physical distance. However, the desire for psychological distance and autonomy can also mark a significant turning point in parent-child relationships. In her study on parents and children, Golish identified "rebellious teenager" as a turning point that occurs when children express a need for autonomy from their parents. Friends also identify turning points associated with proximity and distance. For example, friends often recall that becoming roommates was a significant turning point in their relationship that led to either increased or decreased closeness. Friends who ended their relationship often point to turning points such as not living together anymore and an increase in distance as markers of relationship decline (Johnson et al., 2004).

Crisis and Conflict

The challenges that people face are often significant turning points in their relationships with one another. Bullis and her colleagues identified **disengagement and conflict,** which includes a couple's first big fight, attempts to de-escalate or withdraw from the relationship, and actual relational breakups, as major relational turning points. Conflict is also a significant turning point in friendships (Johnson et al., 2004). Researchers examining turning points in both families and friendships have talked about **times of crisis** as a significant turning point (Baxter et al., 1999; Golish, 2000; Johnson et al., 2004). Crises include illnesses, death, accidents, and major financial problems. In Baxter and her colleagues' study of blended families, 72% of people reported that these crisis-related turning points brought the family closer together. A crisis situation can also lead to the turning point known as **sacrifice or support,** which includes being there to support and comfort each other in crises, such as dealing

with the death of a loved one or helping one regain confidence after an embarrassing failure (Bullis et al., 1993; Johnson et al., 2004). Similarly, although conflict can decrease closeness and commitment, couples sometimes make up and feel more connected than ever. Thus, making up is another important turning point in many relationships. Baxter and Bullis (1986) noted that there is not always a perfect correspondence between conflict and making up. Sometimes the conflict is viewed as more significant than the making-up session or vice versa.

Perceptual Changes

Sometimes people report that a turning point does not have a specific, external cause. Instead they simply report that their attitudes toward the partner changed, even though they cannot figure out exactly why. When attitudes and perceptions become more positive, the turning point is called **positive psychic change** (Bullis et al., 1993). For example, Anne might suddenly see Connor as more physically attractive and sexually appealing (a positive psychic change) without being able to pinpoint why. In other cases, labeled **negative psychic change**, attitudes and perceptions become more negative. A person might suddenly see the relationship as boring and the partner as dull even though nothing else has really changed.

SUMMARY AND APPLICATION

This chapter focused on how people form and develop relationships. Although some of the approaches discussed in this chapter suggest that relationships follow a typical linear pattern, it is important to recognize that every relationship follows a unique trajectory. Social penetration theory and Knapp's coming-together stages give us an idea of what to expect, but the specific paths our relationships travel will usually be filled with unexpected turns. Some relationships are characterized by more linear development than others.

Connor and Anne's relationship provides a good example of how linear stage theories might

work along with the turning-point approach to explain the trajectory of a particular relationship. Their relationship develops smoothly and in a linear fashion for the first two months. Then they have their first big fight followed by a period of withdrawal and then making up. When they resume their relationship, they follow a fairly linear path toward increasing closeness for a while. Then a new turning point occurs when Anne raises the issue of cohabitation. This combination of gradually increasing closeness marked by some turbulence due to turning points is probably fairly common in developing relationships.

It is also important to keep in mind that one person may want to intensify a relationship while the other person may not, so two people could actually want to be in different stages. One person may be trying to reach the intensifying stage of Knapp's model, while the other is content to stay at the experimenting stage. Similarly, two people might map the turning points in their relationship differently. Anne might see the night they spent talking under the stars as the beginning of their romantic relationship, whereas Connor might regard their first kiss as the start of their romance. Anne might also be more ready than Connor to move in together and reach a sort of prebonding stage. If partners hope to develop and sustain a successful relationship, they have to negotiate the path that works well for both individuals. This is especially true when couples reach important relational turning points.

Our fictional couple, Anne and Connor, have reached such a turning point. Should they move in together now or wait until they get married or engaged? The studies we reviewed in this chapter suggest that the reasons Anne wants to cohabitate are important. If she wants to move in together because she is afraid of a stronger commitment (such as marriage) and wants to "test" the relationship, research suggests that cohabitation may not be the best move. Cohabiting couples are most likely to be happy and to stay together if they plan on marrying and if their relationship is characterized by positive rather than negative communication patterns. Of course, Connor has valid concerns. Research suggests that cohabiting can have a negative impact on long-term happiness and stability of relationships, and if Connor has reservations, Anne needs to respect them and not pressure him to cohabitate. Like so many other aspects of relationships, there is no "right" answer to Anne and Connor's dilemma; they need to decide as a couple what is best for them.

In closing, the research on relationship formation and development provides a useful blueprint of how close relationships typically unfold over time. Yet every relationship follows a different path, and rarely will relationships progress smoothly as people move from being strangers to being close friends or lovers. The joy of discovering a new friend or developing a new romantic relationship, however, makes the journey worthwhile.

DISCUSSION QUESTIONS

1. Think about times when you felt uncomfortable because someone engaged in too much or too little self-disclosure. What circumstances caused you to feel uncomfortable? In other words, why is self-disclosure considered inappropriate in some contexts and appropriate in others?

2. Stage theories of relational development suggest that although there is some variation, most relationships follow a fairly predictable trajectory. Do you agree or disagree? Do your relationships typically follow the stages outlined by Knapp's coming-together stages, or do they take a different course?

3. Based on the research reported in this chapter as well as your own personal experiences and observations, what is your position regarding cohabitation before marriage? When do you think it might be harmful to a relationship, and when might it be beneficial? What other variables, besides those mentioned in this chapter, are likely to influence whether people should live together before marriage?

STUDENT STUDY SITE

Visit the study site at **www.sagepub.com/guerrero3e** for e-flashcards, survey and assessments from the chapter, and SAGE journal articles.

6

Communicating Closeness

Affection, Immediacy, and Social Support

Kevin treasures his close relationships. Aside from his family, there are two people he feels especially close to—his girlfriend, Jennifer, and his best friend, Dan. When they are together, Jennifer brightens Kevin's day. They spend a lot of time together talking, touching, comforting, and listening to one another. Best of all, he can tell Jennifer anything and she listens and supports him. If he is sad or upset, she has a way of cheering him up, and she always seems to make him feel good about himself. Kevin's connection with Dan is different but nonetheless special. They have a long history together. In high school, they were teammates on the track and football teams, and in college they were both on their university's debate team. Today they take ski trips and run together, and they have great conversations about everything—business, sports, politics, and life in general. Unlike with his other male friends, Kevin can talk to Dan about anything, even Jennifer. They are like brothers.

As Kevin's relationships with Jennifer and Dan illustrate, close relationships come in many forms. People have close relationships with family members, friends, and romantic partners. All of these relationships play vital roles in people's lives. As Andersen and Guerrero (1998a) put it, "The brightest side of life's experience often occurs in close . . . relationships during the exchange of warm, involving, immediate messages" (p. 303).

Communication helps people develop and sustain feelings of closeness. Communication also reflects the unique qualities associated with people's closest relationships. For example, although Kevin's close relationships with Jennifer and Dan both play vital roles in his life, these two relationships also differ in important ways. If Kevin kept a diary of the behaviors that he used to communicate closeness to Dan and Jennifer, what types of behaviors would likely be similar and different across these two relationships? What behaviors might be more characteristic of his best friendship with Dan? Which might be reserved for his romantic relationship with Jennifer?

To answer these and other questions, this chapter focuses on three specific types of communication that help foster and sustain closeness in relationships—affectionate communication, immediacy, and social support. First, definitions of different types of closeness are provided. Second, research on affectionate communication and affection exchange theory is presented, followed by a discussion of immediacy and cognitive valence theory. Finally, work on social support is reviewed. Together, the literature on affectionate communication, immediacy, and social support paint a picture of how people develop and reinforce feelings of closeness and connection in their relationships.

CLOSENESS IN RELATIONSHIPS

What makes relationships like the ones Kevin shares with Dan and Jennifer so special? It is the **level of closeness** that sets these relationships apart. Closeness is a multifaceted concept that has different meanings. Sometimes the term *close* or *closeness* refers to spatial proximity (e.g., living near or standing next to someone). Other times closeness refers to the type of relationship people share or the way people feel about each other. Researchers have tried to distinguish between various types of closeness, including physical, emotional, and relational closeness.

Physical Closeness

Physical closeness refers to the amount of spatial proximity and physical contact people have. Engaging in behaviors such as touching, sitting next to each other, and putting one's head on another's shoulder all indicate physical closeness. Spending time with someone, even if it is just sitting in a car together listening to the radio, or being reunited at the end of the day contributes to physical closeness. For example, in a study on closeness in married couples, one of the wives said that she "felt that closeness when he [her husband] came back early from work, unexpectedly, and we spent the whole evening together, just the two of us" (Ben-Ari & Lavee, 2007, p. 634). In some relationships, sexual interaction is another common form of physical closeness. However, even in marital relationships, sexual interaction does not appear to be as central to

the concept of closeness as affectionate communication (Ben-Ari & Lavee, 2007).

Emotional Closeness

Emotional closeness has been defined in terms of having a sense of shared experiences, trust, enjoyment, concern, and caring in a relationship (Lee, Mancini, & Maxwell, 1990). Sharing and caring are fundamental to both the experience and the expression of emotional closeness. In Ben-Ari and Lavee's (2007) study of married couples, "Sharing thoughts, experiences, and feelings appeared both as a conception of closeness ('closeness *is* wanting to share with her') and an expression of it ('*when we are close* we have deep conservations')" (p. 633). Caring involves showing concern and providing support for another. Sharing and caring are essential components of emotional closeness and studies have shown that high levels of self-disclosure and social support characterize close friendships (Feeney, 1999; Parks & Floyd, 1996).

Relational Closeness

Relational closeness is the interdependence people share (Kelley et al., 1983). Interdependent partners exchange resources; influence one another's thoughts, behaviors, and emotions; and meet each other's needs. Especially strong, enduring, and diverse levels of interdependence characterize close relationships (Kelley et al., 1983). For example, Kevin and Jennifer might discuss major life decisions together, learn major life lessons from each other, and become emotionally attached to one another's families. In these ways, and more, they have become interdependent. Some scholars have also conceptualized closeness in terms of the degree to which two individuals overlap (Aron & Aron, 1986; Aron, Mashek, & Aron, 2004; see also Chapter 3). In these studies, a circle represents each person. The degree to which two people's circles overlap then indicates their level of closeness. As is the case with emotional closeness, relational closeness is associated with caregiving and social support. Interdependent individuals rely on each other; what matters to one person matters to the other person.

Communicating Closeness

Communication is also an integral part of closeness (Andersen, Guerrero, & Jones, 2006). Ben-Ari and Lavee (2007) asked married couples to describe what closeness meant to them. The participants in this study often mentioned communication. For example, Michael, a 43-year-old man who had been married for 13 years, described closeness this way:

> I had a busy day with meetings one after the other all day long, I knew I would come home late in the evening. I had a small break between meetings in the middle of the day so I rushed home, gave her a big hug, a kiss, and I brought her a flower. . . . For me, this is closeness. (p. 627)

As Michael's response suggests, many forms of physical closeness, such as hugs and rushing home to be with someone, reflect emotional or relational closeness. These three forms of closeness overlap even though they each have their distinct qualities. For example, you can be emotionally close without being physically close. Some of the couples in Ben-Ari and Lavee's study made this point, with one wife saying that "being emotionally close to her husband did not mean that she needed to be around him physically" (pp. 634–636). There are also important distinctions between emotional closeness, which is rooted more in feelings, and relational closeness, which is rooted more in behavioral patterns that foster interdependence.

Closeness is reflected in three specific types of communication: affectionate communication, immediacy behavior, and social support (Andersen & Guerrero, 1998a; Rittenour, Myers, & Brann, 2007; Weigel & Ballard-Reisch, 2002). These three types of communication each highlight a different aspect of closeness. Work on affectionate communication focuses on how people portray feelings of fondness and positive regard to one another. Research on immediacy examines behavior that

increases both physical and emotional closeness. Finally, the literature on social support emphasizes concern and caring. All three areas of research show that communication is vital in creating and sustaining close relationships.

AFFECTIONATE COMMUNICATION

Affection is both a need and an emotion (Pendell, 2002). As noted in Chapter 1, affection is a basic human need. People want to feel accepted and cared for by others. This need for affection is met through interpersonal interaction and forging mutually supportive relationships (Prager & Buhrmester, 1998; Rubin & Martin, 1998). As an emotion, affection is rooted in feelings of fondness, caring, and positive regard that have developed for someone over time (Floyd & Morman, 1998).

Affectionate communication is behavior that portrays feelings of fondness and positive regard to another (Floyd, 2006). Affection and affectionate communication occur in a wide variety of close relationships, including those between friends, family members, and romantic partners (Floyd & Ray, 2003; Pendell, 2002; Salt, 1991). Affectionate communication is a key to establishing relationships and keeping them close. In fact, affectionate communication often acts as a "critical incident" that facilitates the establishment of close relationships (King & Christensen, 1983; Owen, 1987). The absence of affectionate communication, conversely, can reflect decreased emotional closeness and propel a relationship toward de-escalation (Owen, 1987). Floyd (2006) also noted that there is a **paradox of affection** because "although affection is often intended and usually perceived by others to be a positive communicative move, it can backfire for a number of reasons and produce negative outcomes" such as distress and relationship dissolution (p. 2). For instance, showing affection too early in a relationship can scare potential friends and romantic partners away.

There are numerous ways to communicate affection (Pendell, 2002). Floyd and Morman (1998), however, argued that it is useful to categorize affectionate communication into one of three categories: direct verbal behavior, direct nonverbal behavior, or indirect nonverbal behavior. The types of affectionate communication that fall under each category differ in terms of how they are encoded and decoded.

Direct and Verbal Affectionate Communication

Many verbal behaviors, such as saying "I care about you" or leaving a sticky note that says "I love you," are direct ways of communicating affection. People usually encode direct and verbal expressions of affection with the intent of communicating affection to someone, and others easily decode these messages as clear and unambiguous expressions of affection. Verbal statements of affection are also usually more precise than nonverbal expressions. As Floyd (2006) put it, "There is an enormous qualitative difference between saying 'I like you' and 'I'm in love with you,' a distinction that may not be conveyed quite as accurately through nonverbal behaviors" (p. 32). Of course, words are not always completely unambiguous. The statement "I love you" could mean "I love you as a friend" or "I love you as a potential romantic partner" and it could be seen as sincere or insincere, thoughtful or rash. Nonetheless, verbal statements provide people with a channel for communicating affection in a relatively direct and precise manner. Pendell (2002) describes several verbal behaviors that are often direct expressions of affection, including self-disclosure, direct emotional expressions, compliments and praise, and assurances.

Self-Disclosure

Communicating openly about one's feelings and beliefs is called **self-disclosure** (see Chapter 5). Among the many verbal behaviors that create and sustain emotional closeness, self-disclosure is probably the most important (Derlega, Metts, Petronio, & Margulis, 1993). As Prager and Roberts (2004) argued, self-disclosure allows people to develop shared knowledge about one another, and this shared knowledge leads to emotional and relational closeness. In fact, when people are asked to describe how "close" or "intimate" friendships differ from more casual friendships, self-disclosure is the most common response (Monsour, 1992). Self-disclosure is a key indicator of affection and closeness across a variety of relationships, including romantic relationships, women's friendships, and men's friendships (Monsour, 1992; Parks & Floyd, 1996). It is not surprising, then, that self-disclosure figures prominently in all of the basic theories of relational development and closeness, including social penetration theory and Knapp's coming-together stages (see Chapter 5). Although many forms of self-disclosure, such as sharing family history or future career aspirations, do not communicate affection directly, they send messages of trust and liking. Other forms of self-disclosure, such as direct emotional expressions, are especially clear and unambiguous ways of communicating affection.

Direct Emotional Expressions

Sometimes people communicate their positive feelings directly by using phrases such as "I love you," "You make me happy," and "You're fun to be around." These statements are the most direct and least ambiguous way to communicate affection to someone. However, the directness of these expressions also makes them risky. Imagine telling someone "I love you" and then waiting as the recipient of that message hesitates, squirms, and then says "Thank you." When people communicate affection in such a direct manner, they open themselves up for rejection and possibly even ridicule. Yet such expressions are usually necessary if relationships are to become emotionally close. For relationships that are already close, periodic statements that express affection directly may also be essential for sustaining high levels of emotional and relational closeness.

Compliments and Praise

People sometimes communicate their positive regard for someone by giving compliments or praise (Pendell, 2002). Many compliments can be considered direct expressions of affection because they unambiguously communicate positive regard. Compliments can occur in a variety of relationships and send different types of messages depending on the characteristic that is positively regarded. For example, in the course of playing a game of one-on-one basketball together, Dan might tell Kevin that he has always admired his seemingly effortless athletic ability. Later, during a romantic dinner, Jennifer might tell Kevin that he looks especially handsome. Both types of compliments can contribute to overall feelings of emotional closeness; Jennifer's comment may also contribute to feelings of romantic closeness. In both cases, compliments usually make people feel good and therefore strengthen feelings of affection and emotional closeness.

Assurances

Assurances, which have also been termed **relationship talk**, are direct messages about people's commitment level in a relationship. As noted in Chapter 9, assurances have been conceptualized as a relational maintenance behavior but are also expressions of affection. Statements such as "I want to see you again," "I can't imagine my life without you," and "I hope our friendship never ends" are symbols of emotional closeness that reflect how much people care about and value each other (Andersen, 1998a; Floyd, 2006; King & Sereno, 1984). Expressing such sentiments can lead people to define their relationships as closer and more affectionate, but they can also frighten or intimidate a person who does not share that relationship definition or who is not ready for that level of closeness. Similarly, talk about the future of the relationship can create perceptions of greater emotional and relational closeness. For example, romantic partners might start making plans for the next summer or talk about what they might name their future children. Such talk clearly implies a long-term commitment to the relationship, which reinforces interdependence and feelings of emotional closeness. However, as with declarations of love or liking, talk about the future of the relationship can scare partners away if they do not share the same level of commitment, illustrating the paradox of affection mentioned earlier.

Direct and Nonverbal Affectionate Communication

Many nonverbal behaviors, such as hugging someone, are direct and nonverbal expressions of affection because others commonly interpret them as communicating affection (Floyd & Morman, 2001). According to the **social meaning model of nonverbal communication**, some nonverbal behaviors have strong consensual meanings across different contexts (Burgoon & Newton, 1991). For example, smiling usually signals friendliness and hugs usually communicate affection regardless of the situation in which people find themselves. Of course, there are exceptions to these rules. Sometimes a smile is fake, condescending, or sarcastic, and a hug is an obligatory rather than an affectionate move. The social meaning model, however, suggests that people recognize the exceptions to the rule because they do not look only at one nonverbal cue, but rather a constellation of nonverbal cues that work in concert to communicate a message. A condescending smile therefore will look different than a friendly smile, and an obligatory hug will look (and feel) different than a genuinely affectionate hug. Although a wide variety of nonverbal behaviors can communicate affection, three classes of behavior in particular have been found to do so in a relatively unambiguous manner that is consistent with the social meaning model. These three classes of behavior are physical closeness, eye behavior, and vocal behavior.

Physical Contact and Distancing

Touch and close distancing often communicates messages with clear social meanings. Floyd and Morman (1998) created a measure of affectionate communication that includes several types of touch—holding hands, hugging, kissing, massaging someone, and putting one's arm around another's shoulders—as well as sitting close to one another. Similarly, Pendell (2002) listed physical closeness and a wide variety of tactile behaviors as nonverbal indicators of affection, including friendly roughhousing or mock aggression, hand squeezes, shaking hands, cuddling, snuggling, lap sitting, picking someone up, gently cleaning someone, and fondling.

Notice that some of the tactile behaviors identified as communicating affection are most appropriate in romantic relationships. However, many of these behaviors can occur in other types of relationships as well. For example, men sometimes use roughhousing behaviors, such as body slams or slapping one another's butts, to express camaraderie and affection during sporting events. Kevin and Dan likely engaged in these types of behaviors during football games and track meets. Parents and children often snuggle, and parents might pick up a child or gently wipe food off a child's face as ways of expressing affection while also accomplishing tasks.

Eye Behavior

Certain forms of eye behavior also communicate affection in a relatively direct and unambiguous fashion, especially when used alongside other behaviors that reflect positive emotions, such as smiling. Floyd and Morman (1998) listed looking into one another's eyes as an indicator of affection. Pendell (2002) noted that eye contact is most likely to convey affection when it is mutual, prolonged, and focused. Eye contact can also promote affection and relaxation in some situations. In one study, strangers were paired in opposite sex dyads. Each person was told to either look at the partner's hands for two minutes, look into the partner's eyes for two minutes, or count the number of times their partner blinked (Kellerman, Lewis, & Laird, 1989). People reported greater liking when they had both been told to look at each other, which suggests that mutual gaze is related to liking. In another study, men were asked intimate questions by an interviewer with whom they were set up to either like or dislike (Wellens, 1987). During the middle of the interview, the interviewer either started avoiding gaze or began giving continuous eye contact. When people disliked the interviewer, their heart rate went up in response to the interviewer's shift to continuous eye contact. In contrast, there was a small drop in heart rate when a liked interviewer started using continuous eye contact. This study suggests that eye contact may sometimes be related to relaxation as well as liking.

Vocalic Behavior

The way people say words can also communicate affection. Pendell (2002) identified several ways people can express affection using their voices, including speaking tenderly or in a warm voice and laughing with someone. A faster speaking rate and moderate talk time (not speaking too much or too little in comparison to the partner) may also be associated with communicating affection and liking, although people may not be conscious of using these vocal behaviors to communicate affection (Palmer & Simmons, 1995).

In another study, people engaged in "get-acquainted conversations" with a same-sex stranger (Floyd & Ray, 2003). What the participants did not know was that the stranger, who was actually a confederate working for the researchers, was asked to behave as though he or she either liked or really disliked them. After the interaction, the participants in the study were asked to rate how affectionate the confederate had been during the interaction. People rated the confederates as more affectionate if they spoke in a higher pitched voice. Observers watching the interaction rated women as more affectionate if they spoke in higher pitched voices, but men as more affectionate if they spoke in lower pitched voices. Therefore, people may evaluate affection communicated in men's voices differently depending on if they are a participant in a conversation or an observer of that conversation.

Indirect and Nonverbal Affectionate Communication

According to Floyd and Morman (2001), there are two types of affectionate communication that are indirect and nonverbal expressions of affection: support behaviors and idiomatic behaviors. Although these behaviors are frequently interpreted as communicating affection, sometimes they are not. The situation and the relationship people share often help determine whether or not these behaviors are construed as expressions of affection.

Support Behaviors

Support behaviors involve giving someone emotional or instrumental support (Burgoon, Guerrero, & Floyd, 2010). For example, friends and relatives might show support to a new mother by bringing her food, offering to babysit, giving her child care advice, buying savings bonds for the new baby, and listening patiently when she complains about being overly tired. Although these types of actions do not communicate affection directly, they likely let the young mother know that people love and care for her.

Of course, these types of behaviors are not always interpreted as expressions of affection. If Dan helps Kevin fix his car, Dan would likely perceive his help as a gesture that reflects the closeness of their relationship. However, if someone else offers to help, Dan might make a different interpretation. For instance, he might wonder if an acquaintance who offers to help wants something in return. He might even refuse help because he does not want to feel obligated to someone whom he does not know well. Thus, the type of relationship that people share helps shape how indirect nonverbal expressions of support are interpreted. Indirect nonverbal expressions also are used more commonly than direct messages in certain types of relationships, such as those between fathers and sons or male friends (Morman & Floyd, 1999). So it probably wouldn't be a surprise to see Kevin (who is a math whiz) helping Dan with his calculus homework, but it would come as a surprise to hear Kevin tell Dan "I love you" and then embrace him with a big hug.

Idiomatic Behaviors

Idiomatic behaviors "have a specific meaning only to people in a particular relationship" (Burgoon et al., 2010, p. 331). Hopper, Knapp, and Scott (1981) gave several examples of idioms in romantic relationships, including twitching noses to signal "You're special" and twisting wedding rings to warn "Don't you dare do or say that!" For example, Dan might sometimes tease Kevin acting like he is sprinkling something over his head. This gesture may have a special meaning for the two of them because

it leads them to recall an event they attended together where Kevin ended up with cake crumbs all over his head. Other people—even Jennifer—will not understand the meaning of this gesture unless Dan or Kevin shares it with them. And even if Kevin explains it to Jennifer, since she was not there, she might not fully understand its meaning.

Idioms such as these can be a reflection of the level of emotional closeness people share. Knapp (1983) argued that when people first meet, their communication tends to be scripted. In other words, they tend to use conventional language that is widely understood. However, as a relationship becomes close, people develop an idiosyncratic style of communication that reflects the unique characteristics of their personalities and the relationship they share. Idioms are often a part of this unique communication style. In romantic relationships, the primary reason romantic couples use idioms is to communicate affection (Bell, Buerkel-Rothfuss, & Gore, 1987). Couples are especially likely to report using idioms to express affection if their relationships are characterized as satisfying and loving. Idioms are also more likely to be nonverbal than verbal, and to be used in public rather than private (Bell et al., 1987; Hopper et al., 1981).

AFFECTION EXCHANGE THEORY

To better understand how affectionate communication functions in various relationships, Floyd (2001, 2002, 2006) developed **affection exchange theory**. This theory is based on the idea that affectionate communication is a biologically adaptive behavior that evolved because it helps people provide and obtain valuable resources necessary for survival. Thus, the theory draws upon Darwin's (1872) principle of selective fitness, which specifies that people who adapt best to their environment have the best chance to survive, procreate, and pass their genes on to the next generation. Pendell (2002) expressed a similar belief about the adaptive value of affection, stating that "Intimate relationships, pair bonding, and affection are basic human biological adaptations evolved for the purpose of reproduction and protecting the young" (p. 91).

Principles of Affection Exchange Theory

Affection exchange theory contains three overarching principles that illuminate how affectionate communication is adaptive. First, affectionate communication is theorized to facilitate survival because it helps people develop and maintain relationships that provide them with important resources. For example, centuries ago, humans fared better if they had people to help feed them and protect them if attacked. Today, resources gained from one's social network, such as having a friend help with homework or a parent finance one's education, are helpful for surviving daily life as well as gaining the resources necessary to attract potential mates.

Second, people who display affectionate communication are more likely to be perceived as having the skills necessary to be a good parent, thereby increasing their ability to attract potential mates and have reproductive opportunities. As noted in Chapter 3, people are generally attracted to those who are warm and caring. When looking for a long-term romantic partner, both men and women usually want someone who they believe will be a nurturing and responsible parent for any children they might have.

Third, people are motivated to show affectionate communication to people who serve one of two basic evolutionary needs—viability and fertility (Floyd & Morr, 2003). **Viability** relates to the motivation to survive, whereas **fertility** relates to the motivation to procreate and pass on one's genes. At an unconscious level, these needs motivate people to show affection to those with whom they share a genetic or sexual relationship. For example, parents are motivated to show affection to their children because "the benefits associated with receiving affection make the children more suitable as mates, thereby increasing the chances that the children will themselves reproduce and pass on their genes to yet a new generation" (Floyd & Morman, 2001, p. 312). People who grew up in affectionate families are also more likely to be affectionate adults who develop emotionally close relationships with their own spouse and children. People are also motivated to show affection to nieces, nephews, siblings, and cousins who share their genetic material. Thus, the goal is not necessarily to reproduce oneself, but rather to pass on one's genes either directly or indirectly through one's relatives (Hamilton, 1964). Finally, people are motivated to show affection to sexual partners who can help them achieve the goal of procreation. Of course, people can also receive valuable resources from their broader social networks, which include friends, in-laws, and acquaintances, but according to affection exchange theory, the motivation to exhibit affectionate behavior is strongest in relationships that have the most potential to fulfill viability or fertility needs.

Benefits of Giving and Receiving Affection

In affection exchange theory, affectionate communication is cast as a valuable resource that is essential for survival and procreation. One reason affectionate communication helps people survive and attract others is because giving and receiving affection is related to better mental and physical health. In fact, people who regularly receive affection are advantaged in almost every way compared to people who receive little affection; they are happier, more self-confident, less stressed, less likely to be depressed, more likely to engage in social activity, and in better general mental health (Floyd, 2002). Giving affection has similar benefits. People who readily show affection to others report more happiness, higher self-esteem, less fear of intimacy, less susceptibility to depression, and greater relational satisfaction (Floyd et al., 2005).

A substantial body of research also provides compelling evidence that giving and receiving affection is associated with better physical health. Floyd and his colleagues (2005) demonstrated a physiological link between affection and bodily changes. When people gave or received affection, adrenal hormones associated with stress tended to decrease, while oxytocin (a hormone associated with positive moods and behaviors) tended to increase (Floyd, 2006). Other health benefits of affection include lower resting blood pressure, lower blood sugar (Floyd, Hesse, & Haynes, 2007), lower heart rate, a less exaggerated hormonal response to stress (Floyd, Mikkelson, Tafoya et al., 2007), and healthier changes in cortisol levels (Floyd & Riforgiate, 2008). In one study, people in married or cohabiting relationships were either given instructions to kiss more over a six-week period or were given no instructions about how to behave. Those who were told to kiss more reported less stress, more relational satisfaction, and healthier levels of cholesterol at the end of the study (Floyd et al., 2009). Even writing about the affection that one feels toward close friends, relatives, and romantic partners reduces cholesterol levels (Floyd, Mikkelson, Hesse, & Pauley, 2007). To see how affectionate you are, take the test in Box 6.1. People who score higher on the affectionate communication index tend to possess better mental and physical health, even after controlling for the amount of affection received from others.

BOX 6.1 Put Yourself to the Test

The Affectionate Communication Index

Circle the number that represents how much you agree with how each statement describes you. Answer the questions using the following scale: 1 = you strongly disagree, 7=you strongly agree.

	Disagree						Agree
1. I consider myself to be a very affectionate person.	1	2	3	4	5	6	7
2. I am always telling my loved ones how much I care about them.	1	2	3	4	5	6	7
3. When I feel affection for someone, I usually express it.	1	2	3	4	5	6	7
4. I have a hard time telling people that I love them or care about them.	1	2	3	4	5	6	7
5. I'm not very good at expressing affection.	1	2	3	4	5	6	7
6. I am not a very affectionate person.	1	2	3	4	5	6	7
7. I love giving people hugs or putting my arms around them.	1	2	3	4	5	6	7
8. I don't tend to express affection to other people very much.	1	2	3	4	5	6	7
9. Anyone who knows me well would say that I'm pretty affectionate.	1	2	3	4	5	6	7
10. Expressing affection to other people makes me uncomfortable.	1	2	3	4	5	6	7

To calculate your score: First, give yourself 30 points. Second, add up your responses to questions 1, 2, 3, 7, and 9 and put the total on the first line below. Third, add up your responses to questions 4, 5, 6, 8, and 10 and put the total on the second line below. A score at or close to 0 means that you are highly unaffectionate; a score at or close to 60 means that you are highly affectionate.

My score: 30 plus _____ minus _____ = _____

(line 1)   (line 2)

Affectionate Communication in Families

Given the importance of genetic relatedness in affection exchange theory, it is not surprising that much of the research testing this theory has examined family relationships. Studies support the idea that affectionate communication is viewed as a valuable resource for which family members compete. Floyd and Morman (2005) found that children from large families perceive that they receive less affection from their parents than do children from small families. They also found that adult children may hold a **naïve theory of affection**, which means that they see affection as a limited resource for which they must compete. Conversely, parents tend to view affection toward their children as an unlimited resource, regardless of the number of children they have.

As predicted in affection exchange theory, some studies also suggest that people show most affection to those with whom they share a genetic or sexual bond. For example, in one study, fathers reported expressing more affection to their biological sons than their stepsons (Floyd & Morman, 2001). In another study, people reported using more nonverbal, verbal, and supportive affectionate communication with their spouses than their siblings (Floyd & Morr, 2003). They also reported using more of all three forms of affectionate communication with their siblings than their sibling-in-laws. Importantly, Floyd and Morman were able to rule out the possibility that these differences were due to how close and satisfying these different types of relationships were. Specifically, people were more likely to report showing affection in relationships that were closer and more satisfying, but this alone did not explain why spouses reported the most affectionate communication, followed by siblings and then sibling-in-laws. Thus, it appears that emotional and relational closeness only explain part of the reason people display differing amounts of affection across various relationships. Motivations related to viability and fertility may provide an even stronger explanation for these differences.

IMMEDIACY BEHAVIORS

In addition to suggesting that affectionate communication is a resource that helps people survive and pass on their genes, this chapter has also shown that affectionate communication is essential for establishing and sustaining emotional closeness. Immediacy behaviors play a complementary and equally important role in developing and maintaining close relationships. **Immediacy behaviors** are actions that signal warmth, communicate availability, decrease psychological or physical distance, and promote involvement between people (Andersen, 1985). These behaviors have also been called **positive involvement behaviors** (Guerrero, 2004; Prager, 2000) because they show both positive affect and high levels of involvement in an interaction.

Immediacy (or positive involvement) is a broader concept than affection. Affection and affectionate communication are rooted in feelings of fondness and positive regard that have developed toward someone over time (Floyd, 2006). Immediacy, in contrast, is a style of communicating that is used across a wide variety of interactions to express involvement and positivity without necessarily expressing affection. For example, a person who uses behaviors such as eye contact, smiling, and handshaking with a prospective employer during a job interview would probably be labeled as immediate but not affectionate. Nonetheless, increases in immediacy provide a foundation for creating and sustaining close relationships (Andersen, 2008), and there is some overlap between immediacy behavior and affectionate communication.

Verbal Immediacy

Most research on immediacy has focused on nonverbal behaviors. However, certain verbal behaviors also reflect immediacy. **Verbal immediacy** is a function of several stylistic features of language that reflect the closeness of a relationship (see Andersen, 1998a), including word choice, forms of address, depth of disclosure, and relationship indicators.

Word Choice

Inclusive pronouns, such as *we*, are perceived to indicate more interdependence than using exclusive pronouns, such as *I* or *you and me* (Weiner & Mehrabian, 1968). Prager (1995) suggested that more immediate pronoun use (*this* and *these* versus *that* and *those*), adverb use (*here* versus *there*), and verb tense (present versus past), as well as the use of the active as opposed to the passive voice, all contribute to greater verbal immediacy and perceptions of closeness. Bradac, Bowers, and Courtwright (1979) maintained that verbal immediacy builds positive relationships and likewise that being in a close, emotionally connected relationship leads to more verbal immediacy.

Forms of Address

Casual forms of address ("Chris" as opposed to "Dr. Rodriguez") also imply a closer relationship (King & Sereno, 1984), as do nicknames (Bell, Buerkel-Rothfuss, & Gore, 1987; Hopper, Knapp, & Scott, 1981). Using inappropriately informal names or disliked nicknames, however, is not a way to establish a close relationship. For example, calling your boss "Bud" when he prefers "Mr. Johnson" or calling your date by a nickname that might be considered derogatory or sexist, such as "sweet cheeks" or "sugar daddy," is not an effective way to build a strong relationship. As noted earlier, personal idioms can be a way to express affection and emotional closeness in a relationship. Special greetings, secret nicknames, sexual euphemisms, mild teases, and unique labels for the relationship often are a source of emotional closeness that also increases the immediacy level of an interaction (Bell et al., 1987; Hopper et al., 1981). Of course, the use of some of these terms in a public setting may be a source of embarrassment and cause a loss of closeness.

Depth of Disclosure

Close relationships are characterized by deep rather than superficial interactions. In close relationships partners "can communicate deeply and honestly . . . sharing innermost feelings" (Sternberg, 1987, p. 333). Self-revealing statements that convey vulnerable emotions are especially conducive to emotional closeness (Prager & Roberts, 2004). Self-disclosure plays an essential role in relationship development because, as people become closer, they share their innermost thoughts and feelings (see Chapter 5). Only by sharing personal information, thoughts, and feelings

can two people get to know each other well enough to develop an emotionally close relationship and build interdependence. Therefore, the depth with which people explore various topics and self-disclose to one another is sometimes considered to be an indicator of the immediacy level within an interaction (Andersen, 1998a). For example, when responding to a friend who asks, "How've you been?" the level of depth in Kevin's answer may reflect the emotional closeness of the friendship. If the friendship is casual, Kevin might say "fine" even if he has been feeling terrible lately. If the friendship is moderately close, Kevin might say, "not that great, I've been overwhelmed with work and sick with the flu, but I'll be okay." In contrast, if talking to Dan or Jennifer, Kevin would feel free to go into much more depth about his recent trials and tribulations, including asking for help.

Relationship Indicators

The language partners use to refer to each other suggests a certain public, relational image that is an index of the closeness between them. For example, cohabitors may describe themselves along a continuum that includes roommate, friend, boyfriend or girlfriend, and partner—which signals increasing levels of immediacy and emotional closeness. Similarly, when individuals call someone their "best friend" in public, this label sends a strong message about the closeness of the relationship. The first time Kevin publicly referred to Jennifer as his "girlfriend" in public was probably a milestone in their relationship because the nature of their relationship was made clear to both Jennifer and others, suggesting that Kevin and Jennifer are a "pair," have a special bond, and are dating each other exclusively. This type of language is considered immediate because it emphasizes that there is a special level of psychological and physical closeness between Kevin and Jennifer.

Nonverbal Immediacy

Verbal immediacy is undoubtedly important, yet nonverbal immediacy appears to be even more critical for sending messages related to emotional closeness. Some scholars even contend that nonverbal immediacy is a stronger predictor of emotional and relational closeness than self-disclosure. Montgomery (1988) stated, "The nonverbal mode of expression appears to be more closely linked to relational quality than the verbal mode" (p. 348). Similarly, Prager (2000) suggested that nonverbal behavior makes a major contribution to the level of closeness that people experience in their relationships, "probably due to its relatively involuntary character. People's facial expressions, voice tones, postures and gestures can reveal unspoken emotions and intentions and can override efforts at impression management" (p. 232). Clearly, nonverbal communication is a vital component within close relationships.

Although the specific behaviors that communicate nonverbal immediacy are reviewed separately in the following sections, it is important to remember that nonverbal behaviors are often processed as a **gestalt** (Andersen, 1985, 1999). In other words, rather than focusing on single behaviors, people usually take the whole package of nonverbal behaviors into consideration when assigning meaning and determining how much immediacy is being communicated. In addition, nonverbal communication is interpreted within a broader social context. Eye contact reflects closeness sometimes but intimidation other times. Similarly, a smile might be perceived as friendly in one context and condescending in another.

Visual or Oculesic Behaviors

Eye behavior, or **oculesics**, is essential in establishing emotional closeness. The eyes have been said to be "the windows to the soul," and eye contact is widely recognized as an invitation to communicate (Andersen, 2008). Increased eye contact is a sign of intimacy and attraction (Andersen, 1985; Exline & Winters, 1965; Ray & Floyd, 2006). People engage in the highest levels of eye contact with friends, dating partners, and people they like (Coutts & Schneider, 1976; Exline & Winters, 1965). Romantic partners, in particular, appear to use high levels of eye contact to communicate relational and emotional closeness (Guerrero, 1997). Eye contact is also a sign of attentiveness and involvement.

One interesting, although somewhat obscure, oculesic behavior is pupil dilation. Most people are aware that pupils dilate in low light, but do not realize that pupils also dilate in response to any stimuli people find interesting or attractive (Hess, 1965; Hess & Goodwin, 1974). People are also more attracted to individuals with dilated pupils. In an imaginative study, Hess and Goodwin (1974) showed people two virtually identical pictures of a mother holding her baby; however, in one photo, the eyes were retouched to appear dilated, while in the other photo they were constricted. People thought the mother with the dilated pupils seemed to love her baby more. Interestingly, only a few of these people accurately identified the eyes as the source of their attributions, which suggests that pupil dilation is processed as an immediacy cue but only at very low levels of awareness. Of course, low light, candlelit dinners, and dusk have always been associated with romance and closeness, perhaps in part due to subtle cues like pupil dilation.

Spatial or Proxemic Behaviors

Proxemics, or the way people use space in interpersonal communication, signals the level of closeness in a relationship. Hall (1968) identified four distance zones as a function of types of interpersonal interaction. He called the closest of these zones, from touch to 18 inches, *intimate distance*. The people we most often let into this zone are those with whom we have intimate relationships, such as our children, our closest friends, family members, and romantic partners. The other three zones—*personal* (1.5–4 feet), *social* (4–10 feet), and *public* (over 10 feet)—are used for less intimate relationships. When the intimate zone is invaded by someone who is not a close friend or romantic partner, people, often react with defensive behaviors (Andersen, 1985, 1998b; Burgoon, Stern, & Dillman, 1995) including reducing eye contact, drawing back, using arms or objects as buffers, and giving the person "the cold shoulder" by turning away.

Immediacy is also communicated proxemically via body angle. Facing someone directly is immediate, while sitting or standing at a 45-degree angle is less immediate, and positioning oneself side by side with another person is even less immediate. Turning one's back on someone is the opposite of immediate. Interestingly, women are more likely to use a direct, face-to-face body orientation than men (Guerrero, 1997); this is one of several ways that women seem to be more nonverbally immediate than men.

Face-to-face communication between people of very different heights is difficult. When a 6-foot-tall adult communicates with a child, a person in a wheelchair, or a 5-foot-tall person, adjustments must usually be made if the communicators wish to be at eye level. Research has shown that communicating eye to eye increases perceptions of immediacy and closeness (Andersen, 1985). Andersen and Andersen (1982) suggested that getting into an eye-to-eye position is essential for early elementary school teachers to create rapport with their young students. When height discrepancies inhibit interaction, sitting, reclining, or kneeling can increase immediacy. Thus, the 6-foot-tall adult can increase immediacy and perceptions of closeness simply by repositioning to eye-to-eye contact with someone, and shorter individuals can engage in behaviors to raise themselves. For example, toddlers are often placed in high chairs so they are face-to-face with the rest of the family at the dinner table. Such placement increases the overall immediacy level of the family's interaction during dinner.

Tactile or Haptic Behaviors

Physical contact, or **haptics**, is a key immediacy behavior. High levels of touch characterize many of people's closest relationships, such as those between parents and children, childhood friends, and romantic partners. Andersen (1985) observed that "although dependent on cultural norms and the interpersonal relationship, normative touch is usually perceived as a warm, intimate behavior" (p. 10). Touch is an important sign of emotional and relational closeness and is synonymous with physical closeness. In a study of airport arrivals and departures, Heslin and Boss (1980) found a strong association between the amount of tactile intimacy recorded by observers and the closeness of the relationship reported by couples. Another study found that observers perceived higher levels of closeness

for touching couples than for nontouching couples (Kleinke, Meeker, & LaFong, 1974). Similarly, Guerrero and Andersen's (1991) study of couples' tactile communication in theater and zoo lines revealed that high levels of touch were associated with a more serious, accelerating relationship. Emmers and Dindia (1995) found that this was true for private touch as well. Andersen (2008) concluded that in romantic relationships, the most touch occurs when couples are in the process of escalating their relationships from casual to committed. Hugs and kisses are a particularly immediate and affectionate form of communication, as is touch to the face (Andersen, 2008; Andersen et al., 2006; Floyd, 2006; Guerrero & Floyd, 2006).

Body Movement or Kinesics

Kinesics comprises body movements such as smiling, gestures, nodding, posture, and bodily relaxation. The smile is a primary immediacy behavior that helps establish and maintain close relationships. Over several decades, researchers have found that the frequency and intensity of smiling is the single best predictor of interpersonal closeness, liking, and warmth (Argyle, 1972; Bayes, 1970; Ray & Floyd, 2006; Reece & Whitman, 1962). Smiles are a universal sign of positive affect that signal approachability and availability for communication.

Open body positions free of obstruction by objects or limbs are also considered immediate. People are most likely to cross their arms, hide their face, or stand behind objects when they lack trust, feel vulnerable, and do not want to interact. Morris (1977) suggested that these "barrier signals" communicate avoidance and defensiveness in interpersonal interaction. Beier and Sternberg (1977) reported that "close" couples used more open leg positions than did couples who were less close or who were experiencing conflict.

Like good dancers, intimate couples show high levels of coordinated movement, called **body synchrony**. The good "vibes" resulting from smooth interaction with and adaptation to one's partner are a vital part of communicating immediacy and closeness (Guerrero & Floyd, 2006; Morris, 1977).

Andersen (2008) noted, "Although most synchronous patterns are reciprocal, some are not. Some are complementary: one person gives a back rub, and the other receives it; one person discloses, and the other listens and nods attentively" (p. 223). It is not just reciprocity that promotes closeness; it is smooth synchronization of behavior, whether complementary or reciprocal, that creates perceptions of relational closeness. In one study, when people were asked to signal liking to another person, one of the behaviors they employed was postural matching (Ray & Floyd, 2006). Although they are unaware of it, Kevin and his best friend Dan frequently match postures; they lean forward together at a bar, both put their feet up while watching a game, and both throw their heads back when they laugh.

Vocalic Communication

Words have meaning, but changes in pitch, volume, rate, and tone of voice—or **vocalics**—may be more important than words. These nonverbal elements of the voice have important effects on perceptions of emotional closeness. Studies have shown that shifts in vocal pitch, rate, amplitude, and duration are associated with positive interpersonal affect (Beebe, 1980; Scherer, 1979). Certain vocalic behaviors, such as baby talk, are especially immediate. Adults often use baby talk, a high-pitched, highly varied imitation of children's speech, to communicate with infants and small children (Andersen, 2008). Baby talk includes real words ("You're a little sweetie") and nonsense sounds ("kutchy-kutchy-koo"). Such talk has been found to aid the development of conversational skills, as well as more emotionally connected parent-child relationships (Ferguson, 1964). Interestingly, lovers like Kevin and Jennifer sometimes privately employ baby talk during their most intimate interactions perhaps because intimate behaviors related to courtship are often submissive, nonthreatening, and childlike (see Chapter 8).

Chronemic Behaviors

The way people use time, or **chronemics**, communicates a lot about their relationships. In North America and parts of Europe, time is a precious commodity that is spent, saved, wasted, or invested as though it were money. Studies show that chronemic cues send messages related to immediacy and closeness (Andersen, 1984). Spending time with another person sends the message that the person is important and reflects a desire to develop or maintain a close relationship. Egland, Stelzner, Andersen, and Spitzberg (1997) found that the best way to signal relational closeness is to spend time with one's partner. Similarly, being on time, waiting for a late partner, sharing conversation time, and devoting time to work on the relationship all play a role in the level of emotional closeness partners feel for one another.

COGNITIVE VALENCE THEORY

As noted previously, engaging in affectionate or immediate communication carries risks. Sometimes people respond positively to such behavior; other times people respond negatively. **Cognitive valence theory** (CVT) helps explain why people respond to increases in immediacy positively in some cases and negatively in others by examining six cognitive valencers: (1) culture, (2) personality, (3) the rewardingness of the partner, (4) the relationship, (5) the situation, and (6) temporary states. **Cognitive valencers** can be thought of as templates or knowledge structures that people use to help them evaluate behavior as appropriate or inappropriate and welcome or unwelcome. The six cognitive valencers identified in cognitive valence theory also influence how people give and receive affection (Pendell, 2002). The overall theory includes interpersonal perception, physiological arousal, social cognition, and relational outcomes (Andersen, 1985, 1989, 1998a). (See Figure 6.1 for a depiction of the theory.)

Behavior

All close relationships begin with one person increasing immediacy via nonverbal or verbal communication (see the Behavior column in Figure 6.1). As Andersen (1998a) explained, "Relationships do not occur in the absence of human contact. They begin, develop, thrive and disengage as communicative acts" (p. 40). Thus, using Dan and Kevin to help illustrate,

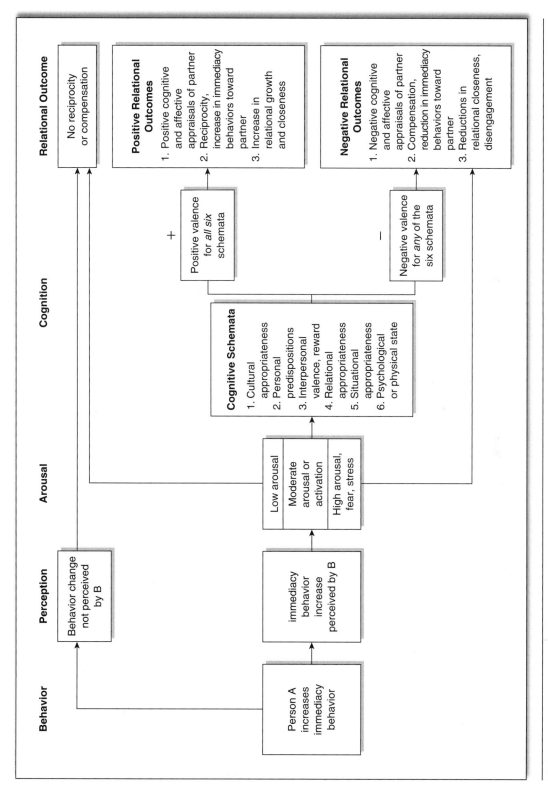

Figure 6.1   Cognitive Valence Theory

139

Dan would try to develop a closer friendship with Kevin by increasing immediacy through verbal or non-verbal communication. As noted earlier, Dan would have a variety of verbal behaviors at his disposal, including personal forms of address and expressions of relational closeness such as telling Kevin that he respects his athletic performance and is glad they are teammates. Usually, nonverbal communication plays a substantial role in promoting relational closeness, so Dan also might engage in behaviors such as smiling, making eye contact, touching, or hanging out with Kevin.

Perception

Behaviors by themselves do not increase close-ness; one's partner must notice the behaviors (see the Perception column in Figure 6.1). Andersen (1989) indicates that expressions of closeness have "no communicative significance" unless perceived by one's partner (p. 8). Such perceptions need not be conscious but must register in the mind of the receiver. Words spoken to no ear and smiles perceived by no eye do not communicate and have no chance of increasing closeness. So, Dan might smile and comment to Kevin that he enjoys being team-mates. But if Kevin's mind is on something else, Dan's attempt to develop a closer friendship will fail.

Arousal

If Kevin notices Dan's immediacy behavior, he will respond physiologically, and possibly cognitively and behaviorally. Nonverbal immediacy behaviors are stimulating and increase physiological arousal (see the Arousal column in Figure 8.3). In his summary of 24 studies on the relationship between immediacy behaviors and arousal, Andersen (1985) concluded, "The research generally supports a positive relationship between immediacy and increases in arousal" (p. 15). Increases in multichanneled immediacy behavior, such as more eye contact, smiles, and touch, increase physiological arousal (Andersen, Guerrero, Buller, & Jorgensen, 1998). Sometimes arousal change is accompanied by positive emotions; other times by negative emotions. Take Kevin and Dan again as an example. If Dan hugs Kevin after he

scores a goal during a soccer game, Kevin might feel heightened arousal, joy, and pride because Dan's gesture affirms that he is highly valued as both a friend and teammate. On the other hand, Kevin might experience a high level of arousal if he is embarrassed by Dan showing him high levels of immediacy in public, especially since heterosexual men are often homophobic and regard such displays of affection as unmasculine (Floyd, 2006).

Many studies have shown that rapid arousal increases are aversive and frightening (see Andersen, 2008, for a summary). For example, a threatening-looking stare by a stranger with a menacing facial expression likely prompts high arousal and the impulse to flee in a receiver. As a consequence, CVT predicts that negative relational outcomes will occur when arousal levels are very high. By contrast, when a friend says hi on the way to class, no arousal will occur because this behavior is highly routine and represents no real increase in immediacy. The most interesting reactions occur in relation to moderate increases in immediacy. For example, when receiving a smile from an attractive person or personal self-disclosure from a friend, moderate arousal is likely to occur. Moderate arousal has been shown to stimulate cognitive processes, which in turn influence how people respond to increases in immediacy behavior.

Cognition

For the sake of example, imagine that Dan's friendly behavior leads Kevin to experience a moderate increase in arousal. In this case, CVT predicts that Kevin's response to Dan's behavior will be contingent on how he cognitively appraises the situation. Specifically, CVT suggests that Kevin will evaluate Dan's increase in immediacy based on how appropriate Dan's behavior is in relation to the six cognitive valencers, as are shown in Figure 6.1.

Culture

Andersen (2008) argued that culture is so foundational in our lives that we often confuse it with human nature itself. We determine if something is appropriate in our culture, and that gives us a basis for reacting to it. For instance, kissing the wife of a friend goodbye would often be appropriate in the United States but not in Arab countries. If a behavior is appropriate, it can be positively valenced; if the behavior is culturally inappropriate, it will be negatively valenced. Within U.S. culture, Dan's smile and self-disclosure would probably be perceived as appropriate and so would be positively valenced. However, if Dan's self-disclosure was too immediate for a male in U.S. culture, it could be valenced negatively.

Personality

Personal predispositions make up one's personality. People differ in their sociability, extroversion, and attitudes toward touch and the degree to which they approach or avoid new experiences or sensations (see Andersen, 1993, 1998a). A hug or a personal disclosure may be appreciated by one person but not by another. Thus, people will valence the same behavior differently based on their personality. If Kevin is an outgoing, friendly person, he might welcome Dan's self-disclosure. However, if Kevin is shy and introverted, he might be nervous and uncomfortable hearing something personal about Dan. In the former case, Kevin would likely react positively to Dan's self-disclosure; in the latter, he would likely react negatively.

Rewardingness

The degree to which people find someone rewarding influences how they react to that person's increase in immediacy behavior (Burgoon & Hale, 1988). Rewardingness, which is also called **interpersonal valence**, refers to the degree to which someone is considered attractive. Recall from Chapter 3 that people can be attractive based on physical attributes (e.g., how beautiful they are or what clothes they wear), social qualities (e.g., how friendly they are), and instrumental qualities (e.g., how good they are at performing certain tasks). In general, people who are physically attractive, have high social standing, possess positive personality traits, and are similar to the receiver are regarded as highly rewarding. Thus, people react differently to changes in immediacy on the basis of who their partner is. Andersen (1993) noted that "positive perceptions of another person's values,

background, physical appearance and communication style are the primary reasons why we initiate and maintain close relationships" (p. 25). For example, a touch from a disliked other is judged very differently from a touch from a highly attractive date. Similarly, if Kevin likes Dan and thinks he is good guy, he is likely to react positively when Dan increases immediacy. By contrast, if Kevin thinks Dan is a pest who is no fun to be around, or has negative qualities such as abrasiveness, he is likely to react negatively.

The Relationship

The most important valencer that influences how people react to increases in immediacy is the relationship (see Andersen, 1998a, 1999). People are able to easily classify relationships with others as friend, coworker, best friend, lover, fiancé, parent, boss, roommate, and so on. These relational definitions create parameters regarding the appropriateness or inappropriateness of immediacy increases. Too much touch or self-disclosure on a first date is often a turnoff, yet the same amount of touch or self-disclosure from a fiancé would be warmly accepted. In the right relationship, almost any immediacy behavior will be valenced positively. In the wrong relationship, even mild displays of immediacy can be negatively valenced and cause adverse relational outcomes. Kevin and Dan have been close friends for years, so Kevin will probably expect a high level of in-depth self-disclosure. But if Kevin did not know Dan at all, Kevin would likely react negatively to Dan's disclosure of personal information to him.

The Situation

The situation, or the context in which immediacy behavior occurs, is vital in determining how people respond to increases in immediacy (Andersen, 1993). High levels of immediacy in the classroom, boardroom, bathroom, and bedroom produce distinctly different reactions. Some settings, such as living rooms, hot tubs, and hotel rooms, are highly conducive to immediacy. Other situations are highly formal with immediacy behaviors limited to handshakes or polite smiles. Passionately kissing one's date goodnight in a private place has entirely different connotations than engaging in the same behavior in front of one's parents. The bottom line is this: Immediacy must be situationally appropriate. If Dan increases immediacy with Kevin during a private conversation, his self-disclosure is likely to be regarded positively. But if he increases immediacy while Kevin is in the middle of an important conversation with Jennifer, his self-disclosure is likely to be regarded negatively.

Temporary States

Everyone has bad days and good days—intellectually, emotionally, and physically. Temporary states are short-term internal conditions that make individuals feel and react differently at various times (Andersen, 1993). Many things affect a person's temporary state or mood, including having a fight with the boss, being criticized (or complimented) by a friend, getting a bad night's sleep, partying too much, and receiving a pay raise. A classic example of negative-state valencing is a person's response to an affectionate spouse: "Not tonight, dear, I have a headache." Negative physical or emotional states generally lead to negative valencing of immediacy behavior, whereas positive states generally lead to positive valencing. Thus, Kevin is more likely to react positively to Dan's increase in immediacy if he is alert, feeling well, and in a good mood.

Relational Outcomes

As noted earlier, relationships are fragile and few relationships reach high levels of emotional and relational closeness. CVT provides one explanation for why this is so. Negative valencing for *any* of the six cognitive valencers can lead to decreased relational closeness. When immediacy increases are valenced negatively, a host of aversive outcomes follow, including appraising one's partner negatively, reducing immediacy behaviorally (perhaps by moving away), and maybe even disengaging from the relationship. Positive valencing of the immediacy behavior, by contrast, results in more favorable appraisals of one's partner, reciprocity of immediacy behaviors, and greater relational and emotional closeness. Thus, increasing immediacy behavior is

not without risk, but the benefits can outweigh the potential costs if a more enjoyable, closer relationship is desired. Dan's original attempt to become friends with Kevin might have resulted in rejection, but luckily Dan ended up developing a rewarding and emotionally close relationship with a new friend.

COMFORT AND SOCIAL SUPPORT

Friends, relatives, and romantic partners also communicate emotional closeness and show interdependence by being there for each other in times of distress. As discussed in Chapter 9, making sacrifices for one another and providing social support are key ways of sustaining closeness and maintaining relationships. When people want to establish a closer friendship, they both give and receive more social support (Sanderson, Rahm, Beigbeder, & Metts, 2005). People feel distress in reaction to a wide variety of situations. In Jones's (2000) study of distressing events among college students, the following were most frequently described as distressing: problems in a romantic relationship, college performance (grades), friend or roommate problems, family problems, work-related stress, family illness, death, and personal illness or injury. A follow-up study by Jones (2006) demonstrated that these situations vary in terms of the type of distress they produce, with sadness related to death and breakups, hurt related to breakups, and helplessness related to personal illness or injury.

Regardless of the type of distress one is experiencing, a key question is: How can people provide the most helpful support to someone who is distressed or in need of help? Support is only likely to relate to emotional and relational closeness when it is effective. Thus far, research suggests that certain types of support are more effective than others. Specifically, the most effective support tends to be invisible, person-centered, and nonverbally immediate.

Invisible Support

As noted earlier, a number of mental and physical health benefits are associated with giving and receiving affection. Thus, it seems logical to expect that receiving social support would have similar benefits. The research on this, however, is mixed. People report better health when they have large social networks and perceive that resources are available, yet people sometimes report worse health when they perceive that their partner provided them with actual support (Bolger & Amarel, 2007). These types of contradictory findings led Bolger, Zuckerman, and Kessler (2000) to propose the **invisible support phenomenon**. This phenomenon suggests support attempts that go unnoticed by recipients are the "most effective in reducing distress" and promoting good health (Bolger & Amarel, 2007, p. 458). This may be because people want to be viewed as autonomous and capable, rather than dependent and needy. Receiving too much support, or receiving support from an unskilled partner, may draw too much attention to a person's problems, thereby exacerbating distress and lowering self-esteem (Shrout, Herman, & Bolger, 2006). The invisible support phenomenon may also reflect that "support is rooted in the everyday fabric of relationships, in the routine interactions that people have with their friends and partners, interactions that are not necessarily viewed as acts of support" (Bolger & Amarel, 2007, p. 459; see also Leatham & Duck, 1990). Thus, affectionate communication may provide indirect forms of support that are superior to more direct expressions of support.

Recent studies have supported but qualified the invisible support phenomenon. Bolger and Amarel (2007) conducted three studies to determine whether invisible support was superior to visible support. In these studies, participants were told that they would be delivering a speech. A confederate who was working for the researcher pretended to be another participant in the study who had been assigned to write an essay rather than a speech. At some point, the researcher walked in and asked, "Do you have any questions for me before we move on?" The confederate then provided either invisible or visible support. In the first study, **practical support**, which entails giving concrete advice (e.g., telling the participant to be sure to summarize the speech at the beginning and the end) was provided in the visible support condition. In the invisible support condition, the confederate simply asked the researcher if summarizing at the beginning and the end was a good idea. The second study focused on **emotional support**, which involves helping the partner feel better without necessarily trying to solve the problem. In the visible support condition, the confederate told the participant, "Look, you've got nothing to worry about, you'll do fine. I'd understand if you were nervous, but really I think it's going to be okay," whereas in the invisible support condition the confederate told the researcher that the participant "is going to do fine, she's got nothing to worry about, but I still don't know what I'm supposed to do" (Bolger & Ameral, 2007, p. 464). As hypothesized, larger increases in distress occurred when people were given visible rather than invisible support. Therefore, invisible support was more effective than visible support.

The third study (Bolger & Amarel, 2007) compared five conditions, four of which are shown in Box 6.2. The fifth condition simply involved having the confederates say "No, not really" when asked if they had any questions. In addition to including both visible and invisible forms of practical support, Bolger and Amarel varied the degree to which the message implied that the participant or the confederate was considered to be effective or ineffective in coping with the situation. They reasoned that practical support is more likely to be perceived as condescending or threatening when it is stated in a way that implies the person is having difficulty coping with something. The results of this study were in line with this reasoning. People reported more distress in response to Message 1 (see Box 6.2) than they did if they received no support message at all. Therefore, visible support messages that imply that the recipient is ineffective actually made the situation worse rather than better. Messages 2 and 4 were not very effective either, with people who received these messages reporting about the same level of distress as those who received no support message at all. Only Message 3 meaningfully decreased participants' distress. This indicates that the best practical support may occur when it is not only invisible, but directed at someone else.

BOX 6.2 Highlights

Examples of Practical Support That Vary on the Basis of Visibility and Efficacy

1. Visible support/recipient inefficacy	"Well, I can tell that you could use some help. I think it's best to summarize what you're going to say at the beginning of a speech and to end with a definite conclusion."
2. Visible support/recipient efficacy	"Well, I don't think you need any help. But, if I had to say something, I've heard that it's best to summarize what you're going to say at the beginning of a speech and to end with a definite conclusion."
3. Invisible support/recipient efficacy & partner inefficacy	"Well, I don't think she needs any help, but I could use some help. Should I structure my essay in a certain way? Like to summarize what I'm going to say at the beginning, and to end with a definite conclusion?"
4. Invisible support/recipient & partner efficacy	"Well, I don't think that she needs any help, and I don't either. I'll just summarize what I'm going to say at the beginning of my essay and end with a definite conclusion."

SOURCE: Adapted from Bolger & Amarel (2007). Effects of social support visibility on adjustment to stress: Experimental evidence. *Journal of Personality and Social Psychology*, 92, 458–475.

Support may also be especially effective when it is perceived as responsive. **Responsiveness** refers to the degree to which a message communicates understanding, caring, and validation of one's partner (Maisel & Gable, 2009). In a study designed to determine whether responsiveness might help explain why some forms of visible support are perceived as ineffective, Maisel and Gable had cohabiting couples complete questionnaires for two weeks every night before they went to bed. Like past work, they found that invisible support was generally more effective than visible support. However, the level of perceived responsiveness also made a difference. In fact, visible support had positive effects when it was considered to be responsive, whereas invisible support had negative effects when it was considered to be unre-sponsive. The worst support occurred when both the recipient and the support provider agreed that the support was low in responsiveness. This study suggests that the way support is communicated is critical, regardless of whether support is visible or invisible.

Person-Centered Messages

One way to provide responsive, high-quality support is to use **person-centered messages** (Applegate, 1980; Burleson, 1982, 2003). When messages are highly person centered, they acknowledge, elaborate on, and validate the feelings and concerns of the distressed person. Comforting messages can be ranked as high or low in quality based on how person centered they are (Applegate, 1990; Burleson, 1982, 1984;

Jones, 2000). Highly person-centered messages help distressed people gain a perspective on their feelings. These messages also legitimize the distressed person's feelings. Suppose that Dan gets a C on his calculus exam even though he studied diligently. If Kevin used a highly person-centered message, he might say something like, "It sure must be frustrating to study hard for a test and then get a C. In fact, that really surprises me because you're smart. Don't you think you'll do better on the next test now that you know the type of questions your professor asks?" Notice that the highly person-centered response conveys understanding ("It sure must be frustrating") and support ("You're smart") while also helping the distressed person think about the event in a different way (perhaps as a learning experience).

Moderately person-centered messages acknowledge the distressed person's feelings, but these messages do not help the distressed person contextualize or elaborate on the situation. For example, Kevin might tell Dan, "I'll bet the test was really hard, and I'll bet most people got Cs or worse, so you shouldn't feel that bad." Or he might say, "It's only one test. You'll do better on the next one. Let's go see a good movie—that will help get your mind off this." Notice that these messages provide simple explanations and solutions that do not allow for much elaboration or reappraisal. These types of messages, which are frequently used by people in the comforter's role, provide support that is okay, but not great.

Finally, messages that are low in person-centeredness (sometimes called *position-centered messages*) implicitly or explicitly deny the legitimacy of the distressed person's feelings, sometimes by blaming the distressed person for the situation and other times by changing the topic or the focus. For example, Kevin might tell Dan, "It's only one test. You shouldn't make such a big deal out of it." Worse yet, he might say, "I'm sure some people got As, so you really don't have anyone to blame but yourself. I helped you as much as I could but I guess calculus is just too hard for you to understand." Or Kevin might also start talking about himself: "I got a C on a test once too. It was a real bummer, but that's life. Hey, do you want to get some lunch or something?"

Not surprisingly, several studies have shown that people who use highly person-centered messages provide the best comfort and are perceived the most positively (Burleson & Samter, 1985a, 1985b; Jones & Burleson, 1997; Jones & Guerrero, 2001). Highly person-centered messages are perceived as the most appropriate, effective, helpful, and sensitive. These messages are likely to be effective in expressing care and concern, but perhaps more important, they might help the distressed person to reevaluate the situation so that the event seems less distressing (Burleson & Goldsmith, 1998; Jones, 2000).

Nonverbal Immediacy

Of course, when comforting someone, it is important to use both nonverbal and verbal strategies. Jones and Guerrero (2001) investigated whether nonverbal immediacy behaviors and verbal person-centeredness work together to influence the quality of comforting behavior. They trained people to enact high, moderate, and low levels of nonverbal immediacy and person-centeredness, and then had them listen and react to people's distressing stories. They found that both nonverbal immediacy behaviors and person-centeredness had strong effects on comforting quality. When distressed people interacted with someone who used high levels of nonverbal immediacy and high levels of person-centeredness, they reported feeling the best. When high person-centered messages were paired with low levels of nonverbal immediacy, or conversely, when low person-centered messages were paired with high levels of nonverbal immediacy, overall comforting quality decreased. Not surprisingly, comforters who used low levels of both nonverbal immediacy and person-centeredness were least effective at alleviating distress.

Other studies have also highlighted the important role nonverbal immediacy plays in providing high-quality, successful comforting (Jones, 2004; Jones & Burleson, 2003). Dolin and Booth-Butterfield (1993) asked students how they would comfort a roommate who was distressed because of a recent relational breakup. The students reported that they would use the following behaviors most frequently, with percentages showing how often a behavior was mentioned in the students' descriptions:

- *Hugs* (41.9%): giving the person a whole body hug or hugging him or her around the shoulder.
- *Close proxemic distancing* (40.9%): sitting down next to the person or leaning closer.
- *Facial expression* (38.7%): looking empathetic, sad, or concerned.
- *Attentiveness* (37.7%): listening carefully and nodding as the person talked about the distressing event.
- *Increased miscellaneous touch* (34.4%): using all forms of touch other than hugs or pats, such as holding the person's hand or stroking the person's hair.
- *Pats* (26.9%): using short, repetitive, movements such as patting the distressed person's arm or shoulder.

- *Eye contact* (23.7%): looking directly at the distressed person, particularly while the person was talking.

In addition to these behaviors, Dolin and Booth-Butterfield found a few other nonverbal comforting strategies that were reported less often. Some students described behaviors related to weeping, such as crying with the distressed person or offering a "shoulder to cry on." Some said that they would engage in emotional distancing behavior, such as trying to remain uninvolved, getting comfortable, or fixing a cup of coffee. Presumably these strategies would keep the individual from experiencing too much negative affect while talking to the distressed person. Other students reported that they would engage in instrumental activities, such as getting the

SOURCE: ©iStockphoto.com.

Giving and receiving social support is a key characteristic of close friendships, and touch is the most common behavior friends use to comfort one another.

distressed person a tissue or something to eat. Still others indicated that they would show concern through warm vocal tones and empathetic gestures. For example, if the distressed person was angry, the individual in the comforting role might clench her or his fist to mirror the distressed person's anger.

Considered together, these studies suggest that when people want to do a good job comforting someone, they should pay attention to both their verbal and nonverbal behavior. In some cases, nonverbal forms of social support may be especially effective because they are somewhat "invisible." In other words, people can comfort someone without directly offering them advice or providing commentary on their situation. When a distressed person wants to talk, it is important for comforters to listen instead of changing the topic or focusing the discussion on themselves. When people can disclose their distressing circumstances freely to others, it helps them vent their negative emotion and possibly think through and reassess the problem, which can contribute to psychological and physical well-being (Burleson & Goldsmith, 1998; Pennebaker, 1989; Pennebaker, Colder, & Sharp, 1990). It is also important to remain positive when comforting a distressed person since people tend to match the affect that their partner expresses using immediacy cues (Jones & Wirtz, 2007).

SEX DIFFERENCES IN THE EXPERIENCE AND EXPRESSION OF CLOSENESS

Sex differences in closeness are important to consider. People sometimes expect women to be more affectionate and to provide more social support than men, and a number of studies confirm that women are generally more nonverbally immediate than men (Burgoon & Bacue, 2003). Yet it should not be presumed that men and women are completely different. Rather, men and women may achieve closeness and appreciate closeness, though in somewhat different ways. Indeed, research shows that men and women are far more similar than different in how they achieve emotional and relational closeness in both same-sex and opposite-sex relationships.

Perceptions of Closeness

Certainly both men and women have the potential to develop very close relationships. Despite popular literature suggesting that men and women are from different planets, research has shown that men and women are far more similar than different. As noted in Chapter 9, according to Dindia, a more apt metaphor than "men are from Mars, and women are from Venus" is "men are from North Dakota, and women are from South Dakota" (Wood & Dindia, 1998). Both men and women believe that emotional communication is more important for developing close relationships than are instrumental or task-oriented skills (Burleson, Kunkel, Samter, & Werking, 1996). Perhaps surprisingly, this appears to be true in male friendships, female friendships, cross-sex friendships, and romantic relationships. As Burleson and fellow researchers (1996) discovered, "Affectively oriented communication skills appear to be important for both genders in the conduct of intimacy—regardless of whether intimacy is realized in same-sex friendship or opposite-sex romances" (p. 218).

Several other studies have demonstrated that there are few, if any, differences in closeness levels for men and women. In one study, college students reported similar levels of closeness in their same-sex versus cross-sex friendships (Johnson et al., 2007). Similarly, a study of committed Canadian couples produced almost identical reports of emotional, social, intellectual, and recreational intimacy for men and women (McCabe, 1999). Emotional intimacy referred to how much individuals felt their partner was there for them, social intimacy referred to how much people enjoyed spending time with their partner, intellectual intimacy referred to how much the partner helped expand and clarify one's thoughts, and recreational intimacy referred to how much they enjoyed doing activities together. In a study of Australian men's and women's friendships, there were no sex differences for behavioral or cognitive closeness, which suggests that men's and women's friendships are equally interdependent (Polimeni, Hardie, & Buzwell, 2002). There was, however, a small sex difference for emotional closeness, with women reporting more trust, affection, and caring in their same-sex friendships compared to men.

Despite the lack of sex differences found in some studies, some scholars have claimed that females have closer relationships than males, starting in childhood (Meurling, Ray, & LoBello, 1999). Others have argued that the finding that females have closer relationships than males may be due to the fact that researchers have employed a "feminine" definition of closeness (Wood & Inman, 1993). Most of the data on differences in closeness between men and women comes from research claiming that in the United States, women disclose more than men (Floyd, 1995). But disclosure is only one type of closeness. Parks and Floyd (1996) pointed out that, for decades, scholars have thought of close relationships as emotional, feminine, and affectionate rather than instrumental, masculine, and logical. Because men's relationships are somewhat lower in emotional expression and self-disclosure, men were thought not to have very close relationships. However, there is little actual evidence for a difference in the closeness of men's and women's friendships. In fact, Parks and Floyd (1996) found no support for the hypothesis that women are more likely than men to label their relationships as "intimate" or "close."

Communication of Closeness

When sex differences do emerge, they tend to revolve around how men and women communicate closeness in their same-sex friendships. Females are more likely to have **expressive friendships** that involve using emotionally charged nonverbal and verbal communication during conversations, showing nonverbal affection, talking about fears, and shopping (Floyd, 1995; Helgeson, Shaver, & Dyer, 1987; Monsour, 1992). Studies also suggest that girls show more trust and loyalty, more dependence on friends, and a greater tendency to discuss their relationships with friends than do boys (Muerling et al., 1999; Sharabany, Gershoni, & Hoffman, 1981). Similarly, Floyd (2006) reported a series of studies that show that, in general, women express more affection than men in same-sex dyads, even though men increase their level of affection to nearly the same level as women in cross-sex friendships. Another study showed that women use more emotional nonverbal cues, such as emoticons and descriptions of nonverbal behaviors (e.g., typing in *sigh*) than men do when providing social support via email (Ledbetter & Larson, 2008).

Males, in contrast, are more likely to have **agentic friendships** that focus on companionship and shared activities (Rawlins, 1982). Sharing adventures, telling stories, doing physical labor, working on a joint project, taking a fishing trip, and serving in the army are all experiences that develop and sustain closeness in their own way. Floyd (1995) found that among college students, males are more likely than females to develop closeness through shaking hands, drinking together, and talking about sex. These action-oriented behaviors may be just as valid a path to high levels of closeness as self-disclosure or emotional expression.

The distinction between expressive and agentic friendships was illustrated in a study by Caldwell and Peplau (1982) who asked men and women to choose whether they would rather "just talk" or "do some activity" with a same-sex friend. Women preferred talking, 57% to 43%, whereas men overwhelmingly preferred activity, 84% to 16%. However, this distinction does not mean that women friends never do activities together; they do. Nor does it mean that men never get together just to talk; sometimes they do. The distinction simply means that given a preference, more women would want to get together just to talk, whereas more men would want to get together to engage in an activity.

Preferences for Same-Sex Versus Cross-Sex Friendships

In much of the research on friendships, there is an implicit assumption that people's closest friendships tend to be with members of the same sex. Recent research casts doubt on this assumption. Specifically, Baumgarte and Nelson (2009) found that college students were just as likely to prefer having a close friendship with someone of the opposite sex as someone of the same sex. Like past work, this study showed that women's same-sex friendships were generally perceived to be higher in closeness, common interests, caring, and trust than men's same-sex friendships. However, this difference disappeared or reversed when preferences for same-sex versus cross-sex friendships were considered. For example, women who preferred cross-sex friendships reported that they were just as interested in sharing activities as talking with their male friends. These women also rated their friendships with men as more caring, supportive, and trusting than their friendships with women. This study suggests that

the increased prevalence of cross-sex friendships may be closing the gap between men's and women's communication styles. As Baumgarte and Nelson (2007) put it, stereotypes of women as expressive and men as agentic may be "relevant primarily to those who hold a strong preference for same-sex friendship. Those who prefer cross-sex friendship either make much weaker distinctions based on the sex of their friends, or they hold values that reflect a reversal of these stereotypes" (p. 915).

SUMMARY AND APPLICATION

As this chapter has emphasized, people communicate closeness in various ways. Kevin is very close to both Jennifer and Dan, but closeness is communicated somewhat differently in these two relationships. Kevin's relationship with Jennifer emphasizes deep conversations, lots of time spent together, long eye contact, and romantic touch as manifestations of emotional and relational closeness. Kevin communicates closeness to Dan in different ways, through playing ball and skiing, debating political issues, discussing their careers, and sharing a ball game and some refreshments on a Sunday afternoon. Although these differences reflect stereotypes about the type of behavior that is appropriate in romantic relationships versus male friendships, there are also many ways that Kevin displays closeness similarly to Dan and Jennifer. He frequently uses immediacy behaviors such as smiling, using idioms, and speaking in a warm, confidential voice with both of them.

Indeed, to have truly close relationships with both Jennifer and Dan, Kevin needs to break away from stereotypical behavior. For example, to sustain emotional closeness with Jennifer, it is essential that Kevin do things that men often forget to do, such as listening during conversations and looking at Jennifer when she is talking. For her part, it is important Jennifer remember to share in Kevin's activities, such as skiing or watching a ball game. She may need to try some activities that Kevin likes even though she never attempted them before. And, Kevin and Dan may need to have periodic talks that

include in-depth self-disclosure. They should also not be afraid to show each other affection through verbal, nonverbal, or supportive behavior.

Kevin may also find himself giving both invisible and visible (but hopefully person-centered and immediate) social support to both Jennifer and Dan. For his attempts at social support to be effective, Kevin should focus on listening to and validating their thoughts and opinions rather that stating what he would do in their situation. He should also offer emotional support without criticism. If practical support is necessary, Kevin should be sure to phrase his advice in a way that implies that Dan or Jennifer is fully capable of dealing with the situation at hand. Finally, the best social support occurs in the context of emotionally close relationships where people feel safe, secure, and supported regardless of whether explicit comfort is given.

Finally, real connection is impossible without communication. As cognitive valence theory suggests, closeness is created by two people through a series of moves and countermoves. Kevin cannot develop or sustain a close relationship by himself; instead, "it takes two to tango." It is also important to remember that close relationships occur in a larger context. Kevin needs to understand that factors such as Dan's or Jennifer's cultural background, the context or situation of their interaction, Dan's and Jennifer's moods and states, their personality, their level of rewardingness, and, of course, the stage of their relationship can all influence whether immediate communication is accepted or rejected. As Kevin and Jennifer become even closer, it may be important for them to define where they are in their relationship. Saying "I love you," giving rings, and planning a future together are important ways to express affection and develop emotional and relational closeness. However, Kevin should avoid making such moves too early in the relationship if they could scare Jennifer off. By understanding the six cognitive valencers, Kevin may be better equipped to know when (and when not) to increase immediacy with Jennifer. Hopefully, this chapter provides many other helpful hints regarding how to best develop and sustain closeness in various types of relationships.

DISCUSSION QUESTIONS

1. Which of the three types of closeness discussed in this chapter—physical, emotional, or relational—do you think is most important within close relationships? Why? Also, how do you think these three types of closeness vary based on relationship type, such as relatives versus friends or lovers?

2. Do you agree or disagree with the principles guiding affection exchange theory? How might the theory explain patterns of affectionate communication in relationships between friends or adopted children and their parents?

3. If you want to give friends or loved ones effective social support, what should you say and do? What might you avoid saying or doing? Do you agree or disagree with the idea that invisible support is often more effective than visible support? Explain your reasoning.

STUDENT STUDY SITE

Visit the study site at **www.sagepub.com/guerrero3e** for e-flashcards, survey and assessments from the chapter, and SAGE journal articles.

7

Making a Love Connection

Styles of Love and Attachment

Gabriela and Brian have been dating for months. Although they care deeply for one another, problems have started to surface in their relationship. Brian wishes Gabriela would show him more affection. Every time they get really close, she seems to pull away. She also seems to put her career ahead of their relationship. Just last week, she cancelled their Saturday night date so she could spend extra time working on an advertising campaign. Sometimes Brian wonders if he cares more for Gabriela than she cares for him. Gabriela, in contrast, wants Brian to give her more space. She doesn't understand why he needs her to say "I love you" so often. Shouldn't he understand how she feels without her having to tell him all the time? After all, she always makes sure to fit some quality time with Brian into her busy schedule, and they do all sorts of activities together—golfing, skiing, and watching old movies. Sometimes Gabriela wonders if she can devote enough time to the relationship to satisfy Brian. Maybe she's just not ready for the level of commitment he wants.

Who do you relate to more—Gabriela or Brian? Gabriela is focused on her career. She expresses love by engaging in activity, and she values her autonomy. Brian, on the other hand, is more focused on the relationship. He expresses his feelings by saying "I love you" and showing affection. Are Gabriela and Brian's attitudes toward love fairly common? What other attitudes do people have about love? How do they know if they are really in love? Finally, can two people such as Gabriela and Brian—who have such different needs, priorities, and communication styles—be happy together? The literature on love and attachment helps answer these questions.

In this chapter, we examine different styles of love and attachment. Before doing so, we define love and discuss the situation of unrequited love. Next, we cover three major perspectives on love: (1) Sternberg's triangle of love, (2) Lee's love styles, and (3) Marston and Hecht's love ways. These three perspectives highlight how people experience and communicate love in different ways. Finally, we discuss attachment theory. Attachment is an important part of various loving relationships, including relationships between family members, romantic partners, and close friends.

WHAT IS LOVE?

When love is shared, it is one of the most wonderful human experiences. When love is not returned, people feel rejected and miserable. Researchers have spent considerable energy investigating love. Some of this research has focused on answering basic questions, addressed in the following sections, and including: Is love a distinctly different experience than liking? Are there different types of love? How do people feel in situations involving unrequited love?

Love Versus Liking

Some researchers have tried to distinguish love from liking. Rubin (1970, 1973, 1974) suggested that there are qualitative, rather than quantitative, differences between love and liking. In other words, liking someone a lot does not necessarily translate into love. Love is more than an abundance of liking, and love and liking are related but distinctly different concepts. People can, in some cases, love others without liking them very much. In general, however, individuals tend to like the people they love. For example, Rubin (1970, 1973) found that people *like* their close friends and dating partners about equally, but *love* their dating partners more than their friends. Romantic partners who are "in love" and plan to marry also report loving each other more

than dating partners who do not have concrete plans for the future. Thus, romance and commitment appear to be important in many love relationships.

Liking and loving can be distinguished from each other by certain feelings and relationship characteristics. Rubin (1973) suggested that liking is characterized by affection and respect, whereas love is a deeper bond characterized by attachment, caring, and interdependence. A series of studies by Davis and colleagues also demonstrated that love is qualitatively different than liking and, again, that love is special because it often includes more caring and passion than liking (Davis & Roberts, 1985; Davis & Todd, 1982, 1985). In these studies, friendship was defined by characteristics such as enjoyment, acceptance, trust, and respect, as well as doing things for one another, disclosing information, understanding each other, and feeling comfortable together. Love was defined by all of these friendship characteristics *plus* caring and passion. Caring includes making supreme sacrifices for the loved one and defending the loved one to others; passion includes being fascinated by the loved one, feeling that the relationship is unique and exclusive, and experiencing strong sexual desire. Of course, love also occurs in nonromantic relationships such as those between parents and children or best friends. In these cases, the level of caring is especially high.

Love as a Triangle

Sternberg's (1986, 1988) triangular theory of love also distinguishes between liking and different types of love. This theory includes three components related to love—intimacy, passion, and commitment—pictured as sides of a triangle. According to Sternberg, liking occurs when a person experiences high levels of intimacy but relatively low levels of passion and commitment in a relationship. Love occurs when intimacy combines with passion or commitment. The most complete type of love, consummate love, is based on having high levels of all three components (see Box 7.1).

BOX 7.1 Highlights

Selected Love Triangles

Types of Love	Intimacy	Passion	Commitment
Liking	+	–	–
Infatuation	–	+	–
Romantic love	+	+	–
Friendship love	+	–	+
Empty love	–	–	+
Consummate love	+	+	+

Intimacy: The "Warm" Component

Intimacy is based on feelings of emotional connection and closeness, and has therefore been called the "warm" part of love. Among the three sides of Sternberg's (1986) triangle, intimacy is seen as most foundational to both love and liking. **Liking** is defined by intimacy alone. When passion is combined with intimacy, people experience **romantic love**. This type of love often characterizes initial stages of dating relationships, when two people are sexually attracted to each other and feel an intimate connection but have not yet fully committed themselves to the relationship. When commitment is combined with intimacy, **friendship love** emerges. This type of love transcends relationship type (Fehr & Russell, 1991). In other words, love for family members and friends fits this description, as does love between romantic partners who have been together for a long time or consider themselves to be best friends more than lovers. Many scholars consider these two types of love to be universal and to have existed throughout time (Berscheid, 2010). When these two types of love are experienced together so that a relationship contains high levels of intimacy, passion, and commitment, people achieve **consummate love**.

Sternberg theorized that intimacy is moderately stable over the course of a relationship. However, he made an important distinction between latent and manifest intimacy. **Latent intimacy** refers to internal feelings of closeness and interpersonal warmth, which are not directly observable by others. This type of intimacy is what we feel inside. **Manifest intimacy** refers to how people communicate affection and closeness to someone, such as disclosing intimate feelings to a partner or spending extra time together. According to Sternberg (1986), latent intimacy is likely to increase but then reach a plateau as a relationship develops. Manifest intimacy, by contrast, is likely to grow during the initial stages of a relationship but then decline over time.

Research has shown some support for Sternberg's predictions. Acker and Davis (1992) found that couples felt more intimacy and closeness as their relationships became more serious; however, behavioral (or manifest) intimacy decreased as the relationship progressed. Guerrero and Andersen (1991) found a similar pattern for touch in public settings. Their observations showed that couples in serious dating relationships touched more than married couples, yet spouses felt just as close to each other as did daters. Emmers and Dindia (1995) found a similar pattern for private touch.

Therefore, even though married couples used less touch to manifest intimacy, they still experienced very high levels of latent intimacy.

Passion: The "Hot" Component

According to Sternberg (1986, 1988), **passion** is the "hot" component of love that consists of motivation and arousal. However, passion is not limited to sexual arousal. Friends can experience excitement though activities or by just being together. Passion also includes motivational needs for affiliation, control, and self-actualization. Thus, parents can feel a passionate love for their children that includes an intense desire for them to achieve success and happiness. In romantic relationships, however, passion is often experienced primarily as sexual attraction and arousal. When people have this type of passion without much intimacy or commitment, they are experiencing **infatuation**. Infatuated individuals idealize the objects of their affection and imagine that their lives would be wonderful if they could develop a relationship with that person. Some researchers also argue that infatuation is blind because people downplay dissimilarities and other potential problems when they are infatuated with someone (McClanahan, Gold, Lenney, Ryckman, & Kulberg, 1990). Because infatuation is based on the "hot" component of the love triangle, it is not surprising that infatuated individuals often fall in and out of love quickly, as their passion heats up and then cools down.

Passion is also relatively unstable as relationships progress, with passion levels often fluctuating greatly during the course of a relationship. Passion and romance tend to be high during the initial stages of a relationship but then level off as the relationship becomes more predictable and less arousing (Hatfield & Sprecher, 1986a; Sternberg, 1986). This is not to say that long-term romantic relationships are devoid of passion. As Sternberg (1986) suggested, highly committed couples are likely to cycle back and forth in terms of passion. A romantic weekend away or a candlelight dinner followed by stargazing in a hot tub can provide an important passionate spark to a long-term relationship. Sternberg's point is that these types of events occur less often in developed relationships because it is hard to sustain a high level of passion all of the time. Acker and Davis (1992) found that people feel and desire less passion as they grow older, which suggests that passion may be more characteristic of young romances and the reproductive years than mature relationships. However, Acker and Davis also found that while women were more passionate in new relationships compared to established relationships, men showed fairly high levels of passion regardless of whether the relationship was new or old.

Commitment: The "Cool" Component

The third component of Sternberg's (1986, 1988) love triangle is commitment/decision. This component refers to the decision to love someone and the commitment to maintain that love. Because commitment is based on cognition and decision making, Sternberg referred to it as the "cool" or "cold" component. Commitment is undoubtedly an important part of love for many people. In a study by Fehr (1988), college-aged students rated how closely various words or phrases, such as "affection" and "missing each other when apart," relate to love. Of the 68 words and phrases Fehr listed, the word *trust* was rated as most central to love. *Commitment* ranked 8th overall, suggesting that it is also highly central to love. The other two components of the triangular theory of love were also important, although less central, with *intimacy* ranking 19th and *sexual passion* rating 40th. Fehr (1988) also had college-aged students rate words and phrases describing the concept of commitment. *Loyalty, responsibility, living up to one's word, faithfulness,* and *trust* were the top five descriptors of commitment, suggesting that commitment involves being there for someone over the long haul.

Of the three components of the love triangle, commitment is most stable over time. In long-term relationships, commitment typically builds gradually and then stabilizes (Acker & Davis, 1992). Commitment also appears to play an important role in keeping a relationship satisfying and stable. In Acker and Davis's study, intimacy, passion, and commitment were all related positively to satisfaction, but commitment, followed by intimacy, were the strongest predictors of satisfaction. Hendrick, Hendrick, and Adler (1988) conducted a study to determine whether commitment, relational satisfaction, or investment of time and effort was the best predictor of relational stability. They found that commitment was the best predictor of whether dating couples would still be together two months later. Thus, commitment is not only a part of most love relationships but also a stabilizing force within these relationships.

Yet commitment alone is not enough to keep a relationship happy. When individuals experience **empty love**, they have commitment but relatively low levels of intimacy and passion. Some long-term relationships fall into this category. For instance, if partners no longer feel attached to each other but stay together for religious reasons or because of the children, their love might be characterized as empty. In other cases, empty love characterizes the beginning of a relationship. For example, spouses in arranged marriages may begin their relationships with empty love. Intimacy and passion may, or may not, emerge later.

Unrequited Love

Sometimes the feelings of friendship, caring, or passion that characterize liking and loving are not reciprocated. Such is the case with **unrequited love**, whereby one person, the would-be lover, wants to initiate or intensify a romantic relationship, but the other person, the rejector, does not (Baumeister & Wotman, 1992; Baumeister, Wotman, & Stillwell, 1993; Bratslavsky, Baumeister, & Sommer, 1998). Unrequited love can characterize several types of situations. Sometimes the two people do not know one another well even though one of them feels "in love" with the other; other times they may be good friends but one person wants to intensify the relationship further and the other person does not; still other times unrequited love occurs in the initial stages of a relationship. For example, after going on a few dates, one person may fall in love but the other might want to stop dating altogether (see Chapter 15). Unrequited love also occurs in established or de-escalating relationships when one partner ceases to love the other. Rejection is usually more unpleasant and hurtful when it comes from a romantic partner as opposed to a friend or acquaintance (Young, Paxman, Koehring, & Anderson, 2008).

When unrequited love is perceived, the would-be lover has two options: (1) to keep quiet about the feelings or (2) to try to win the partner's love (Baumeister et al., 1993). Either way, there are considerable risks for the would-be lover. On the one hand, approaching the loved one could lead to rejection, humiliation, or, in the case of an established friendship, the de-escalation or termination of the relationship. On the other hand, keeping quiet could cost the person any opportunity to win the other person over or escalate the relationship.

Situations of unrequited love are difficult for both people, but perhaps surprisingly, Baumeister and his colleagues discovered that rejectors typically report experiencing more negative emotions than do would-be lovers. According to their research, would-be lovers perceive the situation as having either extremely positive or negative outcomes, whereas most rejectors perceive only negative outcomes. Although it is flattering to be the object of someone's affection, the rejector typically feels guilty for being unable to return the would-be lover's sentiments. If the would-be lover is persistent, the rejector may feel frustrated and even victimized (Baumeister et al., 1993). The appropriate way to communicate rejection is also unclear, since it is difficult to reject the advances without hurting the would-be lover's feelings. Would-be lovers, by contrast, have a much clearer script for how to behave. As Baumeister and colleagues (1993) put it:

> The would-be lover's script is affirmed and reiterated from multiple sources; for example, one can probably hear a song about unrequited love in almost any American house within an hour, simply by turning on the radio. A seemingly endless stream of books and movies has portrayed aspiring lovers persisting doggedly to win the hearts of their beloveds. Many techniques are portrayed as eventually effective. If one is rejected in the end, the familiar script calls for heartbroken lovers to express their grief, perhaps assign blame, accept the failure, and then go on with their lives. (p. 379)

For example, songs like Taylor Swift's 2009 hit, "You Belong to Me," include storylines where the underdog would-be lover eventually prevails. The rejector, however, does not have a clearly defined cultural prescription for how to deal with the would-be lover. Movies and novels often portray rejectors as "aloof, casual, teasing, or sadistic heartbreakers," but in real life, most rejectors are concerned with helping the would-be lover save face (Baumeister et al., 1993, p. 391). Thus, many rejectors resist making harsh statements such as "I'm not attracted to you" and instead rely on polite, indirect communication strategies, such as saying that they value the friendship too much to ruin it by pursuing a romantic relationship or that they are too busy to date anyone at this time. Folkes (1982) found that rejectors try to let other people down easily and avoid hurting their feelings.

The problem with polite or indirect messages is that they can be misinterpreted (Cupach & Metts, 1991). Would-be lovers may cling to the hope that, since the rejector did not dismiss them directly, a love relationship is still possible. For example, would-be lovers who receive a message such as "I'm not interested in dating anyone right now, but I want to say friends" might hear this as "There might be a chance of a love relationship in the future since I like you." Eventually, the rejector may have to resort to harsher and more direct messages if the would-be lover persists (Metts, Sprecher, & Regan, 1998). When clear sexual advances are made, women are likely to be verbally direct, and most men accept their refusals (Metts et al., 1998).

Although there is not a clear script for how to best reject someone, research suggests that some rejection messages are more inappropriate than others depending on the relationship between the would-be-lover and the rejector. Young and fellow researchers (2008) examined several types of rejection messages, including ambiguous or "off-record" strategies (e.g., "I like you but I'm really busy right now"); direct "on-record" strategies that blame situational constraints for the rejection (e.g., "I'm interested in someone else"); and direct "on-record" strategies that blame the self for the rejection (e.g., "It wouldn't work because I'm not right for you").

The would-be lovers in Young and colleagues' (2008) study rated the ambiguous off-record strategies as especially inappropriate for friends to use, perhaps because such messages left them wondering whether or not to pursue a romantic relationship in the future. Friends may also expect more directness in their relationships. When the rejector was a romantic partner, would-be lovers rated on-record strategies that blamed situational constraints as the most inappropriate. Given that they are already in a romantic relationship, would-be lovers are often surprised to have their attempts at escalation rebuffed, and perhaps even more surprised that the rejector blames external factors such as a third party. Finally, would-be lovers rated on-record strategies that blamed the self as the most inappropriate message for acquaintances to use. Since the two people don't yet know one another well, it may seem premature for the rejector to assume that something personal (age, disposition, values, etc.) would stand in the way of the desired relationship. The would-be lover may feel that the potential relationship was rejected without giving it a fair chance.

LOVE STYLES

Just as people vary in terms of the rejection strategies they use, so too do people differ in their styles of loving. Love is also communicated in a variety of ways, including through self-disclosure, emotional responses, and time spent together. Two perspectives in particular prevail on different styles of loving. The first focuses on different ideologies that people hold about the love. The second focuses on different styles of communicating love.

Lee's Love Styles

Lee (1973, 1977, 1988) argued that people have various ideologies when it comes to love. These **ideologies** can be thought of as collections of beliefs, values, and expectations about love. Lee also contended that there are three primary styles of loving, much as there are three primary colors. When mixing paint, the primary colors are red, blue, and yellow. Mixing these three colors can create any color in the rainbow. Lee conceptualized styles of loving in a similar manner. He proposed that the primary love styles are **eros**, or romantic love; **storge**, or friendship love; and **ludus**, or game-playing love. Just as the primary colors can be blended to create a multitude of different hues, Lee theorized that elements of the three primary styles of love can combine to create a vast number of love styles. Of the many possible combinations, Lee suggested that three are the most common: **mania**, or possessive love; **agape**, or compassionate love; and **pragma**, or practical love. Figure 7.1 depicts Lee's love styles as a color wheel.

Each style of love is defined by both positive and negative characteristics. The more strongly and

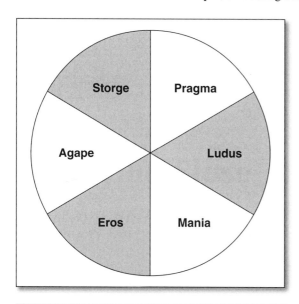

Figure 7.1   Lee's Love Styles Represented as a Color Wheel

NOTE: The primary styles are shaded; the secondary styles are composed of the aspects of the two primary styles adjacent to them.

exclusively a person identifies with a single style, the more likely the person is to experience some of the negative characteristics associated with that style. Most people, however, report identifying with a combination of styles, with one or two styles experienced most strongly. Box 7.2 gives a scale by which you can determine your own love style.

Eros: Romantic Love

Eros, which has also been termed **romantic** or **passionate love**, is rooted in feelings of affection, attraction, and sexual desire. It is also closely related to being "in love." In one study, college students were asked to write the names of members of their social network under four categories: friends, people they love, people they are in love with, and people whom they feel sexual desire toward (Meyers & Berscheid, 1997). The students were told that they could place a person's name in more than one category. Most students only put one person in the "in love" category, and that person was also listed in the

"friend" and "sexual desire" categories, which suggests that being in love is related to both intimacy and passion, as Sternberg (1986, 1988) predicted.

Individuals with the eros style look for partners who are physically attractive and good lovers (Lee, 1988; Levine, Aune, & Park, 2006). They are eager to develop intense, passionate relationships and often experience intense emotional highs and lows. They also feel substantial arousal and desire physical contact. Because they possess strong feelings of attraction, eros lovers develop a sense of intimacy and connectedness relatively quickly. These individuals are "intense communicators" who show high levels of self-disclosure, are able to elicit similarly high levels of self-disclosure from their partners, and display high levels of touch and nonverbal affection (Taraban, Hendrick, & Hendrick, 1998, p. 346). When eros lovers want to intensify their relationships, they tend to use strategies such as increasing contact, giving tokens of affection (e.g., sending gifts or flowers), and changing their behavior to please their partner (Levine et al., 2006). Romantic love is also related to engaging in everyday forms of routine communication, such as asking about each other's day or discussing current events or television shows (Tagawa & Yashida, 2006).

Eros is a central part of many love relationships. This type of love is common in the initial stages of romantic relationships. Eros love can also evolve into a more friendship-based and secure style of love as the relationship progresses (Hendrick, Hendrick, & Adler, 1988). Some level of eros also keeps relationships exciting and passionate. However, too much eros can have negative effects. For example, if you are only interested in someone because of the person's beauty, the attraction may fade quickly. Also, some eros lovers have trouble adjusting after the initial "hot" attraction begins to cool or after they discover that the partner, who seemed perfect at first, cannot possibly live up to their unrealistically high expectations. Still, research suggests that maintaining some degree of eros is beneficial in a relationship. Hendrick and associates (1988) found that dating couples were more likely to stay together if the partners were high in eros and low in the ludic, game-playing style of love, which suggests that passion and commitment are both important in many love relationships.

BOX 7.2 Put Yourself to the Test

What Is Your Love Style?

To determine your dominant love style, rate yourself on each of these statements according to the following scale: 1 = strongly disagree, 5 = strongly agree.

	Disagree				Agree
1. My partner and I were attracted to each other immediately when we first met.	1	2	3	4	5
2. My partner and I have the right physical chemistry.	1	2	3	4	5
3. The physical part of our relationship is intense and satisfying.	1	2	3	4	5
4. My partner and I were meant for each other.	1	2	3	4	5
5. My partner fits my ideal standards of physical attractiveness.	1	2	3	4	5
6. I try to keep my partner a little uncertain about my commitment to her/him.	1	2	3	4	5
7. I believe that what my partner doesn't know about me won't hurt her/him.	1	2	3	4	5
8. I could get over my relationship with my partner pretty easily.	1	2	3	4	5
9. When my partner gets too dependent on me, I back off.	1	2	3	4	5
10. I enjoy playing the field.	1	2	3	4	5
11. It is hard for me to say exactly when our friendship turned into love.	1	2	3	4	5
12. To be genuine, our love first required caring.	1	2	3	4	5
13. Our love is the best kind because it grew out of a close friendship.	1	2	3	4	5
14. Our love is really a deep friendship, not a mysterious or mystical emotion.	1	2	3	4	5
15. Our love relationship is satisfying because it developed from a good friendship.	1	2	3	4	5
16. I considered what my partner was going to become in life before committing myself to her/him.	1	2	3	4	5
17. I tried to plan my life carefully before choosing a partner.	1	2	3	4	5
18. In choosing my partner, I believed it was best to find someone with a similar background.	1	2	3	4	5

	Disagree				Agree
19. An important factor in choosing my partner was whether she/he would be a good parent.	1	2	3	4	5
20. Before getting very involved with my partner, I tried to figure out how compatible our goals were.	1	2	3	4	5
21. If my partner and I broke up, I don't know how I would cope.	1	2	3	4	5
22. It drives me crazy when my partner doesn't pay enough attention to me.	1	2	3	4	5
23. I'm so in love with my partner that I sometimes have trouble concentrating on anything else.	1	2	3	4	5
24. I cannot relax if I suspect that my partner is with someone else.	1	2	3	4	5
25. I wish I could spend every minute of every day with my partner.	1	2	3	4	5
26. I would rather suffer myself than let my partner suffer.	1	2	3	4	5
27. I am usually willing to sacrifice my own wishes to let my partner achieve her/his goals.	1	2	3	4	5
28. Whatever I own is my partner's to use as she/he pleases.	1	2	3	4	5
29. When my partner behaves badly, I still love her/him fully and unconditionally.	1	2	3	4	5
30. I would endure all things for the sake of my partner.	1	2	3	4	5

Add up the following items to get your score on each love style.

Eros: Items 1–5 _____

Ludus: Items 6–10 _____

Storge: Items 11–15 _____

Pragma: Items 16–20 _____

Mania: Items 21–25 _____

Agape: Items 26–30 _____

Higher scores mean that you possess more of a particular love style. The highest possible score for a given style is 25; the lowest possible score is 5.

SOURCE: This is an abbreviated, modified version of Hendrick and Hendrick's (1990) love attitudes scale.

Storge: Friendship Love

This type of love, which is also called **companionate love**, is based on high levels of intimacy and commitment but comparatively low levels of passion (Sternberg, 1986, 1988). Grote and Frieze (1994) defined friendship love as "a comfortable, affectionate, trusting love for a likable partner, based on a deep sense of friendship and involving companionship and the enjoyment of common activities, mutual interests, shared laughter" (p. 275). Friendship love has been called the glue that keeps relationships together because it is thought to be enduring. However, Berscheid (2010) cautioned that storgic love is based on shows of similarity, reciprocal self-disclosure, shared activities, and mutual validation. If these activities wane, so too will friendship love.

Storgic lovers have relationships based on affection, shared values and goals, and compatibility (Lee, 1988). Physical attraction is not as important as security, companionship, task sharing, and joint activity. Indeed, when asked what they find attractive in potential romantic partners, storgic individuals endorse personality characteristics, such as intelligence, understanding, a good personality, compassion, and communication skills rather than physical characteristics (Levine et al., 2006). Although these relationships are not very exciting, they are dependable and stable. Levine and colleagues found that people with a storgic style tended not to report using secret tests, which are indirect, sometimes sneaky ways of trying to find out information, such as asking third parties what they know, seeing if your partner gets jealous when you flirt with someone, or taking a break to find out if your partner will miss you (see Chapter 4 for more on secret tests). Presumably, storgic lovers do not need to use secret tests because their relationships tend to be secure with little uncertainty.

For storgic individuals, love often is framed as a partnership or a lifelong journey. Thus, it is important that the two individuals want the same things—perhaps a home and family, or perhaps independence and the ability to travel together to exotic places. Like a person with an old pair of blue jeans, storgic lovers feel extremely comfortable with each other, and emotions tend to be positive but muted. Unlike some other love styles, storgic lovers do not experience many intense emotional highs or lows. Yet this type of love tends to last. Because storgic lovers trust each other and do not require high levels of emotional stimulation and arousal, they are able to withstand long separations. For example, military couples may be better able to withstand their time apart if they are storgic lovers. Although they are likely to be sad when parted from each other, their trust and relational security keeps them from being distressed. Other types of lovers (e.g., erotic or manic lovers) feel much higher levels of distress because their relationships are fueled by physical attraction and the physical presence of the loved one. Of course, it is important to keep in mind that, although trust and security can provide a safety net for a relationship, too much stability can lead to predictability and boredom. Thus, bringing excitement and emotion to the relationship is often the biggest challenge for storgic lovers.

Ludus: Game-Playing Love

Ludic lovers see relationships as fun, playful, and casual; they view relationships as games to be played. Like eros lovers, they look for partners who are physically attractive and good lovers (Levine et al., 2006). The opening lines ludic lovers report using highlight the game-playing aspect of this love style. Specifically, Levine and associates found that ludus was associated with using cute or flippant opening lines when meeting people, such as saying, "Someone like you should be arrested for being too beautiful." The lack of commitment that characterizes the ludic style is also reflected in their communication; ludic lovers are less likely to report using increased contact, relationship talk, or bids for commitment (e.g., agreeing to have an exclusive relationship) than are people with other love styles (Levine et al., 2006). Instead, ludic lovers intensify their relationships by engaging in more affectionate communication and sexual intimacy. Compared to the other love styles, individuals with the ludic style are also the least likely to value communication skills related to emotional support and comfort within their relationships (Kunkel & Burleson, 2003).

Because they avoid commitment and prefer to play the field rather than settle down with one person (Lee, 1988), ludic lovers are also more likely to have on-again, off-again relationships and to use certain types of secret tests. Levine and fellow researchers (2006) found that, rather than using direct communication, ludic lovers reported trying to get information indirectly by asking third parties, checking for fidelity or jealousy, and increasing the costs in the relationship to see if the partner will still stick around. Ludic lovers also tend to use negative strategies to try to maintain their relationships, such as making the partner jealous or being unfaithful (Goodboy et al., 2010). People with the ludic style also share relatively little personal information with their partners and are slow to develop intimate relationships (Hendrick & Hendrick, 1986). Some ludic lovers are self-sufficient individuals who put personal goals and activities ahead of their relationships, similar to Gabriela described at the beginning of this chapter. Many students and recent college graduates adopt the ludic style, especially if they feel they are not ready for a highly committed romantic relationship. Instead, they may feel that school or career takes precedence over relational involvements. When these individuals are ready and when they meet the right person, they are likely to move out of the ludic style and into a more committed style of loving.

Mania: Possessive Love

The manic style is a combination of eros and ludus, and therefore contains elements related to passion and game-playing. Manic lovers tend to be more demanding, dependent, possessive, and jealous than people with other love styles (Lee, 1973, 1988). They often feel a strong need to be in control and to know everything that the partner is doing. The classic song "Every Breath You Take," by the Police, exemplifies the manic lover's desire to monitor "every breath you take, every move you make, every smile you fake." Manic lovers feel high levels of physical attraction and passion for their partners (Hendrick et al., 1988). Perhaps surprisingly, manic lovers are not interested in finding partners who are intelligent or good lovers; instead they want sensitive

partners who understand their feelings (Levine et al., 2006). Finding a sensitive partner who can cope with the emotional highs and lows that manic lovers often experience may be advantageous. Manic lovers often want to spend every minute with the partner, and any perceived lack of interest or enthusiasm by the partner, or any physical separation, results in extreme emotional lows. By contrast, when the beloved person reciprocates affection, the manic lover experiences an emotional high. A sensitive partner may be equipped to cope with these reactions while satisfying the manic partner's needs.

The emotional highs and lows associated with mania are also reflected in communication. Manic individuals report using a lot of communication aimed at intensifying the closeness within their relationships (Levine et al., 2006). They also report using secret tests relatively frequently, including triangle tests designed to make the partner jealous or see if the partner will be faithful, and endurance tests designed to see if the partner will stay with them even if they behave badly (Levine et al.). In an effort to maintain their relationships, manic lovers also tend to use some negative behaviors, such as trying to make the partner feel jealous, spying on the partner, and engaging in destructive conflict designed to control the partner (Goodboy et al., 2010). Of course, not all manic lovers engage in these potentially destructive behaviors. Many people experience a mild form of mania—they feel jealous when their partners flirt with an ex-boyfriend or ex-girlfriend; they find themselves constantly thinking about the partner; and their happiness seems to depend, at least in part, on having a relationship with the person they love. When these thoughts and feelings become extreme, a more negative form of mania emerges.

Agape: Compassionate Love

Agapic love revolves around caring, concern, and tenderness, and is more focused on giving than receiving (Lee, 1988; Sprecher & Fehr, 2005). The agapic style contains elements of both eros and storge (Lee, 1973). An agapic lover has a deep, abiding, highly passionate love for a partner—although not only in a physical sense. The storge side of agapic love stresses the enduring and secure nature of the relationship, which helps explain why agapic individuals are able to love their partners unconditionally. These individuals look for partners with a host of positive personal characteristics, including a sense of humor, intelligence, understanding, compassion, caring, communication skills, and sensitivity (Levine et al., 2006).

Once in a relationship, agapic lovers are motivated by an intense concern for their partner's well-being. They are willing to make sacrifices for their partner, even at the expense of their own needs and desires. For example, an agapic husband might decide not to pursue having a large family (even though he really wants one) if his wife had a difficult first pregnancy. Agapic love is associated with prosocial behavior, with agapic (as well as manic) lovers reporting that they use the most communication designed to intensify their relationships (Levine et al., 2006). Unlike those with the manic style, however, agapic lovers tend not to use secret tests in their relationships. This pattern of communication reflects the intense, passionate part of agapic love that is related to eros, combined with the stable part of agapic love that is related to storage. Although this description might make agapic love seem ideal, there are some drawbacks to this style. Agapic lovers sometimes seem to be "above" everyone else. Their partners often haven trouble matching their high level of unconditional love, which can lead to feelings of discomfort and guilt. In addition, agapic lovers sometimes put their partners on too high of a pedestal, leading their partners to worry that they cannot live up to such an idealized image. Agapic love may also have an easier time flourishing in relationships that are considered fair and equitable (Berscheid, 2010). So, if one partner is doing all the giving and the other is doing all the receiving, levels of agapic love may drop off.

Pragma: Practical Love

The pragmatic style combines elements of both storge and ludus. As Lee (1988) explained, storge comes into play because pragmatic lovers are seeking a compatible partner. Undertones of the ludus style also are evident in many pragmatic lovers, who typically avoid emotional risk taking and commit to a relationship only after careful thought and considerable time. Pragmatic lovers search for a person who fits a particular image in terms of vital statistics, such as age, height, religion, and occupation, as well as preferred characteristics, such as being a loyal partner or having the potential to be a good parent. In Levine and colleagues' (2006) study, the pragma love style was also associated with looking for a partner who had money and was successful. Lee (1988) used a computer dating service metaphor to help describe the pragma style. If you went to a dating service, you might indicate that you are looking for a petite brunette who is Jewish, likes sports, and has a stable job. Or, you might request a college-educated male who is older than you, has a good sense of humor, and loves children. In either case, you would have specified vital statistics that are most important to you.

Pragmatic lovers have a "common-sense, problem-solving approach to life and love" that is reflected in their communication style (Taraban et al., 1998, p. 346). For example, when meeting a potential partner, individuals with the pragma style tend to use direct opening lines, such as simply stating their name and introducing themselves (Levine et al., 2006). When they want to intensify a relationship, they are likely to engage in social enmeshment strategies, such as getting to know their partner's friends and family. Such a strategy is practical because it gives people insight into how they fit in the partner's social network if the relationship grows serious. Practical lovers also try to present a positive personal appearance when they want to escalate their relationships (Levine et al., 2006). As a way of obtaining additional information to help them decide if a partner is right for them, pragmatic lovers sometimes engage in secrets tests such as seeing if the partner gets jealous, spending time apart to see if they miss each other, and publicly presenting the partner to check others' reactions (Levine et al.). For example, a pragmatic lover might introduce her new love interest as "my really good friend" to see if he objects or wants to be called her "boyfriend." Practical lovers also use spying to get information and try to maintain their relationships (Goodboy et al., 2010). The practical nature of this style has benefits; people tend to match themselves up with those with whom they are compatible. But if love is based only on practical concerns, it can be lifeless and dull. Some level of intimacy and passion is required to put the spark into a relationship. For pragmatic lovers, intimacy and passion sometimes develop after realistic concerns have laid the foundation for the relationship.

Differences Due to Sex and Culture

Lee's original work, as well as subsequent research, suggests that the tendency to identify with the various love styles differs somewhat for men versus women. Studies have shown women from the United States and Portugal score higher than men on pragma (Bernardes, Mendes, Sarmento, Silva, & Moreira, 1999; Hendrick & Hendrick, 1986), while men tend to score higher in ludus and agape (Bernardes et al., 1999; Kunkel & Burleson, 2003; Sprecher & Toro-Morn, 2002). The finding that women tend to be more pragmatic is in line with other research showing that women are rational lovers who are choosier about their partners. The finding that men tend to identify with ludus fits with research showing that men are generally less committed to relationships than are women. Yet studies have also found that men generally fall in love faster than do women (Huston, Surra, Fitzgerald, & Cate, 1981; Kanin, Davidson, & Scheck, 1970) and that they usually say "I love you" first in heterosexual romantic relationships (Owen, 1987; Tolhuizen, 1989), which could help explain why some studies have shown men to be more agapic than women. Together these seemingly contradictory findings suggest that, although men may hesitate to make a strong commitment, when they do fall in love, they do it more quickly and emotionally than do women.

As noted previously, some types of love tend to be experienced similarly across different cultures. For example, Jankowiak and Fischer (1992) tested the idea that romantic (or erotic) love is a product of Western culture. Contrary to this idea, they found romantic love to exist in 147 of the 166 cultures sampled. Based on these data, Jankowiak and Fischer suggested that romantic love is nearly universal. Friendship love also appears to cross cultural boundaries, with many people from many different cultures around the globe embracing the warmth and security that storgic love offers. Another study showed that young adults from the United States, Russia, and Japan were similar in terms of their love styles (Sprecher et al., 1994).

There are some cultural differences in love styles, however. People from cultures that endorse arranged marriages believe more strongly in pragmatic love than do people in cultures in where people marry for love alone. In arranged marriages, the parents, often with the community, match their children based on perceived compatibility and an equitable exchange of resources, which makes practical love highly relevant. Research conducted in India, for example, has shown that people who believe in arranged marriages tend to value the conjugal love that emerges from a socially sanctioned and family-approved union more than they value romantic love (Gupta, 1976). Couples in arranged marriages also report a larger increase in love over time compared to nonarranged marriages (Gupta & Singh, 1982), which suggests that love can develop and grow in some relationships that begin purely on the basis of practical love.

In addition to being more prevalent in countries where arranged marriages are common, pragma is also a popular love style in China, where people tend to endorse both pragmatic and agapic types of love more than people from the United States (Sprecher & Toro-Morn, 2002). Although many people in the United States do identify with the agapic love style (Levine et al., 2006), it is even more prevalent in Asian cultures where people focus on group harmony and cohesiveness rather than individual needs. People in the United States and East Asian countries may also emphasize different aspects of the agapic style, with those from the United States valuing unconditional love, and those from China, Japan, and South Korea valuing caregiving (Kline, Horton, & Zhang, 2008). There are also differences in how love is communicated across cultures, as discussed in Box 7.3.

BOX 7.3 Highlights

Communicating Love American and Non-American Style

Love is a universal emotion, so it should be communicated the same way across different cultures, right? Well, not always. Research has shown that love is communicated both similarly and differently across cultures.

Similarity Across Cultures

Self-disclosure, social support, and shared experiences are related to love across cultures. One study showed that dating relationships characterized by either friendship or romantic love contain higher levels of self-disclosure than same-sex or cross-sex friendships for both U.S. and Japanese college students (Kito, 2005). Another study investigated how people in China, Japan, South Korea, and the United States communicate love to their friends and spouses (Kline et al., 2008). Across all these countries, people reported expressing love to friends by sharing common experiences, being supportive, and engaging in open discussion. With spouses, people also reported communicating love through physical intimacy and verbal statements, such as saying "I love you" and "I miss you."

Differences Across Cultures

Verbal expressions of love may be valued more in certain cultures than others. In individualistic cultures, such as the United States, where self-expression and individual feelings are valued, people are especially likely to verbalize their love by saying "I love you" (Wilkins & Gareis, 2006). People from Latino cultures also appear to say "I love you" to their romantic partners, friends, and family more than do people from other non-U.S. cultures (Wilkins & Gareis). In contrast, nonverbal expressions of love may be valued more in cultures where people pay especially close attention to subtle contextual cues, which is the case in many Asian countries.

Culture may affect the activities people see as expressing love. Activities are valued differently across cultures. People in more developed countries have more leisure time, whereas those in less developed countries may work together more often. One study demonstrated that there are subtle differences in the types of activities that people in the United States versus East Asian countries saw as expressing love in their marriages. For spouses from the United States, sports, food preparation, and shopping were key activities. For East Asians, talking and food preparation were most important.

Marston and Hecht's Love Ways

There is also individual variability in how people communicate love. For example, in addition to thinking about love differently, Gabriela and Brian appear to have different styles of communicating love. Marston, Hecht, and colleagues developed a system for measuring different styles of communicating and experiencing love (Hecht, Marston, & Larkey, 1994; Marston & Hecht, 1994; Marston, Hecht, Manke, McDaniel, & Reeder, 1998; Marston, Hecht, & Robers, 1987). Specifically, they looked at physiological and behavioral responses to love, with behavior encompassing both verbal and nonverbal communication.

To identify different ways of loving, Marston and colleagues (1987) conducted interviews to determine the types of feelings and behaviors that occur when people experience love. First, they asked people to describe physiological changes that occur when they are in love. The most common response was that people feel more energetic and emotionally intense when in love. People also reported feeling (1) beautiful and healthy; (2) warm and safe; (3) nervous, as manifested by butterflies or knots in the stomach; (4) stronger than normal; and (5) less hungry, with a marked loss of appetite. Next, the researchers asked, "How do you communicate love to your partner?" The top five responses were (1) saying "I love you" to the partner; (2) doing special things for the partner; (3) being supportive, understanding, and attentive; (4) touching the partner; and (5) simply being together. Of these, saying "I love you" was the most common response, with 75% of respondents mentioning it. The researchers also asked, "How does your partner communicate love to you?" The top five responses were similar to those listed previously. Saying "I love you" again emerged as the most common answer, with 70% of the participants identifying this strategy. The next most common responses were showing love through touch and sexual contact, being supportive, doing favors or giving gifts, and engaging in behaviors that show togetherness. Other less frequently mentioned behaviors included communicating emotion, engaging in eye contact, and smiling. Together these findings show that love is communicated and received in a variety of ways, but that verbally telling our partners we love them is a particularly important way of expressing love. This may explain why Brian wishes that Gabriela would tell him she loves him more often.

Marston and his colleagues argued that love consists of interdependent thoughts, feelings, attitudes, and behaviors, and the subjective experience of love changes in importance throughout the relationship. They also suggested that relational partners can have similar or complementary styles, and that the degree of similarity versus complementarity often changes as partners adapt to each other (Marston & Hecht, 1994). Thus, love experiences are unique at any given time and for any given person or relationship. Nonetheless, Marston and colleagues (1987) found that the physiological and behavioral responses to love could be grouped into seven categories or love ways, with these **love ways** representing the experiences of over 90% of lovers:

1. *Collaborative love:* Love is seen as a partnership that involves mutual support and negotiation, increases energy, and intensifies emotion.

2. *Active love:* Love is based on activity and doing things together. It also involves feelings of increased strength and self-confidence.

3. *Intuitive love:* Love is a feeling often communicated through nonverbal behavior such as touch and gaze, and experienced through physical reactions such as feeling warm all over, feeling nervous, and losing one's appetite.

4. *Committed love:* Love is based on commitment and involves experiencing strong feelings of connection, spending time together, and discussing the future.

5. *Secure love:* Love is based on security and intimacy. It is experienced through feelings of safety and warmth, and communicated through intimate self-disclosure.

6. *Expressive love:* Love is shown through overt behavior. It involves doing things for the partner and saying "I love you" frequently.

7. *Traditional romantic love:* Love involves togetherness and commitment. When people are in love, they feel beautiful and healthy.

Understanding each other's love style may help partners maintain a happy relationship. Marston and Hecht (1994) provide specific advice for managing love styles in ways that maximize relational satisfaction. First, they suggested that people recognize that their partner's love style might be different from their own. For example, if Brian expresses love through public affection, he should not necessarily expect Gabriela to do the same. In fact, Gabriela might dislike showing affection in public and prefer to cuddle in private or to show her love through shared activities. Second, people should be careful not to overvalue particular elements of their love way. For example, Gabriela seems to have an active love style. Therefore, she might worry if she and Brian start to develop different sports interests or argue about which old movies to watch. If this happens, Gabriela should recognize that other aspects of their relationship may still reflect their love for one another. Finally, people should avoid statements like "If you really loved me, you'd give me more space" (as Gabriela might say) or "If you really loved me, you'd tell me more often" (as Brian might say). Instead, Brian and Gabriela should focus on the various other ways that they express love for one another. Remember that any two people bring different ideologies and expectations about love to the relationship. The key may be to appreciate what each partner brings to the table, rather than wishing that the table was set in a different way.

ATTACHMENT THEORY

So far, we have shown that scholars classify love in many different ways. Lee's six styles of love are based largely on ideology. Marston and Hecht's seven love ways are based on how people experience and express love through verbal and nonverbal communication. Attachment theorists take yet another approach in studying love. According to attachment theorists such as Hazan and Shaver (1987), love is best conceptualized as a process of attachment, which includes forming a bond and becoming close to someone. **Attachment theory** takes a social-developmental approach, stressing how interactions with others affect people's attachment style across the life span. Children first learn to develop attachments through communication with caregivers. As children grow, they develop a sense of independence that is rooted in security. Finally, security in adulthood is based on being self-sufficient when necessary, while also having the ability to provide care and support for another adult in a love relationship that functions as a partnership (Ainsworth & Bowlby, 1991).

Communication plays a central role in attachment theory (Guerrero, 2008). Communication is one of the key causes of attachment style. People's communication with others leads them to think about

themselves and others in ways that lead them to develop particular attachment styles. Communication is also a result of one's attachment style. As discussed later in this chapter, people with different attachment styles vary along a wide array of communication variables, including self-disclosure, emotional expression, caregiving, conflict behavior, and nonverbal behavior, just to name a few. People also report different levels of relational satisfaction depending on their attachment style and the attachment style of their partner. Some research suggests that communication plays an important role here too. Partners with certain attachment styles may be happier in their relationships because they are better communicators.

The Propensity for Forming Attachments

Originally, attachment theory was studied within the context of child-caregiver relationships (Ainsworth, 1969; Ainsworth, Blehar, Waters, & Wall, 1978; Ainsworth & Wittig, 1969; Bowlby, 1969, 1973, 1980). Later, researchers extended the theory to adult romantic relationships (Hazan & Shaver, 1987). Although parent-child and romantic relationships have received the most attention, attachment theory applies to all types of close relationship, including friendships and sibling relationships. Because people usually want to be part of a social group and to be loved and cared for by others, attachment theorists believe that people have a natural tendency to try to develop close relational bonds with others throughout the life span.

In childhood, the need to develop attachments is an innate and necessary part of human development (Ainsworth, 1991). According to Bowlby (1969, 1973, 1980), attachment is an essential component within a larger system that functions to keep children in close proximity to caregivers, which protects children from danger and provides them with a secure base from which to explore their world. For example, toddlers may feel free to try the slides and swings at the playground if they know that a caregiver is close by to act as a **secure base** if they get hurt or need help. Similar to the way soldiers return to a military base to get supplies or reinforcements, children use their caregivers as secure bases that allow them to feel comfortable exploring their surroundings. Exploration of the environment eventually leads to self-confidence and autonomy. Thus, one goal of the attachment system is to give children a sense of both security and independence. Another goal is to help children develop a healthy capacity for intimacy.

In adulthood, attachment influences the type of relationship a person desires. For example, some people (like Gabriela) might want a relationship that is emotionally reserved, while others (like Brian) might desire a relationship that is emotionally charged. Bowlby (1977) and Ainsworth (1989, 1991), who pioneered research on child-caregiver attachments, both believed that attachment typifies intimate adult relationships, with Bowlby (1977) arguing that attachment is characteristic of all individuals from the cradle to the grave. The type of attachment individuals form depends on their cognitive conceptions of themselves and others. These cognitions, or internal working models, influence orientations toward love, intimacy, and interpersonal interaction in adult relationships.

Internal Working Models and Attachment Styles

According to attachment theorists, people have different styles of attachment depending on how they perceive themselves and others. These perceptions, which are called **internal working models**, are cognitive representations of oneself and potential partners that reflect an individual's past experiences in close relationships and help an individual understand the world (Bowlby, 1973; Bretherton, 1988; Collins & Read, 1994). Models of both self and others fall along a positive-negative continuum. A positive self-model is "an internalized sense of self-worth that is not dependent on ongoing external validation" (Bartholomew, 1993, p. 40). Thus, individuals who hold positive self-models view themselves as self-sufficient, secure, and lovable. Those holding negative self-models see themselves as dependent, insecure, and unworthy of love and affection. Positive models of others reflect expectations about how supportive, receptive, and accepting

people are, as well as how rewarding it is to be in an intimate relationship. Individuals with positive models of others see relationships as worthwhile and possess *approach* orientations toward intimacy. Individuals with negative working models of others see relationships as relatively unrewarding and possess *avoidant* orientations toward intimacy.

Depending on individuals' configurations of internal working models—that is, the "mix" of how positive or negative their models of self and others are—they develop different attachment styles. An **attachment style** is a social interaction style that is consistent with the type and quality of relationship one wishes to share with others, based on working models of self and others (Bartholomew, 1990). Attachment styles include one's own communication style, the way one processes and interprets others' behavior, and the way one reacts to others' behavior (Guerrero & Burgoon, 1996). Attachment styles are also associated with "relatively coherent and stable patterns of emotion and behavior [that] are exhibited in close relationships" (Shaver, Collins, & Clark, 1996, p. 25).

Attachment Styles in Childhood

Early communication with primary caregivers shapes children's internal models of themselves and others and sets the stage for later attachments (Ainsworth, Blehar, Waters, & Wall, 1978; Bowlby, 1977). Although new interactions with significant others continue to modify the way people see themselves and relational partners, the first two to three years of life (and especially the first year) are critical in developing these internal models. By the time a baby is about six weeks old, the infant already shows a preference for the primary caregiver—usually the mother. For example, if a 2-month-old baby is crying, she might be best comforted by her mother. At around 14 to 20 months old, toddlers are usually attached to their mothers and feel separation anxiety when they leave. At this time, babysitters may have trouble with their charges, who often become distressed when they realize their mother, who functions as their secure base, is not around. Some of our students have reported experiences like this, where a niece or nephew who used to be fine when alone with them suddenly seems nervous and starts crying or looking around for mom.

Most children emerge from the first two years of life with secure, healthy attachments to caregivers (Ainsworth et al., 1978; Bowlby, 1969). If this is the case, they have developed positive models of both themselves and others. Not all children are so lucky. About 30% of children develop insecure attachment styles because they have negative models of themselves or others. Bowlby's original work showed that children who were raised in institutions and deprived of their mother's care for extended periods of time were more likely to develop insecure attachments (Bowlby, 1969, 1973). Ainsworth and her colleagues later demonstrated that the type of care children receive at home influences their attachment style (Ainsworth, 1969, 1982, 1989; Ainsworth & Eichberg, 1991; Ainsworth et al., 1978; Ainsworth

& Wittig, 1969). They delineated three types of infant attachment: secure, avoidant, and anxious ambivalent.

Secure Children

The majority of children fall into the secure category. Secure children tend to have responsive and warm parents, to receive moderate levels of stimulation, and to engage in synchronized interaction with their caregivers. The fit between the caregiver and the child is crucial. Caregivers may need to adjust their style of communication to accommodate the child. Thus, one child may need a lot of cuddling and reassurance while another may prefer to be left alone. This helps explain why children from the same family environment may develop different attachment styles. Children who develop secure attachments to a caregiver are more likely to feel free to explore, approach others, and be positive

SOURCE: ©iStockphoto.com/RonTech2000.

Although mothers are often considered to be the primary caregiver, the way fathers communicate affection also has profound effects on a child's attachment style.

toward strangers than are insecure types. Secure children are also likely to protest separation and then to show happiness when reunited with their caregivers. These children tend to develop positive models of self and others.

Avoidant Children

Some insecure children develop an avoidant attachment style (Ainsworth et al., 1978). Avoidant children tend to have caregivers who are either insensitive to their signals or try too hard to please. In addition, avoidant children are often either over- or understimulated, which leads to physiological arousal and a flight response. When overstimulated, they retreat from social interaction to avoid being overloaded. When understimulated, they learn how to cope without social interaction. Because their caregivers are not able to fulfill their needs, they develop negative models of others. These children stay within themselves, seldom explore their environment, and are rarely positive toward strangers. They tend not to protest separation from caregivers and show little emotion when the caregiver returns.

Anxious-Ambivalent Children

Other insecure children develop anxious-ambivalent attachment styles (Ainsworth et al., 1978). These children tend to be the product of inconsistent caregiver communication; sometimes the caregiver is appropriately responsive, other times the caregiver is neglectful or overstimulating. Anxious-ambivalent children often have caregivers who are preoccupied with their own problems, such as relational conflict, divorce, or substance abuse. Instead of blaming the caregiver (or the caregiver's situation) for this inconsistency, they blame themselves and develop self-models of doubt, insecurity, and uncertainty. Anxious-ambivalent children often are tentative when exploring their environment in the presence of their caregivers and fearful of exploration if alone. They protest separation from caregivers vehemently, yet are both relieved and angry when the caregiver returns. This contradiction is reflected in their label—they are anxious upon separation and ambivalent when the caregiver returns. Sometimes these children develop positive models

of others because they do receive some comfort and security from caregivers.

Attachment Styles in Adulthood

Attachment styles are also relevant in adult relationships. Hazan and Shaver (1987) conceptualized love as an attachment process that is "experienced somewhat differently by different people because of variations in their attachment histories" (p. 511). Using Ainsworth and colleagues' (1978) three attachment styles as a guide, Hazan and Shaver (1987) proposed that adults can have secure, avoidant, or anxious-ambivalent attachments to their romantic partners. **Secures** are comfortable getting close to and depending on romantic partners, and seldom worry about being abandoned. They strive for a balance of autonomy and closeness in their relationships. **Avoidants** are uncomfortable getting close to or depending on romantic partners. They value autonomy over relational closeness. Finally, **anxious ambivalents** tend to be overinvolved, demanding, and dependent (Collins & Read, 1990; Feeney & Noller, 1991). They value relational closeness over autonomy. As Hazan and Shaver (1987) noted, anxious ambivalents "want to merge completely with another person, and this desire sometimes scares people away" (p. 515). Thus, if interdependence is portrayed as a spider's web, secures would create intimacy webs that are intertwined, avoidants would keep their webs relatively separate, and anxious ambivalents would build webs filled with heavy entanglements.

Shortly after Hazan and Shaver published their groundbreaking work, Bartholomew (1990) proposed a four-category system of attachment. She argued that the working models a person holds about self and others combine to produce four, rather than three, attachment styles: secure, preoccupied, dismissive, and fearful (see Figure 7.2). Research has confirmed that people with these four attachments differ in important ways, including their communication styles. Box 7.4 summarizes some of the key attachment-style differences in communication.

Secure: The Prosocial Style

Secure individuals have positive models of themselves and others ("I'm okay and you're okay").

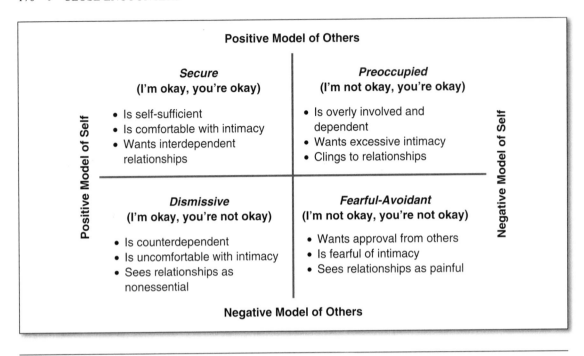

Figure 7.2 Bartholomew's Four Attachment Styles

SOURCE: Adapted from Guerrero (1996).

The secures in Bartholomew's system are essentially the same as those described by Hazan and Shaver. They feel good about themselves and their relationships, and they display "high self-esteem and an absence of serious interpersonal problems" (Bartholomew, 1990, p. 163). These individuals have the capacity for close, fulfilling relationships. They are likely to have realistic expectations, be satisfied with their relationships, and be comfortable depending on others and having others depend on them. Although they value relationships, they are not afraid of being alone.

Secure individuals have a communication style that displays social skill and promotes healthy relationships (Guerrero & Jones, 2005). They seek social support when distressed and know how to provide support and comfort to their relational partners (Kunce & Shaver, 1994; Weger & Polcar, 2002). In general, their communication tends to be pleasant, attentive, and expressive (Guerrero, 1996; Le Poire, Shepard, & Duggan, 1999), and they smile at, laugh with, and touch their romantic partners more than do individuals with other attachment styles (Tucker & Anders, 1998). When secures are distressed they are usually able to express their negative feelings appropriately and seek support from others (Feeney, 1995; Simpson & Rholes, 1994). They cope with feelings of anger, jealousy, and sadness by behaving in ways that bolster their self-esteem and help maintain relationships (Guerrero, 1998; Guerrero, Farinelli, & McEwan, 2009; Sharpsteen & Kirkpatrick, 1997). In conflict situations, secure individuals are more likely than individuals with other attachment styles to compromise and solve problems (Bippus & Rollin, 2003; Pistole, 1989). Secure individuals also employ high levels of relational maintenance behavior, such as engaging in romantic activities, talking about commitment, and sharing activities (Bippus & Rollin, 2003; Guerrero & Bachman, 2008; Simon & Baxter, 1993). A study of married couples also showed that secure individuals were most likely to express positive emotions—such as love, pride, and happiness—to their spouses (Feeney, 1999).

BOX 7.4 Highlights

Attachment-Style Differences in Communication

	Secure	Preoccupied	Fearful	Dismissive
Conflict behavior	Most compromising and adept with problem solving	Demanding, exhibits dominating behavior, nagging, whining	Accommodating, responds passively	Withdrawing, less accommodating, more interrupting
Maintenance behavior	Highest level of maintenance	High level of maintenance	Relatively low level of maintenance	Less maintenance overall, especially less romance and assurances
Emotional expression	Readily expresses emotions in a direct, prosocial manner	Expresses negative emotions using aggression or passive aggression	Inhibits the expression of negative emotions	Experiences and expresses emotions (negative and positive) the least
Self-disclosure	High levels of appropriate disclosure, able to elicit disclosure from others	High levels of disclosure that is sometimes inappropriate or indiscriminate	Low levels of disclosure, especially with strangers or acquaintances	Low levels of disclosure
Nonverbal intimacy	Relatively high levels of facial and vocal pleasantness, laughter, touch, and smiling	Mix of positive and negative nonverbal cues, depending on situation	Relatively low levels of facial and vocal pleasantness, expressiveness, and smiling	Relatively low levels of facial and vocal pleasantness, expressiveness, and smiling
Social skill	Assertive, responsive to others, able to provide effective care and comfort	Overly sensitive, difficulty controlling emotional expression	Trouble expressing self and being assertive, exhibits anxiety cues such as lack of fluency and long response latencies	Trouble expressing self and comforting others

Preoccupied: The Emotional Style

Preoccupied individuals, who are similar to anxious ambivalents, have positive models of others but negative models of themselves ("You're okay but I'm not okay"). These individuals are overly dependent on relationships. As Bartholomew (1990) put it, preoccupied individuals are characterized by "an insatiable desire to gain others' approval and a deep-seated feeling of unworthiness" (p. 163). Their relational identities often are much stronger than their self-identities; they need to have a relationship with someone to feel worthwhile. In fact, preoccupied individuals report feeling lost and unable to cope in the absence of a close relationship. They also are likely to cling to their relationships in times of trouble and to resist any attempts by a partner to de-escalate or terminate close relationships.

Preoccupied individuals exhibit mixed messages that reflect their high need for intimacy coupled with low self-confidence. In everyday interactions, they often appear pleasant, attentive, and expressive (Guerrero, 1996). However, when they become anxious their communication sometimes becomes unpleasant and self-focused. In one study, preoccupied individuals exhibited low levels of enjoyment when talking about relationship issues with their romantic partners (Tucker & Anders, 1998). In another study, preoccupied individuals were expressive but showed low levels of composure and altercentrism (a focus on the partner) when discussing a conflict issue (Guerrero & Jones, 2005). Preoccupied individuals are also overly sensitive and have trouble controlling their emotions (Guerrero & Jones, 2003). In their quest to develop intimacy, they sometimes disclose intimate information too quickly (Bartholomew & Horowitz, 1991; Mikulincer & Nachshon, 1991). Sometimes preoccupied individuals display demanding behavior in an attempt to hang onto their relationship or change their partners (Bartholomew & Horowitz, 1991; Guerrero & Langan, 1999). In conflict situations, they tend to engage in controlling behavior and to nag and whine (Creasey, Kershaw, & Boston, 1999; O'Connell-Corcoran & Mallinckrodt, 2000). Similarly, they tend to express anger using aggressive or passive aggressive behaviors (Feeney, 1995; Guerrero, Farinelli, &

McEwan, 2009). They also avoid discussing deception with their partners, which is perceived as an ineffective communication strategy (Jang, 2008).

Fearful: The Hesitant Style

Fearful individuals have negative models of both themselves and others ("I'm not okay and you're not okay"). Some of the avoidants in Hazan and Shaver's system fall in this category, as do a few of the anxious ambivalents, particularly when they have negative views of both others and themselves. The key characteristic of fearful avoidants is that they are afraid of hurt and rejection, often because they have experienced painful relationships in the past. Fearful individuals usually want to depend on someone but find it difficult to open up to others. As Bartholomew (1990) put it, fearful individuals "desire social contact and intimacy, but experience pervasive interpersonal distrust and fear of rejection" (p. 164).

Fearful individuals tend to avoid social situations and potential relationships because they fear rejection. Even when in relationships, they tend to be hesitant to communicate emotions or to initiate escalation of the relationship. Bartholomew (1990) noted the paradoxical nature of fearful individuals' actions and desires: By refusing to open up to others, they undermine their chances for building the very type of trusting relationship they desire. Their communication style reflects their fear and lack of trust. Guerrero (1996) found that fearful individuals were less fluent and used larger proxemic distances than individuals with other attachment styles. Other studies suggest that fearful individuals possess less social skill than people with other attachment styles. They tend to lack assertiveness (Anders & Tucker, 2000) and to appear uncomposed (Guerrero & Jones, 2005). They also have difficulty expressing emotions and responding to the emotions of others (Guerrero & Jones, 2003). Fearful individuals are both anxious and avoidant, and research shows that people who possess these two characteristics report using less relational maintenance behavior (e.g., showing affection and being positive and cheerful) in their relationships (Guerrero & Bachman, 2006). Fearful individuals also have difficulty confronting conflict issues; instead they tend to withdraw or accommodate the partner (Pistole, 1989).

Dismissive: The Detached Style

Dismissive individuals have positive models of themselves but negative models of others ("I'm okay but you're not okay"). Many of the avoidants in Hazan and Shaver's system would fall here. Dismissives can best be characterized as counterdependent. In other words, they are so self-sufficient that they shun close involvement with others. Some researchers suggest that counterdependence is a defensive strategy that allows people to feel good about themselves without opening themselves up to the criticisms and scrutiny of others. Dismissives neither desire nor fear close attachments, but rather lack the motivation to build and maintain intimate relationships (Bartholomew, 1990). They place a much higher value on autonomy than on relationships and tend to focus on less personal aspects of their lives, such as careers, hobbies, and self-improvement (Bartholomew, 1990).

Not surprisingly, dismissive individuals possess a highly avoidant attachment style. Yet unlike fearful individuals, dismissives are composed and self-confident (Anders & Tucker, 2000; Guerrero & Jones, 2005). Dismissive individuals generally exhibit less disclosure, conversational involvement, and affection than individuals with the secure or preoccupied style (Bartholomew & Horowitz, 1991; Guerrero, 1996). They report relatively low levels of relational maintenance behaviors, such as being romantic and giving assurances that they are committed to the relationship (Guerrero & Bachman, 2008; Simon & Baxter, 1993), and their partners see them as relatively uncaring and unsupportive (Kane et al., 2007). Dismissives also are seen as fairly dominant. They tend to interrupt their partners more than do those with other attachment styles (Guerrero & Langan, 1999), and they report low levels of accommodation and tend to withdraw during conflict (Feeney, Noller, & Roberts, 2000). When dismissives experience emotional distress, they often deny their feelings and insist on handling their problems without help from others (Bartholomew, 1993). As Simpson and Rholes (1994) put it, dismissives "distance themselves from others emotionally. Over time they come to see themselves as fully autonomous and immune to negative events" (p. 84).

Attachment and Relational Satisfaction

As the descriptions of the four attachment styles suggest, security is associated with relational satisfaction. In fact, both one's own security and the partner's security make a difference. In one of the first studies of adult attachment, Hazan and Shaver (1987) found that secure individuals reported having happier and more trusting relationships than insecure individuals. Individuals with negative models of self or others tend to report less satisfaction (Collins & Read, 1990; Feeney, 1994; Feeney, Noller, & Callan, 1994; Feeney, Noller, & Roberts, 1998; Simpson, 1990). In some studies, researchers have asked both partners in romantic couples to rate their own attachment style and relational satisfaction. These studies have shown that one person's attachment style predicts how satisfied the other person is. Specifically, Kane and fellow researchers (2007) found that men were happier when their partners were low in attachment anxiety (which is related to having a positive model of self), and women were happier when their partners were low in attachment avoidance (which is related to having a positive model of others). Guerrero and associates (2009) found that people were most likely to report high levels of relational satisfaction when their partners were high in security and low in both dismissiveness and preoccupation. Other studies have shown that relationships tend to be especially satisfying if both partners are secure (Senchak & Leonard, 1992).

Researchers have also tried to determine why secure attachment is related to being in a happier relationship. Communication provides one answer to this important question. Feeney and colleagues (2000) explained that communication may be "the underlying mechanism" that explains why secure partners have better relationships (p. 198). According to this reasoning, secure individuals engage in patterns of communication that promote closeness and cooperation, whereas insecure individuals engage in communication patterns that are more distant or demanding. Indeed, numerous studies have shown couples that include at least one insecure partner tend to exhibit negative communication patterns (Pearce & Halford, 2008). Several studies also support the idea that communication helps explain the link between attachment and relationship satisfaction. For example, Kane and colleagues (2007) found that security was related to caregiving, and that caregiving helped predict why some partners were more satisfied with their relationships than others. Other studies have shown that the affectionate communication, constructive conflict behavior, and self-disclosure that secure partners use is related to being happier in one's relationship (Feeney et al., 2000; Morrison, Urquize, & Goodlin-Jones, 1997).

Emotional communication provides another explanation for why people are more satisfied with relationships that include secure partners. Feeney and colleagues (1998) found that women reported being happier in relationships with secure men because those men tended to communicate sadness and other emotions directly and openly, allowing them to work out problems. Guerrero and colleagues (2009) found different patterns of emotional communication and relational satisfaction for people who had secure, dismissive, and preoccupied partners. People reported that their secure partners engaged in more prosocial emotional communication, such as discussing feelings in an open and calm manner, which led to more relationship satisfaction. Individuals perceived dismissive partners as using more detached communication, such as avoiding talking about their emotions, which was related to less satisfaction. Finally, people viewed their preoccupied partners as using more aggressive and passive aggressive expressions of anger, which was related to less satisfaction. Thus, the manner in which people communicate emotions helps explain why individuals are more satisfied with secure partners.

BOX 7.5 Put Yourself to the Test

What Is Your Attachment Style?

This questionnaire asks you to think about your general attitudes toward yourself, others, and relationships. Please rate yourself on each of these statements according to the following scale: 1 = strongly disagree, 7 = strongly agree.

	Disagree						Agree
1. I fit in well with other people.	1	2	3	4	5	6	7
2. I worry that people don't like me as much as I like them.	1	2	3	4	5	6	7
3. I would like to trust others, but I worry that if I open up too much people might reject me.	1	2	3	4	5	6	7
4. Sometimes others seem reluctant to get as close to me as I would like.	1	2	3	4	5	6	7
5. I worry a lot about the well-being of my relationships.	1	2	3	4	5	6	7
6. I feel smothered when a relationship takes too much time away from my personal pursuits.	1	2	3	4	5	6	7
7. I worry about getting hurt if I allow myself to get too close to someone.	1	2	3	4	5	6	7
8. I would like to have closer relationships but getting close makes me feel vulnerable.	1	2	3	4	5	6	7

	Disagree						Agree
9. I tend not to take risks in relationships for fear of getting hurt or rejected.	1	2	3	4	5	6	7
10. I rarely worry that I don't "measure up" to other people.	1	2	3	4	5	6	7
11. Achieving personal goals is more important to me than maintaining good relationships.	1	2	3	4	5	6	7
12. I avoid getting too close to others so that I won't get hurt.	1	2	3	4	5	6	7
13. I am confident that other people will like me.	1	2	3	4	5	6	7
14. I worry that others do not care about me as much as I care about them.	1	2	3	4	5	6	7
15. I wonder how I would cope without someone to love me.	1	2	3	4	5	6	7
16. I rarely worry that others might reject me.	1	2	3	4	5	6	7
17. Being independent is more important to me than having a good relationship.	1	2	3	4	5	6	7
18. I am confident that others will accept me.	1	2	3	4	5	6	7
19. I find it relatively easy to get close to people.	1	2	3	4	5	6	7
20. Pleasing myself is much more important to me than getting along with others.	1	2	3	4	5	6	7
21. I need relational partners to give me space to do "my own thing."	1	2	3	4	5	6	7
22. I sometimes worry that my relational partners will leave me.	1	2	3	4	5	6	7
23. It is easy for me to get along with others.	1	2	3	4	5	6	7
24. I frequently pull away from relational partners when I need time to pursue my personal goals.	1	2	3	4	5	6	7
25. I need to be in a close relationship to be happy.	1	2	3	4	5	6	7

Add up the following items and then divide by the number shown to get your score on each attachment style.

Security: Items 1+10+13+16+18+19+23 / 7 = _____

Preoccupation: Items 2+4+5+14+15+22+25 / 7 = _____

Dismissiveness: Items 6+11+17+20+21+24 / 6 = _____

Fearful: Items 3+7+8+9+12 / 5 = _____

Higher scores mean that you possess more of a particular attachment style. The highest possible score for a given style is 7; the lowest possible score is 1.

SOURCE: Adapted from Guerrero et al. (2009).

Stability and Change in Attachment Styles Across the Lifespan

By now, it may not be difficult to guess what attachment styles Brian and Gabriela have. (To assess your own attachment style, take the test in Box 7.5.) Brian appears to be somewhat preoccupied. He worries that he might care more for Gabriela than she cares for him. He also appears to desire high levels of overt affection in his relationships. Gabriela, on the other hand, seems somewhat dismissive. She wonders if she can commit enough time and energy to her relationship, and her priority seems to be her personal goals. If Gabriela and Brian stay together, are their attachment styles likely to change or stay the same during the course of their relationship? Have they had these attachment styles since childhood or could they have developed these styles recently? Finally, do they have the same attachment styles with their friends and family as they have with each other? Research investigating how stable attachment styles are across time suggests that the answer to all of these questions is "it depends." Studies have shown that around 25% to 30% of adults experience changes in their attachment style toward romantic partners (Davila, Burge, & Hammen, 1997; Davila, Karney, & Bradbury, 1999; Feeney & Noller, 1996). Similarly, in a study on adolescent friendships, 35% of high school students reported a change in attachment style from one year to the next (Miller, Notaro, & Zimmerman, 2002). These studies suggest that although attachment styles are fairly stable, they can be modified by new experiences.

Explanations for Stability

At least two forces work to stabilize a person's attachment style. First, communication with caregivers has an especially strong effect on a person's social development, including the attachment style a person develops. Bowlby (1969, 1973) believed that early interactions with caregivers provide a mental blueprint for thinking about oneself and others that carries into adulthood. An avoidant child thus has many obstacles to overcome to develop into a secure adult, including learning to trust others and being comfortable with closeness. Similarly, an anxious-ambivalent child needs to become self-confident and self-sufficient to achieve security. Such changes are possible but require time, effort, and the cooperation and patience of others.

A second source of stability is called the **reinforcement effect** (Bartholomew, 1993). According to this perspective, people communicate in cycles that reinforce their attachment style. For example, because secure individuals are self-confident and readily approach others, they are more likely to make friends and develop relationships, causing them to feel even better about themselves and others. Preoccupied individuals, by contrast, continually reach for higher levels of intimacy. Perhaps you have had a partner like this—someone who wanted to meet your family right away, told you how much she or he loved you on the third date, or wanted to move in with you after your first month together. A common reaction to these premature declarations of love and commitment is to try to de-escalate the relationship, which only makes the preoccupied person engage in more excessive intimacy and closeness. This process reinforces that individual's negative model of self ("My partner doesn't love me as much as I love her") and positive model of others ("Everything would be great if only I could get him to love me").

Fearful and dismissive individuals suffer from similarly paradoxical interaction patterns. More than anything else, fearful individuals need to build a secure, happy relationship to help them feel better about themselves and others. However, their fear of pain and rejection keeps them from reaching out to others and developing the kind of intimate relationship that would bring them out of their protective shells. Dismissives display similarly negative self-reinforcing patterns. If dismissives continually avoid highly committed relationships and refuse to ask others for help and support, they reinforce their view that other people are unnecessary and they should rely only on themselves. They miss the opportunity to discover ways in which committed relationships can enrich, rather than impede, personal satisfaction.

Explanations for Change

There are four primary explanations for change in attachment styles (Feeney et al., 2000). First, significant events such as divorce, marriage, reunion after a long separation, development of a new relationship, or the death of a loved one may modify a person's attachment style. For example, a fearful man may become more secure after reuniting with his ex-wife, and a secure young woman may become more dismissive when she heads off to college and away from those who love her. Second, a person's attachment style may be affected by a partner's style, as several studies have shown (e.g., Guerrero & Bachman, 2008; Le Poire et al., 1999). In the case of Gabriela and Brian, their opposing needs could cause them to become more dismissive and preoccupied, respectively. When Gabriela expresses a need for more space, Brian might feel a lack of closeness and crave more intimacy. When Brian expresses a need for more affection, Gabriela might pull away and retreat into her personal activities.

Third, people may have different attachment styles depending on relationship type (Baldwin & Fehr, 1995; Cozzarelli, Hoekstra, & Bylsma, 2000;

Pierce & Lydon, 2001). For example, Gabriela might have a dismissive attachment orientation toward Brian and her father, but a secure attachment orientation toward her mother and friends. The movie *Good Will Hunting* provides a good example of how attachment orientations sometimes vary on the basis of relationship type. Will exhibits classic fearful behavior with romantic partners—he avoids commitment because he is afraid of being hurt and abandoned as he was as a child in the foster care system. However, within his close-knit group of male friends, Will displays a secure attachment style. Finally, some researchers have suggested that stability (or instability) of attachment style is a personality characteristic, with some people more susceptible to change than others. So, Gabriela's attachment style could be more likely to change based on life events (e.g., what's happening at work) than Brian's.

SUMMARY AND APPLICATION

People approach loving relationships in a variety of ways. Every person has a unique set of perceptions, expectations, and preferences that contribute to that individual's love and attachment styles. When two people's styles interact within the context of a close relationship, another unique relational pattern emerges. Partners should realize that what works in one of their relationships might not necessarily work in others, and that it is difficult for two people to fully meet each other's expectations.

The attitudes Gabriela and Brian have about love and relationships are fairly common. From the description at the beginning of this chapter, Gabriela appears to have an active way of loving and a dismissive attachment style. Brian appears to have an expressive way of loving and a somewhat preoccupied attachment style. Of course, most people do not fall neatly into a love or attachment category. Take another look at Figure 7.2. Where would you fall on the dimensions representing positive versus negative models of self and others? You could fit squarely within a given category or you could fall on the border between categories. For instance, Gabriela might have an extremely positive model of self and only a slightly negative model of others,

and Brian might be on the border between preoccupation and security. Moreover, the interaction between Brian and Gabriela's styles is likely to produce a unique set of behaviors. Styles of love and attachment reflect some important differences in how people approach and communicate in close relationships, but it is crucial to see ourselves and others as complex individuals who do not always fit a particular profile.

People with different relational needs and communication styles, like Brian and Gabriela, can often work together to build happy relationships. One key to a successful relationship is for relational partners to help each other grow as individuals. For example, preoccupied individuals like Brian may need to make an effort to give their partners more space, while dismissive individuals like Gabriela may need to work on showing more affection. At the same time, individuals in relationships with people who have insecure attachment styles should be patient and understanding, rather than demanding more or less intimacy than their partners are comfortable giving. Relational partners should also understand and appreciate each other's ways of loving. For example, Brian may feel more secure if he realizes that Gabriela is showing that she cares for him when she plans activities for them to do together.

In the scenario at the beginning of this chapter, Brian also wonders if Gabriela really loves him. This is a difficult question to answer. Liking and loving differ in both quantitative and qualitative ways. Love is typically characterized by more attachment, caring, and commitment than liking, and love between romantic partners is also usually characterized by feelings of passion. Yet it is hard to quantify love, and there is no simple answer to the seemingly straightforward question, "What is love?" Love is a complex and variable phenomenon that defies simple definition. Indeed, instead of simply asking what love is, it may be more appropriate to ask, "What is love to me and to my partner, and how does love function in the unique relationship we share?" Thinking about these issues may be especially helpful to relational partners like Gabriela and Brian, who have different styles of loving and attachment.

DISCUSSION QUESTIONS

1. How would you distinguish love from liking? Do you think the difference between love and liking is more quantitative or qualitative? Why?

2. Do you think people's love styles change throughout their lives? If so, what factors do you think account for this change? How might culture affect people's love styles beyond what was discussed in this chapter?

3. According to attachment theory, parent-child communication forms the basis for personality development, including the capacity to have close, intimate adult relationships with others. To what extent do you agree or disagree that early communication with parents shapes a person's life? What other events and interactions have shaped your attachment style?

STUDENT STUDY SITE

Visit the study site at **www.sagepub.com/guerrero3e** for e-flashcards, survey and assessments from the chapter, and SAGE journal articles.

8

Communicating Sexually: The Closest Physical Encounter

Although Brittany, Sarah, and Taylor are sisters in the same sorority, their sex lives could not be more different. Brittany has been seeing the same man for four years and has an active sex life. She believes her boyfriend, Chris, is completely faithful but she insisted they both get tested to be sure they do not have STIs. She is on the pill and tries to be as responsible about sex as possible, yet she has never discussed her active sex life with her parents. Although she loves Chris, she is not completely sure he is the "one" for her. Sarah is deeply religious and has chosen to remain a virgin until after marriage. Sometimes she feels strange because most of the girls in the house are not virgins. She enjoys sexual activity with her boyfriend but always makes sure that they stop well short of sexual intercourse. Occasionally, her sisters are a bit unkind and call Sarah frigid or prudish, which makes Sarah feel that her values are out of the mainstream. Taylor dated men in the past but recently admitted to herself and the world that she has always been more attracted to women. She announced to her sisters that she is a lesbian and is in a committed, monogamous relationship with her partner, Leslie. Most of the women in the house accepted her fully; however, she has heard a few homophobic comments and caught some of her sisters exchanging strange glances when she mentions Leslie.

Sex is one of the most rewarding and difficult issues people face. In this chapter, we focus on sexual behavior and its importance in human relationships. Additionally, we examine communication related to the development of sexual attitudes and beliefs, initiation and refusal of sexual activity, coercion and harassment, and safe sex in short- and long-term relationships for both heterosexuals and homosexuals. Although many close relationships are platonic, some of our closest encounters are sexual, including romances and marriages. Most of the research has focused on sexual relationships between men and women; therefore, despite our best efforts to include information about relationships between gay men and lesbians, there is a heterosexual bias evident in the research in general as well as this chapter. Additionally, most studies focus on the attitudes and behaviors of couples in the United States; in other countries, sexual attitudes and behaviors may be quite different. Finally, the physiology of sex and sexual desire is beyond the scope of this chapter, although excellent books on these topics are available (see Rathus, Nevid, & Fishner-Rathus, 1993; Regan & Berscheid, 1999).

SEX IN RELATIONSHIPS

Research has shown that sexual interaction, including physical contact such as intimate kissing and touching, and sexual intercourse, is a vital part of dating and marital relationships. Although people experience some ambivalence about sex in premarital relationships (O'Sullivan & Gaines, 1998), sexual involvement is typical in most dating relationships. For most people sex, attraction, desire, romance, and love are closely intertwined. Differences in sexual interaction often exist based on the type of relationship, sex and gender, and sexual orientation.

Sex in Short-Term and Early Dating Relationships

Short-term sex occurs when a couple has sex once or more without developing an emotionally intimate relationship. Most short-term sex takes the form of hookups or one-night stands. Contrary to the stereotype that only men seek short-term sexual relationships, research shows that women also engage in short-term mating strategies for many of the same reasons as men: sexual desire, sexual experimentation, physical pleasure, and alcohol or drug use. Men are likely to use short-term sex for status and sexual satisfaction, whereas women are more likely to use it as means of trying to establish a long-term commitment or to enhance their economic status (Greitemeyer, 2005; Regan & Dreyer, 1999). For many men, the ideal short-term mate is physically attractive (Buunk, Dijkstra, Fetchenhauer, & Kenrick, 2002; Greitemeyer, 2005; Van Straaten, Engels, Finkenauer, & Holland, 2008), but men are willing to compromise on traits such as intelligence and status. For women, the ideal short-term partner is physically attractive, somewhat older, more experienced, self-confident,

and interpersonally responsive (Buunk et al., 2002; Regan, 1998b). Women are much less likely than men to compromise on these standards.

There is likely a biological basis for seeking short-term sexual encounters. For our ancestors, reproducing frequently was important because life expectancy was short and mortality, especially infant mortality, was high (Andersen, 2006). One strategy for reproductive success, then, was short-term sexual encounters. Throughout the evolution of our species, men could gain a reproductive advantage by impregnating several women, so a common biologically based characteristic of men is to seek frequent mating opportunities with multiple partners even though this underlying motivation is not apparent to men today (Buss & Schmit, 1993; Burt & Trivers, 2006; Willetts, Sprecher, & Beck, 2004). Although women can only have a limited number of offspring, they could potentially increase their chances of having healthy offspring by having children with different biological fathers, and therefore different genes (Tregenza & Wedell, 2002), so short-term sexual encounters may have a biological basis in women as well. Considerable recent research suggests that women are more likely to be attracted to and interested in having a sexual affair with someone other than their partner during the fertile phase that occurs prior to ovulation (Gangestad, Garver-Apgar, & Cousins, 2007). Women also dress better, flirt more, and are more attracted to men other than their partner during their sexually fertile phase (Durante, Li, & Haselton, 2008; Haselton & Gangestad, 2006; Haselton, Mortezaie, Pillsworth, Bleske-Recheck, & Frederick, 2007). Of course, the tendencies that had survival value for our ancestors do not necessarily have the same value today. Most women today do not want to get pregnant through short-term encounters. In addition, men should not use evolution as an excuse for being unfaithful.

Although one-night stands are not uncommon, premarital sex typically occurs in dating relationships between people who share some level of emotional intimacy. In these relationships people seek to experience sexual attraction, sexual arousal, and relational closeness (Mongeau, Serewicz, & Therrien, 2004;

O'Sullivan & Gaines, 1998). Research also suggests that first sex is a turning point in relationships for better or worse (Metts, 2004). Situational factors, such as drinking alcohol, can also prompt sexual involvement (Laumann, Gagnon, Michael, & Michaels, 1994; Morr & Mongeau, 2004; Sprecher & McKinney, 1993), as can special occasions such as going to the senior prom or anniversaries.

Research shows that among dating couples, sexual satisfaction is an important component of relational satisfaction for both men and women (Byers, Demmons, & Lawrence, 1998), although many other factors contribute to relational satisfaction, such as commitment, love, and compatibility. If the relationship is satisfying and if neither partner feels coerced or obligated to have sex, their first experience of sexual intercourse usually has a positive effect on the relationship (Cate, Long, Angera, & Draper, 1993). This is not to say that sex always makes a relationship better, but high-quality sex can contribute to a good relationship.

Sex in Marriage and Other Long-Term Relationships

In long-term love relationships, physical contact—including touching, kissing, and sexual intercourse—is essential (Christopher & Kissler, 2004; Regan & Berscheid, 1999). It is in long-term romantic relationships, not in hookups or dating relationships, where most sexual activity takes place (DeLamanter & Hyde, 2004; Willetts et al., 2004). Married people experience higher levels of sexual satisfaction than dating or cohabiting couples (Sprecher & Cate, 2004). An essential part of heterosexual love, sexual intimacy evolved to keep mates interested in one another (Buss, 1988b; Hendrick & Hendrick, 2002). A couple's ongoing sexual interest promotes bonding, cooperation, a division of labor, and the establishment of a stable environment for childrearing (Buss, 1994; Sprecher & Cate, 2004). Sex is particularly satisfying and enhancing when it results from approach motives such as feeling good about oneself, wanting to please one's partner, or promoting intimacy. Sex is not as pleasurable or relationship enhancing when it is prompted by avoidance motives such as preventing

one's partner from getting upset, avoiding conflict, or preventing one's partner from losing interest (Impett, Peplau, & Gable, 2005).

Although men's sexual desire peaks in their 20s and women's in their 30s, the association between relational and sexual satisfaction is high throughout life, even for seniors (Barr, Bryan, & Kenrick, 2002; Burgess, 2004; Howard, O'Neill, & Travers, 2006; Lawrence & Byers, 1995). The amount of sex declines as couples age, but sexual satisfaction does not (Burgess, 2004; DeLamater & Hyde, 2004, Howard et al., 2006; Willetts et al., 2004). Research shows that as women age into midlife and the senior years, feeling attractive is associated with sexual desire, enjoyment, frequency of sexual activity, and ability to reach orgasm (Koch, Mansfield, Thurau, & Carey, 2005). In long-term relationships, both men and women find a variety of sexual activities important to sexual satisfaction (Lawrence & Byers, 1995).

Both men and women view sexual desire and satisfaction as vital to achieving true romantic love (Regan, 1998a; Regan & Berscheid, 1999; Sprecher & Cate, 2004; Sternberg, 1987). Studies show that people with high levels of sexual desire in their relationships report higher levels of excitement, connection, and love (Christopher & Kissler, 2004; Hendrick & Hendrick, 2002; Sprecher & Regan, 1996). Indeed, when students in the United States were asked to list the persons they sexually desired and the persons with whom they were in love, 85% of the persons named appeared on both lists (Berscheid & Meyers, 1996). Interestingly, the positive association between sexual satisfaction and relational satisfaction also exists in China, suggesting the cross-cultural strength of this association (Reined, Byers, & Pan, 1997).

Criteria for long-term romantic partners differ from those for a first date or short-term sexual encounter. Both men and women place a higher value on qualities such as interpersonal skill, emotional stability, responsiveness, and family orientation, and less value on physical attraction, in long-term opposed to short-term relationships (Buunk et al., 2002; Regan, 1998b). Women throughout the world prefer long-term partners higher in social and economic status than themselves (Buunk et al., 2002). But sex itself is important; in long-term relationships "sexual desire is a distinguishing feature and a prerequisite of the romantic love experience" (Regan & Berscheid, 1999, p. 126). In short-term sexual encounters, by contrast, sexual desire is often present without love or intimacy.

Sex and Gender Differences

Sex is an important part of a good relationship, but men and women are not identical in their sexual inclinations and behaviors. The reproductive roles, sexual behaviors, and mate selection strategies of men and women are different. Biologically, women invest much more time and resources in becoming a parent. For women, reproduction involves finding a mate, having sex, going through pregnancy and childbirth, nursing and nurturing the baby, and in most cases raising the child to adulthood; for men, only finding a mate and having sex are biological imperatives (Trost & Alberts, 2006). In reality, most men stay with their mate during pregnancy and help raise their offspring; this is a choice made by responsible men. As the large number of single moms and deadbeat dads indicates, some men make little investment in their offspring.

Of course, having sex does not mean having babies. Indeed, most couples conscientiously avoid pregnancy during their sexual encounters. Having a baby is a huge commitment of time, money, and resources. Instead, sex is usually about pleasure, commitment, and closeness. The biological imperative of reproduction that makes humans sexual is deeply ingrained, and for most people, sexual desire leads to sexual encounters. Reproduction is far less necessary, if wanted at all.

Men and women also think and act about sex differently. Men have greater expectations for sex on dates than women (Mongeau & Johnson, 1995) and men think about sex more often than women. Some studies have even shown that males think about sex every few seconds (Byers, Purden, & Clark, 1998; Vohs, Catanese, & Baumeister, 2004) and are more likely to look at women longer and more sexually than women look at men (Lykins, Meana, & Strauss, 2008). Women are sexually attracted to men who are relationally oriented, emotionally connected, and who show tenderness and intimacy with them. Men are more likely to experience sexual desire in response to sexy looks, erotic situations, and friendly social behaviors (Benuto & Meana, 2008; Buunk et al., 2002; Cupach & Metts, 1995, Greitemeyer, 2005; Regan, 2004). Studies consistently show that men have a stronger sex drive than women (DeLamater & Hyde, 2004; Holmberg & Blair, 2009; Vohs, Catanese, & Baumeister, 2004), have more sex partners (Willetts et al., 2004), are less monogamous, and are more likely to believe that monogamy is a sacrifice (Schmookler & Bursic, 2007). Men are also more motivated to date and have sexual relations; less willing to live without sex (Mongeau et al., 2004; Regan & Berscheid, 1995); more liberal in sexual attitudes (Benuto & Meana, 2008); more likely to engage in short-term mating opportunities, particularly with physically attractive women (Van Straaten et al., 2008); and are more likely to think of the advantages of sexual relations rather than the disadvantages (Kisler & Christopher, 2008). Studies show that women's sexual desire is more dependent on feelings, the type of relationship they share with the partner, the potential for intimacy and humor, and the status and intelligence of the man (McCall & Meston, 2006), whereas men's desire is more influenced by physical attraction, sexual pleasure, and erotic qualities (Buunk et al., 2002; Greitemeyer, 2005; Metts, 2004; Regan, 2004; Regan & Berscheid, 1995, 1999). Men are more likely than women to regret *not having* a sexual relationship; women regret action and inaction equally (Roese et al., 2006). Interestingly, the first act of sexual intercourse between two people usually has a much more positive effect on the relationship for women than men, assuming that the sex was a voluntary act reflecting love and commitment (Cate et al., 1993).

Research suggests that females exhibit erotic plasticity; their sex drive is more socially flexible, culturally responsive, and adaptable than the male sex drive, which is more predictable and consistent, less shaped by culture, and somewhat stronger (Baumeister, 2000; Vohs et al., 2004; Wells & Twenge, 2005), although recent research suggests that men and women are more similar than different in their sex drives (Benuto & Meana, 2008). Some women seem to do fine without sex, while other women are highly sexual depending on circumstances (Baumeister, 2000) and are more satisfied with their sexual relationships than men regardless of how much sex they are having (Holmberg & Blair, 2009). Numerous studies show individual women vary in sex drive over time. For example, a woman may have a stronger sex drive when she is in an intimate relationship than when she is not involved with anyone. Men, by contrast, have a more consistent sex drive that operates regardless of their relational involvement with someone. Heterosexual women are aroused by a greater variety of stimuli (e.g., affectionate behaviors) than are heterosexual men, who are more likely to be aroused primarily by sights and thoughts of attractive women (Chivers & Bailey, 2005; Chivers, Soto, & Blanchard, 2007). Men masturbate more, are more likely to read pornography, and are more likely to approve of casual sex than women (DeLamater & Hyde, 2004). Of course, the popularity of Viagra and Cialis suggests that men's sex drive is also somewhat variable.

Female sexuality is also more varied across different sociocultural settings than is male sexuality. Baumeister (2000) cited ethnographic studies that report much greater cross-cultural variation in sexual behavior for females than for males. For example, in some cultures women have premarital sex while in others they do not. Studies also show that women are less likely to reveal their true sexual attitudes than are men. This is part of a double standard that still exists, requiring women to hide their sexual interest to a degree so as to not appear "loose" (DeLamater & Hyde, 2004). Finally, women are more likely than men to fake sexual satisfaction to please their partners.

Gay and Lesbian Relationships

Significant minorities of people are not attracted to members of the opposite sex, but rather have same-sex attractions. Like Taylor who we introduced in the opening scenario, most homosexuals have early recollections of same-sex attraction and a clear sense that they were different from the majority as early as preschool (Rathus et al., 1993). Research suggests that throughout the world, most gay men

and lesbians experienced some degree of gender nonconformity as children (Crooks & Baur, 1999).

Because men and women differ in their sexual attitudes and behaviors, it is not surprising that relationships between lesbians, gay men, and heterosexuals also differ to some degree. Yet there are major similarities between heterosexual, gay, and lesbian relationships as well (Holmberg & Blair, 2009). Like heterosexual couples, the vast majority of lesbians and gay men want long-term committed relationships (Peplau, Fingerhut, & Beals, 2004). Indeed, most lesbians and gay men would marry their partner if gay marriage was legally sanctioned (Peplau et al., 2004). Interestingly, gay men and lesbians report higher levels of sexual satisfaction than do heterosexual couples (Holmberg & Blair, 2009).

Despite increasingly progressive attitudes about homosexuality and bisexuality in the United States, gay and lesbian relationships are still not readily accepted or understood by many segments of society (Peplau et al., 2004). Growing up gay in a heterosexual, homophobic world is not easy, and most problems for gay men and lesbians come from adverse reactions of society. Adolescence is a tough time for all young people, as indicated by the high teenage suicide rate. The rate is even higher for gay teens, who may need counseling as they adjust to their sexual orientation and to the attitudes of those around them.

Sex in Lesbian Relationships

Over 75% of lesbian couples are monogamous and research suggests that fidelity is important to lesbians (Blumstein & Schwartz, 1983). Unlike men, lesbians are less attracted to women based on physical attraction. Sexual activity for lesbians declines over time, leading to concerns and even jokes about the "lesbian bed death" (Peplau et al., 2004; Van Rosmalen-Nooijens, Vergeer, Lagro-Jansen, 2008). Although the frequency of sexual relations is associated with increased satisfaction in lesbian couples (Peplau et al., 2004), lesbians have sex less frequently than male gay couples, heterosexual daters, or married couples (Blumstein & Schwartz, 1983). Women are taught to be selective in choosing sexual partners, to take a reactive rather than proactive role in sexual situations, and to act as gatekeepers who decide whether sexual activity will take place. Lesbians must renegotiate these gender roles so that they feel comfortable initiating sex. Moreover, since men have a more consistent sex drive than women (Baumeister, 2000; Julien, Bouchard, Gagnon, & Pomperleau, 1992), with no man to initiate sex, sex is less likely to occur. Among lesbian women, acceptance of oneself as a lesbian is associated with sexual satisfaction (Henderson, Lehavot, & Somoni, 2009). Finally, lesbians may be satisfied with nongenital sex since, like heterosexual women, lesbians value physical contact, such as hugging and cuddling, and are likely to consider these ends in and of themselves rather than a prelude to sex (Blumstein & Schwartz, 1983).

Close to 25% of lesbians are actually married to men (Rathus et al., 1993). Some may be bisexual, others may be testing their heterosexual orientation, and still others may be concealing their homosexual orientation. According to Bell and Weinberg (1978), relational satisfaction is low in such marital relationships and almost all end in separation or divorce. Over 75% of lesbians have had at least one sexual encounter with a man (Reinisch & Beasley, 1990). As discussed previously, research suggests that women are more sexually variable than men and have an easier time accepting various sexual orientations and conditions, including homosexuality or abstinence (Baumeister, 2000).

Sex in Relationships Between Gay Men

According to the Kinsey report, although about one-third of all men have engaged in homosexual behavior at one time in their lives, about 8% have had exclusively gay relationships for three or more years, and only 4% have been exclusively gay throughout their lives. About two-thirds of gay men have had sex with a woman, and 10% to 15% may be more accurately viewed as bisexual (Reinisch & Beasley, 1990).

On average, gay men have a higher number of sex partners and engage in sex more often than lesbians or heterosexuals (Blumstein & Schwartz, 1983; Kelly et al., 2009; Parsons et al., 2008). Because women often act as sexual gatekeepers, the absence of a woman in a relationship probably reduces restraint and increases sexual frequency. Gay men are also more likely than lesbians or heterosexuals to be in nonmonogamous relationships. In 1983, Blumstein and Schwartz reported that 82% of the gay men in their nationwide survey said they were nonmonogamous. Despite this, long-term relationships among gay men are much more common than the media would have us believe. The Kinsey data suggest that virtually all gay men have had a steady, highly committed gay relationship that lasted one to three years (Reinisch & Beasley, 1990). Furthermore, some evidence suggests that gay men, like heterosexual men and women, have become more monogamous since the AIDS epidemic first emerged in the 1980s (Sprecher & Regan, 2000).

Gay men may have difficulty negotiating sexual initiation precisely because it is typically a male prerogative. In short, some gay men resent the other male's initiation and refuse sex, which can lead to conflicts. Gay men have more sex than other couple types since either partner can feel free to initiate sex (Blumstein & Schwartz, 1983; Parsons et al., 2008) and most gay men are highly satisfied with their sexual relationships. How to initiate sex may sometimes be difficult, since kissing, which is a more feminine behavior, is often the gateway to sexual relations and is most likely in lesbian relationships, moderately likely in heterosexual relationships, and least likely in gay relationships between men (Blumstein & Schwartz, 1983).

SEXUAL ATTITUDES AND BEHAVIORS

Deciding if and when to have sex is a personal choice influenced by many factors, including levels of commitment and passion, alcohol consumption, and moral values. Sexual behavior is strongly related to people's attitudes, for people may be born with a number of sexual feelings, preferences, and proclivities, but most attitudes and beliefs about sex are learned. For example, a person might be physically aroused and curious when thinking about having sex, but moral attitudes and beliefs might stop the individual from acting on the impulse to have sex.

Developing Sexual Attitudes and Beliefs

Research has shown that sexual attitudes and knowledge come from many sources, including culture, mass media, parents, peers, and past relationships (Andersen, 1993). These factors influence not only sexual attitudes but also sexual behavior and communication about sex.

Culture

Culture influences relational and sexual attitudes. Andersen (1998a) argued that "the most basic force that molds and shapes human beings, other than our membership in the human race itself, is culture" (p. 48). Culture is resistant to change, and people usually adopt the values and attitudes of their parents and their culture unless very strong countervailing forces come into play. Children of immigrants, for example, are caught between two sets of cultural values—those of their parents and those of their peers. Sexual attitudes change slowly across each generation and still show cultural influences after 100 or more years of cultural assimilation. In the United States, African Americans have the most permissive sexual attitudes, followed by whites, while people from Asian, Latino, and Middle Eastern cultures have the most conservative sexual orientations (Sprecher & McKinney, 1993). Among white Americans, particularly women, and to a lesser degree among African Americans, talking about sexual intimacy is quite common and is believed to be the heart and soul of a good relationship (Crooks & Baur, 1999). By contrast, Asian Americans and Hispanic Americans tend to be more reluctant to discuss their sexual relationship. In interethnic couples, these differences require considerable understanding and adaptation by the partners.

The Mass Media

Media are an important source of information about sex. Research has shown that 29% of interactions on prime-time television depict sexual issues that emphasize male sexual roles and a recreational rather than a procreational orientation toward sex (Ward, 1995). Most of these interactions depict sex as a competition and equate masculinity with being sexual. The media also influences "sexual scripts" for communicating about sex, which are discussed later in this chapter. Magazines are also an important source of information about sex and sexual issues. Starting in 1953 with the publication of *Playboy,* people from the United States were introduced not only to open nudity on newsstands but perhaps more importantly to the "playboy" philosophy that rejected limits on sexual expression, condoned any form of consensual sex, and was critical of the institution of marriage (D'Emilio & Freedman, 1988). Similarly, publication of Helen Gurley Brown's *Sex and the Single Girl* in the early 1960s urged young women to reconsider the taboo against premarital sex. These publications show the impact the media have on sexual attitudes. More recently, sexual material on the Internet has become a concern of parents, educators, and politicians. Cybersex may be a negative influence with increasingly bizarre or violent effects, or it may be a harmless form of safe sex with beneficial cathartic effects.

Parents

Children learn about sex and relationships from their parents both indirectly and directly. Indirectly, parents serve as models for children. If parents are affectionate or sexual toward each other, children will expect their own romantic relationships to include affection or sex. Kids pick up attitudes about sex from their families through modeling and body language. As a result, people raised with more conservative family values are more erotophobic and experience more sexual guilt and anxiety (Simpson, Wilson, & Winterheld, 2004). Parents can also influence their children directly by talking to them about sex, yet parent-child communication about sex is rare (Fisher, 2004; Warren, 1995) and teenagers often feel uncomfortable talking to their partners about sex, primarily because the parents issue orders or warnings rather than frankly discussing sexual thoughts and feelings (Brock & Jennings, 1993; Philliber, 1980; Rozema, 1986). As a result, parents are amazingly unaware of their teenage offspring's sexual behavior (Fisher, 2004). Within families, teens report being most comfortable talking to a same-sex older sibling or same-sex parent about sex (Guerrero & Afifi, 1995b), and mothers and daughters are more likely to talk about sex than are fathers and sons (Fisher, 2004; Philliber, 1980). Children are more likely to delay sexual activity and to use contraception when their parents have talked with them about sex (Fox, 1981), and discussions about sex are most effective when they are integrated into family discussions well before a child is 16 years old (Warren, 1995). Box 8.1 provides information on how parents can communicate effectively with their children regarding sex.

BOX 8.1 Highlights

Ten Tips for How Parents Should Talk to Their Children About Sex

Clay Warren, a communication researcher who has conducted many studies on family sex communication, makes the following recommendations to parents who want to engage in effective communication about sex with their children.

1. *Start talking.* Most parents find it difficult to talk about sex with their children, but the more they initiate discussion about sex, the easier it becomes to talk about it.

2. *Continue talking.* Once discussions about sex are initiated, children expect to hear more. Parents should make an effort to continue talking about sex in more specific detail as their children mature.

3. *Start early.* Discussions about sex should start well before a young person is 16 years old. Early adolescence is often a good time to initiate sex talks. By their mid-teens, children may have outgrown the need to talk about sex with their parents and instead rely more on peers.

4. *Involve both parents if the family has two parents.* If both parents are actively involved in the communication process, neither one should bear the pressure or responsibility alone. Also, teenagers may be more comfortable discussing certain issues with one parent and other issues with the other parent.

5. *Talk to both sons and daughters.* Some research suggests that parents are more likely to talk to their daughters than sons. This double standard needs to be broken so that girls do not always bear the sexual responsibility in teen relationships. It is important for both boys and girls to understand the consequences of sexual activity.

6. *Establish a mutual dialogue.* When parents talk *to* rather than *with* their children about sex, the children are less satisfied with the information they receive. It is important that children feel free to initiate discussions about sex and to ask questions.

7. *Create a supportive environment.* Communication should be open and comfortable rather than defensive. Parents are often tense when discussing sex with their children. Instead, they should be relaxed and open.

8. *Use positive forms of nonverbal communication.* Nonverbal behavior is especially crucial in creating a supportive environment. Behaviors such as a relaxed posture, smiling, vocal warmth, and head nods can all help ease the tension.

9. *Remember that discussing sex does not promote promiscuity.* Knowing this fact might help ease some of the stress parents feel. Many studies have shown that talking about sex and sex-related topics such as contraception does not promote promiscuity. In fact, talking about these issues within the context of a broader discussion of sexual values might even reduce promiscuity.

10. *Don't leave the talking to someone else.* If parents are not successful in influencing their children's sexual attitudes, someone else will be. It might be a boyfriend, girlfriend, peers, teachers, or even the media. Adolescents have questions that need to be answered. If they cannot find the answers at home, they will seek them elsewhere.

SOURCE: Information compiled from Warren (1995).

Peers

Rogers (1995) showed that most diffusion of information about a variety of topics, including sexually related ones, occurs interpersonally between people who are similar to one another. Sprecher and McKinney (1993) reviewed studies showing that peers have a stronger influence on people's sexual standards than parents. Male adolescents are notorious for inculcating male attitudes about what constitutes a physically attractive woman, what constitutes masculine behavior, and the importance of sexual conquests. Females share all manner of relational and sexual information with one another regarding male attractiveness, birth control methods, and the quality of individual males as potential mates. Although these stereotypes of heterosexual men and women are exaggerated, they illustrate that men and women talk about sex with their peers. Sexual attitudes and behaviors are modeled by friends and then imitated.

Past Relationships

Many attitudes about sex result from prior relational experiences. People who have learned to trust others and to be comfortable with closeness tend to be more monogamous in their sexual relationships (Simpson & Gangestad, 1991). Moreover, having a partner who provides consistent, loving physical contact helps build an individual's self-esteem and sets up positive expectations for future relationships (Hazan & Zeifman, 1994). In contrast, people who are uncomfortable with closeness and have had unsatisfying sexual relationships in the past will be more likely to desire short-term, casual sex than committed relationships (Brennan & Shaver, 1995; Stephan & Bachman, 1999) and those who have been hurt in past love relationships are less likely to experience highly passionate or obsessive love in the future (Stephan & Bachman, 1999). Together these findings suggest that people who have had positive sexual experiences in committed relationships are most likely to expect future relationships to be monogamous and sexually satisfying. Past sexual relationships can also affect attraction. Sprecher and Regan (2000) concluded:

> In general, research indicates that low to moderate levels of current or past sexual activity and the restriction of sexual activity to committed relationships are more likely to increase one's desirability as a partner than is a history of many sexual partners or casual sexual activity. (p. 219)

Social Norms and Changing Sexual Attitudes

The social norms of one's culture also influence people's sexual attitudes. Attitudes toward sexuality, particularly premarital and female sexuality, became increasingly permissive and liberal in the United States during the 20th century (Sprecher & McKinney, 1993; Wells & Twenge, 2005). The best data on changes in sexuality come from a study by

Wells and Twenge (2005) that aggregated over 500 studies including over 250,000 participants. Throughout most of the century, premarital sex was considered unacceptable, particularly for women. But "premarital sexual activity has become normative for today's youth. Rates of sexual intercourse for teens have increased dramatically" since the early 1960s" (Christopher & Roosa, 1991, p. 111).

For males and particularly for females, both sexual activity and attitudes in favor of sexuality steadily increased from 1965 to 2005 (Wells & Twenge, 2005). In the 1950s, only 13% of teenage girls were sexually active whereas by the 1990s, 47% were sexually active. Before 1970, the average age for first sexual intercourse for men was 18 and for women was 19; by the late 1990s, this average had dropped to age 15 for both genders (Wells & Twenge, 2005). Similarly, before 1970, less than half of teenagers had engaged in oral sex but by the 1990s over two-thirds of both men and women had engaged in oral sex. In the late 1950s, only 12% of young women approved of premarital sex, and by the 1980s about three-quarters approved. The only sexual behavior not increasing is the number of partners, which has remained fairly constant over the years, especially since news of the AIDS epidemic in the 1980s (Wells & Twenge, 2005). But times have changed; today over 80% of men and women have had premarital sexual intercourse (Willetts et al., 2004).

The revolution in sexual attitudes that began in the 1960s was due to a number of factors. The 1960s was a revolutionary era for all types of values, including those associated with politics, music, the environment, civil rights, and women's rights. In the 1960s images of sexuality were widely depicted in the mass media through magazines, books, and movies, and to a lesser degree, television. Perhaps the biggest factor was the birth control pill—the first simple and effective technology that permitted sex without reproduction. For the first time in human history, women could have sexual relationships without risking pregnancy. Several scholars suggest that the sexual revolution of the 1960s and 1970s was mainly a change in women's values, with men remaining much the same (Baumeister, 2000; Ehrenreich, Hess, & Jacobs, 1986). Today teens and young adults are

much more sexually active than they were before the sexual revolution of the 1960s.

Researchers have identified three types of sexual attitudes held by people today (Sprecher & McKinney, 1993). Some people have a **procreational orientation**, which reflects the belief that producing offspring is the primary purpose of sexual intercourse. Other people have a **relational orientation**, which holds that sexual intercourse is a way of expressing love and affection, and developing greater relational intimacy. Still others have a **recreational orientation**, viewing sex as a primary source of fun, escape, excitement, or pleasure. The procreational orientation, the position taken by most major religions, is associated with traditional, conservative cultural values. The relational orientation, which is equated with moderate sexual values, is widespread in the United States. People with this orientation disapprove of casual sex but usually approve of premarital sex in the context of a committed or loving relationship. The recreational orientation is a sexually liberal view holding that sex is appropriate between consenting adults.

These orientations are not mutually exclusive; many people's sexual attitudes are some combination of procreational, relational, and recreational. Indeed, most married couples in the United States embrace elements of all three values within their relationship at different times. By contrast, attitudes toward premarital sex vacillate between a relational orientation and a somewhat recreational orientation in the United States, but are rarely procreational. Research has shown that couples are more likely to endorse increased sexual activity, including sexual intercourse, as the relationship becomes closer (Sprecher, McKinney, Walsh, & Anderson, 1988). Judging by their behavior, for several decades, people in the United States have subscribed primarily to a relational orientation through the practice of **serial monogamy** (Christopher & Roosa, 1991; Rathus et al., 1993; Sorensen, 1973). In other words, couples are sexually active only with each other (monogamy) and do not engage in other sexual relationships until the current relationship ends. They may, however, move through a series of such relationships.

While a lot of research has focused on the dark side of premarital sex, such as disease, pregnancy, and abortion, positive outcomes also occur. Most premarital sex takes place in an intimate and committed relationship that provides support and often leads to marriage (Christopher & Roosa, 1991). In fact, early research showed that serial monogamists overwhelmingly loved each other and had healthy, caring sexual relationships (Sorensen, 1973). Moreover, serial monogamists had the highest school grades, were most likely to use birth control, enjoyed sex more, and were generally better adjusted than were either promiscuous adventurers or virgins.

Although most college students are sexually experienced, some choose to remain virgins. In a study of sexual behavior of college students, Sprecher and Regan (1996) found that 11% of men and 13% of women were virgins, although virtually all of the virgins reported experiencing sexual desire. Thus, Sarah, who we introduced at the beginning of this chapter, is not alone in her virginity. Women like Sarah give several reasons for being a virgin, including the absence of a long-term or love relationship, fear of negative consequences such as pregnancy or STIs, personal beliefs and values, and feelings of inadequacy or insecurity. All of these reasons were stronger for women than for men. Virgins reported a mixture of pride and anxiety about their status, although positive emotions outweighed negative ones. Women were more likely to be proud and happy about keeping their virginity, while men were more likely to be embarrassed about it. The men and women who were virgins for deep religious or moral reasons, like Sarah, were the most positive about their status.

COMMUNICATION PATTERNS

Research on courtship patterns and flirtation provides insight on how romantic and sexual relationships develop. The literature on sexual scripts examines the communication people employ to initiate and refuse sex at various stages in relationships.

Courtship and Flirtation

When people flirt, they typically use indirect communication strategies to convey their interest and attraction, especially when they are in the early stages of a relationship. Nonverbal flirtation displays are more common than verbal cues (Beres, Herold, & Maitland, 2004). For example, gazes, smiles, warm vocal tones, and close distances are key flirtatious behaviors (Givens, 1978, 1983; Moore, 1985; Muehlenhard, Koralewski, Andrews, & Burdick, 1986). Indirect nonverbal cues are often used because they provide protection from potential rejection. The receiver can simply ignore these nonverbal cues without having to verbally reject the flirtatious person. The flirtatious person can deny flirting and simply feign friendliness. Sometimes, of course, direct verbal strategies are used, such as telling people they look sexy or talking about sex. These more direct strategies, however, are more likely to be used in an established romantic relationship.

Scheflen's (1965, 1974) model of the courtship process sought to explain how various nonverbal behaviors unfold over time to signal availability and sexual interest. Scheflen's model includes five stages, with the earlier stages characterized by the most indirect communication. The courtship behaviors in this model often reflect attentiveness, approachability, and submissiveness. Thus, potential partners must gain one another's attention and signal that they are available or approachable for communication. Submissive behaviors that communicate a desire for intimacy are particularly useful during the courtship process because they are seen as a nonthreatening, playful way to convey sexual interest. Some submissive behaviors, such as stroking someone's hair in a comforting way, also mirror those used in parent-child relationship to convey caring and intimacy.

The Attention Stage

The goal of the first stage in Scheflen's model is to get the other person's attention and to present oneself in the best possible light—either strategically or accidentally. When Taylor met Leslie with a group at dinner, she made sure she was in a good location to converse with her. At the table she made sure that she was seated near her to encourage interaction. Throughout history, people have practiced the art of gaining attention as a precursor to courtship. In 19th-century America, it was common for women to drop something, such as a glove or handkerchief, in front of a man whom they wanted to get to know. The man, if polite, would be obliged to retrieve the dropped item and to turn his attention to the woman. Similarly, men commonly asked to be formally introduced to a woman, often by a relative or friend, before pursuing a conversation. Any place where singles gather, we are likely to see a variety of attention-getting strategies, such as Taylor positioning herself in Leslie's view and trying to catch her eye. These behaviors are indirect, including demure glances, tentative smiles, anxious movement such as twisting the ring on one's finger, and primping behavior such as fixing one's hair, applying lipstick, or straightening one's tie.

The Courtship Readiness Stage

During what is sometimes referred to as the *recognition stage*, the initiator of the flirtation determines whether the other person is approachable for interaction. For example, if Taylor's eye contact and friendliness is met with Leslie's cold stare or annoyed glance, or is ignored, the courtship process will end. Similarly, if Leslie is busy interacting with other people, Taylor will probably hesitate to approach unless she receives a fairly clear signal of interest. Typical flirting behaviors include sustained mutual gaze and smiling, raised eyebrows, more direct body orientation, head tilts in the direction of the other person, and nervous laughter. More grooming behavior also tends to occur in this stage, with people tucking in their stomachs, arranging their clothing and hair, and wetting their lips as they prepare to approach one another.

The Positioning Stage

If Taylor and Leslie are attracted to each other, they will engage in a series of positioning behaviors that signal availability for interaction while indicating to others that they are, at least temporarily, a "couple" and so should be left alone. Close distancing and face-to-face body orientation are typical at this stage, as in forward leans. Partners also gaze

and smile at each other and display interest and animation through gestures and expressive voices. If the relationship is progressing, hand-holding is a common romantic or sexual escalation event (O'Sullivan, Cheng, Harris, & Brooks-Gunn, 2007). If the setting is quiet, Taylor and Leslie may lower their voices to draw each other closer. In this stage, communication becomes more synchronized; that is, turn taking becomes smoother, and partners engage in similar behaviors such as crossing their legs. Although there is a marked increase in the intimacy of communication at this stage, some submissiveness and ambiguity still remain. For example, if Taylor and Leslie gaze for too long into each other's eyes, they might feel embarrassed, avert their eyes, and laugh nervously.

The Invitations and Sexual Arousal Stage

Taylor and Leslie are very attracted to each other and are moving into the fourth stage—sexual intimacy. The beginning of this stage is marked by the first implicit invitation for touch and sexual contact. For example, Taylor might put her hand on Leslie's knee to see how she responds. More subtle signs of intimacy include grooming the partner, performing carrying and clutching activities, and acting sexually provocative (Burgoon, Guerrero, & Floyd, 2010; Givens, 1978; Scheflen, 1965). Grooming behaviors include tucking the tag from someone's clothing back inside the collar and pushing a stray strand of hair out of someone's eyes. Carrying and clutching behaviors include carrying someone's bags or books, holding hands, and leaning on someone's arm for support. Sexually provocative actions include dancing in a suggestive way, revealing body parts by unbuttoning one's shirt or crossing one's leg to expose more thigh, and touching the partner in intimate places.

The Resolution Stage

If Taylor's invitation is accepted and sexual interaction occurs, Taylor and Leslie have reached the final stage. Of course, determining whether the invitation is accepted is not always easy, especially if the behaviors used in the sexual arousal and invitations stage were indirect and ambiguous. When people move through the courtship stages rapidly, the intent of both partners might be unclear. Perhaps Leslie was just being friendly while Taylor was interested in a sexual relationship. Sometimes people engage in sexual teasing, a behavior that is more commonly used by women (Meston & O'Sullivan, 2007) and which can be misconstrued as real sexual interest.

Some studies have shown that men are more likely than women to see flirtatious behaviors as seductive, whereas women often see these same behaviors as ways of being friendly and expressing innocent attraction (Abbey, 1982, 1987; Abbey & Melby, 1986). To complicate matters even further, research has shown that people flirt for a variety of reasons, only one of which is to signal sexual interest. For example, people may flirt because they see it as innocent fun, they want to make a third party jealous, they want to develop their social skills, or they are trying to persuade someone to do something for them (Afifi, Guerrero, & Egland, 1994; Egland, Spitzberg, & Zormeier, 1996; Koeppel, Montagne-Miller, O'Hair, & Cody, 1993). Thus, when someone is flirting, the person may or may not be showing sexual interest.

In longer courtships, couples spend considerable time in the sexual arousal and invitations stage, with sexual intimacy increasing slowly over time. Partners are more likely to be direct about their intentions, but misunderstandings can still occur. Sometimes one person is ready to have sex before the other, and one partner may view intimate touch as a way to express closeness while the other sees it as a prelude to sex. Partners must negotiate if and when sex occurs, often through both verbal and nonverbal communication. If one or both of the partners does not want to have sex, they are entering the first four of Scheflen's stages are referred to as **quasi-courtship** rather than courtship. Misinterpretation of flirtatious cues is likely, given that the first three of four stages often look the same, regardless of whether they are quasi-courtship or true courtship stages.

It is important to note that these courtship stages provide only a rough guide for how people signal romantic interest and increase sexual involvement. Couples are unique and progress at different speeds. A relatively small number of couples have

sex on a first date or shortly after the partners meet; most couples wait until some level of intimacy has developed before having sex. With this in mind, Christopher and Cate (1985) identified four types of couples. **Rapid-involvement couples** have high levels of physical arousal and have sex on the first date or shortly thereafter. For these partners, sexual intimacy often precedes psychological intimacy. **Gradual-involvement couples** let sexual involvement increase gradually as the relationship develops and becomes more psychologically intimate. Sexual involvement moves through stages with sexual involvement increasing as the partners move from a first date, to a casually dating relationship, to a more serious, committed relationship. **Delayed-involvement couples** wait until the two people consider themselves to be a committed couple to become sexually involved. For these couples, psychological intimacy precedes sexual intimacy. **Low-involvement couples** usually wait to have sex until the partners are engaged or married. Research suggests that most couples in the United States define themselves as falling under either the gradual- (31%) or delayed-involvement (44%) category, with around 17% identifying themselves as low involvement and 7% classifying themselves as rapid involvement (Christopher & Cate, 1985; Sprecher & McKinney, 1993). These findings correspond with research showing that most people have a relational orientation toward sex.

Sexual Scripts

Scripts are social information that is deployed in everyday interaction. Cultural forces define with whom, when, where, and in what relationships sexual behavior may appropriately be initiated and conducted (Regan & Berscheid, 1999). **Sexual scripts** most often revolve around the initiation and acceptance or refusal of sexual advances. The North American script casts men as initiators and women as gatekeepers who refuse or accept dates or sexual invitations, particularly in new relationships (Byers, 1996, Mongeau et al., 2004). As Hinde (1984) commented, men seek to propagate widely while women seek to propagate wisely. Research indicates that both men and women are comfortable asking for dates and initiating sexual interaction (Kelley & Rolker-Dolinsky, 1987), although many women think their sexual initiatives might threaten men. However, women are more likely to initiate sexual interaction in well-developed relationships as opposed to developing relationships.

Negotiating sexual activity in a developing relationship can be difficult because both individuals have multiple goals including managing impressions, providing relational definitions, satisfying sexual desire, following sexual standards or morals, and avoiding disease or pregnancy (Cupach & Metts, 1991). Most sexual initiation attempts are indirect and communicated through nonverbal behavior and flirtation (Andersen, 2008). Sometimes, however, friendly behaviors—particularly those by women—are misinterpreted by men as sex-initiating behaviors. To avoid sexually coercive situations (discussed later in this chapter), individuals need to verbally articulate their disinterest, and their partners need to respect their wishes.

Initiation Strategies

Both men and women use persuasive strategies and scripts to initiate dating and sexual relationships. These strategies typically fall into five categories: (1) hinting and indirect strategies, (2) expressions of emotional and physical closeness, (3) pressure and manipulation, (4) antisocial acts, and (5) logic and reasoning (Christopher & Frandsen, 1990; Edgar & Fitzpatrick, 1988, 1993).

Sexual relations are sensitive and ego threatening, so hinting and indirect strategies can be useful. Romantic conversations are full of indirect communication such as compliments, sexual innuendo, hints, and nonverbal communication. Such ploys are safe because if the partner does not respond sexually, little face is lost. As Edgar and Fitzpatrick (1988) noted, when one person wants to have sex, the situation can be emotionally charged, and an opportunity to save face is welcome. Both men and women are most comfortable with sexual involvement if emotional and physical closeness is present; this is particularly true for women. Establishing a close relationship and sending reassuring relational messages results in increased sexual activity (Christopher & Frandsen, 1990). For example,

doing special things for your partner, telling your partner how much you like her or him, flattering your partner, and sharing time and space with your partner are important ways to enhance emotional closeness and initiate sexual activity.

Another sexual influence tactic is logical reasoning by persuading someone that it is advantageous to become sexually involved. This strategy uses logic or negotiates the timing or degree of sexual involvement to overcome a partner's concerns (Christopher & Frandsen, 1990). For example, if Brittany is afraid of getting pregnant or contracting an STI, Chris might make reassuring statements about the effectiveness of condoms or suggest that they both get tested for STIs before having sex. These types of tactics are associated with greater sexual activity in a relationship over the long-term, although they may limit or postpone sexual involvement in the short term (Christopher & Frandsen, 1990).

Not surprisingly, men are more likely to use pressure and manipulation to gain sexual compliance than women (Christopher & Frandsen, 1990). These strategies encompass a wide variety of coercive tactics, such as repeated requests for sex, threats to break off or de-escalate the relationship, the use of drugs or alcohol to reduce resistance to sex, and outright deception. These tactics seldom increase the frequency of sexual activity in a relationship (Christopher & Frandsen, 1990) and can lead to relational dissatisfaction or de-escalation.

Evidence suggests that antisocial acts are similarly unsuccessful in initiating sex in a relationship (Christopher & Frandsen, 1990). These strategies encompass a wide assortment of tactics, including intentionally trying to make the partner jealous (Fleischmann, Spitzberg, Andersen, & Roesch, 2005), pouting or holding a grudge to try to get one's way, and sexual harassment. Such acts may lead to relational termination and even legal action in some cases.

Refusing and Accepting Sexual Invitations

The power to refuse and regulate sex is primarily a woman's prerogative. Throughout the world, women are more judicious and less casual in their choices about sex than men (Buss, 1994). Men are poor at turning down sex and have few refusal strategies in their repertoire; women tend to regard men's refusals as insincere, unexpected, and upsetting (Metts, Cupach, & Imahori, 1992). This does not imply that women have license to ignore men's refusals; men should be taken as seriously as women when they decline to have sex.

Research suggests that women are well prepared with sexual-compliance-resisting scripts and use multiple resistance strategies (Lannutti & Monahan, 2004; Metts et al., 1992). Women often use indirect strategies because these are perceived as polite; however, more direct strategies seem to be more effective for refusing unwanted sex. Moreover, most men have experience receiving sexual rejection messages and find them relatively predictable and not particularly disconcerting (Metts et al., 1992). This is useful information for women who use indirect strategies to refuse sex when they are worried about hurting the partner's feelings. Direct strategies are more effective, and thankfully, they are unlikely to be taken personally by men (Motley & Reeder, 1995).

In steady dating relationships, both men and women accept the majority of sexual initiations by their partner (Byers, 1996). In Byers's study, only about 20% of initiations were refused by the partner with about the same percentage for men and women. These data suggest that sex in steady dating relationships is not adversarial and that, contrary to the stereotype, in developed relationships, women are more likely to be facilitators of sexual interaction than gatekeepers. In investigating sexual activity among heterosexual daters over a one-month period, Byers and Lewis (1988) found that nearly half of the couples reported disagreements caused by the man's desire to increase sexual involvement. However, disagreements occurred during just 7% of all dates. Thus, although disagreements about sex did occur occasionally over the course of a month, most dates were free of such disagreements. When sex is refused from a long-term dating partner, the refusal is both unexpected and viewed negatively (Bevan, 2003).

Once sexual activity becomes fairly regular, shared dyadic scripts emerge to guide sexual interaction. In well-developed relationships, women feel freer to initiate touch, affection, and sexual behavior (Cupach & Metts, 1993; Guerrero & Andersen, 1991). Brown and Auerbach (1981) found that wives increased their initiation of sexual activity by about 1% per year of marriage. Several studies have shown

that stages of sexual involvement are fairly well scripted, starting with kissing, and moving to hand to breast, hand to genitals, oral sex, sexual intercourse, and orgasm in the ideal case (DeLamater & Hyde, 2004; Morris, 1977). This script is generally followed both within a single sexual encounter and across a series of dates with only occasional variation.

Saying no to sex in a long-term relationship is often difficult because partners do not want to hurt one another's feelings, but everyone has the right to refuse sex no matter how close the relationship. It is important for long-term partners to say no in a tender and supportive manner with clear verbal communication. Research has shown that most refusals are done verbally and that the best refusals maintain both the relationship and the partner's face (Cupach & Metts, 1991). For example, telling your partner that you are "really tired" or "not feeling well" is better than saying that you are not feeling much sexual desire for her or him at the moment. When refusals are accompanied by assurances of future activity ("We'll have more time for each other this weekend"), they are also accepted more gracefully.

SEXUAL COERCION AND HARASSMENT

Most people associate sex with pleasure, intimacy, relational closeness, and desire. However, sex has its dark side as well. Negative aspects of sex include sexual dysfunction, sexual abuse, rape, sexual coercion, and sexual harassment. In this section, we focus on coercion and harassment because communication is at the heart of these types of problematic interaction.

Sexual Coercion

Sexual coercion occurs when an individual pressures, compels, or forces another to engage in sexual activity, or practices considered unacceptable by most people, with verbal pressure the least unacceptable and physical force the most unacceptable (Struckman-Johnson & Struckman-Johnson, 1991). Verbal insistence is the most common method of coercion (Murnan, Perot, & Byrne, 1989). In general, women find sexual coercion to be less acceptable than do men (Christopher, Owens, & Strecker,

1993; Struckman-Johnson & Struckman-Johnson, 1991). Additionally, coercive strategies are generally unsuccessful in gaining sexual compliance (Christopher & Frandsen, 1990).

Sexual coercion is far too common. Research has shown that in the majority of sexually coercive situations, a man is the perpetrator and a woman is the victim. For example, over 50% of college women report having been the victim of some form of sexual coercion (Byers, 1996), and over 95% of all women report having engaged in some form of unwanted sexual activity (Muehlenhard & Cook, 1988). Others studies have shown that 22% of college women report having been forced to engage in sexual intercourse, and 35% to 46% of women report having unwanted sex as a result of sexual persuasion or coercion, typically from a partner the woman knew fairly well (Byers, 1996; Muehlenhard

& Cook; 1988; Murnan et al., 1989). Women report experiencing sexual coercion on only about 7% of all dates (Byers & Lewis, 1988). In yet another study, 50% of college women reported that they had engaged in at least one unwanted sexual activity (ranging from hugs to sexual intercourse) over a two-week period, with 20% of the women engaging in unwanted sexual intercourse (O'Sullivan & Allgeier, 1998). Sometimes women have unwanted sex to please their partners; other times they are pressured or forced to have sex. Worst of all, almost two-thirds of sexual assaults occur with regular relational partners (Christopher & Kissler, 2004).

The most common reactions of women to sexual coercion are no response or a strong negative response. In most situations in which men pursue sex and women refuse, men halt their sexual advances (Byers, 1996). About 15% of the time,

SOURCE: ©iStockphoto.com/Stockphoto4u.

You should never assume that someone is using token resistance. "No" means no, and "stop" means stop.

however, the man does not believe the woman's refusal really means no (Byers & Wilson, 1985). In these cases, the man perceives that the woman's saying no is only token resistance (Muehlenhard & Cook, 1988). Clearly, men should not try to second-guess a woman's motivation for saying no. As Andersen (2008) stated, when people misinterpret nonverbal cues or ignore explicit verbal cues in favor of nonverbal cues that erroneously appear positive, sexual harassment or date rape can follow. Therefore, "stop" always means stop and "no" always means no.

When token resistance is used, the situation is unclear, confusing, and dangerous. Both men and women use token resistance, although contrary to the stereotype, men are more likely to use it than women (O'Sullivan & Allgeier, 1994). As noted previously, a sexual initiator should not ignore a request to stop. If, however, an initiator has learned that stop does not really mean stop, "real" requests to stop may be ignored, leading to problems ranging from relational disagreements to sexual assault. Thus, it is best to stop and ask for clarification if you think your partner might be engaging in token resistance. Unless your partner explicitly changes the no into a yes, you should avoid further sexual activity. Similarly, research has shown that men often do not perceive indirect resistance messages on the part of women as real resistance (Motley & Reeder, 1995). Indeed, Motley and Reeder suggested that women need to be much more direct in communicating sexual resistance and that men should listen more carefully to understand women's resistance messages.

Women sometimes fail to send sexual resistance messages because they fear the relational consequences of turning down their partner (Motley & Reeder, 1995). The reality is, men rarely disrupt or terminate a relationship because a woman resists sexual escalation. In fact, Motley and Reeder (1995) found that men rarely are hurt, offended, or angered when women use direct sexual resistance messages, although women erroneously think that men will be offended and de-escalate the relationship if they resist. Because women seldom are turned down in their attempts to sexually escalate a relationship, they are more likely to be hurt and upset if they are

rejected. They project these feelings onto men who do not share their hurt and anger over being sexually rejected. Many men, on the other hand, have considerable experience with sexual rejection and have learned coping strategies to deal with rejection short of relational de-escalation or breakup.

In about 10% of sexually coercive situations, the woman is the aggressor and the man is the target. Among college students, about one-third of all men reported an episode of pressured or forced sex since the age of 16 (Byers, 1996; Struckman-Johnson & Struckman-Johnson, 1994), and in the vast majority of these cases, the perpetrator of coercion was a woman. O'Sullivan and Allgeier (1998) reported that during a two-week period, 26% of college men engaged in an unwanted sexual act and almost 9% had unwanted sexual intercourse. Struckman-Johnson (1988) found that 16% of the men in her sample reported an incident of forced sexual intercourse. Furthermore, Muehlenhard and Cook (1988) studied over 1,000 men and women in introductory college psychology courses and found that more men (62.7%) than women (46.3%) reported having unwanted sexual intercourse. Although men generally have less negative reactions to being the target of coerced sexual encounters than women, one-fifth of the men in a study by Struckman-Johnson and Struckman-Johnson (1994) had a strong negative reaction to the experience.

Overall, studies have shown that women are not very sensitive to male refusals to have sex. O'Sullivan and Byers (1993) found that, when met with a refusal to have sex, 97% of women still tried to influence the man to have sex. Women are not used to being refused, and they find such refusals unpredictable, constraining, and uncomfortable (Metts et al., 1992). In addition, most women have a lot of practice saying no and thus develop good scripts to resist sexual persuasion and coercion. Men, by contrast, may have neither experience in nor well-developed scripts for saying no and believe it is unmanly to refuse sex (Metts et al., 1992). They are also apt to engage in unwanted intercourse due to peer pressure, inexperience, sex-role concerns, and popularity factors (Muehlenhard & Cook, 1988). Of course, both men and women often experience ambivalence about having sex, so some of these cases of unwanted sex probably represent situations in which mixed feelings were present.

Sexual Harassment

Sexual harassment occurs when inappropriate sexual comments, behaviors, or requests create a hostile work or school environment or when a person feels pressure to have sex to avoid negative consequences. Harassment is too common in the workplace, among some friends and acquaintances (Fairhurst, 1986; Keyton, 1996). Although men sometimes experience sexual harassment, research shows that women experience it far more. In fact, studies suggest that one out of every two working women is sexually harassed at some time (Swan, 1997). A study by Hesson-McInnis and Fitzgerald (1997) of 4,385 women employed by the federal government found 1,792 reported they were sexually harassed at least once in the past two years. This problem may be even worse for minority women, as Hargrow (1997) found that over 80% of the working African American women she surveyed reported experiencing some form of sexual harassment. As the research indicates, sexual harassment is a serious problem; it in turn negatively affects job satisfaction, health, and psychological well-being (Glomb et al., 1997).

Describing the behaviors that constitute sexual harassment is complicated. What some people see as harassment, others might see as sexy or innocent fun. Moreover, women sometimes perceive behaviors to be more sexually harassing than do men, especially if they have recently entered the workforce (Booth-Butterfield, 1989). In any case, research suggests that certain verbal and nonverbal behavior should be avoided. Dougherty, Turban, Olson, Dwyer, and Lapreze (1996) noted that some behaviors, such as making lewd comments or grabbing someone's breasts or buttocks, are blatantly harassing. Gutek, Morasch, and Cohen (1983) found that touch behavior (operationalized as a pat on the bottom) and verbal comments about another person's body were perceived as harassing, although touch was perceived even more negatively than verbal comments. Similarly, Marks and Nelson (1993) found that potentially inappropriate touching by professors was seen as more harassing than inappropriate verbal comments. Less sexually oriented forms of touch, such as on the shoulder or around the waist, are not perceived to be as harassing as verbal comments. Doughtery and colleagues (1996) compared people's interpretations of potentially harassing situations involving touch behavior (putting an arm around a female coworker's shoulder) and verbal behavior (asking a female coworker how her love life was and if she'd had any exciting dates lately). They found that the verbal comment was perceived as more harassing than the touch.

More specifically, Lee and Guerrero (2001) compared types of touch to determine which were perceived as most harassing. They excluded blatantly harassing touches, such as grabbing breasts or buttocks or kissing someone on the mouth, and instead focused on more ambiguous forms of touch. Of the eight types of touch they studied, touching the face was perceived as most harassing, followed by an arm around the waist. Lee and Guerrero subsequently theorized that types of touch that invade people's personal space are particularly threatening. The face is an especially vulnerable part of the body, and letting someone touch it requires trust. Interestingly, not everyone saw these types of touch as harassing. In fact, while about one-third of the participants "agreed strongly" that face touch was sexually harassing, another one-third "disagreed strongly." This suggests that some forms of touch are seen as harassing by some people but not others, which leads to confusion and misunderstanding.

When people encounter sexual harassment, they can respond using passive, assertive, or retaliatory strategies. **Passive responses**, also referred to as *indirect strategies*, involve ignoring the harassment or appeasing the harasser. **Assertive responses** involve telling the harasser to stop the behavior, with statements such as "Please stop bothering me," "I'm not interested in you that way," "I'm seeing someone else so I'd appreciate it if you'd stop asking me out," and "Your behavior is inappropriate and unprofessional." Assertive responses also involve issuing warnings, such as threatening to talk to the harasser's supervisor. Finally, **retaliatory responses** involve punishing or getting revenge on the harasser, usually by harassing the person back, making derogatory comments about the harasser to others, or getting the harasser in trouble.

Unfortunately, there is not always an effective way of responding to sexual harassment. Swan (1997) found that people who viewed sexual harassment experiences as highly upsetting were most likely to use coping strategies. When people used assertive strategies, they reported feeling better about their jobs and themselves. By contrast, when people used passive or retaliatory strategies, they reported feeling even worse. Retaliatory responses diminished job satisfaction, and passive responses diminished job satisfaction and psychological well-being. However, some studies also have shown that assertive strategies can exacerbate the problem (Schneider, Swan, & Fitzgerald, 1997). Bingham and Burleson (1989) found that, although sophisticated verbal messages were more effective at stopping sexual harassment than unsophisticated ones, neither type of message was effective. Because sexual harassment often involves a power imbalance, it is a particularly difficult situation. If the victim uses passive strategies, the individual remains powerless, and the harassment is likely to continue. But if the victim uses direct strategies, the powerful person might resent being told how to act and retaliate by demoting the victim or making the work environment even more unpleasant. Even so, research suggests that assertive strategies are most effective. If these strategies do not work, the victim may need to talk with the harasser's supervisor.

SEXUAL SATISFACTION: MISCONCEPTIONS AND REALITIES

People in the United States consider themselves sexually knowledgeable and skilled, but research paints a different picture. Instead, what people learn about sex is often haphazard, unreliable, stereotypic, and incomplete (Strong, DeVault, & Sayad, 1999). The Kinsey Institute tested the basic sexual knowledge of a representative sample of nearly 2,000 adults living in the United States (Reinisch & Beasley, 1990). Unfortunately the participants failed miserably. Applying a standard grading scale, 55% would have

failed, 27% would have received a D, and less than 1% would have received an A. As this study suggests, most people think they know more about sex than they actually do.

To be a good partner in a romantic sexual relationship, it is beneficial to understand sex and sexual interaction. A detailed description of the many aspects of human sexuality is beyond the scope of this book, yet a college course in human sexuality can supplement what is presented in this chapter. Here, we will merely try to correct a few common misconceptions about the connections between sexual interaction and sexual satisfaction.

One misconception is that sexual intercourse is necessary for sexual satisfaction. While having an orgasm is related to sexual satisfaction (Sprecher & Cate, 2004), orgasm can occur through many forms of sexual interaction without sexual intercourse. Indeed, safe sex practices include a form of sexual interaction called *outercourse* that involves less intimate contact and no exchange of bodily fluids. Furthermore, for some people, sexual intercourse alone does not provide satisfaction. Shows of affection such as holding hands, cuddling, and kissing are as important as, and in some cases even more important than, sexual intercourse for some people.

A second misconception is that in an intimate heterosexual relationship, women should not initiate sexual interaction because it may undermine the traditional male role and men will see them as too easy or unfeminine. The reality is that the vast majority of men, particularly those under age 40, think it is not only acceptable for women to initiate sex but desirable (Reinisch & Beasley, 1990). Nonetheless, as the misconception suggests, about half of all wives rarely or never initiate sexual interaction (Reinisch & Beasley, 1990). When women do initiate sex, they do it more subtly than men, so men need to tune in and respond to these understated cues. Of course, men should not assume that every indirect cue is a signal that the woman wants to have sex. Once partners learn each other's signals for sexual initiation, they can be nonverbal and implicit. If a woman (or a man) is not comfortable asking for sex, special signals can be used such as lighting a candle, drinking wine, and playing romantic music in the bedroom (Reinisch & Beasley, 1990).

However, research suggests that men prefer clear, instrumental disclosure about sex because it leads to greater sexual understanding and, in turn, to more sexual satisfaction (MacNeil & Byers, 2005, 2009).

A third misconception is that heterosexual couples are more satisfied with sexual interaction than are gay or lesbian couples. In reality, although the sex lives of heterosexuals, gay men, and lesbians are different in some respects, *all* couple types generally report having satisfying sex lives. Even teens report high levels of satisfaction with their first and most recent sexual encounter and report less stress, less anger, and more well-being following sexual encounters (Shrier, Shin, Hacker, & de Moor, 2007; Wright, Parkes, Strange, Allen, & Bonell, 2008). Some studies have shown that gay and lesbian partners rate the subjective quality of their sexual experiences higher than do heterosexual couples, perhaps because they better understand each other's sexual needs (Crooks & Baur, 1999; Masters & Johnson, 1979; Peplau et al., 2004). In these studies, subjective quality was defined in terms of more psychological involvement, total body contact, enjoyment of sexual activities, and responsiveness to the sexual needs of the partner.

A fourth misconception is that the sight of nudity and touch equally arouse men and women. The reality is that, while each is potentially arousing to members of both sexes, men are visually aroused more than are women. Seeing one's partner in skimpy clothing is more of a turn-on for most men than for women. Conversely, women are much more aroused by touch than are men, particularly nongenital touch. Thus, cuddling and foreplay are important precursors to sexual intercourse for women. In sexual areas of the body, both men and women are highly arousable. Heterosexual couples, in particular, need to learn that what arouses each partner personally might not be as arousing for the other partner and adapt accordingly.

A fifth misconception is that men enjoy sexual intercourse more than women. The reality is that heterosexual men and women both enjoy intercourse. Contrary to the stereotype, research suggests that women may actually enjoy intercourse more than men (Blumstein & Schwartz, 1983). In close, committed relationships, most women enjoy sexual intercourse because of the extreme intimacy and closeness it

reflects. Although some women may not want to have sex as often as men, when they do have high-quality sex, they report finding it extremely pleasurable.

A sixth misconception is that the most important predictor of sexual satisfaction is how often a couple has sex. Nearly 90% of married individuals report that they are sexually satisfied, with couples varying considerably in how often they have sex; indeed, most studies show little or no relationship between amount of sex and satisfaction (Blumstein & Schwartz, 1983; Lauman et al., 1994; Sprecher & Cate, 2004). Frequency of sex thus is not as important as the quality of the sex and the match between two people's needs during sexual activity (Sprecher & Regan, 2000). When partners have similar attitudes about sex, they are happier with their sex lives. Therefore, if they believe that cuddling is more important than sex, they might have sex less often than a couple who believes that sex is the ultimate expression of intimacy; yet both couples would be satisfied. Some support for this line of reasoning also comes from studies comparing heterosexual couples to gay and lesbian couples. On average, gay men place a higher value on sex than do heterosexuals, and heterosexuals place a higher value on sex than do lesbians. These values are reflected in behavior. Rosenzweig and Lebow (1992) found that almost half of gay men reported having sexual relations at least three times a week, while only about one-third of heterosexual couples reported having sex that often. Among lesbian couples, only about one-fifth reported having sex three times a week or more. According to other studies, lesbians spend more time cuddling than do heterosexuals or gay men (Blumstein & Schwartz, 1983). Yet, as discussed previously, relational partners in heterosexual, gay, and lesbian relationships report roughly equal levels of overall sexual satisfaction.

A seventh misconception is that sexual satisfaction is the only key to relational satisfaction. It is true that people who report being happy with their sex lives are also likely to report being happy with their relationships. Although sexual satisfaction and relationship satisfaction are highly associated (Henderson, Lehavot, & Simoni, 2009), sexual satisfaction is not the *best* predictor of relational satisfaction in most relationships. As Sprecher and Regan (2000) put it,

"Neither the quality nor the quantity of sex might be as important as other nonsexual forms of intimacy in the prediction of relationship satisfaction including expressed affection and supportive communication" (p. 223). These authors note that sexual dissatisfaction and incompatibility alone are usually not enough to destroy an otherwise close, caring relationship. Only when these sexual problems are "symptomatic of other relational problems" are they likely to lead to conflict and relational termination. The message here is clear: Sexual satisfaction is an important part of romantic relationships, but other factors, such as love, supportiveness, and compatibility, are usually even more important.

In addition to being knowledgeable about sex, it is important for partners to communicate about sex. Some relational partners think sex is a taboo topic and so do not talk about their sexual desires and preferences (Baxter & Wilmot, 1985). Yet studies suggest that communication about sex is extremely important. Research shows that sexual self-disclosure is associated with a satisfying and rewarding relationship (MacNeil & Byers, 2009).

Frank, Anderson, and Rubinstein (1979) found that about one-half of husbands and three-fourths of wives they studied reported having some sexual difficulty in their marriages, and that these difficulties were increased by poor communication skills. Taking this further, Cupach and Comstock (1990) examined the associations among sexual communication, sexual satisfaction, and overall relational satisfaction. They found that good communication about sex leads to greater sexual satisfaction, which in turn contributes to more relational satisfaction. An earlier study showed that couples are most satisfied with their communication about sex when they are in highly developed, committed relationships. By contrast, couples who are in the early stages of relationship development, or who are in the process of disengaging from the relationship, report being less satisfied with their communication about sex (Wheeless, Wheeless, & Baus, 1984). If you are currently in a sexual relationship, you can access your level of sexual communication satisfaction by taking the test in Box 8.2. Along with this, communication about safe sex is also critical.

BOX 8.2 Put Yourself to the Test

Sexual Communication Satisfaction

Think about a current sexual relationship and rate your communication about sex using the following scale: 1 = strongly disagree, 7 = strongly agree.

	Disagree						Agree
1. I tell my partner when I am especially sexually satisfied.	1	2	3	4	5	6	7
2. I am satisfied with my partner's ability to communicate her or his sexual desires to me.	1	2	3	4	5	6	7
3. I let my partner know things that I find pleasing during sex.	1	2	3	4	5	6	7
4. I do not hesitate to let my partner know when I want to have sex with him or her.	1	2	3	4	5	6	7

(Continued)

(Continued)

	Disagree						Agree
5. I tell my partner whether or not I am sexually satisfied.	1	2	3	4	5	6	7
6. I am satisfied with the degree to which my partner and I talk about the sexual aspects of our relationship.	1	2	3	4	5	6	7
7. I am not afraid to show my partner what kind of sexual behavior I like.	1	2	3	4	5	6	7
8. I would not hesitate to show my partner what is a sexual turn-on for me.	1	2	3	4	5	6	7
9. My partner shows me what pleases her or him during sex.	1	2	3	4	5	6	7
10. My partner tells me when he or she is sexually satisfied.	1	2	3	4	5	6	7
11. I am pleased with the manner in which my partner and I communicate with each other about sex.	1	2	3	4	5	6	7
12. It is never hard for me to figure out if my partner is sexually satisfied.	1	2	3	4	5	6	7

Add up your answers. A score of 84 indicates maximum sexual communication satisfaction. A score of 12 indicates the lowest level of sexual communication satisfaction possible. Since research shows that sexual communication satisfaction increases as relationships develop, you might want to take this test later in the relationship to see if your score changes.

SOURCE: "The Sexual Communication Satisfaction Scale," From Wheeless, Lawrence R., Wheeless, Virginia Eman, and Baus, Raymond (1984). Sexual communication, communication satisfaction, and solidarity in the development stages of intimate relationships, in *Western Journal of Speech Communication. 48* (3, Summer), 217-230. Used with permission of the Western States Communication Association.

COMMUNICATION AND SAFE SEX

The safest form of sex in relationships is no sex. Abstinence is the best way to avoid unwanted pregnancy, AIDS, and other STIs. But total abstinence from sex is unusual, unrealistic, and precludes having romantic relationships or offspring. Thus, additional safe sex practices are imperative. Unfortunately, being in a close relationship inadvertently puts partners at risk since trust is higher and, as a result, safe sex is practiced less in the closest relationships (Noar, Zimmerman, & Atwood, 2004). Worse yet, information and communication about STIs are far less common than they should be, although many publications give excellent advice for safe sex and AIDS prevention (Centers for Disease Control, 1997; Larkin, 1998; Rathus et al., 1993; Student Health Services, 1998). STIs are epidemic in the United States; 65 million Americans have an incurable STI such as genital herpes or HIV (Noar et al., 2004). (For more information about HIV/AIDS, contact your campus health service or county health department.)

Communication is an essential ingredient in promoting safe sex. Unsafe sex can occur with any partner, even one you know well. It is therefore always best to be proactive about safe sex with every partner. This requires communicating with partners about past sexual experiences and talking about safe sex practices, such as those discussed in the following section. Unfortunately, many people are complacent when they have sex with someone they know well (Hammer, Fisher, Fitzgerald, & Fisher, 1996; Noar et al., 2004; Rosenthal, Gifford, & Moore, 1998). They believe that being well acquainted with someone means that they are free of STIs. Recent research suggests that 99% of one college sample were confident in their assessment that their partner did not have an STI, despite research showing that over one-third of college students have an STI (Afifi & Weiner, 2006). Brittany, in our chapter opener, made an intelligent decision; before she got sexually involved with Chris, she insisted they both get tested for STIs. They waited to have sex until they were both found free of sexually transmitted infections.

Many sexually active people believe that they can tell if a partner is lying to them about safe sex behaviors. In actuality, research has shown that people cannot tell when someone is lying about sexual behavior or HIV status (Swann, Silvera, & Proske, 1995). Particularly dangerous is the truth bias, whereby individuals tend to assume that people they like are telling them the truth (see Chapter 13). Trust is important in relationships, but is it worth your life to trust someone who could be wrong about her or his HIV status?

Another danger is people's lack of condom use, even though they know that condoms help prevent STIs. Using condoms consistently, meaning *every time* you have sexual intercourse, is the only effective way to prevent STIs during intercourse (Noar et al., 2004). Studies show that only about one-third of couples use any form of contraception during intercourse (Willetts et al., 2004). Many couples decline to use condoms because they limit spontaneity and reduce sensation (Hammer et al., 1996). Yet about one-third of the males in Hammer and colleagues' study reported that sharing the act of putting on a condom can actually bring the couple closer and is arousing.

Even though logic suggests that people should use condoms to prevent STIs, in real relationships, factors other than logic influence condom use. Managing identity, not wanting to seem promiscuous, not wanting to destroy a romantic moment, not liking the feel of condoms, and believing a partner is "safe" are all factors that influence decision making regarding whether to use condoms (Afifi, 1999; Galligan & Terry, 1993). Galligan and Terry (1993) found that knowledge of the risk reduction effects of condom use was a major motivator for people to use them. However, women were less likely to want to use a condom when they feared it would destroy the romance of the moment. Afifi (1999) reported that when attachment to a partner is high and partners worry that suggesting condom use will be perceived as reflecting a lack of trust, the probability of condom use is decreased. Of course, suggesting condom use may not always be perceived negatively by one's partner; rather, it may be seen as a sign of caring and of responsibility.

These findings underscore the importance of communication; partners should have a frank discussion about safe sex before becoming sexually involved. Interestingly, almost any communication strategy increases the likelihood of condom use, but discussing pregnancy prevention or suggesting condom use "just to be safe" are the most effective strategies, probably because talking about AIDS can make people uncomfortable (Reel & Thompson, 1994). Unfortunately, research has shown that general discussions about AIDS do not promote safe sex. By contrast, discussing the specific sexual history of the partners, negotiating monogamy, and requesting that the partner use a condom can promote safe sex (Cline, Freeman, & Johnson, 1990). Cline and colleagues (1990), however, found that those who discuss safe sex are only a little more likely to engage in safe sex practices than are those who do not. Therefore, it is crucial that partners do more than talk about safe sex practices; they must also take appropriate action to protect themselves. While the following list is likely familiar, here are the rules to follow to avoid AIDS and other STIs:

1. *Practice abstinence.* Although complete abstinence is unlikely for most adults, about 12% of the college-age population are virgins who have had no high-risk sexual activity (Sprecher & Regan, 1996). Abstinence is the most effective policy when it comes to preventing STIs.

2. *Avoid high-risk sex.* HIV and other STIs are transmitted through the exchange of bodily fluids. Intercourse is particularly dangerous. A single episode of unsafe sex with an HIV-positive

person puts you at risk for contracting the virus. Multiple unsafe sex episodes put you at even greater risk (Hammer et al., 1996).

3. *Use condoms.* During sexual intercourse, a new latex condom offers good protection from the transmission of HIV. Old condoms and "off brand" condoms offer poor protection because they may break or leak. Condoms made from animal membranes (skins) are porous and offer less protection against HIV transmission. Although condoms do not offer complete protection, recent studies have shown that when condoms are used properly, they are highly successful in preventing HIV/AIDS even with an infected partner (Centers for Disease Control, 1997; Noar et al., 2004).

4. *Get tested.* If you are uncertain whether you have been exposed to HIV, get tested. Only about 1% of those who are tested show the presence of HIV, so the test is likely to relieve you of concern that you have the virus. If you are HIV positive, you need to get treated immediately. With the proper treatment, many people who are HIV positive live many symptom-free years and even decades. Your campus health center or county department of health typically does HIV tests that are either anonymous or confidential. You can also use an HIV home test kit.

5. *Limit your partners.* Another good preventive technique is to limit yourself to a single partner who was previously a virgin, has been strictly monogamous, or has been tested for HIV since her or his last sexual encounter like Brittany and Chris did. Remember, when you have sex with your partner, you are exposing yourself to risk from every person who has had sex with your partner in the past. Having sex only in the context of a monogamous infection-free sexual relationship provides you with protection and may be the healthiest form of sexual activity (Noar et al., 2006).

6. *Know your partners.* A partner whom you know, respect, and completely trust is the safest kind of person with whom to have a sexual relationship, but this can be misleading. There is great risk with having sex with a new acquaintance, with someone whose sexual history you do not know, or with a long-term partner whom you do not trust. Research has also shown that people make flawed judgments about who is a safe partner. Many people erroneously believe that having sex with healthy looking, physically attractive people, friends, or people similar to themselves is safe (Noar et al., 2004)—sometimes it is not. Research has also shown that many people find it difficult to bring up the topic of safe sex and condom use during a sexual encounter with a new acquaintance (Rosenthal et al., 1998). Again, people who fail to communicate about safe sex are literally risking their lives.

7. *Avoid intoxication.* Research has shown that binge drinkers engage in more sexual activity with a wider variety of partners (Mongeau & Johnson, 1995) than do heavy drug users, yet drug use also increases risk of STIs. Studies also have shown that people are most likely to lapse in their safe sex practices when they are under the influence of alcohol and other drugs. Binging on alcohol is a major predictor of catching STIs (Lindley, Barnett, Brandt, Hardin, & Burcin, 2008). More than one-third of the participants in one study said that they had failed to use condoms on one or more occasions due to the use of drugs or alcohol (Hammer et al., 1996).

8. *Be honest.* It is essential to report any unsafe sex outside your relationship to your partner so that appropriate steps can be taken. Of course, telling your partner about past sexual experiences or recent infidelities can be uncomfortable and harm your relationship. However, in the long run, it is far better to warn your partner of possible dangers than to save yourself from potential discomfort or conflict.

SUMMARY AND APPLICATION

Sex is a vital part of most romantic relationships. Partners who have similar sexual attitudes and high-quality sexual interaction are likely to be satisfied with their sex lives. Sexual satisfaction is associated with relational satisfaction, although it is important to remember that other factors, such as affection, love, and compatibility, are more important. Similarly, partners who are knowledgeable about sex are generally happier with their sex lives.

The research discussed in this chapter can help people like Taylor, Sarah, and Brittany in at least two ways. First, research on sexual attitudes can help them better understand their sexual selves. Second, research on sexual communication can help them improve how they talk about sex with their partners. In terms of sexual attitudes, Taylor has accepted and embraced her homosexuality. Sex is important in lesbian relationships, but nonverbal affection may be even more important to Taylor and Leslie. When Taylor hears homophobic comments and sees strange looks on the faces of her sorority sisters when she mentions Leslie, she has every right to be upset. But Taylor might be consoled by recognizing that people have different attitudes and preferences regarding sex whether they are homosexual or heterosexual. For instance, Sarah sometimes struggles with derogatory comments that people direct at her because she is a virgin.

For her part, Sarah should be comforted by the fact that about 12% of college students (and 13% of women college students) are virgins, and that people who remain virgins because of strong moral beliefs and values are usually happy and proud of their virginity. Indeed, if Sarah gave up her virginity for the sake of pleasing her boyfriend or conforming to social norms, she might very well regret her decision. Research suggests that Sarah should refuse sexual advances in a direct manner, using clear verbal communication. Her boyfriend might use a wide variety of strategies to try to convince her to have sex, including pressure, manipulation, or antisocial behaviors, but research suggests that these strategies are likely to backfire or result in less relational satisfaction, so they should be avoided. Research also suggests that Sarah's boyfriend will accept her decision.

Because she refuses to have sex, Sarah is in the position of being the sexual gatekeeper in her relationship with her boyfriend. Even in relationships that turn sexual, women tend to be in the gate-keeping position at the beginning of the relationship, with men cast in the role of sexual initiator. Socially accepted scripts for sexual communication are typically followed in the early stages of relationships. However, as the relationship develops, women usually feel freer to initiate sex. Unique, individual sexual scripts replace socially normative scripts in developed relationships.

Finally, communication plays an important role in promoting sexual satisfaction. Couples who tell each other their sexual preferences and communicate their needs, desires, and aversions are much more likely to be happier with their sex life. Communication is also critical for promoting safe sex and avoiding STIs or an unplanned pregnancy, as Brittany's communication with her boyfriend exemplifies. Although Brittany does not talk about her sex life with her parents, she learned how to be sexually responsible from them. Parents should talk to their children about sex in a supportive, nondefensive manner rather than issuing warnings. Partners like Brittany and Chris should also talk to each other openly and honestly about their past sexual experiences and the need to practice safe sex. However, it is important to remember that safe sex *talk* is not enough; safe sex *behaviors* save lives.

DISCUSSION QUESTIONS

1. In this chapter, we presented data suggesting that most couples wait until some emotional intimacy or commitment has developed before engaging in sex. We also reported a study indicating that around 10% to 15% of college students are virgins. Based on the conversations you have had with friends, do you think these numbers hold true for your school? Why might these estimates differ depending on the group of people responding?

2. Based on what you learned in this chapter, what strategies would you use to protect yourself from sexual coercion or harassment? Why do you think people misinterpret supposed sexual cues so often?

3. Why do you think people practice unsafe sex even though they know the risks involved? What communication strategies might partners use to ensure that they engage in safe sex?

STUDENT STUDY SITE

Visit the study site at **www.sagepub.com/guerrero3e** for e-flashcards, survey and assessments from the chapter, and SAGE journal articles.

9

Staying Close

Maintaining Relationships

After three years of serious dating, Yasser proposes to Rachel and she accepts. Although she loves Yasser and is excited about the prospect of marrying him, she starts to worry that getting married could change things. When she was in middle school, her parents divorced after several years of bitter fights. To add fuel to her worries, a good friend of hers recently announced that she and her husband were separating after only two years of marriage. Sometimes it seems to Rachel that everyone is getting divorced. Yasser assures her that things will be different for them. After all, they love each other and have a great relationship. And, Yasser's parents have been happily married for nearly 30 years, so he has seen how two people can work together to maintain a successful relationship. Rachel wonders what their secret is. How do Yasser's parents manage to keep their relationship so happy, and can she and Yasser do the same?

In fairy tales, everyone lives "happily ever after," as if happiness was bestowed upon them with the flick of a magic wand. In real life, however, there is no magic recipe for a happy relationship. So what can couples like Rachel and Yasser do to keep their relationships happy? How might getting married change their relationship? Maintaining relationships requires effort and perseverance. The road to a successful relationship can be full of potholes and detours, but "staying on course" and maintaining important relationships is a worthwhile endeavor. In fact, because having a close relationship is a key determinant of overall happiness (Hatfield, 1984), people who have trouble maintaining close relationships with others often are lonely and depressed, and they may doubt their self-worth (Segrin, 1998). Married people tend to report being happier and more satisfied with their lives than do single people (Cargan & Melko, 1982), yet 45% to 50% of first marriages in the United States end in divorce (Lansford, 2009). In 2008, estimates suggested that for every two people who got married in the United States, another person got divorced (Tejada-Vera & Sutton, 2009).

Studies also show that marital satisfaction drops after parenthood, providing another maintenance challenge (Twenge, Campbell, & Foster, 2003). Given these facts, Rachel's concerns are certainly understandable and justified.

The research on relational maintenance provides important information on behaviors that couples like Yasser and Rachel can use to promote relational satisfaction and longevity. In this chapter, we look at two areas of research related to maintenance. First, we discuss specific types of behaviors people use to maintain a variety of close relationships. Second, we focus on two dialectical theories, which describe the tensions that often characterize interpersonal communication and relationships. As described in more detail later, these tensions revolve around various, often competing, meanings that communication can have. For example, imagine that Rachel tells Yasser, "It's good that we spend some extra time with our friends now, but I'm looking forward to the two of us having some quality time alone together after the wedding." What meanings can be derived from Rachel's statement? One meaning might center on the value of autonomy—in this case having time to spend away from one's partner and with one's friends. Another meaning might center on the value of togetherness—in this case having quality time alone to connect with one's partner. Dialectical theories focus on how these types of messages shape meaning and influence how people think about competing forces in their relationships.

DEFINING RELATIONAL MAINTENANCE

People maintain things that they care about. They take their cars in for routine maintenance service and repair mechanical problems when they occur. They maintain their homes by keeping them clean, mowing the lawn, trimming the hedges, and painting the walls. They maintain their good images at work by trying to be punctual, professional, presentable, and well organized. Similarly, people usually try to maintain and mend their relationships with others through contact and communication. As you may already know or will learn, maintaining a relationship is far more challenging than maintaining a car or a home.

Relational maintenance has been defined in various ways. According to Dindia and Canary (1993), there are four common definitions. First, *relational maintenance involves keeping a relationship in existence.* Although some relationships are kept in existence through extensive contact, others require minimal effort. For example, social networking sites such as Facebook and MySpace allow people to keep in touch with one another without having to invest time and effort into communicating with each individual "friend" one-on-one. Similarly, you might send holiday or birthday cards to people who you do not have much contact with during the course of the year as a way of keeping a relationship in existence. Second, *relational maintenance involves keeping a relationship in a specified state or condition, or at stable level of intimacy, so that the status quo is maintained* (Ayres, 1983). For example, friends might work to keep their relationship from becoming romantic, or sisters might try to keep their relationship as close as ever despite living in different cities. Third, *relational maintenance can involve keeping a relationship in satisfactory condition.* Dating and married couples often try to rekindle the romance in their relationships to keep them satisfying. They might have a candlelight dinner or spend a weekend away together. Similarly, friends might plan a weekend ski trip together to catch up with each other and have fun. Fourth, *relational maintenance involves keeping a relationship in repair.* The idea here is that people work to prevent problems from occurring in their relationships, and to fix problems when they do occur.

As Dindia and Canary (1993) stated, these four components of relational maintenance overlap. A critical part of keeping a relationship satisfying is preventing and correcting problems, and an important part of keeping a relationship in existence is keeping it satisfying. In a broad sense, relational maintenance can be defined as *keeping a relationship at a desired level* (Canary & Stafford, 1994). For some relationships, the desired level may be a casual friendship, professional association, or acquaintanceship, with occasional e-mails or contact through social networking sites such as Facebook being all that is necessary. For other relationships, physical and emotional closeness are desired, which typically requires more sustained maintenance efforts. It is also important to recognize that keeping a relationship at a desired level does not necessarily mean that a relationship remains at the same level of closeness over time. As peoples' desires change, the way they define and maintain their relationships also changes. Maintenance is a dynamic process that involves continually adjusting to new needs and demands.

BEHAVIORS USED TO MAINTAIN RELATIONSHIPS

So *how* do people maintain their relationships? Scholars began addressing this important question in the 1980s (Ayres, 1983; Bell, Daly, & Gonzalez, 1987; Dindia & Baxter, 1987; Duck, 1988; Shea & Pearson, 1986). Since then, much has been learned about behaviors people use to maintain various types of relationships. Although various scholars have advanced different lists of behaviors used to maintain relationships, most maintenance behaviors can be characterized based on three distinctions: (1) how prosocial or antisocial they are, (2) their channel or modality, and (3) whether they are employed strategically or routinely.

Prosocial Maintenance Behaviors

The majority of behaviors used to maintain relationships are **prosocial**, positive behaviors that promote relational closeness, trust, and liking. Stafford and Canary (1991) asked dating and married couples what they did to maintain their relationships and keep them satisfying. Five primary maintenance strategies, all of which are prosocial, emerged: (1) positivity, (2) openness, (3) assurances, (4) social networking, and (5) task sharing. Other researchers have identified supportiveness, joint activities, romance, humor, and constructive conflict as common prosocial behaviors used to maintain certain relationships (Afifi, Guerrero, & Egland, 1994; Dainton & Stafford, 1993; Stafford, 2003). These maintenance behaviors are described further in Box 9.1.

Not surprisingly, research suggests that relationships characterized by high levels of prosocial

maintenance tend to be stable and committed. In a study by Guerrero, Eloy, and Wabnik (1993), college-age daters were surveyed near the beginning of the semester and then eight weeks later. People who reported using more prosocial maintenance behaviors at the beginning of the study were more likely to have become more serious or stayed at the same intimacy level by the end of the eight weeks. Those who reported using low levels of prosocial maintenance behavior were likely to have de-escalated or terminated their relationships by the end of the eight weeks. In another study, Ramirez (2008) had married couples complete two surveys that were spaced around two weeks apart. Couples who reported using more prosocial maintenance were more personally committed to their marriage when surveyed two weeks later, with personal commitment defined as the extent to which a person was devoted to the partner and desired to remain in the relationship. Weigel and Ballard-Reisch (2008) also found that spouses use more prosocial maintenance behavior when they are both committed to their marriage.

People who use high levels of prosocial maintenance behavior, then, appear to be more satisfied with their relationships (Stafford, 2003; Weigel & Ballard-Reisch, 2008). **Relational satisfaction** refers to the "pleasure or enjoyment" that people derive from their relationships (Vangelisti & Huston, 1994, p. 173). Positivity, assurances, and social networking all have particularly strong associations with relational satisfaction (Dainton, Stafford, & Canary, 1994; Stafford & Canary, 1991). In one study, people reported being the most satisfied in their relationships when their partners used higher levels of positivity and assurances than they expected them to use (Dainton, 2000). In another study, couples who used high levels of positivity, assurances, and social networking at the beginning of a year-long study were especially likely to be satisfied with their marriages by year's end (Weigel & Ballard-Reisch, 2001). Similarly, young adults report being more satisfied with their family relationships when they use high levels of positivity and social networking (Morr Serewicz, Dickson, Morrison, & Poole, 2007).

The amount of time people spend together is also positively related to satisfaction. Time together creates feelings of companionship and cohesion and opens lines of communication (Egland, Stelzner, Andersen, & Spitzberg, 1997; Reissman, Aron, & Bergen, 1993).

Engaging in joint activities can also promote feelings of togetherness and similarity. Likewise, when partners share tasks in a fair and equitable manner, they tend to feel closer and more satisfied with their relationships (Canary & Stafford, 1994; Guerrero et al., 1993).

BOX 9.1 Highlights

Prosocial Maintenance Behaviors

Behavior	Definition and Examples
Positivity	Making interactions pleasant and enjoyable (e.g., giving compliments, acting cheerful)
Openness and routine talk	Talking and listening to one another (e.g., self-disclosure, sharing secrets, asking how the partner's day went)
Assurances	Giving each other assurances about commitment (e.g., assuring the other you still care, talking about the future)
Social networking	Spending time with each other's social network (e.g., going to family functions together, accepting each other's friends)
Task sharing	Performing routine tasks and chores relevant to the relationship together (e.g., sharing household chores, planning finances together)
Supportiveness	Giving each other social support and encouragement (e.g., providing comfort, making sacrifices for the partner)
Joint activities	Engaging in activities and spending time together (e.g., hanging out together, playing sports, shopping together)
Romance and affection	Revealing positive, caring feelings for each other (e.g., saying "I love you," sending flowers, having a romantic dinner)
Humor	Using inside jokes, humor, and sarcasm (e.g., using funny nicknames, laughing together)
Constructive conflict management	Managing conflict in constructive ways that promote problem-solving and harmony (e.g., listening to one another's positions, trying to come up with acceptable solutions)

Antisocial Maintenance Behavior

In contrast to the prosocial maintenance behaviors that are related to commitment and satisfaction, scholars have identified a set of **antisocial** or negative behaviors that are sometimes used to maintain relationships, although they tend not to increase (and may even decrease) relational satisfaction. These behaviors tend to discourage interaction or try to change the partner in some way; are often coercive, manipulative, or controlling; and include as ultimatums, threats, and becoming distant (Dindia, 1989, 2003; Dindia & Baxter, 1987). Although it might seem puzzling that negative behaviors such as these would be used to try to maintain relationships, keep in mind that antisocial behaviors only qualify as maintenance when they are used specifically for that purpose. Antisocial maintenance behaviors are unlikely to be used to try to keep a relationship satisfying, but they may be used for other maintenance-related reasons, such as trying to control a partner who might break up with you, trying to force someone to see you as more attractive or desirable, or trying to avoid conflict.

Antisocial maintenance behaviors may also be used to try to keep a relationship at a given level of intimacy or closeness, and as Ayres (1983) suggested, is often the case when people use **avoidance** as a maintenance strategy. For example, you might avoid talking about how attracted you are to a friend if you worry that such a revelation could harm your friendship (Afifi & Burgoon, 1998); you might distance yourself from a friend who has a crush on you to signal that you are not interested (Eden & Veksler, 2010); or you might refrain from arguing with your partner on a particular topic if you think it could damage your relationship (see Chapter 11). In other cases, people use avoidance to keep their relationships at a casual level. For instance, if you are uncomfortable becoming close friends with a coworker or classmate, you might avoid personal topics of conversation when talking with this individual. In cross-sex friendships, people sometimes avoid flirting and instead talk about their romantic relationships with others

as maintenance strategies that help keep the relationship platonic (Guerrero & Chavez, 2005; Messman, Canary, & Hause, 2000). Box 9.2 further explains these and other antisocial maintenance behaviors.

Antisocial maintenance behaviors are sometimes designed to alter the partner's feelings or keep the partner in the relationship. At times, people use **jealousy induction** as a maintenance strategy for one or both of these purposes (Dainton & Gross, 2008; Fleischmann, Spitzberg, Andersen, & Roesch, 2005). The idea here is that jealousy might spark feelings of love and possessiveness, making a partner more likely to stay in the relationship. Spying or surveillance may also function to maintain relationships by providing information that reduces uncertainty about rival relationships and helps a jealous person compete with potential rivals (Dainton & Gross, 2008; Guerrero & Afifi, 1999). Dainton and Gross also identified infidelity, allowing control, and destructive conflict as negative behaviors that can be used to try to maintain relationships (see Box 9.2).

Obviously, antisocial behaviors such as jealousy induction, spying, infidelity, and destructive conflict can backfire, leading to more problems or to breakup rather than relational maintenance. Some of these antisocial maintenance behaviors may even represent desperate attempts to hang onto a relationship that is in trouble. For example, jealousy induction is often used when people are worried that their partner is interested in someone else (Guerrero & Andersen, 1998b) and people who do not have the communication skills to solve problems in a constructive manner sometimes use controlling strategies (Christopher & Lloyd, 2000). Not surprisingly, people who report using the antisocial maintenance behaviors of allowing control, destructive conflict, jealousy induction, and infidelity also report low levels of relational satisfaction (Dainton & Gross, 2008). Thus, although behaviors such as avoidance, no flirting, and talking about others can be effective and appropriate at times, and can even lead to more relational satisfaction, many antisocial maintenance behaviors could have destructive effects on relationships.

BOX 9.2 Highlights

Antisocial Maintenance Behaviors

Behavior	Definition and Examples
Avoidance	Evading the partner in certain situations or on certain issues (e.g., planning separate activities, respecting each other's privacy)
No flirting	Refraining from flirting with someone to clearly communicate that you are not interested in pursuing a romantic relationship (e.g., being standoffish when someone flirts with you)
Talking about others	Talking about someone else to signal that you already have a special relationship with another person (e.g., repeatedly mentioning your significant other; explaining why someone is your "best" friend)
Jealousy induction	Attempting to make your partner jealous (e.g., leaving a note from a "secret admirer" out for your partner to see; flirting with someone in front of your partner)
Spying	Getting information about your partner without his or her knowledge (e.g., looking through your partner's text messages; asking your partner's friends for information)
Infidelity	Engaging in sexual activity with someone else (e.g., making out with someone else so your partner knows you have other alternatives; sleeping with someone else to get rewards that you are missing in your current relationship)
Allowing control	Focusing exclusively on the partner (e.g., ignoring your friends so you can spend time with your partner; letting your partner make all the decisions)
Destructive conflict	Using destructive conflict to control the partner (e.g., yelling at your partner if she or he does not do what you want; starting arguments so you can tell your partner how she or he should act)

Modality of Maintenance Behavior

Modality refers to the channel of communication; for example, is a message sent by words, facial expression, voice tone, computer, or letter? Some researchers consider mediated communication, such as e-mail or text messaging, to be a special category of maintenance behavior based on its modality. However, mediated communication is not listed as a separate category in Boxes 9.1 or 9.2 because most maintenance behaviors can be employed in either face-to-face or mediated contexts. For example, friends can call and then catch up by having lunch or they can exchange e-mails. Similarly, individuals can spy on their partners by following them or by checking their Facebook page or e-mails. Mediated forms of maintenance behavior include communicating via social networking services (such as Twitter or Facebook), e-mail, text messaging, the telephone, and cards and letters (Canary, Stafford, Hause, & Wallace, 1993; Marmo & Bryant, 2010; Wright, 2004).

Although people can enact various maintenance strategies through these different modalities, the same behavior may be interpreted differently depending on whether it occurs in face-to-face versus mediated contexts. Various forms of mediated communication may also carry different meanings. Imagine receiving a holiday greeting card from a friend online versus in the mail. Now imagine receiving the card with a pretyped signature versus a real signature. Which card is more personal? All three cards would likely help maintain the friendship, but each card would send a somewhat different message. Some maintenance behaviors are also enacted differently depending on their modality. Take task sharing as an example. People can accomplish some task sharing, such as working together on a written project, through mediated communication. But other forms of task sharing, such as washing and drying the dishes together, can only be accomplished in face-to-face settings.

Mediated forms of communication are especially important for maintaining certain types of relationships, including friendships, online relationships, and long-distance relationships. In terms of friendships, Marmo and Bryant (2010) examined how acquaintances, casual friends, and close friends use Facebook to maintain their relationships. People in all of these friendship groups reported using strategies such as writing on each other's walls and commenting on each other's photos to keep in contact. Facebook users also reported sending messages related to assurances and positivity. For example, if someone posts a comment saying she's having a particularly hard day, her friends are likely to respond with comments expressing support and empathy (Marmo &

Bryant, 2010). The importance of positivity is highlighted by some of the implicit rules that govern how friends interact on Facebook. According to these rules, people expect others to present themselves and their friends positively (in messages, photos, etc.) on Facebook and to refrain from posting anything that could hurt a person's image (Bryant & Marmo, 2010). Another unwritten rule, which is reflected in reports of actual behavior, is that close friends should engage in more maintenance behavior on Facebook than casual friends, who should engage in more than acquaintances (Marmo & Bryant, 2010). However, maintaining a relationship using Facebook alone may not be enough. One study showed that contact via Facebook was sufficient for maintaining acquaintanceships and casual friendships, but close friends and romantic partners also needed to use other means, such as talking face-to-face or on the phone, to maintain the high intimacy levels in their relationships (Bryant & Marmo, in press).

Researchers have also studied relational maintenance in online relationships. Wright (2004) found that openness and positivity were the most frequently used maintenance behaviors in these relationships. Rabby (2007) compared maintenance in four types of relationships: **Virtual relationships** were defined in terms of the partners having communicated only online. **Pinocchio relationships** occur when partners first meet online but then start meeting in person (i.e., they become "real"). **Cyber emigrant relationships** are those in which partners first meet in person, but then start communicating primarily online. Finally, communication in **real world relationships** starts and continues primarily in face-to-face contexts. In Rabby's study, people in the virtual-only group reported using the least maintenance behavior. However, if people in the virtual-only group were highly committed to their partner, they used just as much relational maintenance as did people in the other three groups. This suggests that maintenance behavior is more strongly related to commitment than modality.

Mediated forms of maintenance behavior are also common in long-distance relationships between romantic partners, family members, and friends (Rabby & Walther, 2003; Rohlfing, 1995). In fact,

Communicating with friends using e-mail and social networking sites may be sufficient for maintaining acquaintanceships and casual friendships, but additional modes of communication are usually necessary to maintain our closest relationships.

social networking sites, such as Facebook and Twitter, are marketed as ways to maintain relationships or keep in touch with friends. Mediated communication can also be used to terminate a relationship, as can be the case if someone is "de-friended" on Facebook. Failure to answer an e-mail or even failing to send a greeting card for birthdays or holidays (Dindia, Timmerman, Langan, Sahlstein, & Quandt, 2004) may be also perceived as a sign that someone does not want to maintain a relationship. Some types of maintenance behaviors are especially amenable to mediated communication, and therefore more likely to be used in long-distance relationships. In one study, people reported using computer-mediated forms of communication related to positivity and social networking as ways to maintain their long-distance relationships. In contrast, openness

and shared tasks were more likely to occur in face-to-face contexts (Dainton & Aylor, 2002).

Strategic and Routine Maintenance Behaviors

In addition to modality, maintenance behaviors can be distinguished by how strategic versus routine they are (Canary & Stafford, 1994; Dindia, 2003; Duck, 1986). **Strategic maintenance behaviors** are intentionally designed to maintain a relationship. For example, if you have an argument with your best friend, you might call with the intent of apologizing and repairing the situation. On Mother's Day, you might send your mom a bouquet of flowers so that she knows you are thinking of her. If you live far away from a loved one, you might call twice a week at a designated time or send the loved one an e-mail to keep in touch. These types of actions are deliberate and intentionally designed to maintain a positive relationship with someone.

Routine maintenance behaviors are less strategic and deliberate. They are used without the express purpose of maintaining the relationship, yet they still help people preserve their bonds with one another. Behaviors such as task sharing and positivity are especially likely to be used routinely rather than strategically (Dainton & Aylor, 2002). For example, roommates might share household responsibilities as a routine or habit. One roommate might do grocery shopping, pay bills, and vacuum and dust the apartment, and the other roommate might water the plants, clean the bathroom, and do the cooking. Similarly, Yasser and Rachel might routinely engage in positivity by appearing happy when one partner arrives home from work, and using polite communication such as saying "thank you" when doing favors for one another. Duck (1994) argued that routine talk is more important than strategic behavior for maintaining relationships. Other researchers have demonstrated that routine maintenance is a somewhat better predictor of relational satisfaction and commitment than strategic maintenance (Dainton & Aylor, 2002). Thus, maintaining a relationship does not always require conscious "work." Sometimes maintenance rests in seemingly trivial behaviors that people enact rather mindlessly on a day-to-day basis.

Naturally, the line between strategic and routine maintenance behaviors is sometimes blurred. Many people cannot really tell if a given behavior is strategic or routine. Moreover, the same behavior can be strategic in some situations and routine in others. For example, holding your romantic partner's hand at the movie theater might be a habitual routine; you always hold your partner's hand at the movies. After an argument, however, reaching for your partner's hand might be a strategic move designed to repair the relationship and to restore intimacy. Strategic maintenance behaviors also may be used when people try to prevent a relationship from becoming too intimate, escalate or de-escalate the level of intimacy in the relationship, or restore intimacy to repair a relationship. Both routine and strategic behaviors can contribute to relational maintenance in terms of keeping the relationship close and satisfying.

MAINTENANCE BEHAVIOR IN ROMANTIC RELATIONSHIPS

Maintenance behaviors vary based on the type of relationship people share. People maintain all types of relationships, but most maintenance behavior research has focused on romances. Romantic relationships are high in both emotional and sexual intimacy, so the maintenance behaviors romantic partners use reflect these special types of closeness. Maintenance behaviors of romance and affection are highest in romantic relationships, although people show affection to their friends as well. Openness, assurances, and positivity seem to be more common in romantic relationships than in other types of relationships (Canary et al., 1993). Cohabiting romantic partners use many routine maintenance behaviors, including task sharing, joint activities, and routine talk, more than most friends do. Thus, when Rachel and Yasser move in together after getting married, they may begin to use more routine maintenance behaviors.

Changes in Maintenance Over the Course of Romantic Relationships

Of course, Rachel and Yasser do not have to wait to get married to see changes in how they maintain their relationship. Changes have occurred from the time they first met until they became engaged, and more changes are likely to occur after they get married. Stafford and Canary (1991) compared couples at four relationship stages: casually dating, seriously dating, engaged, and married. They found that (1) married and engaged couples reported using more assurances and task sharing than did dating couples, (2) engaged and seriously dating couples reported using more openness and positivity than married or casually dating couples, and (3) married couples reported the most social networking. Adding to these findings, Dainton and Stafford (1993) compared the reports of maintenance behavior in dating versus marital relationships. They found that spouses shared more tasks than daters. Daters, however, engaged in more mediated communication, such as calling each other on the phone, exchanging cards and letters, and so forth.

These results make sense. As couples become more committed, partners may feel freer to provide assurances, and they may, by necessity, share more tasks, especially if they are living together. Similarly, couples may need to integrate social networks as the relationship becomes more committed and people come to view them as a "couple." However, openness and positivity may peak before romantic partners become fully committed. Once married, spouses may not feel the need to disclose their innermost feelings all the time, in part because they have already told each other so much about themselves. Spouses may also express more negativity once they have the security of marriage. When spouses are still in the "honeymoon stage," they are more likely to be on their best behavior and to "put on a happy face." Moreover, the daily interaction that comes from living together makes it difficult for married couples to be positive all of the time. Complaints and conflicts are likely to occur, even in the best relationships.

In addition to varying across relationship stage, maintenance behaviors appear to change as a function of relationship length. In one study, as their relationships lengthened, couples reported less openness, but more social networking, task sharing, and constructive conflict management (Dainton & Aylor, 2002). Presumably, partners disclose more information in early relationship stages as they get to know one another. As their relationships intensify, they begin to merge social networks and negotiate rules about managing conflict and sharing tasks.

In marriages, relational maintenance may follow a curvilinear pattern; in other words, spouses may use more maintenance behavior in the early and later years of marriage (Weigel & Ballard-Reisch, 1999). One explanation for this finding is that couples put considerable effort in their marriages during the honeymoon stage. Imagine how Rachel might act during the early years of her marriage with Yasser. Because being married is novel and exciting, and because she

is concerned about making her marriage a success, she may be especially likely to engage in maintenance behavior. As the marriage progresses, she and Yasser may become preoccupied with their children and careers, leaving less time to devote to one another. Eventually, however, Weigel and Ballard-Reisch's research suggests that their level of maintenance will rebound, perhaps when their children are older or they settle into a comfortable work routine.

Research by Vangelisti and Huston (1994) on newlyweds suggests that both maintenance behavior and satisfaction levels change during the first years of marriage. The newlyweds were contacted three times—after they had been married three or less months, and shortly after their first and second wedding anniversaries. Spouses generally became less satisfied over time, possibly due to unrealistic expectations at the beginning of their marriages. However, couples who were happy with certain areas of their married lives tended to be more satisfied with their relationships. For both husbands and wives, "communication" and "influence" were very important. Communication referred to how well spouses could talk to each other, while influence referred to the amount of input spouses had in making joint decisions. For wives, four other areas related to satisfaction over the first two and a half years of their marriages included (1) sexual compatibility, (2) fair division of labor, (3) time spent with the spouse, and (4) time spent with friends and family. These findings suggest that communication-related maintenance behaviors such as being open and having a "voice" in the decision-making process are strongly related to marital satisfaction. For wives, sharing tasks in an equitable manner, engaging in joint activities with one's spouse, and social networking also appear to be particularly important.

Maintenance in Gay and Lesbian Relationships

In addition to using the prosocial maintenance behaviors listed earlier, gay and lesbian couples use some unique strategies to maintain their relationships. In the first of two studies they conducted on maintenance behavior in gay male and lesbian relationships, Haas and Stafford (1998) found that partners in same-sex romantic relationships reported that it is important to live and work in environments that are supportive and not judgmental of their relationships. Similarly, gay and lesbian partners emphasized the importance of being "out" in front of their social networks. Spending time with friends and family members who recognize and accept their relationship was a key relational maintenance behavior, as was being able to introduce each other as "my partner." Some gay and lesbian couples also reported modeling their parents' relationships. Gay and lesbian couples tend to see their relationships as similar to heterosexual relationships in terms of commitment and communication, but dissimilar in terms of nonconformity to sex-role stereotypes. Finally, some people proposed that it would be helpful if gay and lesbian couples had the same legal rights as heterosexual couples.

In a second study, Haas and Stafford (2005) found that although same-sex romantic relationships were characterized by many of the same maintenance behaviors as opposite-sex marriages, subtle differences existed. Sharing tasks was the most commonly reported maintenance behavior for both types of relationships. However, gay and lesbian couples reported using more maintenance behaviors that show bonding, such as talking about the commitment level in their relationships. Haas and Stafford argued that bonding communication is more necessary in gay and lesbian relationship because these relationships are not legally validated as are marriages.

MAINTENANCE BEHAVIOR IN SAME-SEX FRIENDSHIPS

Even though our friendships are extremely important, people usually don't work as hard to maintain their friendships as their romantic relationships (Dainton, Zelley, & Langan, 2003; Fehr, 1996). Perhaps this is because people take a more casual approach to friendships. People are taught that romantic relationships require a spark to get started, and that the spark needs to be rekindled from time to time if the relationship is to remain satisfying. Friendships, on the other hand, are expected to be on "cruise control" (see Box 9.3) most of the time. In fact, most people would think it was odd if Rachel was worried about maintaining a relationship with her best friend rather than her future spouse.

BOX 9.3 Highlights

Can Relationships Go Into "Cruise Control"?

Once you are in a committed, long-term relationship, do you still have to work hard to maintain your relationship, or can you go on "cruise control"? This is a complicated question that relational maintenance researchers are still trying to answer: Some researchers take a centrifugal perspective while others take a centripetal perspective (Canary & Stafford, 1994; Duck, 1988).

According to the **centrifugal perspective,** people must work actively to maintain their relationships. Without maintenance, relationships will deteriorate. Think of your car. It might be running great now, but if you never change the oil or check the coolant, it probably won't last very long. Researchers taking the centrifugal perspective see relationships the same way. If you don't put time and energy into maintaining them, they will eventually fall apart.

Researchers taking a **centripetal perspective** believe that people in close, committed relationships stay together unless something pulls them apart. According to this view, there are barriers that prevent people from leaving committed relationships. Unless some outside force makes it easier to break through the barriers, or some problem becomes so big that the couples cannot handle it, people will stay with their

(Continued)

(Continued)

current partners. It is almost like driving in cruise control. You can relax until something unexpected (such as an animal running across the road) happens. For example, a married couple might be content together until one spouse finds a more appealing partner and has an affair. The affair forces the couple out of its routine and has the power to tear the relationship apart.

In this book we take the position that highly committed relationships do run on cruise control some of the time, but that periodic maintenance is necessary to keep them healthy and to adjust to changing needs and demands. Striking a balance between working on a relationship and letting a relationship work for you is best.

Nonetheless, friendships require maintenance. Fehr (1996) suggested that three maintenance behaviors are particularly important in friendships: openness, supportiveness, and positivity. Afifi and colleagues (1994) found that all three of these behaviors are associated with relational closeness in same-sex friendships between both men and women. Several studies have shown that openness, which includes both routine talk and intimate self-disclosure, is the cornerstone of all good friendships (Canary, Stafford, Hause, & Wallace, 1993; Rose, 1985; Rosenfeld & Kendrick, 1984). Other maintenance behaviors, such as joint activities and affection, differ somewhat in importance depending on whether the friends are men or women.

Talking Versus Doing

Many studies have compared, directly or indirectly, how female versus male friends maintain their relationships. One common finding is that women tend to "talk" more while men tend to "do" more (Barth & Kinder, 1988; Sherrod, 1989). Wright (1982) referred to women's friendships as "face-to-face" because of the focus on communication, and men's friendships as "side-by-side" because of the focus on activity. This sex difference, albeit small, appears early in life and extends to mediated communication such as e-mail and phone calls. A study by Crockett, Losoff, and Peterson (1984), for example, found that 85% of eighth-grade girls reported talking to their friends on the phone every day, as opposed to only 50% of the boys. In a study by the Annenberg Public Policy Center, researchers asked 10- to 17-year-old children what activity would be hardest to give up for a week (Stanger, 1997). Over 35% of the girls said that it would be most difficult to give up talking on the telephone. In fact, giving up telephone talk was the top answer for girls, surpassing other activities such as listening to music, playing sports, and watching television. By contrast, over 41% of the boys reported that it would be most difficult to cease playing sports for a week. Only 6.5% of the boys felt that giving up telephone talk would be the most difficult.

However, the talking-versus-doing distinction does not mean that men are insensitive communicators who never share their thoughts and feelings with one another. Nor does it mean that women sit around all day chatting endlessly. Research shows that both men and women value self-disclosure in their relationships (Afifi et al., 1994; Floyd & Parks, 1995; Monsour, 1992; Parks & Floyd, 1996), but women disclose to one another a bit more. Similarly, both men and women value spending time with one another, even though men tend to engage in more focused activities than women. Supporting this, Fehr (1996) reviewed research showing that men and women spend similar amounts of time with their friends. The difference is that men engage in more activities, such as playing sports. In other words, women get together more often just to talk and spend time with another, whereas men get together more often to do something specific, such as surf, play golf, or watch a game. Of course, sometimes men get together just to talk, and sometimes women get together to play sports. In fact, one study found no difference in how much male and female friends reported engaging in shared activities (Floyd & Parks, 1995). The difference between men's and women's activities is more subtle than dramatic; therefore, the talking versus doing distinction may be overstated.

Sex Differences in Emotional Support and Affection

Friendships between men and women also differ somewhat in emotional supportiveness and affection. Fehr (1996) summarized research showing that women's friendships are characterized by more emotional support than men's friendships, although both men and women give one another social support at times. For example, female friends are more positive and supportive than male friends, although this sex difference is small (Afifi et al., 1994). Fehr (1996) also summarized research showing that female friends are more nonverbally affectionate than male friends. This is especially true for elementary school-aged children (Thorne & Luria, 1986), university students (Hays, 1985), and elderly adults (Roberto & Scott, 1986). From a young age, girls in the United States are socialized to be more affectionate toward

their friends than boys. Girls often comb one another's hair, sit so that their arms are touching, and hold hands while skipping or running. By contrast, except in the context of sports, boys rarely touch one another. Similarly, adult women are more likely to hug one another and kiss cheeks than are male friends, especially in the United States and other Western cultures. Male friends show affection in other ways, though, particularly through humor, roughhousing, and shared activities (Fehr, 1996).

Men and Women are From the Same Planet

Taken as a whole, the research suggests that some sex differences exist in how men and women maintain their friendships. However, these differences are not dramatic; men and women are generally more similar than dissimilar, and when differences are found, they tend to be small (Andersen, 1998b; Canary & Hause, 1993). Everyone wants friends to talk to, do things with, and turn to in times of trouble, regardless of gender. In fact, both men and women see their friendships as one of the most important sources of happiness in their lives (Fehr, 1996; Rawlins, 1992). Box 9.4 examines the issue of whether men and women really are from "different planets."

BOX 9.4 Highlights

Are Men and Women Really From Different Planets?

If you watch television talk shows or read popular books on relationships, you have probably been introduced to the idea that men and women are very different from each other and that these differences can cause relational problems. For example, Deborah Tannen's popular 1990 book *You Just Don't Understand: Women and Men in Conversation* is built around the idea that boys and girls grow up in different cultures, with girls learning to communicate in ways that are confirming and create intimacy, and boys learning to communicate in ways that enhance independence and power. According to Tannen, women and men have difficulty communicating with one another because of "cultural misunderstanding."

John Gray's 1992 best seller, discussed in Chapter 1, *Men Are From Mars, and Women Are From Venus*, takes this argument a step further by conceptualizing men and women as inhabitants of different planets. As he put it, "Men and women differ in all areas of their lives. Not only do men and women communicate

(Continued)

(Continued)

differently but they think, feel, perceive, react, respond, love, need, and appreciate differently. They almost seem to be from different planets, speaking different languages and needing different nourishment" (p. 5). According to Gray, these "interplanetary differences" are responsible for all the problems that people have in their opposite-sex relationships.

Most relationship researchers, however, do not take a position as extreme as Gray's. Some take a position similar to Tannen's in that they believe a **different cultures perspective** can help explain communication differences between men and women (see Wood, 1994, 1996). According to this view, boys and girls grow up primarily playing in same-sex groups. Therefore, they learn different sets of rules and values, leading to distinct communication styles.

Some researchers, however, disagree with the different cultures perspective (Dindia, 1997). Instead, they believe that men and women are remarkably similar and that sex differences are small. These researchers are quick to point out that boys and girls grow up in a similar cultural environment, interacting with a variety of people, including teachers and family members, of both sexes. As Dindia has put it, "Men are from North Dakota, and women are from South Dakota."

What do you think? Andersen (1998b) summarized his take on the debate as follows:

> The actual research on sex differences has led to one major, overall conclusion: Men and women are far more similar than different. They are not from different metaphoric planets or cultures. They are all earthlings with goals, hopes, dreams, emotions, fears, and communication behaviors that are a whole lot more similar than they are different. Of course, South Dakotans probably believe that North Dakotans are from another planet. From close range, differences are more obvious than similarities and they are certainty more newsworthy and sensational! From any vantage point other than Dakota, North and South Dakotans look pretty similar. (p. 83)

MAINTENANCE BEHAVIOR IN CROSS-SEX FRIENDSHIPS

Cross-sex friendships can be very rewarding (Werking, 1997). Both men and women like to get the perspective of the "other sex," and many people perceive cross-sex friendships as fun and exciting. However, cross-sex friendships can be confusing and ambiguous at times. Think about your friends of the opposite sex. Do you sometimes wonder if they are physically attracted to you? Do you wonder what it would be like to get involved with them romantically? If one or both of you are heterosexual, these types of questions are likely to surface, even if only in your mind.

Challenges in Cross-Sex Friendships

As a result of this ambiguity, cross-sex friends sometimes face special challenges. O'Meara (1989) discussed four challenges that men and women face when they want to be "just friends" with one another. Three of these challenges—the emotional bond challenge, the sexual challenge, and the public presentation challenge—are especially relevant to maintaining cross-sex friendships.

The Emotional Bond Challenge

This challenge stems from men and women being socialized to see one another as potential romantic partners rather than platonic friends. This can lead to uncertainty regarding whether cross-sex friends have romantic feelings for each other. It may also be confusing to feel close to opposite-sex friends without also feeling romantic toward them. We grow up believing that when we feel close to an age-appropriate person of the opposite sex, we should also be able to fall in love with that person. For example, have you ever had a good friend of the opposite sex whom you thought was wonderful yet for whom you did not have romantic feelings? If so, you may have wondered how you could be so close without becoming romantic. This is because the line between emotional closeness and romantic attraction can be blurred in some cross-sex friendships. In contrast, heterosexual same-sex friends expect emotional closeness without romantic attraction.

The Sexual Challenge

This challenge involves coping with the potential sexual attraction that can be part of some cross-sex relationships. In the classic movie *When Harry Met Sally,* Harry declares that men and women cannot be friends because the "sex thing" always gets in the way. Although Harry's statement is extreme, it is true that cross-sex friends (particularly if both are heterosexual) are likely to think about sexual issues related to each other. In one study (Halatsis & Christakis, 2009), about 50% of the participants reported having experienced sexual attraction toward a cross-sex friend. This percentage is higher for men, who tend to see their cross-sex friends as potential sexual partners far more often than do women (Abbey, 1982; Abbey & Melby, 1986; Shotland & Craig, 1988). Research has also shown that sex among friends is not uncommon. Although most cross-sex friends see themselves as strictly platonic (Guerrero & Chavez, 2005), nearly half of the college students surveyed in one study admitted to having had sex with a nonromantic friend (Afifi & Faulkner, 2000). These students also reported experiencing feelings of uncertainty after having sex with their friend. Later in this chapter, and also touched on in Chapter 1, we discuss the phenomenon of "friends with benefits," which refers to nonromantic relationships between friends who have

sex. Clearly, potential sexual attraction can complicate cross-sex friendships.

The Public Presentation Challenge

This challenge arises when other people assume there is something romantic or sexual going on in a cross-sex friendship. Cross-sex friends are sometimes careful about how they present their friendship to others and may be asked to explain the nature of their relationship to others. If you have a close cross-sex friend, you can probably relate to this. Have people ever asked you questions such as "Are you really just friends?" or "Do you love her or him?" or "Have you ever slept together?" Romantic partners may also be suspicious and jealous of your close cross-sex friends leading to other complications.

Some scholars have criticized O'Meara's four challenges for being applicable only to cross-sex heterosexual friendships. However, these challenges are also applicable to homosexual same-sex friends. Additionally, when one friend is homosexual and the other is heterosexual, these challenges may apply regardless of whether the friends are of the same or the opposite sex.

Coping With Romantic Intent

In cross-sex friendships that include at least one heterosexual partner, these challenges can make relational maintenance a complex and delicate matter (Werking, 1997). Two studies provide a closer look at how **romantic intent**, or the desire to move the friendship toward a romantic relationship, is related to maintenance behavior. The first of these studies (Guerrero & Chavez, 2005) examined four types of cross-sex friendships that differ in terms of romantic intent. Individuals in the **strictly platonic** group said that neither they nor their partner wanted the friendship to become romantic. Individuals in the **mutual romance** group said that both they and their partner wanted the friendship to become romantic. Individuals in the **desires-romance** group said that they wanted the friendship to become romantic but their partner wanted it to stay platonic. Finally, individuals in the **rejects-romance** group said that they wanted the friendship to stay platonic but their partner wanted it to become romantic. In the second of these studies (Weger & Emmett, 2009), both friends reported on the degree of romantic intent that they felt toward their cross-sex friend. Together these studies suggest that cross-sex friends report different levels of some maintenance behaviors depending on their romantic intentions.

Friends who have romantic intentions are especially likely to report using prosocial maintenance behavior. In Guerrero and Chavez's (2005) study, friends in the mutual romance group said they used the most maintenance behaviors, which suggests that increases in maintenance behavior might mark a move from friendship toward romance. Those in the desires-romance group also reported relatively high levels of maintenance, with one notable exception: People who desired romance but believed that their friend did not were the least likely to report talking about the relationship with their friend, perhaps because they feared rejection and worried that confessing their feelings could jeopardize the friendship. In Weger and Emmett's (2009) study, people who had romantic intentions toward their cross-sex friend were likely to report engaging in routine relationship activity, support and positivity, and flirtation, and were unlikely to report talking about the relationship with other people.

Individuals who reported low levels of romantic intent reported somewhat different patterns of maintenance behavior. In Guerrero and Chavez's (2005) study, individuals in both the rejects-romance and strictly platonic groups reported using less joint activity and flirtation, but more talk about outside relationships, such as referring often to their boyfriend or girlfriend. This suggests that individuals who want to keep the relationship platonic refrain from flirting with each other, so as not to lead each other on. They also limit their public appearances by showing up at parties separately and engaging in less joint activity in public settings. This may be a way of managing O'Meara's public presentation challenge; if they limit the amount of time they spend together, others are less likely to see them as a potentially romantic couple. Finally, individuals in the rejects-romance and strictly platonic groups are especially likely to talk about their boyfriends, girlfriends, or spouses (assuming that they are already in another romantic relationship), perhaps as a way of signaling that they are already taken.

Keeping Friendships Platonic

Although some cross-sex friends have to deal with the sexual and romantic challenges O'Meara proposed, most cross-sex friends define their relationships as strictly platonic (Guerrero & Chavez, 2005; Messman et al., 2000). There are at least six reasons why people in cross-sex friendships want to maintain the status quo and keep their relationships platonic (Messman et al., 2000). First, people report that it is important to safeguard the relationship; people worry that a shift toward romance could hurt the quality of their friendship or result in a breakup. Second, people reveal that they are not attracted to their friend in a romantic or sexual way. Third, people say that there would be network disapproval if they became romantically involved with their friend; people in their social network might get upset. Fourth, people keep friendships platonic because one or both members of the friendship are already involved in a third-party romantic relationship. Fifth, people experience risk aversion, which involves feeling uncertain about the partner's reaction and worrying about potentially being hurt or disappointed. Finally, people take a time-out, meaning they do not want a serious romantic relationship with anyone at the present time.

Of these six reasons, safeguarding the relationship was the most common, followed by lack of attraction and network disapproval. Risk aversion and time-out were least common. Sex differences for keeping friendships platonic also exist. Women are more likely than men to want to safeguard the relationship and to say they are not attracted to their friend in a romantic way (Messman et al., 2002).

People also use different maintenance behaviors depending on their reason for keeping the friendship platonic. In particular, people who want to safeguard the relationship are most likely to report using openness, positivity, joint activities, and supportiveness in their friendships. People were most likely to say they used avoidance if they reported risk aversion, network disapproval, and time-out as reasons for keeping the relationship platonic. Finally, people who were unattached to their friend reported that they avoided flirting as a way to maintain the relationship. To determine why you may keep one of your friendships platonic rather than romantic, take the test in Box 9.5.

BOX 9.5 Put Yourself to the Test

Why Do You Keep One of Your Close Cross-Sex Friendships Platonic?

Think about why you have kept a relationship with a good friend (of the opposite sex if you are hetero-sexual, or the same sex if you are gay) platonic. Rate the following reasons using this scale: 1 = you strongly disagree, 7 = you strongly agree.

	Disagree						Agree
I keep our friendship platonic because:							
1. My friend might reject me.	1	2	3	4	5	6	7
2. My friend and/or I are already dating someone else.	1	2	3	4	5	6	7
3. I do not want to risk losing our friendship.	1	2	3	4	5	6	7
4. My friend is not the kind of person I want to be involved with in a romantic way.	1	2	3	4	5	6	7
5. At this time, I am not ready for a romantic relationship with anyone.	1	2	3	4	5	6	7
6. My friend might end up hurting my feelings.	1	2	3	4	5	6	7
7. Other people would be upset if our relationship turned romantic.	1	2	3	4	5	6	7
8. I value this person as a friend too much to change things.	1	2	3	4	5	6	7
9. I think of this person *only* as a friend.	1	2	3	4	5	6	7
10. My friend and/or I are already romantically involved with someone else.	1	2	3	4	5	6	7
11. This person is not sexually attractive to me.	1	2	3	4	5	6	7
12. I don't want to date anyone at this time.	1	2	3	4	5	6	7
13. I am not sure that the romantic feelings I have for my friend are mutual.	1	2	3	4	5	6	7
14. Some of my friends or family would be upset with me if our friendship turned romantic.	1	2	3	4	5	6	7
15. My friend and/or I already have good romantic relation-ships with someone else.	1	2	3	4	5	6	7

(Continued)

(Continued)

	Disagree						Agree
16. Getting romantic could cause problems within our social network.	1	2	3	4	5	6	7
17. Getting romantic could ruin our friendship.	1	2	3	4	5	6	7
18. I'm not interested in a romantic relationship right now.	1	2	3	4	5	6	7

To obtain your results, add your scores for the following items:

Emotional uncertainty: Items 1 + 6 + 13 = _____

Network disapproval: Items 7 + 14 + 16 = _____

Safeguard relationship: Items 3 + 8 + 17 = _____

Not attracted: Items 4 + 9 + 11 = _____

Time-out: Items 5 + 12 + 18 = _____

Third party: Items 2 + 10 + 15 = _____

Higher scores indicate stronger reasons for keeping your friendship platonic.

SOURCE: Adapted from Messman, S. J., Canary, D. J., & Hause, K. S. Motives to remain platonic, equity, and the use of maintenance strategies in opposite-sex friendships, in *Journal of Social and Personal Relationships, 17,* 67-94. Copyright © 2000, SAGE, Inc.

MAINTENANCE CHALLENGES IN OTHER RELATIONSHIPS

Cross-sex friends are not the only individuals who sometimes face special challenges in their relationships. Scholars have also identified friends-with-benefits relationships and long-distance relationships as especially challenging to maintain.

Friends-With-Benefits Relationships

In contrast to platonic friendships, some friends decide to have sex but stay friends rather than become a romantic couple. This type of relationship, which has been called *friends with benefits* in television shows and the popular press, is fairly common on college campuses. Although most studies have examined friends-with-benefits relationships as a form of cross-sex friendship, these relationships also occur between same-sex friends who are gay, lesbian, or bisexual. Across various studies, between 47% and 68% of college students report that they are currently or had previously been involved in at least one relationship characterized as friends with benefits (Afifi & Faulkner, 2000; McGinty, Knox, & Zusman, 2007; Mongeau, Ramirez, & Vorrell, 2003; Reeder, 2000).

College students have described several advantages and disadvantages associated with friends-with-benefits relationships. The overriding theme of the advantages is that a person is able to have "sex with a trusted other while avoiding commitment" (Bisson & Levine, 2009, p. 68). In fact, lack of commitment was mentioned as an advantage by almost 60% of students in Bisson and Levine's study. A smaller percentage of students (7.3%) listed "becoming closer" as an advantage, and nearly 9% said that there were no advantages associated with friends with benefits relationships, even though they had participated in one. In terms of disadvantages, students worried that unreciprocated romantic feelings, jealousy, or hurt might develop, all of which could harm the friendship. Concern about developing romantic feelings was the top disadvantage, with over 65% of students mentioning this possibility. Some students also listed lack of commitment as a disadvantage rather than an advantage, and others noted the possible negative consequences of having sex as a disadvantage.

There may also be differences in how men and women view the advantages and disadvantages associated with friends-with-benefits relationships. In one study, women were more likely to emphasize the "friends" part of the relationship by focusing on emotions, whereas men were more likely to emphasize the "benefits" part of the relationship by focusing on sex (McGinty et al., 2007).

Given that many participants in friends-with-benefits relationships worry about the possibility of developing romantic feelings, it is not surprising that about half the participants in Bisson and Levine's (2009) study experienced some uncertainty about their friends-with-benefits relationship. Sources of uncertainty included how they should label their relationship, how their relationship might change in the future, how they felt about each other now that they were having sex, whether they could stay friends, and how they could maintain their relationship. Despite this uncertainty, 76% of the students in the study said that they did not initiate any discussion about these issues, and 66% reported that they never negotiated any ground rules for the relationship.

When friends with benefits do talk about these issues, they appear to focus on establishing rules that help them maintain their relationship so that neither party gets hurt. According to research by Hughes, Morrison, and Asada (2005), the most common rule in friends-with-benefits relationships involves staying emotionally detached. Friends with benefits often agree not to get jealous or fall in love with one another (Hughes et al., 2005). Other rules for maintaining these friendships include negotiations about sexual activity (e.g., agreeing to use condoms), communication (e.g., making rules about calling one another and being honest about other relationships), secrecy (e.g., agreeing not to tell common friends that they have sex), permanence (e.g., agreeing that the sexual part of the relationship is only temporary), and the friendship (e.g., agreeing to value the friendship over the sexual relationship).

Although many of these maintenance rules help friends with benefits maintain the status quo, this type of relationship sometimes ends completely, returns to friendship only (no sex), or turns into a romantic relationship (Hughes et al., 2005). Although friends with benefits often keep the sexual aspect of their relationship private, Hughes and her colleagues found that these friendships are more likely to continue if their broader network of friends is accepting of the type of relationship they have. Of course, these types of friendships can be fraught with all kinds of challenges, including one friend wanting the relationship to turn romantic while the other person does not. Compared to other types of relationships, the friends-with-benefits relationship is probably one of the most difficult to maintain.

Long-Distance Relationships

Long-distance relationships can also be challenging to maintain. Most people have been in at least one long-distance romantic relationship, and virtually everyone has been in a long-distance relationship of some sort, whether it be with a friend or family member. With more individuals pursuing higher education, more couples having dual professional careers, and more people immigrating to the United States, the number of romantic relationships separated by large distances is increasing. In 1987, Stafford, Daly, and Reske estimated that one-third of dating couples in the United States were separated by sufficient distance to make frequent face-to-face interaction difficult. Within the college student population, between 25% and 40% of romantic relationships are long distance (Dainton & Aylor, 2001).

A primary challenge for maintaining long-distance romantic relationships is the lack of face-to-face communication (Stafford & Merolla, 2007), which is believed to be the glue that holds romantic relationships together. How, then, can couples stay close if partners are unable to engage in much face-to-face communication? Distance also prevents partners in long-distance relationships from displaying nonverbal affection, sharing most activities or tasks, and engaging in the same type of daily routine talk as couples in proximal relationships do. Indeed, studies show that people in long-distance relationships generally use less maintenance behavior, such as openness, assurances, and joint activities, than people in geographically close relationships (Johnson, 2001; Van Horn et al., 1997). Yet many long-distance couples maintain happy relationships. In fact, some studies suggest that individuals in romantic long-distance relationships are happier and more "in love" with their partners than are people in proximal romantic relationships (Stafford & Merolla, 2007; Stafford & Reske, 1990). Similarly, friends in long-distance relationships report as much relational satisfaction as friends in geographically close relationships (Johnson, 2001).

The concept of **idealization** has been offered as an explanation for why some long-distance relationships stay satisfying despite the lack of face-to-face interaction (Stafford & Reske, 1990). Idealization occurs when people describe their relationship and their partner in glowing, overly positive terms that sometimes reflect unrealistic expectations (Stafford & Merolla, 2007). This type of idealization keeps people committed to their relationships; dating couples are more likely to believe that they will get married one day if they idealize each other (Stafford & Reske, 1990). At first, it may seem counterintuitive that long-distance couples would idealize their relationships more than proximal couples would, but considering that people in such relationships usually experienced relational closeness before separating, these findings begin to make sense. Moreover, partners in romantic long-distance relationships often think about how great their lives would be if they could be with their partners more of the time, making idealization more likely (Stafford & Reske, 1990); in this case, "absence indeed makes the heart grow fonder." Idealization may also be fueled by some of the communication patterns that typically occur in long-distance relationships, including reliance on mediated communication and the tendency to be on one's best behavior when together.

Mediated communication may offer a skewed perception of a partner's communication style, in part because people can control their communication in mediated contexts compared to face-to-face contexts (Stafford & Merolla, 2007). For example, partners likely pick up the phone when they feel like talking, something over which each partner has almost complete control. Moreover, if one partner is not in the mood to talk when the other calls, it is easy to listen to a message without answering or to ask the other partner to call back at another time. One of our students described how she sent videotapes to her boyfriend in Iraq. She cut scenes in which she did not look her best and rehearsed her monologue so that she said exactly the right things. Such control over communication is unusual in proximal relationships, where relational partners are face-to-face on a regular basis. Similar findings have been found for Internet-based relationships (Wright, 2004). People who send electronic messages showing positivity and openness tend to be regarded favorably by their Internet partners.

As these examples illustrate, individuals in long-distance relationships are typically on their best relational behavior when they are together. Compared to those in geographically close relationships, people in long-distance relationships tend to engage in less joint activities, task sharing, and social networking (Dainton & Aylor, 2001; Johnson, 2001), especially if they have limited contact with one another. However, when people in a long-distance relationship do get together, they often plan shared activities more carefully, work hard to treat each other in a fair and equitable manner, and have long, in-depth discussions. People in long-distance relationships often prepare well in advance for weekend visits and present an image of themselves that may not be consistent with the day-to-day reality of their lives. Dinner reservations are made, work calendars are cleared, and plans with friends and family are often suspended so the partners can spend quality time alone. Partners in proximal relationships seldom make such accommodations for each other. Thus, compared to partners in proximal relationships, partners in long-distance relationships often perceive that their communication is more restricted but of higher quality (Stafford & Reske, 1990). As Johnson (2001) stated, it may be the quality rather than the quantity of communication that is most important when it comes to maintaining long-distance relationships.

Although idealization helps long-distance partners maintain their relationships, it can also lead to difficulties when the relationship becomes proximal (Stafford & Merolla, 2007). Suddenly, the once seemingly perfect partner needs to study or write a report for work when the other partner wants to spend quality time together, and the sensitive issues that were never discussed over the phone lead to conflict in face-to-face interaction. Stafford and Merolla found that long distance couples who moved close to one another were twice as likely to break up as those who remained apart. The more long-distance couples had idealized each other and their relationship, the more likely they were to break up after they moved near one another. This research suggests that partners in long-distance relationships may need to work to keep their expectations realistic so that they are not disappointed once the relationship becomes proximal. Some level of idealization is healthy in both proximal and long-distance relationships (Murray, Holmes, & Griffin, 1996), but too much idealization in long-distance relationships appears to make the transition to a proximal relationship more difficult (Stafford & Merolla, 2007).

In sum, the good news is that long-distance relationships are as stable and satisfying, and perhaps more emotionally intense, than are proximal relationships (Van Horn et al., 1997). The bad news is that friends and romantic partners in long-distance relationships sometimes get frustrated with their lack of face-to-face communication (Rohlfing, 1995). Romantic partners in long-distance relationships also need to ensure that their positive perceptions of each other are not a function of idealization, perhaps the biggest challenge facing long-distance partners who wish to maintain their romantic relationships.

THE DIALECTICAL PERSPECTIVE

Clearly, many factors are relevant to maintaining close relationships. The road to a happy relationship is not always smooth, and partners do not always travel in the same direction or at the same pace.

Every relationship experiences ups and downs, and no relationship stays the same from start to finish. Theories taking a dialectical perspective capture the dynamic nature of relationships and describe some of the common tensions that are reflected in interpersonal communication.

According to the **dialectical perspective** (see Baxter, 2010; Baxter & Montgomery, 1996), relationships are never completely stable, but are constantly changing. As Baxter (1994) stated, "A healthy relationship is a changing relationship" (p. 234). Think about your close relationships. Wouldn't they be boring if they were always the same? Doesn't communication reflect the changing ways that you think about one another and construct meaning in your relationships? The dialectical perspective embraces the ever-changing nature of relationships. According to this perspective, relationships are managed rather than simply maintained.

Tension is at the heart of the dialectical perspective, with a push and pull toward two seemingly contradictory needs (e.g., autonomy versus closeness) seen as both healthy and inevitable. Some scholars have described dialectic tensions as competing needs within relationships. For example, Fehr (1996) described the tug-of-war of dialectical tensions this way:

> We have to juggle our need for dependence with our need to be independent; wanting to be completely open versus wanting to protect ourselves by not revealing everything; wanting to have a lot in common, but not so much that the relationship feels boring and predictable. (p. 156)

If two people can manage these competing needs successfully, they will be more likely to sustain a happy and healthy relationship.

Other scholars have situated these tensions within communication. Most notably, Baxter's (2010) relational dialectics theory focuses on **discursive tensions**, which can be thought of as messages that have two seemingly contradictory meanings. Baxter and Braithwaite (2008) gave the following example of a college student telling a friend, "Well, I'm kinda, like, seeing him, but we're not, ya know, serious" (p. 26). This statement displays a discursive tension between connection ("I'm seeing him") and autonomy ("but we're not serious"). Importantly, these types of contradictions are not viewed as problematic, but rather as a necessary and inevitable part of communication. Two theories in particular from the dialectical perspective—Baxter's relational dialectics theory and Rawlins's application of dialectics to friendships—allow deeper understanding and application of how these tensions function within relationships.

Relational Dialectics Theory

The central idea in relational dialectics theory is that "all of communication is rife with the tension-filled struggle of competing discourses" (Baxter & Braithwaite, 2008, p. 352). People express different perspectives through their interaction with one another. The meaning-making process then involves communicating and making sense of these differing viewpoints. Within **relational dialectics theory**, communication is viewed as the means by which people make sense of the social world. Thus, communication gives meaning to people's relationships.

There are various discursive tensions in relationships, such as tensions between similarity and dissimilarity (Baxter & West, 2003), old and new family structures in stepfamilies (Braithwaite, Baxter, & Harper, 1998), and fortune and misfortune (Krusiewicz & Woods, 2001). Of the many tensions that exist in

various relationships, Baxter (2006) identified the dialectics of integration, certainty, and expression as "the big three" (p. 137). Each of these dialectics can be expressed as an internal or an external tension, as shown in Figure 9.1. **Internal manifestations** refer to the tensions that people express about their relationships with one another. For example, Rachel may tell Yasser that planning their upcoming wedding has made her feel closer to him in some ways even though they have been too busy to spend much time together. This statement reflects tensions of closeness and separation within their relationship. **External manifestations** refer to tensions that people in a relationship or group (e.g., a family) express in regard to their interaction with others who are outside that relationship or group. Yasser, for example, may tell Rachel that he wants to keep their wedding intimate by limiting the guest list, but he also doesn't want to hurt anyone's feelings. This statement reflects tension between excluding versus including others. The three major discursive tensions—integration, certainty, and expression—manifest both internally and externally.

The Dialectic of Integration

The dialectic of **integration** refers to the tension between social integration and social division. That is, people talk about being connected to relational

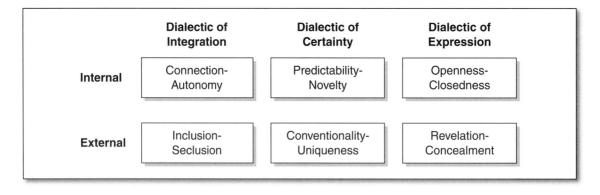

Figure 9.1 Baxter's Dialectical Tensions

SOURCE: From Werner, C. M., Altman, I., Brown, B. B., & Ganat, J. Celebrations in personal relationships: A transactional/dialectical perspective. In S. Duck (Ed.), Social context and relationships (pp. 109–138). Copyright © 1993. Reprinted with permission of SAGE, Inc.

partners and social groups, but they also talk about being self-sufficient and doing things on their own. Baxter (2006) related an effective analogy that one of her students used to describe how the dialectic of integration functions within families. This student "referred to her family as a hand: individual fingers whose strength rests in their capacity to function independently yet which unite to form the strength of a single fist" (Baxter, 2006, p. 135). In this analogy, the fingers represent division (or independence) whereas the hand represents integration.

The internal manifestation of this dialectic has been called the **connection-autonomy** tension (Baxter, 1993). This tension is expressed when people communicate in ways that reflect both closeness and distance (or independence). For example, after they have their first child, Yasser might say, "I'm glad you're always attending to the baby, but I'm starting to feel a bit neglected." Such a statement includes elements related to both autonomy (Yasser realizes Rachel needs to spend time with the baby) and closeness (he wants to feel more connection). The external manifestation of the integration dialectic is the **inclusion-seclusion** tension. Couples or groups often communicate in ways that stress the importance of spending time with other people, but they also communicate in ways that suggest they want to keep to themselves. A study of lesbian couples provides a useful example of this tension (Suter, Bergen, Daas, & Durham, 2006). One couple explained that although they usually celebrate their anniversary alone (seclusion), they invited friends and family to help them celebrate their 10th anniversary (inclusion) because they considered it to be an especially important milestone in their relationship.

The Dialectic of Certainty

This dialectic reflects the tension between the forces of certainty, stability, and routine, and the forces of surprise, change, and newness. The internal manifestation of this dialectic is **predictability-novelty**. For example, Rachel and Yasser might go to the movies together most Saturday nights. One evening while searching the Internet to see what is playing, Yasser might comment "It's nice that we always have a movie date on Saturdays (predictability), but maybe

we should change things up tonight (novelty)." Successfully negotiating the predictability-novelty tension is important because boredom is one of the top reasons couples break up (Hill, Rubin, & Peplau, 1976); thus, excitement is vital in relationships.

The external manifestation of the certainty dialectic is **conventionality-uniqueness**. This tension focuses on how people communicate in ways that show consistency or inconsistency with the larger social group. Baxter (2006) shared an example given by one of her students, who said, "The [Jones] are the [Jones]: the same from one generation to the next, but different, too" (p. 136). This statement reflects some conventionality or sameness across generations, but also some unique aspects of each generation. Similarly, Rachel and Yasser may find themselves adopting some of their parents' traditions for celebrating holidays, while also creating some of their own.

The Dialectic of Expression

This dialectic reflects "the interplay of discourses of openness, disclosure, and candor with the competing discourses of discretion, privacy, and secrecy" (Baxter, 2006, p. 136). The internal manifestation of this dialectic, **openness-closedness**, refers to communication that occurs within a dyad or group. One of Baxter's (2006) students described her family as being able to say anything they want to one another, but as also knowing when they should refrain from saying something. The external contradiction, **revelation-concealment**, refers to the tension between keeping information private and sharing it with the social network. In Suter and colleagues' (2006) study, many lesbian couples expressed this tension. One of these couples discussed how they felt closeted but also wanted to share their relationship with others.

Managing Dialectical Tensions

Relational dialectics theory also addresses how dyads and families manage these tensions. As noted previously, the contradictions that discursive tensions represent should not be viewed as good or bad, but rather as a vibrant and dynamic part of the communication process. Through communication, people can manage these tensions in productive ways that help relationships evolve and change in positive ways. According to work by Baxter (1990), there are four general ways to manage dialectical tensions: selection, separation, neutralization, and reframing.

Selection involves talking about the tensions in a way that values one side of the dialectic over the other. For example, Rachel and Yasser might promise that they will always be completely open and honest about everything with each other. This way of managing a dialectic tension can sometimes be successful, but it can also lead to problems if Rachel or Yasser engages the other side of the dialectic later. For instance, Rachel may say that she doesn't want to talk about something, to which Yasser might reply, "I thought we promised to always be open with each other." As this example illustrates, selection may not always be a very practical way to manage dialectical tensions.

Separation occurs when people favor each side of the dialectic at different times. There are two ways to accomplish this. First, couples can use **cyclic alternation** by moving from one side of the dialectic to the other in a cyclical fashion. For example, if Yasser and Rachel start feeling disconnected from each other, they might say that they need to get away alone together somewhere (and perhaps plan a romantic getaway). Conversely, if they start feeling smothered, one or both of them might stress the importance of spending some time apart. Another way to accomplish separation is through **topical segmentation,** which involves emphasizing different sides of the dialectic depending on the topic or context. Rachel and Yasser might decide to reveal positive information about their relationship to others but conceal negative information. So if Rachel's best friend asks how things are going between her and Yasser, Rachel might say, "Great, we picked out china yesterday" without telling her that they had conflict over which pattern to choose. Couples using topical segmentation might also decide to keep certain activities separate (e.g., playing golf or shopping with friends) while engaging in others together (e.g., going to a favorite restaurant or watching a television program).

Neutralization occurs when couples avoid fully engaging either side of the dialectical tension. There are two strategies for accomplishing neutralization. The first, **moderation,** involves striving to reach a "midpoint" such that couples engage both sides of the dialectic, but only to a certain extent. For example, Rachel might reveal some information about her relationship with Yasser to others, but still keep the details private. She could tell her best friend, "Oh, yeah, we get into some little fights once in a while, but it's nothing that major and we always make up." Second, couples can use **disqualification,** which involves being ambiguous so that neither side of the dialectic is engaged. This includes tactics such as changing the topic or avoiding an issue. For example, Rachel might change the subject when someone asks her about her wedding plans. Or she might avoid engaging in behavior that is either too predictable or too novel when interacting with Yasser.

The final, general way to manage dialectical tension is through **reframing,** a sophisticated strategy that involves talking about tensions so that they seem complementary rather than contradictory. For example, Yasser might tell Rachel, "If we tell each other everything all the time, pretty soon we won't have anything left to say." Or Rachel might say, "I love when you come home after being away on business all weekend. It makes me appreciate our time together more." Such statements demonstrate a recognition that seemingly contradictory forces—like openness and closedness or connection and autonomy—can work together to make relationships healthier and more productive.

Dialectical Tensions in Friendships

Although applicable to a variety of relationships, Baxter's work on dialectics has focused primarily on romantic relationships. Yet researchers have also looked at dialectics within the context of friendships (Bridge & Baxter, 1992; Rawlins, 1989, 1992, 1994). In particular, Rawlins's (1992) investigation of friendship took a dialectical perspective. He argued that six main dialectical tensions characterize friendships, as well as other types of relationships.

Two of Rawlins's dialectics—independent-dependent and expressive-protective—are similar to those identified as autonomy-connection and openness-closedness by Baxter, except that they focus more on needs friends have than discursive tensions. Specifically, the **independent-dependent** dialectic refers to the tension between wanting the freedom to pursue individual activities and depending on someone for help and support. For example, you might want to ask your friend, who is a math major, to help you with your trigonometry homework, but you might also want to prove that you can do the work on your own. The **expressive-protection** dialectic focuses on how much friends express versus keep information private. After interviewing pairs of close friends, Rawlins (1983a, 1983b) concluded that this is a central tension that exists in friendships. In order for a friendship to be close, people must disclose personal information. However, if friends disclose too much, they open themselves up to potential criticism and rejection (see also Chapter 5).

The remaining four dialectics differ from those proposed by Baxter. The **judgment-acceptance** dialectic involves being able to accept friends for who they are versus feeling free to offer criticism and advice. This is a common tension. For example, imagine that a good friend of yours has been in a dead-end job for two years after graduation. Should you accept that your friend isn't very ambitious, or should you suggest that your friend go out and look for something better? You avoid insulting your friend if you do the former, but in the long run you might help your friend if you do the latter. The choice is indeed a dilemma.

The **affection-instrumentality** dialectic refers to whether friends focus more on feelings of warmth or on instrumental tasks. When friendships are based only on instrumental goals (e.g., wanting help with homework), the relationship may seem impersonal. Conversely, when friendships are based on affection without instrumental benefits, people might feel that some of their goals are not being fulfilled. Rawlins (1992) suggested that although both men and woman want both types of benefits, men value instrumentality more, while women value affection more.

The **public-private** dialectic involves how the relationship is negotiated in public versus private. Rawlins (1992) argued that all friendships are negotiated primarily in private, yet some aspects of the relationship are made public. For example, you might call your friend silly nicknames like "bubblehead" or "monkey face" in private but not in public. In high school, if you invited an unpopular person to your house, you might not have told the other kids at school. But if the homecoming king and queen came over, you likely would have told everyone. Cross-sex friends might show affection to one another in private, but not in public because they don't want other people to think they have romantic feelings for one another.

Finally, the **ideal-real** dialectic reflects the tension between what the friendship "ought to be" and what the relationship "really is." People want an ideal friendship, but most people know that the ideal relationship is a fantasy and that no friend is perfect. In high school, some kids wish they could be friends with a certain student who is especially popular, athletic, talented, or beautiful. However, their "real" friends have a mix of positive and negative characteristics. There may also be tension between trying to live up to idealistic expectations and wanting to be oneself.

SUMMARY AND APPLICATION

The literature on relational maintenance offers couples such as Rachel and Yasser advice about how to keep their relationship strong. Both routine and strategic maintenance are related to satisfaction, but routine behavior may be a little more important. Therefore, it is essential that Yasser and Rachel settle into a routine that includes prosocial maintenance behaviors, such as asking about each other's day and sharing tasks in a fair and equitable manner. For married couples, positivity and assurances appear to be especially effective maintenance behaviors. Rachel therefore might try to compliment Yasser once in a while and to act cheerful and optimistic. Rachel might periodically offer Yasser assurances that she loves him and is committed to their relationship. Yasser should do the same. The couple should also focus on doing things together through maintenance behaviors such as joint activities and social networking. Engaging in these activities creates a partnership, reinforces similarity, and allows couples to have fun together.

Rachel wondered if getting married would change their relationship. It likely would. Long-term committed relationships, such as marriage, tend to contain less openness, but more social networking, task sharing, and constructive conflict management. Although Rachel and Yasser may engage in especially high levels of maintenance at the beginning of their marriage, these levels are likely to drop over time, especially if they have children. Later in life, however, maintenance behaviors may show a resurgence when they retire or their children leave the nest, giving Rachel and Yasser more time to spend together. Relational dialectics theory also suggests that Rachel and Yasser's marriage, like any relationship, is constantly changing, as evidenced in part by the discursive tensions they are likely to communicate. For example, after getting married, they might feel more constrained by the conventional rules associated with marriage, and they may feel pressure to merge their social networks.

It may also be harder to be spontaneous and novel or to keep things private because they have daily contact with one another.

As the dialectical perspective suggests, relationships cycle through periods of highs and lows. The ebb and flow of relational closeness is a normal process (Wilmot, 1994). When things are not going well, it is a signal that a change needs to be made so that the relationship can be rejuvenated—this is comforting. An argument might help solve a problem, and a temporary feeling of being smothered by the relationship might lead to some valued time alone. Couples like Yasser and Rachel should remember that strategic maintenance behavior is likely to vary throughout the course of their marriage. This is why routine maintenance is so important: Routine patterns of positive behavior help sustain relationships even when couples have little time to focus on one another. Using maintenance behavior may be one of the secrets that helps couples like Yasser's parents maintain a happy relationship across the years.

DISCUSSION QUESTIONS

1. In this chapter, we discussed sex differences in relational behaviors such as self-disclosure and sharing activities. Do you agree with our conclusion that, although some sex differences exist, they are actually quite small? What do your everyday experiences tell you about sex differences in relational maintenance behaviors?

2. Which of the following statements do you think is truer: "Relationships stay together unless something tears them apart" or "Relationships require effort or else they fall apart"?

3. Based on the information in this chapter, what five pieces of advice do you think would be most important to share with someone like Rachel who wants to maintain a relationship? How might your advice change based on the type of relationship (friendship, romantic, long distance, proximal) that people wish to maintain?

STUDENT STUDY SITE

Visit the study site at **www.sagepub.com/guerrero3e** for e-flashcards, survey and assessments from the chapter, and SAGE journal articles.

10

Exchanging Rewards and Costs

Interdependence and Equity in Relationships

Brent and Josh have been best friends since sixth grade. Because they went through the sometimes turbulent adolescent years together, they share an especially close bond. Throughout middle school and high school, their friendship seemed almost ideal. They enjoyed the same activities, they could talk to each other about almost anything, and most of all, they knew they could count on each other through thick and thin. Now in college, the two men decide to share an apartment. Suddenly their normally tranquil relationship is filled with tension. Brent thinks Josh is taking advantage of him. Josh eats all of Brent's food, has friends over all the time without asking first, and worst of all, never pays his bills on time. It seems to Brent that Josh is getting all the benefits of having an apartment near campus without having to be responsible or courteous. Brent wonders why becoming roommates has wreaked such havoc on their friendship. Would it be better if he moved out—or should he stick it out and hope that things will change?

f you were in Brent's place, would you consider moving out? What other options does Brent have for addressing the problems that have surfaced in his friendship with Josh? As this scenario illustrates, it is important that relationships are rewarding and fair. Like a seesaw that is too heavy on one side, if one partner is putting more effort into the relationship and still getting less out of it, this person will feel weighted down and, as a result, the relationship could come crashing down. Indeed, in some ways, relationships are like balancing acts. Both partners need to give and take in a fair manner. For partners to stay satisfied with their relationship,

the scales also need to be tipped so that rewards outweigh costs and both people believe they are getting a fair deal.

In this chapter, we examine three social exchange theories that focus on this delicate balancing act. **Social exchange theories** focus on how people exchange rewards (or benefits) and costs (or contributions) in their relationships (Stafford, 2008). First, we discuss interdependence theory, which explains how costs and rewards work in conjunction with our expectations about relationships to affect satisfaction and commitment. Second, we look at the investment model, which is an extension of interdependence theory, followed by a discussion of barriers that keep people in relationships. Next, we discuss equity theory, which focuses on whether rewards and costs are distributed fairly between relational partners. In addition, we discuss the fair division of household labor as an especially important part of maintaining equitable relationships.

INTERDEPENDENCE THEORY

Interdependence theory is based on the idea that interaction between partners is "the essence of all close relationships" (Rusbult, Drigotas, & Verette, 1994). Through communication and the exchange of resources, relational partners become interdependent and committed to one another (Kelley, 1979). Every relationship has a unique pattern of interdependence that is based on the specific rewards and costs partners exchange, as well as the degree to which they are dependent on one another to reach their goals.

According to interdependence theory and other social exchange theories, people are motivated to be in relationships that provide them with high levels of rewards and low levels of costs. Using accounting as an analogy, people want to maximize their "profits" and minimize their "losses" in relationships (Blau, 1964; Homans, 1961, 1974; Thibaut & Kelley, 1959). Rewards and costs are weighed against each other, against people's standards and expectations for relationships, and against the alternative rewards and costs that people could have in other relationships or on their own. When these comparisons are favorable, people are generally satisfied with and committed to their relationships. When these comparisons are unfavorable, as in Brent's case, satisfaction and commitment tend to suffer. Various components of interdependence theory further illustrate these comparisons in the context of relationships.

Rewards and Costs

Different types of rewards and costs characterize relationships. Sprecher (1998b) defined **rewards** as "exchanged resources that are pleasurable and gratifying" and **costs** as "exchanged resources that result in a loss or punishment" (p. 32). Rewards and costs play an important role in both friendships and romantic relationships. In one study, people rated their friendships as especially close when they felt they were receiving rewards such as affection and support (Tornblom & Fredholm, 1984). For romantic couples, exchanging love and information is related to increased intimacy and satisfaction (Lloyd, Cate, & Henton, 1982). At a more general level, rewards and costs are exchanged at four levels: emotional, social, instrumental, and opportunity based.

Emotional Rewards and Costs

Perhaps ironically, our closest relationships are most likely to contain the greatest emotional rewards, but also the most intense emotional costs. People we are close to can make us feel happy, excited, and loved, but also angry, hurt, and disappointed. **Emotional rewards**, then, include all the positive feelings we experience in a relationship, whereas **emotional costs** include all the negative feelings. Emotional rewards are critical within close relationships. When partners experience emotions such as joy and warmth in connection with each other, they tend to feel closer and to be happier with their relationship (Feeney, Noller, & Roberts, 1998; Prager & Buhrmester, 1998). Nonverbal expressions of affection and joy are part of the emotional fabric that keeps relationships satisfying. In fact, Kelly, Fincham, and Beach (2003) observed that happy couples are not necessarily defined by the verbal content of their communication, but rather by the positive emotions they experience and express through smiles, laughter, hugs, and warm vocal tones. In contrast, relationships that contain more negative emotion than positive emotion are considered costly and dissatisfying. For Brent, the frustration he has been feeling since he moved in with Josh may be starting to overshadow the positive aspects of their relationship.

Social Rewards and Costs

We obtain social rewards and costs from a variety of people within our social networks. **Social rewards** revolve around two main themes—being able to meet and interact with people we like and enjoy being around, and being seen in a positive light because of our association with someone. For example, if Josh is popular and has a lot of friends, Brent may benefit from having Josh as his friend and roommate. Josh can introduce Brent to interesting people and invite him to participate in fun activities that he would otherwise not get to do. **Social costs** revolve around the same two themes—having to engage in unpleasant social activities or being cast in a negative light because of an association with someone. Examples include having to attend your partner's boring company picnic and being embarrassed when your partner criticizes you in front of others. For Brent, a social cost is that he sometimes has to endure having Josh's friends come over unexpectedly when he'd rather have quiet time to read or do homework.

Instrumental Rewards and Costs

Since becoming roommates, Brent has also perceived an increase in instrumental costs in his relationship with Brent. Instrumental rewards and costs revolve around tasks. With **instrumental rewards**, partners help one another get things done. For example, if you have a partner who manages the household finances well, you enjoy an instrumental reward. By contrast, **instrumental costs** are incurred when being in a relationship causes someone more work or increased responsibility, or when one partner impedes the other's progress in relation to a specific task. Having to do the majority of the housework, paying off your partner's debt, and helping your partner with a project are all examples of instrumental costs. Notice, however, that what constitutes an instrumental cost for one partner often constitutes an instrumental reward for the other partner. This is why Brent feels like Josh is taking advantage of him. Brent fronts the rent money until Josh can pay him back, he pays for groceries that Josh eats, and he cleans the apartment after Josh messes it up. In all these instances, Brent is incurring a cost while Josh is receiving a reward.

Opportunity Rewards and Costs

Finally, being in relationships provides people with some opportunities while taking away others. **Opportunity rewards** involve being able to do something that one could not otherwise do. For instance, by moving in together, Brent and Josh can probably afford a nicer apartment than each of them could if living alone (assuming that Josh contributes enough

financially). Similarly, pooling financial resources often gives married couples the opportunity to purchase a nicer home than either partner could afford individually. **Opportunity costs** involve having to give up something one wants for the sake of the relationship. For example, if you have to quit your job and move across the country to remain with your partner, you have given up the opportunity to advance in a particular organization, which is an opportunity cost. When a romantic relationship is exclusive, both people give up the opportunity to pursue relationships with other people. And, when Brent signed a lease and moved in with Josh, he gave up the opportunity to live with someone else.

Outcomes

In every relationship, whether it is between friends, romantic partners, family members, coworkers, or employees and their supervisors, there are both rewards and costs. According to interdependence theory, people mentally account for rewards and costs so they can evaluate the outcome of their relationship as either positive or negative. When rewards outweigh costs, the outcome is positive; when costs outweigh rewards, the outcome is negative. Put another way, rewards minus costs equal the **outcome**. To illustrate, suppose that Brent perceives that he is receiving 10 rewards and 20 costs in his friendship with Brent. According to interdependence theory, Brent then has a negative outcome ($10 - 20 = -10$). In economic terms, his friendship with Josh is characterized by a deficit. In contrast, Josh may perceive that he is receiving 30 rewards and incurring only 10 costs. His outcome would then be positive ($30 - 10 = +20$); Josh would be getting a profit from being friends and roommates with Brent. Of course, in real life, rewards and costs are very hard to quantify, and some rewards and costs are more important than others. The critical point here is that people mentally compare costs and rewards to determine whether they are in a positive or negative relationship.

Certain rewards and costs may be weighted especially heavily. A good example of this is found in the classic television show *Friends* when Ross discovers that Rachel is romantically interested in him. Ross has had a crush on Rachel since high school, but he is currently in a happy relationship with a woman named Julie. Trying to decide which woman to date, Ross makes a list of Rachel's and Julie's good and bad qualities. Even though he lists more rewards and less costs in the "Julie column," Ross ultimately chooses Rachel for one reason—she's Rachel. Complications occur, however, when Rachel finds the list, sees all the bad qualities Ross listed about her, and questions why someone would make such a list in the first place. This example illustrates two points. First, a single reward (or cost) can outweigh other rewards and costs. Second, trying to quantify one's feelings is difficult. In Rachel's case, she is insulted by Ross's list as well as the idea that he needs a "list" to decide if he prefers her to Julie. To get a general idea of how rewarding one of your relationships is, complete the scale found in Box 10.1.

BOX 10.1 Put Yourself to the Test

How Rewarding Is Your Relationship?

To determine how rewarding one of your current relationships is, answer the following questions using this scale: 1 = very unrewarding, 7 = very rewarding.

	Unrewarding					Rewarding	
1. How rewarding is your partner in providing you with affection and warmth?	1	2	3	4	5	6	7
2. How rewarding is your partner in contributing material goods, such as gifts and possessions?	1	2	3	4	5	6	7
3. How rewarding is your partner in being comforting and supportive of you?	1	2	3	4	5	6	7
4. How rewarding is your partner in contributing money, such as letting you borrow money or paying for you?	1	2	3	4	5	6	7
5. How rewarding is your partner is helping you accomplish your goals related to work or school?	1	2	3	4	5	6	7
6. How rewarding is your partner socially, in terms of having common friends and liking to do things together?	1	2	3	4	5	6	7
7. When you think about everything that your partner has to offer you and your relationship (in the areas above as well as other areas), how rewarding is he or she?	1	2	3	4	5	6	7

To calculate your score, add the numbers you circled for each of the first six questions. Multiply your response to Question 7 by 2, and then add this to the sum. The total can range from 8 to 56. Higher scores mean that you perceive your relationship to be especially rewarding in a variety of ways.

SOURCE: Adapted from Sprecher, S., A comparison of emotional consequences of and changes in equity over time using global and domain-specific measures of equity, in *Journal of Social and Personal Relationships, 18,* 477–501. Copyright © 2001, SAGE, Inc.

Comparison Level

Knowing whether the relationship has a positive or negative outcome is not enough. Some people expect highly rewarding relationships, so outcomes have to be particularly positive for them to be happy. Other people expect their relationships to be unrewarding, so a slightly positive outcome, or even an outcome that is not as negative as expected, might be all that is needed to make them happy.

To account for the influence of expectations, interdependence theory includes the concept of **comparison level**, which involves the expectation of the kinds of outcomes a person expects to receive in a relationship (Thibaut & Kelley, 1959). This expectation is based on the person's past relational experiences and personal observations of other people's relationships. For example, if you have had really good relationships in the past, and your parents and friends all tend to have happy relationships, you are likely to have a high comparison level. Thus, you could be in a relationship in which the rewards outweigh the costs, but not enough to exceed your comparison level, leading you to be dissatisfied. Consistent with the idea of comparison levels, one study demonstrated that women are less likely to rate their current relationship as committed and satisfying if their past relationships were especially close (Merolla, Weber, Myers, & Booth-Butterfield, 2004).

The history of one's current relationship can also influence comparison levels. For example, based on how their friendship operated in the past, Josh expected his rewards to continue to outweigh his costs by about 5 to 1 in his friendship with Brent. However, after becoming roommates, Josh started to perceive an increase in costs. They began arguing more and Brent always seemed to be nagging him to clean up after himself. As a result, Josh now perceives that he is getting about 3 rewards for every cost in his friendship with Brent. Josh's friendship still has a positive outcome because he is getting more rewards than costs. However, because the outcome does not meet his expectation, he is likely to be dissatisfied with his relationship.

The opposite can be true when a person has a low comparison level. For example, imagine that a friend of yours has a history of really bad relationships. Your friend's current relationship might have 5 rewards versus 10 costs, leading to a negative outcome (of -5 if we quantify it). However, if your friend expects to have to incur at least 20 costs to receive 5 rewards, your friend's outcome of -5 would actually be better than the low comparison level of -15, so your friend should be fairly satisfied with the relationship.

As these examples suggest, people will be satisfied when their outcomes meet or exceed their comparison levels. This can be written as an equation: satisfaction equals the outcome minus the comparison level. Thus, the comparison level and the outcome work together to predict how satisfied people are in their relationships (Sabatelli, 1984). Comparison levels also influence how much positive behavior people expect from their partners. Dainton (2000) conducted two studies looking at comparison levels, relational satisfaction, and maintenance behaviors. Maintenance behaviors included actions such as showing commitment to the partner, being positive and cheerful around the partner, and sharing tasks in a fair manner (see Chapter 9). These behaviors can be thought of as "rewards" within the context of the relationship. Dainton's research showed that people tended to be satisfied with their relationships when they perceived their partner to use high levels of rewarding maintenance behavior. Satisfaction was also higher when people reported that their partner used more maintenance behavior than they expected them to. In other words, people were happiest when their partner engaged in lots of rewarding behavior that met or exceeded their comparison level.

Quality of Alternatives

Although satisfaction and commitment often go together, it is possible for people to be in satisfying relationships that are uncommitted or in committed relationships that are unsatisfying. You can probably think of relationships that fit these categories. Perhaps you know people who do not seem to want to commit to their relationships even though they seem happy. Perhaps you also know people who seem to be stuck in relationships that have no future and are unsatisfying. **Quality of alternatives** helps explain these situations, and refers to the types of alternatives that people perceive they have outside of a current relationship (Thibaut & Kelley, 1959). Alternatives might include pursuing other relationships or being on one's own. Some people perceive that they have several good alternatives. Perhaps many other attractive people would be interested in them, and perhaps they would be happier alone than in their current relationship. Other people perceive that they have poor alternatives. Perhaps they are dependent on their partner for financial support and cannot afford to leave the relationship, or they can envision no attractive alternative relationships, or they view themselves as unlovable and think that if they leave their partner they will be alone for the rest of their lives.

When people have good alternatives, they tend to be less committed to their relationships. By contrast, when people have poor alternatives, they tend to be highly committed to their relationships (Crawford, Feng, Fischer, & Diana, 2003). A simplistic example of the way alternatives function might be observed during the month before the senior prom. Suppose that Rosa, a high school senior, has been dating Carlos for the past year. She is considering breaking up with him sometime before they both leave for college, but she is not sure when. If Rosa thinks that two or three boys she finds attractive are likely to ask her to the prom, she might break up with Carlos sooner (assuming that going to the prom is important to her). But if Rosa thinks that no one "better" than Carlos is going to ask her to the prom, she is likely to stay with him, at least temporarily.

On a more serious note, some individuals stay in unsatisfying and even abusive relationships because they have poor alternatives. For example, a man might decide that it is better to stay in his unhappy marriage rather than risk losing custody of his children. In a study on predictors of divorce, people reported being much more likely to leave their spouses when they had appealing alternatives (Black, Eastwood, Sprenkle, & Smith, 1991). Research also suggests that abused women who are dependent on their husbands for financial support are more likely to stay in their abusive relationships (Pfouts, 1978; Rusbult & Martz, 1995). These women, many of whom have little education, few work skills, and no means of transportation, often see their abusive relationships as a better alternative

than being poor, hungry, and unable to support their children (Rusbult & Martz, 1995).

Combining Comparison Level and Quality of Alternatives

Whereas the comparison level is a measure of satisfaction, the quality of alternatives is a measure of dependency and (at least temporary) commitment. These two factors combine to create different types of relationships, as shown in Figure 10.1.

Here are examples for each of the boxes in Figure 10.1:

Box 1: The committed and satisfying relationship. Joe perceives Darren to be the best relational partner he has ever had. He is more considerate and caring than all of his past boyfriends, and they also have a lot in common. Therefore, Joe's relationship exceeds his comparison level, and he is very satisfied. Furthermore, Joe cannot imagine being with anyone who makes him happier than Darren. When he considers his alternatives (which he rarely does), he thinks he is better off staying with Darren than pursuing a new relationship. Joe tells Darren, "I love you. Let's make our relationship exclusive."

Box 2: The uncommitted but satisfying relationship. After her divorce, Kristen was really depressed. She thought dating would be really difficult, and she didn't think she'd ever find anyone she liked. Then she met

		Alternatives Are:	
		Poor	Good
The Relationship:	Meets or Exceeds CL	**Box 1:** Joe Satisfied Committed	**Box 2:** Kristen Satisfied Uncommitted
	Fails to Meet CL	**Box 3:** Caroline Dissatisfied Committed	**Box 4:** Jose Dissatisfied Uncommitted

Figure 10.1 The Combined Influence of Comparison Level and Quality of Alternatives

Tim, who exceeded her expectations in nearly every way. He was easy to talk to, fun to be with, and very attractive. He definitely made her happy. Lately, however, several other attractive men have shown an interest in Kristen, and she wonders if it would be a mistake to "settle" for the first man to come along after her divorce. She tells Tim, "I really want to keep seeing you, but I think we should both see other people as well."

Box 3: The dissatisfying but committed relationship. Caroline and Diana are partners who have been living together for almost a year. When they first moved in together, everything was great. But in recent months they have started arguing more, and they seem to be drifting apart. Sometimes Caroline dreads coming home at night because she is so worried that they will argue. Diana no longer meets her expectations; Caroline has been in happier relationships than this. Yet Caroline feels trapped. She has not met anyone else she is remotely interested in dating, and she is terrified of being alone. She hopes that despite her unhappiness things will eventually get better, so she says to herself, "I'll stick it out a little while longer— at least until something better comes along."

Box 4: The dissatisfying and uncommitted relationship. Jose feels that his relationship with Cecilia is at a standstill. At first, Cecilia seemed like the perfect woman—intelligent, fun loving, easygoing, and beautiful. Six months into their relationship, however, Jose started focusing on Cecilia's flaws. Cecilia seems to use her intelligence to try to prove that she is always right, and she never wants to do anything fun anymore. In fact, Jose can think of many past girlfriends with whom he had much more fun. Lately Jose has noticed that a coworker he finds more attractive than Cecilia has started to pay extra attention to him. He is sure she will accept if he asks her out. Jose tells Cecilia, "I'm sorry, but I don't think this is working out anymore. I think we need to break up."

As these four types of relationships illustrate, the comparison level and the quality of alternatives shape the type of relationship people share. Some people stay in unhappy relationships because they do not have better alternatives, while others leave happy relationships to pursue even more appealing alternatives. Indeed, Donovan and Jackson (1990) argued that interdependence theory "may well be the theory most frequently used to explain the cause of divorce" (p. 24).

THE INVESTMENT MODEL

The investment model is an extension of interdependence theory. In the original **investment model**, Rusbult (1980, 1983) theorized that quality of alternatives, relational satisfaction, and investment size affect commitment. Commitment, in turn, determines whether people stay together or break up. Later Rusbult and her colleagues developed an expanded investment model that focused on relational maintenance (Rusbult et al., 1994). According to this expanded model, commitment has a profound influence on whether people use positive, relationship-maintaining behaviors and survive the problems, conflicts, and temptations that threaten their relationships.

Within the investment model, relational satisfaction is seen as a product of the choices and behaviors that *both* people in the relationship make. Consistent with other interdependence models, this model suggests that, when relationships are characterized by behavior that is rewarding and fulfills expectations, satisfaction is likely. But satisfaction is only part of the story. According to the investment model, commitment is influenced not only by level of satisfaction but also by the quality of alternatives and the investments that people put into their relationships. Figure 10.2 depicts the components of this model.

Investments

As shown in Figure 10.2, the investment model includes many of the same elements as interdependence theory but adds the concept of investments. **Investments** are "resources that become attached to a relationship and would decline in value or be lost if the relationship were to end" (Rusbult et al., 1994, p. 119). Investments can be classified as either intrinsic or extrinsic (Rusbult, 1983). **Intrinsic investments** are those that are put directly into the relationship, including time, effort, affection, and disclosure. **Extrinsic investments** are resources or benefits that are developed over time as a result of being in the relationship, such as material possessions, enmeshment within a common social system, and an identity that is attached to being in a relationship. People put more investments into relationships to which they feel a

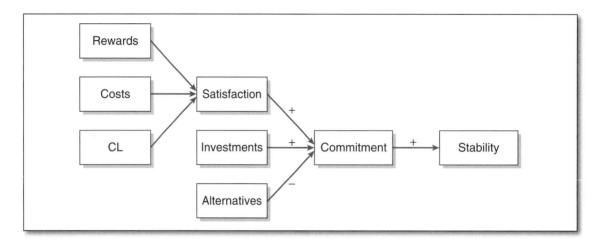

Figure 10.2   Rusbult's Original Investment Model

SOURCE: From Rusbult, C. E., Drigotas, S. M., & Verette, J., The Investment Model: An Interdependence Analysis of Commitment Processes and Relationship Maintenance Phenomena. In Daniel J. Canary & Laura Stafford (eds.), *Communication and Relational Maintenance.* Used with permission from Elsevier.

strong commitment (Matthews, 1986). These investments then make it difficult to walk away from a relationship, which strengthens commitment even more. If two people do end a highly invested relationship, they probably will feel that all the time and effort they put into their relationship was a waste. They also might feel that they now have to start over, find someone new, and make adjustments to their identity and social image. These challenges make the prospect of ending a long-term, committed relationship a daunting one.

The basic idea behind the investment model is that satisfaction (which is influenced by rewards, costs, and comparison level), quality of alternatives, and investment size work together to produce commitment (as shown in Figure 10.2). When satisfaction and investments are high, and the quality of alternatives is low, people are likely to be highly committed to their relationships. By contrast, when satisfaction and investments are low, and the quality of alternatives is high, people are likely to be highly uncommitted to their relationships. Rusbult and her colleagues (1994) noted that a high level of commitment can be good or bad. High commitment can keep a satisfying relationship strong, but it can also trap people in unsatisfying relationships—especially if their alternatives are poor. Therefore, according to the

investment model, satisfaction and commitment are related but distinctly different.

Several studies have demonstrated that investments help predict commitment (Le & Agnew, 2003). These studies have shown that investments, along with satisfaction and the quality of alternatives, influence whether people are committed to and stay in their relationship with friends and romantic partners (Drigotas & Rusbult, 1992; Duffy & Rusbult, 1986; Guerrero & Bachman, 2008; Rusbult, 1980, 1983), as well as whether people stay at their jobs (Farrell & Rusbult, 1981; Rusbult & Farrell, 1983). For example, Rusbult (1983) looked at dating relationships over a seven-month period. She found that daters who reported increases in satisfaction and investment, as well as decreases in the quality of alternatives, were the most committed to their relationships. These people were also likely to be together at the end of the seven-month period. By contrast, daters who reported decreases in satisfaction and investment, as well as increases in the quality of alternatives, tended to experience less commitment and to voluntarily leave the relationship sometime during the seven-month period.

Another study examined abusive relationships by interviewing women at shelters (Rusbult & Martz, 1995). Women who went back to their

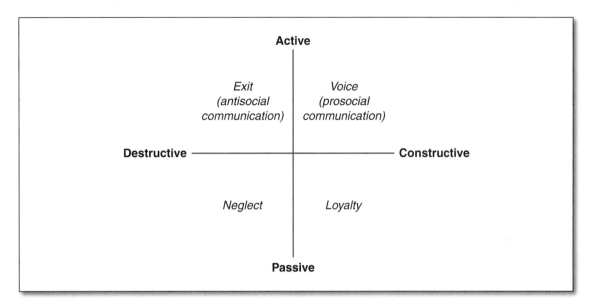

Figure 10.3   Responses to Dissatisfaction

SOURCE: From Rusbult, Caryl E., Drigotas, Stephen M. & Verette, Julie, The Investment Model: An Interdependence Analysis of Commitment Processes and Relationship Maintenance Phenomena. In Daniel J. Canary & Laura Stafford (eds.), *Communication and Relational Maintenance.* Used with permission from Elsevier.

abusive partners usually had large investments in the relationship and low-quality alternatives. Women in this situation may believe that it is better to stay in the relationship than to be alone or to move on to another, potentially worse, relationship. They may be dependent on their partner for financial resources or self-esteem. They also may not want to face the possibility that they have put a lot of time and effort into a bad relationship. Therefore, they may work even harder to improve their relationship by trying to change their own and their partner's behavior. This continuous investment, however, keeps them trapped within the dissatisfying relationship. Thus, while high levels of investment keep people in relationships, it does not always ensure that relationships are satisfying.

Responses to Dissatisfying Events

All relationships go through tough times. To complement the investment model, Rusbult and her colleagues (Rusbult, Johnson, & Morrow, 1986;

Rusbult, Verette, Whitney, Slovik, & Lipkus, 1991) advanced a **model of accommodation** that describes how people respond to problems or dissatisfying events in their relationships. According to this model, people have a natural tendency to respond to negative events with more negativity. For example, if Brent yells at Josh to stop leaving toothpaste residue all over the sink, Josh might be tempted to yell back and call Brent "a neat freak" or some other more colorful sentiment. However, if people are in a highly committed and satisfying relationship, they will often refrain from engaging in a negative response and instead act constructively in an effort to maintain the relationship. According to the model of accommodation, people have four basic response choices when it comes to dealing with problems in their relationships: exit, neglect, voice, and loyalty (Rusbult, 1987; Rusbult & Zembrodt, 1983). As Figure 10.3 shows, each of these responses is defined by whether it is constructive or destructive and whether it is passive or active.

The two destructive behaviors tend to exacerbate problems. **Neglect** behaviors involve standing by and letting conditions in the relationship get worse—for example, ignoring the partner, spending less time together, treating the partner poorly, and avoiding any discussion of relational problems. **Exit** behaviors include actions such as threatening to break up, moving out of the house, and getting a divorce. Some communication scholars have argued that exit and neglect are not the only behaviors that fall under the destructive side of Rusbult's model. Antisocial communication, such as insulting or punishing one's partner, are also destructive, active strategies for responding to dissatisfying events in relationships (Bachman & Guerrero, 2006a; Brandau-Brown & Ragsdale, 2008).

The two constructive behaviors, by contrast, help people repair and maintain their relationships. Partners who use **voice** attempt to improve conditions in the relationship by engaging in prosocial communication, such as discussing problems in a polite manner, seeking help from others, and changing negative behavior. Partners who use **loyalty** optimistically wait for positive change by hoping that things will improve, standing by the partner during difficult times, and supporting the partner in the face of criticism. Although voice and loyalty behaviors may help preserve the relationship, it is important to keep in mind that sometimes it is better to exit a bad relationship than work to improve it (Rusbult, Arriaga, & Agnew, 2001). Also, voice is a better strategy for repairing relationships than loyalty. Voice involves directly confronting issues and solving problems, whereas loyalty often leaves issues unresolved (Guerrero & Bachman, 2008; Rusbult et al., 2001).

The investment model helps predict how people attempt to repair their relationships following dissatisfying events. A study by Brandau-Brown and Radsdale (2008) showed that people who are highly committed to their relationships are especially likely to use strategies such as being open, emphasizing the importance of their relationships, and spending time together as ways of repairing their relationships. Two other studies investigated communication following betrayals, such as a partner lying or being unfaithful. Guerrero and Bachman (2008) focused on how the betrayed person reacts. Betrayed individuals were likely to respond with prosocial communication when they were satisfied with and invested in the relationship, and antisocial communication when they were dissatisfied with the relationship. Betrayed individuals were also less likely to respond with revenge if they were highly invested in their relationship. Another study on betrayal suggested that offenders are more likely to use prosocial repair strategies such as apologizing and promising to change if they are in committed relationships, and that people are most likely to stay with their partners following betrayals if they still regard their relationship as satisfying (Ferrara & Levine, 2009). Together these studies suggest that satisfaction, investment, and commitment are all related to prosocial communication and relationship stability.

Another study looked at the investment model within the context of romantic jealousy (Bevan, 2008). This study showed that people were likely to report discussing jealousy in a prosocial manner when they were highly invested in and committed to their relationship. People were more likely to report communicating about jealousy in a direct but antisocial manner (called *distributive communication*) when they had invested into their relationship but the relationship was dissatisfying. This antisocial response may reflect the frustration that often stems from investing in a relationship that is no longer satisfying.

These studies on jealousy (Bevan, 2008) and betrayal (Ferrara & Levine, 2009; Guerrero & Bachman, 2008) also suggest that the investment model may not always operate the way that it is depicted in Figure 10.2. Take another look at that figure. Notice how satisfaction, investment, and low quality of alternatives are supposed to lead to commitment, and then commitment is supposed to lead to relational stability. The accommodation model makes a similar prediction. Satisfaction, investment, and low quality of alternatives are theorized to lead to more commitment, which then leads to more prosocial (and less antisocial) communication. However, the studies on jealousy and betrayal all demonstrate that satisfaction, investment, quality of alternatives, and commitment all lead *directly* to prosocial communication. In other words, satisfaction can have a positive effect on communication that is separate from commitment. Indeed, these studies suggest that satisfaction, in particular, tends to be a stronger predictor of whether couples communicate constructively and stay together following betrayals than commitment.

The Investment Model of Relationship-Maintaining Behavior

A later version of the investment model (Rusbult et al., 1994) merged and expanded upon the original investment model and the model of accommodation by suggesting that people in highly committed relationships get through difficult times by employing five types of prorelationship behavior, as shown in Figure 10.4. In addition to accommodating the partner, this model suggests that people in committed relationships also decide to remain in the relationship, derogate alternatives, show a willingness to sacrifice, and perceive relationship superiority.

Deciding to Remain

The first and perhaps most important step is the decision to remain in the relationship. People who choose the exit or neglect responses have often stopped believing in the relationship. Without a commitment by the partners to stay in the relationship and work through problems, the relationship is unlikely to survive. In one study, couples who were committed to one another were less likely to report exiting the relationship following a relational transgression, such as their partner betraying or lying to them (Menzies-Toman & Lydon, 2005). In the studies reported earlier on betrayal, couples were less likely to de-escalate their relationships if they had reported high levels of satisfaction and investment earlier (e.g., Guerrero & Bachman, 2008).

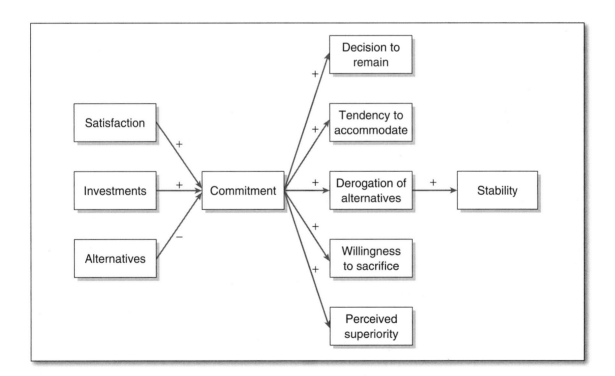

Figure 10.4 Rusbult's Expanded Investment Model of Relationship-Maintaining Behavior

SOURCE: From Rusbult, C. E., Drigotas, S. M., & Verette, J., The Investment Model: An Interdependence Analysis of Commitment Processes and Relationship Maintenance Phenomena. In Daniel J. Canary & Laura Stafford (eds.), *Communication and Relational Maintenance.* Used with permission from Elsevier.

Derogating Alternatives

Commitment also leads people to derogate their alternatives. In other words, committed people tend to find reasons to downgrade potential alternative partners. For example, in a study by Johnson and Rusbult (1989), when highly committed individuals were matched up with attractive partners via computer-assigned dates, they found ways to derogate their computer dates and, interestingly, especially if they were highly attractive. Although derogating alternatives is probably most relevant to romantic relationships, people in friendships and work relationships might also derogate attractive alternatives. Imagine, for example, that Brent and Josh work out the issues that have been causing tension in their friendship so that satisfaction and commitment are restored. If an acquaintance, Paul, who owns a nicer apartment and has a stable income, approaches Brent about becoming roommates, Brent would likely find fault with Paul's offer. For example, Brent might think "Josh is a lot more fun than Paul," even though Paul is known to have a great sense of humor. Of course, if nothing has changed and Brent still feels frustrated about the costs in his relationship with Josh, he would be likely to take Paul's offer.

Being Willing to Make Sacrifices

People in highly committed relationships are also more willing to make sacrifices for each other. Sacrifices can be thought of as special types of investments that involve putting aside one's own immediate self-interest and focusing on the best interests of the relationship. The willingness to make sacrifices has been found to be an important factor in maintaining high-quality relationships. People are more likely to make sacrifices for their partner or their relationship when they are committed and satisfied, have made large investments, and have low-quality alternatives (Van Lange et al., 1997). Making sacrifices sometimes involve helping a relational partner through a crisis situation. One study showed that college students see their closest friends as a significant source of comfort, encouragement, and social support (Burleson & Samter, 1994). Willingness to sacrifice is also important because it is difficult for two people to get everything

each one wants within the constraints of the relationship. For example, spouses have to make hard decisions regarding their careers, children, and so forth. If the wife's new promotion means that the family will have to move somewhere that is unappealing to the husband, the couple will have to make some type of compromise or sacrifice. Or, if the husband wants to have only one child and the wife wants at least three, something will have to give. In short, because both people cannot always have everything their own way, it is essential that relational partners be willing to sacrifice their own preferences for the overall good of the relationship.

Perceiving Relationship Superiority

Relational partners who are highly committed to each other perceive their relationship to be superior to other relationships. This can be thought of as a "relationship-enhancing illusion" (Rusbult et al., 1994, p. 129). For highly committed relationships, "the grass is rarely greener" on the other side. People tend to see their own relationships as having more positive and fewer negative characteristics than the relationships of others. This bias is particularly strong in highly committed relationships (Rusbult, Van Lange, Wildschut, Yovetich, & Verette, 2000). People might say and think things like, "We give each other a lot more freedom than most couples do" and "Our relationship doesn't have as many problems as the average relationship has." This type of thinking leads to positive attitudes about the relationship and sets the tone for behaving constructively and making more sacrifices. In relationships that are low in commitment and satisfaction, such positive thinking is less likely—the "grass on the other side" may indeed seem greener.

The investment model has proven to be a powerful theory for explaining the role that commitment plays in the process of relational maintenance. Two people are most likely to become committed to each other when they are satisfied with the relationship, have low-quality alternatives, and have made sizable investments. Once a couple is highly committed, the relationship is maintained through several types of prorelationship activities, including accommodating the partner by resisting the urge to retaliate, remaining in the relationship through good times and bad, derogating alternatives, being willing to sacrifice for the good of the relationship, and perceiving the relationship to be superior to the relationships of others. These forces combine to help maintain the relationship.

Barriers That Keep Relationships Together

Barriers, another factor that helps keep relationships together, can be thought of as all the forces that stop people from terminating a relationship. As Johnson (1982) stated, "People stay in relationships for two major reasons: because they want to; and because they have to" (pp. 52–53). Many of the barriers that keep people together are related to rewards, costs, and investments. For example, attraction, love, and other rewards make people want to stay in relationships. Social pressures, financial considerations, and the fear of being alone are factors that make people feel that they have to stay in a relationship, whether they want to or not. Similarly, when people make investments into a relationship, they also create a barrier that prevents breakup, because ending the relationship would mean losing those investments.

Researchers have identified many barriers to relational dissolution that help people maintain their relationships. Attridge (1994) grouped these barriers into two overarching categories: (1) internal psychological barriers and (2) external structural barriers. **Internal psychological barriers** are personal factors that keep people from ending a relationship; **external structural barriers** are outside forces that keep people in a relationship together.

Internal Psychological Barriers

Internal psychological barriers include commitment, investments, obligations, religious or moral beliefs, and identity. Consistent with interdependence theory and the investment model, commitment, which refers to how much a person feels attached to the partner and desires to remain in the relationship (Rusbult, Johnson, & Morrow, 1986), keeps relationships stable. For example, because Brent and Josh have been friends for a long time, Brent wants to work through problems and stay friends despite his frustrations. Longitudinal studies

of relationships show that commitment, and specifically a long-term relationship orientation, is a key to relational maintenance (Arriaga & Agnew, 2001). Investments, which were defined earlier as resources that have been deposited into the relationship and would lose value or be lost if the relationship ended, are also considered to be an internal psychological barrier. Since Brent and Josh are in a long-term, committed friendship, they have likely made considerable investments into their relationship, including time, effort, and personal sacrifices. If they manage their problems and remain roommates, their investment levels will likely increase even more.

Obligations refer to the extent to which people feel they owe something to someone. In close relationships, people usually feel a sense of personal obligation to one another. For instance, Brent may feel obligated to Josh because of all the things that Josh did for him in the past. Perhaps Josh provided him with invaluable support after his father died and was loyal to him at a time when few other people were. This sense of history and personal obligation makes it likely that Brent will try to make their friendship work despite their recent problems. Another type of obligation, parental obligation (Attridge, 1994), would not apply to Brent and Josh, but does apply to many spouses, unmarried couples, and divorced couples. The presence of children keeps relational partners together even when marital satisfaction is relatively low. Attridge (1994) reviewed research showing that couples without children may be as much as six times more likely to divorce than couples with two children. Moreover, as the number of children increases, the likelihood of divorce decreases (see also Greenstein, 1990). Some couples may even postpone a divorce until they believe the children are old enough to handle it. Some couples with children are reluctant to divorce because the spouses remember how devastated they were when their own parents divorced. In addition, even if parents do divorce, if they have children, they are likely to maintain some kind of renegotiated relationship, such as being friends or partners in raising their children.

Strong religious or moral beliefs might also act as barriers that keep people in some relationships, especially marriages. Some people believe that marriage is sacred and divorce is not an option. In fact, Attridge (1994) reviewed research showing that, the more religious people were, the less likely they were to divorce. People who reported that they never attended church were two to three times more likely to divorce than were people who reported attending church at least once a week. Thus, religiosity is one variable that might explain why some people decide to remain in a relationship, whereas others use exit or neglect strategies.

The final internal psychological barrier revolves around the meshing of people's self-identity and relational identities. Many people see their relationships as an important part of their self-identity. For example, Brent and Josh may see themselves as supportive, loyal, fun, and easygoing, in part because they act that way when they are with each other (or at least they used to). Brent's role as a loyal and steadfast friend is entwined within his broader image of himself as an engineering student, son, brother, Democrat, and so forth, but his image of himself as a good friend is nonetheless likely to be a central role. If his friendship with Josh ended and he had to move out of the apartment, he might have to adjust how he views himself as a friend. Self-identity is also connected to how partners reflect upon each other. For example, Brent might enjoy having Josh as a friend because he is popular and makes people laugh, which creates a positive atmosphere for him as well. For his part, Josh might be proud that his best friend is a straight-A student and a good athlete. If their friendship ends, they would lose the "reflected glory" they gain from being best friends. The bottom line here is that, the more central the relationship is to a person's self-identity, the more difficult it is to end the relationship.

External Structural Barriers

External structural barriers include financial considerations, legal issues, and social pressures. Financial considerations could be a barrier in Brent and Josh's friendship if either of them cannot afford to live on his own. But even more so, finances are an especially strong structural barrier that prevent breakup for married couples and cohabitors who have to resolve a myriad of financial issues if they end their relationships. Many couples cannot afford

two separate mortgages so they must sell their home and move into less luxurious homes. Couples also may have joint savings accounts and credit cards that need to be changed to separate accounts. Possessions can also act as barriers. It is often difficult to decide who should keep joint property such as furniture, exercise equipment, art, CD collections, computers, and so forth. Separation can also lead to increased financial obligations if alimony or child support payments must be made. And, of course, one spouse may be financially dependent upon the other—typically the wife because, unfortunately, women still tend to earn less money than men, even for the same work (Greenstein, 1990). Greenstein reported that women are less likely to divorce if they are financially dependent on their husbands. Women who earned less than 25% of their household income were least likely to divorce, while women who earned more than 75% of their household income were most likely to divorce. All of these considerations—household income, possessions, alimony, child support, and financial dependency—make it costly, in more ways than one, to end the relationship.

For married couples, the legal process also acts as an external structural barrier to relational dissolution. (The lease that Brent and Josh signed may also function as a sort of barrier preventing the disintegration of their roommate arrangement.) Depending on the state where a couple resides, the legal process can be easy or difficult, but the fact remains that spouses have to go through a formal process to divorce. This process may cause them to stop and think before ending the relationship. In fact, some spouses go through marriage counseling en route to a divorce, only to find that they would rather stay together after all. Interestingly, some states have drafted legislation to try to make it more difficult to obtain a divorce. The reasoning is that if the legal process is more time consuming and draining, spouses might try harder to work their problems out before filing for a "quickie divorce."

Finally, a number of social pressures act as external structural barriers to ending relationships. People's relationships are embedded in a larger social structure that includes their families and friends, and sometimes their communities and churches. The breakup of a long-term relationship often leads to disruption of the larger social network. For example, common friends may feel uncomfortable inviting both members of an estranged couple to a party. Members of the social network might also exert pressure on the couple to stay together. Brent and Josh have also built up an integrated friendship network over the years. What would happen if they stopped being friends? Would they still hang out with the same group of common friends or would they need to branch off and make new friends? Their parents may even encourage them to work things out and stay friends since they have all known each other since Brent and Josh were kids.

EQUITY THEORY

Like interdependence theory and the investment model, equity theory has been used to explain why some couples are more satisfied with their relationships than others. **Equity theory** focuses on determining whether the distribution of resources is fair to both relational partners (Deutsch, 1985). Equity is measured by comparing the ratio of contributions and benefits for each person. The key word here is *ratio*. Partners do not have to receive equal benefits (e.g., receiving the same amount of love, care, and financial security) or make equal contributions (e.g., investing the same amount of effort, time, and financial resources) as long as the ratio between these benefits and contributions is similar.

For example, in the past, Brent and Josh had an unequal but equitable friendship. Brent put more into the friendship than Josh—even then. He helped Josh with homework on a regular basis, financed a lot of their ski trips and other social activities, and even moved so they could go to the same college with group of their other high school friends. But the relatively high level of rewards Brent received from Josh balanced these contributions. In contrast to his own shy and introverted personality, Josh had always been outgoing and popular, which helped Brent meet and develop relationships with a lot of friends. Josh was also Brent's rock during difficult times, such as his father's death and the breakup of his romantic relationships. So even though Brent felt like he was

putting a little more into the relationship, he also felt he was getting a little more out of it. Now, however, the balance seems to have tipped so that Brent is putting more in and getting less out of the relationship compared to Josh. Because of this, Brent feels frustrated and dissatisfied.

When determining how equitable or inequitable a relationship is, it is also important to consider that both equity and inequity occur at general levels as well as specific levels (Henningsen, Serewicz, & Carpenter, 2009). **General equity** (or inequity) represents an overall assessment of balance between two people's benefits and contributions. **Specific equity** focuses on the balance between people's benefits and contributions in a specific area, such as physical attractiveness, financial resources, social status, ability to influence each other, and supportiveness. A relationship can be unbalanced in terms of specific equity, but balanced overall. For example, over the history of their friendship, Brent may have been underbenefited in terms of sharing financial resources and helping with homework, but overbenefited in terms of social status and supportiveness, making the overall relationship balanced and satisfying until recently.

Principles of Equity Theory

As the example of Brent and Josh illustrates, equitable relationships are usually characterized by more satisfaction and commitment than inequitable relationships, largely because people feel distress when inequity is perceived to exist (Adams, 1965; Walster, Berscheid, & Walster, 1973; Walster, Walster, & Berscheid, 1978). Five principles help explain why rewards and equity are associated with relational satisfaction and commitment (Canary & Stafford, 2001; Guerrero, La Valley, & Farinelli, 2008; Walster, Walster, & Berscheid, 1978):

1. Individuals try to maximize their outcomes so that relational rewards outweigh relational costs.

2. People in groups and dyads develop rules for distributing resources fairly.

3. Within groups and dyads, people will reward those who treat them equitably and punish those who treat them inequitably.

4. When individuals are in inequitable relationships, they will experience distress. This distress will lead them to try to restore equity, such that the more distress they experience, the harder they will try to alleviate that stress.

5. Individuals in equitable relationships experience more satisfaction. They also engage in more prosocial communication than do individuals in inequitable relationships.

These principles have been tested and supported for people in the United States and other Western cultures. In other cultures, equity may operate differently (see Box 10.2).

BOX 10.2 Highlights

Equity Across Different Cultures

Some researchers have suggested that equity and equality are valued differently depending on how fairness is conceptualized within a culture. People in Australia, North America (excluding Mexico), and Western Europe prefer **equity**, which means that they believe resources should be distributed based on the contributions people make. In contrast, people in Asia and Eastern Europe prefer **equality**, which means that they believe resources should be distributed equally among people regardless of their contributions (Carson & Banuazizi, 2008; Leung, 1988; Powell, 2005). For example, one study showed that people from the United States preferred equity more than people from Korea (Kim, Park, & Suzuki, 1990). Another study showed that inequity was related to anger and decreased liking for people from the United States, but not for people from Korea (Westerman, Park, & Lee, 2007). Yum and Canary (2009) examined the link between equity and relational maintenance behavior, such as being positive and open, in six countries—China, the Czech Republic, Japan, South Korea, Spain, and the United States. This link was strongest in the United States, followed by Spain. In these countries, people reported using more prosocial communication to maintain relationships that were perceived as equitable. However, equity was not related to maintenance behavior in China, the Czech Republic, Japan, or South Korea. These findings highlight that while equity is an important concept in the United States and other Western cultures, it is somewhat less important in other cultures.

When relationships are inequitable, one individual is overbenefited and the other is underbenefited (Walster, Walster, & Berscheid, 1978). The overbenefited individual receives more benefits or makes fewer contributions, or both, than does the partner, so that the ratio between them is unbalanced. In simple terms, this person is getting the "better deal." In the scenario with Brent and Josh, Josh is overbenefited. The underbenefited individual, by contrast, receives fewer benefits or makes greater contributions than does the partner, so that the ratio between them is not balanced. This person (Brent in our scenario) is getting the "worse deal."

Theoretically, inequity should always entail one person being overbenefited and the other person being underbenefited. However, perception does not always match reality. Because people tend to overestimate their own contributions to relationships, both dyadic members might think they are underbenefited even though this is not actually the case. For example, in a classic study by Ross and Sicoly (1979), husbands and wives rated the degree to which they had responsibility for various activities, such as caring for the children, washing the dishes, and handling the finances, on a scale from 0 (no responsibility) to 150 (complete responsibility). Thus, if a husband and wife split the task of doing the dishes evenly, both should have rated their responsibility at the 75-point midpoint. However, the results suggested that 73% of the spouses overestimated the amount of work they did; when their ratings were summed and averaged across all the activities, they totaled over 150 points. (Apparently a lot of dishes were being cleaned twice!) As this example illustrates, relational partners like Josh and Brent might both perceive themselves to be underbenefited; but in reality it would be impossible for each person to be getting a "worse deal" than the other. To see if you and a relational partner overestimate the extent to which you contribute to the relationship, take the test in Box 10.3.

BOX 10.3 Put Yourself to the Test

How Much Do You and Your Partner Contribute to the Division of Labor?

Think about a relationship you have with a person with whom you live. It could be a romantic relationship, a roommate relationship, or a family relationship. (If you are currently living alone, you can report on a past relationship.) Make two copies of this page so that you and your partner can each fill it out separately at first.

What percentage of the time, from 0% to 100% do you do the following things? If you and your partner do a particular chore separately, mark 50%. For example, you and your roommate might each do your own laundry. If something is not relevant to your relationship, leave it blank.

	% of time I do this	% of time my partner does this	Total %
1. Dishes.	_____	_____	_____
2. Household laundry.	_____	_____	_____
3. Writing checks or using e-mail to pay the bills.	_____	_____	_____
4. Contributing money to pay for bills and household expenses.	_____	_____	_____
5. Cleaning the bathroom(s).	_____	_____	_____
6. Vacuuming the floors.	_____	_____	_____
7. Cleaning noncarpeted floors.	_____	_____	_____
8. Going grocery shopping.	_____	_____	_____
9. Dusting the furniture and other household goods.	_____	_____	_____

(Continued)

(Continued)

	% of time I do this	% of time my partner does this	Total %
10. Taking care of a pet or pets.	_____	_____	_____
11. Taking out the trash.	_____	_____	_____
12. Cooking meals.	_____	_____	_____
13. Setting and clearing the table.	_____	_____	_____
14. Going out and getting prepared meals (e.g., from a restaurant).	_____	_____	_____
15. Mowing lawns and doing landscaping.	_____	_____	_____
16. Doing maintenance on cars (including washing and repairs).	_____	_____	_____
17. Helping children with homework.	_____	_____	_____
18. Taking basic care of children, such as getting them dressed and brushing their teeth.	_____	_____	_____
19. Driving children places.	_____	_____	_____
20. Purchasing clothing and supplies for people in the household.	_____	_____	_____

After each person fills out this form separately, add up the percentages and put them under the "Total %" column. Percentages over 100% indicate that one or both of you overestimates the extent to which you do a chore, whereas percentages under 100% indicate that one of both of you underestimates the extent to which you do a particular chore.

Benefits of Equity

Around half of spouses report that their marriages are equitable (Peterson, 1990). Partners who perceive equity tend to be satisfied with and committed to their relationships. Early work on equity theory showed that individuals who perceived their dating relationships to be equitable reported being happier and more content than those who perceived their dating relationships to be inequitable (Walster, Walster, & Traupmann, 1978). Later work on married couples showed that people who perceive equity or themselves as overbenefited are happier than those who perceive themselves as underbenefited (Buunk & Mutsaers, 1999; Guerrero et al., 2008). Couples who perceive equity also tend to report more commitment to their relationships (Crawford et al., 2003).

Equity in specific areas is also related to satisfaction and commitment. For example, one study showed that when partners are equitable in how much they influence one another, they report more satisfaction and commitment in their relationship (Weigel, Bennett, & Ballard-Reisch, 2006).

Communication patterns may contribute to the satisfaction that couples in equitable relationships experience. For instance, couples and friends in equitable relationships report using more relational maintenance behavior than those in inequitable relationships (Canary & Stafford, 2001; Messman, Canary, & Hause, 2000; Stafford & Canary, 2006). Maintenance behaviors help couples keep their relationship satisfying. Several specific maintenance behaviors have been found to associate with equity, including positivity, openness, and assurances. **Positivity** involves making interactions pleasant and enjoyable by engaging in behavior such as acting cheerful and optimistic and complimenting the partner. **Openness** involves disclosing personal information, as well as engaging in more routine, mundane talk. **Assurances** involve making statements that show commitment to the relationship, such as talking about the partners' future together. (See also Chapter 9.) Couples in equitable relationships also say that they express anger, guilt, and sadness in more constructive ways than do couples in inequitable relationships (Guerrero et al., 2008). For example, they talk about their anger in an assertive manner without resorting to aggression.

Consequences of Underbenefited Inequity

According to equity theory, whether people are over- or underbenefited, they experience increases in distress and decreases in satisfaction and happiness (Walster, Walster, & Berscheid, 1978). Of course, underbenefited individuals experience a different kind of stress than overbenefited individuals. As you might suspect, underbenefited individuals are usually more distressed than overbenefited individuals (Canary & Stafford, 1994). They also report the least relational satisfaction (Buunk & Mutsaers, 1999; Guerrero et al., 2008). When people are underbenefited, they tend to feel cheated, used, and taken for granted, and they

experience anger or sadness (Walster, Walster, & Traupmann, 1978). Men may be particularly likely to be angry when they are underbenefited, while women may be especially likely to be sad, disappointed, or frustrated (Sprecher, 1986, 2001). Both men and women report expressing anger more aggressively when they are in the underbenefited position (Guerrero et al., 2008).

Underbenefited individuals also report that both they and their partners use less prosocial forms of communication. In a study on relational maintenance behaviors, underbenefited husbands reported that their wives used less positivity, offered fewer assurances, and shared fewer tasks than did overbenefited husbands and husbands in equitable relationships (Canary & Stafford, 1992). Therefore, people may feel underbenefited if they do not receive adequate amounts of relational maintenance. A study on comforting behavior suggested that people who are underbenefited in terms of supportiveness or physical attractiveness put less effort into comforting their partners when they are distressed (Henningsen, Serewicz, & Carpenter, 2009). This suggests that people who feel underbenefited might not feel like exerting much effort into maintaining a dissatisfying or unfair relationship. Doing so could make them even more underbenefited.

Consequences of Overbenefited Inequity

Overbenefited individuals tend to experience less distress than their underbenefited counterparts, but more distress than individuals who are in equitable relationships (Guerrero et al., 2008; Sprecher, 1986, 2001; Walster, Walster, & Traupmann, 1978). People who perceive themselves as overbenefited may also feel smothered and wish that their partner would spend less time doing things for them. One study showed that overbenefited wives tend to express guilt by apologizing and doing nice things for their husbands (Guerrero et al., 2008). Another study showed that people who are overbenefited in terms of the balance of supportiveness in their relationship report using the most sophisticated comforting strategies when their partner is distressed (Henningsen et al., 2009). Thus, when people perceive themselves to be overbenefited, they might use prosocial behaviors to try to balance their relationships by increasing their partner's rewards. Yet some research shows that women in the overbenefited position use less relational maintenance behavior (Canary & Stafford, 1992). These women may not feel much need to maintain their relationships because their husbands are already providing them with high levels of rewards. However, if they feel guilty about something or their partner is distressed, they may be likely to engage in positive behavior that prevents the relationship from becoming too out of balance.

Not surprisingly, some overbenefited men and women feel quite content with their relationships and not guilty at all (Hatfield, Greenberger, Traupmann, & Lambert, 1982; Traupmann, Hatfield, & Wexler, 1983). One study even showed that people are increasingly happy the more overbenefited they are (Buunk & Mutsaers, 1999). People may need to be highly overbenefited before they experience distress and guilt. By contrast, being even somewhat underbenefited can lead to anger and frustration. In any case, if people perceive enough inequity, feelings of anger, sadness, and guilt may pervade the emotional fabric of the relationship.

Reducing Distress in Inequitable Relationships

What happens when relational partners experience inequity and distress? According to Walster, Walster, and Berscheid (1978), they will be motivated to reduce inequity and the accompanying distress. There are three general ways to do this. People can restore actual equity, adjust their perceptions, or leave the relationship.

Restoring Actual Equity

People can attempt to restore actual equity by changing their behavior. For example, the overbenefited partner might contribute more to the relationship, whereas the underbenefited partner might do less. Alternatively, the underbenefited partner might ask the overbenefited partner to do more. Some research suggests that underbenefited people are more likely to ask their partners to change their behaviors to restore equity, whereas overbenefited people are more likely to change their own behavior (Westerman, Park, & Lee, 2007). This makes sense from an equity theory standpoint. Underbenefited individuals probably feel that they are already in a disadvantaged position, so why should they change their behavior? Overbenefited individuals, on the other hand, may change their behavior to make the relationship more equitable, thereby protecting the benefits they gain from being in the relationship.

Adjusting Psychological Equity

People can also attempt to restore psychological equity. Recall that equity is "in the eye of the beholder" in that perceptions are as important as actions. To restore equity, people sometimes reassess their costs and benefits and decide that they are actually getting a fairer deal than they first thought. For instance, on reflection, Brent might realize that Josh actually does a lot for him, and that it isn't his fault he is broke all of the time and that his mom used to always pick up after him. Sometimes mental adjustments such as these represent the situation more accurately. However, there is also a potential danger. Individuals might continually readjust their perceptions even though the situation has remained unchanged. If this happens, they might remain stuck in the underbenefited or overbenefited position.

Leaving the Relationship

Sometimes people temporarily leave as a way to try to restore equity. For example, Brent could leave for a few days so that Josh realizes how messy the place would be if he was not there to clean it up. Overworked moms might go "on strike" for a week so that their family will see how hard it would be for them to function without her. Another way to restore equity, which is sometimes a last resort, is to end the relationship entirely. As the investment model suggests, this option is most likely when people have made low investments into the relationship and have high-quality alternatives outside of the relationship. When this is the case, there is little incentive to stay in a relationship that is inequitable and distressing.

People are also more likely to exit inequitable relationships if their costs outweigh their rewards.

Combined Influence of Reward-Cost Ratios and Equity

Although equity relates to a host of positive processes in relationships, equity alone does not capture how interdependence affects a relationship. To be highly satisfied, a couple also needs to be in a relationship in which rewards outweigh costs. In fact, studies by Cate and his associates showed that the overall level of reward value associated with a relationship is more important than equity (Cate & Lloyd, 1988; Cate, Lloyd, & Henton, 1985; Cate, Lloyd, & Long, 1988). Some level of inequity might be inconsequential if both partners are receiving high levels of rewards. Thus, relationships that are characterized by equity as well as positive outcomes (rewards outweigh costs) are most likely to be satisfying. Relationships that are inequitable with rewards outweighing costs should also be satisfying, especially if the rewards are high and the inequity is fairly small. By contrast, relationships that are equitable with costs outweighing rewards are likely to be perceived as fair but somewhat dissatisfying. Finally, inequitable relationships in which costs outweigh rewards are the least satisfying.

Let's take a look at some examples that illustrate how equity and reward-cost levels work together. Earlier we introduced Joe and Darren, who are in a satisfied, committed relationship. Suppose that Joe receives 25 benefits for every 5 contributions he makes to his relationship with Darren. This means that Joe has a benefit-contribution ratio of 25:5. Darren has a ratio of 50:10. Is their relationship equitable or inequitable? Because both Joe and Darren are receiving 5 benefits per contribution, their relationship is equitable. Notice that for the relationship to be equitable, Joe and Darren do not have to be receiving the exact same number of benefits, nor do they have to be making the same number of contributions. Instead, the ratios between each person's benefits and contributions must be the same. Notice also that their outcome value (rewards minus costs) is positive. Thus, Darren and Joe's relationship is equitable and rewarding, and as a consequence, satisfying.

In other cases, relationships can be equitable without being particularly rewarding. Imagine one partner having a benefit-contribution ratio of 15:30 while the other partner has a benefit-contribution ratio of 10:20. Both individuals are getting 1 benefit for every 2 contributions they make, so the relationship is equitable. But would such a couple have a satisfying relationship? The answer seems to be yes and no. They might be satisfied in that both are getting a fair deal but dissatisfied because they are not maximizing their rewards, which, as discussed previously, is the first principle of equity theory. It would be better to be in a relationship where rewards outweigh costs even if that relationship was somewhat inequitable.

Equity in the Division of Household Labor

Before leaving the topic of equity, it is important to discuss how issues of equity and fairness are related to the division of household labor. Couples who share tasks in a fair manner report being happier and more committed (Canary & Stafford, 1993, 1994). They also report giving and receiving more social support to one another (Van Willigen & Drentea, 2001). Yet research suggests that it is hard for many couples to achieve a fair division of labor (Steil, 2000). When it comes to household work, women are typically underbenefited and men are typically overbenefited. In fact, according to Steil's (2000) careful review of the literature, working women do about two-thirds of the household chores and even more of the child care. It may seem that the division of household chores would be more equitable for working than nonworking women, since working women's husbands might be expected to do more. However, Berk (1985) found that men in dual-career couples spend only four more minutes a day engaged in household tasks than do men in traditional single-career relationships. Even among dual-career partners who report splitting household tasks evenly, women still do far more in terms of caring for children (Rosenbluth, Steil, & Whitcomb, 1998). The situation is no better for wives who earn more

Why does this mom looked more stressed out than the rest of her family? Research suggests that if she is doing more than two-thirds of the household work, she is likely to feel stressed and to see her relationship as inequitable and unsatisfying.

than their husbands. In fact, Biernat and Wortman (1991) found that men actually do fewer household chores when their wives earn more than they do, perhaps because they see their wives as highly capable of handling multiple tasks or because they are resentful. On the basis of these results, it is not surprising that wives are more likely to feel underbenefited than husbands (e.g., Guerrero et al., 2008).

Ironically, although women usually air their relational grievances to their husbands (Gottman & Carrere, 1994), in the case of unfair division of household labor, they are often silent (Thompson & Walker, 1989). Unless their share of household work exceeds the two-thirds mark, they typically do not perceive that the division of labor is unfair, nor do they complain. Instead they deal with the inequity by adjusting their perceptions or comparing themselves to other women who have a worse situation than

themselves (e.g., Himsel & Goldberg, 2003). Steil (2000) labeled this problem "the paradox of the contented wife" (p. 127). Women want equality, yet even when they are aware that they do more household tasks than their husbands, they often end up reporting that their relationship is fair, equitable, and satisfying.

Even though women are fairly satisfied in marriages in which inequities (up to the two-thirds share mark) occur, working mothers become less satisfied as the gap between their husband's and their own share of the household tasks widens (Barnett & Baruch, 1987; Staines & Libby, 1986). At this point, women begin to feel underbenefited. Based on these findings, Gottman and Carrere (1994) made the following recommendation: Most men need to do more housework, care for their children more, and show their wives more affection and appreciation if they want their wives to be truly happy.

Unlike their heterosexual counterparts, most gay and lesbian partners do roughly the same amount of household tasks. Peplau and Spalding (2000) provided a comprehensive review of the literature on the division of labor in homosexual households. In their review, they noted that most gay men and lesbians are in dual-career relationships, "so that neither partner is the exclusive bread-winner and each partner has some measure of economic independence. The most common division of labor involves flexibility, with partners, sharing domestic activities or dividing tasks according to personal preferences" (p. 117). Kurdek (1993a) compared the division of household labor in heterosexual, gay male, and lesbian couples. Consistent with other research, he found that women did a larger portion of household work than men in heterosexual relationships. Gay men and lesbians were more likely to do an equal amount of household tasks. But whereas gay men divided the chores up so that each man routinely did certain tasks more than the other, lesbians tended to share tasks, often by doing chores together. Thus, opposite-sex couples might take a lesson from same-sex couples when it comes to sharing household chores in a fair, equitable manner.

SUMMARY AND APPLICATION

People exchange resources with one another in all types of relationships. Parents provide children with love and a secure home, and children give their parents affection and feelings of self-worth. Friends exchange companionship and do favors for one another, and romantic partners exchange financial resources, household responsibilities, and love. Social exchange is even part of work relationships, wherein employers provide rewards such as praise and raises, and subordinates contribute productivity and loyalty to the company (Farrell & Rusbult, 1981).

Certain circumstances can change the balance of rewards, costs, and equity in relationships. For Brent and Josh, becoming roommates introduced a new set of costs into their friendship. Issues revolving around financial responsibility and the division of household tasks, which were once irrelevant to their relationship, now threaten to ruin their long-standing friendship. These types of shifts in reward-cost ratios can occur in all types of relationships. For instance, a new baby might change the division of labor for a married couple, and a wife's big promotion at work might alter how financial resources are distributed between spouses.

Whether relational partners experience a change in their reward-cost ratios or not, it is important for them to exchange resources in a fair and equitable manner. People report being happier in relationships characterized by equity, perhaps because partners in equitable relationships experience less distress, and perhaps because they use more maintenance behaviors and express emotion in more positive ways. In contrast, people who are underbenefited tend to experience distress in the form of anger, frustration, and disappointment, whereas people who are overbenefited tend to experience distress in the form of guilt. Other times, people who are overbenefited try to balance the relationship by engaging in behaviors that appease or comfort their partner.

Brent and Josh have several options for relieving the distress they are feeling. They could negotiate new rules so that Josh keeps the house cleaner and contributes more financially. This would decrease Brent's costs. Josh could also provide Brent with more benefits by doing special things for him, like cleaning his car or picking up dinner for them more often. Or, Brent could agree to continue doing more around the house in exchange for Josh finding a job and paying more rent. They could even decide that it is better to stop being roommates so they can preserve their friendship.

Although it is possible that the tension in their roommate relationship could end up destroying their friendship, there are several reasons to be optimistic for the future of Brent and Josh's relationship. First, given their long history together, it would appear that Brent and Josh have made considerable investments into their friendship. It would be difficult for either man to build the same kind of friendship with someone else, especially in the short term. Second, they are likely to evaluate the current state of their relationship in the context of their broader friendship. For years, they have been satisfied with their friendship and loyal to one another. According to Rusbult's investment model, being invested and committed to someone provides a buffer against relationship termination; they are more likely to use voice strategies to deal with their problems than exit strategies. Other factors, such as their joint social network and overlapping identities, also act as barriers that keep them from ending their friendship. Thus, although Brent and Josh are experiencing some dissatisfaction in their relationship, they are likely to engage in accommodation and make sacrifices for one another. They are also likely to derogate alternatives (e.g., living with someone else would be worse) and to see their friendship as superior (e.g., our friendship is stronger than most so we can work this out).

Married and cohabiting couples often deal with some of the same issues as Brent and Josh. The fair division of household labor is often a contentious issue in marriage, as are issues related to the distribution of financial resources (see Chapter 14). Couples with children also exchange resources related to parenting, and their parental obligations and legally sanctioned bond act as barriers that keep them from separating. Thus, across various types and stages of relationships, the balance of rewards and costs plays a critical role in determining our feelings toward others. The next time you think that one of your relationships has become unfair or less rewarding, we hope that this chapter will give you some insight into the causes of, and possible remedies for, your distress.

DISCUSSION QUESTIONS

1. People obtain various types of rewards and costs in their relationships, including those related to emotions, tasks, social needs, and opportunities. Based on your experience, which types of rewards do you think are most important within relationships? Are some costs especially detrimental to relationships? How might the importance of various rewards and costs differ by relationship type (e.g., married couples, roommates, siblings)?

2. Which theory do you think does a better job explaining why people are more satisfied and committed to some relationships than others—interdependence theory, the investment model, or equity theory? Why? How might these theories work together to provide an even better explanation of satisfaction and commitment in relationships?

3. Why do you think working women still do two-thirds of the household work, and, perhaps more important, why don't most women complain until their share of the work exceeds this two-thirds mark?

STUDENT STUDY SITE

Visit the study site at **www.sagepub.com/guerrero3e** for e-flashcards, survey and assessments from the chapter, and SAGE journal articles.

11

Influencing Each Other

Dominance and Power Plays in Relationships

Tyler is a pretty laid-back individual who really loves his girlfriend, Ashley. Ashley feels the same toward Tyler, although she would like him to get a better job and go back to school. Their love life is good in all respects except when Ashley hassles him about school and work. Tyler defends his lifestyle and his current job, but when Ashley's persuasion becomes more strident, Tyler withdraws, Ashley gets mad and shops excessively, and their sex life goes downhill. Ashley is smart and beautiful and Tyler worries that she has better alternatives, especially since she is about to graduate with a communication degree from college and already has better job offers than his current entry-level position.

As illustrated by Ashley and Tyler's situation, power struggles characterize many relationships, with one or both partners striving to influence or change the other. Power is a crucial aspect of social relationships. The philosopher Bertrand Russell (1938) once remarked, "The fundamental concept in social science is Power in the same sense that Energy is the fundamental concept in Physics" (p. 10). But there is a dark side to power; as historian Lord Acton (1887/1972) famously observed, "Power corrupts and absolute power corrupts absolutely" (p. 335). Whether power is force for good or evil, power abhors a vacuum, and close relationships are no exception. Power

exists in all relationships: Someone takes the initiative to start a relationship, or decide how to spend money, initiate sex, accept or reject the initiation, take out the garbage, or clean the bathroom. At some level, power exists in every friendship, romance, marriage, and family.

Power is so prevalent in relationships that some scholars have labeled dominance and submission as a basic dimension of interpersonal communication (Burgoon & Hale, 1984). When power imbalances exist, couples like Ashley and Tyler need to find ways to communicate their needs in constructive rather than controlling ways. What options do they have for influencing one another?

Are some forms of communication more effective than others? And perhaps most important, how can they achieve a more balanced, egalitarian relationship? This chapter addresses these and other questions by examining how issues of power, control, and influence play out in close relationships. First, we define power and outline six principles of power. Next, we review the literature on influence goals and examine specific verbal tactics and nonverbal power behaviors. Finally, we focus on issues of power and equality in families.

Defining Power and Related Terms

Power refers to an individual's ability to influence others to do what the individual wants (Berger, 1985; Henley, 1977), as well as a person's ability to resist the influence attempts of others (Huston, 1983). People often exert power by controlling valuable resources (Ellyson & Dovidio, 1985). In relationships, people control resources in several ways. First, relational partners can grant or withhold resources, such as money and possessions, affection, sex, and time spent together (Fitzpatrick & Badzinski, 1994). For example, Ashley gives her partner extra affection to reinforce his good behavior and withholds affection to punish his negative behavior. Second, power is part of the decision-making process when relational partners determine how to spend valuable resources such as time and money. Relational partners exercise power when they distribute tasks such as washing the dishes, balancing the checkbook, and doing the driving on a road trip. Relational partners also exercise power when they decide what type of car to buy, how to spend their time together, and where to go on vacation. In interpersonal relationships, power reflects the ability to affect the behavior, emotions, or decisions of one's partner (Berger, 1985).

Power is a basic feature of relationships because humans want to control their lives and be their own free agents. A free agent is said to have **agency**, an empowering aspect of experience where a person is able to freely control the surrounding environment, including social interaction and relationships (McAdams, 1985). This is why people often feel the need to "change" their relational partners so they fit their conceptions of how a perfect partner should behave. Uncontrolled agency leads to dominance. Ideally, power motivates, energizes, and enables a person without diminishing or enslaving other people. Negative forms of power, such as harassment or coercion, usually destroy intimacy and produce unstable and dissatisfying relationships. The key to using power productively is for partners to use their influence for the good of the relationship and to keep the decision-making process fair and equitable. In other words, both people in a relationship should have a voice.

Dominance refers to the display or expression of power through behavior (Burgoon, Buller, & Woodall, 1996). As we will discuss in this chapter, dominant behaviors include verbal communication such as commands and other "one-up" messages ("*We* are going to *my* family's home for Thanksgiving this year"), as well as nonverbal communication such as using a loud voice while maintaining high levels of eye contact. However, using a particular behavior does not determine if someone is dominant. Instead, dominance is determined by people's submissive responses; it is not dominance unless it works (Burgoon et al., 2010). So, if the demand to spend Thanksgiving with one's family is met with a response such as "I'm not going—you can go by yourself," or if the strategy of using a loud voice while maintaining steady eye contact fails to get a partner's attention, dominance has not occurred.

Social influence involves changing someone's thoughts, emotions, or behaviors (Burgoon et al., 2010). Sometimes social influence is the result of strategic communication, whereby one person actively uses communication to try to change the other person's attitudes, beliefs, feelings, or behaviors. In other cases, indirect influence occurs. Dominant behaviors can be part of the social influence process, although they do not have to be. The person who ultimately affects a change in the other person is influential and has exerted power, either directly or indirectly.

POWER PRINCIPLES

Whether power is exercised through dominance or more subtle forms of influence, it occurs within a social and relational context. Six principles of power describe how power functions within our interactions with others.

Power as a Perception

The first principle is that *power is a perception*. As suggested earlier, people can engage in powerful communication, but if others do not perceive their power, their behavior is not dominant. Others are powerful only to the extent that we believe they are powerful. Some people have objective power but still have trouble influencing others. **Objective power** is the authority associated with factors such as position, strength, weaponry, and wealth. For example, presidents, defensive linemen, nuclear powers, and millionaires have objective power, but they have real power only if other people perceive their power and are influenced by these perceptions. People who use power cues and act powerfully and proactively tend to be perceived as powerful by others (Hall, Coates, & LeBeau, 2005; Magee, 2009). However, peoples' perceptions about power are more exaggerated than actual power cues because these stereotypes are important social knowledge, taught by culture even though they may contain only a "kernel" of truth (Hall et al., 2005). For instance, using direct gaze while talking is a powerful behavior but people often think it is more powerful than it really is. People who seek power overestimate the power motivations of other people and are hyperaware of power cues (Mast, Hall, & Ickes, 2006). Powerful people often look for power cues so that they can use communication skill to acquire or resist power.

The opposite can occur as well; some people become influential and dominant even though they do not overtly use powerful behavior. The lives of people such as Mahatma Gandhi, Martin Luther King Jr., and Mother Teresa suggest that people of humble means and little objective power can be very influential and wield real power when they stand for

something in which large groups of people believe. Similarly, our relational partners are only as powerful (or as powerless) as we perceive them to be, regardless of their level of objective power.

The way people perceive themselves is also important. Thinking of one's self as powerful does not ensure that someone will be powerful, but thinking one is powerless virtually guarantees powerlessness. People who are confident and appear self-assured are likely to manifest more power and are more able to influence others than people who lack confidence (Burgoon et al., 2010; Dunbar & Burgoon, 2005). People who feel powerless often get trapped in bad relationships because they do not have the confidence to assert themselves to change the situation.

Power as a Relational Concept

A second principle is that *power exists in relationships*. Power is always a relational concept; one individual cannot be dominant without someone else being submissive. In relationships, the issue is often how much **relative power** a person has in comparison to one's partner. Most romantic relationships are characterized by small imbalances of power (Dunbar, Bippus, & Young, 2008; Dunbar & Burgoon, 2005). In heterosexual relationships, men are more likely to be perceived as the more powerful partner (Felmlee, 1994; Sprecher & Felmlee, 1997). Research suggests that people are happiest in equalitarian relationships and least happy in relationships where the woman has considerably more power than the man (Gray-Little & Burks, 1983). However, the balance of power in relationships is often dynamic. Partners in close and satisfying relationships often influence each other at different times in various arenas. For example, in a single day, a wife may influence her husband to invest in a certain stock and meet her at a particular restaurant for dinner, while he may decide what movie they see that night and which babysitter to call. Interestingly, men are more likely than women to perceive the world to be hierarchical and organized in pecking orders and power structures (Mast, 2005). Box 11.1 provides a way of determining how much relative power you have in one of your relationships.

BOX 11.1 Put Yourself to the Test

How Much Relative Power Do You Have?

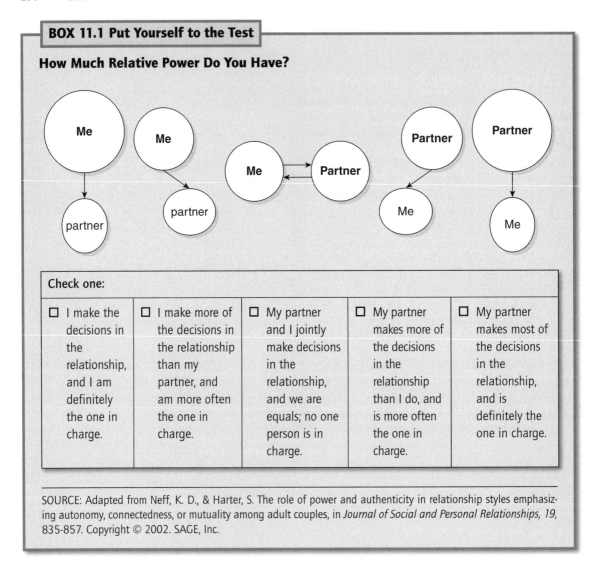

Check one:				
☐ I make the decisions in the relationship, and I am definitely the one in charge.	☐ I make more of the decisions in the relationship than my partner, and am more often the one in charge.	☐ My partner and I jointly make decisions in the relationship, and we are equals; no one person is in charge.	☐ My partner makes more of the decisions in the relationship than I do, and is more often the one in charge.	☐ My partner makes most of the decisions in the relationship, and is definitely the one in charge.

SOURCE: Adapted from Neff, K. D., & Harter, S. The role of power and authenticity in relationship styles emphasizing autonomy, connectedness, or mutuality among adult couples, in *Journal of Social and Personal Relationships, 19,* 835-857. Copyright © 2002. SAGE, Inc.

In close relationships, influence is inevitable—even desirable. Partners who exercise little influence over each other may not really be a couple, but virtual strangers in the same household. Partners in close relationships are interdependent; the action of one person affects the other. As we will see in this chapter, the way in which power is used and communicated is crucial. When partners perceive that power is fairly distributed and they are receiving adequate resources from each other, they are more likely to experience relational satisfaction (see Chapter 10).

Power as Resource Based

A third principle is that *power usually represents a struggle over resources. The more scare and valued resources are, the more intense and protracted are power struggles.* People bring many resources to their relationships. Most early research on power focused on money and social standing as powerful resources (Berger, 1980), and when resources are defined in this way, men typically have more power than women. More recently, as the gap between men's and women's earnings narrows, more women than men are graduating from college, and most of these women are pursuing well-paying careers. As women bring more financial resources to relationships, their level of power is increasing. Research from numerous countries shows that when married men and women have more equal income, women have more decision-making power, share in money management, and do less housework (Kan, 2008; Yodanis & Lauer, 2007). Similarly, unequal access to money in a marital relationship and keeping money in separate accounts for the partners is associated with more male control and less female relationship satisfaction (Vogler, Lyonette, & Wiggins, 2008).

Income also appears to be an important source of power for gay men. Studies have shown that in gay relationships, the man who is older and earns more money typically has more power (Blumstein & Schwartz, 1983; Harry, 1984; Harry & De Vall, 1978). For lesbians as well, some research has shown that the woman who earns more has more power (Peplau & Fingerhut, 2007; Reilly & Lynch, 1990), but Blumstein and Schwartz's (1983) extensive study found no differences in power based on income. Instead, lesbians reported that it was important for both partners to earn money so that neither partner would be financially dependent on the other.

Of course, money is only one resource that people bring to relationships. The research on power in families has been criticized for focusing too much on income and social prestige (Berger, 1980; McDonald, 1981). Other resources—such as communication skill, physical attractiveness, advice, social support, a sense of humor, parenting ability, sexual rewards, affection, companionship, and love—are exchanged in relationships (see Chapter 10).

When resources are defined as more than financial, women wield considerable power in their relationships. Gottman and Carrere (1994) argued that in public interactions, or interactions with strangers, men typically act more dominant and are more influential than women. However, in private interactions, especially with relational partners, women typically are more dominant and influential. As Gottman and Carrere (1994) put it, "Women's public tentativeness and deference, the acceptance of a subordinate role and politeness in stranger groups does not hold in

marriages" (p. 211). In close relationships, women have considerable influence in that they confront conflict more readily and are more demanding, expressive, and even coercive (Gottman, 1979). Thus, women are *not* passive in marriages, as gender stereotypes may suggest. Interestingly, in high-status positions, men and women exhibit few power differences but in low-status positions, men are much more likely to employ power strategies than women (Kesher et al., 2006).

Women also tend to be more powerful during sexual interactions. The decision to escalate or not escalate a relationship sexually in almost all societies has been a women's prerogative (Byers, 1996). Virtually every theory, based on either biology or socialization, suggests that women have more negative attitudes toward casual sex than men (Browning, Kessler, Hatfield, & Choo, 1999). Studies have shown that the more powerful partner can refuse sex and this finding is true in gay, lesbian, and heterosexual romances (Blumstein & Schwartz, 1983). Thus, in dating relationships, sexual escalation and access is an arena where women exert considerable power. However, more submissive women were more likely to consent to casual sexual behavior, particularly unusual sexual behavior (Browning et al., 1999).

In relationships, some resources are scarcer than others. According to the **scarcity hypothesis,** people have the most power when the resources they possess are hard to come by or in high demand. For example, you may be attracted to several different people, but if you are in love with one of them, that person will have the most power. Of course, a scarce resource leads to power only if it is valued within a relationship. For one person, money and position may be important, so a partner who is rich and successful is seen as possessing a scarce and valuable resource. For another person, religious beliefs and family values might be perceived as scarce and therefore valuable resources for a relational partner to possess.

The Principle of Least Interest and Dependence Power

A fourth principle is that *the person with less to lose has greater power*. People who are dependent on their relationship or partner are less powerful, especially if they know their partner is uncommitted and might leave them. This phenomenon has been termed **dependence power** (Samp & Solomon, 2001). Dependence power is also related to a person's alternatives. According to interdependence theory, **quality of alternatives** refers to the types of relationships and opportunities people could have if they were not in their current relationship (see Chapter 10). In the opening example, if Ashley is attractive to many other men, but Tyler is not as attractive to other women, Ashley is the scarcer resource and has more power than Tyler.

The **principle of least interest** suggests that if a difference exists in the intensity of positive feelings between partners, the partner who feels most positive is at a power disadvantage (Safilios-Rothschild, 1970; Sprecher, Schmeeckle, & Felmlee, 2006; Waller & Hill, 1951). For example, if you are in love with your partner but your partner is not in love with you, your partner has more power. If you are not interested in the relationship and your partner is interested, you have more power. There is an inverse relationship between your interest in the relationship and how much relational power you have. When the least interested partner makes requests, such as requesting money or sex, the more interested partner is likely to comply rather than risk losing the relationship. By contrast, when the more interested partner makes a request, the less interested partner does not have to give in to maintain the relationship.

Research on both heterosexual and lesbian couples confirms the principle of least interest (Caldwell & Peplau, 1984; Peplau & Campbell, 1989; Sprecher et al., 2006; Sprecher & Felmlee, 1997). Sprecher and Felmlee found that for both men and women, the partner with less emotional involvement in the relationship had greater power and control in the relationship. They also found that men are generally less emotionally invested in their relationships than women, which suggests the balance of power generally favors men. In lesbian relationships, Caldwell and Peplau found that women who were more committed and involved in the relationship than their partners tended to have less power. Longitudinal research has shown that a

partner with less emotional involvement does have more power, but equal emotional involvement was associated with greater relational satisfaction and stability (Sprecher et al., 2006).

In line with the principle of least interest, when one person in a relationship values autonomy over closeness, that person tends to have more power. Harter and her colleagues (1997) described three relationship orientations: self-focused autonomy, other-focused connection, and mutuality. People who emphasize autonomy value their independence over closeness. Those who emphasize connection do the opposite—they value closeness over independence. Finally, people who have a mutuality orientation value balancing independence with relational closeness. Around 74% of people report having a mutuality orientation. Most of the other 26% of couples are characterized by one partner having a mutuality orientation and the other partner having either an autonomy- or connection-focused style. Neff and Harter (2002) showed that people tend to be more subordinate if their partner values self-focused autonomy. Conversely, people are more likely to be dominant if their partner values other-focused connection. Equality was most likely in relationships where both partners value mutuality.

Power as Enabling or Disabling

A fifth principle is that *power can be enabling or disabling*. People can use power to achieve success; power is part of the human spirit that infuses us with agency and potency. However, excessive power or frequent power plays often cripple close relationships. Few people like being dominated or manipulated and often respond to power plays with resistance, stubbornness, and defiance (McAdams, 1985). As we will learn, large power discrepancies in a relationship tend to be unhealthy. Overall, research has shown that men with very high power needs often have problems in love relationships; both men and women with high power needs have less intimate friendships (McAdams, 1985) and their partners experience increased negative emotions (Langner & Keltner, 2008). Like powerful nations, powerful people must be careful not to overuse their power. Research has shown that people are more likely to have an enduring influence on others when they engage in dominant behavior that reflects social skill rather than intimidation (Guerrero & Floyd, 2006). Personal power is also protective against pressure and excessive influence by others and situational stress (Galinsky, Magee, Gruenfeld, & Whitson, 2008). People who communicate power through self-confident, expressive, and composed behavior tend to be successful in achieving their goals and maintaining good relationships.

In contrast, power can be disabling when it leads to destructive patterns of communication. Two such patterns are the chilling effect and the demand-withdrawal pattern. According to the **chilling effect**, the less powerful person often hesitates to communicate grievances to the partner (Roloff & Cloven, 1990). Researchers have identified the conditions conducive to the chilling effect related to the power dynamics within the relationship. First, people are susceptible to the chilling effect when they are dependent on their relationship but perceive that their partner is uncommitted (Cloven & Roloff, 1993; Roloff & Cloven, 1990; Solomon, Knobloch, & Fitzpatrick, 2004). The chilling effect is less likely to occur in committed relationships. Second, people who are afraid of losing their partners often respond to relationship problems by withdrawing support and withholding complaints (Roloff, Soule, & Carey, 2001). Third, partners are likely to withhold grievances to avoid negative relational consequences, such as conflict or partner aggression (Cloven & Roloff, 1993). These conditions are related to dependence power (Solomon & Samp, 1998). Indeed, research on both European Americans and Mexican Americans show that power discrepancies are associated with a lack of self-expression that negatively impacted physical health (Neff & Suizzo, 2006). The chilling effect has harmful effects on relationships; problems habitually stay unsolved, power differentials increase, stress increases, and relational satisfaction erodes.

Power dynamics can also lead to a **demand-withdrawal pattern**, which can be disabling and destructive (Christensen & Heavey, 1990; see also Chapter 14). This pattern occurs when one person makes demands and the other person becomes defensive and withdraws. When people feel powerless, they sometimes enact demanding behavior to try to change their partner's behavior. In the scenario at the beginning of this chapter, Ashley is portrayed as the "demander." She is frustrated that Tyler lacks ambition, so she tries to get him to go back to school and find a better job. Tyler is portrayed as the "withdrawer" who unsuccessfully tries to defend himself and then withdraws, perhaps to avoid further conflict. Although Ashley might have other types of power in her relationship, she seems powerless when it comes to influencing Tyler on an issue.

Research shows that people are most likely to be in the demanding position when, like Ashley, they are seeking compliance or change from their partner (Sagrestano, Heavey, & Christensen, 2006). Women are more likely than men to seek such change, as well as to be in a less powerful position; therefore, they tend to be in the demanding role. Patterns of demand-withdraw are found in both satisfying and dissatisfying relationships, but when such patterns occur repeatedly, they erode relational satisfaction (Heavey, Christensen, & Malamuth, 1995). Research shows that the demand withdrawal pattern results in short-term decreases in relational satisfaction for both partners, though in the long run it can actually increase relational satisfaction for women (Caughlin, 2002). So there is still much to learn about demand-withdrawal patterns.

Power as a Prerogative

The sixth principle is that *the partner with more power can make and break the rules.* According to this **prerogative principle**, powerful people can violate norms, break relational rules, and manage interactions without as much penalty as powerless people. In fact, in many cases, powerful individuals actually enhance their positive images when they display power (Guerrero & Floyd, 2006). In organizations, people with higher status and power usually can arrive late to a meeting

SOURCE: Jupiterimages/Getty Images/ThinkStock.

Patterns such as the chilling effect and demand-withdrawal sequences often reflect power imbalances in relationships. When couples stop talking, they are unable to manage problems and restore an equitable balance of power.

without penalty, while subordinates may be reprimanded. Similarly, high-status individuals, such as presidents or CEOs, can dress casually if they want (Burgoon et al., 2010). In families, parents may be able to eat while sitting on the new leather sofa, but children might be told to eat their food at the table. In romantic relationships, the person who cares the least may be able to get away with arriving late for dates, forgetting birthdays or anniversaries, or even dating other people. These actions may reinforce the powerful person's dependence power; such actions show that one person is more dedicated to the relationship than the other.

The more powerful person also has the prerogative to manage both verbal and nonverbal interactions.

As discussed later in this chapter, powerful people can initiate conversations, change topics, interrupt others, and terminate discussions more easily than less powerful people. For instance, imagine that you are in a hurry to get to your next class and someone stops you and starts to initiate a conversation. Would you be likely to chat for a moment or to brush them off and rush to class? According to the prerogative principle, you would be much more likely to stop and chat with someone you found powerful or attractive (e.g., your professor or someone you want to date). Similarly, in high school, the popular kids get to decide where to go and what to talk about, with the less popular kids following their lead. In romantic relationships, the person with the most power may decide which relational topics can be discussed and which are taboo.

The power prerogative is evident in nonverbal behavior as well (Andersen, 2008; Burgoon et al., 2010). Take touch as an example. Think about interactions between teachers and students, supervisors and subordinates, or lawyers and clients. Who has the prerogative to initiate touch in these relationships? Research suggests that the teachers, superiors, and lawyers will be most likely to initiate touch because they typically have more power in these relationships. By contrast, if students, subordinates, or clients initiate touch, it will be perceived as inappropriate. Some research suggests that in heterosexual romantic relationships, men typically have more power in the initial stages of the relationship. As a result, they have the prerogative to ask the woman out and to initiate behavior such as hand-holding and sex. For example, Guerrero and Andersen (1994) found that men were more likely than women to initiate touch in casual dating relationships but women tend to initiate touch more than men in married relationships.

Together, these six principles indicate that power relational partners negotiate power based on perceptions of each other and characteristics of their relationship. In close relationships, partners often share power, with each person exerting influence at certain times and accommodating the partner's wishes at other times. Thus, designating one person as "powerful" and the other as "powerless" can be misleading. In addition, when trying to influence each other, relational partners have goals that will affect the power dynamic.

INTERPERSONAL INFLUENCE GOALS

Most communication is influential. Thus, when we ask someone to do us a favor, when we advertise a product, or when we campaign for a political office, we are trying to influence people's attitudes and change their behavior. Other times, we try to resist such influence. This is particularly true in close relationships—for example, parents try to prevent their kids from smoking; dating partners initiate or refuse sexual involvement; and spouses influence

each other about when and whether to have children or to buy a new house. As Dillard (1989) stated, "Close personal relationships may be the social arena that is most active in terms of sheer frequency of influence attempts" (p. 293). Most interpersonal influence attempts are goal driven. In other words, people enact influence attempts to try to achieve particular goals (Berger, 1985). Dillard's (1989) research suggests that most influence goals fall into the six categories.

Making Lifestyle Changes

The most frequent influence attempt in close relationships involves the desire to change the behavior patterns of a partner, friend, or family member, which Dillard (1989) called giving advice about lifestyles. Examples of these types of influence goals might include trying to prevent conflict between your partner and your friends, getting a close friend to terminate a romantic relationship that you think is bad for her, convincing your brother not to move to Ohio for a job, and persuading a friend to reconcile differences with his parents. In addition to being common in relationships, influence attempts that revolve around lifestyle changes are also some of the most important. Dillard's (1989) research indicated that lifestyle-change messages are usually logical, positively presented, and direct.

Gaining Assistance

A more routine but important kind of influence attempt involves gaining assistance. Examples of these influence attempts might include getting your spouse to proofread your term paper, getting a friend to drive you to another city to see your girlfriend, borrowing money from your parents, and getting the university to accept your petition for readmittance. These influence attempts may be less significant than lifestyle changes, but they are personally and relationally important. For example, when romantic partners, friends, or family members assist you, their actions say something powerful about your relationship with them—namely, that they are willing to aid and support you. Messages designed to gain assistance are often indirect.

People often attempt to gain assistance through the use of hints or suggestions (Dillard, 1989). Instead of saying, "Get me a blanket and a bowl of popcorn," the person might hint by saying, "I'm kind of cold and hungry. A soft blanket and some warm popcorn would really feel good right now."

Sharing Activities

A critical type of relational influence attempt involves offers to share time and space (see Egland, Stelzner, Andersen, & Spitzberg, 1997). As discussed in Chapter 9, shared activities play a critical role in maintaining relationships. Joint activities enable people to spend time together, show common interests, enjoy companionship, and develop intimacy. Shared activities are a particularly important form of intimacy in many male friendships because men do not generally develop intimacy by disclosing personal information. Examples of these influence attempts might include running or biking together, partying together, or taking a vacation together. Many of these activities reflect attempts to increase the closeness of a relationship, and if the other person agrees to the persuasive overture, the relationship can escalate. This is particularly true of activities that require people in romantic relationships to spend time together, especially time alone together, and activities that signal commitment or exclusivity, like to a romantic partner's home for Thanksgiving. Sometimes requests for shared activity are direct, but more often they are indirect and appeal more to emotion than logic (Dillard, 1989).

Initiating Sexual Activity

One common form of interpersonal influence is initiating sexual relationships. This is true in dating, cohabiting, marital, gay, and lesbian couples (see Chapter 8 for a longer discussion of sex including sexual resistance strategies). The principle of least interest discussed above means that the person who desires sex the most will have the least power and the person who can take it or leave it has the most power. In dating and cohabiting relationships, men usually initiate sex (Morgan & Zurbriggen, 2007), though in marital relationships the woman may suggest or request sex more (see Chapter 8). Lesbian relationships may have less sex because sexual initiation not in most women's sexual scripts.

Condom use is another situation where power and sexuality intersect. More powerful partners can put their partner at risk by coercing or persuading a partner to have unprotected sex. Research shows that teenage women, particularly African American and Hispanic women, who experience partner dominance and intimate violence are less likely to use condoms consistently (Teitelman, Ratliff, Morales-Aleman, & Sullivan, 2008). Empowering young women and keeping them free of abusive partners may be one area where power is a matter of life and death.

Changing Political Attitudes

Some people are more political than others, but nearly everyone gets involved in political issues at one time or another. Convincing someone to take stands, support causes, or join movements are acts of political persuasion. Examples include talking someone into joining a union, persuading someone to vote for a political candidate, getting someone to register to vote, or convincing someone to boycott a sexist movie. By participating with you, friends or partners show their support for your cause and demonstrate that their attitudes align with yours, which can contribute to relational satisfaction. When relational partners seek to change each other's political attitudes, they often use indirect appeals for involvement that are low in coerciveness so they do not threaten each other's autonomy (Dillard, 1989).

Giving Health Advice

One important reason for exerting power and influence in close relationships is to help partners improve their mental and physical health. For example, we may want our romantic partners to get more exercise or to take vitamins. We may advise a friend to abandon an abusive relationship or tell our teenage brother to drive carefully and to party safely. We might tell a troubled colleague to seek counseling or recommend that a sick friend go to the doctor.

Of course, the way people give health advice may make a difference in terms of whether the advice is followed. If the persuader is too judgmental or demanding, the receiver may resist exercising, refuse to seek help, or rebel by engaging in dangerous behavior. **Psychological reactance** or **boomerang effects** occur when a parent, friend, or spouse is controlling or demanding (see Shen & Dillard, 2005). When this occurs, the influence attempt may cause the other person to become defensive and resistant. As a result, the person continues engaging in unhealthy behavior, or even worse, engages in more unhealthy behavior than before. One study showed that wives' social control efforts on their husband's cancer treatments had no positive effects and some negative effects on his health behavior and negative effects on the couple's interactions (Helgeson, Novak, LePore, & Eton, 2004). In fact, research on inconsistent nurturing suggests that partners who alternate patterns of punishing or reinforcing their partners may actually perpetuate drug and alcohol abuse (Le Poire, Hallett, & Erlandson, 2000). Conversely, socially supportive communication had positive effects. Messages that express concern without being critical may be best. Dillard (1989) found that most successful messages aimed at giving health advice are direct and logical.

Changing Relationships

A common form of influence among close friends is relationship advice. For instance, you may suggest that a friend dump her unfaithful boyfriend, or ask a friend to join your church community, or suggest to a romantic partner that we "just be friends." Because the stakes are so high, such influence attempts can be problematic, and whether they are accepted or not, they signal major changes in a relationship. Think about times when you wanted to change either your own or a friend's relationship. Maybe you wanted a platonic friendship to turn romantic but were afraid that communicating your romantic desire might ruin your friendship (see Chapter 9). Or, perhaps you were

afraid to give relational advice to a friend because you thought you might get caught in the middle. The prototypical example of this is when you see a friend's romantic partner out with someone else. If you tell your friend what you saw, your friend might side with her or his partner and accuse you of being jealous or making things up. But if you keep silent, your friend might be more hurt in the long run. As these examples suggest, giving relational advice can be a tricky proposition. When people try to influence others to change their relationships, they usually use direct communication, logical appeals, and large amounts of positivity (Dillard, 1989).

VERBAL POWER PLOYS

Traditionally, power and persuasion have been thought of as verbal activities. But in reality, communication that is powerful and persuasive consists of a combination of verbal and nonverbal cues.

Verbal Influence Strategies

Research has shown that relational partners can choose from an assortment of strategies that help influence each other. These strategies are often called **compliance-gaining strategies** (Miller & Boster, 1988; Miller, Boster, Roloff, & Siebold, 1977; Wiseman & Schenck-Hamlin, 1981) or **influence strategies** (Falbo & Peplau, 1980). Skilled communicators have a diverse arsenal of strategies at their disposal. In given situations, they select the strategies that are most likely to be influential for particular people and purposes. However, research has shown that people in more stable and equitable relationships use fewer power strategies than do people in unstable and inequitable relationships (Aida & Falbo, 1991), presumably because there is less that they want to change. Research has also shown that powerful people are more likely to be persuasive than less powerful people, regardless of the strategies they use (Levine & Boster, 2001). For individuals who are low in power, the best strategy may be to phrase requests using a positive, polite tone (Levine & Boster, 2001).

Direct Requests

One of the most obvious interpersonal influence strategies is the **direct request** (Wiseman & Schenck-Hamlin, 1981), also known as the **simple request** or **asking** (Falbo & Peplau, 1980). Research shows that this is the most common strategy for both men and women, most likely used by a person who feels powerful and supported (Levine & Boster, 2001; Morgan & Zurbriggen, 2007; Sagrestano, 1992). Examples of direct requests include asking your boyfriend or girlfriend, "Could you turn down the stereo, please?" or saying, "I really wish you wouldn't swear in public." While they are not very sophisticated or strategic messages, they are usually effective, particularly in relationships with high levels of mutual respect and closeness. Indeed, in a study of unmarried heterosexual and gay couples, Falbo and Peplau (1980) found that the most satisfied couples typically use direct strategies. Similarly, in a study of married couples, Aida and Falbo (1991) found that satisfied couples used more direct and fewer indirect strategies than did unsatisfied couples.

Bargaining

A **bargaining strategy** involves agreeing to do something for someone if the person does something in return. In addition to bargaining (Falbo & Peplau, 1980; Howard, Blumstein, & Schwartz, 1986), this type of influence attempt has been called *promising* (Miller et al., 1977; Wiseman & Schenck-Hamlin, 1981) and the *quid-pro-quo strategy*. For example, if one partner agrees not to watch football on Sunday if the other gives up smoking, each partner is giving up something in return for a concession by the other. Sometimes individuals using the bargaining strategy to persuade a partner will recall past favors or debts owed by the partner (Wiseman & Schenck-Hamlin, 1981). Other times people using the bargaining strategy to reward their partner prior to a persuasive request; this is called *pregiving* (Miller et al., 1977). Howard and fellow researchers (1986) found that more occupationally and relationally equal couples tended to bargain more than unequal ones. In unequal relationships, the person

with more power does not need to bargain to get compliance, while the person with less power does not have as many resources to use in the bargaining process. However, less powerful people may be more likely to negotiate and bargain than more powerful people (Levine & Boster, 2001).

Aversive Stimulation

Also called the **negative affect strategy** (Falbo & Peplau, 1980), **aversive stimulation** (Miller et al., 1977; Wiseman & Schenck-Hamlin, 1981) involves whining, pouting, sulking, complaining, crying, or acting angry to get one's way. The idea here is that the receiver will eventually comply merely to stop the aversive behavior. This strategy is not very sophisticated and is often thought of as childish because it is so widely employed by toddlers and small children. Although this strategy is sometimes effective, individuals who use it may be seen as spoiled or immature, and other people will avoid them if they use this strategy frequently. In fact, Sagrestano (1992) reported that people perceived aversive stimulation as the second most negative and unpleasant power strategy among the 13 strategies she tested (withdrawal, which we will discuss, ranked first). Recent research on adolescent couples reveals that girls often use shaming or humiliating behaviors on their immature partner as power ploys, though final decisions are more often made by the male partner in adolescent dyads (Bentley, Galliher, & Ferguson, 2007).

Ingratiation

Often called **positive affect** (Falbo & Peplau, 1980), liking (Miller et al., 1977), **ingratiation** (Wiseman & Schenck-Hamlin, 1981), "kissing up," or "sucking up," this strategy involves using excessive kindness to get one's way. A husband buying his wife flowers before asking for forgiveness or an athlete repeatedly complimenting her coach are examples of ingratiation. The person using the ingratiation wants to be perceived as friendly and likable so that the other person will want to be helpful and compliant. Of course, ingratiation strategies can backfire if the person using them is perceived as insincere. Canary and Cody (1994) discussed the concept of **illicit ingratiation**, which occurs when a person acts nice merely to gain compliance. Ingratiation can be persuasive only if it is seen as honest rather than manipulative.

Hinting

Called **indirect requests**, **suggesting** (Falbo & Peplau, 1980), or **hinting** (Wiseman & Schenck-Hamlin, 1981), this strategy involves implying a request without ever coming out and stating one. For example, Ashley might hint to Tyler that lots of people are returning to college this fall after taking a break from school. A wife who mentions to her husband how nice it would be to take a vacation may be hinting that she wants to go somewhere for their anniversary. While this is a polite strategy, its effectiveness depends on the perceptiveness of one's partner. If the partner does not pick up on the hint, this strategy will fail. In other cases, the partner might understand what the sender is hinting at but nonetheless ignore the request. In addition, when the request is made in such an indirect manner, the partner's responsibility for responding diminishes.

Moral Appeals

These compliance-gaining messages, which are also called **positive** and **negative altercasting** (Miller et al., 1977), take one of two forms. **Positive moral appeals** suggest that a good or moral person would comply with the request ("An understanding partner wouldn't nag me about school," says Tyler). **Negative moral appeals** suggest that only bad or immoral people would fail to comply ("Only an unambitious or unintelligent person would pass up the opportunity to complete his education," says Ashley). Both positive and negative moral appeals associate certain behaviors with the basic "goodness" of the receiver. Such a strategy also ties into an individual's identity as a basically good person. As discussed in Chapter 2, people generally prefer to act consistent with their positive self-identities. So, if Ashley sees herself as an understanding girlfriend and Tyler sees himself as an ambitious and intelligent person, they might be more likely to comply in

response to moral appeals. But, such appeals can also exacerbate conflict and lead to defensiveness, especially if a receiving partner perceives being attacked at a personal level (see Chapter 14).

Manipulation

Manipulation is set of strategies that involves getting one's way through attempts to make the partner feel guilty, ashamed, or jealous (Fleischmann, Spitzberg, Andersen, & Roesch, 2005; Wiseman & Schenck-Hamlin, 1981). These often include passive-aggressive strategies (see Chapter 12). Examples of such strategies may include making a relational partner feel guilty for going on vacation without you or ashamed for flirting with another person. Suggesting that alternative partners are available is also manipulative and threatening, and can occasionally be an effective manipulation strategy if the person becomes jealous. For instance, if your partner is not spending enough time with you at a party, you might flirt with someone in the hope that your partner will get jealous and be more attentive to you. Certainly, such strategies can backfire because people do not like to be manipulated. Manipulative strategies can also be thought of as a special kind of aversive stimulation. Strategies that cause people to experience negative affect often are seen as childish. Moreover, instead of stopping the offending behavior, some people avoid the person administering the aversive stimulation as a way of alleviating negative affect. So, if you start flirting with someone at a party, your partner simply might ignore you or leave with someone else rather than giving you the attention you want.

Withdrawal

Closely related to both aversive stimulation and manipulation are a set of strategies called **distancing, avoidance** (Guerrero et al., 1995), **withdrawal** (Falbo & Peplau, 1980), or **passive aggression** that occur when people withdraw, and give partners the silent treatment, ignore them, or limit communication with them. A young woman in one of our classes gave a good example of how withdrawal can be used as an influence strategy. She had been dating her fiancé for six years and thought she would be getting an engagement ring for Christmas. When she failed to get a ring, she gave her fiancé the silent treatment until he asked what was wrong; eventually he bought her the ring. This might not be the best way to become engaged. Over time, she might begin to wonder whether he would have proposed if she had not manipulated him in this way. Furthermore, this strategy does not always work. Sometimes the partner gets used to being ignored or grows tired of dealing with negativity and moves on. In fact, Sagrestano (1992) found that people perceived withdrawal as the most negative of the 13 power strategies she examined. Still, the withdrawal strategy can be effective in some situations. Sometimes people might be hesitant to bring up a sensitive subject, and by withdrawing they let the partner be the one who initially asks, "What's wrong?" and starts the conversation. Other times, people might miss their partner and appreciate them more after spending time apart.

Deception

Some people use lies and **deception** as a compliance-gaining strategy (Wiseman & Schenck-Hamlin, 1981). People may make false promises, such as saying that they will do something in exchange for compliance, when they actually have no intention of doing so. People may also exaggerate or make up information to try to gain compliance. For example, a teenager who wants his curfew extended might tell his parents that all of his friends get to stay out past midnight when only a handful of them actually do. Aside from the ethical issues associated with this strategy, it is a risky relational maneuver. Discovery of deception may result in a loss of trust and the general deterioration of the relationship (see Chapter 13). Even if the relationship survives the discovery of deception, the partner may become suspicious and guarded, making it difficult for the deceiver to successfully gain compliance later.

Distributive Communication

With **distributive** or **antagonistic strategies**, people attempt to blame, hurt, insult, or berate their partner in an effort to gain compliance (Guerrero et al., 1995; Sillars, Coletti, Parry, & Rogers, 1982; Wiseman & Schenck-Hamlin, 1981). These strategies are sometimes called **bullying** (Howard et al., 1986) and are usually ineffective and often lead to escalated conflict (see Chapter 14) and relational deterioration. Howard and associates (1986) reported that, contrary to some stereotypes, both men and women and both masculine and feminine people are likely to use distributive strategies.

Threats

Threats, or tactics such as threatening to walk out on the partner, failing to cooperate with the partner until the partner gives in, or threatening to withhold resources such as money or information, are usually ineffective. Howard and colleagues (1986) found that men and women equally use asserting authority through self-serving threats. People also may engage in mock violence or issue violent warnings, acting as if they are going to hurt their partner but then not do so. For example, a girl might make a fist and shake it in front of her brother's face without hitting him to illustrate what might happen if he does not stop teasing her. People are more likely to use threats such as these when the partner is perceived to be low in power (Levine & Boster, 2001).

Relational Control Moves: One-Ups and One-Downs

Rogers and her associates developed a classic method to determine dominance and control in relational communication (Rogers & Farace, 1975; Rogers & Millar, 1988). In any conversation, messages can be coded as dominant and controlling, or **one-up messages**; deferent or accepting, or **one-down messages**; or neutral, **one-across messages**. The focus is on the *form* of the conversation, not the content. Consider the following interaction between teenage sisters:

Marissa: You've been on the phone for an hour—get off! (one-up)

Nicole: Okay. (one-down)

Marissa: Now! (one-up)

[Nicole tells her friend she will call her later and hangs up.]

Marissa: Thank you. (one-down)

Nicole: Ask a little more nicely next time. (one-up)

Coding a person's verbal behavior can reveal whether the individual is domineering or submissive. Researchers can also study how the behavior of one partner impacts the relationship. For example, Rogers and Millar (1988) reported that when wives were domineering, both husbands and wives tended to experience less relational satisfaction.

More significant, by looking at patterns of one-up and one-down messages, we can determine the nature of the relationship between two people. This coding method represented a major conceptual breakthrough. A pair of utterances, called a **transact**, can be coded as symmetrical or complementary. If people engage in a pattern in which one person uses mostly one-ups and the other person uses mostly one-downs, the pattern is **complementary** with one person in the dominant position and the other person in the submissive position. If both people use the same moves, it is **symmetrical**. When two people repeatedly use one-up moves, the pattern is termed **competitive symmetry**. When two people repeatedly use one-down moves, the pattern is termed **submissive symmetry**. Along with these variations, a considerable portion of conversation is neutral in terms of control. When both partners exchange these one-across messages, the pattern is termed **neutral symmetry**. And, when a one-up or one-down message is paired with a one-across message, a **transition** has occurred. Box 11.2 provides examples of these five interaction patterns. Research has shown that spouses who report dyadic inequality in their marriages have higher proportions of competitive symmetry (Rogers & Millar, 1988).

BOX 11.2 Highlights

Examples of Transacts

Complementarity

Ashley: If you really don't want to go back to school, it's okay. (one-down)

Tyler: I won't go back no matter what you say. (one-up)

Marissa: We should pool our money together to buy something for Mom and Dad's anniversary. (one-up)

Nicole: Okay. How much do you think I should give? (one-down)

Competitive Symmetry

Tyler: Stop nagging me about school. (one-up)

Ashley: Then get off your butt and look for a better job. (one-up)

Submissive Symmetry

Nicole: What should we buy Mom and Dad for their anniversary? (one-down)

Marissa: I don't know. You decide. (one-down)

(Continued)

(Continued)

Neutral Symmetry

Marissa: They have been married 23 years. (one-across)

Nicole: Grandma and Grandpa were married for over 50 years before Grandpa died. (one-across)

Transition*

Tyler: I wish you would stop talking about graduation all the time. (one-up)

Ashley: Hey, did you see *American Idol* last night? (one-across)

Nicole: I wonder if there are tickets left for that concert Mom said she'd like to go to. (one-across)

Marissa: If you want me to, I can check. (one-down)

*Transitions include all combinations of one-across messages paired with one-up or one-down messages, regardless of order.

Of course, some interactions do not fall neatly into these categories. Take the interaction between Marissa and Nicole. At the beginning of the interaction, Marissa is the dominant sister, but by the end of the interaction, Nicole asserts herself. It is also important to consider the nonverbal communication and the context when interpreting one-up and one-down statements. A statement such as "You sure are in a good mood today" could be interpreted as a one-down message in most cases, but as a one-up message if delivered in a sarcastic tone of voice.

Powerful and Powerless Speech

Researchers have identified the characteristics associated with **powerful speech**, which occurs when speakers focus mainly on themselves rather than others, dominate conversations, redirect the conversation away from topics others are discussing, and interrupt others (Fitzpatrick & Badzinski, 1994). Research suggests that men are somewhat more likely than women to use these forms of powerful speech (Kalbfleisch & Herold, 2006), though it is highly dependent on the topic (Palomares, 2009). Falbo and Peplau (1980) found that women used more indirect strategies such as hinting, whereas men used more direct strategies such as open communication. Moreover, women were more likely to use unilateral strategies such as pouting or negative affect, whereas men were more likely to use bilateral strategies such as debate or negotiation. Timmerman's (2002) review of 30 studies supported the claim that men use more powerful language than women, particularly when addressing other men. However, the effect of sex on powerful language tends to be small, which brings into question the practical importance of these differences. In a recent study of e-mail language use, Palomares (2009) reported no sex difference in the use of powerful language on gender-neutral topics. Nonetheless, research has shown that more powerful speech creates more credibility and persuasive power, enabling those who use it and hindering those who do not (Burrell & Koper, 1998).

It is important to note that differential use of strategies appears to be less a function of sex or gender than one of power or powerlessness. Cowan, Drinkard, and MacGavin (1984) found that both men and women use more indirect and unilateral strategies when communicating with a power figure.

By contrast, both females and males are more direct and bilateral when communicating with a power equal. Kollock, Blumstein, and Schwartz (1985) found that the more powerful person in the relationship interrupts the partner more, regardless of sex or sexual orientation. Moreover, whether men or women use powerful verbal behavior depends on the topic. A study by Dovido, Brown, Heltman, Ellyson, and Keating (1998) revealed that on traditionally male topics, such as working on a car, men engage in more verbal power strategies, such as speech initiation and total time speaking. However, women use more of these verbal power strategies when discussing traditionally female topics such as cooking or raising children.

Some studies have also found that women use more **powerless speech** than men (Giles & Wiemann, 1987). Powerless speech occurs when people use tag questions and hedges. Tag questions involve asking people to affirm that one is making sense or that they understand. For example, you might ask, "You know what I mean, don't you?" Hedges refer to statements that give the sender or receiver an "out." Statements such as "I'm not sure this is right but. . ." and questions such as "You did say you'd help me with this, didn't you?" exemplify hedges. Although studies show that women use these forms of powerless speech more often than men, studies also suggest that these forms of speech are not always submissive. Sometimes women use tag questions and hedges in creative ways to get more information, accomplish goals, and improve their relationships (Giles & Wiemann, 1987). In addition, speaking is a skill that can be taught and many women have learned to use more powerful speech (Timmerman, 2002).

NONVERBAL POSITIONS OF POWER

Verbal communication carries messages of power, but nonverbal communication is an even richer source of power messages. The animal kingdom, which is a nonverbal world, is replete with dominance displays and pecking orders. Competition for mates, food, and territory is fierce and can be deadly. Animals evolved with power cues that establish dominance hierarchies without the need for deadly combat, and these pecking orders are all established nonverbally. Humans have even more complex power structures, and these are mostly nonverbal in nature (Andersen, 2008). Moreover, research suggests that perceptions of power are more influential than the actual power people possess (Hall et al., 2005).

Power is communicated via many forms of nonverbal communication, as introduced in Chapter 1. Thus, it is important to remember that the context and the relationship between people help determine if these behaviors are perceived as powerful.

Physical Appearance

Before a word is ever uttered, people make judgments about power from others' physical appearance. Research suggests that more physically attractive people are more influential, and that women in particular are more likely to use physical attraction as a power or persuasion behavior (Davies, Goetz, & Shackleford, 2008). Formal, fashionable, and expensive dress is also indicative of power and dominance (Andersen, 2008; Bickman, 1974; Morris, 1977). Recent research suggests that wearing high-status brand clothing induces more submissive behavior in interaction partners in both male and female dyads (Fennis, 2008). Similarly, expensive shoes, as well as the trendiest workout or basketball shoes, are major status symbols that connote power (Andersen, 2008). Women's clothing, once inflexibly prescribed, is now quite varied. Women can dress informally or formally, in modest or sexy attire, and in a feminine or masculine style. Men's clothing, by contrast, is proscribed more rigidly and generally must be modest, masculine, and appropriate to the occasion (Kaiser, 1997). Despite the variability of women's clothing, when women violate norms by dressing in inappropriate attire perceived as too trendy, sexy, nerdy, or masculine, they produce more negative reactions than men who violate clothing norms. Uniforms can convey the power associated with an occupation (surgeon, police officer), but uniforms can also convey powerlessness because they strip away individuality and other status symbols (e.g., jewelry) (Joseph & Alex, 1972). Clothing color also makes a difference. Black athletic uniforms, for instance, may be associated with power and aggression (Frank & Gilovich, 1988).

Studies have shown that the mesomorphic or muscular body is associated with power. Likewise, height is related to power and confidence (Andersen, 2008; Burgoon et al., 2010). This **principle of elevation** (Guerrero & Floyd, 2006) suggests that, fair or not, height or vertical position is associated with power. This is why powerful people are often seated in elevated positions. Kings and queens sit on thrones, and judges often sit above the courtroom. By contrast, people bow to show submission. In interpersonal interactions, people can exercise power by looming over someone who is seated (Andersen, 2008). Height differentials are also related to the use of space. For example, moving in close and simultaneously standing over someone is often perceived as intimidating. Interestingly, the greater height and muscle mass of men compared to women is one explanation for the traditional dominance and oppression women have experienced at the hands of men. Traditional ideals of the tall, dark, and handsome man and the petite women have perpetuated this stereotype (Andersen, 2004). It is important to note that physical appearance is most important during initial interactions; once a relationship is established, its effects diminish (Andersen, 2008).

Spatial Behavior

The study of interpersonal space and distance, proxemics, reveals that the way we use space reflects and creates power in interpersonal relations. Invading someone's space and "getting in someone's face" are powerful and intimidating behaviors. In the United States, most people interact at about arm's length, but powerful people, such as superiors communicating with subordinates, or parents talking to children, are afforded the right to invade another's space (Carney, Hall, & LeBeau, 2005; Henley, 1977; Remland, 1981). Subordinates, by

contrast, must respect the territory of their superiors. As the prerogative principle suggests, powerful individuals can violate personal space norms by invading other people's space or by remaining spatially aloof. Others, in turn, view these violations as dominance displays (Burgoon & Dillman, 1995; Hall et al., 2005).

A higher status person can give someone the "cold shoulder" by adopting an indirect body orientation and not facing that person. For example, the husband who reads the paper during a conversation with his wife or the teenager who won't even look at his parents when they are talking to him might be seen as powerful, but also rude. Body angle often interacts with another form of nonverbal communication, eye behavior, to create messages of power. Open body positions have been found to convey intimacy (see Chapter 6) but also are an indicant of confidence and power (Carney et al., 2005; Hall et al., 2005).

Eye Behavior

The study of eye behavior, oculesics, has revealed numerous behaviors associated with power, including staring, gazing while speaking, and failing to look when listening. People who are perceived as powerful are also looked at more by others, a principle we call **visual centrality**. Although eye contact is usually affiliative and friendly, staring is powerful, rude, and intrusive (LaFrance & Mayo, 1978). Looking less while listening is the prerogative of the powerful; low-status individuals must remain visually attentive. Direct eye contact while speaking is perceived as a dominant, even intimidating, behavior (Andersen, 2004; Carney et al., 2005; Hall et al., 2005). Although eye contact while speaking is dominant, eye contact while listening is a submissive behavior. This finding led Exline, Ellyson, and Long (1975) to develop the **visual dominance ratio**, which is a function of the time spent looking while speaking divided by the time spent looking while listening. A high score indicates interpersonal dominance. Shy, submissive people tend to break eye contact when confronted with direct gaze (Andersen, 2004). Similarly, excessive blinking is perceived as a weakness and submissive (Mehrabian, 1971).

Body Movements

The study of body movement, kinesics, reveals that several body positions, facial expressions, and gestures communicate power and status. Expansive body positions with arms and legs apart and away from the body, and the hands-on-hips positions, convey considerable power and dominance (Andersen, 2004; Hall et al., 2005; LaFrance & Mayo, 1978; Remland, 1982). Superiors can sprawl and even get into another person's personal space (Andersen, 2008). Powerful people can lean back to relax or lean forward to make a point; submissive people usually must remain still and attentive. In most situations, relaxation rules (Andersen, 2004).

Gestures, especially grand, sweeping ones and those directed at other people, are perceived as powerful and create perceptions of dynamism and panache (Burgoon, Johnson, & Koch, 1998; Carney et al., 2005; Hall et al., 2005). Purposeful gestures communicate power and confidence. Pointing at someone or wagging one's finger in another person's face is a powerful but hostile move (Remland, 1981; Scheflen, 1972). Such gestures are intrusive acts, much like invading a person's space or, as we discuss next, brashly or rudely touching another person.

Some facial expressions, such as a deep frown or a scornful sneer, are dominant and threatening. A jutting jaw, narrowed eyes, and a face reddened with anger are facial expressions that communicate dominance (Andersen, 2008; Carney et al., 2005; Henley, 1977). Conversely, expressions of fear and sadness are believed to be signs of lower power (Carney et al., 2005). Overall facial expressiveness and skill at facial expressiveness is perceived as more dominant and powerful (Carney et al., 2005; Hall et al., 2005) and is associated with more power (Dunbar & Burgoon, 2005). Because smiling is sometimes designed to convey the absence of threat, it is often perceived as a submissive, appeasing gesture in both humans and other primates (Andersen & Guerrero, 1998b; Hall et al., 2005). Women smile more and by doing so, send friendly, nonthreatening messages (Andersen, 2008). Smiling women are also more likely to be interrupted by their interaction partner than are either unsmiling women or men (Kennedy & Camden, 1983). However, it is important to recognize that smiling can convey dominance in some situations. When smiling is used alongside other dominance cues, smiles convey confidence, power, and social skill (Burgoon & Bacue, 2003; Hall et al., 2005, 2006).

Touch

The study of interpersonal touch, haptics, has shown that, while touch is usually an affectionate, intimate behavior, it can also be used to display one's power (Andersen, 2008). First, the initiation of touch is perceived as more dominant than receiving or reciprocating touch, because the person who initiates touch is controlling the interaction (Carney et al., 2005; Hall et al., 2005; Major & Heslin, 1982). Among casual daters, men are more likely to initiate touch, presumably because social norms dictate that men have the prerogative to try to escalate intimacy in the early stages of relationships. Women, however, initiate touch more often in marital relationships (Guerrero & Andersen, 1994; Stier & Hall, 1984). Guiding another person through a door, physically restraining an individual, and touching someone in an intimate place are all indicative of high power (Andersen, 2008). But caution is advised; charges of sexual harassment and even sexual assault can be the consequences of excessive or inappropriate touch (Lee & Guerrero, 2001). Even when the sender means to send a message of affiliation, the receiver can perceive touch as inappropriate or harassing. While early research (Henley, 1977) indicated that touch was a highly dominant, powerful behavior, more recent research suggests that touch is more affiliative than dominant (Andersen, 2008; Burgoon & Dillman, 1995; Hall et al., 2005; Stier & Hall, 1984). Longitudinal research suggests that receiving intrusive and negative forms of touch early in life is associated with poor romantic relationship quality, conflict, and aggression later in life (Ostrow & Collins, 2007).

The Voice

The content of spoken words is the subject of verbal communication, but voice tones and intonations are in the realm of nonverbal communication, called *vocalics* or *paralinguistics*. Social status can be detected from one's voice fairly accurately (Andersen, 2008), with higher-class speakers having clearer articulation and sharper enunciation of consonants. Similarly, fewer filled pauses, like *ah* and *um* and other speech errors, are associated with greater status and power (Carney et al., 2005; Hall et al., 2005). Listeners can make fairly accurate judgments about people's levels of dominance by listening to samples of their voices (Scherer, 1972). Vocal variation, which is perceived as an immediate, affiliative behavior (see Chapter 6), is also perceived as more powerful (Hall et al., 2005). Louder, deeper, and more varied voices are perceived as more dominant (Andersen, 2008; Hall et al., 2005). However, research suggests that male speakers sometimes rate higher pitched voices as more dominant (Tusing & Dillard, 2000), and that for both men and women, louder and slower speech rates are viewed as more dominant than softer or faster speech rates. More expressive speech was also rated as more dominant. When people are making an important point, they might vary their pitch and talk slowly but loudly and deliberately. Other research suggests that moderately fast voices are perceived as reflecting confidence and power because they suggest that the speaker knows about the subject and does not need time to think (Burgoon et al., 2010; Hall et al., 2005). Together this research suggests that both slower and faster voices can be considered dominant under certain circumstances. In close relationships, departures from normal modes of interaction may signal dominance. For instance, when people who are normally soft spoken raise their voices, even slightly, dominance is communicated.

Time

The study of the interpersonal use of time, chronemics, has revealed that the way people employ time tells a lot about how powerful and dominant they are. Speaking time is related to dominance, especially for men (Mast, 2002). Powerful people are allowed to speak longer and have more speaking turns, which gives them more opportunity to influence others. Waiting time also reflects power; waiting is the fate of the powerless, as people are generally waiting for the powerful. The powerless wait in long lines for welfare checks and job interviews while the rich and powerful have reservations and can relax in luxurious lounges on the rare occasions when they must wait (Henley, 1977). Doctors are notorious for exercising their power prerogative to keep patients waiting, and many executives let people "cool their heels" as a power ploy before negotiating a business deal. However, keeping relational partners waiting may be a bad idea because it signals their lack of importance and could be perceived as inconsiderate.

In contrast, spending time with relational partners is one of the most meaningful signs of love. Time spent together shows that a relationship is valued. Egland and colleagues (1996) found that among all the behaviors that convey understanding, equality, and intimacy, spending time together is the most important. Conversely, like being late, people who spend little time with children, friends, or spouses are communicating that the relationship is of little importance to them.

Artifacts

Artifacts are the ultimate status symbols. Having a big house, luxury cars, and expensive toys are signs of power, particularly in our status-conscious, materialistic society. Some status symbols are subtle, such as the largest office, the reserved parking space, and the most expensive and slimmest briefcase (Korda, 1975). Similarly, giving expensive, unique, or rare gifts to loved ones is a sign of their status and importance in one's life.

POWER AND INFLUENCE IN FAMILIES

Power is part of the fabric of family relationships. Although equality is often the goal, parents sometimes have more knowledge than their children, and one spouse sometimes has more financial resources than the other. Some of the main power issues that surface in parent-child relationships, in romantic relationships, and in marriage reveal significant considerations for our close relationships.

Parent-Child Relationships

Parents need power. No one believes that a two-year-old is capable of making important decisions. Parents must control the behavior of their young children, but control should be inversely related to age. Clearly, the youngest children need the most control. Teenagers still need considerable control and guidance, but parents are kidding themselves if they believe they can start to become strong parents during the teen years. Indeed, most parents decrease their power and dominance over their children from early to late adolescence (De Goede, Branje, & Meeus, 2009). Attempts to crack down on an unruly teen who has developed no moral foundation will usually result in conflict and defiance. A strong foundation laid in early childhood helps children to become good decision makers and responsible teens. Indeed, the whole enterprise of parenting involves the gradual relinquishing of authority, from total control over an infant or toddler to minimal control over a young adult. As Gibran (1923/1970) famously said:

> Your children are not your children. They come through you but not from you. And though they are with you, yet they belong not to you. You are the bows from which your children as living arrows are sent forth. Let your bending in the archer's hand be for gladness. (pp. 18–19)

Gibran's quote highlights two junctures at which power can be especially important in parent-child relationships: (1) at the beginning, when parents are raising infants and very young children, and (2) during the teenage years, when children often assert their independence. Although parents need to control young children, they certainly are not the only agents of influence in early parent-child interactions. As anyone who has seen a mother trying desperately to calm a crying infant or a father trying to get his toddler to eat her vegetables can attest,

young children can have a huge impact on their parents' behavior. Yingling (1995) put it this way:

> That parents influence their infants is beyond dispute, but infants' influence on parents has begun to receive attention as well. . . . At some point in the first year, infants begin to recognize the power of their interactive behaviors to influence the primary relationship. However, interactive effects begin even before that recognition. (p. 35)

Without consciously intending to, newborns persuade parents to feed them in the middle of the night, change their diapers around the clock, and soothe them when they are upset. As infants get older, they learn to manage social interactions through crying, cooing, and smiling, and by the time they are toddlers, they are particularly good at using the word *no* to assert themselves (Lewis & Rosenblum, 1974).

Naturally, parents use much more sophisticated influence strategies than their young children. Classic work by Baumrind (1971, 1991) suggests that there are three general approaches to parenting: authoritarian, permissive, and authoritative. **Authoritarian parents** are demanding, directive, and nonresponsive. They control and monitor their children's behavior continuously, so that it conforms to strict standards of order. In being nonresponsive, they expect their children to obey them without question. Authoritarian parents do not believe that they need to explain reasons behind disciplinary actions to their children—their word is "law" and is not to be questioned.

Permissive parents, by contrast, are undemanding, nondirective, and responsive. These parents relinquish most of their authority and let their children regulate their own behavior in most situations. If they punish their children, which happens rarely, they are lenient. Permissive parents try to be responsive to their children by showing them support and giving them encouragement. Unlike the authoritarian parent, who acts like a dictator, the permissive parent acts more like a friend and the child is given considerable, often excessive power.

Authoritative parents blend aspects of the authoritarian and permissive styles. These parents are demanding and directive, but also responsive. Authoritative parents have clear standards and expectations for how their children should behave, and these standards are communicated to the children in terms they can understand. These parents set limitations, but they also allow their children some freedom and privacy. Authoritative parents are responsive in that they generally avoid harsh punishments and focus instead on reasoning with their children and providing support. The authoritative parent is more like a benevolent teacher than either a dictator or friend. Although the parent has more power than the child, the child still has a voice in the decision-making process, and parents and children mutually influence each other.

Hoffman's (1980) work identified two similar styles of parenting: power assertion and induction. **Power assertion**, similar to the authoritarian style, refers to parents who believe that they should be in complete control and can demand compliance without having to explain why. The prototypical dialogue that characterizes this style is when a parent issues a directive ("You cannot go to Olivia's party"), the child asks for an explanation ("Why not?"), and the parent asserts authority without giving an explanation ("Because your father and I say you can't go—that's why not"). Power assertion strategies can also include threats, spankings or other physical punishment, and harsh verbal reprimands.

The **inductive philosophy** of parenting is similar to the authoritative style. When parents use induction, they believe that it is critical that they provide their children with reasons for their disciplinary actions. They provide explanations for their decisions in the hope that the children will learn how to make good decisions on their own. For example, if Lauren was told that she could not go Olivia's party, her parents would explain why. Perhaps Lauren's parents know that Olivia's parents will not be home and that some of the kids are bringing beer, or perhaps Lauren had violated her curfew the last three times she went to a party. In any case, Lauren's parents would explain their thinking, and Lauren would have the opportunity to reason with them.

Inductive parenting strategies are usually more effective because they involve explanation and reasoning. Burleson, Delia, and Applegate (1992) argued that such strategies are also **reflection enhancing** because they encourage children to think about their misconduct, including how their actions affect themselves and others. Numerous studies show that children, from preschoolers to teenagers, who are disciplined using the authoritative or inductive style have higher self-esteem, are more morally mature, engage in more prosocial and cooperative behavior, show greater communication competence, and are more accepted by their peers than are children who are disciplined using other styles (Baumrind, 1991; Buri, Louiselle, Misukanis, & Mueller, 1988; Burleson et al., 1992; Hart, DeWolf, Wozniak, & Burts, 1992; Hoffman, 1970; Kennedy, 1992).

Of course, authoritarian or power assertive strategies might be necessary in some cases. Steinmetz (1979) found that power strategies often lead to more rapid compliance than to inductive strategies. Similarly, studies have shown that power assertive strategies are efficient when parents are seeking immediate, short-term compliance (Grusec & Kuczynski, 1980; Kuczynski, 1984). Thus, when a mother is worried that her son might hurt himself by crossing the street without looking or by using drugs, an authoritarian strategy might be most effective in the short term, with inductive explanations given later.

Separation and Individuation

As children grow older and become more independent, a moral foundation based on explanations and reasoning rather than commands helps them make better decisions. Such a foundation is particularly important during adolescence when teenagers become more independent and sometimes rebel against their parents' authority (Andersen, 2004; De Goede et al., 2009). By their early teens, most children depend more on their friends than their parents when it comes to making decisions and asking for advice (Steinberg & Silverberg, 1986). Similarly, teens yield much less to their parents and insist on making their own decisions much more often when they reach midadolescence (Steinberg, 1981). The teen years are a transition between the time when children are heavily dependent on their parents and the time when teenagers become responsible, independent young adults. Scholars have referred to this transition period as a process of **separation and individuation** whereby teenagers distance themselves, to some degree, from their parents and develop an individual identity apart from the family structure (Guerrero & Afifi, 1995b).

During this transition period, power struggles between parents and teenagers are almost inevitable. Teenagers are ready to express independence before parents are ready to relinquish authority or before the teens can make responsible adult decisions. This can lead to a period of "storm and stress" characterized by emotional distance between parents and children and increased conflict (Kidwell, Fischer, Dunham, & Baranowski, 1983; Paikoff & Brooks-Gunn, 1991; Steinberg, 1987). Researchers have found that parent-child interaction during the teen years is often marked by less warmth (Paikoff & Brooks-Gunn, 1991; Steinberg, 1981), more interruptions by teens (Jacob, 1974), and less open communication (Guerrero & Afifi, 1995b).

Some adolescent-parent relationships, indeed, are stormier than others. If children gradually show that they are responsible enough to make their own decisions and parents gradually relinquish authority, the transition from child to young adult can be marked by more cooperation and mutual respect than rebellion. Along these lines, Hill and Holmbeck (1986) argued that adolescence is a time of family regrouping, as parents and teenagers renegotiate rules and role relationships. Hill and Holmbeck also argued that the process of separation and individuation does not preclude close relationships between parents and children. Instead, this period of transition often leads to a redefinition of the parent-child relationship from an authority-based relationship characterized by unequal power to one characterized by mutual friendship and respect. Furthermore, Grotevant and Cooper (1985) found that by age 17, most teens had begun renegotiating relational rules and roles with their parents. The key to a successful transition lies partially with the parents, who need to let adolescents become more individuated while still providing a supportive and caring environment (Campbell, Adams, & Dobson, 1984; Papini, Sebby, & Clark, 1989).

Traditional Versus Egalitarian Marriages

Relationships are complex, and maintaining any long-term relationship is difficult (see Chapter 9). Although there is no one formula for an ideal romantic relationship, evidence suggests that peer relationships characterized by respect and relative equality are healthier, more satisfying, and more likely to succeed. This is true for both friendships and dating relationships (Roiger, 1993). However, equality may be harder to achieve in marriages than in many friendships or dating relationships because spouses typically share money and possessions and have to divide household chores. As discussed in Chapter 10, this division is not usually equitable; most working married women in the United States are still responsible for around two-thirds of household chores and an even larger percentage of child care. Interestingly, most women think their relationships are equitable despite their greater contributions to household labor (Braun, Lewin-Epstein, Stier, & Baumgartner, 2008). Trying to find a fair way to share resources and divide labor can lead to power struggles within even the best of marriages.

When studying issues of equality, social scientists have described two different types of marriages: traditional and egalitarian (Steil, 2000). According to Steil, **traditional marriages** are "based on a form of benevolent male dominance coupled with clearly specialized roles. Thus, when women are employed, the responsibility for family work is retained by the women, who add the career role to their traditionally held family role" (p. 128). Of course, some women in traditional marriages are not employed or only work part-time, so that they can devote considerable time to managing the house and raising the children.

Some couples are very happy in traditional marriages (Fitzpatrick, 1988). However, in the 21st century, most women are not satisfied with traditional gender roles, and dual-career households are the rule rather than the exception. In dual-career marriages (as well as other close relationships in which people live together), partners need to negotiate roles related to household responsibilities rather than rely on traditional gender roles. Thus, although various types of marriages can be fulfilling, research shows that the best chance for happiness occurs in marriages in which the balance of power is nearly equal (Aida & Falbo, 1991; DeMaris, 2007; Schwartz, 1994; Steil, 2000; Thompson & Walker, 1989. In **egalitarian marriages**, also called **peer marriages** or **sharing marriages** (Schwartz, 1994), "Both spouses are employed, both are actively involved in parenting, and both share in the responsibilities and duties of the household" (Steil, 2000, p. 128). Combining money into a single pool and making collaborative decisions on how to spend it are also associated with more relational satisfaction (Vogler, Lionette, & Wiggins, 2008).

Egalitarian marriages are often more intimate than traditional marriages. Most egalitarian marriages are deep and true friendships, as well as romances. Furthermore, emotionally bonded spouses are likely to achieve equality in their relationships. Research conducted in Scandinavia by Thagaard (1997) showed that "close emotional ties between spouses are linked to the interpretation of the relationship in terms of equality. The perception of equality is based on the ability to influence the relationship beginning with one's own values" (p. 373). Aida and Falbo (1991) found that partners in egalitarian marriages used fewer dominant power strategies than partners in traditional marriages, perhaps because they could influence each other without power plays. In addition, in a recent study of relationships in 32 countries, female empowerment linked to more equal division of household chores (Knudsen & Waerness, 2008). When partners influence each other in equal, independent relationships, they use more diverse and egalitarian influence strategies than do traditional couples (Mannino & Duetsch, 2007; Witteman & Fitzpatrick, 1986).

Partners in traditional, unequal relationships, by contrast, are more likely to use blatant power strategies such as verbal aggression and less likely to use compliance-gaining strategies (Witteman &

Fitzpatrick, 1986). They also use less open communication. One study compared couples in interdependent, egalitarian marriages to those in more separate, isolated marriages (Solomon et al., 2004). Those in egalitarian marriages were more likely to express complaints and talk about relational problems than those in separate or traditional style marriages.

Equality has also been associated with better mental health, whereas inequality is sometimes associated with lesser mental health. Among couples with troubled marriages, inequality is likely to be associated with depression symptoms in the less powerful partner (Bagarozzi, 1990). Even people in troubled marriages who have an equal power structure are less likely to have severe mental or emotional problems. Halloran (1998) suggested that inequality in close relationships is a cause of both depression and low-quality marriages. Moreover, this pattern leads to a vicious cycle. As one spouse becomes depressed, the other spouse must take over more control of the family, leading to greater inequality. In their major review of justice and love relationships, Hatfield, Rapson, and Aumer-Ryan (2008) conclude:

> In the end, fairness and equity matter, Scientists have found this to be the case for most couples—single, living together, married; affluent or poor, dating for a few weeks or married for 20 years. In all of these groups, the degree of reward, fairness, and equity are linked to sexual satisfaction, marital happiness, contentment, satisfaction, and marital stability. (p. 425)

Equality of marriage does not simply "happen." It takes commitment on the part of partners. As Schwartz (1994) observed, "Social forces and psychological processes tenaciously maintain marriage along the old guidelines. Women still look to men to provide larger and more predictable income that establishes the family's social class and creature comforts" (p. 8). Several forces conspire against equality. At the turn of the century, women in the United States still earned less than 80% of what men earn, creating a power discrepancy and dependence on the part of many wives. Childbearing typically impacts a woman's career and earning power more than her husband's. Perhaps even more important, in terms of household labor, most so-called egalitarian relationships are not really so equal after all. As reported in Chapter 10, in heterosexual relationships, women still tend to do more of the household work than men, when even both partners are working. Centuries of hierarchical relationships do not disappear overnight, nor do the power structures that exist in most families. While great progress has been made in elevating the status of women, sources of inequality still exist that will take additional years and effort to break down.

In the marriages and relationships between gay men and especially between lesbians, sharing of tasks is more equal (Goldberg & Perry-Jenkins, 2007; Kurdek, 2007; Shechory & Ziv, 2007). Like heterosexual couples, more equal division of labor is associated with greater relational satisfaction in both gay and lesbian couples (Kurdek, 2007). This is in contrast to heterosexual couples, where women still do the majority of household tasks (see Chapter 10).

SUMMARY AND APPLICATION

Power and influence are present in almost every human relationship, including Tyler and Ashley's. Whether somebody is persuading a roommate to take out the trash, asking one's child to be home at a certain time, or deciding if and when to marry a dating partner, some level of interpersonal influence is present. Power is a perception. But people do not automatically have power; rather, power is granted to people. Resources such as money, social standing, and love give people the ability to be powerful, especially when these resources are scarce, but ultimately, people are only as influential as others let them be.

In Tyler and Ashley's relationship, they can assert power and try to influence one another using a variety of verbal and nonverbal strategies. Some are ineffective, like Tyler's withdrawal behavior when he refuses to discuss relationship issues, or like Ashley's constant nagging, which she knows does no good. Tyler and Ashley are at their best when they use the large assortment of influence strategies they have in their repertoire and when they select appropriate strategies in a given situation that are the most effective at persuasion.

Power is tied to issues of authority and equality. Child dependence and parental authority initially mark parent-child relationships. Gradually, however, parents relinquish control and children assert their independence—a process that prepares children to be responsible young adults. In marriage, the husband typically has more concrete resources (e.g., income and occupational status) than the wife, which can reduce her power base. Ashley, however,

has better job offers than Tyler and will be more independent and powerful as a result. In fact, Ashley's ambition and Tyler's laziness may create a power imbalance and threaten the equality and stability of the relationship. Ashley thus has dependence power that makes her more powerful in the relationship. Hopefully they will resolve this power discrepancy, as research shows that both men and women are usually happier and the relationship is stronger in egalitarian marriages than in traditional marriages where one partner is more powerful.

Power and equality certainly are important in relationships. As discussed in Chapter 10, relationships function best when people experience more rewards than costs and when they feel that they are being treated fairly. Ashley feels that Tyler is not trying hard enough and that the relationship sometimes has a poor cost-benefit ratio. This is true not in just heterosexual relationships, but gay men and lesbians also believe that it is important to have an egalitarian relationship. Achieving equality, however, is a difficult task. Ashley and Tyler need to equally value the different resources they bring to the relationship. One strength in Ashley and Tyler's relationship is that they have the power to influence decisions without getting their way at the expense of the partner. And, if Tyler is less ambitious about his career, perhaps he can do more of the household tasks such as cleaning and home repair to provide balance between the partners.

It is important for Tyler and Ashley to realize some facts about power. Power is a perception that is simultaneously a reality for a person. If Tyler believes Ashley is too powerful or controlling in the relationship, they both have to deal with that perception and either the perception or behavior must change to resolve that discrepancy.

Tyler is right to be concerned about the future of the relationship. People with considerable resources—like Ashley's beauty, occupational sta- tus, and intelligence—have more power since they have more alternatives. And like so many women today, who are graduating from college in greater numbers, her excellent job offers give her the abil- ity to be self-sufficient and powerful in ways beyond traditional sources of feminine power such as sex and beauty.

DISCUSSION QUESTIONS

1. Think about whom you consider the three most powerful famous people. Now think about the three most powerful people you have known personally. What characteristics make (or made) these individuals powerful?

2. In your relationships, do you agree or disagree with some scholars that men have more power than women? On the basis of what you have read in this chapter, how do you think relative power, and sex differences in power, influence relationship satisfaction and decision making? Does this seem to apply to your own romantic relationships?

3. In this chapter, we discussed a number of strategies people use to gain compliance in their relationships. Which persuasive strategies do you personally think are most effective? Is your experience consistent with the research?

STUDENT STUDY SITE

Visit the study site at **www.sagepub.com/guerrero3e** for e-flashcards, survey and assessments from the chapter, and SAGE journal articles.

12

Getting Too Close for Comfort

Privacy and Secrets in Relationships

Khaled is secretly in love with his best friend's girlfriend, Tara. He wishes he could tell her he loves her and see if there is a chance she might reciprocate his feelings, but he values his relationship with his best friend Randy too much to put their friendship in jeopardy.

Samantha was sexually abused by her uncle as a child but has never told anyone; she just accepted her boyfriend's marriage proposal and is feeling guilty that even he doesn't know. She also hasn't told him that her family was on welfare when she was in elementary school, in part because she is embarrassed about it, but mostly because it is a family secret that her mother and sisters don't like to talk about. She would feel like she was betraying them if she told her fiancé.

Tyrone and Suzanne suspect that their teenage son, John, is starting to experiment with drugs and alcohol. They sit down with John and have a long talk about the dangers of doing drugs and drinking. During the conversation, Tyrone carefully avoids telling John that he smoked pot in college and Suzanne avoids telling him that she used to have a drinking problem—a topic she has never even disclosed to Tyrone.

These situations reflect disclosure and privacy decisions that people make every day. Who among these people is "right" in their decision to withhold information? Who, in your opinion, is "wrong"? The research in this area makes one thing clear: The popular idea that we should always be 100% open with our romantic partners, family, and friends is neither followed nor typically well advised.

Several studies have shown that the times people seek privacy and avoid sharing information with others are just as important to personal and relational health as disclosure and connectedness. Parks (1982) was one of the first scholars to recognize this. He argued that the ideology of complete intimacy is overrated—too much openness can be smothering and people need privacy. Altman, whose work on social penetration theory (see Chapter 5) helped popularize the notion that self-disclosure is essential for relationship development, has also touted the importance of balancing needs for expression with needs for privacy (Altman, Vinsel, & Brown, 1981). Rosenfeld (2000) echoed these sentiments when he stated, "Self-disclosure is a scary notion! It can explain our existence, reveal who we are to ourselves and others as we disclose and engage in an act of 'becoming,' and, more fundamentally, *allow* us to exist in the world" (p. 4). It is no wonder, then, that people value their privacy. Yet too much privacy can also be problematic. Most people also need some openness and connection with others.

In this chapter, we review some of the research on the importance of privacy in our relationships with others. First, we examine communication privacy management (CPM) theory, which explains how people manage information in ways that maintain privacy (Petronio, 1991). Second, we discuss privacy violations, including obsessive relational intrusion. Finally, we discuss patterns of topic avoidance and secret keeping in relationships.

COMMUNICATION PRIVACY MANAGEMENT THEORY

Communication privacy management (CPM) theory helps explain how individuals cope with the need to maintain privacy boundaries (Petronio, 1991, 2002). The theory is rooted in the assumption that people set up **boundary structures** as a way to control the risks inherent in disclosing private information. These boundary structures are based on two elements associated with private information: ownership and permeability.

Ownership

When people feel that they have **ownership** over information, they believe they also have the "right" to control who has access to it. For example, if Suzanne thinks that the topic of her drinking habits in college is private, she will be upset if one of her old college friends starts talking about it with others around. Indeed, the notion of information ownership and its consequences is at the heart of

CPM and is a big reason why the theory if so useful for understanding privacy management decisions.

Permeability

The information people own also comes with varying levels of **permeability**. Permeability is similar to a barometer measuring how freely people allow others to share information they disclosed about themselves. The information within each instance of disclosure comes with particular levels of permeability. Relatively permeable boundaries are ones where the sharing filter is thin, and we are comfortable with the person sharing the information widely. In contrast, impermeable boundaries are set around disclosures that we make in confidence and expect the recipients to keep to themselves. Importantly, permeability is an aspect of the information, not a characteristic of a relationship. In other words, we tell our partners things that we are comfortable being public knowledge, as well as other things that we expect to be kept absolutely private. Of course, if we suspect that someone can't or won't keep a secret, we are only likely to disclose information that has permeable boundaries; in other words, we won't share information that we want kept private.

Levels of permeability are one important feature of boundaries, but what are the basic principles that go into shaping the nature of the boundaries we set around the information we disclose? Three principles stand out as being particularly important to the way that CPM views the disclosure process.

Influences on Rules for Boundary Management

The first principle specifies that *the rules for communication boundary management are influenced by five main factors, including (1) culture, (2) personality, (3) the relationship, (4) biological sex, and (5) motivations.* First, each *culture* has different rules regarding privacy and self-disclosure (see Box 12.1). For example, some cultures have relatively loose rules regarding what topics are appropriate to discuss with strangers; other cultures are more restrictive. For example, cultures differ in terms of ownership over health information. Certain cultures, including in some Asian and Middle Eastern countries, have a family-centric tradition of health information disclosure, whereby physicians give information about a patient's health only to a patient's family. The family then decides what, if anything, to tell the patient. In contrast, countries such as the United States have strict laws that ensure that health information belongs only to the patient.

Second, *personality* guides disclosure decisions. Some people are highly self-disclosive and expressive, whereas other people are much more private. Third, a host of *relational factors*, such as attraction, closeness, and relationship type (friends versus coworkers), impact the dynamics of privacy and self-disclosures. As mentioned in Chapter 5, people tend to disclose more with individuals they like than with those they dislike. Fourth, *sex differences*, although usually small, can nonetheless influence privacy boundaries. As discussed previously, women's rules for disclosing information sometimes differ from men's; women tend to disclose somewhat more than men, particularly on intimate topics (see Chapter 6). Finally, individuals' *motivations* can affect how they manage privacy boundaries. For instance, people who are motivated to make friends may disclose more than those who are motivated to accomplish a task, and people who worry about getting hurt or rejected might avoid self-disclosure that could make them vulnerable. CPM recognizes that the ways in which we create disclosure boundaries are influenced by these many factors, which shape when, where, and to whom we disclose information.

BOX 12.1 Highlights

Privacy Management and Culture

Cultures vary dramatically in the extent to which individuals' privacy is promoted. One dimension that seems to separate cultures on this front is communal-individual norms. In communal cultures, individuals play a secondary role to the good and rights of the community (e.g., the family). In contrast, individualistic cultures generally prioritize individuals over community members. This difference affects privacy expectations and disclosure norms in many ways. For example, studies have shown that some communal cultures treat an individual's health information and health decisions as community owned. Physicians either withhold diagnosis information or first inform family members who then decide what to reveal to the patient (Hamadeh & Adib, 1998). Compare that to norms in the United States, where laws require the disclosure of medical information to the patient, and only the patient.

Privacy may also be difficult to maintain in cultures that are highly communal because of the realities of the living contexts. Communal cultures often expect all family members to live under one roof, often with very little space. Under these conditions, the privacy of one's bedroom evaporates. When one shares a room with four or more siblings or relatives, it is difficult to maintain privacy. Famously, some people from communal cultures share generally private marital successes and challenges with family members. For instance, sheets taken from the bed after the first marital sexual episode may be displayed publicly, as evidence that the marriage has been consummated. Uncles or aunts may also be brought in as mediators to help solve marital conflicts in the family. Clearly, privacy maintenance is difficult in these contexts. A norm is established where community members, typically all with close connections to one another, look out for each other. So, a teenager who tries to escape with a girlfriend to a remote location for privacy often discovers that the rendezvous was far less private than he expected, because others in the community saw them going to that location, and then immediately shared the information with the parents.

(Continued)

(Continued)

Given the decreased status of the individual, vis-à-vis the community, in communal cultures, individuals' perceptions of the appropriateness of revealing personal struggles is very different than those of people from more individualistic cultures. Therapists have long been aware of the need to be sensitive to cultural differences on this front (Sue & Zane, 1987). People often consider therapists in the United States to be safe havens to reveal dark personal secrets, and research has shown that such disclosures to therapists can be very beneficial. This benefit, though, is unlikely to be realized in communal cultures, where therapists' offices are not shielded from the strongly held notion that personal disclosures and the difficulties they sometimes reveal are selfish and inappropriate. In other words, even people who go to therapists for help may be unwilling to engage in the necessary disclosure because of a sense, accurate or not, that they will be perceived by the therapist as overly focused on themselves.

Finally, much of our understanding of family strengths comes from an assumption that parents and children should disclose to one another. While that may be true in individualistic cultures, some communal cultures are founded on a premise of a certain distance between parent and child. As such, both parents and their children may perceive personal disclosures to one another as too intimate of an exercise. The patterns we have discussed here point out an interesting reality: We have argued that disclosure is linked to privacy—the less one discloses, the more privacy one has. However, we have also pointed to the reality of communal cultures, where both privacy and disclosure are low in some cases. What gives? What is the relationship between privacy and disclosure? These are interesting and important questions that do not yet have clear answers, but one thing is clear: People's experience with privacy goes beyond simple disclosure patterns.

Cooperation

The second principle is that *successful boundary management often requires cooperation between people.* People often must involve others in their information-boundary management. These people become **boundary insiders** (Petronio & Reirseon, 2009). For example, secrets held by an entire family (like Samantha's family secret regarding welfare) require that all family members agree to keep the relevant information private, which means that they must coordinate their boundary structures and rules on that particular issue. In a similar vein, someone who cheats on a romantic partner must either implicitly (and naively) assume or explicitly discuss a degree of boundary coordination with the sexual partner to keep the incident a secret. To help maintain coordinated boundary structures, people usually develop penalties for group or dyad members who violate the boundary structure (Petronio, 1991, 2002). Boundary coordination becomes especially salient when the information is revealed to someone who is not a part of the original group. For example, Samantha's family secret about welfare may eventually be divulged to her fiancé when they marry and he officially becomes a member of the family. The addition of a new member into the secret-keeping group necessitates additional boundary structure coordination, and the rules must often be made explicit to the new member.

Boundary Turbulence

The third principle is that *co-owners of information sometimes undergo boundary turbulence.* **Boundary turbulence** occurs when new events force renewed boundary management (Petronio, 1991). There are situations in which old boundary structures may need to be either fortified or renegotiated. For example, when people's lives change, topics previously avoided (e.g., the future of the relationship) may become acceptable topics (e.g., after a marriage proposal). Similarly, once a previous boundary structure is violated (e.g., when a secret is first disclosed), a radical change in the nature of the new structure may occur (e.g., the once-secret information becomes a commonplace disclosure). When the boundary expectations held by the original owner of the information are violated, confidentiality is considered to have been compromised. This breach is the sort of event that creates boundary turbulence.

Although medical settings are not contexts where most people expect confidentiality breaches, Petronio and Reirseon (2009) identified several examples of such violations by medical personnel. For instance, patients are sometimes frustrated by the loss of control over their medical information once it enters the realm of a medical team, especially within teaching hospitals where the case may become an occasion to test medical students' knowledge. Patients may feel violated by a loss of control over sensitive information. The result may be boundary restructuring in future encounters with physicians—a dangerous outcome since it may involve concealment of important information as a way to prevent a potential privacy breach. The ways in which individuals negotiate privacy boundaries thus can be both complex and challenging.

NEGOTIATING PRIVACY BOUNDARIES IN RELATIONSHIPS

The central feature of CPM is its recognition that we cherish our rights to privacy and our ability to control information. But perhaps the most interesting questions revolve around information ownership issues. Ask yourself: What information does your romantic partner (present or future) have a right to know—your past dating history, financial status, job history, whether you have a sexually transmitted infection, details about your parents' relationship, or none of the above? Do you have the right to decide whether to disclose these types of information or not? Now ask yourself this: What information about your parents do you have the right to know—the quality of their relationship, their health and well-being, or what they did in college? Put yourself in John's shoes (see the examples that opened the chapter). Does he have a right to know about his parents' past experiences with

drugs and alcohol since they are judging him for engaging in similar behavior? Or do Tyrone and Suzanne have a right to keep this information private?

Types of Privacy Violations

To address real-world privacy right challenges that people face, Petronio, Sargent, Andea, Reganis, and Cichocki (2004) used CPM to study family and friends who serve as informal health care advocates for patients. Their results showed some of the privacy-related difficulties that physicians, patients, and extended family members face in these situations. Physicians in the United States are often uncomfortable giving information to someone other than the patient, and advocates sometimes worry that the information they receive could depress or worry the patient, and undermine the treatment. Advocates also struggle about whether to keep certain patient information private (by not divulging it to the physician) or whether to reveal private information for the sake of the patient's health. In the end, most advocates put the patient's health needs over their privacy needs.

This struggle for privacy emerges in many different contexts and relationships. Given that adolescence is a time when we generally try to establish our own identities separate from that of our family, it is not surprising that privacy struggles occur with some frequency in families with teenage children. Teenagers may believe they have a right to be independent and to maintain their privacy, but parents may believe that their teens still need guidance and protection. In this sense, the boundary coordination rules in families can be complex, and their negotiation can be very difficult. In general, though, these privacy struggles decrease once children "leave the nest" (e.g., for college). Parents' privacy violations at that stage reflect a failure to recognize the children's "right" to independence at a time when their sense of autonomy is beginning to flourish (McGoldrick & Carter, 1982). The consequences of privacy violations at that stage may be particularly damaging to the parent-child relationship, but how common are they, and what form do they take?

To answer these questions, Petronio and Harriman (1990) asked college students to describe recent instances of privacy violations by their parents and how they responded. All of the students were able to describe at least one example, and 96% of them described at least three such incidences, suggesting that parents' privacy violations are a fairly common occurrence for college students. Eight types of parental privacy violations were reported: (1) asking personal questions about the student's life, (2) giving unsolicited advice, (3) making unsolicited remarks about the student's life, (4) opening the student's mail without permission, (5) going through the student's belongings without permission, (6) entering the bathroom without knocking, (7) eavesdropping on face-to-face conversations with others, and (8) using a second telephone line to listen in on a phone conversation without permission. Moreover, two general reactions were reported: **confrontation**, where the child openly challenges the guilty parent (asking the parent to stop the privacy violation, confronting the parent with evidence), and **evasion**, where the child changes the behavior to protect privacy but does not discuss it directly with the parents. Petronio and Harriman found that students were more likely to react in a confrontational manner when they caught their parents secretly trying to invade their privacy than when their parents invaded their privacy by asking questions or giving unsolicited advice. Not surprisingly, the authors noted that these sorts of privacy violations and the resultant confrontation were related to decreased trust and a drop in the quality of the parent-child relationship.

Responses to Privacy Violations

In another effort to understand people's responses to privacy violations, Koehler (2005) identified four general types of reactions to privacy violations, varying in directness. **Verbal assertion** involves communicating with the person who violated one's privacy in a direct and cooperative manner (e.g., asking the person to stop engaging in the behavior). **Passive aggression and retaliation** involves trying to retaliate against a person through behaviors such as making the person feel guilty and getting revenge by violating their privacy. **Tempered tolerance** is outwardly accepting the privacy violation through responses such as "grinning and bearing it" and "acting like the incident never happened." Finally, **boundary restructuring** occurs when people adjust their public boundaries to prevent future privacy violations. These types of strategies are also likely used in our relationships with friends, family, and romantic partners. To get an idea of which of these strategies you tend to use within a given relationship, take the test in Box 12.2.

BOX 12.2 Put Yourself to the Test

How Do You React to Privacy Violations?

Think about the times that someone you know has violated your privacy by doing things such as listening to your conversations with others, asking you overly personal questions, or borrowing something of yours without permission. How do you typically react to these types of privacy violations? Answer the questions using the following scale: 1 = you almost never react that way, 7 = you almost always react that way.

When a certain person violates my privacy, I:	Almost Never						Almost Always
1. Ask this person to stop engaging in such behavior.	1	2	3	4	5	6	7
2. Tell this person that her or his actions are inappropriate.	1	2	3	4	5	6	7

	Almost Never					Almost Always	
3. Ask for an apology.	1	2	3	4	5	6	7
4. Ask for assurances that it won't happen again.	1	2	3	4	5	6	7
5. Make this person feel guilty.	1	2	3	4	5	6	7
6. Give this person the silent treatment.	1	2	3	4	5	6	7
7. Invade this person's privacy to get revenge.	1	2	3	4	5	6	7
8. Get back at this person somehow.	1	2	3	4	5	6	7
9. Act like the incident never happened.	1	2	3	4	5	6	7
10. Try to forget about it.	1	2	3	4	5	6	7
11. Just grin and bear it.	1	2	3	4	5	6	7
12. Pretend that I'm not upset about it.	1	2	3	4	5	6	7
13. Make sure not to have private conversations in front of this person.	1	2	3	4	5	6	7
14. Hide personal belongings.	1	2	3	4	5	6	7
15. Lock the door or otherwise prevent this person from entering private space.	1	2	3	4	5	6	7
16. Become more careful not to talk about certain topics in front of this person.	1	2	3	4	5	6	7

Add up your responses:

Verbal assertion: Items 1–4   _____

Passive aggression and retaliation: Items 5–8   _____

Tempered tolerance: Items 9–12   _____

Boundary restructuration: Items 13–16   _____

Higher scores indicate that you use more of a particular response within a particul
(The highest score possible is 21, and the lowest is 4.) You might want to try taking this
different people to see if your privacy management strategies vary on the basis of the r

SOURCE: Used with permission of Milissa Koehler.

One of the most difficult aspects of maintaining privacy stems from how the need for privacy is often interpreted as a desire to separate from others (see Mehrabian, 1981). For example, it is sometimes hard to separate friends or partners' requests for alone time from a desire to distance themselves from us. Of course, as discussed in previous chapters, the need for privacy is completely normal and, in fact, is critical to healthy relationships (Baxter & Montgomery, 1996). As dialectics theory suggests, people have needs for both autonomy and connection, and for both privacy and interaction (see Chapter 9). Still, the reality is that communicating privacy needs, especially in relationships, can be difficult. The management of privacy is even more challenging when others are either unaware of the signals we send or willfully ignore them.

OBSESSIVE RELATIONAL INTRUSION

Another challenge occurs when people continue to invade someone's privacy even when the other person clearly wants to be left alone. Such is the case with **obsessive relational intrusion (ORI)**, which occurs when someone knowingly and repeatedly invades another person's privacy boundaries by using intrusive tactics to try to get closer to that person (Cupach & Spitzberg, 1998). ORI includes a host of behaviors, including what may be considered annoying behavior, such as repeated calls or texts; malicious behavior, such as spreading false rumors; stalking behaviors, such as following someone; and even violent behavior, such as kidnapping or assault. Box 12.3 contains a sample of ORI behaviors.

BOX 12.3 Highlights

Types of Obsessive Relational Intrusion (ORI)

Cupach and Spitzberg (1998) surveyed 876 people to determine the types of ORI behaviors they had experienced. Some of the behaviors they found are listed below, along with the percentage of people who reported experiencing these types of ORI.

Called and argued with me (73%).

Called and hung up when I answered (70%).

Constantly asked for "another chance" (64%).

Watched or stared at me from a distance (62%).

Made exaggerated claims about affection for me (61%).

Drove by my house or work (57%).

Used third parties to spy or keep tabs on me (55%).

Performed large favors for me without my permission (52%).

Spread false rumors about me to my friends (49%).

Left notes on my car windshield (45%).

Sent me unwanted cards or letters (42%).

Increased contact with my family members to stay connected to me (37%).

Went through private things in my room (34%).

Physically shoved, slapped, or hit me (32%).

Made obscene phone calls to me (30%).

Damaged my property or possessions (26%).

Forced me to engage in unwanted sexual behavior (16%).

Called radio station and devoted songs to me (15%).

Cluttered my e-mail with messages (11%).

Broke into my home or apartment (8%).

SOURCE: Spitzberg and Cupach (1998).

The circumstances surrounding ORI behaviors vary. For example, in Chapter 7, we discussed situations of unrequited love, wherein one person (the would-be lover) is interested in another person who does not return her or his affection (the rejector). Some would-be lovers use ORI. Sometimes ORI is also used when one person wants the relationship to turn romantic and the other person wants to remain only friends (Cupach & Spitzberg, 2008). In other cases, ORI occurs after a breakup. Cupach and Spitzberg have identified the primary reasons that individuals may use these behaviors.

Reasons People Use ORI Behavior

Cupach and Spitzberg (2004) developed **relational goal pursuit theory** to help explain ORI. According to this theory, people expend energy to develop or reinitiate relationships to the extent that they perceive a relationship is desirable and attainable. When a relationship is perceived to be unattainable, people abandon their original goal and seek an alternative. Unfortunately, however, people sometimes continue to believe that a relationship is attainable even though it is not. In these cases, ORI is likely to occur. In fact, episodes of ORI typically increase in intensity as the object of attention tries to fortify privacy boundaries, for example, by taking pains to avoid the pursuer. At first, ORI behaviors are usually prosocial, indirect, and only mildly annoying (Cupach & Spitzberg, 2004, 2008). The pursuer might act flirtatious, try to spend time with the desired partner, and

telephone or e-mail frequently. If these ORI behaviors are unsuccessful, the pursuer will sometimes employ more invasive violations of privacy, such as surveillance, harassment, and infiltration into the desired person's social network. Such behaviors are typically perceived as aggravating and inconvenient. Finally, in some cases, ORI becomes particularly volatile, frightening, and creepy, with pursuers stalking their victims and engaging in coercive and even violent behavior (Cupach & Spitzberg, 2004).

So, why do some pursuers continue to use ORI behaviors rather than abandoning their goal and seeking an alternative relationship? Cupach and Spitzberg (1998, 2004, 2008) suggest four general reasons: cultural scripts, the ambiguity of communication, rumination, and a shift in motivation. First, **cultural scripts** often portray people as "playing hard to get." Cultural scripts also suggest that if people try hard enough, they will eventually win the affection of the person they love. Together, these cultural scripts work against the realization that a relationship is unattainable.

Second, **ambiguous communication** related to the initiation, reinitiation, and rejection of relationships may also keep hope alive. As noted in Chapter 6, during courtship people engage in ambiguous flirtatious behavior that is safe and helps them save face if they are rejected. Similarly, people often use indirect strategies to reject people because they worry about hurting their feelings. Rather than seeing these strategies as polite ways of rejecting them, pursuers may fail to correctly interpret rejection signals and continue to believe that the desired relationship is attainable.

Third, when people are having trouble obtaining a goal, they often ruminate about it. In these cases, the **rumination** may lead pursuers to redouble their efforts to get close to the desired partner as a way to alleviate the negative affect they are feeling.

Finally, a **shift in motivation** for ORI behaviors can occur, from relationship pursuit to the desire for revenge if the pursuer feels humiliated. This shift sometimes marks the beginning of more aggressive ORI behaviors (Cupach & Spitzberg, 2008). When this shift occurs, ORI sometimes escalates to stalking, wherein someone repeatedly harasses another person in a way that threatens the individual's safety (Meloy & Gothard, 1995). A recent summary of studies suggests that anywhere from 2% to 13% of men and 8% to 32% of women have been stalked in their lifetime (Cupach & Spitzberg, 2004). This wide range is likely a function of the various definitions given for stalking in different studies. For example, Kohn, Flood, Chase, and McMahon (2000) found that 15% of the women in their sample reported that they had been "stalked, harassed, or threatened with violence for more than one month by someone who would not leave [them] alone." In comparison, 45% of Elliott and Bradley's (1997) sample reported having been "stalked or harassed with obscene phone calls." Studies also suggest that the vast majority of stalkers (e.g., about 75%) have had a previous relationship with their victims (Cupach & Spitzberg, 2004). And, strikingly, the average stalking episode lasts nearly two years. One individual described her experience as "pure hell" that "just kept going on and on and on and on" (Draucker, 1999, p. 478).

Consequences of ORI Behavior

Not surprisingly, the toll that this sort of constant threat takes on victims' psychological and physiological health is tremendous. Even moderate forms of ORI, though, can have devastating psychological consequences for the person being pursued (Cupach & Spitzberg, 2000). The most obvious consequence of ORI episodes is extreme and repeated experiences of fear associated with the target's loss of control over individual physical and psychological

privacy (Mullen & Pathe, 1994). This fear often results in the target making drastic attempts to regain this privacy, including equipping house and car with alarm systems, changing phone numbers and addresses, and even changing jobs. In fact, Wallace and Silverman (1996) argued that the effects of stalking are often similar to those experienced by victims of post-traumatic stress disorder.

A key question, then, is how can the desired person thwart ORI behavior? Cupach and Spitzberg (2008) identified five general ways that people cope with ORI behavior: **passive** (waiting for the pursuer to tire of the target, lose interest, or give up), **avoidant** (not answering phone calls and staying away from the pursuer), **aggressive** (being mean or rude, threatening to harm the pursuer if the target is not left alone), **integrative** (communicating disinterest directly, negotiating relationship rules and boundaries), and **help seeking** (asking others for assistance in preventing ORI behavior). Cupach and Spitzberg (2008) concluded that the success of each strategy varies dramatically, but found that confrontation and the clear outlining of relationship rules and boundaries (i.e., integrative strategies) had the greatest likelihood of success.

Another potentially intrusive behavior has become common during the past few years. Facebook stalking—although, in itself, not an ORI behavior (partly, at least, because it is hidden from the target)—often occurs as part of a pattern of obsessive relational intrusion and is something that sometimes provides a gateway to ORI behaviors or sustains them. In two studies involving more than 400 Facebook users, Joinson (2008) found that "virtual people watching" was the second most common use for Facebook (after maintaining contact with friends) and that the motivation of "social investigation," which includes "stalking other people," was among the best predictor of both frequency of visits to Facebook and number of Facebook friends.

Most recently, Phillips and Spitzberg (in press 2009; see also Phillips, 2009) have carefully examined the use of social networks (e.g., Facebook) for social surveillance. Their examination of social network's use for prying electronically (SNUPE-ing) has revealed several noteworthy trends. First, Phillips's (2009) analysis of over 450 students revealed three general types of surveillance: obsessive (e.g., "I could seem preoccupied with checking on my partner's social network site"), covert (e.g., "I have asked friends to use their cameras or phones to photograph my partner and tag a photo of my partner to a social networking site so I would know what my partner was up to"), and problematic (e.g., "My partner and I have had conflicts about what I discovered on his or her social network site") surveillance. These types of SNUPE-ing are not mutually exclusive—someone who overtly or covertly engages in surveillance may very well discover something that leads to conflict—but they do help us better understand some of the methods for, and outcomes of, prying on Facebook.

It is worth noting that this sort of SNUPE-ing has dark-side implications beyond the context of relationships. For example, in March 2010, it was revealed that a member of the Israeli Defense Force (IDF) was disciplined after he updated his Facebook status with specifics about his involvement in an upcoming offensive, including dates and location of the offensive. Once discovered, the IDF had to change their plans for the offensive. In another example, a newspaper reported in November 2009 that the wife of the then-incoming head of the British Secret Intelligence Agency had posted details of their children and their friends, along with address information on her Facebook page without privacy restrictions, causing very real security concerns and requiring a reexamination of security and protection procedures. While this case was due to a failure to include tighter privacy settings, it brings to light the fact that these sites create a false aura of privacy among members. Even the designation of strict privacy settings does not make one immune to SNUPE-ing activity. As a case in point, albums that include a photo in which a friend is tagged or on which a friend comments may become accessible well beyond the original restrictions. In that sense, privacy restrictions lose much of their meaning and SNUPE-ing opportunities are especially insidious.

Of course, it is also worth noting that individuals often engage in what some have called *lurking* on friends and family members' social network sites without the sort of preoccupation or manipulative covert behaviors described here. For instance, you might look at your friends' newly uploaded photo albums simply as a way to keep in touch with their lives. Or, you might glance though someone's friend list to see if there is anyone whom you want to befriend on Facebook. In fact, these sorts of lurking behaviors, and the relationship maintenance function they serve, are exactly what many users say they most appreciate about social networking sites and likely do not fit in the category of intrusive behaviors.

TOPIC AVOIDANCE AND SECRET KEEPING

So far, we have discussed how people react to privacy violations that are either mildly or highly intrusive. However, people often manage privacy proactively rather than reactively by either avoiding discussion or keeping something secret. These two information-management strategies—topic avoidance and secret keeping—are related in that they are both efforts to erect privacy barriers around information, but they are different in that they often involve varying degrees of shared knowledge. **Topic avoidance** simply reflects cases where someone intentionally avoids discussing a particular topic. People in relationships avoid discussing topics of which they are both aware—Khaled and Randy may avoid talking about the time during sophomore year when they both tried out for their college basketball team but only Khaled made it beyond the first cut. **Secret keeping**, in contrast, involves intentional efforts to keep information away from others. Such is the case now since Randy does not know that Khaled is secretly in love with Randy's girlfriend. Khaled's keeping quiet about his feelings is considered secret keeping. Khaled may also practice topic avoidance to avoid slipping up and leaking his true feelings. So, whenever Randy starts talking about his girlfriend, Khaled might listen without saying much or try to change the subject (See Afifi, Caughlin, & Afifi, 2007, for further discussion of the difference between topic avoidance and secrets).

Both topic avoidance and secret keeping are common in all types of close relationships. Baxter and Wilmot (1984) found that over 95% of the college students in their study could name at least one topic that they considered to be "taboo" or off limits in their friendships or dating relationships. Relatedly, most studies of secret keeping have found that nearly everyone keeps at least some information secret from partners, family members, or friends (see Finkenauer, Kubacka, Engels, & Kerkhof, 2009; Vangelisti, 1994a; Wegner, 1992). Given the similarities between topic avoidance and secret keeping, the research in the two domains together is reviewed together, but periodically focuses on each separately, as appropriate.

Topics Commonly Avoided or Kept Secret

Although people can avoid talking about almost anything, some topics are more likely to be avoided than others. Guerrero and Afifi's (1995a, 1995b) summary of the available research revealed six general topics that are commonly avoided in close relationships: relationship issues (e.g., relationship norms, the state and future of the relationship, the amount of attention to the relationship), negative experiences or failures (e.g., past experiences that may be considered socially unacceptable or were traumatic), romantic relationship experiences (e.g., past or present romantic relationships and dating patterns), sexual experiences (e.g., past or present sexual activity or sexual preferences), friendships (e.g., current friendships with others, the qualities of the friendship, and the activities engaged in together), and dangerous behavior (e.g., behaviors that are potentially hurtful to oneself). Golish and Caughlin's (2002) study of avoidance between parents and their children led to the addition of six more topics: everyday activities (e.g., school, daily events), other family members (e.g., talking about the other parent or stepparent, siblings), money, deep conversations, drinking or drugs, and religion. Of course, no one study will likely capture all the possible issues that may be avoided in relationships, so it is best to think of these as ones that are commonly avoided. For example, given that most studies in this area used college students, adolescents, and young married couples, they likely underrepresent some of the topics avoided by older adults.

If we turn to common topics that people keep as secrets, we find that they fit within the same category types described for avoided topics. For instance, one-night stands, a socially stigmatized illness, an alcoholic father's behavior, or a real dislike for someone are all among the sort of things one might keep as a

secret. Of course, it is also worth noting that the content of secrets may be positive, although probably not the first thing we think of when discussing secrets. Yet, you may keep secret the surprise birthday party you are planning for your best friend, the vacation plans you made for yourself and your romantic partner, or a gift you purchased for your child. These are positive examples of secret keeping.

Consistent with the notion that most information kept secretive is negative in some way, Caughlin, Afifi, Carpenter-Theune, and Miller's (2005) study of secret keeping in romantic relationships and friendships revealed that the three most common secrets were dating or sexual history (22% kept this secret from a dating partner or friend), an affair (held by 18% of the sample), and personality or opinion conflicts (held by 14% of the people in the study). In a study of family secrets, Vangelisti and Caughlin (1997) showed that finances—which include issues related to money, business holdings, and other assets owned by family members—were the most often kept secrets by families, followed by substance abuse, and then premarital pregnancy.

Families are a common context for secret keeping. Karpel (1980) discussed three forms of secrets particularly relevant to family units that differ in the complexity of the required boundary coordination (to use CPM terminology). The first form of secrets is whole-family secrets, which are held by the entire family and kept from outsiders. For example, sadly, Armstrong (1978) described a common tendency to keep a child's sexual abuse by a family member secret from all those outside the immediate family, assuming that the family is aware of the abuse.

Karpel's (1980) second form of secrets, intrafamily secrets, occurs when some family members have information they keep from other members. For instance, John's brother may have known for a while that John drinks and smokes pot, but he may have intentionally concealed this information from their parents. Or, Samantha's sexually abusive uncle may have originally told her to "keep it our little secret," thereby hiding the abuse from other family members (Cottle, 1980).

The third form of secrets, individual secrets, occurs when information is held by a single individual and kept secret from other family members, such as Suzanne hiding the fact that she is a recovered alcoholic from her husband, children, and other relations (Karpel, 1980). Individual secrets may or may not be shared outside of the family. Suzanne's best friend from college and her cohort from Alcoholics Anonymous might know her secret, even though her family members do not.

Reasons for Topic Avoidance and Secret Keeping

People engage in topic avoidance and secrecy for a myriad of reasons. Many of these reasons fall under three general motivations (Afifi & Guerrero, 2000; Caughlin & Vangelisti, 2009).

Relationship-Based Motivations

Paradoxically, people can use topic avoidance to strengthen or to disengage from a relationship. In fact, contrary to research conducted in the 1970s and early 1980s that touted the benefits of complete openness and self-disclosure, more recent studies on topic avoidance suggest that one of the most important reasons for maintaining individual boundaries around information is a concern for maintaining the relationship (Afifi & Guerrero, 2000; Parks, 1982). Baxter and Wilmot (1985) found that the desire for **relationship protection** was the single biggest motivator leading to avoidance of a particular issue with a relational partner. Similarly, Hatfield (1984) and Rosenfeld (1979) noted that fear of abandonment often explained someone's decision to avoid certain topics or keep something a secret. In other words, if people are worried that their dating partner will disapprove, they will likely keep something to themselves.

This motivation is not restricted to romantic relationships. Like Khaled, people sometimes withhold information that could harm their friendships. Although Khaled would like to see if Randy's girlfriend, Tara, shares his romantic feelings, he puts his friendship with Randy above his feelings for Tara. Afifi and Guerrero (1998) found that males were more likely than females to claim relationship protection as a reason for topic avoidance in their friendships and that people avoided certain topics with male friends more than with female friends because of this concern. In family relationships, Guerrero and Afifi (1995a) found

that individuals were more likely to be driven by a desire to protect the relationship when avoiding topics with their parents, as opposed to their siblings. In an extension of this research, Golish and Caughlin (2002) found that relationship protection was more often a reason underlying avoidance with stepparents than with fathers, and with fathers than with mothers. Thus, although relationship protection is an important reason underlying decisions to avoid disclosure, it seems especially relevant to some close relationships.

In contrast to the desire to protect and sustain the relationship, some people avoid discussing certain topics or keep secrets in hopes of destroying the relationship or preventing it from becoming closer. This motivation has been labeled **relationship destruction** or **relationship de-escalation** (Afifi & Guerrero, 2000). Although much less work has focused specifically on this motivation, several lines of research support the idea that people use topic avoidance or secrets to terminate a relationship or to prevent it from becoming more intimate. For instance, during the breakup stages of relationships, partners may distance themselves from the other by shutting down communication and keeping information that was previously shared (see Chapter 15). Another way to think about this motivation is how it works, for example, when someone you dislike wants to become friends with you. You might strategically avoid discussing personal topics with this person so that intimacy cannot develop.

Individual-Based Motivations

People also avoid discussing certain issues to protect themselves. Chapter 2 highlighted the importance people place on protecting their public identities. Literally hundreds of studies have shown that people work hard to project and maintain a positive image. Not surprisingly, then, one of the main reasons people avoid discussing certain issues is that disclosure on certain topics may make them "look bad." Afifi and Guerrero (2000) labeled this motivation **identity management**. In fact, across four studies—spanning sibling, parent-child, stepparent-child, friendship, and dating relationships—the fear of embarrassment and criticism, fueled by feelings of vulnerability, was the leading reason given for topic avoidance (Afifi & Guerrero, 1998; Guerrero & Afifi, 1995a, 1995b; Hatfield, 1984). Together, these studies suggest that the primary reason people avoid discussing certain issues is the fear that disclosure will threaten their identities. Relationship protection is a close second. Apparently people decide that it is better not to talk about something if it might make others perceive them negatively. If a person's identity is on the line, disclosure oftentimes is not worth the risk.

Besides this concern over public identity, people may avoid specific topics as a way to maintain privacy. This motivation, which Afifi and Guerrero (2000) termed **privacy maintenance**, is rooted in individuals' needs for privacy and autonomy. Given the importance of privacy maintenance in people's lives, one way that people maintain privacy is to avoid disclosure about certain topics. For example, you may become annoyed with a friend who wants to know all the details about your romantic relationship or who constantly asks you how well you did on exams or term papers. In response, as a way to protect your privacy, you may refuse to answer your friend's questions and avoid bringing up any related topics in the future.

Information-Based Motivations

The final set of reasons people choose to avoid disclosure or keep information to themselves is based on the information they expect to receive from the other person. In particular, people may choose to avoid disclosure because they suspect that the other person will find the disclosure trivial, not respond in a helpful way, or lack the requisite knowledge to respond. Afifi and Guerrero (2000) labeled these types of motivations **partner unresponsiveness**. For example, if you have a problem for which you need advice, but you think your friend will be unable to provide you with much help or will not care enough to really listen, you will likely avoid discussing that problem with your friend. Studies have found that people are especially likely to avoid discussing problems with men for this reason (Afifi & Guerrero, 1998; Guerrero & Afifi, 1995a, 1995b). In fact, a study by Burke, Weir, and Harrison (1976) found that 23% of wives, compared to only 10% of husbands, avoided disclosure because of a belief that their spouse would

be unresponsive. This finding is consistent with research on social support, which shows that women generally are better listeners than men (Derlega, Barbee, & Winstead, 1994).

People also engage in topic avoidance or secret keeping when they believe that talking about a particular topic would be futile or a "waste of time." Afifi and Guerrero (2000) labeled this motivation **futility of discussion**. Although this motivation has received less attention than the others, it may play an important role in people's decisions to withhold information. For example, believing that your partner or friend is so entrenched in her or his position as to make discussion meaningless certainly will motivate topic avoidance, but it may also be especially detrimental to relational success. Knowing that your partner will never understand why you loaned a lot of money to a friend, for instance, may make you keep that information secret.

Recent research has revealed another important information-based motivation for avoidance and secrecy—but one that is less focused on failings of the "other" and more on the self. This motivation revolves around one's own **communication inefficacy** (Afifi & Afifi, 2009; Afifi, 2010; Afifi & Steuber, 2009). Specifically, people often avoid a topic or keep something secret because they don't feel they have the communication skills to bring up the topic or maintain discussion in a competent and effective manner. They may not know how to start the conversation or think they'll freeze once the discussion starts. In either case, the motivation to just stay quiet in these cases is strong.

Collectively, these motivations account for many of the reasons that people maintain strict information boundaries within their relationships; Box 12.4 gives a real-life example of each. It is also important to keep in mind that people often avoid topics or keep secrets for several reasons, not just one, and that the reasons are often related. Knobloch and Carpenter-Theune (2004) found that people who avoided topics with their partner because of concerns that discussion would damage their image also worried that talking about the issue would harm the relationship. Indeed, these two motivations—identity management and relationship protection—are the most commonly cited reasons for information management and tend to work together to prohibit disclosure. Other research has uncovered more specific reasons why people keep information to themselves. For example, Golish and Caughlin (2002) found several specific reasons why parents and children use topic avoidance with one another, including lack of contact (especially in the case of divorced families), the emotional pain of discussion, and simple dislike for the person.

BOX 12.4 Highlights

Examples of Different Motivations for Topic Avoidance*

Relationship-Based Motivations

Relationship protection: A member of a cross-sex friendship discussed avoiding talk about the "state of the relationship" by stating that "if you bring that stuff back up, you don't know what it's going to cause, you know . . . so it's safer to just avoid it . . . safer on the relationship."

Relationship destruction: A 15-year-old girl wrote the following account: "My mom remarried about a year ago. I don't like my stepdad at all. He is always trying to act like my real dad and boss me around. I resent this. He will never be my dad. I already have a dad. I really hate it when he tries to get all close to me be asking about my life. He'll try to cozy up to me and ask all about my friends and stuff like he's my buddy or something. I make sure I don't tell him anything but he never gets the hint."

Individual-Based Motivations

Identity management: A college student wrote the following about her actions on a first date: "He asked about school and started talking about grades and stuff. I tried to switch the topic because I am not a very good student and I didn't want him to think I'm dumb or something."

Privacy maintenance: A 17-year-old girl wrote this account: "My mom wants me to tell her everything. She thinks she has to know everything about me all the time. I get sick of it. Sometimes I want to tell her it's just not her business. I am almost an adult. I have my own life. I need my privacy."

Information-Based Motivations

Partner unresponsiveness: A college student wrote this account: "My husband sometimes asks me about school, but I know that he is only asking out of politeness. He is not really interested and doesn't really understand what it is like to go back to school when you are in your 40s. Once when I was stressed out about a final, he told me it was 'only an exam.' Since then, I haven't talked about school with him much at all."

Futility of discussion: A 17-year-old boy wrote the following: "It is a total waste of time to talk to my dad about my SAT scores. We have been over it a million times and no matter how much we talk about it, it doesn't change anything. My college applications are in and I'm going to have to live with my score."

Communication inefficacy: A college student noted that "there is a student in my group communication class who is not doing his share on our project. I want to tell him to do more, but I don't know how to say it without sounding like I'm whining, so I'm hoping someone else will bring it up instead of me."

---

*These are actual accounts written by teenagers and college students who reported topic avoidance (see Afifi & Guerrero, 2000; Afifi, Guerrero, & Egland, 1994).

How People Engage in Topic Avoidance

Most studies of topic avoidance have involved asking people to rate how much they avoid discussing a certain topic with a particular person on a scale that ranges from "I always avoid discussing this issue with this person" to "I never avoid discussing this issue with this person." Recently, however, scholars have started investigating specific ways people practice topic avoidance rather than just measuring the degree of topic avoidance.

Dailey and Palomares (2004) identified eight general strategies for avoiding disclosure, varying in directness and politeness. Examples of avoidance tactics perceived as direct and impolite include abruptly saying something like "you should go" or simply leaving the conversation when a topic comes up. Other strategies for avoiding disclosure are more subtle and polite, such as using an idiom to avoid expressing true feelings (e.g., "that's the way the ball bounces") or giving a hesitant response to signal discomfort about the topic, hoping the other helps out by switching topics. In another study, college students who had frequent contact with their parents recalled their response when their parent last asked them about a topic they wanted to avoid (Mazur & Hubbard, 2004). Participants offered 10 different avoidance strategies, ranging from telling a lie (i.e., avoiding through deception), to showing anger or irritation, to appearing disinterested or uncomfortable.

Topic Avoidance During Relationship Transitions

People can engage in topic avoidance at any time. Sometimes topic avoidance is embedded in a relationship, such as spouses avoiding talking about politics because they know they cannot change each other's minds and will only argue. Other times, topic avoidance is a one-time occurrence. For instance, perhaps you are in a bad mood and don't want to talk about something, but later you end up sharing everything with your partner. Even though topic avoidance can occur at any time, there appear to be certain transition points in relationships, and two in particular, that are marked by higher overall levels of topic avoidance.

Topic Avoidance in Escalating Romantic Relationships

Researchers have examined how relationship stage affects the times when people are most likely to avoid certain topics. The assumption for a long time was that people most avoided disclosure in the beginning stages of dating relationships, when intimacy was still somewhat low and topics were considered sensitive. Knobloch and Carpenter-Theune (2004), however, found that the most avoidance in dating relationships usually occurs in the middle stages of development, when intimacy is moderate. Their rationale is that people are most likely to fear that discussing a topic will harm the relationship, make them look bad, or have other negative consequences when a relationship is shifting from casual to serious. They also reasoned that this transition time is accompanied by increased uncertainty about the relationship and how one's partner might react to certain disclosures. Their findings supported these predictions: People who reported moderate levels of intimacy were the most uncertain about their relationships and also the most likely to avoid topics with their partner.

Topic Avoidance During Family Transitions

Studies of family communication have also shown times in the parent-child relationship when avoidance is particularly high. Not surprisingly, young people are most likely to avoid topics with their partners during their middle teenage years (Guerrero & Afifi, 1995b). Mid-adolescence is a time when teens try to separate themselves from their parents, and keeping information private from parents is an important way for teens to develop a unique sense of self. Less avoidance occurs when children go to college or leave their parent's home. Another time when avoidance is high is during and shortly after a divorce. Tamara Afifi (previously Golish) has conducted several studies of topic avoidance in divorced families and found children from divorced families are more likely to avoid issues with their parents than those from intact families, especially if the child feels caught between loyalties to each of the parents. A common reaction in these cases is for the child to shut down and avoid expressing feelings so as not to betray either parent (Afifi, 2003; Afifi & Schrodt, 2003; Golish & Caughlin, 2002).

Consequences of Topic Avoidance

Avoidance is common, but what about the consequences of avoidance? Can avoidance have positive consequences for individuals and relationships? As mentioned earlier in the chapter, some scholars say yes (Altman et al., 1981; see also dialectics theory, Chapter 9), but most researchers still find that avoidance is a symptom of an unsatisfying relationship. For example, Dailey and Palomares (2004) studied three different relationship types—dating relationships, mother-child relationships, and father-child relationships—and found lower satisfaction across all three relationships when individuals avoided discussing their concerns about the relationship with their partner. Importantly, though, avoidance on another topic—personal failures—was not associated with lower satisfaction. Therefore, one possibility is that avoidance is harmful to relationships only when it is about issues that are directly relevant to the relationship itself. The conclusion here would be that avoidance about relationally relevant issues harms the relationship while avoidance of nonrelationally relevant issues has little effect. However, in complete contrast to that prediction, Caughlin and Afifi (2004) found that people who avoided a topic in order to protect their relationship tended not to experience negative consequences.

One explanation for these seemingly contradictory findings may lie in Afifi and Joseph's (2009) **standards for openness hypothesis**. This hypothesis extends earlier work (Caughlin & Golish, 2002) showing that a person's perception of how much the partner is avoiding influences satisfaction more than the partner's actual avoidance. In this most recent explanation, Afifi and Joseph (2009) argue that the perception of a partner's avoidance is harmful to relationship satisfaction to the extent that it comes across as a sign of a bad relationship. In other words, if people associate openness with having a good relationship, they will think there is a problem if they perceive their partner to be less than open. Since women often have higher expectations of openness in relationships than men, and are often more attuned

to shifts in their partner's openness, women are more likely to become unsatisfied in the face of perceived partner avoidance than men. Thus, women may be more likely than men to perceive topic avoidance and to experience negative relationship consequences associated with topic avoidance. The effects for topic avoidance hold both similarities and differences to those found for secret keeping.

Consequences of Secret Keeping

Secret keeping can have positive or negative consequences. Sharing a secret can communicate trust and show that a relationship is close. On the other hand, having a secret kept from us can make someone feel left out. Thus, there are both negative and positive consequences involved in secret keeping, with complexities related to various relationship contexts.

Negative Consequences of Secret Keeping

Research on the effects of secret keeping on individuals has focused on how keeping information secret influences people's thought patterns through a process called **hyperaccessibility** (Wegner, 1989, 1992; Wegner & Erber, 1992; Wegner, Lane, & Dimitri, 1994). Because secrets require people to avoid disclosing information to others, people often try to suppress the information and thoughts related to that secret. The reasoning here is that, if people suppress thoughts about a secret, they will be less likely to disclose secret information because it will not be "on their minds." However, thought suppression is not usually successful, and it can even backfire. The strong impact of thought suppression can be illustrated by a simple example. Here it goes: *Do not think of dancing elephants.* Now that you have been asked not to think about dancing elephants, you will probably have dancing elephants on your mind as you read this section. The simple request for people to suppress a thought about a particular thing, regardless of how innocent the request or how irrelevant the thing, has been shown to increase their thinking about it. In fact, that information is often all they can think about.

In their study of thought suppression, Wegner, Schneider, Carter, and White (1987) asked students not to think of a white bear and then had them ring

SOURCE: ©iStockphoto.com/cthoman.

Are you still thinking of dancing elephants?

a bell every time they thought of the bear. Rather than suppress the thought of the white bear, the students, on average, thought of the bear more than once per minute over a five-minute period. Several subsequent studies have confirmed that the desire to suppress a thought does the exact opposite, bringing it to the forefront of our thoughts and thus making it *hyperaccessible*.

Studies have also examined why thought suppression leads to hyperaccessibility. Think of Khaled, from the chapter opening. He is purposely concealing his feelings for Randy's girlfriend from everyone. Wegner's (1992) work helps explain how keeping such a secret might intensify Khaled's feelings. First, Khaled might try to distract himself from thoughts about Tara and his need to keep his feelings secret (attempts at thought suppression). Next, he might try to think of something else to talk to Randy about, such as how school and his new job are going. So, he starts thinking in earnest about those aspects of his life, but soon thoughts about Tara, his secret, and how it might affect his friendship with Randy pop into his head. Even though he is trying to suppress

those thoughts, they are hard to get out of his head, so he tries to think about something else, such as his mother's birthday party the next week. But whatever Khaled thinks about, the same cycle kicks in, and he thinks about how difficult it is to be around Randy when Tara is around. In sum, he keeps going back to the thought he is trying to ignore.

But is this hyperaccessibility permanent? Don't those thoughts eventually fade? According to Wegner and associates (1987), the hyperaccessibility of the suppressed thought decreases over time if one removes oneself from contact with the relevant information or secret. This makes Khaled's case doubly problematic since he wants to be around Randy, but being around Randy reminds him of Tara. Even if Khaled distanced himself from Randy and Tara for a while, his thoughts about them and his secret would likely come back with a vengeance at first contact with anything that reminds him of them. This scenario can also be applied to Samantha's situation. Children who were sexually abused may eventually stop thinking about the "secret" if they are separated from the abusing adult for long enough, but the thoughts will come flooding back as soon as the possibility of seeing that adult surfaces.

This **rebound effect** may also make it difficult for infidelity to remain a secret in relationships. The unfaithful person may be away from the partner or lover at work long enough to successfully suppress the thought of infidelity, but seeing the partner or lover will immediately serve as a reminder of the thought being attempted to suppress. The hyperaccessibility of the thought will make it difficult for the unfaithful person to keep the infidelity a secret. As a result of repeatedly thinking about the affair, the unfaithful person may also experience more guilt about the affair or anxiety about being caught.

The **fever model of self-disclosure** (Stiles, 1987; Stiles, Shuster, & Harrigan, 1992) can explain these effects. According to this model, people who are distressed about a problem or who think about a problem a lot are much more likely to reveal thoughts and feelings about the problem than are those who are not experiencing anxiety about an issue. If given the opportunity, people who are feeling highly anxious about something are likely to disclose more about it than people who are not. This model, when combined with Wegner's research on the hyperaccessibility of secrets, may explain why people so often reveal secrets to others. Their hyperaccessibility (especially during times when the secret information is "rebounding") makes the level of stress and anxiety so high that individuals have to find an outlet. The result frequently is the selection of someone they consider to be a confidant.

Afifi and Caughlin's (2006) research has shown another consequence of the secret keeping and rumination mix. At two points in time, they asked students about a secret they were keeping from a friend or dating partner and found secret keeping was harmful for self-esteem. Although it was the first study to show this link, the association makes sense, especially for individually held secrets, in which the information being concealed is often something that people regret and something that makes them question themselves. Given the negative impact that low self-esteem has on individuals and relationships, the fact that secret keeping promotes rumination about a negative aspect of self may be one of its most damaging consequences.

The maintenance of secrets has been shown to have additional negative consequences. First, keeping secrets negatively impacts the quality of interactions with the person from whom the secret is being kept (e.g., Brown-Smith, 1998). For example, imagine that John and his brother vowed not to tell their parents that they recently smoked pot together after school. The brothers are likely to experience considerable anxiety when the family sits together at the dinner table, especially if their parents ask them what they have been doing after school lately. Any topic related to afterschool activities or how they have been getting along is likely avoided, making for awkward family interactions. That, in turn, is likely to make the parents question their children, further leading to awkwardness and often promoting conflict.

Second, secrets encourage concealment of relational problems and related deception. Hiding a secret from others requires the secret keepers to put on an "air" that everything is fine and that the secret keepers share a happy relationship. This pretense can cause personal and relational stress (Karpel, 1980). For example, growing up, Samantha may have had to act as if she didn't fear her uncle when the extended family got together. Concealing her feelings would likely add even more stress to her life. In Khaled's case, he may feel he has to act indifferently yet polite when around Tara so as not to betray his true feelings. Obviously, the effort it takes to project these fake feelings can hinder development of healthy relationships and prevent partners from addressing problems in or outside of their relationship. A related problem, then, is that the maintenance of secrets often results in the spinning of lies to cover up the information. For instance, Khaled might pretend to be interested in another woman. The consequence often is a web of deception that must be continuously tended. If discovered, the deception is often considered a serious relational transgression that erodes trust (see Chapter 13). Yet, in some cases, such as Samantha's, uncovering a secret can be the first step toward recovering from a traumatic event. Her fiancé and parents would likely understand why she kept the information secret and help her deal with the scars left from the sexual and emotional abuse.

Family researchers have also uncovered negative consequences of keeping secrets. Researchers in the Netherlands demonstrated that 10- to 14-year-olds who keep secrets from their parents suffer lower self-esteem; elevated levels of depression; and high levels of stress, aggression, and delinquency (Frinjs, Finkenauer, Vermulst, & Engels, 2005). Family-held secrets also interfere with family dynamics in important ways. First, such secret keeping can create power imbalances. Given that knowledge often is equated with power, family members who know the secrets have power over those who do not (Imber-Black, 1993). When children know secret information about their parents, the typical power structure in families is sometimes irreversibly altered, changing the family dynamics forever (Brown-Smith, 1998). For example, imagine a child knowing about a parent's adulterous affair and holding that parent hostage with the information. Any disciplinary power that the parent has over that child is undermined by the fear that the secret will be disclosed.

The power structure of families has been studied to better understand to whom children are likely to disclose individual secrets (see Chapter 11). Afifi and Olson (2005) found that children were least likely to disclose secrets to the parent whom they saw as having the greatest punitive power. So, while holding a parent's secret may decrease the parent's power, children who hold individual secrets are especially likely to fear repercussions from powerful family members and, as such, continue concealment from those people.

Another possible consequence of family secrets is the development of what Karpel (1980) called a *split loyalty pattern*. Secret keepers are often put in a bind of having to choose between being loyal to other secret holders or being loyal to friends or family members who may be hurt by not knowing the secret. Samantha is caught in this bind. She feels guilty that she keeps the family welfare secret from her fiancé, yet she would also feel guilty if she told her fiancé and betrayed the "family secret." Split loyalties can also occur outside the family. For example, imagine that you were a college friend of Suzanne's who knew that Suzanne was a recovering alcoholic. Another friend of yours, Jill, was going to drive with Suzanne to and from a party. You would have to decide whether to warn Jill about Suzanne's past drinking problem. Should you help maintain Suzanne's positive identity by keeping the alcoholism secret, or should you protect Jill by giving her information that might help her determine whether it is safe to drive with Suzanne? Split loyalties create lose-lose situations, ruin relational dynamics, tear families apart, and destroy friendships.

Positive Consequences of Secret Keeping

Although most of the research points to negative effects of secrets, there are cases when secret keeping has positive consequences. Although studies have shown it harmful for early adolescents to keep secrets from their parents, other studies have found secret keeping beneficial in middle adolescence. Specifically, 14- to 18-year-olds are usually in the midst of developing their own identities. As discussed in research on avoidance, an important developmental event is the ability of children this age to form their own identities separate from their parents. Keeping secrets seems to perform that function and, as such, some types of secret keeping may

SOURCE: Digital Vision/ThinkStock.

Secrets can serve a bonding function. Even young children feel privileged and special when someone shares a secret with them.

be developmentally advantageous for children at this stage (Finkenauer, Engels, & Meeus, 2002).

Another way that secret keeping may be beneficial is that it sometimes increases cohesion among holders of the secret. Secrets kept by a whole family, spouses, dating partners, or members of a group may bring the secret holders closer together because of the bond and trust they share. Research by Vangelisti (1994a) and Vangelisti and Caughlin (1997) seems to support this conclusion. Students in these studies reported that the existence of familywide secrets often improved relationships, perhaps by creating a special bond between members who were trusted to keep secrets. Thus, secret keeping can sometimes be beneficial rather than harmful to relationships.

Consequences of Revealing Secrets

There are no doubt various consequences of keeping a secret, but what are the consequences of revelation? Derlega and Grzelak (1979) noted five reasons why people eventually reveal private information: (1) to achieve catharsis, (2) to clarify their own interpretation of events, (3) to get validation from others that they are still a good person, (4) to make the relationship closer, or (5) to control others. Each of these reasons has different consequences—positive and negative.

Positive Consequences of Revealing Secrets

Although it is impossible to say with certainty when someone should or should not disclose a secret, Kelly and McKillop (1996) made several recommendations for when to do so. Their research led them to identify three reasons people might want to consider revealing secrets; these include if the secret (1) reduces psychological or physical problems, (2) helps deter hyperaccessibility, or (3) leads to resolution of secrets.

First, there is considerable evidence that secret keeping is stressful and wears on secret keepers psychologically and physiologically (see Pennebaker, 1990). Spiegel (1992) has found that individuals with life-threatening illnesses who reveal private information in therapy sessions have a longer life expectancy than those who do not. Pennebaker's research on social support also suggests that the mere act of disclosing distressful information makes people feel better.

Second, as noted previously, keeping information secret makes secrets salient. As Wegner and colleagues (1994) put it, "The secret must be remembered, or it might be told. And the secret cannot be thought about, or it might be leaked" (p. 288), thus creating the two conflicting cognitive processes discussed earlier. Disclosing the secret frees the secret keeper from having to suppress it and makes it no longer hyperaccessible, thereby decreasing anxiety.

Third, without disclosing the secret, secret keepers cannot work toward a resolution of issues underlying the secret. Sharing the information may provide the individual with insight into the secret and allow a much-needed regained sense of control over life events (see Pennebaker, 1990). The secret keeper often has an unbalanced view of the situation and may benefit from the perspective of the recipient of the disclosure. Silver, Boone, and Stones (1983) found that female victims of incest who were able to reveal the secret to a confidant were much more likely to feel better about themselves and their lives than those who were unable to do so. Afifi and Caughlin (2006) showed that those who revealed their secret across an eight-week period experienced a significant increase in self-esteem. It is also worth noting that Caughlin and fellow researchers (2005) found that those who revealed secrets often reported partner reactions that were less negative than they had originally feared. So, one benefit of disclosing may be that one gains the advantages of catharsis and resolution without the feared destruction of the relationship.

Negative Consequences of Revealing Secrets

These positive consequences of revealing a secret should be weighed against the possible negative consequences. Specifically, three considerations can be assessed: Kelly and McKillop (1996) suggested that people might consider keeping a secret if revelation would (1) elicit a negative reaction from the listener or (2) help a person maintain a privacy boundary; and Petronio (1991) suggested that people might decide to keep secrets if revealing private information would (3) be seen as a betrayal by others.

First, given the typically negative nature of secrets, there is always a possibility that the recipient of the information will react with disapproval or shun the discloser. In fact, Lazarus (1985) reported that confidants often distance themselves following the disclosure of a negative secret. Coates, Wortman, and Abbey (1979) showed that people who disclose secret problems to others are considered less attractive than those who suppress such disclosure. When people have kept negative information to themselves as a way to manage their identities, they are especially likely to put stock in the listener's reaction when they finally reveal the secret. Disconfirming reactions may worsen what is likely an already diminished sense of self.

Work on disclosure of abuse demonstrates this point especially well. Dieckman (2000) interviewed female victims about their decision to tell others about their abuse. Her interviews highlighted the difficulty associated with disclosure and the importance of the response. Victims of abuse often hesitate to tell others about their experience because they fear being perceived as "weak" or being ridiculed for staying in the relationship. Indeed, Crocker and Schwartz (1985) found that many people responded to disclosures of abuse by telling the discloser that they "would never put up with that kind of treatment" and asking them why they didn't "just leave." Since victims typically disclose past abuse for the purpose of self-expression or validation, responses like those can diminish the discloser's ability to cope with the situation. Rather than helping disclosers, such responses often lower their self-esteem and discourage future disclosure. Their already low sense of self falls even lower because the response they feared the most—ridicule—is the response they received. Worse yet, the discloser might decide to keep the information secret once again, rather than risking more ridicule. As this example illustrates, the listener's response to sensitive self-disclosure is of paramount importance.

Second, preserving personal boundaries is critical to people's identities, as conveyed in the communication boundary management theory discussed in this chapter. To the extent that secrets make up part of the personal boundaries of individuals, secret keeping may help people maintain a sense of independence. Some scholars have even argued that secret keeping serves a developmental function by helping people manage their personal identity (Hoyt, 1978).

By contrast, revealing the secret erodes the personal boundaries being tightly held by the secret keeper. In a related vein, keeping secrets greatly increases a person's control over the information. By contrast, the decision to disclose a secret requires boundary coordination and leaves the individual vulnerable to betrayal of confidences. The information is no longer solely the person's own, and the individual has less control over how the information is spread.

Third, sometimes secrets are shared between two or more people, and revealing the secret to someone outside the dyad or group will be seen as a betrayal. Indeed, research reported in Chapter 13 suggests that betraying confidences is one of the most common relational transgressions in friendships, romantic relationships, and family relationships. If a confidence has been betrayed, revealing a secret often has a significant cost. Trust is eroded, and future self-disclosures from the person who feels betrayed are less likely. As such, another negative consequence of revealing secrets may be severe sanctions by other secret keepers. To ensure that a member of a group of secret keepers is not tempted to disclose the secret, groups will often make explicit boundary rules or threaten individuals with severe penalties for revealing the secret (Petronio, 1991).

The diversity of potential positive and negative consequences makes it difficult to determine when to disclose a secret and when not to do so. Kelly and McKillop (1996) developed a decision-making model for revealing secrets that takes into account the primary consequences associated with the revelation of individually held secrets; Figure 12.1 shows the model. In a similar vein, Petronio (1991) noted that the answers to five questions typically determine what people will disclose and to whom they will disclose it: (1) How badly do you need to reveal the information? (2) What do you think will be the outcome of the disclosure? (3) How risky will it be to tell someone the information? (4) How private is the information? and (5) How much control do you have over your emotions? These questions reflect a variety of issues raised in this chapter, as well as capturing the essence of Kelly and McKillop's model. Clearly, then, issues of anxiety, hyperaccessibility, and informational control play a key role in determining whether the revelation of secrets is likely to produce positive or negative outcomes.

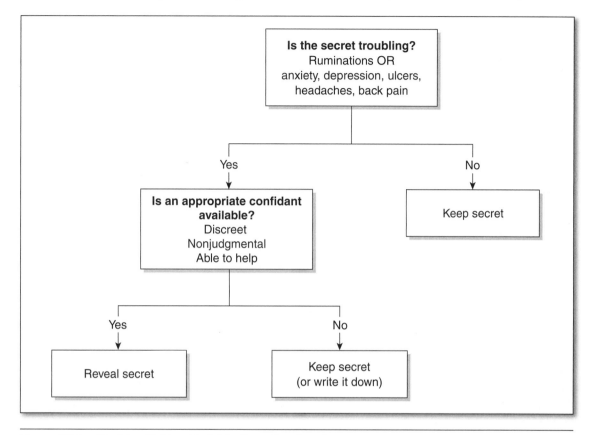

Figure 12.1   Decision-Making Model for Revealing Secrets

SOURCE: From Kelly, A. E., & McKillop, K. G., Consequences of revealing personal secrets, in *Psychological Bulletin,* 120. Copyright © 1996, the American Psychological Association. Reprinted with permission.

SUMMARY AND APPLICATION

This chapter started with examples from three people struggling with decisions to keep information from significant others. Hopefully this chapter provides you with the background to help you understand how needs for privacy operate in your relationship and the relationships of others.

Several factors affect whether people decide to disclose or avoid sharing information. As such, people practice topic avoidance for a variety of reasons. Understanding what those motivations are may be the first step in deciding whether to reveal a secret or not. For instance, Samantha might realize that when she was a child she avoided talking about the sexual abuse that she suffered because she was afraid of her uncle and was deeply ashamed. Now that she is an adult, however, Samantha may no longer fear her uncle and she may understand that she was an innocent victim. She may also recognize that now her main motivation for keeping the abuse a secret is that she does not want to relive the emotional pain. Through these types of realizations, Samantha may come to believe that she can trust her fiancé with her secret, and that he will support her through the emotional pain and help her heal old wounds. However, if Samantha decides to continue to keep this information a secret, it is her right to do so.

The research in this chapter also provides other helpful information about when to reveal a secret. If Khaled is feeling high levels of uncertainty and ruminating about his situation with Randy and Tara all the time, he might consider telling his secret to someone to help relieve his stress. Whether he decides to tell Randy or not may depend on how supportive and nonjudgmental he thinks Randy will be. If Khaled thinks Randy's feelings for Tara will make it difficult for him to understand, he may talk to a trusted third party about his dilemma. Similarly, Tyrone's decision about whether to tell John that he smoked pot in college may come down to how he thinks John will react. If Tyrone believes John will think he is a hypocrite who doesn't have any right to tell him what to do, he is likely to avoid disclosure about his pot-smoking days. On the other hand, if Tyrone believes that John will think he better understands the allure and risk of smoking pot because he once did it himself, he would be much more likely to share his past experiences with his son.

As these examples illustrate, privacy dilemmas are common in relationships. Even in the closest relationships, people desire and defend their privacy. In this chapter, we reviewed many studies showing the impact of privacy boundaries on our relationships and day-to-day lives. By contrast, Chapter 5 highlighted the many ways in which privacy loss through self-disclosure affects our relationships. Together, these chapters provide a peek into the dialectical struggles between openness and closedness that shape our lives. People need both privacy and expression (Altman et al., 1981), and managing privacy boundaries to accommodate both of these needs is a delicate process.

This process can be even more delicate and complex in the context of close personal relationships, because many people subscribe to an ideology of intimacy. In other words, many people think that openness is the hallmark of close relationships and that any attempts to maintain privacy will hinder the development and maintenance of intimacy. Samantha probably feels this way since she is experiencing guilt about not revealing certain information to her fiancé. The research in this chapter, however, suggests that it is normal and healthy to erect privacy boundaries. Individuals need privacy as well as connection. Relational partners who are always together and constantly sharing every bit of information with each other may lose their individual identities and become engulfed by the relationship. Thus, the hallmark of satisfying relationships may be the maintenance of individual identities in the midst of a close, connected relationship.

DISCUSSION QUESTIONS

1. On television and in the news, we often hear about cases involving obsessive relational intrusion or stalking. Have you or people you have known ever experienced this problem? What strategies might you use to stop such behavior?

2. Researchers have debated whether topic avoidance is related to more or less satisfaction in relationships. In what situations do you think topic avoidance would increase satisfaction? In what situations is it more likely to decrease satisfaction? Why?

3. How hard is it for you to keep a secret? Do you agree with the idea that attempts to suppress thoughts about it actually make it harder to keep the secret?

STUDENT STUDY SITE

Visit the study site at **www.sagepub.com/guerrero3e** for e-flashcards, survey and assessments from the chapter, and SAGE journal articles.

13

Hurting the Ones We Love

Relational Transgressions

Tia and Jamal are deeply in love and plan to marry after Tia finishes graduate school. During a conversation with a mutual friend, Jamal finds out that Tia had lunch with her ex-boyfriend, Robert, a week earlier. Jamal is flooded with negative thoughts and emotions. He always suspected that Robert regretted breaking up with Tia. Worse yet, Robert has become successful over the past couple of years, whereas Jamal's career has been stalled. Jamal can't help but wonder if Tia prefers Robert to him. And, why hadn't she told him that they had lunch? Is she trying to hide something? Perhaps even an affair? When Jamal confronts Tia later that evening, she tells him that she is completely "over" Robert, that they met by chance and decided to have a quick lunch to "catch up," and that she didn't tell him because it didn't mean anything and she knew he'd get upset. Tia declares, "I told him that I love you and we are engaged." Tia's words provide Jamal with some comfort, but he still can't seem to stop worrying.

I f you were in Jamal's place, would you still be worried about Robert? Research on the "dark side" of relationships suggests that Jamal's situation is not at all unusual. People commonly experience problems such as jealousy, deception, and infidelity in their close relationships (Cupach & Spitzberg, 1994; Spitzberg & Cupach, 1998). The question becomes, how can people cope with such situations most effectively? For example, should Jamal continue communicating his jealous feelings to Tia, or should he pretend that nothing is wrong? What about Tia? Was her explanation for not telling

Jamal about her lunch with Robert plausible? And what can she do or say to convince Jamal that she loves him and has been faithful?

In this chapter, we focus on understanding how relational partners hurt one another, as well as how people respond to being hurt. First, we discuss hurt feelings in the context of relationships. Then we review research related to three especially hurtful events—infidelity, jealousy, and deception—followed by a review of research on hurtful messages. The last part of the chapter focuses on communication and forgiveness following hurtful events.

HURT FEELINGS IN RELATIONSHIPS

Think about the last few times you felt emotional pain. Chances are that you had close relationships with the people who directly or indirectly inflicted that pain. In one study, people described a situation that led them to experience hurt feelings (Leary, Springer, Negel, Ansell, & Evans, 1998). Of the 168 participants in this study, only 14 described situations involving strangers or acquaintances; the other 154 all described situations involving close relational partners, such as romantic partners, family members, or good friends. Scholars have noted the paradoxical nature of hurt—the people with whom we share the strongest emotional connection have the power to hurt us in ways that other people cannot. As Dowrick (1999) put it:

> It is one of life's most terrible ironies that betrayal can be as connective as love. It can fill your mind and color your senses. It can keep you tied to a person or to events as tightly as if you were bound, back to back—or worse, heart to heart. The person you want to think of least may become the person you think of constantly. (p. 46)

Types of Hurtful Words and Events

The most intense hurt feelings arise when a partner's words or actions communicate devaluation (Feeney, 2005). **Devaluation** involves feeling unappreciated and unimportant. A person can feel devalued at the individual or relational level. For example, if a good friend says she's not surprised that you failed an exam because you're not very smart, you might feel hurt because your friend does not value your intellect. At a relational level, devaluation is a perception that one's partner does not perceive the relationship to be as close, important, or valuable as one would like (Leary et al., 1998). Examples of relationship devaluation include someone breaking up with you, saying "I don't love you anymore," or choosing to spend time with other people instead of you.

Relational transgressions and hurtful messages are forms of behavior that inflict hurt feelings.

Relational transgressions occur when people violate implicit or explicit relational rules (Metts, 1994). For example, many people believe that romantic partners should be sexually faithful and that all close relational partners should be emotionally faithful, loyal, and honest. When people violate these standards of faithfulness, loyalty, and honesty, they also devalue the partner and the relationship (Feeney, 2005). The top relational transgressions identified by college students are (1) having sex with someone else, (2) wanting to or actually dating others, and (3) deceiving others about something significant (Metts, 1991). Other transgressions include flirting with or kissing someone else, keeping secrets from the partner, becoming emotionally involved with someone else, and betraying the partner's confidence (Jones & Burdette, 1994; Roscoe, Cavanaugh, & Kennedy, 1988). **Hurtful messages** refer to words that elicit psychological pain. As Vangelisti (1994b) argued:

> [Words] have the ability to hurt or harm in every bit as real a way as physical objects. A few ill-spoken words (e.g., "You're worthless," "You'll never amount to anything," "I don't love you anymore") can strongly affect individuals, interactions, and relationships. (p. 53)

Effects of Hurtful Words and Events

It follows that hurtful words and events often have negative effects on relationships. In Jones and Burdette's (1994) study, 93% of people who had been betrayed by their partners said that their relationships had been harmed as a result of the transgression. Leary and his colleagues (1998) examined a wider variety of hurtful events than betrayals. Nonetheless, 42% of their participants said that the hurtful event had permanently damaged their relationships. In friendships, betrayal leads to less acceptance, trust, and respect (Davis & Todd, 1985). In fact, when people are betrayed by a friend, they often recast the friend's entire personality to frame the friend in a more negative light (Wiseman, 1986). Situations involving infidelity, jealousy, deception, and hurtful messages provide a framework to better understand some of the events that lead to hurt feelings and relational problems.

INFIDELITY

Infidelity is especially hurtful. Feeney (2004) studied a number of hurtful events and found infidelity to have a particularly strong negative effect on relationships. In another study, sexual infidelity, along with relationship breakup, were rated as the least forgivable of several hurtful events in dating relationships (Bachman & Guerrero, 2006b). The way people discover sexual infidelity also makes a difference. Afifi, Falato, and Weiner (2001) compared four methods of discovery: (1) finding out from a third party, (2) witnessing the infidelity firsthand, such as walking in on the partner with someone else, (3) having the partner admit to infidelity after being questioned, and (4) having the partner confess without being asked. People who found out through a third party or by witnessing the partner's infidelity firsthand were the least likely to forgive their partners and the most likely to say that their relationships had been damaged. People were most likely to forgive their partners when they confessed on their own.

Types of Infidelity

Researchers have made a distinction between sexual and emotional infidelity. **Sexual infidelity** refers to "sexual activity with someone other than one's long-term partner" (Shackelford & Buss, 1997, p. 1035). Most people in the United States disapprove of sexual infidelity (Weinbach, 1989; Weis & Slosnerick, 1981), yet studies suggest that around 20% to 40% of dating and cohabiting relationships are marked by at least one incident of sexual infidelity (Guerrero, Spitzberg, & Yoshimura, 2004; Wiederman & Hurd, 1999). Rates of sexual infidelity are lower for married couples, with estimates suggesting that between 13% and 18% of married individuals admit to having at least one extramarital affair over the course of their marriage (Blow & Hartnett, 2005). Across all types of romantic relationships, men are more likely than women (Blow & Hartnett, 2005; Sprecher & McKinney, 1993), and gay men are more likely than lesbians or heterosexuals, to have sexual affairs (Blumstein & Schwartz, 1983). **Emotional infidelity**, on the other hand, refers to emotional involvement with another person, which leads one's partner to channel "emotional resources such as romantic love, time, and attention to someone else" (Shackelford & Buss, 1997, p. 1035). Suspecting that your partner loves or confides in someone else more than you, if confirmed, is an example of emotional infidelity.

Researchers have also discussed the concept of communicative infidelity (Spitzberg & Tafoya, 2007). **Communicative infidelity** occurs when people engage in sexual activity with a third party to communicate a message to their partner. People sometimes use communicative infidelity to send messages related to jealousy, sex, or revenge (Tafoya & Spitzberg, 2007). For example, Jamal might try to make Tia jealous by engaging in sexual activity with an old girlfriend, and then Tia might get revenge on Jamal by sleeping with Robert. Other times, people engage in communicative infidelity as a way to signal to their partner that they are dissatisfied with the sexual activity in their current relationship. Tafoya and Spitzberg's work also showed that communicative infidelity is more acceptable and justifiable under certain circumstances—such as engaging in infidelity in response to one's partner having sex with someone else or partners saying that they are no longer in love.

Given the prevalence of infidelity, it is important to ask why people engage in acts of infidelity in the first place. Research on sexual infidelity suggests that dissatisfaction with the current relationship is the leading cause (Hunt, 1974; Roscoe et al., 1988; Sheppard, Nelson, & Andreoli-Mathie, 1995). Other common causes of infidelity include boredom, the need for excitement and variety, wanting to feel attractive, sexual incompatibility with one's partner, and trying to get revenge against the partner (Buunk, 1980; Fleischman, Spitzberg, Andersen, & Roesch, 2005; Roscoe et al., 1988; Wiggins & Lederer, 1984). Less research has examined causes of emotional infidelity, yet it is likely that emotional infidelity is related to feeling dissatisfied with the communication and social support a person is receiving in the current relationship.

Behavioral Cues to Infidelity

Researchers have uncovered specific behavioral cues that trigger suspicion about infidelity. In one study (Shackelford & Buss, 1997) undergraduate students described the cues that would lead them to suspect that their partners were (1) being sexually unfaithful (sexual infidelity), or (2) falling in love with someone else (emotional infidelity). Fourteen types of behavior were found to trigger suspicion. As illustrated in Box 13.1, some of these cues were associated more with suspicions of sexual infidelity, while others were associated more with suspicions of emotional infidelity. Still other cues were associated with sexual and emotional infidelity about equally.

BOX 13.1 Highlights

Examples of Cues to Infidelity

Behaviors Leading Primarily to the Suspicion of Sexual Infidelity	
Indirect physical signs	Smelling someone's perfume or cologne on the partner's clothing.
Direct revelations	Walking in on the partner with someone else or the partner confesses.
Changes in sexual behavior	Noticing that the partner acts differently during sex.
Exaggerated affection	Perceiving that the partner is acting especially affectionate because he or she feels guilty about being with someone else.
Sexual disinterest	The partner seems less interested and excited about having sex.
Behaviors Leading Primarily to the Suspicion of Emotional Infidelity	
Relationship dissatisfaction	The partner reveals that she or he is no longer in love or wants to pursue other alternatives.
Emotional disengagement	The partner seems to be distancing herself or himself emotionally.
Passive rejection	The partner becomes more inconsiderate or inattentive than usual.
Negative communication	The partner is uncharacteristically angry, critical, or argumentative.
Reluctance to spend time together	The partner starts to spend less time one-on-one and to separate his or her social network.
Reluctance to talk about a certain person	The partner seems reluctant or nervous to talk about a particular person.
Guilty communication	The partner acts like he or she has done something wrong.
Behaviors Leading to the Suspicion of Both Sexual and Emotional Infidelity	
Apathetic communication	The partner seems to be putting less effort into the relationship.
Increased contact with third party	The partner seems to be focusing more time and attention on another person.

SOURCE: Information compiled and adapted from Shackelford and Buss (1997).

While most of the behaviors that trigger suspicion about sexual infidelity are related to observed changes in a partner's sexual behavior, most of the behaviors that trigger suspicion about emotional infidelity are the opposite of those that people use to maintain their relationships. As discussed in Chapter 9, self-disclosure, routine talk, and positivity are key behaviors that help keep a relationship satisfying. Thus, when partners stop using these behaviors, and instead act emotionally distant, apathetic, and argumentative, people suspect that something is amiss. Integrating social networks and spending time together are also important maintenance behaviors (see Chapter 9), so when partners start spending more time with a third party (and less time with you), suspicions are likely to arise. In short, it appears that when people feel their partners are no longer working to maintain the relationship, they may suspect this lack of effort is due to emotional infidelity, or worse yet, both emotional and sexual infidelity. If Jamal notices changes in Tia's behavior that reflect a lack of effort and interest in their relationship, his worries about possible emotional or sexual infidelity might grow.

There are also sex differences in how people perceive possible cues to infidelity. In Shackelford and Buss's (1997) study, women were more likely than men to see suspicious behaviors as indicative of infidelity (see Box 13.1). Perhaps this is because, in the United States, men are somewhat more likely than women to have extradyadic affairs (Sprecher & McKinney, 1993) or because women are better encoders of information than men (Burgoon, Guerrero, & Floyd, 2010).

Sex Differences in Reactions to Infidelity

Research has also examined sex differences in reactions to sexual versus emotional infidelity. Much of the research in this area takes a social evolutionary perspective (Buss, 1989, 1994; see also Chapter 10), suggesting that men and women react to emotional and sexual infidelity differently because they have different priorities related to reproduction. Women know they are the parent of a child, but men are sometimes uncertain about paternity and therefore are more concerned about sexual infidelity. Women, on the other hand, according to this perspective, should be more worried about emotional infidelity because they are especially concerned with protecting their most important resource, their relationship. Thus, the **evolutionary hypothesis** predicts that men should get more upset over sexual infidelity than emotional infidelity, whereas women should get more upset over emotional infidelity than sexual infidelity.

Studies supporting this evolutionary hypothesis have generally used one of two methods (Guerrero et al., 2004). The first of these methods involves having men and women imagine that their partner either engaged in sexual activity or was in love with someone else, and then measuring their level of distress. In these studies, men show greater psychological and physiological distress when they imagine their partner engaging in sexual infidelity, whereas women display more distress when they imagine their partner in love with someone else (Buss, Larsen, Westen, & Semmelroth, 1992; Wiederman & Allgeier, 1993). The second method involves having people choose which would make them more upset—their partner having a one-night stand or their partner falling in love with someone else. When this method is used, men identify sexual infidelity as more upsetting whereas women identify emotional infidelity as more upsetting (Becker, Sagarin, Guadagno, Millevoi, & Nicastle, 2004; Trost & Alberts, 2006).

Despite these findings, the evolutionary hypothesis has been challenged. Some researchers have argued that sex differences in reactions to sexual and emotional infidelity are better explained by the **double-shot hypothesis** than the evolutionary hypothesis (DeSteno & Salovey, 1996). According to this view, both men and women get most upset when their partners have engaged in both sexual and emotional infidelity. Therefore, when people are forced to choose between whether sexual or emotional infidelity is more upsetting, they will choose the event that is most likely to imply that both types of infidelity are occurring. Men choose sexual infidelity as more upsetting because they assume that their girlfriends or wives would not have sex with a man unless they were also connected to him emotionally. Women, on the other hand, choose emotional infidelity because they believe that their boyfriends or husbands are likely to have had sex with a woman with whom they have a strong emotional attachment.

Researchers supporting the double-shot hypothesis have also argued that the sex difference only emerges when using a forced-choice format (DeSteno, Bartlett, Salovey, & Braverman, 2002). In other words, if people report how jealous or upset they are on a scale (e.g., from 1 to 10 with 10 being the most jealous), instead of choosing which type of infidelity is more upsetting, then the sex difference disappears. DeSteno and associates had people use scales and found that both men and women reported more jealousy in response to sexual infidelity than emotional infidelity. Similarly, Parker (1997) found that both women and men perceived sexual infidelity as more threatening than verbal intimacy when people rated the degree of threat for each situation using a scale.

JEALOUSY

When people suspect or discover infidelity, jealousy is a common reaction. Interestingly, jealousy is often the result of a relational transgression such as a partner having an affair or spending extra time with someone else. But jealousy is also seen as a transgression in its own right when a partner's suspicions are unwarranted (Metts, 1994). For example, if Tia has been completely emotionally and sexually faithful to Jamal, but Jamal continues to act suspicious and possessive, Tia is likely to become upset by his behavior. To Tia, Jamal's lack of trust may very well be seen as a relational transgression.

Characteristics of Jealousy

Tia and Jamal's scenario highlights an important point: Jealousy can be a reaction to an imagined threat or to an actual threat. There are also different types of jealousy. The first two forms of jealousy shown in Box 13.2 pertain to romantic relationships. The remaining five forms of jealousy, which

Jealousy always involves at least three people. Jealousy also tends to involve multiple emotions. What emotions do you think the woman in this photo is feeling?

were identified by Bevan and Samter (2004), can occur in romantic relationships, friendships, and family relationships.

Jealousy is different than two related constructs, envy and rivalry (Bryson, 1977; Guerrero & Andersen, 1998a; Salovey & Rodin, 1986, 1989). **Jealousy** occurs when people worry that they might lose something they value, such as a good relationship or high-status position, due to interference from a third party. The prototypical jealousy situation involves fearing that someone will "steal" a romantic partner away. **Envy**, by contrast, occurs when people want something valuable that someone else has. Prototypical envy situations involve feelings of resentment toward someone who seems to have a better life, often because the

---

BOX 13.2 Highlights

Different Types of Jealousy

Romantic jealousy	Worrying that a potential rival might interfere with the existence or quality of the romantic relationship.
Sexual jealousy	Worrying that a rival is having or wants to have sex with one's partner.
Friend jealousy	Feeling threatened by the partner's relationships with friends, such as worrying that your closest friend has a new "best friend."
Family jealousy	Feeling threatened by the partner's relationships with family, such as worrying that your spouse is closer to her or his mother than you.
Activity jealousy	Worrying that the partner's activities, such as work, hobbies, or school, are interfering with the relationship.
Power jealousy	Perceiving that one's influence over the partner is being lost to others.
Intimacy jealousy	Believing that one's partner is engaging in more intimate communication, such as disclosure and advice seeking, with someone else.

---

person has stronger relationships, is better looking, is intelligent and talented, or has more stature, money, or possessions. Rivalry occurs when two people are competing for something that neither one of them has. A prime example of rivalry involves siblings who are competing to be seen as "best" in the eyes of their peers, parents, and other adults (Dunn, 1988a, 1988b). As these examples and Figure 13.1 illustrate, who possesses the desired relationship or commodity differentiate jealousy, envy, and rivalry.

The triangle of Jamal, Tia, and Robert helps illustrate the differences between jealousy and envy. On the basis of the descriptions above, would you characterize Jamal as jealous or envious? It seems clear that Jamal is experiencing jealousy because he is worried that he might lose Tia to Robert. However, Jamal might also be experiencing envy because he wishes to possess some of the things Robert has, such as a successful career. Assuming that Robert is still in love with Tia, he might be envious of Jamal's relationship with her. Now pretend that Tia is not currently in a relationship with either man, and that they both want to date her exclusively. If this was the case, Jamal and Robert would be experiencing rivalry. As this example shows, jealousy, envy, and rivalry sometimes coexist within the same set of relationships.

Experiencing Romantic Jealousy

When people perceive a third-party threat to their romantic relationships, they are likely to experience a number of cognitions and emotions. On the cognitive side, jealous individuals typically make appraisals regarding the source and severity of the threat. On the emotional side, jealous individuals tend to experience a cluster of jealousy-related emotions.

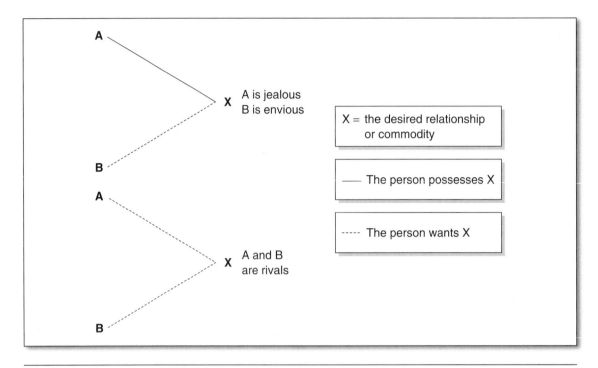

Figure 13.1 Differences Between Jealousy, Envy, and Rivalry Based on Possession of a Desired Relationship or Commodity

Jealous Thoughts

White and Mullen (1989) described primary and secondary cognitive appraisals that tend to occur as jealous feelings develop. **Primary appraisals** involve general evaluations about the existence and quality of a rival relationship, including the degree of the threat from the third party. For example, Jamal might ask himself questions like: "Has Tia been seeing Robert behind my back?" and "Could Tia love Robert more than me?" **Secondary appraisals** involve more specific evaluations of the jealousy situation, including possible causes and outcomes. White and Mullen (1989) described four types of secondary appraisals that people use to gather information and interpret the situation. First, jealous people assess motives ("Why did Tia have lunch with Robert?"). Second, they compare themselves to the rival ("Robert is more successful than I am, but I'm

more intelligent and caring"). Third, they evaluate their alternatives ("If Tia dumps me for Robert, whom would I want to date? Would I rather be on my own than date someone who has been unfaithful to me?"). These questions would help prepare Jamal, or anyone else dealing with jealousy or infidelity, for a possible breakup or reconciliation. Finally, jealous people assess their potential loss ("How devastating would it be to lose Tia?").

According to White and Mullen (1989), jealous individuals like Jamal make appraisals so that they can plan coping strategies and assess outcomes. For example, if Jamal decides that Tia could be attracted to Robert because of his success, he might compensate by putting more effort into his own career. If Tia responded favorably to Robert's intensified career pursuits, Jamal would likely continue those behaviors. But if Jamal's behavior change does not have the desired effect (perhaps Tia complains that Jamal is so focused on his career that he is ignoring her), he is likely to try a different strategy.

Jealous Emotions

In addition to making cognitive appraisals, jealous individuals usually experience combinations of emotions. The emotions most central to jealousy are fear and anger (see Guerrero & Andersen, 1998a, 1998b; Sharpsteen, 1991). People are jealous because they fear losing their relationship, and they are often angry at their partner for betraying them. Sometimes jealous individuals are also angry at the rival, particularly if the rival is someone they know; other times, they feel irritated or annoyed but not really angry (Guerrero, Trost, & Yoshimura, 2005).

Beyond fear and anger, other aversive emotions such as sadness, guilt, hurt, and envy often mark jealousy (Fitness & Fletcher, 1993; White & Mullen, 1989). Sadness occurs near the end of some jealousy episodes when people are feeling gloomy and lonely because a breakup seems inevitable or has just occurred (Sharpsteen, 1991). Sometimes jealous individuals feel guilty because they wrongly accused their partners of misdeeds, as Jamal might feel if he discovers he mistakenly suspected Tia of any improprieties. Other times, people feel guilty because they think that their own negative qualities caused the partner to become interested in someone else. For example, Jamal might think that if he had paid more attention to Tia, she might not be attracted to someone else. Envy can be part of the jealousy experience, especially when the rival has positive qualities that the jealous person does not possess.

Sometimes jealousy leads to positive emotions such as increased passion, love, and appreciation (Guerrero & Andersen, 1998b; Guerrero et al., 2005). For example, think about how you might feel if you saw someone flirting with your romantic partner. The fact that someone else sees your partner as attractive might make you feel more passionate and loving toward your partner (Pines, 1992; White & Mullen, 1989). Recent research shows that people sometimes intentionally induce jealousy to achieve

two goals: to make their partner value the relationship more, and to get revenge (Fleischmann et al., 2005). Pines (1992) also argued that jealousy can lead partners to appreciate their partners more, to become more committed to the relationship, and to work harder to maintain the relationship. Other researchers have argued that jealousy is closely related to love because people would not get jealous if they did not care about their partners (Salovey & Rodin, 1985). However, inducing jealousy is a dangerous strategy because jealousy often leads to relationship dissatisfaction and sometimes even violence (Guerrero & Andersen, 1998a).

Communicative Responses to Jealousy

Just as jealousy can involve a wide range of thoughts and emotions, so, too, can jealousy be expressed in many different ways. Guerrero and her colleagues have identified many different communicative responses to jealousy, which are summarized in Box 13.3 (Guerrero, Andersen, Jorgensen, Spitzberg, & Eloy, 1995; Guerrero, Hannawa, & Gallagher, 2008). The most commonly reported responses are integrative and negative communication. In addition to these specific responses, it is important to consider how much emotion people express when communicating jealousy. For example, a person could be cold and stoic when using integrative communication, or show anxiety and sadness.

People use different communicative responses to jealousy based on their goals and emotions (Bryson, 1977; Guerrero & Afifi, 1998, 1999; Guerrero et al., 2005). When people want to maintain their relationships and feel annoyance rather than anger, they report using constructive responses. People who fear losing their relationships tend to report compensatory restoration. In contrast, people who are more concerned with maintaining their self-esteem report denying their jealous feelings. When people are motivated to reduce uncertainty about their relationship, they report using integrative communication, surveillance, and rival contacts, which all represent ways of seeking information. People tend to use destructive responses when they feel jealous anger and want revenge against their partners.

BOX 13.3 Highlights

Communicative Responses to Jealousy

Constructive Responses	
Integrative communication	Direct, nonaggressive communication about jealousy with the partner (e.g., disclosing feelings and trying to reach an understanding).
Compensatory restoration	Behavior aimed at improving the primary relationship or oneself (e.g., trying to look more physically attractive, giving the partner gifts or extra attention).
Destructive Responses	
Negative communication	Direct and indirect aggressive communication with the partner (e.g., arguing, being sarcastic, giving cold or dirty looks, withdrawing affection).
Violent communication	Threats or actual physical violence against the partner (e.g., threatening to harm the partner, hitting).
Counterjealousy induction	Engaging in actions to make the partner feel jealous (e.g., flirting with others, talking about a rival in front of the partner).
Avoidant Responses	
Denial	Pretending not to be jealous (e.g., denying jealousy, acting like nothing is wrong).
Silence	Decreasing communication (e.g., getting quiet, not talking as much as usual).
Rival-Focused Responses	
Signs of possession	Publicly displaying the relationship so people know the partner is "taken" (e.g., kissing the partner in front of rivals, introducing the partner as one's "girlfriend" or "boyfriend").
Derogating competitors	Negative comments about potential rivals to the partner and to others (e.g., telling the partner about the rival's bad traits).
Surveillance	Behavioral strategies designed to find out about the rival relationship (e.g., checking the partner's cell phone or e-mail, spying on the partner).
Rival contacts	Direct communication with the rival about the jealousy situation or rival relationship (e.g., telling the rival the partner is already in a relationship).

SOURCE: Adapted from Guerrero, Hannawa, and Gallagher (2008).

Jealousy and Relational Satisfaction

Although jealousy can be a sign of love and attachment, it can also be both a symptom and a cause of relational distress. In fact, research has shown that jealous thoughts and feelings generally are associated with relational dissatisfaction (Andersen, Eloy, Guerrero, & Spitzberg, 1995; Buunk & Bringle, 1987; Guerrero & Eloy, 1992; Salovey & Rodin, 1989). However, jealousy is experienced in many relationships that remain satisfying. The key seems to be managing jealousy in a productive way such that the jealous individual shows care and concern without seeming overly fearful, aggressive, or possessive.

Among the many communicative responses to jealousy listed in Box 13.3, only the two constructive responses appear to be consistently associated with relational satisfaction. All the other responses usually make the problem worse, although some studies have shown that counterjealousy induction and signs of possession can be effective in certain circumstances (Buss, 1988a; Fleishmann et al., 2005). Integrative communication involves talking about jealousy in a constructive manner, often by disclosing feelings and renegotiating relational rules and boundaries. Rusbult and Buunk (1993) suggested that this type of communication is critical for maintaining relationships after jealousy is felt. Similarly, Afifi and Reichert (1996) found a positive association between integrative communication and relational satisfaction in jealous situations. Research by Andersen et al. (1995), however, found that integrative communication was only associated with relational satisfaction when people expressed their emotions while communicating with their partner. Showing that one is hurt and upset, but still making an effort to talk issues over in a fair and rationale manner, may be the key to preserving relational satisfaction in the face of a jealous threat. Expressing negative emotions honestly and openly may also cause the partner to feel empathy. Unless used too excessively and seen as a desperate move, compensatory restoration is also associated with relational satisfaction. Individuals who try to improve themselves and their relationships may become more desirable to their partners. Indeed, Buss (1988a) reported that strategies such as demonstrating love and caring for one's partner were highly effective in keeping couples together after jealousy had occurred.

Sex Differences in Jealous Emotions and Communication

Research findings on sex differences in jealous emotions are mixed, but some studies suggest that women experience more hurt, sadness, anxiety, and confusion than men, perhaps because they blame themselves for the situation more often (Becker et al., 2004; Bryson, 1976). By contrast, men have been found to deny jealous feelings and to focus on bolstering their self-esteem more than women (Buunk, 1982; White, 1981). These differences are small, but they suggest that women are somewhat more focused on the relationship, whereas men are more focused on individual concerns.

Sex differences in communicative responses to jealousy are more consistent, although relatively small. Jealous women report using integrative communication, expressing emotion, enhancing their appearance, and using counterjealousy inductions more often than jealous men. In contrast, jealous men more often contact the rival, restrict the partner's access to potential rivals, and give gifts and spend extra money on the partner (Buss, 1988a; Guerrero & Reiter, 1998). An evolutionary perspective can partially explain these findings: Men focus on competing for mates and showing resources, whereas women focus on creating social bonds and showcasing their beauty (Buss, 1988a).

DECEPTION

Like jealousy, deception is a major relational transgression that often leads to feelings of betrayal and distrust (O'Hair & Cody, 1994). Deception violates both relational and conversational rules, and is often considered to be a negative violation of expectancies (Aune, Ching, & Levine, 1996). Most people expect friends and loved ones, as well as strangers, to be truthful most of the time. In fact, McCornack (1992) argued that expecting others to be truthful is a basic feature of conversations (see also Grice, 1989). If people did not expect that most conversations are truthful, talking to others would simply be too difficult and unproductive. For example, if you were always suspicious and had to question the veracity of every statement you heard, it would be virtually impossible to get to know people.

On a given day, however, it is highly likely that you or someone you are talking to will engage in some form of deception. Studies have found that people report lying in approximately 25% of their daily interactions in both face-to-face (DePaulo, Kashy, Kirkendo, Wyer, & Epstein, 1996) and computer-mediated communication situations (George & Robb, 2008). In another study that defined deception more broadly, people were asked to keep a log of their conversations. Remarkably, only one-third of these conversations were completely truthful (Turner, Edgley, & Olmstead, 1975). Some degree of lying, exaggeration, or intentional concealment of information characterized the other two-thirds of conversations.

Types of Deception

Lying is only one way relational partners deceive each other. Deception includes all communications or omissions that serve to distort or omit the truth. Buller and Burgoon (1994) defined **deception** as intentionally managing verbal or nonverbal messages so that a receiver will believe or understand something in a way that the sender knows is false. Notice that the word intentionally is part of this definition. For example, if you truly believe that the big basketball game between your college and a rival school starts at 6:00 p.m. when it really starts at 7:00 p.m., it would not be deception if you told your friend the incorrect time. Instead, this type of misinformation might be termed a *mistake.* But when people intentionally mislead others or conceal or misrepresent the truth, deception has occurred.

There are five primary types of deception: lies, equivocations, concealments, exaggerations, and understatements. **Lies**, also called *falsifications* or *fabrications*, involve making up information or giving information that is the opposite of (or at least very different from) the truth (Ekman, 1985). For example, if you are single and someone you find unattractive approaches you at a bar and asks if you

are married, you might say you are. **Equivocation** or evasion (Bavelas, Black, Chovil, & Mullett, 1990; O'Hair & Cody, 1994) involves making an indirect, ambiguous, or contradictory statement, such as saying that your friend's new hairstyle (which you hate) is the "latest fashion" when you are asked if you like it. **Concealment** or omission involves omitting information one knows is important or relevant to a given context (Buller & Burgoon, 1994; O'Hair & Cody, 1994; Turner et al., 1975). This is what Tia did. She decided not to tell Jamal about having lunch with Robert even though she knew he might think the information was relevant to their relationship.

The last two forms of deception are opposites. **Exaggeration** or overstatement involves stretching the truth a little—often to make oneself look better or to spice up a story (O'Hair & Cody, 1994; Turner et al., 1975). The prototypical example of exaggeration involves job interviews, in which people often make their skills and experiences sound better than they actually are. **Understatement** or minimization, on the other hand, involves downplaying aspects of the truth. For instance, Tia might have told Jamal that she ran into Robert and they had a casual chat, when actually they had lunch together and talked for over an hour about deep topics.

Motives for Deception

People engage in deception for many reasons. Metts (1989; Metts & Chronis, 1986) described three major motivations for deception in close relationships. First, relational partners have **partner-focused motives**, such as using deception to avoid hurting the partner, to help the partner maintain self-esteem, to avoid worrying the partner, and to protect the partner's relationship with a third party. For example, if you say that your best friend's new hairstyle looks great when you really think it looks awful, your deceptive behavior probably has a partner-focused motive. Sometimes partner-motivated deception is seen as socially polite and relationally beneficial. Indeed, not engaging in deception when you hate your friend's new hairstyle might violate relational expectations and hurt your friend's feelings. Partner-focused deceptions also tend to be altruistic. In other words, they benefit someone else rather than the deceiver. People report using more partner-focused lies with close relational partners than strangers (Ennis, Vrji, & Chance, 2008). Similarly, people are more likely to use partner-focused lies in relationships characterized by high levels of interdependence (Kam, 2004).

Second, people deceive due to **self-focused motives**, such as wanting to enhance or protect their self-image, or wanting to shield themselves from anger, embarrassment, criticism, or other types of harm. So, if a job applicant exaggerates his qualifications during an employment interview, or a child avoids telling her mother that she failed an exam because she doesn't want to be punished, deception is based on self-focused motives. This type of deception is usually perceived as a much more significant transgression than partner-focused deception because the deceiver is acting for selfish reasons rather than for the good of the partner or the relationship. Indeed, across different cultures, self-motivated deception is perceived as more unacceptable than partner-motivated deception (Mealy, Stephan, & Urrutia, 2007; Seiter, Bruschke, & Bai, 2002). People also report feeling more guilt and shame when deceiving to benefit themselves rather than their partner (Seiter & Bruschke, 2007).

Finally, people have **relationship-focused motives** for deceiving a partner. Here the deceiver wants to limit relational harm by avoiding conflict, relational trauma, or other unpleasant experiences. For example, Tia might have concealed having lunch with Robert because she thought it would lead to an unnecessary argument or, at the very least, a misunderstanding. Notice that in this case, as well as in other cases involving relationship-focused motives, partner- and self-focused motivations may also come into play. By not telling Jamal about her lunch with Robert, Tia might also be protecting herself from false accusations (a self-focused motive) while protecting Jamal from feeling hurt and jealous (a partner-focused motive). The key is whether someone is using deception primarily to protect the relationship, rather than only to protect either oneself or the partner.

Sometimes, relationally motivated deception is seen as beneficial within a relationship. Other times,

however, such deception only complicates matters. Metts (1994) used the following excerpt from an advice column to illustrate how deception can make a bad situation even worse:

> Dear Abby: My husband and I were planning a 40th anniversary celebration, but I called it off three months ago when I learned from someone that my husband had had an affair with a young woman while he was stationed in Alameda, California, during World War II. The affair lasted about a year while he was waiting to be shipped out, but never was. When I confronted him with the facts, he admitted it, but said it was "nothing serious." . . . I am devastated. I feel betrayed, knowing I've spent the last 37 years living with a liar and a cheat. How can I ever trust him again? The bottom has fallen out of my world. (p. 217)

In this situation, even if the deception was motivated by relational concerns, such as wanting to avoid conflict and even divorce, it compounded the problem in the long run. As Metts (1994) observed, "In this case, the act of infidelity is only the first blow; the 37 years of omission is the second, and probably more devastating, hit" (p. 217). Jamal might feel the same, although on a smaller scale. Even if Tia had a good motive for not telling Jamal about her lunch with Robert, Jamal might feel betrayed because she didn't trust him enough to confide in him. Jamal may also question Tia's motivations and wonder if she didn't tell him because she really does have something to hide.

Deception Detection

The letter about the husband who cheated on his wife might spark questions about how he got away with deceiving her for so long. One might think that there must have been clues that he had had an affair or that he was concealing something from her. In reality, however, it is difficult to detect deception in everyday conversations with relational partners unless one partner says something that is blatantly false or that contradicts information the other partner knows. This is not to say that most people can successfully deceive their partners all the time. In fact, it is difficult to hide serious relational transgressions such as infidelity over a long period. However, in day-to-day conversations about relatively minor issues, deception often occurs without one partner suspecting that anything is amiss.

Detecting deception is difficult because there are no completely reliable indicators of deception. Although behaviors such as speech hesitations and body shifts often accompany deception, these behaviors can indicate general anxiety, shyness, or discomfort in addition to deception (Andersen, 2008; Burgoon, Guerrero, & Floyd, 2010). Also, stereotypic behaviors such as eye behavior are often controlled during deception. When people lie to you, for instance, they know to look you straight in the eye, which makes eye contact an unreliable cue for detecting deception (Hocking & Leathers, 1980). Perhaps the most reliable method for detecting possible deception is to compare a person's normal, truthful behavior with that individual's current behavior. If the person's behavior is noticeably different—either more anxious or more controlled—perhaps deception is occurring. There is not, however, a fool-proof method for detecting deception.

People often assume they are better able to detect deception by close relational partners than strangers or acquaintances. Research, however, suggests that this is not the case. Comadena (1982) found that friends and spouses are better at detecting deception than acquaintances. However, Comadena also found that friends are superior to spouses, suggesting that the ability to detect deception does not increase as a relationship becomes closer. Other studies have shown that romantic partners have trouble detecting deception, with accuracy rates only slightly better than chance (Levine & McCornack, 1992; Stiff, Kim, & Ramesh, 1992). In one study, people reported that their romantic partners accepted about half of their deceptive messages as truthful (Boon & McLeod, 2001). People in close relationships experience both advantages and disadvantages when it comes to detecting deception.

Advantages of Relational Closeness

Because comparing "normal" behavior to deceptive behavior is important in the deception detection process, close relational partners have an advantage over strangers: They have knowledge of the partner's typical communication style. Burgoon and her colleagues (2010) called this type of knowledge **behavioral familiarity**. Close friends, family, and romantic partners are familiar with one another's honest behavior; therefore, deviations from this behavior can tip them off that something is amiss. Relational partners also have the advantage of **informational familiarity** (Burgoon et al., 2010). In other words, you know certain information about your relational partner, so your partner cannot lie to you about that information. You can tell a stranger that you have three children instead of one, but obviously you cannot get way with telling such a lie to family members or friends.

Disadvantages of Relational Closeness

Despite these advantages, deception is difficult to detect in close relationships for at least two reasons. First, people have a **truth bias**. People expect others to be honest, so they enter conversations without suspicion and do not look for deceptive behavior. Truth biases are especially strong within close relationships and with people whom we like. People who are socially attractive are generally seen as less deceptive, and when they are caught deceiving, people usually attribute their motives for deception to more benign causes (Aune et al., 1996). McCornack and Parks (1986) argued that the truth bias makes close relational partners overly confident in the truthfulness of each other's statements, causing them to miss much of the deception that occurs. Even in the face of seemingly deceptive information, relational partners can be influenced by the truth bias (Buller, Strzyzewski, & Comstock, 1991; McCornack & Parks, 1986). Indeed, Kam (2004) found that relationship interdependence was associated with a stronger truth bias and lower accuracy in detecting deception.

The second reason close relational partners might have trouble detecting deception is that the deceiver may exert **behavioral control**. People try to control their nervous or guilty behaviors to appear friendly and truthful. Several deception researchers have demonstrated that, regardless of whether deceivers are interacting with friends or strangers, they try to control their behavior so that they seem honest (see Ekman & Friesen, 1969; Zuckerman, DePaulo, & Rosenthal, 1981). However, this may be particularly true for close relational partners, who have more to lose if the deception is discovered. Buller and Aune (1987) found that when people deceived friends or romantic partners, they became friendlier and showed less anxiety as the interaction progressed than when they deceived strangers. In comparison to deceiving strangers, people tried harder to look truthful when deceiving relational partners, in part by "putting on a happy face" and hiding nervousness.

Effects of Deception on Relationships

Paradoxically, research shows that deception can help people develop and maintain relationships, but it can also lead to conflict and relationship breakup. Most people believe that honesty is an absolutely essential ingredient in the recipe for close, healthy relationships. Yet people can identify situations where it is important, even ethical, to deceive their partner (Boon & McLeod, 2001). For example, if Jamal overhears someone saying something really negative about Tia, he might decide not to tell her because it would hurt her feelings too much. Partner-focused deceptions such as these are often regarded as acceptable and appropriate, and can help maintain positive relationships.

Cole (2001) discussed two other ways that deception is associated with the development and maintenance of relationships. First, deception may help couples avoid arguments, thereby promoting relational harmony. For example, a mother who is mediating an argument between her two sons may try to sound evenhanded even though she thinks one of the sons is more to blame. Similarly, your best friend might understate how hurt she feels when you receive an honor that she wanted so you won't feel badly.

Second, deception allows people to downplay their faults and accentuate their virtues, which may help them develop and maintain relationships (Cole, 2001). Two lines of research support this idea. Work on the benefit of positive illusions (Murray, Holmes,

& Griffin, 1996) suggests that people who hold idealized images of one another are most satisfied in their relationships. So, if Tia exaggerates by telling Jamal, "You are ten times more attractive than Robert," her exaggeration would contribute to his positive illusions and perhaps lead him to feel more secure about her having lunch with Robert.

Work on date initiation also supports the idea that people use deception to emphasize their positive qualities and minimize their negative qualities. In one study, 46% of men and 36% of women admitted that they have lied to initiate a date with someone (Rowatt, Druen, & Miles, 1999). In another study on deception in the early stages of dating (Tooke & Camire, 1991), men were more likely than women to exaggerate (or lie about) how successful they were, and to act more committed and sincere than they actually were. Women, in contrast, were more likely to try to enhance their appearance by engaging in behaviors such as wearing clothing that made them look thinner and using makeup to exaggerate desirable facial features. Furthermore, people are most likely to lie when initiating dates with potential partners who are very physically attractive (Rowatt, Cunningham, & Druen, 1999). With Internet dating on the rise, people may have more opportunities than ever before to deceive dating prospects on these issues.

Of course, deceiving a partner about one's positive versus negative qualities can backfire. Eventually a deceiver is seen more truthfully, which may lead to disappointment and disillusion. It is thus important to remember that deception can have negative consequences for relationships. When people uncover a significant deception, they usually feel a host of negative emotions, including anxiety, anger, and distress (e.g., McCornack & Levine, 1990). People who use deception frequently in their relationships report lower levels of commitment, intimacy, and closeness. Similarly, when people perceive their partners as dishonest, they report less relational satisfaction and commitment (Cole, 2001). Deception is also a leading cause of conflict and relationship breakup (see Chapters 14 and 15). Finally, some deceptions are not only harmful to people's relationships, but also to their health. Lucchetti (1999) found that one-third of sexually

udents avoided talking about their
ith their partners, even though many
hat doing so would help them have
nd 20% of these same college stu-
dents ... that they had intentionally misrepre-
sented their sexual history to their partner.

HURTFUL MESSAGES

Deception is one of many forms of hurtful messages. As noted previously, messages that communicate devaluation are especially hurtful. Such messages are associated with less satisfying relationships. Specifically, people report more distancing and less relational closeness when their partner frequently uses hurtful messages (Vangelisti, 1994b; Vangelisti & Young, 2000). Messages perceived to be intentional are especially hurtful and damaging to relationships (McLaren & Solomon, 2008; Mills, Nazar, & Farrell, 2002; Vangelisti, 1994b; Vangelisti & Young, 2000). For example, if you think someone said something to purposely hurt your feelings, you are likely to be more upset than if you thought the comment was not intended to hurt you. You are also more likely to distance yourself from someone who frequently uses hurtful messages (McLaren & Solomon, 2008). Messages are also more or less hurtful based on the topic they address, and the form of communication they take. One study showed that hurtful messages are less psychologically painful when they are lightened through humor (Young & Bippus, 2001). Another study suggested that messages focusing on relationship issues are even more hurtful than those focusing on personality traits (Vangelisti, 1994b).

Types of Hurtful Messages

To determine the specific types of messages people find hurtful, Vangelisti (1994b) identified 10 types of hurtful messages (see Box 13.4) from college students' reports. The most common were evaluations, accusations, and informative statements (Vangelisti, 1994b). Research has also examined hurtful messages between parents and children. In one study, children (age 7 to 10) and parents were asked to describe a time when a hurtful message had occurred in the context of their parent-child relationship (Mills et al., 2002). Children described situations involving discipline or disregard, whereas mothers described situations involving misconduct or disregard. Under the category of disregard, children mentioned issues such as sibling favoritism, teasing, criticism, rebuffs, and statements showing disrespect. Similarly, mothers wrote about times they felt criticized, rebuffed, or disrespected. Together, these studies demonstrate that feeling devalued is a central component of hurtful messages for young children as well as adults.

BOX 13.4 Highlights

Hurtful Messages

Evaluation	Negative judgments of worth, value, or quality (e.g., "This relationship has been a waste of my time").
Accusation	Charges about a person's faults or actions (e.g., "You are a selfish and rude person")
Informative statement	Disclosure of unwanted information (e.g., "I only dated you because I was on the rebound").
Directive	Directions or commands that go against one's desires or imply negative thoughts or feelings (e.g., "Don't call me anymore").

Expressions of desire	Statements about one's preferences or desires (e.g., "I wish you were more like your brother").
Threat	A declaration of intent to inflict punishment under certain conditions. (e.g., "If you see him again I'll break up with you")
Question	Inquiry or interrogation that implies a negative judgment (e.g., "Aren't you finished with school yet?").
Joke	A witticism or prank that insults the partner (e.g., "I guess your wife wears the pants in the family and you wear the skirt").
Deception	A statement that is untrue or distorts the truth (e.g., One partner says, "Trust me, I didn't do it" when the other partner knows this is false).

SOURCE: Definitions adapted from Vangelisti (1994b).

Responses to Hurtful Messages

Research has examined three general ways people respond to hurtful messages: active verbal responses, acquiescent responses, and invulnerable responses. These responses occur in both adult relationships (Vangelisti & Crumley, 1998) and parent-child relationships (Mills et al., 2002).

Active Verbal Responses

Active verbal responses focus on confronting one's partner about hurtful remarks. Some active verbal responses are more positive than others. For example, questioning the partner and asking for an explanation are active verbal responses that may help partners understand one another. Other active verbal responses, such as sarcasm and verbal attacks on the partner, can lead to an escalation of negativity. Active verbal responses are the most frequently reported response in both adult relationships and parent-child relationships (Mills et al., 2002). People may be especially likely to use active verbal responses when they are in satisfying relationships (Vangelisti & Crumley, 1998). Couples in satisfying relationships may talk to one another more, which could help them repair the psychological damage caused by hurtful messages. Couples in happy relationships may also be better able to withstand the use of more negative active verbal responses than those in unhappy relationships.

Acquiescent Responses

Instead of talking about the hurtful message, people sometimes use **acquiescent responses**, which involve giving in and acknowledging the partner's ability to inflict hurt. For example, people might cry, apologize ("I'm sorry I make you feel that way"), or concede ("Fine, I won't see him anymore"). People use acquiescent responses when they are deeply hurt by something a close relational partner said (Vangelisti & Crumley, 1998). To that end, the quickest way for people to stop emotional pain may be to give in and acknowledge their feelings.

Invulnerable Responses

Invulnerable responses also avoid talking about the hurtful message and involve acting unaffected by the hurtful remark. For instance, you might ignore the hurtful message, laugh it off, become quiet, or withdraw. Both acquiescent and invulnerable responses may be more likely than active verbal strategies when people become flooded with emotion and have difficulty talking about their feelings.

THE AFTERMATH OF HURTFUL EVENTS

As we discuss in Chapter 15, issues related to jealousy, infidelity, and deception, along with negative spirals of hurtful messages, often cause relational breakups. Yet many romantic couples and friends survive and even thrive after experiencing transgressions. Doing so, however, is a challenging enterprise. Fincham (2000) used the metaphor of "kissing porcupines" to describe this challenge:

> Imagine two porcupines huddled together in the cold of an Alaskan winter's night, each providing life-sustaining warmth to the other. As they draw ever closer together the painful prick from the other's quills leads them to instinctively withdraw—until the need for warmth draws them together again. This "kiss of the porcupines" is an apt metaphor for the human condition, and it illustrates two fundamental assumptions . . . humans harm each other and humans are social animals. (p. 2)

As Fincham put it, acceptance of these two assumptions results in the following challenge: "how to maintain relatedness with fellow humans in the face of being harmed by them" (p. 2). It follows, then, to explore how partners use forgiveness, forgiving communication, and remedial strategies to try and meet this challenge.

Forgiveness

Forgiveness plays a critical role in repairing a relationship after a transgression occurs (Emmers & Canary, 1996). But what does it mean to forgive someone? Waldron and Kelley (2008) defined **forgiveness** as a relational process that has four characteristics: (1) acknowledgment of harmful conduct, (2) an extension of undeserved mercy, (3) an emotional transformation, and (4) relationship renegotiation.

Harmful Conduct

For forgiveness to even be necessary, one or both partners must acknowledge that there has been wrongdoing. Behavior that requires forgiveness in one relationship may be acceptable in another

relationship. For example, Tia decided not to tell Jamal about her lunch with Robert because she thought he might get upset. This tells us that Tia understood that the unwritten (and perhaps unspoken) rules of their relationship dictated that she should not spend extended time with Robert. If, however, there was no such "rule," and both Tia and Jamal instead had an understanding that they could spend as much time with ex-boyfriends and ex-girlfriends as they wanted, then there would be no need for forgiveness because no wrongdoing occurred.

Extension of Undeserved Mercy

Second, the hurt person must make a decision to extend mercy to the partner. The idea that such mercy is undeserved is highlighted by Freedman and Enright (1996), who stated, "There is a decidedly paradoxical quality to forgiveness as the forgiver gives up the resentment, to which he or she has a right, and gives the gift of compassion, to which the offender has no right" (p. 983). The decision to forgive sets the process of forgiveness in motion and makes statements such as "I forgive you" meaningful (Fincham, 2000). You have probably been in a situation, for instance, when someone told you "I forgive you" but you did not really believe it. When this happens, people doubt that the hurt person has truly made the decision to forgive them.

Emotional Transformation

Forgiveness involves an emotional transformation that allows hurt individuals to let go of negative feelings (Boon & Sulsky, 1997; Waldron & Kelley, 2008). When individuals are hurt, their natural reaction is to get revenge, seek restitution, or avoid the person who hurt them (McCullough, Worthington, & Rachal, 1997). Forgiveness entails getting rid of these impulses and instead feeling positively about oneself and the partner. In line with this emotional transformation, hurt individuals report engaging in more positive forms of communication, such as talking over issues and calmly renegotiating relationship rules, once they have forgiven their partner (Bachman & Guerrero, 2006b; McCullough et al., 1998). In contrast, when people do not forgive their partners, they tend to engage in more vengeful communication (e.g., arguing and name-calling), de-escalation (e.g., breaking up or dating others), and avoidance. Being able to transform one's emotions also has benefits for the hurt person. As one of the participants in Kelley's (1998) study on forgiveness wrote, "I began to realize that this anger was not only torturing him, but myself as well. It was eating me up inside and making me more of an angry person. Why should I suffer for what he has done?" (p. 264).

Relationship Renegotiation

Sometimes the hurt individual is motivated to reconcile with the partner. Other times the relationship de-escalates or ends even though forgiveness is granted. Either way, forgiveness entails renegotiating the nature of one's relationship, including rules and expectations for future behavior. In a study examining the relational consequences of forgiveness, Kelley (1998) found that around 28% of participants indicated that their relationship had returned to "normal" after forgiveness was granted, around 36%

reported that their relationship had deteriorated, and around 32% reported that their relationship had strengthened. Thus, forgiveness does not always entail reconciliation. For example, you might forgive your friend for lying to you but still not feel as close to her as you once did. Reconciliation can also occur without forgiveness. Jamal might not forgive Tia if she has lunch with Robert again, but he might value their relationship enough to stay with her anyway.

Forgiving Communication

The way people communicate forgiveness is connected to how partners renegotiate their relationships following hurtful events. People communicate forgiveness in a variety of ways. Waldron and Kelley (2005) identified five specific ways people show forgiveness following a partner's relational transgression: (1) explicit forgiveness, (2) nonverbal display, (3) minimization, (4) discussion, and (5) conditional forgiveness. To determine the strategy you used to grant forgiveness the last time you forgave someone after being hurt, take the test in Box 13.5.

BOX 13.5 Put Yourself to the Test

Forgiveness-Granting Strategies

Think about the last time you forgave a relational partner (e.g., a good friend, family member, or romantic partner) after he or she hurt your feelings. Use the following scale to determine which strategies you used the most: 0 = not used at all, 4 = used moderately, 7 = used extensively.

	Moderately				Extensively		
1. I gave my partner a look that communicated forgiveness.	0	1	2	3	4	5	6	7
2. I told my partner I had forgiven him or her but I really didn't forgive my partner until later.	0	1	2	3	4	5	6	7
3. I joked about it so my partner would know he or she was forgiven.	0	1	2	3	4	5	6	7
4. I initiated discussion about the transgression.	0	1	2	3	4	5	6	7

(Continued)

(Continued)

	Moderately						Extensively	
5. I told my partner I forgave her or him.	0	1	2	3	4	5	6	7
6. I gave my partner a hug.	0	1	2	3	4	5	6	7
7. I told my partner not to worry about it.	0	1	2	3	4	5	6	7
8. I discussed the transgression with my partner.	0	1	2	3	4	5	6	7
9. The expression on my face said "I forgive you."	0	1	2	3	4	5	6	7
10. I told my partner I would forgive him or her only if things changed.	0	1	2	3	4	5	6	7
11. I told my partner it was no big deal.	0	1	2	3	4	5	6	7
12. I touched my partner in a way that communicated forgiveness.	0	1	2	3	4	5	6	7
13. I told my partner I would forgive her or him if the transgression never happened again.	0	1	2	3	4	5	6	7

To obtain your results, average your scores for the following items:

Nonverbal display: Items (1+6+9+12) / 4 = _____

Conditional forgiveness: Items (2+10+13) / 3 = _____

Minimization: Items (3+7+11) / 3 = _____

Discussion: Items (4+8) / 2 = _____

Explicit forgiveness: (5) = _____

Higher scores indicate that you used more of a particular strategy.

SOURCE: Adapted from Waldron, V. R., & Kelley, D. L., Forgiving communication as a response to relational transgressions, in *Journal of Social and Personal Relationships, 22*, 723–742. Copyright © 2005, SAGE, Inc.

Explicit Forgiveness

Explicit forgiveness, which is the most common way to communicate forgiveness (Kelley, 1998), involves making a direct statement, such as "I forgive you." Making such a statement appears to have positive consequences for relationships. Explicit forgiveness is the clearest way to communicate forgiveness to a transgressor and convey that one wants to repair the relationship (Scobie & Scobie, 1998). When the hurt person verbally says, "I forgive you" (or something similar), both partners also have more closure and the relationship has a better chance of strengthening instead of declining (Waldron & Kelley, 2005).

Nonverbal Display

Sometimes people display forgiveness nonverbally through behaviors such as smiles, hugs, or head nods. These types of nonverbal displays are likely to be used when people want to repair the relationship, indicate that a transgression is not that serious, or avoid confrontation (Gracyalny, Jackson, & Guerrero, 2008; Kelley, 1998). Nonverbal displays often occur as part of a conciliatory pattern of communication with the transgressor engaging in constructive communication such as making apologies and showing affection, and the victim reciprocating by showing forgiveness nonverbally (Gracyalny et al., 2008).

Discussion

The discussion-based approach involves "explicit acknowledgment of the transgression, mutual perspective-taking, and dialogue" (Waldron & Kelley, 2005, p. 735). People who use this strategy often grant forgiveness within the context of a deeper discussion of the hurtful event and its consequences for the relationship. Thus, discussion can include renegotiating relationship rules, explaining why and how the transgression occurred, and expressing feelings to one another.

Minimizing Approach

When people use the minimizing approach, they emphasize that the hurtful event was not that "big of a deal" and that the partner should not worry about it anymore. Minimization is most likely when the transgression is not very serious (Guerrero & Bachman, 2008). So, Jamal might be likely to use minimization ("Okay, it doesn't seem like that big of a deal") if he believes Tia's lunch with Robert was innocent. People may also use minimizing strategies when they do not want to invest any more time and energy into dealing with the issue (Waldron & Kelley, 1998). Jamal might decide that he has thought enough about Robert and wants to move on. If, on the other hand, he continues to be suspicious of Tia's motives, he might use conditional forgiveness ("It's okay, as long as you promise not to see him again").

Conditional Forgiveness

Conditional forgiveness is used when people grant forgiveness contingent upon the partner's behavior. As such, conditional forgiveness is an "if/then" strategy. The victim may make statements such as "I will only forgive you if you do X or Y." Conditional forgiveness was shown in a classic episode of the popular television series *Friends* when Ross's new wife, Emily, told Ross that she would only forgive him for saying Rachel's name during their wedding ceremony if he promised to never see Rachel again. Some scholars have pointed out that conditional forgiveness is often a temporary state, and that relationship deterioration is more likely when forgiveness is granted with conditions (Waldron & Kelley, 2005), as it was for Ross and Emily. Yet conditional forgiveness may be the only appropriate course of action, at least initially, when a person has been deeply hurt. As Fincham (2000) noted, forgiveness is contingent not only on the hurt person's change in motivation but also on the offending person's change in behavior. If a person does not believe that the relational partner will change the hurtful behavior, that person is unlikely to be forgiving.

Conditions That Promote or Impede Forgiveness and Forgiving Communication

As Fincham's porcupine quote suggests, forgiveness is not always easy, nor should it be. Forgiveness can help heal a relationship, but it cannot always save it. And, in some cases it may be better not to save the relationship. For instance, people who forgive too readily might stay in abusive relationships (Katz, Street, & Arias, 1995). So how do people determine—consciously or unconsciously—whether to forgive or not, and which, if any, forms of forgiving communication they should use? Some research suggests that women may generally be more forgiving than men (Miller, Worthington, & McDaniel, 2008). Research also demonstrates that victims are more likely to grant forgiveness and use positive communication with their partner if (1) the seriousness of the transgression does not prohibit forgiveness and (2) the relationship was of high quality prior to the transgression.

The Seriousness of the Transgression

It probably goes without saying that people are less forgiving when a transgression is especially serious (Bennett & Earwaker, 1994; Girard &

Mullet, 1997). But what might be less obvious is that victims sometimes reassess the transgression as less serious if they decide to stay in the relationship. In Kelley's (1998) study, 44% of victims forgave their partners after reframing the situation so that the transgression seemed less severe. For example, they came to understand why the transgressor had behaved in a certain way or realized that the transgressor had not intended to hurt them.

The seriousness of a transgression also relates to how much a behavior violates relationship expectations. For example, hurtful events vary in the extent to which someone considers them unacceptable. When people consider a hurtful event to be a highly negative violation of their expectations, they are less likely to forgive their partner and less likely to engage in positive forms of communication, including explicit forgiveness, nonverbal displays, and minimization (Bachman & Guerrero, 2006a; Guerrero & Bachman, 2010). Even if people do forgive their partner, they are likely to do so with conditions (Guerrero & Bachman, 2010; Waldron & Kelley, 2005). Recall the situation between Jamal and Tia. Jamal might be upset that Tia concealed information from him, but he is unlikely to regard this transgression as one of the worst things Tia could do. Therefore, he would be more likely to forgive Tia for her deception. On the other hand, if Tia really was having an affair with Robert, Jamal would be much more likely to see that as a highly negative violation of a relationship rule—and as a consequence, be much less likely to forgive her.

Relationship and Partner Characteristics

People are also more likely to forgive their partners and engage in positive communication when they are in high-quality relationships with rewarding partners. In Kelley's (1998) study, 35% of victims indicated that forgiveness was granted because they wanted to repair their relationship. Love was a motivation behind forgiveness for another 15% of the participants. People are also likely to evaluate transgressions as less serious, to forgive their partners, and to engage in more positive communication, such as nonverbal displays of forgiveness, if they perceive their partner to be socially attractive and rewarding (Aune et al., 1996; Bachman & Guerrero,

2006a; Guerrero & Bachman, 2010). Forgiveness may also be especially likely when victims perceive their partner to be more rewarding than they perceive themselves to be (Sidelinger & Booth-Butterfield, 2007). In addition, people are more likely to report using positive communication and discussion-based forgiveness following relational transgressions when their relationships are highly committed and emotionally involved (Guerrero & Bachman, 2010; Menzies-Toman & Lydon, 2005; Roloff, Soule, & Carey, 2001). Finally, people in committed, satisfying relationships tend to evaluate their partner's transgressions as less serious than do those in less satisfying, less committed relationships (Menzies-Toman & Lydon, 2005; Young, 2004).

Remedial Strategies

Remedial strategies also influence whether or not forgiveness is forthcoming. **Remedial strategies** are attempts to correct problems, restore one's positive face, or repair the relationship. To illustrate, if you are the transgressor, what strategies can you use to try to save your relationship? The answer is far from simple; you cannot erase your offense with the wave of a magic wand, and your relationship might never again be the same even if your partner forgives you. However, research on discovered deception (Aune, Metts, & Hubbard, 1998), sexual infidelity (Mongeau, Hale, & Alles, 1994), social predicaments (Cupach, 1994), and forgiveness (Kelley, 1998) suggests that people use various remedial strategies when they have committed a transgression.

Apologies and Concessions

Apologizing and admitting guilt is one of the most obvious and frequently used remedial strategies. However, not all apologies are equal. Apologies can vary from a simple statement such as "I'm sorry" to more elaborate forms of apology that include expressing guilt and remorse, derogating oneself, promising to make up for the bad behavior, and promising never to engage in the transgression again (Cupach, 1994; Schlenker & Darby, 1981). When people have committed serious transgressions, elaborate apologies are more successful than simple ones (Darby & Schlenker, 1982, 1989). In general, apologies are most effective when they are perceived as sincere, elicit empathy, and are given voluntarily.

Sincere apologies can lead the victim to perceive the transgressor as a generally good and thoughtful person despite the hurtful event. In Kelley's (1998) study, 31% of victims indicated that they forgave their partners because they acted in ways that showed remorse or accepted responsibility, such as apologizing for their actions. Victims are also more likely to say that they used explicit forgiveness and engaged in positive communication toward the transgressor if the transgressor made a sincere apology (Bachman & Guerrero, 2006b; Gracylyn et al., 2008).

Apologies are most likely to be effective if the victim feels empathy for the transgressor. It may seem odd that a victim should feel empathy when the victim is the one who was hurt. However, if the transgressor expresses negative emotions—such as guilt, remorse, and even fear of losing the partner— the victim might feel badly for the transgressor. As McCullough and colleagues (1997) put it, empathy can lead to "an increased caring" for the transgressor that "overshadows the salience" of the hurtful action and leads to forgiveness (p. 333). The relationships between apologies, empathy, forgiveness, and communication are depicted in Figure 13.2.

Finally, it is important that the apology is perceived as voluntary rather than forced. Studies have shown that people are more likely to forgive their partners for engaging in infidelity if they confess on their own and concede their guilt (Afifi et al., 2001; Mongeau et al., 1994). In fact, in Mongeau and associates' study, concessions emerged as the most effective strategy for repairing a relationship following infidelity. However, if the apology and accompanying confession are offered after someone is accused of a transgression, the apology loses its effectiveness because it seems forced rather than honest. Of course, many people do not want to apologize and admit guilt if their partner does not know about the transgression (Mongeau & Schulz, 1997). But if they wait until the partner accuses them (as would be the case if Tia apologizes), their apology might be seen as the result of being caught rather than a free admission of guilt.

Appeasement

Types of appeasement, or compensation, behaviors have appeared in the literature on remedial strategies (Waldron & Kelley, 2008). For instance, people who seek forgiveness often use ingratiation strategies such as promising to make up

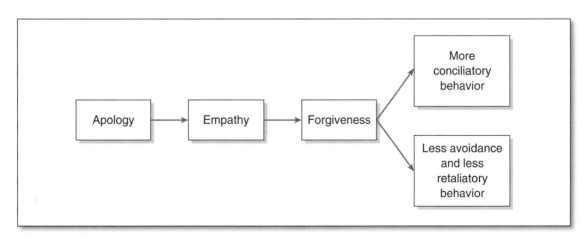

Figure 13.2 Model of the Forgiveness Process

SOURCE: From McCullough, M. E., Worthington, E. L., & Rachal, C., Interpersonal forgiving in close relationships, in *Journal of Personality and Social Psychology, 73*, p. 327. Copyright © 1997, the American Psychological Association. Reprinted with permission.

for what they did (Kelley, 1998). When people are caught deceiving their partners, they sometimes use soothing strategies that are designed to appease the target. Specifically, Aune and his colleagues (1998) found that people used remedial strategies such as complimenting the partner, trying to be more attentive to the partner, spending more time with the partner, saying "I love you" more often, and buying the partner gifts and flowers. With all of these strategies, the transgressor seeks to "compensate" for the hurtful behavior by being particularly nice and helpful. Tia uses an indirect appeasement strategy when she says: "I told him [Robert] that I love you and we are engaged." She might also show Jamal more affection to convince him that he is the one she loves. Appeasement has been found to be a fairly effective strategy, although some research suggests that apologies are even more effective (Waldron & Kelley, 2008). When people report that their partner used appeasement, they are more likely to say that they granted forgiveness using nonverbal displays, such as hugs or smiles (Gracylyn et al., 2008). However, they are also more likely to say that forgiveness was conditional (Gracylyn et al., 2008). Waldron and Kelley (2008) suggested that appeasement (or compensation) is sometimes used as part of the bargaining process that is associated with conditional forgiveness. So, if Jamal says that he will forgive Tia if she is sure that it is him whom she loves, Tia might engage in appeasement strategies (e.g., spending extra time with him or giving him a special gift) to meet his conditions and prove her love for him.

Explanations

When transgressors try to explain why they engaged in an untoward act, they are using excuses or justifications to account for their behavior. When transgressors use **excuses,** they try to minimize responsibility for their negative behavior by focusing on their inability to control their own actions or by shifting the blame to others (Aune et al., 1998; Cupach, 1994; Mongeau & Schulz, 1997). For example, Tia might offer an excuse by saying, "I didn't know I was going to run into Robert; it just happened." Tia could also blame Robert by saying,

"He insisted that we have lunch and I was afraid of hurting his feelings." When transgressors use **justifications**, they try to minimize the negative implications of the transgression by denying their behavior was wrong or that the transgression was severe (Aune et al., 1998; Cupach, 1994; Mongeau & Schulz, 1997). Tia offers a justification when she says that having lunch with Robert didn't really mean anything to her.

Explanations can play an important role in repairing relationships, yet the degree to which they are effective varies. Waldron and Kelley (2008) argued that explanations provide information that "is crucial in deciding whether forgiveness is warranted and whether the relationship can be mended" (p. 115). However, explanations are generally not as effective as apologies or appeasements, and can even be negatively related to forgiveness (Gracylyn et al., 2008). The quality of the explanation makes a difference. Some explanations are more plausible and forgivable than others. Explaining that you talked with an ex-lover at a party because he or she seemed depressed, for instance, is probably a better explanation than saying you were so drunk you couldn't help flirting with her or him.

Denials

With explanations, transgressors admit some responsibility for their hurtful actions. However, with denials, or refusals, transgressors argue that they should not be held accountable for their behavior or that a transgression never occurred. Some scholars believe denials are a special type of excuse, one that is good enough for the transgressor to feel that a relational rule has not been broken. Again, the television show *Friends* provides a great example of denial as a remedial strategy. Ross and Rachel have been dating for some time when they get into an argument and agree to "take a break." That night, Ross has sex with another woman. When Rachel finds out about Ross's one-night stand, she is very upset. Ross, however, denies he has done anything wrong because they were "on a break." Ross refuses to take any blame because he does not see his behavior as a transgression. This example illustrates the complexity of relational transgressions—what is perceived as a transgression by one party might not necessarily be perceived as a transgression by the other. Not surprisingly, Mongeau and his colleagues (1994) found refusals to be an ineffective remedial strategy that was likely to aggravate rather than repair the relationship. Gracylyn and her associates (2008) also found that denials were associated with more de-escalation and a greater likelihood of relationship breakup.

Avoidance and Evasion

Avoidance and evasion, or silence, involve efforts to avoid discussing the transgression. Transgressors who use this strategy often report that talking about the problem only makes it worse and it is better to let the transgression fade into the background of the relationship and be minimized (Aune et al., 1998). Transgressors using this strategy might also refuse to give an explanation for their behaviors. If avoidance and evasion are used after an apology and forgiveness has been granted, it may be effective. But, if the primary strategy is avoidance and evasion, the problem might be left unresolved and could resurface in the future. Because relational transgressions often lead to relational change, which sometimes includes the altering of rules and boundaries, avoidance and evasion may not be a particularly effective strategy in the long run. Indeed,

Mongeau and colleagues (1994) found that avoidance (or silence) was an ineffective strategy for repairing relationships after infidelity had occurred.

Relationship Talk

Relationship talk involves talking about the transgression within the larger context of the relationship. Aune and associates (1998) discussed two specific types of relationship talk. The first, which they called **relationship invocation**, involves expressing attitudes or beliefs about the relationship, or using the qualities of the relationship as a backdrop for interpreting the transgression. For example, transgressors might say, "Our relationship is strong enough to survive this," or "I love you too much to lose you over something like this." In Tia's case, she might tell Jamal that their relationship is much better than Robert and hers ever was. The second type of relationship talk, **metatalk** (Aune et al., 1998), involves explicitly discussing the transgression's effect on the relationship. For instance, after conceding that she was wrong not to tell Jamal about her lunch with Robert, Tia might say that she wants Jamal to trust her. This might lead Tia and Jamal into a discussion about rules of honesty in their relationship. They might also discuss the future of their relationship, and the type of marriage they want to have.

SUMMARY AND APPLICATION

In a perfect world, people would never hurt one another. But the world is full of imperfect people leading imperfect lives. Coping with relational transgressions and hurt feelings is a difficult challenge that many relational partners face. Sometimes the damage from infidelity, deception, or other transgressions is too great, and the relationship ends. Other times, like Fincham's kissing porcupines, people decide to draw back together despite the pain, hoping that they will not be "pricked" again.

So what advice can communication researchers give to people like Jamal, who are hurt because their partners engaged in relational transgressions? (At minimum, Tia conceals the fact that she had

lunch with Robert from Jamal. More seriously, she could be hiding an affair.) When coping with transgressions, it is important for partners to weigh the severity of the offense against how much they value the relationship. When a transgression destroys trust in a relationship, the relationship may not recover. However, many transgressions can be repaired by renegotiating the rules and boundaries of the relationship or by offering apologies and explanations for one's actions. For example, open discussion might reaffirm to Jamal that Tia is completely committed to him. Jamal may also learn that she concealed her lunch with Robert to protect him from hurt feelings. For her part, Tia might learn not to conceal such information from Jamal in the future. She might also apologize for not telling Jamal about her lunch with Robert, and she might use appeasement strategies and relationship invocation to show Jamal how much he and their relationship mean to her.

If Jamal continues to feel jealous, he should use integrative communication and express his feelings rather than destructive responses such as negative communication and violent behavior. He should also appraise the situation to determine the level of threat that Robert actually poses. Perhaps he is overreacting and should trust Tia rather than continuing to be suspicious. Or, perhaps he has real reason to be jealous. In either case, it is important for people to remember that romantic jealousy can stem from a real or imagined (or sometimes exaggerated) relationship between a loved person and a rival.

If Jamal decides to forgive Tia for deceiving him, research suggests that he should tell her explicitly "I forgive you." If he regards her transgression as serious, he might add that it is important that she is honest with him when similar situations arise in the future. If the relationship is to be repaired, Jamal needs to move from feeling a need to retaliate against or avoid Tia, to using positive, conciliatory forms of communication. A transgression can be a bump in the relationship road or a detour sign; it depends on the seriousness of the offense, the strategies used to cope with the problem, and the willingness or unwillingness of the victim to forgive the transgressor.

DISCUSSION QUESTIONS

1. Think about the hurtful events that you have experienced. Why did you choose to forgive some people and not others? Are some hurtful events more forgivable than others? What variables do you think are most important in determining whether or not you forgive someone?

2. Think about the last time you or someone you know was jealous. Which of the communicative responses to jealousy did you or the person you know use? Did these responses make the situation better or worse?

3. Under what circumstances, if any, do you think it is okay to deceive a friend or relational partner? When would you feel betrayed if your friend or partner deceived you?

STUDENT STUDY SITE

Visit the study site at **www.sagepub.com/guerrero3e** for e-flashcards, survey and assessments from the chapter, and SAGE journal articles.

14

Coping With Conflict

When Relational Partners Disagree

Mary and Doug catch their teenage daughter, Amanda, smoking after school with her friends. Because Mary is convinced that Amanda's friends are a bad influence on her, she wants to ground Amanda for a month, making her come home immediately after school. Doug, however, thinks grounding will be more of a punishment for the parents than Amanda, because she will be moping around the house complaining all the time and arguing with her twin sister, Megan. Instead, Doug proposes that they deduct the cost of a carton of cigarettes from Amanda's weekly allowance for the next six months. Mary objects, saying that she does not want Amanda to be motivated to change her behavior because of money. Both parents feel strongly that their punishment is best, leading to a disagreement.

I f you were Amanda's parent, how would you want to handle this situation? From Amanda's perspective, which punishment would most likely be effective? Are there other types of punishment—besides grounding or reducing Amanda's allowance—that might actually be more effective? What conflict management styles might Mary and Doug use to deal with this situation, and are there any conflict behaviors that are especially destructive? The literature on interpersonal conflict demonstrates that people have a variety of options for dealing with conflict. Some of these options involve cooperating and managing conflict productively and effectively. Other options lead to distress, competition, and sometimes exacerbation of the problem.

In this chapter, we examine how relational partners cope with disagreement. First, we define conflict and discuss the role conflict plays in close relationships, including those between spouses, family members, friends, and romantic partners. Next, we turn our attention to how people communicate during conflict situations. We review six conflict styles—competitive fighting, compromising, collaborating, indirect fighting, avoiding, and yielding. We also discuss patterns of communication, such as negative reciprocity and demand-withdrawal sequences. The chapter ends with practical rules for constructive conflict management.

CONFLICT IN RELATIONSHIPS

Think about all the positive and negative experiences you have had with close friends, family members, and romantic partners. As you reflect on these experiences, can you think of a close relationship of yours that has not included some conflict or disagreement? If you can, that relationship is the exception to the rule.

Defining Conflict

Notice that we asked you to try and think of a close relationship that did not include some level of conflict or disagreement. When people think about "conflict" in their relationships, they usually imagine angry voices, name-calling, and relationship problems. However, conflict is more synonymous with the term *disagreement* than with yelling or arguing. People can engage in conflict by using positive forms of communication during disagreements, such as collaboration and compromise. Voices can be calm, negative emotions muted,

positions can be validated, and relationships can be strengthened instead of weakened.

Most scholars define **conflict** broadly as disagreement between two interdependent people who perceive that they have incompatible goals (Cahn, 1992; Hocker & Wilmot, 1998). Because the people are interdependent, lack of compatibility can interfere with each person's ability to reach personal goals. Understandably, some forms of incompatibility are more important than others. Hocker and Wilmot (1998) argued that incompatibility will likely lead to a struggle when rewards are scarce. In short, conflict is most likely when incompatible goals are important to both people and hard to obtain. The various issues linked to conflict in different relationships, as listed in Box 14.1, highlight incompatibility as the central theme. For example, you can imagine Amanda (a teenager) wanting to stay out later than her parents want her to (curfew), Amanda and her sister arguing about who gets more space in the bedroom closet they share (territory), and Amanda's parents arguing over how to best discipline her for smoking (children).

BOX 14.1 Highlights

Common Conflict Issues in Various Relationships

Parents and Young Children	Parents and Teenagers	Siblings	Married Couples
possessions	curfew	possessions	household labor
caretaking*	friends	privacy	money and possessions
hurtful behavior**	dating patterns	parental attention	jealousy/possessiveness
rules and manners	privacy	territory	sex
need for assistance***	lifestyle choices		children

SOURCES: Canary et al. (1995); Dunn (1983); Dunn & Kendrick (1982); Eisenberg (1992); Gottman (1994); Mead, Vatcher, Wyne, & Roberts (1990).

*Caretaking refers to tasks such as having to take a bath; **hurtful behavior refers to behaviors such as calling a sibling names; ***need for assistance refers to demands to be helped or left alone, such as a child not wanting any help brushing teeth.

Conflict is most likely to occur in the context of close relationships. In a study by Argyle and Furnham (1983), people rated different relationships in terms of frequency of conflict and degree of emotional and relational closeness. Spouses reported the most closeness but also the most conflict. Family relationships, including parents and children or siblings, were also high in both conflict and closeness. Conversely, relationships between neighbors were low in both conflict and closeness. Lloyd and Cate (1985) found that conflict increased as relational partners became more committed and interdependent. Their study makes an important point: Conflict is a normal part of many close relationships.

Frequency and Characteristics of Conflict in Various Relationships

Across the life span, conflict is more likely to occur within family and romantic relationships than friendships or work relationships (Sillars, Canary, & Tafoya, 2004). In parent-child relationships, the most conflict tends to occur when children are toddlers or teenagers. One study showed that disputes between mothers and their 18- to 36-month-old children occurred around seven times per hour, with about half of these disputes being brief and the other half lasting longer and being more competitive (Dunn & Munn, 1987). During the teenage years, around 20% of parents and adolescents complain that they have too much conflict with one another, with conflict frequently revolving around issues such as curfews, friends, dating patterns, privacy, and other lifestyle choices (Canary et al., 1995). When children reach late adolescence and early adulthood, conflict typically declines (Paikoff & Brooks-Gunn, 1991).

Like conflict between parents and children, conflict between siblings is often intense during early childhood and adolescence (Arliss, 1993). Same-sex siblings of about the same age are particularly likely to engage in frequent, competitive fighting. In fact, adolescent siblings are also unlikely to compromise with one another. Instead, their conflict often ends in a standoff or in intervention by another family member or friend (Laursen & Collins, 1994). Sibling relationships also tend to involve violence. Around 36% of siblings report

engaging in acts of moderately severe violence, such as kicking and hitting with objects. Even more siblings (around 64%) report that they have engaged in less severe forms of violence, such as shoving and pushing (Straus & Gelles, 1990). Yet siblings also share a unique bond. They usually know each other most of their lives; the sibling relationship predates romantic relationships and typically outlives parent-child relationships. Many siblings not only survive stormy periods of conflict but also develop a close and special bond as adults.

Disagreement appears to be common in romantic relationships as well. Most romantic couples have between 1 and 3 disagreements per week, with 1 or 2 disagreements per month being particularly unpleasant (Canary et al., 1995). Unhappy couples often experience much more conflict; one study found that distressed couples reported having 5.4 conflicts over a five-day period (see Canary et al., 1995). Although most couples manage conflict without resorting to violent behavior, some disagreements escalate into violence. Research suggests that about 16% of married couples, 35% of cohabiting couples, and 30% of dating couples can recall at least one incidence of interpersonal violence in their relationship over the past year (Christopher & Lloyd, 2000). Gay and lesbian couples report violence rates that are about the same as married couples, although they appear to report using milder forms of violence than straight couples (Rohrbaugh, 2006). The most common types of interpersonal violence include pushing or shoving one's partner, forcefully grabbing one's partner, and shaking or handling one's partner roughly (Marshall, 1994).

Effects of Conflict on Relationships

Conflict that is accompanied by hostile communication, such as yelling, name-calling, sarcastic comments, and pointedly ignoring the partner, has a negative impact on relationships. Along with this, Caughlin and Vangelisti (2006) summarized a substantial body of research showing that negative conflict is associated with relational dissatisfaction. Couples who argue frequently and in an aggressive manner also report less relational stability and reduced commitment (Knee, Patrick, Vietor, & Neighbors, 2004; McGonagle, Kessler, & Gotlib, 1993).

Marital conflict can have harmful effects on children as well as spouses. Children who witness their parents engaging in frequent, aggressive conflict are more likely to have trouble interacting with their peers and performing at their full potential in school (Buehler et al., 1997; Sillars et al., 2004). Research on this **spillover effect** suggests that these negative effects arise because parents who engage in dysfunctional conflict are also likely to have dysfunctional parenting styles (Davies & Cummings, 1994). A **socialization effect** is also likely to occur, with children adopting conflict styles similar to their parents' conflict styles (Koerner & Fitzpatrick, 2002; Reese-Weber & Bertle-Haring, 1998). A study by Kitzmann and Cohen (2003) examined several aspects of interparental conflict: frequency (how often parents argue in front of them), intensity (how mad parents get when they argue with each other), perceived threat (how scared children get when their parents argue), and resolution (how long parents stay mad at each other beyond the actual argument). Their results showed that children in Grades 3 through 6 were less likely to report having a high-quality relationship with a best friend if their parents had trouble resolving their conflicts. Frequency, intensity, and threat were less predictive of poor friendship quality than resolution, underscoring how important it is for parents to manage conflict rather than holding grudges and remaining angry. Studies have also shown that children actually fare better when feuding parents divorce compared to when they stay together and engage in increasingly negative patterns of conflict communication (Caughlin & Vangelisti, 2006).

Despite these negative effects, conflict can be beneficial when it is managed productively. Gottman's (1979, 1994) research shows that satisfied couples are more likely to discuss issues of disagreement, whereas dissatisfied couples are likely to minimize or avoid conflict. By confronting disagreement, relational partners can manage their differences in ways that enhance closeness and relational stability (Braiker & Kelley, 1979; Canary, Cupach, & Messman, 1995; Lloyd & Cate, 1985). A study by Siegert and Stamp (1994) examining the effects of a couple's "first big fight" also underscores the important role that conflict plays in relationship development. Partners who stayed together after the fight gained a greater mutual understanding of their feelings, felt they could solve problems together, and were confident that they would both be willing to make sacrifices for each other. By contrast, partners who broke up after the fight reported feeling uncertain about their relationship. During the fight, many people discovered negative information about their partners, and many felt that future interaction would be tense and uncomfortable. More than anything, however, the way partners perceived and handled conflict predicted whether their first big fight would signal the end of their relationship or a new beginning. In addition, the way partners manage conflict is a better predictor of relational satisfaction than is the experience of conflict itself. Being able to resolve conflict so that both parties are satisfied with the outcome is also predictive of relational satisfaction (Cramer, 2002).

CONFLICT STYLES

Considerable research has focused on the strategies or styles that people use to deal with conflict in organizations (Blake & Mouton, 1964; Putnam & Wilson, 1982; Rahim, 1986; Rahim & Bonoma, 1979) and in relationships between friends, lovers, and roommates (Fitzpatrick & Winke, 1979; Klein & Johnson, 1997; Sillars, 1980; Sillars et al., 2004). Research in both these areas suggests that conflict styles can be distinguished by two dimensions: cooperation and directness (Rahim, 1986; Sillars et al., 2004). Cooperative conflict takes both partners' goals into account, whereas uncooperative conflict focuses on one person trying to win the argument. Direct conflict involves engaging in conflict and talking about issues, whereas indirect conflict involves avoiding discussion of conflict. Researchers have developed several typologies of conflict styles from these dimensions, with some scholars identifying three styles (e.g., Putman & Wilson, 1982; Sillars, 1980), other scholars finding four styles (e.g., Klein & Johnson, 1997; Sillars et al., 2004), and still other scholars discovering five styles (e.g., Blake & Mouton, 1964; Rahim, 1986). A review of the strategies in these typologies suggests that there are six styles of conflict: competitive fighting, compromising, collaborating, indirect fighting, avoiding, and yielding (see Figure 14.1). To determine your own conflict style, complete the scale in Box 14.2.

Competitive Fighting

Competitive fighting is characterized by an uncooperative orientation and a direct style of communication (Blake & Mouton, 1964). This style has been called *direct fighting* (Sillars et al., 2004), *distributive* (Sillars, 1980), *dominating* (Rahim, 1986), *controlling* (Putnam & Wilson, 1982), and *contentious* (Klein & Johnson, 1997; Pruitt & Carnevale, 1993). As these labels suggest, people with a competing style try to control the interaction so they have more power than their partner. They attempt to achieve a win-lose situation, wherein they win and their partner loses. In their attempts to achieve dominance, individuals who employ competing strategies use several tactics: confrontational remarks, accusations, personal criticisms, threats, name-calling, blaming the partner, sarcasm, and hostile jokes (Sillars et al., 2004).

Imagine that Mary and Doug both used competitive fighting when trying to determine how to punish Amanda. They might cling stubbornly to their own perspectives, with each arguing that their method is superior to the other partner's. Mary might accuse Doug of being too selfish to put up

with Amanda being at home all the time because she is grounded, and Doug might claim that Mary's past attempts at grounding Amanda have been unsuccessful and that "everyone knows" she is too lenient. The conflict could very well escalate, with Mary and Doug yelling at each other and calling each other names. Even if one of them eventually yields, the desired win-lose outcome likely will be only temporary (Kilmann & Thomas, 1977). In the long run, Mary and Doug's relationship could be harmed, leading to a lose-lose situation for both.

As this example illustrates, the competing strategy is usually associated with poor communication competence and reduced relational satisfaction (Canary & Spitzberg, 1987, 1989, 1990; Gross & Guerrero, 2000; Sillars, 1980). People who use competing strategies are typically ineffective in meeting their goals and inappropriate in their treatment of their partner. There are exceptions to this, however. In relationships where a power differential exists, such as those between managers and employees or between parents and children, strategies related to competitive fighting are sometimes effective. For instance, if a father wants to prevent his son from engaging in dangerous behavior, he might force him to stay home while his friends attend a rowdy party. The competing strategy is most useful when immediate compliance is necessary (Hocker & Wilmot, 1998). The competing strategy may also be useful when it is important to deal with a particular conflict issue. For instance, if

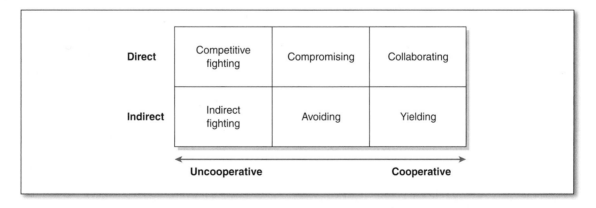

Figure 14.1   Interpersonal Conflict Styles

one partner does not want to talk about a critical problem (e.g., how to deal with the financial fallout of the wife being laid off from her job), the other partner may engage in competing behaviors to force the partner to confront the issue. In other cases (e.g., finding out one's partner flirted with an ex-lover all night at a party), people may be justified in expressing anger or leveling accusations at their partners. Usually, however, competitive fighting leads to a conflict escalation and harms relationships, especially if positive communication does not counterbalance verbal aggression (Canary & Lakey, 2006).

Collaborating

The collaborating style involves having a cooperative orientation and using direct communication (Blake & Mouton, 1964). Collaboration involves considering each other's goals and opinions. This style has been called *integrating* (Rahim, 1986; Sillars, 1980), *solution oriented* (Putnam & Wilson, 1982), *problem solving* (Klein & Johnson, 1997; Pruitt & Carnevale, 1993), and *negotiation* (Sillars et al., 2004). As these labels suggest, the collaborating style focuses on cooperative problem solving that leads to a win-win situation. Collaboration involves trying to find creative solutions to problems that incorporate both partners' needs. This style opens lines of communication, increases information seeking and sharing, and maintains relationships for future interaction (Hocker & Wilmot, 1998). Tactics associated with the collaborating style include expressing agreement, making descriptive or disclosive statements, being supportive, accepting responsibility, brainstorming ideas, and soliciting partner opinions (Sillars et al. 2004).

BOX 14.2 Put Yourself to the Test

What Is Your Conflict Style?

Think about the last few times you and a relational partner disagreed. How did you behave? Use the following scale to determine your typical conflict style: 1 = disagree strongly, 7 = agree strongly.

	Disagree						Agree
1. I discuss the problem to try to reach a mutual understanding.	1	2	3	4	5	6	7
2. I keep arguing until I prove my point.	1	2	3	4	5	6	7
3. I show my partner that I am angry or upset without saying a word.	1	2	3	4	5	6	7
4. I sometimes sacrifice my own goals so my partner can meet her or his goals.	1	2	3	4	5	6	7
5. I try to find a new solution that will satisfy both our needs.	1	2	3	4	5	6	7
6. I usually try to win arguments.	1	2	3	4	5	6	7
7. I do not like to talk about issues of disagreement.	1	2	3	4	5	6	7
8. I am willing to give up some of my goals in exchange for achieving other goals.	1	2	3	4	5	6	7

	Disagree					Agree	
9. I try to get all my concerns and my partner's concerns out in the open.	1	2	3	4	5	6	7
10. I try to get back at my partner by giving the silent treatment or holding a grudge.	1	2	3	4	5	6	7
11. I usually try to forget about issues of disagreement so I don't have to confront my partner.	1	2	3	4	5	6	7
12. I try to think of a solution that satisfies some of both our needs.	1	2	3	4	5	6	7
13. Sometimes I find myself attacking my partner.	1	2	3	4	5	6	7
14. I use facial expressions to let my partner know I am angry or upset.	1	2	3	4	5	6	7
15. It is important to get both our points of view out in the open.	1	2	3	4	5	6	7
16. Sometimes I criticize my partner to show that he or she is wrong.	1	2	3	4	5	6	7
17. I try to meet my partner halfway.	1	2	3	4	5	6	7
18. If the issue is very important to my partner, I usually give in.	1	2	3	4	5	6	7
19. I attempt to work with my partner to find a creative solution we both like.	1	2	3	4	5	6	7
20. I tend to show negative feelings through nonverbal communication, such as rolling my eyes.	1	2	3	4	5	6	7
21. I usually let my partner take responsibility for bringing up conflict issues.	1	2	3	4	5	6	7
22. I would rather not get into a discussion of unpleasant issues.	1	2	3	4	5	6	7
23. I give in to my partner to keep my relationship satisfying.	1	2	3	4	5	6	7
24. I try to make my partner see things my way.	1	2	3	4	5	6	7
25. I avoid bringing up certain issues if my arguments might hurt my partner's feelings.	1	2	3	4	5	6	7

(Continued)

(Continued)

	Disagree						Agree
26. I might agree with some of my partner's points to make my partner happy.	1	2	3	4	5	6	7
27. I am likely to give my partner cold or dirty looks as a way of expressing disagreement.	1	2	3	4	5	6	7
28. I avoid talking with my partner about disagreements.	1	2	3	4	5	6	7
29. I try to find a "middle ground" position that is acceptable to both of us.	1	2	3	4	5	6	7
30. I believe that you have to "give a little to get a little" during a disagreement.	1	2	3	4	5	6	7

To obtain your results, add your scores for the following items:

Yielding: Items 4+18+23+25+26 = _____

Avoiding: Items 7+11+21+22+28 = _____

Collaborating: Items 1+5+9+15+19 = _____

Competitive fighting: Items 2+6+13+16+24 = _____

Compromising: Items 8+12+17+29+30 = _____

Indirect fighting: Items 3+10+14+20+27 = _____

Higher scores indicate that you possess more of a particular conflict style.

So, how might Mary and Doug use a collaborating style? A starting point would be to share their concerns and search for a creative way to teach Amanda about the dangers of smoking. By using collaborative tactics, Doug might discover that Mary's main motivation is to keep Amanda away from the "bad" crowd she has been spending time with lately. Mary might discover that Doug's main objection to grounding is that it will not teach Amanda anything about the negative consequences of smoking. Doug might also realize that reducing Amanda's allowance by the cost of several cartons of cigarettes will only teach Amanda about the monetary cost of smoking, not the health risks. They might agree that it would

be better if they required Amanda to volunteer some time after school at the local hospital, where she can help patients with lung cancer. Such a disciplinary action will keep Amanda away from her new friends (meeting Mary's needs) while also teaching Amanda about the risks associated with smoking (meeting Doug's needs). In fact, this new solution might address each of their concerns better than their original plans would have.

It is likely no surprise that the collaborating style is evaluated as effective and appropriate in managing conflict (Canary & Spitzberg, 1987, 1989, 1990; Gross & Guerrero, 2000; Gross, Guerrero, & Alberts, 2004). Couples who use collaborating styles and show positive affect during conflict are likely to be happier, and children benefit from parents who use this conflict style (Caughlin & Vangelisti, 2006; Koerner & Fitzpatrick, 2006). Collaboration is related to perceptions of competence and relational satisfaction because it gives each individual access to the partner's views of so-called incompatible goals, allowing disputants to reach understanding and to coconstruct meaning. When such understanding occurs, problems can be defined, and a solution that integrates the goals and needs of both parties can be reached (Tutzauer & Roloff, 1988). In one study, parents and children reported being more satisfied with their relationships if they reported using the collaborating style to cope with conflict (La Valley & Guerrero, 2010).

Compromising

Like the competing and collaborating styles, the compromising style involves direct communication between partners. The compromising style is also moderately cooperative (Blake & Mouton, 1964; Kilmann & Thomas, 1977; Rahim, 1986). Compromise involves searching for a fair, intermediate position that satisfies some of both partner's needs. There is a key difference between collaboration and compromise. With collaboration, the solution is especially satisfactory because both people have met their goals. With compromise, people need to give something up to reach a solution that will meet at least some of their goals. Thus, compromise usually leads to a part-win-part-lose situation. Indeed, people who compromise talk about "splitting the difference" and "meeting the partner halfway." According to Hocker and Wilmot (1998), compromising behaviors include appealing to fairness, suggesting a trade-off, maximizing wins while minimizing losses, and offering a quick, short-term resolution to the conflict.

Suppose that Mary and Doug are unable to come up with a better solution than either of them originally proposed. Maybe there is no hospital in their area. Or perhaps their goals are so radically different that a solution that will satisfy both of their needs does not exist. In this case, compromise may be a good choice. They could decide to ground Amanda for two weeks instead of a month and deduct cigarette money from her allowance for three months instead of six. This way, Mary and Doug both get to administer the punishment they perceive as appropriate, but neither applies the punishment for as long as they originally proposed. In short, they get to keep something but they also have to give up something. Notice that compromising usually involves modifying preexisting solutions, whereas collaborating involves creating new solutions.

Research suggests that the compromising style is generally perceived to be moderately appropriate and effective (Gross & Guerrero, 2000). Although this style is not as effective or appropriate as collaborating, there are situations in which compromising is best. Suppose a couple is arguing over whom to ask to be godparents for their son. The husband wants his sister and brother to be godparents, while the wife prefers her favorite aunt and uncle. Assuming their son can only have two official godparents, the couple might decide to put names in a hat, with one slip of paper appointing the aunt and brother as godparents and the other designating the sister and uncle. Such a compromise is likely to be seen as fair by all parties. As Hocker and Wilmot (1998) described, most people perceive compromising to be a reasonable, fair, and efficient strategy for managing conflict, even though it requires some sacrifice and hampers the development of creative alternatives. When a compromise is seen as unfair, it can lead to dissatisfaction. In one study, violent couples actually used more compromise than satisfied couples (Morrison, Van Hasselt, & Bellack, 1987). Thus, although compromise is usually a moderately effective conflict strategy, if couples have to compromise too often, they may feel that their needs are not being met and their problems are never truly resolved.

Yielding

The yielding style is cooperative and indirect (Klein & Johnson, 1997; Pruitt & Carnevale, 1993; Sillars, 1980). People who use this style forgo their own goals and desires in consideration of the partner

(Kilmann & Thomas, 1977). This style has also been labeled *obliging* (Rahim, 1986) and *accommodating* (Blake & Mouton, 1964). Papa and Canary (1995) noted that this type of response is adequate and comfortable; it does not cause further disagreement or escalation of conflict. However, the yielding style glosses over differences, plays down disagreements, and trivializes conflict, making effective conflict management difficult. Hocker and Wilmot (1998) described several specific yielding tactics, including putting aside one's own needs to please the partner, passively accepting the partner's decisions, and making conciliatory statements.

Mary or Doug might engage in any or all of these tactics as part of a yielding response. Suppose Doug decides to give in to Mary and grounds Amanda. He might tell Mary that she is right, that he'll just have to deal with having Amanda at home, that he loves his family and hopes it works out. Doug may yield for many different reasons. Perhaps he really does believe that Mary knows best when it comes to disciplining Amanda. Or perhaps he decides that it is not worth arguing over and he will simply let Mary have her way. Yet another possibility is that he feels threatened or coerced. In their research on the **chilling effect**, Cloven and Roloff (1993) found that people are likely to avoid voicing their opinions and complaints when they feel powerless or fear that their partner will act aggressively toward them (see also Chapter 12).

Yielding occurs for many different reasons, so it can be perceived as both competent and incompetent (Gross & Guerrero, 2000). Yielding behavior is cooperative and appropriate when one person feels strongly about an issue and the other person does not. In such cases, it is appropriate for the person who feels less strongly to give in to the partner. Yielding may also be an appropriate strategy when two people cannot agree but a decision must be made. For instance, if Mary and Doug are arguing over who is going to pick Amanda up after a party (each believes it is the other's turn), one of them might give in so that Amanda will have a safe ride home.

However, most research suggests that, although the yielding style is sometimes appreciated by one's partner, it is generally ineffective (Gross & Guerrero, 2000; Papa & Canary, 1995). People who use the yielding style are unlikely to achieve personal goals, which could strain their relationship. According to Hocker and Wilmot (1998), repeatedly yielding puts a person in a powerless position. Perhaps this is why people seldom report yielding when the conflict issue is important to them. Sillars (1980) examined how often roommates reported using yielding strategies. He had students recall significant disagreements with their roommates and describe how they and their roommates communicated. Only 2% of the students reported using yielding strategies during their most significant roommate disagreements. By contrast, 33% of students perceived their roommates to have yielded during these same disagreements. Sillars suggested that the discrepancy occurred because students reported on a disagreement that was significant to them, which made it less likely that they would yield. Their roommates, conversely, may not have seen these disagreements as significant and so were willing to concede the issue. This finding suggests that yielding is more common when people do not care much about an issue.

Avoiding

Like accommodation (a cooperative strategy) and indirect fighting (an uncooperative strategy), avoiding is an indirect style of conflict. Avoiding is regarded as somewhat neutral in terms of how cooperative versus uncooperative it is. This style has also been called *inaction* (Klein & Johnson, 1997; Pruitt & Carnevale, 1993) and *nonconfrontation* (Putnam & Wilson, 1982). When using the avoiding style, people refrain from arguing and refuse to confront their partners in any meaningful way. Avoiding tactics are fairly common. Studies have shown that roommates frequently report using the avoiding style in their conflicts (Sillars, 1980), and 63% of college students report withholding at least one complaint from their dating partners (Roloff & Cloven, 1990). People who use the avoiding strategy engage in tactics such as denying the conflict, being indirect and evasive, changing or avoiding topics, acting as if they don't care, making irrelevant remarks, and joking to avoid dealing with the conflict (Hocker & Wilmot, 1998).

Imagine that Mary and Doug deal with their disagreement through avoidance. Neither of them wants to confront the issue, so they avoid talking about how to best handle the situation with Amanda. Perhaps they both punish Amanda their own way, without consulting the other, making Amanda suffer two punishments instead of one. Or perhaps they both decide not to do anything, letting Amanda "off the hook" for smoking. Either way, the use of avoidance would lead to a lose-lose situation, with little being accomplished. Consistent with this example, several studies have shown that the avoiding style is evaluated as inappropriate and ineffective (Canary & Spitzberg, 1987, 1989, 1990; Gross & Guerrero, 2000; Gross et al., 2004).

Occasionally, though, avoidance may be beneficial. Roloff and Ifert (2000) described five conditions that influence whether avoidance has a positive or negative effect on relationships. First, avoidance may be an effective strategy for certain types of couples. Couples who find it difficult to engage in conflict without resorting to aggression may find avoidance preferable to engagement. Second, avoidance is more acceptable when accompanied by expressions of positive affect. So, if Doug says "I'm too tired to talk about this anymore, honey" with a warm voice and genuine smile, Mary might empathize with him rather than feeling dismissed. Third, people are most likely to respond positively to avoidance when the topic is of little importance to both people. As Hocker and Wilmot (1998) noted, the avoidant style can be used to acknowledge that a relationship is more important than a particular issue (Hocker & Wilmot, 1998).

Fourth, individuals are more likely to find avoidance acceptable if it is their decision to avoid discussion about a particular topic. When people feel their partners are pressuring them to keep quiet about relational issues that are bothering them, avoidance may have an especially harmful effect on the relationship. Finally, when people are socially skilled communicators, they may be able to recognize when avoidance is appropriate versus inappropriate.

For example, imagine that Doug is staunchly conservative and Mary is extremely liberal. If they are socially skilled, they might be flexible enough to "agree to disagree" when it comes to political issues, but to confront conflict issues revolving around Amanda and her twin sister, Megan.

Indirect Fighting

Sillars and his colleagues (2004) refer to conflict behaviors that are indirect and uncooperative as indirect fighting. These behaviors have also been called *passive aggression* (Guerrero & La Valley, 2006) and *active distancing* (Bachman & Guerrero, 2006a) and are related to patterns of negative withdrawal (Gottman, 1994). Examples of indirect fighting include failing to acknowledge or validate the partner's concerns, ignoring the partner, holding a grudge, using a whiny voice, giving the partner cold or dirty looks, angrily leaving the scene, rolling one's eyes, and administering the silent treatment (Guerrero & La Valley, 2006; Sillars et al., 2004). All of these behaviors express aggression or disagreement in an indirect manner that could shut down discussion about the conflict issue.

For instance, rather than discussing optimal punishment in a calm manner that facilitates cooperation, Doug and Mary might show hostility through indirect behaviors. Doug might try to explain his philosophy—that Amanda needs to learn there are consequences associated with smoking—in a condescending tone that makes Mary feel he is talking to her as if she is a child. Mary's response may be to sigh, roll her eyes, and cross her arms over her chest in a defensive manner. Doug might then complain, in a hostile voice, that Mary isn't even listening. Such tactics could result in one or both of the partners leaving the scene in frustration. In this type of scenario, the indirect behaviors often provoke metaconflict, which we earlier defined as conflict about how people disagree. Mary might demand, "Stop talking to me as if I'm a child," and Doug might complain, "We never get anywhere because you don't listen to me." Metaconflict often sidetracks partners away from discussing the issue at hand—in this case, how to best teach Amanda a lesson about smoking.

Indirect fighting may be especially destructive when partners use these behaviors to avoid confronting problems (Sillars et al., 2004). A study of conflict in parent-child relationships showed that people report using more indirect fighting when their partner has an avoidant personality type (La Valley & Guerrero, 2010). Therefore, people may resort to indirect fighting when they feel that they are being dismissed or ignored by their partners. Indirect fighting reflects a level of hostility that is not found in other indirect styles of conflict management. In comparison, yielding is much more cooperative, and avoiding is more neutral. Indirect fighting is related to many of the same negative outcomes as the competing style, including relationship dissatisfaction and a failure to resolve conflicts. However, indirect fighting may be even more detrimental to relationships than competitive fighting because it is an indirect strategy. At least competitive fighting involves engaging in direct, verbal communication that might bring important issues to the forefront. As you will learn later in this chapter, behaviors associated with indirect fighting, such as rolling one's eyes, sounding disgusted or fed up, and ignoring one's partner, have been identified as signs of unproductive conflict that can lead to relationship decline (Gottman, 1994). People who employ indirect fighting are also perceived as less effective and appropriate than are those who use cooperative strategies (Guerrero & La Valley, 2006).

PATTERNS OF CONFLICT INTERACTION

Although people have tendencies to manage conflict in particular ways, many people use several strategies depending on the situation and the type of conflict. Conflict strategies are not mutually exclusive. In other words, people can use more than one strategy during a single conflict interaction. For example, Doug and Mary may begin with the intention of communicating in a cooperative, direct manner, but become increasingly competitive as they both stubbornly hang on to their original positions. They might also exhibit different conflict styles altogether. Perhaps Mary favors indirect fighting whereas Doug prefers to yield. As these examples illustrate,

understanding various conflict styles in isolation does not paint a very good picture of how conflict interaction unfolds. This is why researchers have sought to understand common patterns of conflict within relationships. Five such patterns, in particular, include negative reciprocity, common couple violence the demand-withdrawal pattern, the four horsemen of the apocalypse, and accommodation.

Negative Reciprocity

Despite the fact that indirect and competitive fighting usually have negative effects on relationships, people use these strategies more frequently than cooperative strategies (Canary et al., 1995; Sillars, 1980). This may be because of the **principle of negative reciprocity**, a pattern whereby aggression begets more aggression. Once one person uses competitive or indirect fighting, the other person is likely to follow suit. Hostile nonverbal behaviors tend to be reciprocated during conflict (Gottman, 1994; Krokoff, Gottman, & Roy, 1988), and relational partners also tend to reciprocate verbal communication such as complaints and criticisms. Alberts and her colleagues (Alberts, 1989; Alberts & Discoll, 1992) found that if a partner launches a complaint, the other partner is likely to fire back with a countercomplaint. Moreover, individuals in dissatisfying relationships were twice as likely as individuals in satisfying relationships to respond to complaints by denying the validity of the complaint or by escalating the hostility of the interaction (Alberts & Discoll, 1992). Patterns of negative reciprocity also distinguish couples who are dissatisfied and violent from those who are dissatisfied but nonviolent. Violent couples are most likely to engage in high levels of negative reciprocity and low levels of positive reciprocity (Smith, Vivian, & O'Leary, 1990).

In conflict interaction, negative reciprocity appears to be more common than positive reciprocity. In a classic study, Gaelick, Brodenshausen, and Wyer (1985) studied how perceptions of a partner's behavior influence patterns of reciprocity during conflict. They found that people enact positive behaviors when they perceive their partner is expressing affectionate emotions, and negative behavior when they perceive their partner is expressing hostile emotions. However, negative reciprocity was the main pattern for two reasons. First, people exhibit more negative than positive emotion in conflict situations. Second, and perhaps more importantly, people perceived their partners were expressing hostility even when they were not. For instance, imagine that Mary offers her view using a neutral voice, but Doug interprets her tone to be condescending. This could set off a chain of negativity, even though Mary's initial comment was not meant to be hostile.

Patterns of negative reciprocity can be set off by a variety of hostile behaviors, including sarcasm, personal criticism, name-calling, yelling, and unfair accusations. Three other tactics have been found to be especially likely to divert attention away from the conflict issue while escalating negativity—gunnysacking, kitchen sinking, and bringing third parties into the argument. **Gunnysacking** occurs when people store up old grievances and then dump them on their partner during a conflict (Bach & Wyden, 1970). Rather than discussing each issue when it first surfaces, issues are placed in a metaphorical gunnysack and presented all at once. **Kitchen sinking** is similar to gunnysacking. However, instead of storing up complaints, people rehash their old arguments when they get into a new argument (Bach & Wyden, 1970). Because gunnysacking and kitchen sinking involve multiple attacks, partners are likely to feel defensive and overwhelmed, making it difficult to discuss any of the issues productively.

Bringing third parties into an argument can also promote defensiveness. There are at least three ways that people bring third parties into their arguments. First, people mention things that other people said as a form of evidence ("Your sister warned me you can be really picky"). Such comments are especially hurtful and hard for receivers to defend because they cannot confront the person who supposedly made them. Second, people can badmouth the partner's friends or family by making comments such as "I guess your erratic behavior shouldn't surprise me— your whole family acts that way." Statements like these make people particularly defensive. Not only do they have to defend themselves, but they have to defend their friends or family. Third, individuals

compare their partner unfavorably to other people ("None of my other girlfriends ever complained about that"), which is an especially frustrating type of personal attack.

Couples who engage in patterns of negative reciprocity, such as joint gunnysacking and sequences of complaints followed by countercomplaints, report less relational satisfaction (Gottman, 1979). Dissatisfied couples also become increasingly hostile during discussions about problems or conflict issues, while satisfied couples maintain a consistently lower level of hostility (Billings, 1979; Gottman & Levenson, 1992). This does not mean that couples in satisfying relationships never display negative reciprocity. On the contrary, research suggests that negative reciprocity is a fairly common pattern in conflict interaction. The key appears to be the percentage of behaviors that are negative versus positive. Gottman's (1994) research demonstrates that happy couples tend to engage in about five positive behaviors for every negative behavior, whereas the ratio of negative-to-positive behaviors was about one to one for unhappy couples.

Common Couple Violence

Common couple violence is a form of negative reciprocity that occurs when conflict spins out of control and partners resort to using violence as a way to vent their emotions and try to control the conflict (Johnson, 1995; McEwan & Johnson, 2008). This type of violence tends to be reciprocal, with one person committing a violent act and the other person retaliating with more violence (Hamel, 2009; Johnson, 1995). Because common couple violence is reciprocal, men and women tend to engage in this type of violence about equally (Graham-Keven & Archer, 2003; Hamel, 2009; Johnson, 1995; Olson, 2002b). Most of the time, common couple violence includes less severe forms of violent behavior, such as throwing objects, grabbing, shoving, pushing, or slapping (Johnson & Leone, 2005; Olson, 2004). Other times, common couple violence gets out of control, escalating into more severely violent behaviors, including hitting, beating, or using a weapon against the partner (Johnson & Leone, 2005).

Violence is always unacceptable. Research suggests that people sometimes resort to violent behavior when they lack the interpersonal skills necessary to solve relational problems.

There appear to be two general patterns of common couple violence in relationships. Some couples show a pattern of **repeated common couple violence**, with episodes of this type of violence occurring once every two months or so in their relationships (Johnson, 1995). For these couples, conflicts that are especially serious tend to escalate into violence on a fairly regular basis. More couples, however, report a pattern of **isolated common couple violence**. To examine these patterns, a large national survey about violence against women was conducted. Only 1% of people who reported that common couple violence had occurred at some point in their relationship said that an incident had occurred within the past 12 months (Johnson & Leone, 2005). In other words, some people could recall at least one time when they had experienced common couple violence in their relationship, but it was rare enough that it had not occurred in the past year. Some of the couples who experience isolated common couple violence discuss their violent behavior, deem it inappropriate, and vow that it will not happen again. These types of discussions decrease future episodes of common couple violence (Olson, 2002b).

Common couple violence often occurs alongside other aggressive forms of communication, such as competitive fighting and indirect fighting. It can also happen when people feel ignored or want to stop someone from leaving during a conflict episode (Olson, 2002a, 2002b; Olson & Braithwaite, 2004). Hamel (2009) concluded that common couple violence occurs when partners are motivated to communicate rather than control their anger, but have trouble communicating effectively. Similarly, Olson argued that people often resort to this form of violence when they get frustrated and feel that they cannot communicate what they want to their partner (Olson, 2002b; Olson & Braithwaite, 2004). Sometimes violence occurs in response to withdrawing behavior. For example, Olson's work has shown that people sometimes use violence to gain their partner's attention and keep their partner from leaving the scene of the conflict (Olson, 2002a, 2002b; Olson & Braithwaite, 2004). Common couple violence has also been associated with the demand-withdrawal pattern.

Demand-Withdrawal

Researchers have identified another common but dysfunctional conflict sequence called the **demand-withdrawal interaction pattern** (Gottman & Levenson, 1988; Sagrestano, Heavey, & Christensen, 2006). This pattern occurs when one person wants to engage in conflict or makes demands on a partner and the other wants to avoid it. The person in the demanding position is likely to be in a less powerful position (relative to the partner) and tends to be dissatisfied with something. By contrast, the person in the withdrawing position is likely to be in a more powerful position and to be happy with the status quo. Married couples are more likely to engage in the demand-withdrawal pattern when one partner desires more closeness or involvement in the home and the other partner desires more autonomy (Sagrestano et al., 2006).

The demand-withdrawal pattern can move in both directions—increased demands can lead to more withdrawal, but increased withdrawal can also lead to more demands (Klinetob & Smith, 1996). In fact, couples who use the demand-withdrawal pattern may have problems of **punctuation** (Watzlawick, Beavin, & Jackson, 1967), with each partner "punctuating" the cause of the conflict differently. One partner might say "I have to nag you all the time because you always withdraw," whereas the other partner might say, "I have to withdraw because you are always nagging me." Notice that both partners blame the other for their behavior.

The demand-withdrawal pattern is most likely to occur when the conflict engager uses either competitive or indirect fighting. Engagers who use cooperative strategies are rarely perceived as demanding (Heavey, Christensen, & Malamuth, 1995). Because the demand-withdrawal pattern consists of uncooperative behavior, it is generally seen as an incompetent form of dyadic communication (Christensen & Shenk, 1991; Gottman & Levenson, 1988). Yet the effect this pattern of conflict communication has on

relationships is not clear. Some studies have shown that couples characterized by the demand-withdrawal pattern are more likely to be dissatisfied with their relationships and, eventually, to break up. Yet other studies have shown that couples who use the demand-withdrawal sequence are likely to report increased relational satisfaction over time (Caughlin & Vangelisti, 2006). It may be that couples who break free from this sequence end up reporting more satisfaction because important changes were made in their relationships, whereas those who repeatedly follow this pattern become increasingly dissatisfied.

A more consistent finding is that women are more likely to do the demanding whereas men are more likely to do the withdrawing (Caughlin & Vangelisti, 1999; Christensen & Shenk, 1999; Gottman, 1994; Heavey, Layne, & Christensen, 1993). Imagine if Doug approaches Mary to discuss Amanda's punishment, but Mary tells him she does not want to talk about it anymore. Would this situation seem more believable if it were reversed—with Mary wanting to talk about the problem and Doug retreating? The research suggests it would. However, this sex difference reverses if the conflict involves something the man wants to change (Kluwer, de Dreu, & Buunk, 1998; Sagrestano, Heavey, & Christensen, 1998). For example, if Doug thinks it is unfair that he always ends up having to tell his daughters what their punishments are, he might be cast in the demanding role when he and Mary discuss who will tell Amanda that she must volunteer at the hospital. Women may be in the demanding role more often because they are more likely to want to institute change in their relationships. Finally, some evidence suggests that couples characterized by husband-to-wife violence are more likely than nonviolent couples to exhibit rigid patterns of husband demand and wife withdrawal (Caughlin & Vangelisti, 2006). Olson (2002b) also found that individuals who engage in common couple violence were often caught in a demand-withdrawal conflict pattern.

Overall, then, research has shown that the demand-withdrawal pattern is more prevalent in relationships where violence is present and, in such relationships, men are just as likely to be the demanders and women are just as likely to be the withdrawers

(Babcock, Waltz, & Jacobson, 1993; Berns, Jacobson, & Gottman, 1999; Holtzworth-Munroe, Smutzler, & Stuart, 1998; Ridley & Feldman, 2003). To manage conflict constructively and maintain a happy relationship, couples must learn to break this cycle. The person in the demanding role needs to be patient and persistent without becoming aggressive or violent. The person in the withdrawing role needs to listen and try to understand and empathize with the partner. With effort, the cycle can be broken and the relationship can become more satisfying.

The Four Horsemen of the Apocalypse

Gottman's extensive research on the causes of divorce uncovered another especially destructive pattern of conflict called the **four horsemen of the apocalypse**. According to Gottman (1994), couples who divorce are likely to exhibit a conflict pattern that includes the following four behaviors: (1) complaints and criticisms, (2) contempt or disgust, (3) defensiveness, and (4) stonewalling. Gottman proposed that the four horsemen of the apocalypse form a "cascade" or sequence, with complaining and criticizing leading to contempt, "which leads to defensiveness, which leads to listener withdrawal from interaction" (p. 110); Figure 14.2 depicts this process. For unhappy couples, the most common pattern is as follows: wives' complaints are perceived as criticisms by husbands, then both husbands and wives become contemptuous and defensiveness, followed by the husband stonewalling. Although this

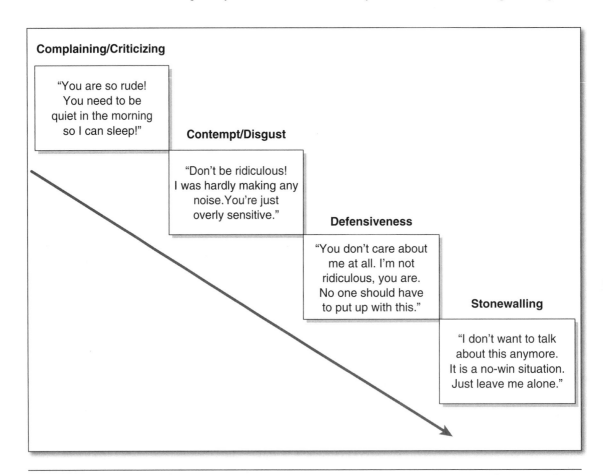

Figure 14.2   Gottman's Cascade Process of Relational Dissolution: The Four Horsemen of the Apocalypse

is the most common pattern in Gottman's work, this sequence can occur in various ways (e.g., the husband's complaint could start the process and both the husband and wife might end up stonewalling).

Complaints and Criticisms

The cascade starts when one person complains or criticizes. Gottman (1994) noted that some complaints are actually healthy. If relational partners never complained, they would be unable to improve their relationships by changing problematic behavior. However, if complaints continue over long periods, if they turn into criticisms or are perceived as criticisms, Gottman's research suggests that the partner will start to feel contempt.

There are at least five types of complaints (Alberts, 1988, 1989). The first and most common type of complaint is about behavior. For instance, Amanda might complain that her twin sister, Megan, is gloating because she got punished. This type of complaint focuses on the behavior rather than the person and is specific in terms of the kind of action a person has to take to remedy the problem; in this case, Megan should stop gloating. The second most common type of complaint revolves around personal characteristics ("You are an inconsiderate and rude sister"). This type of complaint almost always constitutes a character attack and often leads to negative reciprocity (Gottman, 1994). Third, people can complain about performance. In this case, they dislike the way something was done. For example, Amanda and Megan might complain that Doug forgot to put oil in the pot when cooking spaghetti, leading to sticky noodles. This type of complaint can be frustrating because it implies that someone is not doing something the proper way. (Indeed, Doug might respond by telling his daughters to cook themselves next time.) Fourth, people can complain about personal appearance. Alberts (1988) provides an example of this type of complaint from her data: "You have a fat butt and better lose weight" (p. 188). Clearly this kind of complaint is also a personal attack. Finally, people can make **metacomplaints**, which involve complaining about the partner's complaining. For example, Doug might tell his daughters to "stop whining about the spaghetti and eat." Alberts (1988) found that satisfied couples were more likely than dissatisfied couples to

use behavioral complaints. Dissatisfied couples, by contrast, were more likely to use personal characteristic complaints.

Contempt and Disgust

According to Gottman (1994), when complaints are interpreted as criticism they often lead to feelings of contempt and disgust, which are usually communicated to the partner. As Gottman (1994) put it, "Disgust typically is communicated by sounding fed up, sickened, and repulsed" (p. 25). For example, you might say, "I've had enough" or "I'm not going to take it anymore." When people who have been criticized feel disgust, they may be particularly prone to making both real and empty relational threats, such as threatening to leave the partner. Contempt is communicated in similarly negative ways. Gottman (1994) stated:

> Contempt is also easy to identify in speech. It involves any insult, mockery, or sarcasm or decision, of the person. It includes disapproval, judgment, derision, disdain, exasperation, mockery, put downs, or communicating that the other person is absurd or incompetent. Three types of contempt are hostile humor, mockery, or sarcasm. In this form of contempt, there may be derision, a put down, or cold hate. There is often a definite sense of distance, coldness, and detachment in this category of behavior. (p. 25)

Defensiveness

People become defensive when they feel a need to protect themselves and ward off personal attacks. Gottman (1994) listed several communicative behaviors related to defensiveness, including denying responsibility for a problem, issuing counter-complaints, whining, making accusations, and reading minds. According to Gottman, when people begin mind reading, this is a sign that they are becoming defensive. **Mind reading** occurs when people assume that they know their partner's feelings, motives, and behaviors. Gottman (1994) gave the following examples to illustrate mind reading: "You don't care about how we live," "You get tense in situations like this one," and "You have to spend whatever we save" (p. 25). Gottman also noted that mind reading statements often include words such as "always" or "never." As such, mind reading violates two principles of fair fighting: (1) it often is based on jumping to conclusions and (2) it usually is based on overgeneralizations.

Mind reading is common in marital interaction, yet seldom accurate, and it usually escalates conflict (Gottman, 1994). Conversational data collected by Alberts and Driscoll (1992) on complaints illustrates this point. For example, imagine that Charles was upset because Cindy assumed that if he did a favor for her he would hold it against her in some way. He told her that he did not mind doing favors for her and would not expect anything in return. Eventually, Charles said to Cindy:

> When you tell me what I was going to say, it's almost always wrong. I mean it's wrong, and it's infuriating and it drives me nuts. Like you really know me so well, that you know exactly what I'm going to say. And it's never ever true. It's never the correct answer. It's what you want to believe I'm going to decide. (p. 404)

Stonewalling

Stonewalling falls at the end of Gottman's cascade of negative conflict behavior. After people have been attacked, experienced contempt, and tried (often unsuccessfully) to defend themselves, they often stonewall, or withdraw from the interaction. At this point, interaction seems futile. Partners no longer are trying to work problems out, as disagreements escalate into negative conflict interactions, and both partners are hurt and defensive. As mentioned previously, however, typically men tend to stonewall more frequently than women (Gottman, 1994). This often leads to the demand-withdrawal cycle, with wives insisting on talking about problems and husbands refusing to engage in such a dialogue. If stonewalling persists, Gottman's research suggests that relationships become stagnant and couples are likely to break up.

Patterns of Accommodation

The conflict patterns discussed so far tend to increase negativity or avoidance rather than promoting positive, open communication about contentious issues. Rusbult's work on accommodation helps explain why some couples are more likely to break away from patterns of negativity and avoidance than others (Rusbult, Bissonnette, Arriaga, & Cox, 1998; Rusbult, Verette, Whitney, Slovik, & Lipkus, 1991). The **accommodation principle** rests on three ideas. First, people have a tendency to retaliate when their partner engages in destructive behavior. Second, accommodation occurs when people are able to overcome this initial tendency and engage in cooperative rather than uncooperative communication to maintain their relationships. Third, couples in satisfying, committed relationships more often use accommodation than couples in uncommitted or dissatisfying relationships (Rusbult, Olsen, Davis, & Hannon, 2001).

Several studies have supported the accommodation principle (e.g., Campbell & Foster, 2002; Duffy & Rusbult, 1986; Guerrero & Bachman, 2008; Rusbult & Zembrodt, 1983; Wieselquist, Rusbult, Foster, & Agnew, 1999). These studies demonstrate that accommodation is most likely to occur in relationships characterized by high levels of commitment, satisfaction, and trust. However, accommodation may not always have positive effects on relationships. Rusbult and her colleagues (2001) noted that accommodation can cause relational problems, including power imbalances. As with the yielding strategy, if only one person is doing the accommodating (or yielding), that person may be in a powerless position that could eventually lead to relational dissatisfaction. Thus, the key to successful accommodation may be that it prompts a pattern of **positive reciprocity**, with both partners eventually engaging in cooperative strategies. This does not mean that all conflict behaviors need to be cooperative; indeed, it may be hard to refrain from using some uncooperative forms of communication when a conflict issue is particularly contentious. It does mean, however, that it is critical for partners to break escalating cycles of negativity by engaging in and responding positively to accommodation. Some research has even shown that couples who fail to reciprocate positive messages are more likely to report interpersonal violence (Smith et al., 1990).

There are many ways to accommodate a partner's negative behavior, including refraining from reacting angrily, using appropriate humor, or showing positive affect. Alberts and Driscoll's (1992) data on conversational complaints provide a nice example of accommodation that leads to a more productive interaction. They gave an example of a man (we'll call him Aaron) who complains to a woman (we'll call her Beth) that he cannot find his possessions because she always moves them when she cleans the house. The end of their conversation went this way:

Aaron: But, I mean, it's not like you do it on purpose. It's because you're absentminded.

Beth: Uh-huh. Yeah.

Aaron: And it's not like I don't do it either.

Beth: Yeah, I mean, I agree that things have to have their place . . . if you put them in their place, then you know where they are and it saves you a lot of worry.

Aaron: Well, then, there's really no disagreement.

Beth: Yeah, that's the way things should be. It's just that sometimes we do things that are contrary to the things we agree on.

Notice that Aaron engaged in a personal attack when he called Beth "absentminded." Yet instead of reciprocating his hostility, Beth accommodated by expressing agreement (perhaps because she agreed that she did not do it "on purpose"). This led Aaron

to admit that he sometimes does the same thing, which paved the way to ending the disagreement.

Being able to respond to negativity with positivity promotes relational satisfaction. In one study, couples in which people were nice only when the partner was nice were more likely to separate either one and half, two and a half, or five years later than were couples in which the two people were nice regardless of whether their partners acted positively or negatively. As this study demonstrated, it is important for people to be positive when the partner is sad, angry, or inexpressive, as well as when the partner is happy. Gottman's (1994) recommendation that couples counterbalance every one negative statement with five positive statements appears to be very sound advice.

EXPLANATIONS FOR CONFLICT PATTERNS

Questions likely follow as to why patterns such as negative reciprocity and demand-withdrawal are so common. If people care about their relationships, why don't they try to defuse a negative situation by accommodating and reacting with positivity? Sometimes people do respond positively, but often they find it hard to refrain from negativity because of emotions they feel, attributions they make, or their lack of communication skills. Complementing the discussion in this section, Box 14.3 provides rules for fair fighting that help people avoid falling into the trap of negative reciprocity during conflict.

BOX 14.3 Highlights

Ten "Rules" for Constructive Conflict Management

Based on the situation, there are various ways to manage conflict effectively. However, based on the research reviewed in this chapter, the following 10 "rules" should serve people well in most conflict situations.

1. Avoid gunnysacking or bringing in everything but the kitchen sink.

2. Do not bring other people into the conflict unless they are part of the conflict.

3. Attack positions, not people (no name-calling, button pushing, or violence).

(Continued)

(Continued)

4. Avoid making empty relational threats.

5. If necessary, postpone conflict until your emotions cool down.

6. Try to understand your partner's position by practicing active listening and avoiding mind reading.

7. Use behavioral complaints rather than personal criticisms.

8. Try to accommodate rather than get defensive when you feel like you are being attacked.

9. Try to validate your partner's position by expressing agreement and positive affect rather than stonewalling or escalating conflict.

10. For every one negative statement or behavior, use five positive statements or behaviors.

Emotional Flooding

During conflict situations, people often naturally experience aversive emotions, such as anger, hurt, and guilt (Guerrero & La Valley, 2006). Earlier in this chapter, we defined conflict as occurring when people have incompatible goals. Similarly, people feel negative emotion when someone or something blocks or disrupts their goals. So, if Mary feels that Doug's plan for punishing Amanda interferes with her goal to teach Amanda the "right" kind of lesson about smoking, Mary is likely to feel frustrated and perhaps even angry. Interestingly, moderate levels of emotion may be helpful during conflict situations (Jones, 2000). When people feel low levels of emotion, they are unlikely to put much effort into resolving conflict issues. On the other hand, especially intense emotion is counterproductive during conflict interactions.

During conflict situations, negative emotions may become so intense that people automatically resort to the fight-or-flight response. Gottman (1994) suggested that **emotional flooding** occurs when people become "surprised, overwhelmed, and disorganized" by their partner's "expressions of negative emotion" (p. 21). When this happens, people often experience high levels of physiological arousal (including increased heart rate and higher blood pressure), have difficulty processing new

information, rely on stereotyped thoughts and behaviors, and respond with aggression (fight) or withdrawal (flight). Thus, flooding contributes to negative patterns of communication that involve both uncooperative behavior and avoidance.

Several communication behaviors are associated with flooding. According to Gottman's (1994) research, if one partner becomes defensive, stubborn, angry, or whiny, the other partner is likely to experience emotional flooding. Other behaviors act as buffers against emotional flooding. If one partner expresses joy, affection, or humor during a conflict interaction, the other partner is less likely to experience emotional flooding. Situational variables also play a role. Zillman's (1990) work on the excitation transfer suggests that people who are highly aroused (due to either stress or physical exertion) before engaging in conflict are more likely to react aggressively, presumably because they are experiencing emotional flooding. When people experience emotional flooding, they sometimes say things they don't really mean, or things they wish they could take back. For example, relational partners who are experiencing intense emotion might call each other names or make statements such as "I hate you" or "I wish I never met you." In the moment, such statements seem true because people are filled with negative emotion. However, when they calm down, they realize they actually care deeply for each other. Other times, people make these kinds of statements to get a kind of emotional revenge. They know that they don't really hate the partner, but by saying "I hate you" they hope to hurt the partner the way they themselves feel hurt.

When feeling hurt and uncertain, people sometimes lash out by engaging in button pushing or making empty relational threats. When people engage in **button pushing**, they purposely say or do something they know will be especially hurtful to the partner. This could entail bringing up a taboo topic, insulting the partner with an offensive name, or looking away when the partner is talking. The key is that the button pusher knows the words or behavior will bother the partner.

Empty threats involve suggestions to do something that the speaker does not really intend to do. For instance, someone might say, "If you see her again, I'll break up with you," or "I can't stand this anymore; I want a divorce" when the speaker in each case actually has no intention of terminating the relationship. Empty threats have at least two negative consequences. First, if someone does not follow through on these threats, the person will lose face, and the partner may think the person is bluffing during future interactions when this time the individual is really serious. As the old fairy tale warns, it is not wise to "cry wolf" too many times. Second, if someone threatens to end a relationship without really intending to, this could plant a seed for relationship termination. Research suggests that people go through a cognitive process of psychological separation before terminating close relationships (Duck, 1988). Therefore, if one partner continues talking about ending the relationship, the other partner might think about being single or about better relational alternatives. If this happens, the partner who delivered the threats moved the possibility of breaking up to the forefront of the other partner's mind. Thus, empty relational threats are more likely to backfire than to solve problems.

Because people tend to become defensive or aggressive when they are emotionally flooded, it is advisable to avoid discussing conflict issues until both partners have calmed down. However, conflict should not be put off indefinitely. If necessary, couples might need to schedule a time to talk about issues that are bothering them. In the interim, each partner might want to write down their feelings. To illustrate, one of our students once told us about a writing technique that she and her husband used when they were feeling really angry with each other. From their past experiences, they knew it was likely that conflict would escalate if they confronted each other when their emotions were running high. They thus decided to vent their negative emotions by going to different rooms and writing letters to each other. Later, after they had calmed down, they would each read the letters to themselves and decide whether to share them with the spouse. This student said that neither of them ever ended up sharing the letters, but instead always tore them up. The letters were usually filled with things they did not really mean, such as exaggerations, name-calling, or unfair accusations. But, these letters helped her and her husband put their conflict issues in perspective and enabled them to move on and discuss their problems in a calmer fashion.

Attributions

People like to be able to explain the behavior of others, particularly during significant events such as conflict episodes. To do this, people make attributions. In their book on interpersonal communication, Fisher and Adams (1994) defined an **attribution** as "a perceptual process of assigning reasons or causes to another's behavior" (p. 411). This definition is consistent with Heider's (1958) conception of people as "naive scientists" who study one another's behavior and make judgments about why they act the way they do. People are especially likely to make attributions about negative behavior, including the uncooperative types of behaviors that often occur during conflict (Roloff & Miller, 2006).

Three specific types of attributions have been studied extensively (Kelley, 1973). First, people attribute a person's behavior to personal versus situational causes. When people make personal attributions, they believe that the cause of another person's behavior is rooted in their personality. By contrast, when people make situational attributions, they believe that the other person's behavior was affected by external factors, such as context or situation. For example, Doug might be upset because Mary ran out and got his birthday present at the last minute, causing them to be late for their dinner reservation. He could attribute Mary's behavior to personality factors (Mary is forgetful and disorganized) or to situational factors (Mary has been especially busy with work and has had to drive Amanda to the hospital every day after work).

Second, people make attributions about behavior being stable versus unstable. In other words, is Mary usually too busy to prepare for Doug's birthday? After many years of marriage, Doug might determine that her last-minute behavior is atypical and that she usually finds the time to buy him a nice gift no matter how busy she gets. Third, people make attributions about how global versus specific the cause of a behavior is. The more global a cause is, the greater number of behaviors and situations it applies to. For instance, the extra tasks with which Mary has been occupied might have caused her to put off doing things she normally does, or perhaps she just forgot about getting Doug a present.

Research on the **attribution hypothesis** has shown that patterns of attribution are related to conflict escalation and lower levels of satisfaction (Fincham, Harold, & Gano-Phillips, 2000). As Figure 14.3 shows, people in happy relationships tend to make **relationship-enhancing attributions** by attributing negative behavior such as complaints, whining, and nagging to causes that are external, unstable, and specific. By contrast, people in unhappy relationships tend to make **distress-maintaining attributions** by attributing negative behavior to internal, stable, and global causes (Bradbury & Fincham, 1990; Brehm & Kassin, 1990; Harvey, 1987; Holtzworth-Munroe & Jacobson, 1985). In general, people make more positive attributions about their own behavior than their partner's behavior during conflict, but partners in dissatisfying relationships are especially likely to blame their partners (Sillars, Roberts, Leonard, & Dun, 2000).

Since Doug and Mary are happily married, their pattern of attributions would most likely be relationship enhancing. For instance, if Mary becomes aggressive when Doug doesn't agree with her, he might think, "She's just especially upset because her grandfather died of lung cancer and she's worried about Amanda. We can usually talk about disciplining our daughters without getting into a heated argument." On the other hand, if they were a dissatisfied couple, Doug might think, "Mary is so stubborn. She always thinks she's right! We never agree about how to discipline our daughters—or anything else for that matter!"

As these examples suggest, when people attribute negative behavior to internal, stable, and global causes (as people in dissatisfying relationships tend to do), they are more likely to use uncooperative conflict behaviors, such as indirect and competitive fighting (Davey, Fincham, Beach, & Brody, 2001; Schweinel, Ickes, & Bernstein, 2002). This can lead to negative spirals in dissatisfying relationships. Couples in dissatisfying relationships are also more likely to pay attention to negative behaviors than positive behaviors, and to attribute positive behaviors to negative causes. In some cases, these attributions represent habitual but inaccurate ways of perceiving the partner's behavior.

In other cases, negative attributions may be accurate. Amanda might resist her parents' advice about smoking because she is stubborn and rebellious (a personal cause), and Megan and Amanda might continually fight over family possessions, such as the phone and computer, because they both want privacy and autonomy (a stable cause). In conflict situations such as these, identifying the causes may be essential for managing the conflict (Roloff & Miller, 2006). Therefore, it is essential—although difficult—to sort out inaccurate attributions from accurate attributions so that the true causes of conflict can be identified.

Communication Skill Deficits

In addition to emotional flooding and cognitive attributions, some people simply do not have the communication skills necessary to engage in constructive conflict. These individuals are likely to feel helpless and defensive when attacked by others because they cannot respond effectively. Thus, they resort to aggressive behaviors or withdrawal, which

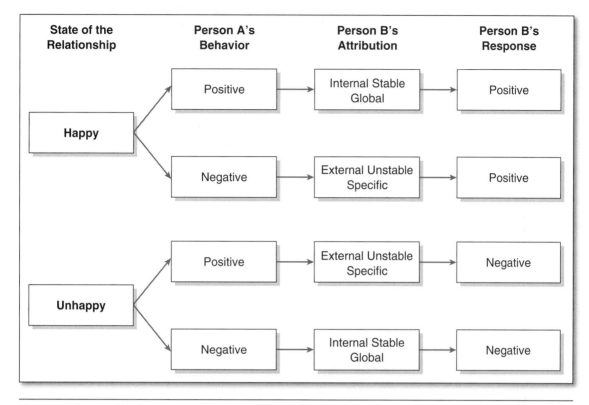

State of the Relationship	Person A's Behavior	Person B's Attribution	Person B's Response
Happy	Positive	Internal Stable Global	Positive
	Negative	External Unstable Specific	Positive
Unhappy	Positive	External Unstable Specific	Negative
	Negative	Internal Stable Global	Negative

Figure 14.3   Attribution Patterns in Happy Versus Unhappy Couples

can contribute to negative spirals of behavior. People with communication or social skill deficits are also more likely to report using violence in their relationships (Christopher & Lloyd, 2000). These deficits include having difficulties in the following areas: general emotional expression, anger management, social support seeking and giving, and problem solving. Men with communication skill deficits are also less likely to make relationship-enhancing attributions for their partner's behavior (Holtzworth-Munroe & Hutchinson, 1993; Holtzworth-Munroe & Smutzler, 1996).

Argumentativeness Versus Aggressiveness

Another important communication skill is the ability to engage in logical argument. Infante and his colleagues distinguished between argumentativeness and verbal aggressiveness (Infante, 1987; Infante, Chandler, & Rudd, 1989; Infante & Rancer, 1982). **Argumentativeness** refers to conflict styles that focus on logical argument and reasoning: People with argumentative styles confront conflict directly by recognizing issues of disagreement, taking positions on controversial issues, backing up claims with evidence and reasoning, and refuting views contrary to their own. Argumentativeness is an important social skill. People who are skilled in argument do not have to resort to name-calling, accusations, or other negative tactics. Instead, they can present their positions in a skilled and convincing manner. Rather than attacking their partner, they attack their partner's position.

Verbal aggressiveness involves attacking the other person's self-concept, often with the intention of hurting the other person. Verbally aggressive people engage in such tactics as teasing, threatening, and criticizing the partner's character or appearance (Infante, Sabourin, Rudd, & Shannon, 1990). Infante's research has shown that people resort to these types of tactics when they are unskilled in argumentation. Partners in violent marriages are more likely to report high levels of verbal aggression and low levels of argumentativeness than are those in nonviolent marriages (Infante et al., 1989, 1990).

The following example illustrates how difficult it is to deal with someone who is verbally aggressive: Amanda and Megan are starting to think about where to apply for college, so they watch a news report on admission requirements at various universities. After the report, the sisters begin discussing their differing opinions on affirmative action.

Amanda: I can't believe they are going to prohibit affirmative action at State.

Megan: If you ask me, it's about time they did.

Amanda: You mean you are against affirmative action?

Megan: Let's put it this way: I think people should be admitted to universities based on their qualifications rather than their skin color.

Amanda: So you are a racist who hates minorities.

Megan: That's not true. I don't like discrimination in any form. I just think universities should make exceptions based on factors other than race. Poor white students are also disadvantaged. Maybe a policy that admits students based on where they rank in their particular high school would be fairer. That way, all students who are economically disadvantaged, including minority students, would get help.

Amanda: And I suppose you think that white men are discriminated against too. I thought you were smarter than that. How can you be so gullible?

If you did not have a strong opinion about affirmative action policies before reading Amanda and Megan's comments, you may have been persuaded by Megan's arguments because they focused on her position rather than attacking Amanda as a person. In short, Megan used argumentative communication. By contrast, Amanda used verbal aggression when she called Megan a racist, implied she was unintelligent, and asked how she could be so gullible. If Amanda had used argumentative communication, you might have been persuaded by her argument rather than Megan's. This example also illustrates how verbally aggressive communication can lead to negative spirals. Put yourself in Megan's place. If the conversation continued, and you kept being attacked personally, would you have been tempted to retaliate by using verbal aggression yourself? Most people have a hard time remaining neutral in the face of personal attacks, partly due to emotional flooding.

Effective Listening

The ability to listen to others is another critical skill for effective conflict management. When people practice effective listening, they are better able to understand their partner's thoughts and feelings, and, ultimately, to empathize with their concerns. Such understanding plays a vital role in collaboration and compromise. In fact, studies have shown that people with listening and decoding skills (the ability to figure out what the partner is feeling) tend to be more satisfied in their relationships (Guerrero & Floyd, 2006).

Active listening is very challenging in conflict situations. For instance, think about the last heated argument you had with someone. How carefully did you listen to what the person said? If you felt attacked or became defensive, chances are that you did not really listen to the other person very carefully. Instead, you were probably thinking about what you would say next. Your mind may have been racing as you thought about how to defend yourself, and your emotions may have been so turbulent that you became preoccupied with your own thoughts and feelings and "tuned the other person out." Ironically, if the other person was not practicing active listening either, all the counterarguments you spent so much time creating would never really be heard.

Active listening thus requires effort and concentration. The experts on listening and negotiation give the following advice for improving active listening skills (Stark, 1994; Steil, Barker, & Watson, 1983; Stiff, Dillard, Somera, Kim, & Sleight, 1988):

1. *Let your partner speak.* Refrain from arguing your case or interrupting until your partner finishes stating her or his position. If you spend noticeably more time talking than your partner, this probably means that you need to talk less and encourage your partner to talk more.

2. *Put yourself in your partner's place.* Enter a conflict situation with specific goals regarding what you would like to learn from your partner. As Gottman (1994) emphasized, if people want to understand and empathize with each other, they need to create **mental maps** of each other's thoughts and feelings. By listening actively, people can see things from their partner's perspective.

3. *Don't jump to conclusions.* Don't assume you know what your partner will say or why they will say it. Making such assumptions can lead you to interpret your partner's statements in a way that is consistent with your preexisting beliefs, even if your preexisting beliefs are wrong.

4. *Ask questions.* Ask questions that allow your partner to clarify and explain her or his position. Be sure to phrase these questions in a positive manner so you don't sound sarcastic or condescending.

5. *Paraphrase what your partner says.* Paraphrase what you hear to confirm that you have really heard what your partner is trying to tell you. When partners paraphrase, they summarize each other's positions. This way partners the opportunity to correct misinterpretations and to further clarify their positions.

SUMMARY AND APPLICATION

Conflict is inevitable in close relationships. The closer you are to someone, the more likely you will encounter disagreements. Disagreements also have both positive or negative effects on relationships. When differences are handled cooperatively, conflict can improve relationships by helping partners solve problems and understand each other. But when negative patterns of conflict communication become pervasive, including those involving common couple violence, relational partners are likely to become less satisfied and committed, and to feel less emotional closeness. When spouses argue, their conflict style can also impact their children's well-being. Children whose parents repeatedly engage in hostile patterns of conflict are less likely to have good peer relationships and more likely to use uncooperative conflict styles themselves. Conflict between parents and children also has a socializing effect on children. So, if Amanda disagrees with her parents regarding her punishment, the way her parents communicate with her will likely influence how Amanda deals with conflict in other relationships in the future.

Doug and Mary have many options for dealing with conflict. They could engage in communication that is cooperative or uncooperative, direct or indirect. Although six separate styles of conflict are described in this chapter, Doug and Mary could use a variety of styles during a conflict interaction and each could use different styles of communication. Mary might be more direct than Doug, and Doug might be more cooperative than Mary. In addition, conflict interaction is a two-way street. It takes two people to escalate conflict; it also takes two people to cooperate.

Engaging in cooperative conflict requires communication skills. Many people use uncooperative strategies, such as competitive fighting and indirect fighting, that cause conflicts to escalate. It follows that negative patterns of conflict communication can develop in relationships. For example, some relational partners get caught in patterns of negative reciprocity, demand-withdrawal, or the four horsemen of the apocalypse. Others resort to common couple violence as they get increasingly frustrated and flooded with emotion. If Doug and Mary notice that their conflict interactions are characterized by plenty of personal criticism, contempt, defensiveness, or stonewalling, their relationship could be in trouble. Violence is another red flag. Patterns of accommodation, which involve responding to negative behavior with positive behavior, help diffuse negativity and promote cooperation.

Using the collaborating style would provide Mary and Doug with the best option for disciplining Amanda effectively. Mary and Doug would be more likely to reach a collaborative solution if they avoided destructive patterns of conflict communication and remained focused on their goals. The studies reviewed in this chapter point to several rules for constructive conflict management, which Mary and Doug would be advised to follow. These rules are summarized in Box 14.3 and provide a blueprint for communicating effectively during conflict situations.

Although these rules probably make sense to you, it may be hard for Mary and Doug (or any two people) to follow them all of the time. Even if you have good intentions and know how you *should* act during a conflict situation, when your emotions are running high, it is difficult not to violate some of these rules. If you find yourself engaging in some destructive tactics during conflict situations, do not panic—even experts in negotiation make mistakes. Recognizing these mistakes is a first step toward managing conflict in ways that keep your relationships satisfying.

DISCUSSION QUESTIONS

1. Think about your long-term relationships. How often do you have disagreements with these relational partners? Did the number and types of conflict change as the relationship became more serious?

2. Do you tend to avoid or engage in conflict? Which of the six conflict styles discussed in this chapter best fits you? Does your style of communication stay fairly consistent, or does it vary a lot depending on the situation and the partner?

3. When people are in the midst of interpersonal conflict, they often are flooded with emotions. This makes it difficult to "fight fairly." Which of the rules for constructive conflict management do you think is most difficult to follow? Do you have any additional suggestions that might help your classmates learn to manage conflict in more constructive ways?

STUDENT STUDY SITE

Visit the study site at **www.sagepub.com/guerrero3e** for e-flashcards, survey and assessments from the chapter, and SAGE journal articles.

15

Ending Relationships

Disengagement and Termination

Katelyn is crushed. "I've never been hurt so badly in my life," she tells her friend Tamika. "I am a complete basket case since Sean left me. It was so out of the blue." Since Sean broke up with Katelyn last week, she has suffered greatly. She can't sleep at night. She has missed work. She can't study. Worse, she left desperate pleading messages on Sean's answering machine that must make him think she is psycho. The only thing that seems to help is having long talks with Tamika while they go shopping or have lunch. For Sean, the breakup was building for years. He thinks that Katelyn is too traditional, too religious, not spontaneous enough, and too preoccupied with money. When they talked about these differences, it became clear to Sean that they were just too different. The gap between their values and goals was just too wide to bridge. He even started feeling like he was losing his "real self" by trying to be someone he is not just to please Katelyn. Finally, he decided to end the relationship despite the fact that he felt terrible about hurting someone he loved. Sean wished there had been a nicer way to break up. At first, he thought Katelyn would get the hint when he spent more time with his friends and withdrew affection from her. When she didn't get the hint, he eventually had to tell her straight out that he wanted to break up. Katelyn insisted that they could work it out, but Sean was firm in telling her that his decision was made and it was definitely over.

In Paul Simon's classic song "Fifty Ways to Leave Your Lover," breakups sound so easy. We are told to "walk out the back, Jack, just make a new plan Stan, don't need to by coy, Roy, just set yourself free." Rarely, however, is it that easy. For a person in either Katelyn's or Sean's position, breakups are some of the most difficult episodes in life. Relationship researchers who have been examining the ends of relationships for several decades have come to understand how and why relationships end and the central role played by communication before, after, and during relationship breakups.

The goal in this chapter is to provide a better understanding of the relational disengagement process. Think about the relationships in your own life that have ended. Some probably ended abruptly, whereas others disintegrated slowly. You and your partner may have had different perceptions of how and why the relationship ended, like Katelyn and Sean. It is likely that it was painful to end some relationships and a relief to end others. Relational disengagement is a complex phenomenon. To help unravel this complexity, this chapter focuses on four areas of relational disengagement research. First, we examine the reasons relationships end. Second, we review models of the disengagement process. Third, we discuss 15 communication strategies people use to leave their partners. Finally, we take a look at the aftermath of relational disengagement.

WHY RELATIONSHIPS END

All relationships end. Regardless of whether they are brief or close encounters, last 50 days or 50 years, or are friendships or marriages, all relationships end at one time or another. Sometimes they end voluntarily through our personal choice. Other times they end involuntarily because someone breaks up with us, moves away, or dies. Conville (1991) suggested that "disintegration is everywhere. . . . Disintegration is a process that is triggered when the relationship is out of kilter" (p. 96). Baxter (1982) stated: "The breaking up of a relationship is a phenomenon known to most and dreaded by all. It accounts for some of our most intense and painful social experiences" (p. 223). Worse, it is relatively common; 85% of adults in the United States have experienced a romantic relationship breakup (Battaglia, Richard, Datteri, & Lord, 1998) . The deep positive and negative feelings we experience in our relationships are connected: There are no highs without lows. Gibran (1923) described these two sides of love:

> When love beckons to you follow him, though his ways are hard and steep, and when his wings enfold you, yield to him, though the sword hidden among his pinions may wound you. And when he speaks to you believe in him, though his voice may shatter your dreams as the north wind lays waste the garden. Even as love crowns you so shall he crucify you. Even as he is for your growth so is he for your pruning. (p. 12)

The fact that relationships end, often painfully, prevents some people from developing close relationships. By denying themselves the opportunity to feel both the joys and the sorrows of relationships, these people miss an important secret of life: Not feeling anything at all may be worse than feeling bad. Avoiding relationships prevents them from experiencing the deepest involvements and emotions humans can have.

People become deeply enmeshed in their close relationships (Baxter, 1982). Relationships exist in a web of close ties, emotional involvements, financial arrangements, sexual relations, friendship networks, possessions, memories, identities, families, and sometimes offspring. When a relationship dies, many of these ties die as well. The loss of these other relationships, resources, and connections compounds the emotional pain of relational loss. Given how painful the end of relationships can be, you might wonder, why do relationships end? What are the common causes for relationship breakup?

Relationships end in many ways, but research suggests that most couples, unmarried or married, straight or gay, show more similarity than difference in the way they break up (Kurdek, 1991). In their massive study of couples living in the United States, Blumstein and Schwartz (1983) were surprised to find that lesbians were most likely to break up, followed by gay men, and then heterosexual cohabitors. Married couples were the most stable of these four couple types, but when they did break up, they separated for many of the same reasons as did other couples. Interestingly, some variables one would think are associated with relational breakups, such as self-esteem and amount of conflict, have not been shown to predict breakups very well (Cate, Levin, & Richmond, 2002). What, then, does predict breakups?

National data from a 17-year study of married individuals gives us some clues (Amato & Previti, 2003). Individuals who had divorced at some point during this study were asked why their marriage ended. Box 15.1 shows the top 10 reasons they gave for divorcing. Women were more likely to report that their divorce was due to infidelity, drinking or drug abuse, physical or psychological abuse, and her partner not meeting his family obligations. Men were more likely to report divorcing due to personality problems, lack of communication, or loss of love.

BOX 15.1

The Top 10 Reasons People Give for Divorcing

1. **Infidelity/interest in a third party** (21.6%) "I wouldn't put up with his cheating."

2. **Incompatibility/lack of shared interests** (19.2%) "We didn't agree on sex, friends, goals, or anything."

3. **Drinking or drug use** (10.6%) "He drank too much."

4. **Grew apart** (9.6%) "Our priorities changed; we weren't the same people."

5. **Partner's personality** (9.1%) "She was selfish and only thought of herself."

6. **Lack of communication** (8.7%) "We didn't talk anymore."

7. **Physical or psychological abuse** (5.8%) "Our relationship started to get violent."

8. **Loss of love** (4.3%) "I guess I didn't love him anymore."

9. **Not meeting family responsibilities** (3.4%) "He didn't do his share around the house or with the kids."

10. **Work problems** (3.4%) "He was too preoccupied with work all the time."

SOURCE: Amato, P. R., & Previti, D. (2003). People's reasons for divorcing: Gender, social class, the life course, and adjustment. *Journal of Family Issues, 24,* 602–626.

Several other predictors of divorce emerged in this study, including being generally unhappy in one's marriage and wishing to pursue better alternatives, undergoing personal change (e.g., therapy or a midlife crisis) that leads one to want to do new things, financial problems, interference from family or one's social network, physical or mental illness, and immaturity (e.g., getting married too young). Other studies have also focused on these issues. For example, several researchers have identified money or financial problems as a cause of divorce (Bradford, 1980; Parker & Drummond-Reeves, 1993; Safron, 1979) and problems in gay and lesbian separations (Kurdek, 1991). Few relational problems revolve around how much money a couple makes. Instead, problems seem to stem from money management, with the values surrounding spending and saving producing considerable turmoil for couples (Blumstein & Schwartz, 1983).

Several issues related to social networks also contribute to breakups. Dating partners are more likely to break up if their social networks or parents disapprove of their relationship (Felmlee, Sprecher, & Bassin, 1990; Sprecher & Felmlee, 1992). Having separate friendship networks that do not intermix can also signal that a relationship is in danger of termination (Metts & Cupach, 1986; Vaughn, 1986), as can problems getting along with in-laws (Safron, 1979).

Finally, there are several reasons why getting married young is more likely to result in divorce, including immaturity, lack of financial resources, perceptions of being tied down too early in life, and marrying to escape an unhappy home environment (Huston, 2009). Indeed, the probability of divorce within a few years after marrying decreases from 40% for 18- to 19-year-olds to 24% for individuals 25 or older (Clarke-Stewart & Brentano, 2006). In relationships, experience does matter.

Although not mentioned in Amato and Previti's (2003) study, boredom or lack of excitement has also been cited as a reason for breakup, especially in dating relationships (Hill et al., 1976). Nearly 10% of the participants in one study noted the absence of magic and romance as a primary cause for relational termination (Baxter, 1986). Interestingly, this was a factor for 19% of the men but only 5% of the women, suggesting that men are less practical partners who may disengage if the magic is no longer there. Honeycutt, Cantrill, and Allen (1992) also reported that one of the most common thoughts that disengagers have about a relationship is that it has become boring. Considering that our interpersonal relationships are one of our greatest sources of joy and excitement, when they begin to bore us, the end may be near.

Needs for autonomy may also be a more prominent reason for breakups in dating relationships than marriages. Studies have repeatedly shown that wanting to maintain one's autonomy is a major reason for relationship disengagement among daters. People often complain that the relationship is "smothering" or "suffocating" them and they need their "space" and "freedom." In studies on dating relationships, needs for autonomy and independence are often one of the top three predictors of breakup (Baxter, 1985; Hill et al., 1976). In Baxter's study, this was the primary reason given by around 24% of men and 44% of women. Similarly, one of the five most common general issues leading to relational breakups in gay and lesbian couples was excessive fusion, which is a loss of individuality due to the relationship (Kurdek, 1991).

Although all the factors mentioned here can lead to breakups, some of the major contributors to divorce identified in Amato and Previti's (2003) study—infidelity and interest in a third party, incompatibility, drinking or drug use, growing apart, loss of love, and equity issues related to family responsibilities—are particularly relevant alongside communication. Communication, or lack of communication, is also a significant factor related to breakups.

Infidelity and Interest in a Third Party

Extramarital or extrarelational sex is often detrimental to a relationship and may lead to termination, although the reverse is sometimes true; that is, unhappy relationships lead to extrarelational sex. Research suggests that sexual betrayal is common in all type of relationships but particularly during dating (Feldman & Cauffman, 1999). For every type of couple, gay or straight, the relationship is less likely to survive when one partner is having sex outside the relationship (Blumstein & Schwartz, 1983). Gagnon (1977) reported that nearly 40% of extramarital sexual relationships had an important effect on the decision to divorce, and 14% to 18% of the time, these affairs had a major effect. In other studies, extramarital affairs were a factor in the breakups of 21% to 55% of the couples studied (Amato & Previti, 2003; Bradford, 1980; Parker & Drummond-Reeves, 1993).

As Amato and Previti's study suggests, women cite infidelity as a reason for breakup more than men. Cupach and Metts (1986) found that, while extrarelational affairs were a problem associated with breakups for both married and unmarried couples, affairs were a more salient concern for women than for men. They suggested that, for men, an affair is a form of self-gratification, whereas women see affairs as a violation of the relationship, and thus a more central cause of relationship disengagement. On the other hand, consistent with a social-evolutionary hypothesis about sex differences between men and women, the type of the affair is critical. People can engage in sexual infidelity (having sex with someone else), emotional infidelity (falling in love with someone else), or both. Relative to women, men find it more difficult to forgive sexual infidelity than emotional infidelity and are more likely to terminate a relationship following a partner's sexual infidelity (Shackelford, Buss, & Bennett, 2002). The reverse was true for women, who were more likely than men to break up as a result of their partner's emotional infidelity. Of course, both forms of infidelity can be a reason for break up for either men or women.

As the idea of emotional infidelity suggests, rivals threaten relationships whether or not sexual infidelity has occurred. Perhaps this is why jealousy is such a widespread emotion and a major cause of relational violence (see Chapter 13). Hill and colleagues (1976) reported that one of the top 10 reasons for terminating a dating relationship for both men and women was interest in someone else. Similarly, Metts and Cupach (1986) reported that one of the most common disengagement themes was third-party involvement, particularly for women. Furthermore, failure to be faithful was a primary reason for terminating relationships in 16% of the accounts in Baxter's (1986) study on breakups, and the availability of attractive alternative partners makes relational breakups more likely (Felmlee et al., 1990; Rusbult, Zembrodt, & Gunn, 1982). Interestingly, when people have few good prospects as alternative partners or are unaware of alternative partners, they are more likely to stay with their current partner (Miller, 1997; Simpson, 1987). These findings correspond with social exchange theory principles (see Chapter 10). Young couples are particularly vulnerable to breakups caused by infidelity (Huston, 2009), though it is not the only reason why younger couples break up more frequently.

Incompatibility

Despite the oft-repeated folk wisdom that "opposites attract," a more valid cliché is: "Birds of a feather flock together" (see Chapter 3). Dozens of studies show that the more two people have in common, the more likely they are to stay together. For example, think of your close friends. Chances are that you have many things in common, including hobbies and interests, political opinions, and religious values. Similarities are also important in romantic relationships. Studies have shown that similarities in personality lead to longer relationships and fewer breakups, with spouses who are more alike in extraversion, attractiveness, and interest in art less likely to divorce (Bentler & Newcomb, 1978, Cody, 1982). In Baxter's (1996) study of heterosexual dating relationships, the second most common reason for breakups was a discrepancy in beliefs, attitudes, and values—a factor mentioned by nearly one-third of the respondents. Likewise, Metts and Cupach (1986) found that value dissimilarity commonly led to relational disengagement. In a major statistical summary of factors leading to divorce, Karney and Bradbury (1995) concluded that attitude dissimilarity was one of the most important factors leading to both relational dissatisfaction and divorce.

Although interethnic dating relationships and marriages can be very successful and rewarding, they are at greater risk for breakups. Lack of similarity in attitudes, activities, and interests, as well as differences in ethnic, religious, and socioeconomic backgrounds, can precipitate relational breakups (Cate et al., 2002; Felmlee, Sprecher, & Bassin, 1990). This may be primarily due to the prejudiced influences of family, friends, and society in general that puts greater strain on an interethnic couple (Williams & Andersen, 1998). In a classic study on dating relationships, Hill and associates (1976) found that the fourth most important factor leading to breakups was differences in background. Similarly, although age-discrepant relationships can be very happy, large age differences are statistically related to breakups (Bentler & Newcomb, 1978).

Differences in educational background, intelligence, and health may also pose problems for relationships. In Hill and colleagues' (1976) study, differences in intelligence were among the top reasons for dating relationship breakup. Similarly, when one partner continues education and the other partner does not, the couple sometimes finds that they have less and less in common (Scott & Powers, 1978). Although personal health is not associated with divorce, *differences* in partners' health status dramatically increase the chance of divorce, particularly among otherwise satisfied couples (Wilson & Waddoups, 2002).

Relationships also benefit from similar levels of emotional involvement in the relationship. In over half of dating relationships, people report that one person is more emotionally involved in the relationship, tracing to the principle of least interest that makes breakups easier for the least interested person (see Chapter 12). Such asymmetrical levels of emotional involvement are thus a risk factor for relational breakups (Sprecher, Schmeeckle, & Felmlee, 2006).

Sexual incompatibility is also important. Conflicting sexual attitudes have been identified as a key contributor to breakups in heterosexual dating relationships (Hill et al., 1976), marriages (Cleek & Pearson, 1985; Safron, 1979), and gay and lesbian relationships (Kurdek, 1991). As discussed in Chapter 8, sex is a central, personal feature of marriages, romances, and many dating relationships that can lead to several types of relational problems. Relational partners may differ over the desired frequency of sexual relations, the type of sexual behaviors, and the initiation of sex. In dating relationships, engagements, marriages, and gay relationships, fighting about sex is associated with relational breakups (Blumstein & Schwartz, 1983), although there is little association between how much sex a couple has and how long the partners stay together. Apparently frequency is not as important as compatibility. In other words, some couples may be satisfied with less sex than others.

Alcohol and Drugs

Alcohol and drugs play a role in many relational breakups. These problems have been cited as one of the top 10 reasons for marital breakup in several studies (e.g., Amato & Previti, 2003; Safron, 1979). Similarly, alcohol and drugs were reported to be a factor in 45% of the divorces in a study by Parker and Drummond-Reeves (1993). Alcohol and drugs may lead to violence, addiction, problems with the law, the squandering of money, and problems at work—any of which can greatly strain a relationship.

Research suggests that alcohol and drugs can also lead to codependency in relationships. Le Poire, Hallett, and Giles (1998), for example, argued that the partners of alcoholics and drug addicts often become **codependent**, letting their partner's behavior greatly affect their own behavior. Many codependents become obsessed with controlling their partner's negative behaviors and with nurturing the partner. According to Le Poire and colleagues (1998), codependents often show a mix of punishing and reinforcing behaviors. Sometimes, they try to get their partner to stop using drugs or alcohol through punishment (e.g., verbal confrontation, threats to leave the relationship). Other times, however, they reinforce the partner's behavior by doing things such as keeping the children out of the way and taking care of the partner when the partner is ill. Although codependency may keep people in relationships for a while, in the long run, codependent behavioral patterns may put considerable strain on relationships.

Growing Apart

Some relationships wither away (Metts & Cupach, 1986). This could result from different interests, such as the dissimilarities between Katelyn and Sean discussed at the beginning of this chapter. Relationships also deteriorate due to decreased quality and quantity of communication, distance, reduced efforts to maintain the relationship, or competition from the hundreds of relationships in today's fast-paced world. In marriages, people often cannot pinpoint when they started growing apart. This type of atrophy is a gradual process. Sometimes spouses get absorbed in the business of their everyday lives—working and raising children—to the point that they forget to give each other the attention they need and deserve. Growing apart is an even more common cause for relationship termination among friends and partners in long-distance relationships who do not interact with one another as frequently as spouses.

In marriages characterized by atrophy, marital happiness slowly declines over time (Sternberg, 1987). Feelings of intimacy and passion may diminish and then disappear as partners grow further and further apart. Owen (1993) found that many relationship breakups were characterized by atrophy or decay. Typical metaphors for relationship endings were "It was like a flower that blossomed and then withered," "I could see the relationship rot each day," and "The relationship faded into the sunset" (pp. 271–272).

Loss of Love

There are many reasons why partners stop loving each other. Sometimes people experience **chronic dissatisfaction** in their relationships. Although temporary dissatisfaction may cause couples to attempt to repair and maintain their relationship (see Chapter 9), couples with a long history of dissatisfaction are more likely to be at risk for marital dissolution and divorce (Kurdek, 1993b). Love is associated with feelings of joy, warmth, contentment, and passion. We want to be around people we love so we can experience these positive feelings. Chronic dissatisfaction eats away at these feelings, making us more likely to seek happiness elsewhere. Longitudinal research on dating couples suggests that the vast majority of daters with steady levels of satisfaction remained in their relationships, while few daters with fluctuating levels of satisfaction remained in their relationships (Arriaga, 2001).

Loss of love is also related to disillusionment. **Relationship disillusionment** occurs when people's positive illusions about their partners and their relationships start to fade (Huston, 2009; Niehuis & Bartell, 2006). During courtship when people are falling in love, they often see their partners and their relationships through "rose-colored glasses." For example, some researchers have suggested that people have positive illusions about their partners during courtship and early marriage, but that it is hard to maintain idealized images once the honeymoon stage is over (Murray, Holmes, & Griffin, 1996; Swann, De LaRonde, & Hixon, 1994). The process of disillusionment is more highly predictive of divorce and dating breakups than is either antagonism or contentiousness (Huston, 2009; Niehuis & Bartell, 2006; Niehuis & Huston, 2002). Disillusionment is accompanied by decreases in love and affection, loss of emotional attachment, and disappointment in the relationship and the partner. Disillusionment is especially strong when people have unrealistic expectations and perceptions about their relationship during courtship or early marriage. In fact, Neihuis and Huston (2002) found that people were most likely to experience disillusionment during the first two years of marriage when they had reported particularly high levels of premarital affection and passion. To see if your relationship is characterized by disillusionment, take the test in Box 15.2.

BOX 15.2 Put Yourself to the Test

Relationship Disillusionment Scale

Circle the number that best represents how much you agree or disagree with each statement, using the following scale: 1 = strong disagreement, 7 = strong agreement.

	Disagree					Agree	
1. I am very disappointed in my relationship.	1	2	3	4	5	6	7
2. I am very disappointed in my partner.	1	2	3	4	5	6	7
3. My partner used to be my best friend, but now I sometimes don't like her or him as a person.	1	2	3	4	5	6	7
4. This relationship is not at all what I expected it to be; I feel very disappointed.	1	2	3	4	5	6	7
5. I used to think I was lucky to be with someone like my partner; now I'm not so sure that I am so lucky.	1	2	3	4	5	6	7
6. I used to love spending time with my partner, but now it is starting to feel like a chore.	1	2	3	4	5	6	7
7. I feel tricked, cheated, or deceived by love.	1	2	3	4	5	6	7
8. The relationship is not as enjoyable as I had expected it to be.	1	2	3	4	5	6	7

(Continued)

(Continued)

		Disagree				Agree		
9. If I could go back in time, I would not have gotten involved with my partner.	1	2	3	4	5	6	7
10. My partner used to be on her or his best behavior when with me, but now he or she doesn't bother trying to impress me.	1	2	3	4	5	6	7
11. My partner seems to be an entirely different person now.	1	2	3	4	5	6	7

Add up your responses. A score of 11 represents a lack of disillusionment, whereas a score of 77 represents the highest possible level of disillusionment.

SOURCE: From Niehuis, S., & Bartell, D., The marital disillusionment scale: Development and psychometric properties. *North American Journal of Psychology 8*, 69–83. Copyright © 2006. Reprinted and adapted with permission of the North American Journal of Psychology and the author.

Equity Issues Related to Family Obligations

Issues related to equity or fairness in meeting family responsibilities are often cited as a reason for marital breakups (Amato & Previti, 2003), with some studies casting this as an equality issue for women (Safron, 1979). Indeed, in Amato and Previti's study, women cited having a partner who do not meet family obligations as a reason for divorce about three and a half times more than men did. Equity is also important in dating relationships (see Chapter 10). In Baxter's (1986) study of heterosexual dating relational breakups, equity was a primary factor in the breakup for 17% of the women and 5% of the men. In Blumstein and Schwartz's (1983) study, a major factor in relational breakups revolved around men's opinions about working women. Specifically, if the man objected to the woman working, or if he was unhappy about her job, the couple was more likely to terminate their relationship. Moreover, research suggests that employment may make women more independent and increase their likelihood of leaving a troubled marriage (Kalmijn & Poortman, 2006).

Working women are also likely to be under considerable stress, especially if they have children and are trying to run a household. In the popular press, this problem is referred to as the *superwoman syndrome*. Women are supposed to do their jobs and then to go home and tend to their families and homes. Because women are expected to be the caregivers at home, they are always working—at the office and at home. Hochschild (1997; Hochschild & Machung, 1989), for example, has shown that women typically do about 70% of the household chores. Moreover, only 20% of dual-career couples report a fair distribution of labor exists in their home. For the other 80% of couples, the woman is nearly always responsible for the majority of homemaking and child care chores. When this type of inequity exists, it is a primary source of tension in the relationship. A longitudinal study of marital breakups found that women's perception of inequality and a sense of being underbenefitted increased the risk of divorce significantly (DeMaris, 2007). The association between women's perceived inequity held even when more objective indicants such as actual contributions to the relationship were controlled.

COMMUNICATION AS A CAUSE OF RELATIONAL BREAKUP

Poor communication is also a common culprit predicting relational breakup, with several studies reporting poor communication as the number one problem leading to divorce (Bradford, 1980; Cleek & Pearson, 1985; Parker & Drummond-Reeves, 1993). This includes too much communication, too little communication, low-quality communication, communication that is too negative, and communication that is less mutually constructive. In Amato and Previti's (2003) study, the lack of communication as psychological abuse (which involves engaging in hurtful communication) was among the top predictors of divorce. Gottman and Levenson (2000, 2002) found that the type of communication that predicts divorce differs depending on the length of one's marriage. Specifically, couples who divorce within 5 to 7 years tend to report high levels of destructive conflict in their marriages, whereas those who divorce within 10 to 12 years report a loss of intimacy and connection. It follows that several patterns of communication are related to breakup. (See Chapter 14 for a more detailed discussion of destructive communication patterns used during conflict.)

Withdrawal

Studies have shown that withdrawal is a common reason for relationship breakups that can reflect a lack of intimacy and connection. Baxter (1986) found that low levels of supportiveness, and particularly a lack of listening, was a major factor in over one-fourth of the relational breakups she studied. As discussed in Chapter 14, stonewalling occurs when individuals fail to discuss important issues with their partners (Christensen & Shenk, 1991; Gottman, 1993; Gottman & Levenson, 1992). Men have been found to use this type of dysfunctional communication more often than women (Clements, Cordova, Markman, & Laurenceau, 1997).

A number of studies have also examined the demand-withdrawal sequence (also discussed in Chapter 14), which is associated with separation (Christensen & Shenk, 1991). This sequence occurs when one person makes a demand and the partner responds by withdrawing from communication. People are likely to be in the demanding position if they are dissatisfied and want to change something about their relationship. Children of divorced parents are more likely to report that their mother and father engaged in demand-withdrawal patterns than are children of nondivorced parents (Afifi & Schrodt, 2003). Further, Honeycutt, Cantrill, and Allen (1992) had disengaged couples recall and describe behaviors that aided in the process of relational disengagement. These behaviors included spending less time together, avoiding each other in public settings, and making excuses for not going out together.

Negative Communication

All couples have conflicts and disagreements. In fact, as dating partners become more loving and committed, conflict increases, presumably because of their increased interdependence (Lloyd & Cate, 1985). Research has shown that it is not primarily the presence or absence of conflict that determines whether a couple will be satisfied and stay together; it is how the partners deal with conflict that is more important (see Chapter 14). In a series of studies spanning 15 years, Clements and colleagues (1997) reported that, in their earliest interactions, partners who were destined to break up dealt with their disagreements in a destructive fashion characterized by fights, name-calling, criticisms, and accusations. Research by Filsinger and Thomas (1988) found that negative communication during interpersonal interaction was predictive of disengagement a year and a half later. In a major statistical summary of the research on divorce, Karney and Bradbury (1995) reported that one of the most prevalent factors leading to divorce was negative behavior. One study found that a common path to relational disengagement was rules violation, whereby one partner engages in behavior inappropriate to the relationship (Metts & Cupach, 1986). For example, if relational partners have agreed to call when they are going to be late and not to swear at each other during disagreements, repeated violations of these rules can lead to dissatisfaction and, perhaps, disengagement.

Conflict increases as dating relationships become more committed, and it rises even more sharply for partners who are contemplating a breakup or have decided to terminate their relationships (Lloyd & Cate, 1985). Thus, there may be an optimal level of conflict in a committed relationship beyond which the relationship is threatened. In other words, some conflict may be normal and even healthy for relationships. But high levels of conflict may be detrimental, particularly if issues of contention keep resurfacing because they have not been discussed in a constructive manner.

Increased negative emotional expression and decreased positive emotional expression also put couples at risk for dissolution (Dailey, Pfiester, Jin, Beck, & Clark, 2009; Gottman, 1993; Gottman & Levenson, 1992; Karney & Bradbury, 1995). Karney and Bradbury (1995) found that the reciprocity of

negative behaviors was the most detrimental factor in a marriage. Honeycutt and fellow researchers (1992) reported that couples recalled various forms of aversive communication—such as arguing about little things, disagreeing, verbally fighting, criticizing the partner, and making sarcastic comments—as sets of behaviors that led to the breakup of their relationships. Surprisingly, Gottman (1993) reported that husbands' anger was unrelated to divorce. However, husbands who became defensive, showed contempt, and used stonewalling were more likely to divorce. Similarly, wives who criticized, became defensive, and showed contempt were more likely to see their relationships end. Recently, Gottman and his colleagues have focused on communication patterns that prevent rather than predict divorce (Gottman, Gottman, & DeClaire, 2006). Some of their advice for preventing divorce is presented in Box 15.3.

BOX 15.3

Communication That Helps Prevent Divorce: The Marriage Masters

Based on research conducted in his "love lab" at the University of Washington, John Gottman, along with coauthors Julie Schwartz Gottman and Joan DeClaire, explain that some people are "marriage masters" while others are "marriage disasters." The difference between being a master versus a disaster rests, in large part, on how people communicate. If you are a marriage master, you are more likely to do the following:

- *Soften the start up.* Gottman and colleagues note that it would be ludicrous to expect two people to live together without complaining, but that complaints can be communicated in a respectful manner that expresses your needs without criticizing your partner. When complaints are posed gently and without insults, the partner is more likely to listen and compromise.

- *Tell your partner what you want, rather than what you don't want.* It is easy to tell your partner, "I hate when you leave your dirty socks everywhere" or, "You are so rude when you roll your eyes at me." But it is more constructive to tell your partner that you would like some help keeping the house clean and want to be taken seriously when you are talking.

- *Listen for statements of need and respond with open-ended questions.* Active listening can be a challenge during arguments, but try to look beyond the complaints and criticisms and focus on what your partner needs. Ask your partner questions such as, "What's bothering you?" or, "How can I help?" when appropriate. This can get productive discussion rolling.

- *Accept your partner's emotional bids.* Your partner reaches out for emotional connection in various ways, including giving compliments, smiling, and sitting next to you while watching TV. Marriage masters turn toward their partners and reciprocate positivity, rather than turning away (ignoring) or turning against (reacting with hostility) them, even when they aren't in the best of moods.

- *Express appreciation.* We all have a natural tendency to retaliate or get angry when we are criticized or attacked, but we don't always reward our partner's positive behavior. If your partner is being attentive or putting effort into your relationship, take the time to thank your partner or offer a compliment.

- *Repair conversations.* If a conversation is getting difficult, marriage masters know how to diffuse the negativity by engaging in behaviors such as apologizing, smiling, or making a funny comment. Marriage masters also know how to cool down when they are flooded with negative emotions, sometimes by taking a break from the conversation.

- *Establish rituals for connection.* Some of the most common complaints that couples have are that they do not have enough time for one another because they are busy with work, children, household chores, and other responsibilities. Therefore, it is important to set aside time to be together alone as a couple—just to talk or to get away on a romantic date or getaway.

- *Accept influence.* Marriage masters are also open to accepting advice and being persuaded by their partners. Stubbornly holding on to one's own positions can be harmful, especially if it prevents partners from growing at both a personal and a relational level. Gottman's research suggests marriages are happier when husbands are willing to listen to and be influenced by their wives.

SOURCE: Information compiled from Gottman et al. (2006).

Lack of Openness and Intimacy

Even though couples need some degree of autonomy and privacy (see Chapter 12), open disclosure is still imperative for relationships. Partners who stay together rather than break up report much higher levels of self-disclosure early in their relationships (Berg & McQuinn, 1986). Sprecher (1987) found that dating couples who engaged in more self-disclosure were much more likely to be together four years later. Openness is particularly important to women's evaluation of their partners. In Baxter's (1986) study, 31% of the women, compared to only 8% of the men, mentioned lack of openness as a major factor in relational termination. In a study on memories of relationships breakups, Honeycutt and

his colleagues (1992) reported that many people remember decreases in verbal and nonverbal intimacy as the starting point for relational decline. Couples at risk for eventual disengagement may stop expressing intimate feelings and decrease acts of physical intimacy such as hugs, kisses, and touches.

Abusive Communication

Researchers have tested the "common sense hypothesis" that people are more likely to break up with partners who are physically or psychologically abusive than those who are not (Rhatigan & Street, 2005). **Physical abuse** refers to violent behaviors such as grabbing, pushing, kicking, biting, slapping, and punching, whereas **psychological abuse** refers to hurtful communication, such as insults, name-calling, and personal criticisms. Not surprisingly, research has shown that physical and psychological abuse are related to less relational satisfaction, less commitment, and greater likelihood of relationship termination (Rhatigan & Street, 2005). Physically battered women are more likely to report that they intend to leave their violent partners when they are also psychologically abused (Arias & Pape, 2001), which suggests that both physical and psychological abuse are important determinants of breakups. People are also likely to break up with partners who abuse their children (Amato & Previti, 2003).

Unfortunately, some people stay in abusive relationships. A study that focused specifically on why battered women stay with their husbands uncovered three reasons consistent with past research: financial dependency, family history of violence, and psychological factors such as having low self-esteem and blaming oneself for the partner's violence (Kim & Gray, 2008). Another study uncovered similar reasons, with women more likely to stay in violent relationships if they were financially dependent, needed their spouse to help with child care, were afraid of being lonely or of being harmed if they left, thought the breakup would be socially embarrassing, had poor support from their social network, or hoped the relationship would change for the better (Hendy, Effen, Gustitus, McLeod, & Ng, 2003).

Sometimes, people use abuse to try to control their partner and prevent a breakup. Such is the case with **intimate terrorism**, which is the intentional use of violence as a means of intimidating and controlling one's partner (Johnson, 1995). This type of violence is chronic and tends to be more severe than more common forms of violence that occur occasionally when people lose control during the heat of an argument (see Chapter 14). Intimate partner violence is also asymmetrical—one partner is the perpetrator and the other partner is the victim—whereas many other forms of violence in relationships are reciprocal. Although intimate terrorism can be used by either men or women, studies suggest that women are more likely to be victims than men (Johnson, 1995). This type of violence also tends to be more

severe and enduring that the violence that arises spontaneously during conflict (Graham-Kevan & Archer, 2003; Johnson & Ferraro, 2000). Although victims of intimate terrorism often fear their partner's reaction, they are more likely to end their relationship than are victims of more common forms of violence (Johnson & Leone, 2005).

MODELS OF THE DISENGAGEMENT PROCESS

Logically following the factors that contribute to relational breakups are questions surrounding *how* people end their relationships. Researchers have tackled these questions in two ways: (1) They have examined the general process by which relationships end, and (2) they have uncovered specific communication strategies that people use to terminate their relationships.

Researchers have created several models of how relationships come apart. Most thinking in this area has suggested that relationships pass through several phases—as if descending a staircase from close relationships to breakups. These are stage models of disengagement. Alternatively, many relationships go through sudden changes more akin to falling off a balcony than descending stairs. These are catastrophe theory approaches to disengagement. The leading stage models are the process model of relational dissolution (Duck, 1982, 1988; Rollie & Duck, 2006) and the reversal hypothesis (Knapp & Vangelisti, 2005).

A Process Model of Relational Dissolution

One of the leading models of relational breakups was developed by Duck (1982, 1988), who initially viewed relational dissolution as a set of distinct but connected phases. Recently, this model was revised to focus more on the communication processes that occur during relationship breakups (Duck, 2005). According to Duck's model, five processes are likely to occur as people disengage from relationships—intrapsychic processes, dyadic processes, social processes, grave-dressing processes, and resurrection processes. Moreover, couples can go through several of these processes (particularly the first two) without breaking up. In fact, many couples recognize and resolve relational problems as a function of intrapsychic and dyadic processes that help them re-evaluate their relationships. When partners find themselves embroiled in social processes, however, the relationship might be ready to derail.

Intrapsychic Processes

Feelings of relational dissatisfaction often trigger intrapsychic processes that involve reflecting on the negative aspects of the relationship, and comparing these flaws with the cost of leaving the relationship. Part of the intrapsychic process also involves determining one's own feelings about the relationship, as well as preparing to talk to the partner about problems. Duck (2005) noted that these processes "not only provide a psychological engine for rumination but also affect communicative activity; in particular, they promote a social withdrawal, so that the person can nurse perceived wounds and take stock of the partner and the relationship" (p. 211). At this point, people sometimes realize that their problems are not as bad as they once thought. However, mulling about relational problems can make them worse rather than better (Cloven & Roloff, 1993; Saffrey & Ehrenburg, 2007). Vaughn (1986) claimed that "uncoupling begins with a secret. One of the partners starts to feel uncomfortable with the relationship" (p. 11). This is exactly what happened to Sean, who we introduced at the start of this chapter. The relationship was changing him in ways that made him feel uncomfortable. Dissatisfied partners face a dilemma of whether to discuss these feelings and thoughts with their relational partner or to withdraw. Often they withdraw initially while they are mulling problems over and deciding what to do. A breakup is certainly not inevitable at this stage; the partner is usually seeking to resolve problems and maintain the relationship. However, when people begin to believe that withdrawing from the relationship would be justified, they are likely to engage in dyadic processes that could either repair the relationship or propel it toward dissolution.

Dyadic Processes

These processes occur when dissatisfied partners begin to communicate negative thoughts and feelings with each other. Partners attempt to negotiate and sometimes reconcile the differences to avert a relationship breakup. Fights, arguments, and long discussions often characterize this phase. According to Rollie and Duck (2006), people sometimes experience shock and surprise when a partner airs concerns. Partners can also experience a dramatic reconciliation as a result of dyadic processes. Specific topics related to conflict and expectations for future behavior are often discussed as individuals continue to weigh the costs and rewards associated with being in the relationship. Partners may also renegotiate rules, promise to change, or improve their behavior. In other cases, they may decide the relationship is not worth saving. This is what happened for Sean. He tried to talk to Katelyn about their differences, but he eventually concluded that they were just too different to be able to make their relationship work.

Social Processes

"Going public" about the distress and problems within one's relationship marks social processes (Rollie & Duck, 2006). Couples begin talking to their social networks and investigating alternatives to the current relationship. They attempt to save face and receive support by telling their side of the story to friends and family members, as Katelyn did when she turned to Tamika for comfort. They are also likely to develop a story to convince their network, and themselves, that they are doing the right thing (Duck, 1982). Often nonverbal behaviors such as looking depressed or sounding upset reveal to others that something is wrong in the relationship. Thus, the breakup initiator not only starts to complain publicly but also displays discontentment about the partner to others (Vaughn, 1986). Initially the individual's network may try to prevent a breakup, but when the outcome seems inevitable, they help facilitate the breakup by providing interpersonal and emotional support and taking the initiating partner's side in any disputes. When members of the person's social network take their friend's side, it helps convince the breakup initiator that breaking up is the right decision. A word of caution is in order here, though: If people complain too loudly about their partners to others, the social network may have a hard time accepting them back into the fold if the partners change their minds and get back together. As Rollie and Duck (2006) explain, it is difficult to backtrack and repair the relationship once people have engaged in these types of social processes.

Grave-Dressing Processes

This set of processes focuses on coping with the breakup in a socially acceptable manner. For instance, think about the stories you tell around a relationship breakup. If you are the one who initiated the breakup, you might emphasize that you handled the breakup in a sensitive and caring manner. If you are the person who was dumped, you might assure people that you are strong and will be okay. In other cases, you might note that the breakup was inevitable or mutual. Rollie and Duck (2006) noted that people create and tell plausible stories about the breakup as a way of letting other people know that they are still desirable partners. Rather than there being only one breakup story, people alter their stories based on the audience. So, although Katelyn confesses to Tamika that she is crushed Sean broke up with her, her story may change when she is communicating with a group that includes an attractive man. Now she might downplay her hurt feelings saying something like, "Yeah, I was surprised and hurt, but I'll get over it. I guess it just wasn't meant to be. Something better must be out there waiting for me." These types of accounts are vital for obtaining closure and engaging in resurrection processes.

Resurrection Processes

As Rollie and Duck (2006) explained, the end of a relationship often marks the beginning of something new. After a breakup, people often visualize what their future will look like without their old relationship. To prepare for that future, they often construct and communicate a new image of themselves as wiser as a result of their experiences. For example, Katelyn may eventually realize that she would be better off finding a partner who shared her values. Sean may have learned that he should not have strung Katelyn on for as long as he did. Both may emerge with a sense that they are now better equipped to find a compatible partner and to communicate their needs more clearly. Resurrection processes also include revising stories about the former relationship and the breakup. Right after the breakup there are often bitter feelings, but as time passes people often reframe their partner and the relationship in more positive terms. So while Sean might still acknowledge that he and Katelyn had grown apart, he might also note that she is one of the sweetest and most genuine women he has ever known. Such an account paints both Katelyn and Sean in a positive light, since it shows that Sean does not hold a grudge and can appreciate Katelyn's good qualities despite their differences.

Knapp's Reversal Hypothesis: The "Coming-Apart" Stages

One of the earliest stage models of disengagement was Knapp's (1978) model of interaction stages, which became known as the **reversal hypothesis**. Knapp posited that five stages characterize "coming-apart": differentiating, circumscribing, stagnating, avoiding, and terminating. These stages are the reverse of Knapp's stages of coming together discussed earlier (see Chapter 5). Hence, this part of Knapp's model is called the *reversal hypothesis*.

Differentiating

Differentiating occurs when people begin to behave as individuals rather than as a couple and stress differences at the expense of similarities. Partners start to do things separately, and they may also argue about their differences. Sean, for example, started noticing that he and Katelyn had radically different opinions regarding religion. Of course, many relational partners go through the differentiation phase without proceeding toward relational termination. Sometimes people simply need to assert their individuality and autonomy. Extended differentiation, however, can lead couples to feel disconnected.

Circumscribing

Circumscribing occurs when communication becomes constricted in both depth and breadth. The superficial communication that takes place during this stage is similar to small talk, except that the communicators are using talk (and avoidance of talk) to distance themselves from each other instead of to learn more about each other. Communication can be constricted at any stage of a relationship. However, when partners begin to feel that they have nothing to talk about, it could be a sign that the relationship is declining.

Stagnating

In the third stage, the relationship seems to be stalled. In the **stagnating stage**, communication is tense and awkward, and the relationship is virtually a taboo subject. At this point, people often feel that they already know what their partner will say or that the outcome of interaction will be negative. Thus, communication is seen as unproductive and unpleasant. Some couples who reach this stage find a way to revive the relationship. Others, however, give up hope and move to the next stage.

Avoiding

The **avoiding** stage is best characterized by physical separation. If possible, relational partners move into separate physical environments and try not to encounter each other. If physical separation is not possible, the partners simply ignore each other. For example, spouses who have young children and cannot afford to live apart might move into separate bedrooms until a permanent solution can be reached. In any case, the goal in the avoidance stage is to achieve as much physical and psychological distance as possible.

Terminating

In this final stage, **terminating**, relational partners end contact, and the relationship is over.

Although the partners may quickly be able to separate from each other physically, it might take longer to separate psychologically. Individuals develop their own self-interests and social networks as a way to distance themselves from their past relationship and move on with their lives. If communication does occur at this stage, it is usually tense, awkward, and hesitant.

Knapp's model makes intuitive sense, but it has not been tested extensively. One study partially supported Knapp's reversal prediction regarding self-disclosure. Tolstedt and Stokes (1984) found that during breakups, self-disclosure decreased in breadth and became negatively valenced, consistent with Knapp's model. However, contrary to the reversal hypothesis, depth of disclosure actually increased. This may be because some couples have intense arguments and discussions as they move toward relational termination. Other critics have argued that Knapp's model fails to accurately represent most breakups because it focuses almost exclusively on patterns of avoidance and distancing, rather than on conflict and relational discussion.

A study of undergraduate breakup scripts by Battaglia, Richard, Datteri, and Lord (1998) suggests most breakups recycle through a 16-step sequence: lack of interest, noticing other people, acting distant, trying to work things out, avoidance, lack of interest, considering a breakup, communicating feelings, trying to work things out, noticing other people, acting distant, dating others, getting back together, considering breaking up, moving on, and breaking up.

Recent research also suggests relationships commonly experience rebirth and reconciliation (Dailey et al., 2009) since over half of people report "on-again, off-again" or cyclical relationships. Instead of a linear path from dating to disengagement, many relationships are on-again, off-again where couples break up and get back together, sometimes multiple times. Not surprisingly, on-again, off-again relationships are characterized by less positivity, less validation, less love, and less approval from their social network than noncyclical relationships. Reconciliations probably occur frequently because breakups are usually asymmetrical, so one partner is more motivated to renew the relationship (Cupach & Metts, 2002; Dailey et al., 2009).

Catastrophe Theory

Catastrophe theory is an alternative to the stage models of relational disengagement such as the reversal hypothesis. Critics of stage models believe stages are artificial conceptualizations that fail to capture the real nature of relational dissolution. First, many breakups skip steps. Not every relationship goes through the stages of circumscribing or stagnation; some go straight to avoidance or termination. In the latest versions of the model (see Knapp & Vangelisti, 2005), the researchers address the process of skipping steps. Second, stages occur nonlinearly, in various orders. For instance, reconciliation, temporary bonding, stagnation, and then avoidance may follow termination. Derlega, Metts, Petronio, and Margulis (1993) contended that cyclical movements characterize most relationships as they swing between periods of stability and change. Likewise, couples may go in and out of a stage several times prior to a stable period. Third, the stages of dissolution are not simply the reverse of the acquaintance process. Derlega and colleagues (1993) argued that during dissolution, partners cannot "unknow" each other and are still capable of predicting each other's behavior.

The **catastrophe model** of disengagement suggests that relationships break up in a radically different way; they do not gradually unwind through stages of relational dissolution, but instead via sudden death (Davis, 1973). Like earthquakes along a silent fault line or the violent storm near the quiet eye of a hurricane, relationship stability can be shattered by sudden cataclysmic events. Of course, fault lines are never completely silent, and subtle signs such as falling air pressure and increased humidity accompany impending hurricanes. Likewise, signs of an impending relational catastrophe exist, but people often fail to see them or deny them, as did Katelyn in the opening vignette of the chapter. As Vaughn (1986) stated, "Partners often report that they are unaware, or only remotely aware, even at the point of separation, that the relationship is deteriorating. Only after the other person is gone are they able to look back and recognize the signals" (p. 62).

Breakups are often precipitated by a critical incident leading to rapid disengagement (Baxter, 1984; Bullis et al., 1993; Cupach & Metts, 1986; Rosen & Stith, 1995). These incidents range from discovering infidelity, to big arguments or physical violence, to finding differences in values, such as the realization that one partner hates pets and the other person loves them. In about 25% of the relationships in Baxter's (1984) study, partners reported that a single critical incident led to a breakup. Interestingly, Bullis and associates (1993) reported that few disengagements were intentional. Instead, disengagements often are nonstrategic turning points in relationships that occurred quickly, more in line with a catastrophe model of breakups than a stage model.

Even when no critical incident can be singled out, relationships sometimes dissolve rapidly. Wilmot (1995) discussed the "point of no return" in every relationship, where one or both of the partners know for sure it's over. Wilmot maintained that in these cases "sometimes people just disappear, without any warning or indication of their discomfort with the relationship" (p. 119). Similarly, Davis (1973) talked about sudden relational death, which occurs when a person abruptly decides the relationship is over, falls in love with someone else, or suffers a trauma such as partner abuse. According to Wilmot (1995), sudden death can be likened to an execution rather than a slow death of the relationship. The breakup often occurs without face-to-face communication, but the initiator may enlist the help of a friend to tell the partner the relationship is over, or terminate the relationship via a letter, phone call, or text message.

Catastrophe theory, positing that events are discontinuous rather than linear, explains many events in nature (Isnard & Zeeman, 1977; Tesser & Achee, 1994). Sometimes human behavior, including behavior in relationships, flows along a smooth, geometric plane. Like hikers on a path next to a cliff, the relationship can slip off the edge of the trail to a lower level, with catastrophic discontinuities for the relationship. Catastrophe theory has been successfully applied in many contexts, including mood changes, conflict during arguments, stock market behavior, and hostilities among nations (Zeeman, 1977). Relational researchers could thus benefit from catastrophe theory to predict sudden death of relationships.

FIFTEEN WAYS TO LEAVE YOUR PARTNER

People separate from relationships in many ways. Though there are not 50 ways to leave your lover, as in the Paul Simon song, research found at least 15 strategies by which people terminate relationships. These strategies differentiate based on whether they are direct or indirect, and whether they are unilateral or bilateral (Baxter, 1982, 1984). Direct strategies rely mainly on face-to-face verbal communication, whereas indirect strategies employ more subtle, indirect communication, including nonverbal communication. Unilateral strategies involve one person deciding to break up, whereas bilateral strategies are a joint decision to terminate the relationship.

More breakups are unilateral not bilateral, and more people end their relationships using indirect, not direct, strategies. Baxter (1979b) found that 71% of all disengagement strategies were indirect and implicit. Similarly, in a study of disengagement accounts, Baxter (1984) found that 76% of couples employed indirect as opposed to direct communication strategies. Baxter (1979a) found that when direct strategies were used, they were more commonly unilateral "dumps" than negotiated dialogues. Most sex differences regarding breakups are minimal, but Wilmot, Carbaugh, and Baxter (1985) reported that females are more likely to use direct strategies than males.

Although indirect strategies are used often to end both casual and close relationships, they are particularly likely to be used in casual relationships when couples have less to negotiate (Baxter, 1979b, 1982, 1984, 1992; Perras & Lustig, 1982; Thieme & Rouse, 1991; Wilmot, Carbaugh, & Baxter, 1985). Breakups are stressful, and disengagers try to minimize their pain and anxiety through indirect rather than direct communication. In light of the fact that "ending a relationship is perhaps one of the most face-threatening situations we encounter" (Cupach & Metts, 1994, p. 81), people

are most likely to use indirect strategies that minimize guilt and embarrassment.

Indirect strategies send neither clear nor kind messages. In Baxter's (1984) study, only 22% of recipients of indirect disengagement messages believed the relationship was over. Worse, relational partners were most likely to express regrets about the relationships when indirect rather than direct disengagement strategies were employed (Baxter, 1979b). Baxter (1979b) suggested that "hints" and other indirect disengagement strategies may actually create uncertainty, prolong the termination process, and be more painful for the participants.

Individuals can terminate their relationships using a single strategy or a complex array of both direct and indirect strategies. For people like Sean, who are concerned about hurting their partner, finding a strategy that is both effective and sensitive can be challenging. As you read about the strategies presented in Figure 15.2, you will likely recognize some of them from your own relational breakups. We do not intend for this section to be a "how-to" guide for breaking up with relational partners. As the research presented in this chapter shows, breakups can be emotionally distressing and the strategies you use to end a relationship can contribute to distress. We hope, however, that by learning about the ways that people break off relationships you will be better able to understand the disengagement process—and perhaps will be a little more sensitive the next time you find yourself initiating a breakup.

Unilateral and Indirect Strategies

Avoidance

The most common and least direct relational disengagement strategy is **avoidance**, whereby people literally "just slip out the back, Jack." A number of studies have reported avoidance as a primary disengagement strategy (Baxter, 1982; Cody, 1982; Emmers & Hart, 1996; Perras & Lustig, 1982), which can range from complete evasion to decreased contact. Baxter (1979a) found decreased frequency of contact with a partner to be one of the

	Unilateral	Bilateral
Indirect	• Avoidance • Relational ruses • Withdrawal of support and affection • Pseudo de-escalation • Cost escalation	• Fading away
Direct	• The direct dump • Dating other people • Justification • The relationship-talk trick • Threats and bullying • Positive tone • De-escalation	• The blame game • The negotiated farewell

Figure 15.2   Disengagement Strategies

two most common indirect disengagement strategies. In Baxter's (1984) study of disengagement accounts, 66% of the couples using indirect strategies reportedly used avoidance-based withdrawal strategies. Research has shown that avoidance tactics are likely when there is little likelihood of maintaining a friendship in the future, when intimacy is low, when there are fewer formal ties, and when the perceived faults of the partner are high (Banks, Altendorf, Greene, & Cody, 1987).

Not surprisingly, research shows that avoidance is a fairly ineffective way to end a relationship. Both parties experience a loss of face (Metts, 1997), and it is difficult for former relational partners to experience closure. When avoidance strategies are used, "the breakup is particularly dissatisfying for the disengager and the partner," even in short-term or relatively casual relationships (Metts, 1997, p. 387). Several studies have found that avoidance strategies are the least effective, most protracted, and most distressing way to end a relationship (Baxter & Philpott, 1980). Sean's initial use of this strategy may have unwittingly extended the breakup process because Katelyn failed to recognize his indirect attempts to end their relationship.

Relational Ruses

Unfortunately, disengagers sometimes use strategies that are downright unethical or manipulative, such as **relational ruses**. In one of Baxter's (1982) studies, a common indirect communication strategy labeled "manipulation attempts" included behaviors such as leaking the impending breakup to a friend or asking a third party to announce the disengagement. Other forms of manipulation include pretending to be interested in someone else and asking friends to persuade the partner to end the relationship first. Manipulation is less likely to be used as a disengagement strategy in close relationships (Baxter, 1982). Research also has shown that relationships that are ended through manipulation are unlikely to evolve into cordial postromantic relationships, such as a friendship (Metts, Cupach, & Bejlovich, 1989).

Withdrawal of Supportiveness and Affection

A common disengagement strategy is to withdraw positive forms of communication such as social support, emotional support, affection, and immediacy. **Social support withdrawal** means the disengager is less available to discuss problems or provide comfort and compassion. One study reported that the withdrawal of social support was the most common relationship disengagement strategy in relationships of less than two years (Baxter, 1979b). As noted in Chapters 9 and 10, social support is an important part of close relationships. We expect our friends and loved ones to be there when we need them. If they are unavailable or make no effort to help us, they send an indirect but clear message that they do not value the relationship. Likewise, we expect our close friends and romantic partners to provide us with positive, affectionate communication. During relational disengagement, nonverbal communication becomes less warm, involving, and immediate (Wilmot, Carbaugh, & Baxter, 1985). In healthy interpersonal relationships, relational partners touch, engage in eye contact, employ positive facial expressions, and maintain close interpersonal distances (see Chapter 8). Conversely, a lack of these behaviors provides a powerful, implicit message that psychological distance is widening. Increasingly nonimmediate behavior is a virtually certain sign of relational distress and movement toward disengagement. Unfortunately, Katelyn did not see these signs and was surprised at what she considered the "suddenness" of the breakup with Sean.

Pseudo De-Escalation

This strategy is a false declaration to the other party that the relationship would profit from some distance that masquerades as de-escalation, but is usually a disguised relational breakup (Baxter, 1985) and can result in a "break" rather than a "breakup" (Dailey et al., 2009). A person might say, "Let's just put a little space into the relationship" or, "Let's just be friends for a while" when the person really means, "This relationship is over." The intent is often to let the other party down easily. However, though this strategy may be more humane than the relational ruses described above, **pseudo de-escalation** is essentially a deceptive, unethical behavior that shows little regard for one's partner. Baxter (1984) found this strategy comprised 22% of indirect breakup strategies; but pseudo de-escalation

was highly ineffective since only 9% of the receivers of such a message got the clue that the relationship was actually over. The rest of the participants harbored false hope that the relationship would eventually be revitalized.

Cost Escalation

Also called **Machiavellianism strategies** (Baxter, 1979c; Perras & Lustig, 1982), **cost escalation** (Baxter, 1984; Emmers & Hart, 1996; Thieme & Rouse, 1991) is an attempt to make the relationship unattractive to one's partner. Disengagers may drink or smoke excessively, or be deliberately messy, obnoxious, rude, argumentative, demeaning, or disloyal so that the partner comes to dislike the disengager and becomes more amenable to a breakup. In one account of a breakup, the "dumper" stated: "I thought I would be an 'asshole' for a while to make her like me less" (Baxter, 1985, p. 249). In one study, cost escalation was the most commonly used disengagement strategy, employed by 31% of the respondents (Thieme & Rouse, 1991). But in Baxter's (1984) study, cost escalation was employed by only 12% of the couples using indirect strategies. Ironically, cost escalation can be beneficial in some breakups, especially if the "dumpee" is happy to break off the relationship after the costs have been escalated.

Unilateral and Direct Strategies

The Direct Dump

The most common direct communication strategy is the simple statement that the relationship is over (Baxter, 1984; Dailey et al., 2009; Thieme & Rouse, 1991). This strategy is sometimes called the **open-and-honest approach**, where people forthrightly communicate their desire to end the relationship (Baxter, 1982; Perras & Lustig, 1982). Most commonly called the **fait accompli approach** (Baxter, 1979b, 1984), this tactic gives the partner little choice or chance for a response. Often this strategy emphasizes the negative consequences of not breaking up, which helps the partner accept the breakup. Baxter (1984) reported that fait accompli resulted in 81% of the receivers of such messages accepting the breakup and offering no resistance, probably because of the perceived futility of countering such a direct message. It is very disconcerting to receive the direct dump—to suddenly be told that the relationship is over. This is what Katelyn perceived to have happened, when actually Sean had been trying to signal that he wanted to break up. As the scenario between Katelyn and Sean illustrates, people sometimes use the direct dump after other more subtle strategies have failed.

Dating Other People

Sometimes, rather than break up completely, a disengager recommends dating other people. This strategy, which is sometimes called **negative identity management** (Banks et al., 1987; Cody, 1982; Metts, 1997), imposes one person's solution on the other person, at the expense of the recipient's feelings. For example, the person initiating the breakup might say, "I told him that I was going to date other people and that he should also date other people." In this strategy, the dumper at least communicates directly to the partner. However, even though this strategy is direct, its underlying meaning is less clear. Sometimes dating other people represents a temporary hiatus from an intense, intimate relationship that will rekindle. Often, however, this announcement is a disengagement message.

Justification

This commonly used strategy includes explanations for why the relationship is ending, why the partner is dissatisfied, or for changes that have occurred in the individuals or in the relationship (Banks et al., 1987; Cody, 1982; Dailey et al., 2009). Unlike the direct dump, **justification** acknowledges the need to provide a rationale for the breakup to one's partner. It is an attempt to protect the face of both partners. This strategy is often used in highly intimate and committed relationships where friendship networks of the partners overlap (Banks et al., 1987). Justification is likely when the disengager feels that the rejected partner has many faults.

Research has shown that justifications are important to the rejected partner's ability to accept the relationship's end. Thieme and Rouse (1991) found a significant association between the number of reasons given for a breakup and the rebuffed person's ability to accept the end of the relationship. Of course, if the justification focuses on the rejected individual's personal faults, hurt feelings and lowered self-esteem are likely to follow. But when justifications focus on the initiator of the breakup and general relationship issues, more positive outcomes are likely.

One common type of justification in dating relationships revolves around desire for autonomy. Sometimes people feel too much dependence on each other and that they are losing independence and individuality. As a result, they de-escalate or disengage from the relationship using a strategy Cody (1982) called **relationship faults** or **appeals to independence**. Young lovers often give this reason because they are unsure they are ready to settle down with one person just yet. Partners may also point to external factors, such as needing to concentrate more on school or one's career, as reasons for decreasing interdependence. This strategy is often less threatening than others because it centers on the needs of the breakup initiator (for more space or freedom) or external events (e.g., school or work) rather than on faults of the person who is being left. Often the reason for leaving the relationship is framed in situational terms—"At this point in my life I'm not ready to settle down yet" or "Right now I only have time for school."

The Relationship-Talk Trick

Some disengagers talk about "problems" in the relationship as a guise for a relationship breakup. Baxter (1984) found that this strategy was incorporated in 27% of direct breakups. Sometimes this strategy is an honest attempt to discuss and solve problems in the relationship. More often, however, it is an insincere attempt to discuss problems and solutions in a manner that leads to the conclusion that the problems are insurmountable and justify a breakup. In other words, the breakup initiator intentionally structures the relational talk to show that the partners are better off going their separate ways. Like cost escalation, this strategy can be hurtful in some instances but beneficial in others. If the person initiating the breakup can convince the partner that the relationship is not worth saving, both partners can walk away feeling that although they tried, the relationship just could not be saved.

Threats and Bullying

Another direct and unilateral strategy involves threatening the partner. Baxter (1984) identified threats and bullying as manipulation attempts that people use to get a partner to break up. Sometimes people use these strategies when a partner refuses to break up with them. For example, if a wife wants a divorce and her husband stubbornly refuses, she might threaten to take the children out of state if he doesn't comply with her wishes. Sometimes threats are also part of the fabric of the breakup itself, with people telling their soon-to-be former partner not to divulge certain information about them or the breakup to others, and threatening to get revenge against them if they do. Obviously, these types of breakup strategies are very destructive. Threats and bullying can make the "dumped" person feel powerless at a time when the individual's self-esteem is likely to be very fragile. These types of strategies are also likely to destroy any chances a couple has to remain friends following the breakup.

Positive Tone

Sometimes unilateral breakups are accomplished using a **positive-tone strategy** that is designed to lessen the "dumped" person's hurt feelings and make them feel better about the breakup (Banks et al., 1987; Baxter, 1982; Cody, 1982; Perras & Lustig, 1982). For instance, Sean could have told Katelyn that even though their relationship is ending, he has no regrets about the time he spent with her. He might also have appealed to fatalism by saying things such as "It's nobody's fault; it just wasn't meant to be." Other times, the fairness approach is adopted. Sean might have said sometime like, "If I stayed in this relationship it wouldn't be fair to you. You deserve someone who loves you the way you deserve to be loved." Apologies and compliments can also be part of a positive-tone

strategy. Sean might tell Katelyn that he is sorry and doesn't want to hurt her, but his heart simply isn't in the relationship anymore. He might also tell her that he still thinks she is a beautiful and intelligent woman and wishes that it could have worked out. Like some of the indirect strategies discussed earlier, one danger of using the positive-tone strategy is that the person being dumped may hold onto hope that the relationship might somehow survive—or at least rebound. Thus, it is important to emphasize that the breakup is imminent for this strategy to be both effective and sensitive.

De-Escalation

De-escalation strategies avoid a complete breakup, at least initially, by proposing relationship de-escalation. Unlike pseudo de-escalation, these strategies are an honest attempt to improve the relationship by de-escalating it (Banks et al., 1987; Cody, 1982). Usually the de-escalator recommends relational separation for a while or recommends that "we just be friends" (Cody, 1982)—a strategy most people, especially men, hate to hear (Hill et al., 1976). Other options include trial separation, moving out of the same living space, or spending less time together. Sometimes people think if they spend time away from each other, they will appreciate each other more. Other times, they think they might get along better if they didn't live together. De-escalation provides a new beginning for some relationships as couples transition from romantic partners to friends or from cohabitors to dating partners living apart, but research suggests de-escalation is usually a giant step along the path of complete disengagement. Indeed, research suggests that most married couples who legally separate end up getting divorced.

Bilateral and Indirect Strategy

Fading Away

In Baxter's research, only one strategy emerged as both bilateral and indirect. This strategy is called **fading away**. Sometimes both people in a relationship recognize that the relationship is at a standstill, and they gradually drift apart and lose contact. This is very common in the case of friends who lose touch over the years (Baxter, 1979b) and when relational partners are separated from each other for long stretches of time. In long-distance relationships, people sometimes come to feel like strangers due to the limited contact they have with one another. Words may not be necessary to end the relationship; instead, the couple may simply sense that it is over. For example, one of our students told the following story of her relational breakup:

> We only saw each other a couple times since moving away from our hometown to attend different colleges. At first, we called each other frequently, but over time the calls slowed down, and we seemed to have less and less to say to each other. After spending some awkward time together during Thanksgiving weekend, he drove me to the airport. When I left to board the plane, we hugged briefly, and it was clear that the relationship was not the same—it was over.

In some ways, fading away is the antithesis of catastrophic breakups. Fading away has no dramatic incident preceding the breakup, but rather a slow and gradual descent.

Bilateral and Direct Strategies

The Blame Game

In some cases, dissatisfaction leads to a competitive blame game that eventually results in a breakup. Cycles of negativity become the prevalent pattern, with both partners dissatisfied and the relationship charged with negative emotion. When partners try to talk about their problems, they end up complaining and blaming each other rather than taking responsibility. Eventually, when they agree to break up, they argue over the reasons and blame each other for the relationship's demise (Cody, 1982; Dailey et al., 2009). Both partners may claim that the impending breakup is the other's fault, and both may feel justified in ending the relationship. In fact, partners who use the blaming strategy may set each other up so that leaving the relationship is an option that helps them save face. This type of strategy can be beneficial in that it provides both

partners with a good reason to exit the relationship. However, breakups of this kind are messy, since conflict and disagreement are likely to prevail to the bitter end.

The Negotiated Farewell

Another common method of relational disengagement, particularly for long-term couples, employs strategies of integrative communication and negotiation (Dailey et al., 2009; Emmers & Hart, 1996; Metts, 1997). Some of these couples may also need to divide up possessions, negotiate child custody and financial issues, and determine how they can both reside comfortably within a joint social network. The key to the negotiated farewell is that both parties are willing to try to be fair to each other during the disengagement process (which is in direct contrast to the attitude of those playing the blame game). The goal of the negotiated farewell is to leave the relationship "well" rather than on a sour note. This strategy is most often used when there are high levels of relational intimacy and commitment, and the partners' interpersonal networks are overlapping (Baxter, 1982; Cody, 1982). When negotiating the breakup, couples using this strategy may also use the positive-tone strategy we discussed earlier. Not surprisingly, this is one of the least distressing ways to end a relationship.

Relational Redefinition: Let's Be Friends

Some romantic relationships are able to shift from a romance to a friendship. If there is a great deal of mutual respect and admiration between relational partners, a friendship may serve to preserve the relationship while recognizing it does not have romantic potential any longer. Traditional relational dissolution models have failed to explain relationships that remain after the romance has ended, although some researchers have studied post-dissolution relationships (Lunnutti & Cameron, 2002; Masheter, 1997). Lunnutti and Cameron's research on gay, lesbian, and heterosexual couples demonstrated that all three couple types employ relational redefinition and many are able to transition to nonsexual relationships. Gay and lesbian couples report higher levels of satisfaction, contact, and emotional intimacy with their former partners than heterosexual couples, who report lower satisfaction, closeness, and contact with their former partners. Research shows that even 10 years after divorce, half of all divorced couples report contact with their former spouse (Fischer, De Graaf, & Kalmijn, 2005). Contact is especially likely if the couple had joint children, had a relatively longer marriage, or holds more liberal social values.

The relationship that former spouses develop can take many different forms, including being coparents without being friends and having a unilateral friendship (i.e., only one of the former spouses regards the other as a friend). Many former spouses stay connected through a social network that includes joint children and family get-togethers. Some former spouses become (or remain) good friends after their divorce. Ahrons (1994) use the concept of *perfect pals* to describe postdivorce friendships that are close and satisfying. Most of these couples who described themselves as perfect pals reported that although their divorces were not amicable, they had also not been adversarial. Many of these couples also said that they grew closer in some ways after the divorce. They reported confiding in and doing favors for each other, regularly talking, and actively coparenting their children; they also saw their friendship as close and irreplaceable. According to Ahrons, about 12% of coparents describe themselves as having this type of friendship five years after their divorce. Masheter's (1997) research showed that some former spouses without children also develop or maintain close friendships after divorce.

OUTCOMES: THE RESULTS OF RELATIONSHIP ENDINGS

Losing a relational partner is a devastating experience. During the breakup, the world looks bleak and hopeless. While the experience is usually negative, most people do move on with their lives and eventually may find positive outcomes associated with the loss, with various emotional and relational outcomes following the breakup of close relationships.

Negative Outcomes of Relational Breakups

Most relational breakups are usually characterized by some degree of distress. In fact, most short-term reactions to relationship breakup are negative. Relational partners often feel as if the world is about to end. Even some long-term negative consequences may persist.

Negative Emotions

A common result of a relational breakup is the presence of negative emotions. A relational breakup is one of the most distressing, traumatic events we experience, particularly for the unwilling partner in the breakup. As Duck (1988) stated, "There is very little pain on earth like the pain of a long-term personal relationship that is falling apart" (p. 102).

Studies have shown that depression, anger, hurt, guilt, confusion, and frustration are common feelings during a relational breakup. In one-sided breakups, a sizable majority of partners experience negative emotions, regardless of whether they initiated the breakup and whether they are female or male (Boelen & Reijntjes, 2009; Hebert & Popadiuk, 2008; Kurdek, 1991; Simpson, 1987; Ugbah & DeWine, 1986; Wilmot et al., 1985). In Owen's (1993) study of relationship accounts, respondents described breakups as emotional injuries: "He left a huge hole in my heart," "My heart felt like a dart board," and "I was torn to shreds." Contrary to intuition, some research has found that men experience more initial distress than women after an unwanted breakup (Hill et al., 1976). This is not to minimize women's distress after breakups. Studies have found *both* sexes experience emotional distress following unwanted breakups (Metts, Cupach, & Bejlovec, 1989; Perilloux & Buss, 2008; Wilmot et al., 1985). Indeed, women who were rejected experienced more sadness, confusion, and fear than men who were rejected (Perilloux & Buss, 2008). Nonetheless, breakups are one of life's most traumatic experiences for men and women alike.

Several factors predict how much distress people experience after a relational breakup. Social support; connectedness to other people, especially peers; and economic resources can cushion the distress (Moller, Fouladi, McCarthy, & Hatch, 2003; Vangelisti, 2002).

People are more depressed by a breakup when their love for their partner was deep, they were highly committed to the relationship, their partner was physically attractive, when they didn't want the relationship to end, when their partner did want the relationship to end, and when they brood or ruminate excessively about the relationship (Mearns, 1991; Saffrey & Ehrenberg, 2007; Sprecher et al., 1998). Recent research indicates that negative thoughts about the breakup, particularly self-blame, were highly associated with grief, depression, and anxiety following a breakup (Boelen & Reijntjes, 2009). Also, people in romantic relationships who felt emotionally close to their partner, had high relational satisfaction, were in the relationship for a long time, and had little control over the breakup experienced the most distress from the breakup (Frazier & Cook, 1993; Simpson, 1987; Sprecher et al., 1998). Chapter 2 illustrated how relationships create self-expansion; during breakups, individuals who experienced the greatest self-expansion as a result of their relationship suffered the greatest contraction, loss of possibilities, and reduced self-esteem during a breakup (Lewandowski, Aron, Bassis, & Kunak, 2006).

While distress typically is greater for the victim of an unwanted breakup (Perilloux & Buss, 2008), the emotional distress experienced by the initiator of the breakup should not be underestimated. Like Sean, many people feel badly about having to initiate a breakup. Initiators may feel guilt, shame, embarrassment, stress, and ambivalence about the breakup. Also, they may repeatedly be reminded of the breakup by their social network and may have to provide numerous accounts and justifications for their actions.

Loneliness

The loss of a relationship is very likely to produce intense feelings of loneliness. In a study of gay and lesbian relationships, Kurdek (1991) found that loneliness was the second most common emotional reaction following a breakup. Moreover, a breakup is a double whammy: Not only have the partners lost one of the most important people in their lives; they have lost the person they would normally have turned to for comfort following such a loss.

It is natural for people to feel lonely after a significant relationship breakup. According to Segrin (1998), loneliness is the result of a discrepancy between one's actual and desired level of social interaction with others. When an intimate relationship ends, this discrepancy may increase. Suddenly there is a wider gap between how much intimacy someone wants and how much intimacy the person receives. But individuals are likely to feel less loneliness after a breakup if they are surrounded by friends and family members who care about them (Segrin, 1998).

Interestingly, loneliness can also be a motivation for breaking off a relationship. As discussed previously, people sometimes initiate breakups because they are dissatisfied or bored with their relationships. They long for the connection that they felt early in their relationships when they were first getting to know each other and everything was exciting and new. Breaking up an old relationship and searching for a new one that better fulfills one's needs is often an impetus for breakup. Indeed, one reason for divorce is the hope of finding a happier relationship, and most divorced people do remarry. Unfortunately, a divorce is even more likely in a second marriage than a first (Argyle & Henderson, 1988).

Financial Consequences

Divorce or separation commonly becomes a financial disaster. The costs of maintaining dual residences, paying lawyers, selling a home quickly, to mention but a few problems, makes divorce one of the worst things a person can experience financially. Single moms and "deadbeat dads" are a major source of poverty in this country. Also, men who pay alimony and child support often feel financially trapped (Hendrick & Hendrick, 1992); it is difficult to start a new family with financial burdens of one's old family still on one's shoulders.

Unfortunately, one factor keeping many long-term partners in negative and even abusive relationships is financial dependency (see Chapter 9). Just as with married couples, Kurdek (1991) found that one of the problems facing gay and lesbian couples after a breakup involved finances. Cohabitors, regardless of their sexual orientation, are particularly likely to experience financial difficulties as they move out of each other's homes and lives. Like emotional dependency, financial dependency often traps people in unhealthy relationships.

Effects on Children

What effect does the breakup have on the children of the divorcing couple? Sadly, children seem to fare worse in divorced families than in families in which their parents were continuously and happily married. Amato and Keith (1991) published a statistical summary of prior research on the effects of parental divorce on children's well-being as adults. Based on information from 81,000 people, they reported that divorce is generally associated with a host of negative consequences. Adults from divorced homes are more likely to be depressed, less satisfied with life, less likely to have satisfying relationships, more likely to get divorced themselves, and more likely to have lower socioeconomic status, less income, and poorer physical health than adults from nondivorced families. The authors concluded: "These results lead to a pessimistic conclusion: the argument that parental divorce presents few problems for children's long-term development is simply inconsistent with the literature on this topic" (Amato & Keith, 1991, p. 54). Even worse news is that these negative effects are consistent across dozens of studies. The good news, though, is that the effects tend to be small, and when both parents maintain positive relationships with their children, the effects are smaller still. There is some evidence that boys cope better if they live with their father and that girls cope better if they live with their mother (see Hendrick & Hendrick, 1992, for a summary). Despite these gloomy findings, research suggests that it is often better for a child to suffer through a divorce than to live with parents who are constantly fighting (Booth & Edwards, 1989; see also Chapter 14).

Research has also supported the **intergenerational transmission of divorce**, which refers to the fact that children of divorced parents are about one to two times more likely to get divorced than children of nondivorced couples (Amato, 1996; Gahler, Hong, & Bernhardt, 2009; Segrin, Taylor, & Altman, 2005; Wolfinger, 1999). Segrin and his colleagues (2005) summarized some of the reasons

why this occurs. First, children of divorced parents may have negative attitudes toward commitment and marriage; they may learn that "marriage is a miserable experience, and . . . therefore avoid the behavior" (p. 362). Second, children of divorced parents are likely to have witnessed negative, dysfunctional conflict, which only adds to the perception of marriage as a stressful experience. Third, some research suggests that couples who divorce are less likely to have effective communication skills than are couples who stay together. Certainly this is not always the case—some couples are communicatively competent and simply realize they are not compatible. Nonetheless, children of divorced parents may not have learned as many skills related to successful marital communication, making them more susceptible to divorce and other failed relationships. All three of these explanations—negative marital attitudes, dysfunctional parental conflict, and lack of communication skills—have been shown by researchers to relate to the intergenerational transmission of divorce; the study by Segrin and his colleagues suggests that negative attitudes toward marriage and commitment may be the most important.

Research also suggests that "feeling caught" between one's parents leads to negative outcomes such as anxiety and depression (Buchanan, Maccoby, & Dornbusch, 1991, 1996). As Afifi and Schrodt (2003) explained, "Children who feel caught between their parents often describe themselves as being 'put in the middle,' 'torn,' or forced to defend their loyalty to each of their parents" (p. 142). Children are more likely to feel caught in the middle when their parents argue in front of them and disclose negative information about one another. When children feel caught in the middle between divorced parents, they are likely to avoid talking about the state of their family in front of their parents (Golish & Caughlin, 2002), presumably because they do not want to start conflict or appear to be supporting one parent over the other. Children who feel caught in the middle report less satisfaction and closeness in their relationships with their parents (e.g., Afifi & Schrodt, 2003). These findings suggest that it is critical for parents to avoid having their children take sides. Parents who talk to and about one another in a respectful, positive manner

SOURCE: Pixland/ThinkStock.

Some research suggests that witnessing parents engaging in frequent, aggressive conflict is more damaging to children than divorce.

are likely to foster a postdivorce environment that is more comfortable for themselves and their children.

Health Consequences

Studies have also shown that separation and divorce threaten people's health. Divorced people have a higher incidence of heart problems, cancer, liver disease, pneumonia, and a host of other diseases (Argyle & Henderson, 1988). Divorce has also been linked to a variety of emotional and physical disorders, psychiatric illness, suicide, and interpersonal violence (Hendrick & Hendrick, 1992). The breakup of dating relationships can also lead to psychological stress. Monroe, Rohde, Seeley, and Lewinsohn (1999) found that relational breakups were predictive of the onset of a major depressive disorder during adolescence. Najib and colleagues (2004) documented changes in brain activity after a romantic relationship breakup consistent with the pattern associated with chronic depression. Similarly, the death of a partner can affect the grieving person's physical health. When people are depressed, stressed, or grieving, their bodies may be more susceptible to physical ailments, such as ulcers, heart problems, and even the common cold.

Healing After a Separation

Because relationship loss can be personally devastating, it is important to understand what factors influence recovery from the distress, loneliness, and depression that often accompanies a breakup.

Mutually negotiated breakups result in the fewest bad feelings (Wilmot et al., 1985) and generally are the easiest from which to recover. Men and women employ similar strategies after they are dumped, including discussions about the breakup, crying, pleading with the ex-partner, and avoiding the ex-partner; the only sex difference is that women tend to go shopping more than men during their recovery (Perriloux & Buss, 2008). Recovery from a unilateral breakup is difficult or impossible when one person wants the relationship to continue (Frazier & Cook, 1993). Thus, if a relationship is really over, it is important to stop dwelling on it and to move on with one's life. Of course, this is more easily said than done. Research has found that the most anxiously attached and insecure people, who have difficulty detaching from a former relationship, may benefit from the prospect of dating a new partner (Speilmann, McDonald, & Wilson, 2009). For these individuals, dating someone on the rebound can substantially promote recovery following a breakup. Studies also suggest that breakups are more protracted and distressing when more indirect termination strategies are employed (Baxter & Philpott, 1980). Lack of closure about a relational termination is associated with less recovery from the breakup, more preoccupation with the breakup, and more relational regret (Saffrey & Ehrenberg, 2007). It is more humane and honest to tell someone, in direct and positive terms, that the relationship is over, as Sean eventually did. Only then can the recovery process begin. Research suggests that disclosing one's feelings to others, or even writing about them, is a therapeutic activity that can aid recovery from a breakup (Lepore & Greenberg, 2002; Pennebaker, 1990). Therefore, Katelyn is taking a step in the right direction by shopping with Tamika while they discuss her core feelings about the breakup.

Positive Outcomes of Relational Breakups

Despite the trauma associated with breakups, it is not unusual for one or both partners to actually have positive feelings about a separation (Wilmot et al., 1985). One of the most common outcomes in Kurdek's (1991) study of gay and lesbian relationships was increased happiness following the breakup.

Indeed, often it is a relief to be out of a bad or dangerous relationship. Sometimes a breakup can provide relief from relational ambiguity or conflict. Not infrequently, a person moves on to a more satisfying relationship following a breakup. Kurdek (1991) reported that relief from conflict was one of the most common outcomes of separation in gay and lesbian relationships. In addition, Kurdek found that personal growth was the most commonly cited positive outcome of relational breakups. Of course, some relationships continue to be problematic after the breakup, especially if one person cannot let go. For example, in our opening scenario, Katelyn leaves pleading messages on Sean's answering machine. Such messages are highly unlikely to change the situation. Instead, they make Sean feel guiltier and Katelyn feel even worse about herself.

One positive outcome of relationship breakups is personal growth that can occur in the relationship's aftermath (Hebert & Popadiuk, 2008; Tashiro & Frazier, 2003). Several kinds of postrelational growth include **personal positives**, such as increased self-confidence and being able to handle life on one's own; **relational positives**, such as having learned how to communicate in a relationship and the importance of not jumping into a relationship too quickly; **environmental positives**, such as concentrating more on school or work or relying on friendship networks more, and **future positives**, such as knowing what one wants in a relational partner (Tashiro & Frazier, 2003). Eventually, Katelyn may experience some of these benefits following her breakup. She may learn that she can cope temporarily without a romantic partner, and perhaps she'll devote more time to other activities that she finds personally rewarding.

Ending any relationship, especially a bad relationship, also represents an opportunity to form a new relationship. But many people make the mistake of leaping head first into a new relationship, which can land them in another relationship destined to fail. Thus, rapid expressions of love and affection in a new relationship are often a turnoff because people doubt whether someone can already like them that much (Sternberg, 1987) and suspect whether they are just being used to recover from the loss. New relationships, then, should evolve slowly and naturally.

SUMMARY AND APPLICATION

Relationships end for a variety of reasons. Sometimes people make a conscious choice to take their lives in a new direction. Other times relationships slowly wither away, partners physically separate from each other due to school or career choices, or death occurs. In each case, coping with the loss of a significant relationship is difficult. Both Katelyn and Sean will feel badly that their relationship has ended. Sean is likely to feel guilty since he initiated the breakup, but he may also feel relief because Katelyn finally got the message that the relationship is over. Katelyn is likely to have a more difficult time, in part because the breakup seemed sudden to her. Seeking social support from friends like Tamika is a first step toward understanding the breakup and moving forward.

Understanding why you broke up can also be helpful. Researchers have identified various specific reasons for relationship breakups. Often, communication is the culprit. Avoidance, negative communication, and lack of openness are three common communication problems that cause breakups. Gottman's research shows that stonewalling (or avoidance) is an especially strong harbinger of divorce. Katelyn or Sean may have noticed some of these communication patterns in their relationship. If they had worked on their communication, it is possible (although not at all certain) that their relationship could have improved. Dissimilarity and sexual incompatibility can also precipitate relational breakups, as can financial issues, inequity, disillusionment, and alcohol or drug abuse. The most common reason for the termination of dating relationships is boredom. People simply miss the excitement that once was present in their relationships but that somehow dimmed over time. Sometimes this boredom leads people to look elsewhere and to develop an interest in alternative partners. Still others feel smothered by their relationships and break up to achieve autonomy and independence.

Regardless of why a relationship ends, research has shown that people usually experience a host of negative outcomes following relational termination, including emotional, physical, and financial distress. If a person did not want the relationship to end, the individual might feel rejected and fearful of starting a new relationship. A person who initiated the relational breakup often feels guilt. The strategy people use to end their relationships can make a difference. Direct strategies are usually preferred, especially if they include positive communication. Thus, the best way for Sean to break up may have been to use the positive-tone strategy. He could have told Katelyn that their relationship meant a lot to him, complimented her, and told her how sorry he was that it wasn't going to work out. Of course, for this strategy to be effective, Sean would need to communicate his desire to break off the relationship—despite his positive regard for her—very clearly. Direct, definitive statements delivered with a positive tone may be the best strategy when breakups are unilateral. The negotiated farewell is the optimal strategy when breakups are bilateral. Such strategies allow a person to get over the breakup more quickly, which opens up the possibility of finding new partners and exploring uncharted relational territory.

DISCUSSION QUESTIONS

1. How are the stage models developed by Duck and Knapp similar and different? Which of these models describes the disengagement process better? Why?

2. Of the 15 specific breakup strategies mentioned in this chapter, which do you think are the least pleasant or ethical? Why?

3. How might you help a friend get over a relationship breakup?

STUDENT STUDY SITE

Visit the study site at **www.sagepub.com/guerrero3e** for e-flashcards, survey and assessments from the chapter, and SAGE journal articles.

REFERENCES

Abbey, A. (1982). Sex differences in attributions for friendly behavior: Do males misperceive females' friendliness? *Journal of Personality and Social Psychology, 42,* 830–838.

Abbey, A. (1987). Misperceptions of friendly behavior as sexual interest: A survey of naturally occurring incidents. *Psychology of Women Quarterly, 11,* 173–194.

Abbey, A., & Melby, C. (1986). The effects of nonverbal cues in gender differences in perceptions of sexual intent. *Sex Roles, 15,* 283–298.

Aboud, F. E., & Mendelson, M. J. (1998). Determinants of friendship selection and quality: Developmental perspectives. In W. M. Bukowski & A. F. Newcomb (Eds.), *The company they keep: Friendships in childhood and adolescence* (pp. 87–112). New York: Cambridge University Press.

Acker, M., & Davis, M. E. (1992). Intimacy, passion, and commitment in adult romantic relationships: A test of the triangular theory of love. *Journal of Social and Personal Relationships, 9,* 21–50.

Acton, L. (1972). *Essays on freedom and power.* Gloucester, MA: Peter Smith. (Original work published in 1887.)

Adams, J. S. (1965). Inequity in social exchange. In L. Berkowitz (Ed.), *Advances in experimental psychology* (Vol. 2, pp. 267–299). New York: Academic Press.

Afifi, T. D. (2003). "Feeling caught" in stepfamilies: Managing boundary turbulence through appropriate privacy coordination rules. *Journal of Social and Personal Relationships, 20,* 729–756.

Afifi, T. D., & Afifi, W. A. (Eds.). (2009). *Uncertainty, information management, and disclosure decisions: Theories and applications.* New York: Routledge.

Afifi, T. D., Caughlin, J., & Afifi, W. A. (2007). The dark side (and light side) of avoidance and secrets. In B. H. Spitzberg & W. R. Cupach (Eds.), *The dark side of interpersonal communication* (2nd ed., pp. 61–92). Mahwah, NJ: Lawrence Erlbaum.

Afifi, T. D., & Joseph, A. (2009). The standards for openness hypothesis: A gendered explanation for why avoidance is so dissatisfying. In T. D. Afifi & W. A. Afifi (Eds.), *Uncertainty, information management, and disclosure decisions: Theories and applications* (pp. 341–362). New York: Routledge.

Afifi, T. D., Olson, L., & Armstrong, C. (2005). The chilling effect and family secrets: Examining the role of self protection, other protection, and communication efficacy. *Human Communication Research, 31,* 564–598.

Afifi, T. D., & Schrodt, P. (2003). "Feeling caught" as a mediator of adolescents' and young adults' avoidance and satisfaction with their parents in divorced and non-divorced households. *Communication Monographs, 70,* 142–173.

Afifi, T. D., & Steuber, K. (2009). The revelation risk model (RRM): Factors that predict the revelation of secrets and the strategies used to reveal them. *Communication Monographs, 76,* 144–176.

Afifi, W. A. (1999). Harming the ones we love: Relational attachment and perceived consequences as predictor of safe-sex behavior. *Journal of Sex Research, 36,* 198–206.

Afifi, W. A. (2009). Uncertainty and information management in interpersonal contexts. In S. W. Smith & S. R. Wilson (Eds.), *New directions in interpersonal communication research* (pp. 94–114). Thousand Oaks, CA: Sage.

Afifi, W. A. (2010). Uncertainty and information management in interpersonal contexts. In S. W. Smith & S. R. Wilson (Eds.), *New directions in interpersonal communication research* (pp. 94–114). Thousand Oaks, CA: Sage.

Afifi, W. A., & Afifi, T. D. (2009). Avoidance among adolescents in conversations about their parents' relationship: Applying the theory of motivated information management. *Journal of Social and Personal Relationships, 26,* 488–511.

Afifi, W. A., & Burgoon, J. K. (1998). "We never talk about that": A comparison of cross-sex friendships and dating relationships on uncertainty and topic avoidance. *Personal Relationships, 5,* 255–272.

Afifi, W. A., & Burgoon, J. K. (2000). The impact of violations on uncertainty and the consequences for attractiveness. *Human Communication Research, 26,* 203–233.

Afifi, W. A., & Caughlin, J. P. (2006). A close look at revealing secrets and some consequences that follow. *Communication Research, 33,* 467–488.

Afifi, W. A., Dillow, M., & Morse, C. (2004). Seeking information in relational contexts: A test of the theory of motivated information management. *Personal Relationships, 11,* 429–450.

Afifi, W. A., Falato, W. L., & Weiner, J. L. (2001). Identity concerns following a severe relational transgression: The role of discover method for the relational outcomes of infidelity. *Journal of Social and Personal Relationships, 18,* 291–308.

Afifi, W. A., & Faulkner, S. L. (2000). On being "just friends": The frequency and impact of sexual activity in cross-sex friendships. *Journal of Social and Personal Relationships, 17,* 205–222.

Afifi, W. A., & Guerrero, L. K. (1995, June). *Maintenance behaviors in same-sex friendships: Sex differences, equity and associations with relational closeness.* Paper presented at the meeting of the International Network on Personal Relationships, Williamsburg, VA.

Afifi, W. A., & Guerrero, L. K. (1998). Some things are better left unsaid II: Topic avoidance in friendships. *Communication Quarterly, 46,* 231–249.

Afifi, W. A., & Guerrero, L. K. (2000). Motivations underlying topic avoidance in close relationships. In S. Petronio (Ed.), *Balancing the secrets of private disclosures* (pp. 165–180). Mahwah, NJ: Lawrence Erlbaum.

Afifi, W. A., Guerrero, L. K., & Egland, K. L. (1994, June). *Maintenance behaviors in same- and opposite-sex friendships: Connections to gender, relational closeness, and equity issues.* Paper presented at the annual meeting of the International Network on Personal Relationships, Iowa City, IA.

Afifi, W. A., & Metts, S. (1998). Characteristics and consequences of expectation violations in close relationships. *Journal of Social and Personal Relationships, 15,* 365–392.

Afifi, W. A., & Morse, C. R. (2009). Expanding the role of emotion in the theory of motivated information management. In S. W. Smith & S. R. Wilson (Eds.), *New directions in interpersonal communication research* (pp. 87–105). Thousand Oaks, CA: Sage.

Afifi, W. A., & Reichert, T. (1996). Understanding the role of uncertainty in jealousy experience and expression. *Communication Reports, 9,* 93–103.

Afifi, W. A., & Weiner, J. L. (2004). Toward a theory of motivated information management. *Communication Theory, 14,* 167–190.

Afifi, W. A., & Weiner, J. L. (2006). Seeking information about sexual health: Applying the theory of motivated information management. *Human Communication Research, 32,* 35–57.

Agassi, A. (2009). *Open: An autobiography.* New York: Knopf.

Ahrons, C. R. (1994). *The good divorce.* New York: HarperCollins.

Aida, Y., & Falbo, T. (1991). Relationships between marital satisfaction, resources, and power strategies. *Sex Roles, 24,* 43–56.

Ainsworth, M. D. S. (1969). Object relations, dependency, and attachment: A theoretical review of the infant-mother relationship. *Child Development, 40,* 969–1025.

Ainsworth, M. D. S. (1982). Attachment: Retrospect and prospect. In C. M. Parkes & J. Stevenson-Hinde (Eds.), *The place of attachment in human behavior* (pp. 3–30). New York: Basic Books.

Ainsworth, M. D. S. (1989). Attachments beyond infancy. *American Psychologist, 44,* 709–716.

Ainsworth, M. D. S. (1991). Attachments and other affectional bonds across the life cycle. In C. M. Parkes, J. Stevenson-Hinde, & P. Marris (Eds.), *Attachment across the life cycle* (pp. 33–51). New York: Tavistock/Routledge.

Ainsworth, M. D. S., Blehar. M. C., Waters, E., & Wall, S. (1978). *Patterns of attachment: A psychological study of the strange situations.* Hillsdale, NJ: Lawrence Erlbaum.

Ainsworth, M. D. S., & Bowlby, J. (1991). An ethological approach to personality development. *American Psychologist, 46,* 333–341.

Ainsworth, M. D. S., & Eichberg, C. (1991). Effects of infant-mother attachment of mother's unresolved loss of an attachment figure, or other traumatic experience. In C. M. Parkes, J. Stevenson-Hinde, & P. Marris (Eds.), *Attachment across the life cycle* (pp. 160–186). New York: Tavistock/Routledge.

Ainsworth, M. D. S., & Wittig, B. A. (1969). Attachment and the exploratory behaviour of one-year-olds in a strange situation. In B. M. Foss (Ed.), *Determinants of infant behavior* (pp. 113–136). London: Methuen.

Alain, M. (1985). Help-seeking and attractiveness in cross-sex dyads. *Canadian Journal of Behavioral Science, 17,* 271–275.

Albada, K. F., Knapp, M. L., & Theune, K. E. (2002). Interaction appearance theory: Changing perceptions of physical attractiveness through social interaction. *Communication Theory, 12,* 8–40.

Albas, D., & Albas, C. (1988). Aces and bombers: The post-exam impression management strategies of students. *Symbolic Interaction, 11,* 289–302.

Alberts, J. K. (1988). An analysis of couples' conversational complaints. *Communication Monographs, 55,* 184–197.

Alberts, J. K. (1989). A descriptive taxonomy of couples' complaint interactions. *Southern Communication Journal, 54,* 125–143.

Alberts, J. K., & Driscoll, G. (1992). Containment versus escalation: The trajectory of couples' conversation complaints. *Western Journal of Communication, 56,* 394–412.

Altman, I., & Ginat, J. (1996). *Polygamous families in contemporary society.* New York: Cambridge University Press.

Altman, I., & Taylor, D. A. (1973). *Social penetration: The development of interpersonal relationships.* New York: Holt, Rinehart & Winston.

Altman, I., Vinsel, A., & Brown, B. B. (1981). Dialectical conceptions in social psychology: An application to social penetration and privacy regulation. In L. Berkowitz (Ed.), *Advances in experimental social psychology* (Vol. 14, pp. 107–160). New York: Academic Press.

Amato, P. R. (1996). Explaining the intergenerational transmission of divorce. *Journal of Marriage and the Family, 58,* 628–640.

Amato, P. R., & Keith, B. (1991). Parental divorce and adult well-being: A metaanalysis. *Journal of Marriage and the Family, 53,* 43–58.

Amato, P. R., & Previti, D. (2003). People's reasons for divorcing: Gender, social class, the life course, and adjustment. *Journal of Family Issues, 24,* 602–626.

Amodio, D. M., & Showers, C. J. (2005). "Similarity breeds liking" revisited: The moderating role of commitment. *Journal of Social and Personal Relationships, 22,* 817–836.

Anders, S. L., & Tucker, J. S. (2000). Adult attachment style, interpersonal communication competence, and social support. *Personal Relationships, 7,* 379–389.

Andersen, J. F. (1984, April). *Nonverbal cues of immediacy and relational affect.* Paper presented at the annual convention of the Central States Speech Association, Chicago.

Andersen, P. A. (1982, November). *Interpersonal communication across three decades.* Paper presented at the annual convention of the Speech Communication Association, Louisville, KY.

Andersen, P. A. (1985). Nonverbal immediacy in interpersonal communication. In A. W. Siegman & S. Feldstein (Eds.), *Multichannel integrations of nonverbal behavior* (pp. 1–36). Hillsdale, NJ: Lawrence Erlbaum.

Andersen, P. A. (1989, May). *A cognitive valence theory of intimate communication.* Paper presented at the International Network on Personal Relationships Conference, Iowa City, IA.

Andersen, P. A. (1991). When one cannot communicate: A challenge to Motley's traditional communication postulates. *Communication Studies, 42,* 309–325.

Andersen, P. A. (1993). Cognitive schemata in personal relationships. In S. Duck (Ed.), *Individuals in relationships* (pp. 1–29). Newbury Park, CA: Sage.

Andersen, P. A. (1998a). The cognitive valence theory of intimate communication. In M. T. Palmer & G. A. Barnett (Eds.), *Progress in communication sciences: Vol. 14. Mutual influence in interpersonal communication: Theory and research in cognition, affect and behavior* (pp. 39–72). Stamford, CT: Ablex.

Andersen, P. A. (1998b). Researching sex differences within sex similarities: The evolutionary consequences of reproductive differences. In D. J. Canary & K. Dindia (Eds.), *Sex differences and similarities in communication* (pp. 83–100). Mahwah, NJ: Lawrence Erlbaum.

Andersen, P. A. (2000). Cues of culture: The basis of intercultural differences in nonverbal communication. In L. Samovar & R. E. Porter (Eds.), *Intercultural communication: A reader* (pp. 258–270). Belmont, CA: Wadsworth.

Andersen, P. A. (2004). *The complete idiot's guide to body language.* New York. Alpha.

Andersen, P. A. (2006). The evolution of biological sex differences in communication. In K. Dindia & D. J. Canary (Eds.), *Sex differences and similarities in communication* (2nd ed., pp. 117–135). Mahwah, NJ: Lawrence Erlbaum.

Andersen, P. A. (2008). *Nonverbal communication: Forms and functions* (2nd ed.). Prospect Heights, IL: Waveland Press.

Andersen, P. A., & Andersen, J. F. (1982). Nonverbal immediacy in instruction. In L. L. Barker (Ed.), *Communication in the classroom: Original essays* (pp. 98–120). Englewood Cliffs, NJ: Prentice Hall.

Andersen, P. A., Eloy, S. V., Guerrero, L. K., & Spitzberg, B. H. (1995). Romantic jealousy and relational satisfaction: A look at the impact of jealousy experience and expression. *Communication Reports, 8,* 77–85.

Andersen, P. A., & Guerrero, L. K. (1998a). The bright side of relational communication: Interpersonal warmth as a social emotion. In P. A. Andersen & L. K. Guerrero (Eds.), *Handbook of communication and emotion: Research, theory, applications, and contexts* (pp. 303–329). San Diego, CA: Academic Press.

Andersen, P. A., & Guerrero, L. K. (1998b). Principles of communication and emotion in social interaction. In P. A. Andersen & L. K. Guerrero (Eds.), *Handbook of communication and emotion: Research, theory, applications, and contexts* (pp. 49–96). San Diego, CA: Academic Press.

Andersen, P. A., Guerrero, L. K., Buller, D. B., & Jorgensen, P. F. (1998). An empirical comparison of three theories of nonverbal immediacy exchange. *Human Communication Research, 24,* 501–535.

Andersen, P. A., Guerrero, L. K., & Jones, S. M. (2006). Nonverbal intimacy. In V. Manusov & M. L. Patterson (Eds.), *The handbook of nonverbal communication* (pp. 259–277). Thousand Oaks, CA: Sage.

Applegate, J. L. (1980). Person-centered and position-centered teach communication in a day care center. *Studies in Symbolic Interactionism, 3,* 59–96.

Archer, J. (1989). The relationship between gender-role measures: A review. *British Journal of Social Psychology, 28,* 173–184.

Argyle, M. (1972). Non-verbal communication in human social interaction. In R. A. Hinde (Ed.), *Non-verbal communication* (pp. 248–268). Cambridge, UK: Cambridge University Press.

Argyle, M., & Dean, J. (1965). Eye contact, distance, and affiliation. *Sociometry, 28,* 289–304.

Argyle, M., & Furnham, A. (1983). Sources of satisfaction and conflict in long-term relationships. *Journal of Marriage and the Family, 45,* 481–493.

Argyle, M., & Henderson, M. (1984). The rules of friendship. *Journal of Social and Personal Relationships, 1,* 211–237.

Argyle, M., & Henderson, M. (1985). The rules of relationships. In S. Duck & D. Perlman (Eds.), *Understanding relationships: An interdisciplinary approach* (pp. 63–84). London: Sage.

Argyle, M., & Henderson, M. (1988). *The anatomy of relationships.* London: Penguin Books.

Arias, I., & Pape, K. T. (2001). Psychological abuse: Implications for adjustment and commitment to leave violent partners. In D. K. O'Leary & R. D. Maluro (Eds.), *Psychological abuse in violent domestic relations* (pp. 137–151). New York: Springer.

Arliss, L. P. (1993). *Contemporary family communication: Messages and meanings.* New York: St. Martin's Press.

Armstrong, L. (1978). *Kiss daddy goodnight: A speak-out on incest.* New York: Doubleday.

Aron, A., & Aron, E. N. (1986). *Love as the expansion of self: Understanding attraction and satisfaction.* New York: Hemisphere.

Aron, A., & Aron, E. N. (1996). Self and self-expansion in relationships. In G. J. O. Fletcher & J. Fitness (Eds.), *Knowledge structures in close relationships: A social psychological approach* (pp. 325–344). Mahwah, NJ: Lawrence Erlbaum.

Aron, A., Mashek, D., & Aron, E. W. (2004). Closeness, intimacy, and including other in the self. In D. Mashek & A. Aron (Eds.), *Handbook of closeness and intimacy* (pp. 27–41). Mahwah, NJ: Lawrence Erlbaum.

Aron, A., Paris, M., & Aron, E. N. (1995). Falling in love: Prospective studies of self-concept change. *Journal of Personality and Social Psychology, 69,* 1102–1112.

Aron, E. N., & Aron, A. (1996). Love and expansion of the self: The state of the model. *Personal Relationships, 3,* 45–58.

Aronson, E., & Linder, D. (1965). Gain and loss of esteem as determinants of interpersonal attraction. *Journal of Experimental Social Psychology, 1,* 156–171.

Arriaga, X. B. (2001). The ups and downs of dating: Fluctuations in satisfaction in newly formed romantic relationships. *Journal of Personality and Social Psychology, 80,* 764–765.

Arriaga, X. B., & Agnew, C. R. (2001). Being committed: Affective, cognitive, and cognitive components of relationship commitment. *Personality and Social Psychology Bulletin, 27,* 1190–1203.

Attridge, M. (1994). Barriers to dissolution of romantic relationships. In D. J. Canary & L. Stafford (Eds.), *Communication and relational maintenance* (pp. 141–164). San Diego, CA: Academic Press.

Aune, R. K., Ching, P. U., & Levine, T. R. (1996). Attributions of deception as a function of reward value: A test of two explanations. *Communication Quarterly, 44,* 478–486.

Aune, R. K., Metts, S., & Hubbard, A. S. E. (1998). Managing the outcomes of discovered deception. *Journal of Social Psychology, 138,* 677–689.

Ayres, J. (1983). Strategies to maintain relationships: Their identification and perceived usage. *Communication Quarterly, 31,* 62–67.

Babcock, J. C., Waltz, J., Jacobson, N. S., & Gottman, J. M. (1993). Power and violence: The relationship between communication patterns, power discrepancies and domestic violence. *Journal of Consulting and Clinical Psychology, 61,* 40–50.

Bach, G. R., & Wyden, P. (1970). *The intimate enemy: How to fight fair in love and marriage.* New York: Avon Books.

Bachman, G. F., & Guerrero, L. K. (2006a). An expectancy violations analysis of relational quality and communicative responses following hurtful events in dating relationships. *Journal of Social and Personal Relationships, 23,* 943–963.

Bachman, G. F., & Guerrero, L. K. (2006b). Forgiveness, apology, and communicative responses to hurtful events. *Communication Reports, 19,* 45–56.

Back, M. D., Schmukle, S. C., & Egloff, B. (2010). Why are narcissists so charming at first sight? Decoding the narcissism-popularity link at zero acquaintance. *Journal of Personality and Social Psychology, 98,* 132–145.

Bagarozzi, D. A. (1990). Marital power discrepancies and symptom development in spouses: An empirical investigation. *American Journal of Family Therapy, 18,* 51–64.

Baldwin, M. W., & Fehr, B. (1995). On the instability of attachment style ratings. *Personal Relationships, 2,* 247–261.

Bandura, A. (1986). *Social foundations of thought and action: A social cognitive theory.* Englewood Cliffs, NJ: Prentice Hall.

Banks, S. P., Altendorf, D. M., Greene, J. O., & Cody, M. J. (1987). An examination of relationship disengagement: Perceptions, breakup strategies and outcomes. *Western Journal of Speech Communication, 51,* 19–41.

Barnett, R., & Baruch, G. (1987). Mothers' participation in child care: Patterns and consequences. In F. Crosby (Ed.), *Spouse, parent, worker: On gender and multiple roles* (pp. 63–73). New Haven, CT: Yale University Press.

Barr, A., Bryan, A., & Kenrick, D. T. (2002). Sexual peak: Socially shared cognitions about desire, frequency, and satisfaction in men and women. *Personal Relationships, 9,* 287–299.

Barth, R. J., & Kinder, B. N. (1988). A theoretical analysis of sex differences in same-sex friendships. *Sex Roles, 19,* 349–363.

Bartels, A., & Zeki, S. (2004). The neural correlates of maternal and romantic love. *Neuroimage, 21,* 1155–1166.

Bartholomew, K. (1990). Avoidance of intimacy: An attachment perspective. *Journal of Social and Personal Relationships, 7,* 147–178.

Bartholomew, K. (1993). From childhood to adult relationships: Attachment theory and research. In S. Duck (Ed.), *Learning about relationships* (pp. 30–62). Newbury Park, CA: Sage.

Bartholomew, K., & Horowitz, L. M. (1991). Attachment styles among young adults: A test of a four-category model. *Journal of Personality and Social Psychology, 61,* 226–244.

Bateson, G. (1951). Conventions of communication. In J. Ruesch & G. Bateson (Eds.), *Communication: The social matrix of psychiatry* (pp. 212–227). New York: Norton.

Battaglia, D. M., Richard, F. D., Datteri, D. L., & Lord, C. G. (1998). Breaking up is (relatively) easy to do: A script for the dissolution of close relationships. *Journal of Personal and Social Relationships, 15,* 829–845.

Baumeister, R. F. (1982). A self-presentational view of social phenomena. *Psychological Bulletin, 91,* 3–26.

Baumeister, R. F. (Ed.). (1986). *Public and private self.* New York: Springer-Verlag.

Baumeister, R. F. (2000). Gender differences in erotic plasticity: The female sex drive as socially flexible and responsive. *Psychological Bulletin, 126,* 347–374.

Baumeister, R. F., & Wotman, S. R. (1992). *Breaking hearts: The two sides of unrequited love.* New York: Guilford Press.

Baumeister, R. F., Wotman, S. R., & Stillwell, A. M. (1993). Unrequited love: On heartbreak, anger, guilt, scriptlessness, and humiliation. *Journal of Personality and Social Psychology, 64,* 377–394.

Baumgarte, R., & Nelson, D. W. (2009). Preference for same- versus cross-sex friendships. *Journal of Applied Social Psychology, 39,* 901–917.

Baumrind, D. (1971). Current patterns of parental authority. *Developmental Psychology Monographs, 4*(1, Pt. 2), 1–103.

Baumrind, D. (1991). Parenting styles and adolescent development. In R. M. Leder, A. C. Petersen, & J. Brooks-Gunn (Eds.), *Encyclopedia of adolescence* (Vol. 2, pp. 746–758). New York: Garland.

Bavelas, J. B., Black, A., Chovil, N., & Mullett, J. (1990). *Equivocal communication.* Newbury Park, CA: Sage.

Baxter, L. A. (1979a). Self-disclosure as a relational disengagement strategy. *Human Communication Research, 5,* 215–222.

Baxter, L. A. (1979b, February). *Self-reported disengagement strategies in friendship relationships.* Paper presented at the annual convention of the Western Speech Communication Association, Los Angeles.

Baxter, L. A. (1979c, November). *Relational closeness, relational intent and disengagement strategies.* Paper presented at the annual meeting of the Speech Communication Association, San Antonio, TX.

Baxter, L. A. (1982). Strategies for ending relationships: Two studies. *Western Journal of Speech Communications, 46,* 223–241.

Baxter, L. A. (1984). Trajectories of relationship disengagement. *Journal of Social and Personal Relationships, 1,* 29–48.

Baxter, L. A. (1985). Accomplishing relational disengagement. In S. Duck & D. Perlman (Eds.), *Understanding personal relationships: An interdisciplinary approach* (pp. 243–265). London: Sage.

Baxter, L. A. (1986). Gender differences in the heterosexual relationship rules embedded in breakup accounts. *Journal of Social and Personal Relationships, 3,* 289–306.

Baxter, L. A. (1990). Dialectical contradictions in relationship development. *Journal of Social and Personal Relationships, 7,* 69–88.

Baxter, L. A. (1993). The social side of personal relationships: A dialectical perspective. In S. Duck (Ed.), *Understanding relationship processes* (pp. 139–165). Newbury Park, CA: Sage.

Baxter, L. A. (1994). A dialogic approach to relationship maintenance. In D. J. Canary & L. Stafford (Eds.), *Communication and relational maintenance* (pp. 233–254). San Diego, CA: Academic Press.

Baxter, L. A. (2006). Relational dialectics theory: Multivocal dialogues of family communication. In D. O. Braithwaite & L. A. Baxter (Eds.), *Engaging theories in family communication: Multiple perspectives* (pp. 130–145). Thousand Oaks, CA: Sage.

Baxter, L. A. (2010). *Voicing relationships: A dialogic perspective.* Thousand Oaks, CA: Sage.

Baxter, L. A., & Braithwaite, D. O. (2008). Relational dialectics theory. In L. A. Baxter & D. O. Braithwaite (Eds.), *Engaging theories in interpersonal communication: Multiple perspectives* (pp. 349–361). Thousand Oaks, CA: Sage.

Baxter, L. A., Braithwaite, D. O., & Nicholson, J. (1999). Turning points in the development of blended families. *Journal of Social and Personal Relationships, 16,* 291–313.

Baxter, L. A., & Bullis, C. (1986). Turning points in developing romantic relationships. *Human Communication Research, 12,* 469–493.

Baxter, L. A., & Montgomery, B. M. (1996). *Relating: Dialogues and dialectics.* New York: Guilford Press.

Baxter, L. A., & Philpott, J. (1980, November). *Relational disengagement: A process view.* Paper presented at the annual meeting of the Speech Communication Association, New York.

Baxter, L. A., & Pittman, G. (2001). Communicatively remembering turning points of relationship development. *Communication Reports, 14,* 1–18.

Baxter, L. A., & Simon, E. P. (1993). Relationship maintenance strategies and dialectical contradictions in personal relationships. *Journal of Social and Personal Relationships, 10,* 225–242.

Baxter, L., A., & West, L (2003). Couple perceptions of their similarities and differences: A dialectical perspective. *Journal of Social and Personal Relationships, 20,* 491–514.

Baxter, L. A., & Wilmot, W. W. (1984). "Secret tests": Social strategies for acquiring information about the state of the relationship. *Human Communication Research, 2,* 171–201.

Baxter, L. A., & Wilmot, W. W. (1985). Taboo topics in close relationships. *Journal of Social and Personal Relationships, 2,* 253–269.

Bayes, M. A. (1970). An investigation of the behavioral cues of interpersonal warmth (Doctoral dissertation, University of Miami, 1970). *Dissertation Abstracts International, 31,* 2272B.

Becker, D. V., Sagarin, B. J., Guadagno, R. E., Millevoi, A., & Nicastle, L. D. (2004). When the sexes need not differ: Emotional responses to the sexual and emotional aspects of infidelity. *Personal Relationships, 11,* 529–538.

Beebe, S. A. (1980). Effects of eye contact, posture and vocal inflection upon credibility and comprehension. *Australian Scan: Journal of Human Communication, 7–8,* 57–70.

Beier, E. G., & Sternberg, D. P. (1977). Marital communication: Subtle cues between newlyweds. *Journal of Communication, 27,* 92–97.

Beland, N. (2005, October). Catch her eye. *Men's Health, 8,* pp. 164, 166–167.

Bell, A. P., & Weinberg, M. A. (1978). *Homosexualities: A study of diversity among men and women.* New York: Simon & Schuster.

Bell, R. A., & Buerkel-Rothfuss, N. L. (1990). S(he) loves me, s(he) loves me not: Predictors of relational information-seeking in courtship and beyond. *Communication Quarterly, 38,* 64–82.

Bell, R. A., Buerkel-Rothfuss, N. L., & Gore, K. E. (1987). "Did you bring the yarmulke for the cabbage patch kid?" The idiomatic communication of young lovers. *Human Communication Research, 14,* 47–67.

Bell, R. A., Daly, J. A., & Gonzalez, C. (1987). Affinity-maintenance in marriage and its relationships to women's marital satisfaction. *Journal of Marriage and the Family, 49,* 445–454.

Bem, S. L. (1974). The measurement of psychological androgyny. *Journal of Consulting and Clinical Psychology, 42,* 155–162.

Ben-Ari, A., & Lavee, Y. (2007). Dyadic closeness in marriage: From the inside story to a conceptual model. *Journal of Social and Personal Relationships, 24,* 627–644.

Bennett, M., & Earwaker, D. (1994). Victims' responses to apologies: The effects of offender responsibility and offense severity. *Journal of Social Psychology, 134,* 457–464.

Bennett, N. G., Blanc, A. K., & Bloom, D. W. (1988). Commitment and the modern union: Assessing the link between premarital cohabitation and subsequent marital stability. *American Sociological Review, 53,* 127–138.

Bentler, P. M., & Newcomb, M. D. (1978). Longitudinal study of marital success and failure. *Journal of Consulting and Clinical Psychology, 46,* 1053–1070.

Bentley, C. G., Galliher, R. V., & Ferguson, T. J. (2007). Associations among aspects of interpersonal power and relationship functioning in adolescent romantic couples. *Sex Roles, 57,* 483–495.

Benuto, L., & Meana, M. (2008). Acculturation and sexuality: Investigating gender differences in erotic plasticity. *Journal of Sex Research, 45,* 217–224.

Beres, M. A., Herold, E., & Maitland, S. B. (2004). Sexual consent behaviors in same-sex relationships. *Journal of Sexual Behavior, 33,* 475–486.

Berg, J. H., & Clark, M. S. (1986). Differences in social exchange between intimate and other relationships: Gradually evolving or quickly apparent? In V. J. Derlega & B. A. Winstead (Eds.), *Friendship and social interaction* (pp. 101–128). New York: Springer-Verlag.

Berg, J. H., & McQuinn, R. D. (1986). Attraction and exchange in continuing and noncontinuing dating relationships. *Journal of Personality and Social Psychology, 50,* 942–952.

Berger, C. R. (1979). Beyond initial interaction: Uncertainty, understanding, and the development of interpersonal relationships. In H. Giles & R. N. St. Clair (Eds.), *Language and social psychology* (pp. 122–144). Oxford, UK: Basil Blackwell.

Berger, C. R. (1985). Social power and interpersonal communication. In M. L. Knapp & G. R. Miller (Eds.), *Handbook of interpersonal communication* (pp. 439–499). Beverly Hills, CA: Sage.

Berger, C. R. (1987). Communicating under uncertainty. In M. E. Roloff & G. R. Miller (Eds.), *Interpersonal processes: New directions in communication research* (pp. 39–62). Newbury Park, CA: Sage.

Berger, C. R. (1988). Uncertainty and information exchange in developing relationships. In S. Duck (Ed.), *Handbook of personal relationships* (pp. 239–256). Chichester, UK: Wiley.

Berger, C. R. (1993). Uncertainty and social interaction. In S. A. Deetz (Ed.), *Communication yearbook 16* (pp. 491–502). Newbury Park, CA: Sage.

Berger, C. R., & Calabrese, R. J. (1975). Some explorations in initial interactions and beyond: Toward a developmental theory of interpersonal communication. *Human Communication Research, 1,* 99–112.

Berger, C. R., & Douglas, W. (1981). Studies in interpersonal epistemology III: Anticipated interaction, self-monitoring, and observational context selection. *Communication Monographs, 48,* 183–196.

Berger, C. R., & Kellermann, K. (1983). To ask or not to ask: Is that a question? In R. N. Bostrom (Ed.), *Communication yearbook 7* (pp. 342–368). Beverly Hills, CA: Sage.

Berk, S. (1985). *The gender factory.* New York: Plenum Press.

Bernardes, D., Mendes, M., Sarmento, P., Silva, S., & Moreira, J. (1999, June). *Gender differences in love and sex: A cross-cultural study.* Poster presented at the International Network on Personal Relationships Young Scholars Preconference, University of Louisville, KY.

Berns, S. B., Jacobson, R. W., & Gottman, J. M. (1999). Demand/withdraw interaction patterns between different types of batterers and their spouses. *Journal of Marital and Family Therapy, 25,* 337–348.

Berscheid, E. (2010). Love in the fourth dimension. *Annual Review of Psychology, 61,* 1–25.

Berscheid, E., Dion, K., Walster, E., & Walster, G. W. (1971). Physical attractiveness and dating choice: A test of the matching hypothesis. *Journal of Experimental Social Psychology, 7,* 173–189.

Berscheid, E., & Meyers, S. A. (1996). A social categorical approach to questions about love. *Personal Relationships, 3,* 19–43.

Berscheid, E., & Peplau, L. A. (1983). The emerging science of relationships. In H. H. Kelley, E. Berscheid, A. Christensen, J. H. Harvey, T. L. Huston, G. Leaving, et al. (Eds.), *Close relationships* (pp. 1–19). New York: Freeman.

Berscheid, E., & Walster, E. H. (1969). *Interpersonal attraction.* Reading, MA: Addison-Wesley.

Berscheid, E., & Walster, E. H. (1974). A little bit about love. In T. L. Houston (Ed.), *Foundations of interpersonal attraction* (pp. 355–381). New York: Academic Press.

The best dating service? Try the workplace! (1988, February 12). *New York Post,* p. 14.

Bevan, J. L. (2003). Expectancy violation theory and sexual resistance in close, cross-sex relationships. *Communication Monographs, 70,* 68–82.

Bevan, J. L. (2008). Experiencing and communicating romantic jealousy: Questioning the investment model. *Southern Journal of Communication, 73,* 42–67.

Bevan, J. L., & Samter, W. (2004). Toward a broader conceptualization of jealousy in close relationships: Two exploratory studies. *Communication Studies, 55,* 14–28.

Bickman, L. (1974). The social power of a uniform. *Journal of Applied Social Psychology, 4,* 47–61.

Biernat, M., & Wortman, C. B. (1991). Sharing of home responsibilities between professionally employed women and their husbands. *Journal of Personality and Social Psychology, 60,* 840–860.

Billings, A. (1979). Conflict resolution in distressed and nondistressed married couples. *Journal of Consulting and Clinical Psychology, 47,* 368–376.

Bingham, S. G., & Burleson, B. R. (1989). Multiple effects of messages with multiple goals: Some perceived outcomes of responses to sexual harassment. *Human Communication Research, 16,* 184–216.

Bippus, A. M., & Rollin, E. (2003). Attachment style differences in relational maintenance and conflict behaviors: Friends' perceptions. *Communication Reports, 16,* 113–123.

Bisson, M. A., & Levine, T. R. (2009). Negotiating a friends with benefits relationship. *Archives of Sexual Behavior, 38,* 66–73.

Black, L. E., Eastwood, M. M., Sprenkle, D. H., & Smith, E. (1991). An exploratory analysis of the construct of leavers versus left as it relates to Levinger's social exchange theory of attractions, barriers, and alternative attractions. *Journal of Divorce and Remarriage, 15,* 127–139.

Blake, R. R., & Mouton, J. S. (1964). *The managerial grid.* Houston, TX: Gulf.

Blau, P. M. (1964). *Exchange and power in social life.* New York: Wiley.

Blow, A. J., & Hartnett, K. (2005). Infidelity in committed relationships II. A substantive review. *Journal of Marital & Family Therapy, 31,* 217–233.

Blumstein, P., & Schwartz, P. (1983). *American couples: Money, work, sex.* New York: Morrow.

Bochner, A. P. (1984). The functions of human communication in interpersonal bonding. In C. C. Arnold & J. W. Bowers (Eds.), *Handbook of rhetorical and communication theory* (pp. 544–621). Boston: Allyn & Bacon.

Boelen, P. A., & Reijntjes, A. (2009). Negative cognitions in emotional problems following romantic relationship breakups. *Stress and Health, 25,* 11–19.

Bolger, N., & Amarel, D. (2007). Effects of social support visibility on adjustment to stress: Experimental evidence. *Journal of Personality and Social Psychology, 92,* 458–475.

Bolger, N., Zuckerman, A., & Kessler, R. C. (2000). Invisible support and adjustment to stress. *Journal of Personality and Social Psychology, 79,* 953–961.

Boon, S. D., & McLeod, B. A. (2001). Deception in romantic relationships: Subjective estimates of success at deceiving and attitudes toward deception. *Journal of Social and Personal Relationships, 18,* 463–476.

Booth, A., & Edwards, J. N. (1989). Transmission of marital and family quality over the generations: The effect of parental divorce and unhappiness. *Journal of Divorce, 13,* 41–58.

Boon, S. D., & Sulsky, L. M. (1997). Attributions of blame and forgiveness in romantic relationships: A policy-capturing study. *Journal of Social Behavior and Personality, 12,* 19–44.

Booth-Butterfield, M. (1989). Perceptions of harassing communications as a function of locus of control, work force participation, and gender. *Communication Quarterly, 37,* 262–275.

Bowlby, J. (1969). *Attachment and loss: Vol. 1. Attachment.* New York: Basic Books.

Bowlby, J. (1973). *Attachment and loss: Vol. 2. Separation.* New York: Basic Books.

Bowlby, J. (1977). The making and breaking of affectional bonds. *British Journal of Psychiatry, 130,* 201–210.

Bowlby, J. (1980). *Attachment and loss: Vol. 3. Loss, sadness, and depression.* New York: Basic Books.

Boyden, T., Carroll, J. S., & Maier, R. A. (1984). Similarity and attraction in homosexual males: The effects of age and masculinity-femininity. *Sex Roles, 10,* 939–948.

Bradac, J. J., Bowers, J. W., & Courtwright, J. A. (1979). Three language variables in communication research: Intensity, immediacy and diversity. *Human Communication Research, 5,* 257–269.

Bradac, J. J., Hosman, L. A., & Tardy, C. H. (1978). Reciprocal disclosures and language intensity: Attributional consequences. *Communication Monographs, 45,* 1–14.

Bradbury, T. N., & Fincham, F. D. (1990). Attributions in marriage: Review and critique. *Psychological Bulletin, 107,* 3–33.

Bradford, L. (1980). The death of a dyad. In B. W. Morse & L. A. Phelps (Eds.), *Interpersonal communication: A relational perspective* (pp. 497–508). Minneapolis, MN: Burgess.

Braiker, H. B., & Kelley, H. H. (1979). Conflict in the development of close relationships. In R. L. Burgess & T. L. Huston (Eds.), *Social exchange in developing relationships* (pp. 135–168). New York: Academic Press.

Braithwaite, D. O. (1995). Ritualized embarrassment at "coed" wedding and baby showers. *Communication Reports, 8,* 145–157.

Braithwaite, D. O., Baxter, L. A., & Harper, A. M. (1998). The role of rituals in the management of the dialectical tension of "old" and "new" in blended families. *Communication Studies, 49,* 101–120.

Bramlett, M. D., & Mosher, W. D. (2002). *Cohabitation, marriage, divorce, and remarriage in the United States* (Vol. 23). Hyattsville, MD: National Center for Health Statistics.

Brandau-Brown, F. E., & Ragsdale, J. D. (2008). Personal, moral, and structural commitment and the repair of marital relationships. *Southern Communication Journal, 73,* 68–83.

Brashers, D. E. (2001). Communication and uncertainty management. *Journal of Communication, 51,* 477–497.

Bratslavsky, E., Baumeister, R. F., & Sommer, K. L. (1998). To love or be loved in vain: The trials and tribulations of unrequited love. In B. H. Spitzberg & W. C. Cupach (Eds.), *The dark side of close relationships* (pp. 307–326). Mahwah, NJ: Lawrence Erlbaum.

Braun, M., Lewin-Epstein, N., Stier, H. & Baumgartner, M. K. (2008). Perceived equity in the gendered division of household labor. *Journal of Marriage and the Family, 70,* 1145–1156.

Brehm, S. S., & Kassin, S. M. (1990). *Social psychology.* Boston: Houghton Mifflin.

Brennan, K. A., & Shaver, P. R. (1995). Dimensions of adult attachment, affect regulations, and romantic relationship functioning. *Personality and Social Psychology Bulletin, 21,* 267–283.

Bretherton, I. (1988). Open communication and internal working models: Their role in the development of attachment relationships. In R. A. Thompson (Ed.), *Nebraska symposium on motivation* (pp. 57–113). Lincoln: University of Nebraska Press.

Bridge, K., & Baxter, L. A. (1992). Blended friendships: Friends as work associates. *Western Journal of Communication, 56,* 200–225.

Brock, L. J., & Jennings, G. H. (1993). Sexuality education: What daughters in their 30s wish their mothers had told them. *Family Relationships, 42,* 61–65.

Brown, D. E. (1991). *Human universals.* Philadelphia, PA: Temple University Press.

Brown, M., & Auerbach, A. (1981). Communication patterns in the initiation of marital sex. *Medical Aspects of Human Sexuality, 15,* 105–117.

Brown, P., & Levinson, S. (1987). *Politeness: Some universals in language usage.* Cambridge, UK: Cambridge University Press.

Brown, R. (1965). *Social psychology.* New York: Free Press.

Brown, S. L. (2000). Union transitions among cohabitors: The significance of relationship assessments and expectations. *Journal of Marriage and the Family, 62,* 833–846.

Brown, S. L., & Booth, A. (1996). Cohabitation versus marriage: A comparison of relationship quality. *Journal of Marriage and the Family, 58,* 668–678.

Browning, J. R., Kessler, D., Hatfield, E., & Choo, P. (1999). Power, gender and sexual behavior. *The Journal of Sex Research, 36,* 342–347.

Brownridge, D. A., & Halli, S. S. (2000). "Living in sin" and sinful living: Toward filling a gap in the explanation of violence against women. *Aggression and Violent Behavior, 5,* 565–583.

Brown-Smith, N. (1998). Family secrets. *Journal of Family Issues, 19,* 20–42.

Bryson, J. B. (1976, September). *The nature of sexual jealousy: An exploratory paper.* Paper presented at the annual meeting of the American Psychological Association, Washington, DC.

Bryson, J. B. (1977, September). *Situational determinants of the expression of jealousy.* Paper presented at the annual meeting of the American Psychological Association, San Francisco.

Buchanan, C. M., Maccoby, E. E., & Dornbusch, S. M. (1991). Caught between parents: Adolescents' experience in divorce homes. *Child Development, 62,* 1008–1029.

Buchanan, C. M., Maccoby, E. E., & Dornbusch, S. M. (1996). *Adolescents after divorce.* Cambridge, MA: Harvard University Press.

Buehler, C., Anthony, C., Krishnakumar, A., Stone, G., Gerad, J., & Pemberton, S. (1997). Intraparental conflict and youth problem behaviors: A meta-analysis. *Journal of Child and Family Studies, 6,* 233–247.

Buhrmester, D., Furman, W., Wittenberg, M. T., & Reis, H. T. (1988). Five domains of interpersonal competence in peer relationships. *Journal of Personality and Social Psychology, 55,* 991–1008.

Buller, D. B., & Aune, R. K. (1987). Nonverbal cues to deception among intimates, friends, and strangers. *Journal of Nonverbal Behavior, 11,* 269–290.

Buller, D. B., & Burgoon, J. K. (1994). Deception: Strategic and nonstrategic communication. In J. A. Daly & J. M. Wiemann (Eds.), *Strategic interpersonal communication* (pp. 191–223). Hillsdale, NJ: Lawrence Erlbaum.

Buller, D. B., Strzyzewski, K. D., & Comstock, J. (1991). Interpersonal deception: I. Deceivers' reactions to receivers suspicious and probing. *Communication Monographs, 58,* 1–24.

Bullis, C., Clark, C., & Sline, R. (1993). From passion to commitment: Turning points in romantic relationships. In P. J. Kalbfleisch (Ed.), *Interpersonal communication: Evolving interpersonal relationships* (pp. 213–236). Hillsdale, NJ: Lawrence Erlbaum.

Bumpass, L. L., & Sweet, J. A. (1989). National estimates of cohabitation. *Demography, 26,* 615–625.

Burgess, E. O. (2004). Sexuality in midlife and later. In J. H. Harvey, A. Wenzel, & S. Sprecher (Eds.), *The handbook of sexuality in close relationships* (pp. 427–454). Mahwah, NJ: Lawrence Erlbaum.

Burgoon, J. K. (1978). A communication model of personal space violations: Explication and an initial test. *Human Communication Research, 4,* 129–142.

Burgoon, J. K., & Bacue, A. (2003). Nonverbal communication skills. In B. R. Burleson & J. O. Greene (Eds.), *Handbook of communication and social interaction skills* (pp. 179–219). Mahwah, NJ: Lawrence Erlbaum.

Burgoon, J. K., & Dillman, L. (1995). Gender, immediacy and nonverbal communication. In P. J. Kalbfleisch & M. J. Cody (Eds.), *Gender, power, and communication in human relationships* (pp. 63–81). Hillsdale, NJ: Lawrence Erlbaum.

Burgoon, J. K., Guerrero, L. K., & Floyd, K. (2010). *Nonverbal communication.* New York: Pearson.

Burgoon, J. K., & Hale, J. L. (1984). The fundamental topoi of relational communication. *Communication Monographs, 51,* 193–214.

Burgoon, J. K., & Hale, J. L. (1987). Validation and measurement of the fundamental themes of relational communication. *Communication Monographs, 54,* 19–41.

Burgoon, J. K., & Hale, J. L. (1988). Nonverbal expectancy violations: Model elaboration and application to immediacy behaviors. *Communication Monographs, 55,* 58–79.

Burgoon, J. K., Johnson, M. L., & Koch, P. T. (1998). The nature and measurement of interpersonal dominance. *Communication Monographs, 65,* 308–335.

Burgoon, J. K., & Langer, E. (1995). Language, fallacies, and mindlessness-mindfulness. In B. R. Burleson (Ed.), *Communication yearbook 18* (pp. 105–132). Thousand Oaks, CA: Sage.

Burgoon, J. K., & Newton, D. A. (1991). Applying a social meaning model to relational message interpretations of conversational involvement: Comparing observer and participant perspectives. *Southern Communication Journal, 56,* 96–113.

Burgoon, J. K., Parrott, R., Le Poire, B. A., Kelley, D. L., Walther, J. B., & Parry, D. (1989). Maintaining and restoring privacy through communication in different types of relationships. *Journal of Social and Personal Relationships, 6,* 131–158.

Burgoon, J. K., Stern, L. A., & Dillman, L. (1995). *Interpersonal adaptation: Dyadic interaction patterns.* New York: Cambridge University Press.

Buri, J. R., Louiselle, P. A., Misukanis, T. M., & Mueller, R. A. (1988). Effects of parental authoritarianism and authoritativeness on self-esteem. *Personality and Social Psychology Bulletin, 14,* 271–282.

Burke, R. J., Weir, T., & Harrison, D. (1976). Disclosure of problems and tensions experienced by marital partners. *Psychological Reports, 38,* 531–542.

Burleson, B. R. (1982). The development of comforting communication skills in childhood and adolescence. *Child Development, 53,* 1578–1588.

Burleson, B. R. (1984). Comforting communication. In H. Sypher & J. L. Applegate (Eds.), *Communication by children and adults* (pp. 63–104). Beverly Hills, CA: Sage.

Burleson, B. R. (1998). Similarities in social skills, interpersonal attraction, and the development of personal relationships. In J. S. Trent (Ed.), *Communication: Views from the helm for the twenty-first century* (pp. 77–84). Boston: Allyn & Bacon.

Burleson, B. R. (2003). The experience and effects of emotional support: What the study of cultural and gender differences can tell us about close relationships, emotion, and interpersonal communication. *Personal Relationships, 10,* 1–23.

Burleson, B. R., Delia, J. G., & Applegate, J. L. (1992). Effects of maternal communication and children's social-cognitive and communication skills on children's acceptance by the peer group. *Family Relations, 41,* 264–272.

Burleson, B. R., & Goldsmith, D. J. (1998). How the comforting process works: Alleviating emotional distress through conversationally induced reappraisals. In P. A. Andersen & L. K. Guerrero (Eds.), *Handbook of communication and emotion: Theory, research, contexts, and applications* (pp. 246–275). San Diego, CA: Academic Press.

Burleson, B. R., Kunkel, A. W., Samter, W., & Werking, K. J. (1996). Men's and women's evaluations of communication skills in personal relationships: When sex differences make a difference—and when they don't.

Journal of Social and Personal Relationships, 13, 201–224.

Burleson, B. R., & Samter, W. (1985a). Consistencies in theoretical and naive evaluations of comforting messages. *Communication Monographs, 52,* 104–123.

Burleson, B. R., & Samter, W. (1985b). Individual differences in the perception of comforting messages. *Central States Speech Journal, 36,* 39–50.

Burleson, B. R., & Samter, W. (1994). A social skills approach to relationship maintenance: How individual differences in communication skills affect the achievement of relationship functions. In D. J. Canary & L. Stafford (Eds.), *Communication and relational maintenance* (pp. 61–90). San Diego, CA: Academic Press.

Burrell, N. A., & Koper, R. J. (1998). The efficacy of powerful/powerless language on attitudes and source credibility. In M. Allen & R. Preiss (Eds.), *Persuasion: Advances through meta-analysis* (pp. 203–216). Creskill, NJ: Hampton Press.

Burt, A., & Trivers, R. L. (2006) *Genes in conflict: The biology of selfish genetic elements.* Cambridge, MA: Belknap Press.

Buss, D. M. (1988a). From vigilance to violence: Tactics of mate retention in American undergraduates. *Ethology and Sociology, 9,* 291–317.

Buss, D. M., (1988b). Love acts: The evolutionary biology of love. In R. J. Sternberg & M. L. Barnes (Eds.), *The psychology of love* (pp. 100–117). New Haven, CT: Yale University Press.

Buss, D. M. (1989). Sex differences in human mate preferences: Evolutionary hypotheses tested in 37 cultures. *Behavioral and Brain Sciences, 12,* 1–49.

Buss, D. M. (1994). *The evolution of desire: Strategies of make selection.* New York: Basic Books.

Buss, D. M., Larsen, R. J., Westen, D., & Semmelroth, J. (1992). Sex differences in jealousy: Evolution, physiology, and psychology. *Psychological Science, 3,* 251–255.

Buss, D. M., & Schmitt, D. P. (1993). Sexual strategies theory: An evolutionary perspective on human mating. *Psychological Review, 100,* 204–232.

Buunk, B. P. (1980). Extramarital sex in the Netherlands: Motivations in social and marital context. *Alternative Lifestyles, 3,* 11–39.

Buunk, B. P. (1982). Strategies of jealousy: Styles of coping with extramarital involvement of the spouse. *Family Relations, 31,* 13–18.

Buunk, B., & Bringle, R. G. (1987). Jealousy in love relationships. In D. Perlman & S. Duck (Eds.), *Intimate relationships: Development, dynamics, and deterioration* (pp. 123–147). Newbury Park, CA: Sage.

Buunk, B. P., Dijkstra, P., Fetchenhauer, D., & Kenrick, D. T. (2002). Age and gender differences in mate selection criteria for various involvement levels. *Personal Relationships, 9,* 271–278.

Buunk, B. P., & Mutsaers, W. (1999). Equity perceptions and marital satisfaction in former and current marriage: A study among the remarried. *Journal of Social and Personal Relationships, 16,* 123–132.

Byers, E. S. (1996). How well does the traditional sexual script explain sexual coercion? Review of a program of research. *Journal of Psychology and Human Sexuality, 8,* 7–25.

Byers, E. S., Demmons, S., & Lawrence, K. (1998). Sexual satisfaction within dating relationships: A test of the interpersonal exchange model of sexual satisfaction. *Journal of Social and Personal Relationships, 15,* 257–267.

Byers, E. S., & Lewis, K. (1988). Dating couples' disagreements over the desired level of sexual activity. *Journal of Sex Research, 24,* 15–29.

Byers, E. S., Purden, C., & Clark, D. A. (1998). Sexually intrusive thoughts of college students. *Journal of Sex Research, 35,* 359–369.

Byers, E. S., & Wilson, P. (1985). Accuracy of women's expectations regarding men's responses to refusals of sexual advances in dating situations. *International Journal of Women's Studies, 4,* 376–387.

Bryant, E. M., & Marmo, J. (2010, November). *Using Facebook to maintain friendships: Examining the differences between acquaintances, casual friends, and close friends.* Paper presented at the annual meeting of the National Communication Association, San Francisco.

Bryant, E. M., & Marmo, J. (in press). Relational maintenance strategies on Facebook. *Kentucky Journal of Communication.*

Byrne, D. (1961). Interpersonal attraction and attitude similarity. *Journal of Abnormal and Social Psychology, 62,* 713–715.

Byrne, D. (1971). *The attraction paradigm.* New York: Academic Press.

Byrne, D. (1992). The transition from controlled laboratory experimentation to less controlled settings: Surprise! Additional variables are operative. *Communication Monographs, 59,* 190–198.

Byrne, D. (1997). An overview (and underview) of research and theory within the attraction paradigm. *Journal of Social and Personal Relationships, 14,* 417–431.

Byrne, D., & Clore, G. L. (1970). A reinforcement model for evaluative responses. *Personality: An International Journal, 1,* 103–128.

Cahn, D. (1992). *Conflict in intimate relationships.* New York: Guilford Press.

Caldwell, M. A., & Peplau, L. A. (1982). Sex differences in same-sex friendship. *Sex Roles, 8,* 721–732.

Campbell, E., Adams, R., & Dobson, W. R. (1984). Familial correlates of identity formation in late adolescence: A study of the predictive utility of connectedness and individuality in family relationships. *Journal of Youth and Adolescence, 13,* 509–525.

Campbell, W. K. (1999). Narcissism and romantic attraction. *Journal of Personality and Social Psychology, 77,* 1254–1270.

Campbell, W. K., & Foster, C. A. (2002). Narcissism and commitment in romantic relationships: An investment model analysis. *Personality and Social Psychology Bulletin, 28,* 484–495.

Canary, D. J., & Cody, M. J. (1994). *Interpersonal communication: A goals-based approach.* New York: St. Martin's Press.

Canary, D. J., Cupach, W. R., & Messman, S. J. (1995). *Relationship conflict.* Thousand Oaks, CA: Sage.

Canary, D. J., & Hause, K. G. (1993). Is there any reason to research sex differences in communication? *Communication Quarterly, 41,* 129–144.

Canary, D. J., & Lakey, S. G. (2006). Managing conflict in a competent manner: A mindful look at events that matter. In J. Oetzel & S. Ting-Toomey (Eds.), *The SAGE handbook of communication and conflict* (pp. 185–210). Thousand Oaks, CA: Sage.

Canary, D. J., & Spitzberg, B. H. (1987). Appropriateness and effectiveness perceptions of conflict strategies. *Human Communication Research, 14,* 93–118.

Canary, D. J., & Spitzberg, B. H. (1989). A model of perceived competence of conflict strategies. *Human Communication Research, 15,* 630–649.

Canary, D. J., & Spitzberg, B. H. (1990). Attribution biases and associations between conflicts strategies and competence outcomes. *Communication Monographs, 57,* 139–151.

Canary, D. J., & Stafford, L. (1992). Relational maintenance strategies and equity in marriage. *Communication Monographs, 59,* 243–267.

Canary, D. J., & Stafford, L. (1993). Preservation of relational characteristics: Maintenance strategies, equity, and locus of control. In P. J. Kalbfleisch (Ed.), *Interpersonal communication: Evolving interpersonal relationships* (pp. 237–259). Hillsdale, NJ: Lawrence Erlbaum.

Canary, D. J., & Stafford, L. (1994). Maintaining relationships through strategic and routine interaction. In D. J. Canary & L. Stafford (Eds.), *Communication and relational maintenance* (pp. 3–22). San Diego, CA: Academic Press.

Canary, D. J., & Stafford, L. (2001). Equity in the preservation of personal relationships. In J. Harvey & A. Wenzel (Eds.), *Close romantic relationships: Maintenance and enhancement* (pp. 133–151). Mahwah, NJ: Lawrence Erlbaum.

Canary, D. J., Stafford, L., Hause, K. S., & Wallace, L. A. (1993). An inductive analysis of relational maintenance strategies: Comparisons among lovers, relatives, friends, and others. *Communication Research Reports, 10,* 5–14.

Cappella, J. N. (1988). Personal relationships, social relationships and patterns of interaction. In S. Duck (Ed.), *Handbook of personal relationships: Theory, research and interventions* (pp. 325–342). Chichester, UK: Wiley.

Cargan, L., & Melko, M. (1982). *Singles: Myths and realities.* Beverly Hills, CA: Sage.

Carney, D. R., Hall, J. A., & LeBeau, L. S. (2005). Beliefs about the nonverbal expression of social power. *Journal of Nonverbal Behavior, 29,* 105–123.

Carson, A., & Banuazizi, A. (2008). It's not fair!: Similarities and differences in resource distribution between American and Filipino fifth graders. *Journal of Cross-Cultural Psychology, 39,* 493–514.

Carson, J. W., Carson, K. M., Gil, K. M., & Baucom, D. H. (2007). Self-expansion as a mediator of of relationship improvements in a mindfulness intervention. *Journal of Marital and Family Therapy, 33,* 517–528.

Caspi, A., & Gorsky, P. (2006). Online deception: Prevalence, motivation, and emotion. *Cyberpsychology and Behavior, 9,* 54–59

Cate, R. M., Levin, L. A., & Richmond, L. S. (2002). Premarital relationship stability: A review of recent research. *Journal of Social and Personal Relationships, 19,* 261–284.

Cate, R. M., & Lloyd, S. A. (1988). Courtship. In S. Duck (Ed.), *Handbook of personal relationships* (pp. 409–427). New York: Wiley.

Cate, R. M., Lloyd, S. A., & Henton, J. M. (1985). The effect of equity, equality, and reward level on the stability of students' premarital relationships. *Journal of Social Psychology, 125,* 715–721.

Cate, R. M., Lloyd, S. A., & Long, E. (1988). The role of rewards and fairness in developing premarital relationships. *Journal of Marriage and the Family, 50,* 443–452.

Cate, R. M., Long, E., Angera, J. J., & Draper, K. K. (1993). Sexual intercourse and relational development. *Family Relations, 42,* 158–164.

Caughlin, J. P. (2002). The demand/withdrawal pattern if communication as a predictor of marital satisfaction over time: Unresolved issues and future directions. *Human Communication Research, 28,* 49–85.

Caughlin, J. P., & Afifi, T. D. (2004). When is topic avoidance unsatisfying? Examining moderators of the association between avoidance and dissatisfaction. *Human Communication Research, 30,* 479–513.

Caughlin, J. P., Afifi, W. A., Carpenter-Theune, K. E., & Miller, L. E. (2005). Reasons for and consequences of revealing personal secrets in close relationships: A longitudinal study. *Personal Relationships, 12,* 43–60.

Caughlin, J., & Golish, T. (2002). An analysis of the association between topic avoidance and dissatisfaction: Comparing perceptual and interpersonal explanations. *Communication Monographs, 69,* 275–296.

Caughlin, J. P., & Vangelisti, A. L. (1999). Desire for change in one's partner as a predictor of the demand/withdraw pattern of marital communication. *Communication Monographs, 66,* 66–89.

Caughlin, J. P., & Vangelisti, A. L. (2006). Conflict in dating and marital relationships. In J. G. Oetzel & S. Ting-Toomey (Eds.), *The SAGE handbook of conflict communication* (pp. 129–157). Thousand Oaks, CA: Sage.

Caughlin, J. P., & Vangelisti, A. L. (2009). Why people conceal or reveal secrets: A multiple goals theory perspective. In T. D. Afifi & W. A. Afifi (Eds.), *Uncertainty, information management, and disclosure decisions: Theories and applications* (pp. 279–299). New York: Routledge.

Centers for Disease Control and Prevention. (1997, May 2). Contraceptive practices before and after an intervention promoting condom use to prevent HIV infection and other sexually transmitted diseases among women—Selected U.S. sites, 1993–1997. *MMWR Weekly, 46*(17). Retrieved from http://www.cdc.gov/mmwr/

Chaikin, A. L., & Derlega, V. J. (1974). Liking for the norm breaker in self-disclosure. *Journal of Personality, 42,* 117–129.

Chaiken, S. (1979). Communicator physical attractiveness and persuasion. *Journal of Personality and Social Psychology, 37,* 1387–1397.

Chelune, G. J., Rosenfeld, L. B., & Waring, A. E. (1985). Spouse disclosure patterns in distressed and nondistressed couples. *American Journal of Family Therapy, 13,* 24–32.

Christensen, A., & Heavey, C. L. (1990). Gender and social structure in the demand/withdrawal pattern of marital conflict. *Journal of Personality and Social Psychology, 59,* 73–81.

Christensen, A., & Shenk, J. L. (1991). Communication, conflict, and psychological distance in nondistressed, clinical, and divorcing couples. *Journal of Consulting and Clinical Psychology, 59,* 458–463.

Christopher, F. S., & Cate, R. M. (1985). Premarital sexual pathways and relationship development. *Journal of Social and Personal Relationships, 2,* 271–288.

Christopher, F. S., & Frandsen, M. M. (1990). Strategies of influence in sex and dating. *Journal of Social and Personal Relationships, 7,* 89–105.

Christopher, F. S., & Kissler, T. S. (2004). Exploring marital sexuality: Peeking inside the bedroom and discovering what we don't know—but should. In J. H. Harvey, A. Wenzel, & S. Sprecher (Eds.), *The handbook of sexuality in close relationships* (pp. 371–384). Mahwah, NJ: Lawrence Erlbaum.

Christopher, F. S., & Lloyd, S. A. (2000). Physical and sexual aggression in relationships. In C. Hendrick & S. S. Hendrick (Eds.), *Close relationships* (pp. 331–343). Thousand Oaks, CA: Sage.

Christopher, F. S., Owens, L. A., & Strecker, H. L. (1993). An examination of single men's and women's sexual aggressiveness in dating relationships. *Journal of Social and Personal Relationships, 10,* 511–527.

Christopher, F. S., & Roosa, M. W. (1991). Factors affecting sexual decisions in premarital relationships of adolescents and young adults. In K. McKinney & S. Sprecher (Eds.), *Sexuality in close relationships* (pp. 111–133). Hillsdale, NJ: Lawrence Erlbaum.

Chivers, M. L., & Bailey, J. M. (2005). A sex difference in features that elicit genital response. *Biological Psychology, 70,* 115–120.

Chivers, M. L., Soto, M. C., & Blanchard, R. (2007).Gender and sexual orientation differences in sexual response to sexual activities versus gender of actors in sexual films. *Journal of Personality and Social Psychology, 93,* 1108–1121.

Cialdini, R. B. (1984). *The psychology of influence.* New York: Quill.

Cialdini, R. B. (1988). *Influence: Science and practice* (2nd ed.). New York: HarperCollins.

Clarke-Stewart, A., & Brentano, C. (2006). *Divorce: Causes and consequences.* New Haven, CT: Yale University Press.

Cleek, M. G., & Pearson, T. A. (1985). Perceived causes of divorce: An analysis of interrelationships. *Journal of Marriage and the Family, 47,* 179–183.

Clements, M. L., Cordova, A. D., Markman, H. J., & Laurenceau, J. (1997). The erosion of marital satisfaction over time and how to prevent it. In R. J. Sternberg

& M. Hojjat (Eds.), *Satisfaction in close relationships* (pp. 335–365). New York: Guilford Press.

Cline, R. J. W., Freeman, K. E., & Johnson, S. J. (1990). Talk among sexual partners about AIDS: Factors differentiating those who talk from those who do not. *Communication Research, 17,* 792–808.

Clore, G. L., & Byrne, D. (1974). A reinforcement-affect model of attraction. In T. L. Huston (Ed.), *Foundations of interpersonal attraction* (pp. 143–170). New York: Academic Press.

Cloven, D. H., & Roloff, M. E. (1993). The chilling effect of aggressive potential on the expression of complaints in intimate relationships. *Communication Monographs, 60,* 199–219.

Coates, D., Wortman, C. B., & Abbey, A. (1979). Reactions to victims. In I. H. Frieze, D. Bar-Tal, & J. S. Carroll (Eds.), *New approaches to social problems* (pp. 21–52). San Francisco: Jossey-Bass.

Cody, M. (1982). A typology of disengagement strategies and an examination of the role intimacy and relational problems play in strategy selection. *Communication Monographs, 49,* 148–170.

Cole, T. (2001). Lying to the one you love: The use of deception in romantic relationships. *Journal of Social and Personal Relationships, 18,* 107–129.

Collins, N. L., & Miller, L. C. (1994). The disclosure-liking link: From meta-analysis toward a dynamic reconceptualization. *Psychological Bulletin, 116,* 457–475.

Collins, N. L., & Read, S. J. (1990). Adult attachment, working models, and relationship quality in dating couples. *Journal of Personality and Social Psychology, 58,* 644–663.

Collins, N. L., & Read, S. J. (1994). Cognitive representations of attachment: The structure and function of working models. In K. Bartholomew & D. Perlman (Eds.), *Attachment processes in adulthood: Advances in personal relationships* (Vol. 5, pp. 53–90). Bristol, PA: Kingsley.

Comadena, M. E. (1982). Accuracy in detecting deception: Intimate and friendship relationships. In M. Burgoon (Ed.), *Communication yearbook 6* (pp. 446–472). Beverly Hills, CA: Sage.

Conville, R. L. (1991). *Relational transitions: The evolution of personal relationships.* New York: Praeger.

Cooley, C. H. (1922). *Human nature and the social order.* New York: Scribner.

Cottle, T. J. (1980). *Children's secrets.* Reading, MA: Addison-Wesley.

Coutts, L. M., & Schneider, F. W. (1976). Affiliative conflict theory: An investigation of the intimacy equilibrium and compensation hypothesis. *Journal of Personality and Social Psychology, 34,* 1135–1142.

Cowan, G., Drinkard, J., & MacGavin, L. (1984). The effects of target, age, and gender on power use strategies. *Journal of Personality and Social Psychology, 47,* 1391–1398.

Cozzarelli, C., Hoekstra, S. J., & Bylsma, W. H. (2000). General versus specific mental models of attachment: Are they associated with different outcomes? *Personality and Social Psychology Bulletin, 26,* 605–618.

Cramer, D. (2002). Linking conflict management behaviours and relational satisfaction: The intervening role of conflict outcome satisfaction. *Journal of Social and Personal Relationships, 19,* 431–438.

Crawford, D. W., Feng, D., Fischer, J. L., & Diana, L. K. (2003). The influence of love, equity, and alternatives on commitment in romantic relationships. *Family and Consumer Sciences Research Journal, 13,* 253–271.

Creasey, G., & Jarvis, P. (2008). Attachment theory and research: A special focus on relationship initiation. In S. Sprecher, J. Harvey, & A. Wenzel (Eds.), *Handbook of relationship initiation* (pp. 75–94). New York: Taylor & Francis.

Creasey, G., Kershaw, K., & Boston, A. (1999). Conflict management with friends and romantic partners: The role of attachment and negative mood regulation expectancies. *Journal of Youth and Adolescence, 28,* 523–543.

Critchley, H. D., Mathias, C. J., & Dolan, R. J. (2001). Neural activity in the human brain relating to uncertainty and arousal during anticipation. *Neuron, 29,* 537–545.

Crocker, J., & Schwartz, I. (1985). Prejudice and ingroup favoritism in a minimal intergroup situation: Effects of self-esteem. *Personality and Social Psychology Bulletin, 11,* 379–386.

Crockett, L., Losoff, M., & Peterson, A. C. (1984). Perceptions of the peer group and friendship in early adolescence. *Journal of Early Adolescence, 4,* 155–181.

Croghan, R., Griffin, C., Hunter, J., & Phoenix, A. (2006). Style failure, consumption, identity, and social exclusion. *Journal of Youth Studies, 9,* 463–478.

Crooks, R., & Baur, K. (1999). *Our sexuality.* Pacific Grove, CA: Brooks/Cole.

Cunningham, J. D., & Antill, J. K. (1994). Cohabitation and marriage: Retrospective and predictive comparisons. *Journal of Social and Personal Relationships, 11,* 77–93.

Cunningham, J. D., & Antil, J. K. (1995). Current trends in marital cohabitation: In search of the POSSLQ. In J. T. Wood & S. Duck (Eds.), *Understudied relationships: Off the beaten track* (pp. 148–172). Thousand Oaks, CA: Sage.

Cupach, W. R. (1994). Social predicaments. In W. R. Cupach & B. H. Spitzberg (Eds.), *The dark side of interpersonal communication* (pp. 159–180). Hillsdale, NJ: Lawrence Erlbaum.

Cupach, W. R., & Comstock, J. (1990). Satisfaction with sexual communication in marriage: Links to sexual satisfaction and dyadic adjustment. *Journal of Social and Personal Relationships, 7,* 179–186.

Cupach, W. R., & Metts, S. (1986). Accounts of relational dissolution: A comparison of marital and non-marital relationships. *Communication Monographs, 53,* 311–334.

Cupach, W. R., & Metts, S. (1991). Sexuality and communication in close relationships. In K. McKinney & S. Sprecher (Eds.), *Sexuality in close relationships* (pp. 93–110). Hillsdale, NJ: Lawrence Erlbaum.

Cupach, W. R., & Metts, S. (1994). *Facework.* Thousand Oaks, CA: Sage.

Cupach, W. R., & Metts, S. (1995). The role of sexual attitude similarity in romantic heterosexual relationships. *Personal Relationships, 2,* 287–300.

Cupach, W. R., & Metts, S. (2002, July). *The persistence of reconciliation attempts following the dissolution of romantic relationships.* Paper presented at the International Conference on Personal Relationships, Halifax, Nova Scotia.

Cupach, W. R., & Spitzberg, B. H. (Eds.). (1994). *The dark side of interpersonal communication.* Hillsdale, NJ: Lawrence Erlbaum.

Cupach, W. R., & Spitzberg, B. H. (1998). Obsessive relational intrusion and stalking. In B. H. Spitzberg & W. R. Cupach (Eds.), *The dark side of close relationships* (pp. 233–264). Mahwah, NJ: Lawrence Erlbaum.

Cupach, W. R., & Spitzberg, B. H. (2000). Obsessive relational intrusion: Incidence, perceived severity, and coping. *Violence and Victims, 15,* 357–372.

Cupach, W. R., & Spitzberg, B. H. (2004). *The dark side of relationship pursuit: From attraction to obsession and stalking.* Mahwah, NJ: Lawrence Erlbaum.

Cupach, W. R., & Spitzberg, B. H. (2008). "Thanks but no thanks . . .": The occurrence and management of unwanted relationship pursuit. In S. Sprecher, A. Wenzel, & J. Harvey (Eds.), *Handbook of relationship initiation* (pp. 409–424). New York: Taylor & Francis.

D'Emilio, J., & Freedman, E. B. (1988). *Intimate matters: A history of sexuality in America.* New York: Harper & Row.

Dailey, R. M., & Palomares, N. A. (2004). Strategic topic avoidance: An investigation of topic avoidance frequency, strategies used, and relational correlates. *Communication Monographs, 71,* 471–496.

Dailey, R. M., Pfiester, A., Jin, B., Beck, G., & Clark, G. (2009). On-again/off-again dating relationships: How are they different from other dating relationships? *Personal Relationships, 16,* 23–47.

Dainton, M. (2000). Maintenance behaviors, expectations for maintenance, and satisfaction: Linking comparison levels to relational maintenance strategies. *Journal of Social and Personal Relationships, 17,* 827–842.

Dainton, M., & Aylor, B. (2001). A relational uncertainty analysis of jealousy, trust, and maintenance in long-distance versus geographically close relationships. *Communication Quarterly, 49,* 172–188.

Dainton, M., & Aylor, B. (2002). Routine and strategic maintenance efforts: Behavioral patterns, variations associated with relational length, and the prediction of relational characteristics. *Communication Monographs, 69,* 52–66.

Dainton, M., & Gross, J. (2008). The use of negative behaviors to maintain relationships. *Communication Research Reports, 25,* 179–191.

Dainton, M., & Stafford, L. (1993). Routine maintenance behaviors: A comparison of relationship type, partner similarity and sex differences. *Journal of Social and Personal Relationships, 10,* 255–271.

Dainton, M., Stafford, L., & Canary, D. J. (1994). Maintenance strategies and physical affection as predictors of love, liking, and satisfaction in marriage. *Communication Reports, 7,* 88–98.

Dainton, M., Zelley, E., & Langan, E. (2003). Maintaining friendships throughout the lifespan. In D. J. Canary & M. Dainton (Eds.), *Maintaining relationships through communication: Relational, contextual, and cultural variations* (pp. 79–102). Mahwah, NJ: Lawrence Erlbaum.

Daly, J. A., Hoggs, E., Sacks, D., Smith, M., & Zimring, L. (1983). Sex and relationship affects social self-grooming. *Journal of Nonverbal Behavior, 7,* 183–189.

Daly, J. A., & Kreiser, P. O. (1994). Affinity seeking. In J. A. Daly & J. M. Wiemann (Eds.), *Strategic interpersonal communication* (pp. 109–134). Hillsdale, NJ: Lawrence Erlbaum.

Darby, B. W., & Schlenker, B. R. (1982). Children's reactions to apologies. *Journal of Personality and Social Psychology, 43,* 743–753.

Darby, B. W., & Schlenker, B. R. (1989). Children's reactions to transgressions: Effects of the actor's apology, reputation, and remorse. *British Journal of Social Psychology, 28,* 353–364.

Davey, A., Fincham, F. D., Beach, S. R. H., & Brody, G. H. (2001). Attributions in marriage: Examining the entailment model in dyadic context. *Journal of Family Psychology, 15,* 721–734.

Davidson, B., Balswick, J., & Halverson, C. (1983). Affective self-disclosure and marital adjustment: A test of equity theory. *Journal of Marriage and the Family, 1,* 93–102.

Davies, P. T., & Cummings, E. M. (1994). Marital conflict and adjustment: An emotional security hypothesis. *Psychological Bulletin, 116,* 387–411.

Davila, J., Burge, D., & Hammen, C. (1997). Why does attachment style change? *Journal of Personality and Social Psychology, 73,* 826–838.

Davila, J., Karney, B. R., & Bradbury, T. N. (1999). Attachment change processes in the early years of marriage. *Journal of Personality and Social Psychology, 76,* 783–802.

Davis, A. P. C., Goetz, J. C., & Shackelford, T. K. (2008). Exploiting the beauty in the eye of the beholder: The use of physical attraction as a persuasive tactic. *Personality and Individual Differences, 45,* 302–306.

Davis, K. E., & Roberts, M. K. (1985). Relationship in the real world: The descriptive approach to personal relationships. In K. J. Gergen & K. E. Davis (Eds.), *The social construction of the person* (pp. 144–163). New York: Springer-Verlag.

Davis, K. E., & Todd, M. J. (1982). Friendship and love relationships. In E. E. Davis (Ed.), *Advances in descriptive psychology* (Vol. 2, pp. 79–122). Greenwich, CT: JAI Press.

Davis, K. E., & Todd, M. J. (1985). Assessing friendships: Prototypes, paradigm cases, and relationship description. In S. Duck & D. Perlman (Eds.), *Understanding personal relationships: An interdisciplinary approach* (pp. 17–38). London: Sage.

Davis, M. (1973). *Intimate relations.* New York: Free Press.

De Goede, I. H. A., Branje, S. J. T., & Meehus, M. H. J. (2009). Developmental changes in adolescents' perceptions of relationships with their parents. *Journal of Youth and Adolescence, 38,* 75–88.

Dechesne, M., & Kruglanski, A. W. (2009). Motivated cognition in interpersonal contexts: Need for closure and its implications for information regulation and social interaction. In T. D. Afifi & W. A. Afifi (Eds.), *Uncertainty, information management, and disclosure decisions: Theories and applications* (pp. 128–142). New York: Routledge.

Deikman, A. J. (1973). The meaning of everything. In R. E. Ornstein (Ed.), *The nature of human consciousness* (pp. 317–335). New York: Viking Press.

DeLamater, J., & Hyde, J. S. (2004). Conceptual and theoretical issues in studying close relationships. In J. H. Harvey, A. Wenzel, & S. Sprecher (Eds.), *The handbook of sexuality in close relationships* (pp. 7–30). Mahwah, NJ: Lawrence Erlbaum.

DeMaris, A. (1984). A comparison of remarriages with first marriages on satisfaction in marriage and its relationship to prior cohabitation. *Family Relations, 33,* 443–449.

DeMaris, A. (2007). The roles of relationship inequity in marital disruption. *Journal of Social and Personal Relationships, 24,* 177–195.

DeMaris, A., & Leslie, G. R. (1984). Cohabitation with the future spouse: Its influence upon marital satisfaction and communication. *Journal of Marriage and the Family, 46,* 77–84.

DePaulo, B. M. (1992). Nonverbal behavior and self-presentation. *Psychological Bulletin, 111,* 203–243.

DePaulo, B. M., Kashy, D. A., Kirkendol, S. E., Wyer, M. M., & Epstein, J. A. (1996). Lying in everyday life. *Journal of Personality and Social Psychology, 70,* 979–995.

Derlega, V. J., Barbee, A. P., & Winstead, B. A. (1994). Friendship, gender, and social support: Laboratory studies of supportive interactions. In B. R. Burleson, T. L. Albrecht, & I. G. Sarason (Eds.), *Communication of social support: Messages, interactions, relationships, and community* (pp. 136–151). Thousand Oaks, CA: Sage.

Derlega, V. J., & Grzelak, J. (1979). Appropriateness of self-disclosure. In G. Chelune (Ed.), *Self-disclosure: Origins, patterns, and implications of openness in interpersonal relationships* (pp. 151–176). San Francisco: Jossey-Bass.

Derlega, V. J., Harris, M. S., & Chaikin, A. L. (1973). Friendship and disclosure reciprocity. *Journal of Personality and Social Psychology, 9,* 277–284.

Derlega, V. J., Metts, S., Petronio, S., & Margulis, S. T. (1993). *Self-disclosure.* Newbury Park, CA: Sage.

DeSteno, D., Bartlett, M. Y., Salovey, P., & Braverman, J. (2002). Sex differences in jealousy: Evolutionary mechanism or artifact of measurement? *Journal of Personality and Social Psychology, 83,* 1103–1116.

DeSteno, D., & Salovey, P. (1996). Evolutionary origins of sex differences in jealousy? Questioning the "fitness" of the model. *Psychological Science, 7,* 367–372.

Deutsch, M. (1985). *Distributive justice: A social-psychological perspective.* New Haven, CT: Yale University Press.

Dieckman, L. E. (2000). Private secrets and public disclosures: The case of battered women. In S. Petronio (Ed.), *Balancing the secrets of private disclosures* (pp. 275–286). Mahwah, NJ: Lawrence Erlbaum.

Dillard, J. P. (1989). Types of influence goals in personal relationships. *Journal of Social and Personal Relationships, 6,* 293–308.

Dillard, J. P., & Witteman, H. (1985). Romantic relationships at work: Organizational and personal influences. *Human Communication Research, 12,* 99–116.

Dindia, K. (1989, May). Toward the development of a measure of marital maintenance strategies. Paper presented at the annual meeting of the International Communication Association, San Francisco.

Dindia, K. (1997, November). *Men are from North Dakota, women are from South Dakota.* Paper presented at the annual meeting of the Speech Communication Association, Chicago.

Dindia, K. (2003). Definitions and perspectives on relational maintenance communication. In D. J. Canary & M. Dainton (Eds.), *Maintaining relationships through communication: Relational, contextual, and cultural variations* (pp. 1–28). Mahwah, NJ: Lawrence Erlbaum.

Dindia, K., & Allen, M. (1992). Sex differences in self-disclosure: A meta-analysis. *Psychological Bulletin, 112,* 106–124.

Dindia, K., & Baxter, L. A. (1987). Strategies for maintaining and repairing marital relationships. *Journal of Social and Personal Relationships, 4,* 143–158.

Dindia, K., & Canary, D. J. (1993). Definitions and theoretical perspectives on relational maintenance. *Journal of Social and Personal Relationships, 10,* 163–173.

Dindia, K., Fitzpatrick, M. A., & Kenny, D. A. (1997). Self-disclosure in spouse and stranger interaction: A social relations analysis. *Human Communication Research, 23,* 388–412.

Dindia, K., Timmerman, L., Langan, E., Sahlstein, E. M., & Quandt, J. (2004). The function of holiday greetings in maintaining relationships. *Journal of Social and Personal Relationships, 21,* 577–593.

Dion, K. K. (1972). Physical attractiveness and evaluations of children's transgressions. *Journal of Personality and Social Psychology, 24,* 207–213.

Dion, K. K. (1986). Stereotyping based on physical attractiveness: Issues and conceptual perspectives. In C. P. Herman, M. P. Zanna, & E. T. Higgins (Eds.), *The Ontario symposium: Vol. 3. Physical appearance, stigma, and social behavior* (pp. 7–21). Hillsdale, NJ: Lawrence Erlbaum.

Dion, K. K., Berscheid, E., & Walster, E. (1972). What is beautiful is good. *Journal of Personality and Social Psychology, 24,* 285–290.

Dolin, D. J., & Booth-Butterfield, M. (1993). Reach out and touch someone: Analysis of nonverbal comforting responses. *Communication Quarterly, 41,* 383–393.

Donald, M. (1991). *Origins of the modern mind: Three stages in the evolution of culture and cognition.* Cambridge, MA: Harvard University Press.

Donovan, R. L., & Jackson, B. L. (1990). Deciding to divorce: A process guided by social exchange, attachment, and cognitive dissonance theories. *Journal of Divorce, 13,* 23–35.

Dougherty, T. W., Turban, D. B., Olson, D. E., Dwyer, P. D., & Lapreze, M. W. (1996). Factors affecting perceptions or workplace sexual harassment. *Journal of Organizational Behavior, 17,* 489–501.

Douglas, W. (1990). Uncertainty, information-seeking, and liking during initial interaction. *Western Journal of Speech Communication, 54,* 66–81.

Dovido, J. F., Brown, C. E., Heltman, K., Ellyson, S. L., & Keating, C. F. (1988). Power displays between men and women in discussions of gender-linked tasks: A multichannel study. *Journal of Personality and Social Psychology, 55,* 580–587.

Dowrick, S. (1999, March–April). The art of letting go. *Utne Reader, Issue 92,* 46–50.

Draucker, C. B. (1999). "Living in hell": The experience of being stalked. *Issues in Mental Health Nursing, 20,* 473–484.

Drigotas, S. M., & Rusbult, C. E. (1992). Should I stay or should I go? A dependence model of breakups. *Journal of Personality and Social Psychology, 62,* 62–87.

Driscoll, R., Davis, K. E., & Lipetz, M. E. (1972). Parental interference and romantic love: The Romeo and Juliet effect. *Journal of Personality and Social Psychology, 24,* 1–10.

Duck, S. (1982). A topography of relational disengagement and dissolution. In S. Duck (Ed.), *Personal relationships 4: Dissolving personal relationships* (pp. 1–30). London: Academic Press.

Duck, S. (1986). *Human relationships.* Newbury Park, CA: Sage.

Duck, S. (1988). *Relating to others.* Monterey, CA: Brooks/Cole.

Duck, S. (1994). Steady as (s)he goes: Relational maintenance as a shared meaning systems. In D. J. Canary & L. Stafford (Eds.), *Communication and relational maintenance* (pp. 45–60). San Diego, CA: Academic Press.

Duck, S. W. (2005). How do you tell some one you're letting go? A new model of relationship breakup. *The Psychologist, 18,* 210–213.

Duffy, S. M., & Rusbult, C. E. (1986). Satisfaction and commitment in homosexual and heterosexual relationships. *Journal of Homosexuality, 12,* 1–21.

Dunbar, N. E., Bippus, A. M., & Young, S. L. (2008). Interpersonal dominance in relational conflict: A view from dyadic power theory. *Interpersona, 2*(1), 1–33.

Dunbar, N. E., & Burgoon, J. K. (2005). Perceptions of power and dominance in interpersonal encounters. *Journal of Social and Personal Relationships, 22,* 207–233.

Dunn, J. (1983). Sibling relationships in early childhood. *Child Development, 54,* 787–811.

Dunn, J. (1988a). Connections between relationships: Implications of research on mothers and siblings. In R. A. Hinde & J. Stevenson-Hinde (Eds.), *Relationships within families: Mutual influences* (pp. 168–180). New York: Oxford University Press.

Dunn, J. (1988b). Relations among relationships. In S. W. Duck (Ed.), *Handbook of personal relationships* (pp. 193–209). New York: Wiley.

Dunn, J., & Kendrick, C. (1982). *Siblings: Love, envy, and understanding.* Cambridge, MA: Harvard University Press.

Dunn, J., & Munn, P. (1987). Development of justification in disputes with another sibling. *Developmental Psychology, 23,* 791–798.

Durante, K. M., Li, N. P., & Haselton, M. G. (2008). Changes in women's choice of dress across the ovulatory cycle: Naturalistic and laboratory task-based evidence. *Personality and Social Psychology Bulletin, 34,* 1451–1460.

Dutton, D. G., & Aron, A. P. (1974). Some evidence for heightened sexual attraction under conditions of high anxiety. *Journal of Personality and Social Psychology, 30,* 510–517.

Eden, J., & Veksler, A. E. (2010, April). *He likes me, he loves me not (Part II): Relational maintenance in the context of unrequited attraction.* Paper presented at the Eastern Communication Association Convention, Baltimore.

Edgar, T., & Fitzpatrick, M. A. (1988). Compliance-gaining and relational interaction: When your life depends on it. *Southern Speech Communication Journal, 53,* 385–405.

Edgar, T., & Fitzpatrick, M. A. (1993). Expectations for sexual interaction: A cognitive test of the sequencing of sexual communication behaviors. *Health Communication, 5,* 239–261.

Egland, K. L., Spitzberg, B. H., & Zormeier, M. M. (1996). Flirtation and conversational competence in cross-sex platonic and romantic relationships. *Communication Reports, 9,* 105–118.

Egland, K. L., Stelzner, M. A., Andersen, P. A., & Spitzberg, B. H. (1996). Perceived understanding, nonverbal communication and relational satisfaction. In J. Aitken & L. Shedletsky (Eds.), *Intrapersonal communication processes* (pp. 386–395). Annandale, VA: Speech Communication Association.

Ehrenreich, B., Hess, E., & Jacobs, G. (1986). *Remaking love: The feminization of sex.* Garden City, NY: Anchor/Doubleday.

Eisenberg, A. R. (1992). Conflicts between mothers and their young children. *Merrill-Palmer Quarterly, 38,* 21–43.

Ekman, P. (1985). *Telling lies.* New York: Norton.

Ekman, P., & Friesen, W. V. (1969). Nonverbal leakage and clues to deception. *Psychiatry, 32,* 88–106.

Elliott, L., & Bradley, C. (1997). *Sex on campus: The naked truth about the real sex lives of college students.* New York: Random House.

Ellison, N., Heino, R., & Gibb, J. (2006). Managing impressions online: Self-presentation processes in the online dating environment. *Journal of Computer-Mediated Communication, 11,* 415–441.

Ellyson, S. L., & Dovidio, J. F. (1985). Power, dominance, and nonverbal behavior: Basic concepts and issues. In S. L. Ellyson & J. F. Dovidio (Eds.), *Power, dominance, and nonverbal behavior* (pp. 1–27). New York: Springer-Verlag.

Emmers, T. M., & Canary, D. J. (1996). The effect of uncertainty reducing strategies on young couples' relational repair and intimacy. *Communication Quarterly, 44,* 166–182.

Emmers, T. M., & Dindia, K. (1995). The effect of relational stage and intimacy on touch: An extension of Guerrero and Andersen. *Personal Relationships, 2,* 225–236.

Emmers, T. M., & Hart, R. D. (1996). Romantic relationship disengagement and coping rituals. *Communication Research Reports, 13,* 8–18.

Emmers-Sommer, T. M. (2004). The effect of communication quality and quantity indicators on intimacy and relational satisfaction. *Journal of Social and Personal Relationships, 21,* 399–411.

Emmons, R. A. (1989). Exploring the relations between motives and traits: The case of narcissism. In D. M. Buss & N. Cantor (Eds.), *Personality psychology: Recent trends and emerging directions* (pp. 32–44). New York: Springer.

Ennis, E., Vrij, A., & Chance, C. (2008). Individual differences and lying in everyday life. *Journal of Social and Personal Relationships, 25,* 105–118.

Exline, R. V., Ellyson, S. L., & Long, B. (1975). Visual behavior as an aspect of power role relationships. In P. Pliner, L. Krames, & T. Alloway (Eds.), *Nonverbal communication of aggression* (pp. 21–52). New York: Plenum Press.

Exline, R. V., & Winters, L. C. (1965). Affective relations and mutual glances in dyads. In S. Tomkins & C. E. Izard (Eds.), *Affect, cognition, and personality* (pp. 319–350). New York: Springer.

Fairhurst, G. T. (1986). Male-female communication on the job: Literature review and commentary. In M. McLaughlin (Ed.), *Communication yearbook 9* (pp. 83–116). Beverly Hills, CA: Sage.

Falbo, T., & Peplau, L. A. (1980). Power strategies in intimate relationships. *Journal of Personality and Social Psychology, 38,* 618–628.

Farrell, D., & Rusbult, C. E. (1981). Exchange variables as predictors of job satisfaction, job commitment, and turnover: The impact of rewards, costs, alternatives, and investments. *Organizational Behavior and Human Performance, 27,* 78–95.

Feeney, J. A. (1995). Adult attachment and emotional control. *Personal Relationships, 2,* 143–159.

Feeney, J. A. (1999). Adult attachment, emotional control, and marital satisfaction. *Personal Relationships, 6,* 169–185.

Feeney, J. A. (2004). Hurt feelings in couple relationships: Toward integrative models of the negative effects of hurtful events. *Journal of Social and Personal Relationships, 21,* 487–508.

Feeney, J. A. (2005). Hurt feelings in couple relationships: Exploring the role of attachment and perceptions of personal injury. *Personal Relationships, 12,* 253–271.

Feeney, J. A., & Noller, P. (1991). Attachment style and verbal descriptions of romantic partners. *Journal of Social and Personal Relationships, 8,* 187–215.

Feeney, J. A., & Noller, P. (1996). *Adult attachment.* Thousand Oaks, CA: Sage.

Feeney, J. A., Noller, P., & Callan, V. J. (1994). Attachment style, communication and satisfaction in the early years of marriage. In K. Bartholomew & D. Perlman (Eds.), *Attachment processes in adulthood: Advances in personal relationships* (Vol. 5, pp. 269–308). Bristol, PA: Kingsley.

Feeney, J. A., Noller, P., & Roberts, N. (1998). Emotion, attachment and satisfaction in close relationships. In P. A. Andersen & L. K. Guerrero (Eds.), *Handbook of communication and emotion: Research, theory, applications and contexts* (pp. 273–505). San Diego, CA: Academic Press.

Feeney, J. A., Noller, P., & Roberts, N. (2000). Attachment and close relationships. In C. Hendrick & S. S. Hendrick (Eds.), *Close relationships: A sourcebook* (pp. 185–201). Thousand Oaks, CA: Sage.

Fehr, B. (1988). Prototype analysis of the concepts of love and commitment. *Journal of Personality and Social Psychology, 58,* 281–291.

Fehr, B. (1996). *Friendship processes.* Thousand Oaks, CA: Sage.

Fehr, B. (2008). Friendship formation. In S. Sprecher, A. Wenzel, & J. Harvey (Eds.), *The handbook of relationship initiation* (pp. 29–54). Thousand Oaks, CA: Sage.

Fehr, B., & Russell, J. A. (1991). The concept of love viewed from a prototype perspective. *Journal of Personality and Social Psychology, 60,* 425–438.

Feingold, A. (1988). Matching for attractiveness in romantic partners and same-sex friends: A meta-analysis and theoretical critique. *Psychological Bulletin, 104,* 226–235.

Feingold, A. (1991). Sex differences in the effects of similarity and physical attractiveness on opposite-sex attraction. *Basic and Applied Social Psychology, 12,* 357–367.

Feldman, S. S., & Cauffman, E. (1999). Sexual betrayal among late adolescents: Perspectives of the perpetrator and the aggrieved. *Journal of Youth and Adolescence, 228,* 235–258.

Feldman, R., Weller, A., Zagoory-Sharon, O., & Levine, A. (2007). Evidence for a neuroendocrinological foundation of human affiliation: Plasma oxytocin levels across pregnancy and the postpartum period predict mother-infant bonding. *Psychological Science, 18,* 965–970.

Felmlee, D. H. (1994). Who's on top? Power in romantic relationships. *Sex Roles, 31,* 275–295.

Felmlee, D. H. (1995). Fatal attractions: Affection and disaffection in intimate relationships. *Journal of Social and Personal Relationships, 12,* 295–312.

Felmlee, D. H. (1998). "Be careful what you wish for . . .": A quantitative and qualitative investigation of "fatal attraction." *Personal Relationship, 5,* 235–254.

Felmlee, D. H., Sprecher, S., & Bassin, E. (1990). The dissolution of intimate relationships: A hazard model. *Social Psychology Quarterly, 53,* 13–30.

Fennis, B. M. (2008). Branded into submission: Brand attributes and hierarchization behavior in same-sex and mixed-sex dyads. *Journal of Applied Social Psychology, 38,* 1993–2009.

Ferguson, C. A. (1964). Baby talk in six languages. *American Anthropologist, 66,* 103–114.

Ferrara, M. H., & Levine, T. R. (2009). Can't live with them or can't live without them? The effects of betrayal on relational outcomes in college dating relationships. *Communication Quarterly, 57,* 187–204.

Festinger, L., Schachter, S., & Back, K. (1950). *Social pressures in informal groups: A study of human factor in housing.* New York: Harper.

Filsinger, E. E., & Thomas, S. J. (1988). Behavioral antecedents of relational stability and adjustment: A five-year longitudinal study. *Journal of Marriage and the Family, 50,* 585–595.

Fincham, F. D. (2000). The kiss of the porcupines: From attributing responsibility to forgiving. *Personal Relationships, 7,* 1–23.

Fincham, F. D., Harold, G. T., & Gano-Phillips, S. (2000). The longitudinal association between attributions and marital satisfaction: Direction of effects and role of efficacy expectations. *Journal of Family Psychology, 14,* 267–285.

Finkenauer, C., Engels, R. C. M. E., & Meeus, W. (2002). Keeping secrets from parents: Advantages and disadvantages of secrecy in adolescence. *Journal of Youth and Adolescence, 31,* 123–136.

Finkenauer, C., Kubacka, K. E., Engels, R. C. M. E., & Kerkhof, P. (2009). Secrecy in close relationships: Investigating its intrapersonal and interpersonal effects. In T. D. Afifi & W. A. Afifi (Eds.), *Uncertainty, information management, and disclosure decisions: Theories and applications* (pp. 300–319). New York: Routledge.

Fischer, T. F. C., De Graaf, P. M., & Kalmijn, M. (2005). Friendly and antagonistic contact between former spouses after divorce: Patterns and determinants. *Journal of Family Issues, 26,* 1131–1163.

Fisher, B. A., & Adams, K. L. (1994). *Interpersonal communication: Pragmatics of human relationships* (2nd ed.). New York: McGraw-Hill.

Fisher, H., Aron, A., & Brown, L. L. (2005). Romantic love: An fMRI study of a neural mechanism for mate choice. *Journal of Comparative Neurology, 493,* 58–62.

Fisher, T. D. (2004). Family foundations of sexuality. In J. H. Harvey, A. Wenzel, & S. Sprecher (Eds.), *The handbook of sexuality in close relationships* (pp. 385–409). Mahwah, NJ: Lawrence Erlbaum.

Fitness, J., & Fletcher, G. J. O. (1993). Love, hate, anger, and jealousy in close relationships: A prototype and cognitive appraisal analysis. *Journal of Personality and Social Psychology, 65,* 942–958.

Fitzpatrick, M. A. (1988). *Between husbands and wives: Communication in marriage.* Newbury Park, CA: Sage.

Fitzpatrick, M. A., & Badzinski, D. M. (1994). All in the family: Interpersonal communication and kin relationships. In M. L. Knapp & G. R. Miller (Eds.), *Handbook of interpersonal communication* (2nd ed., pp. 726–771). Thousand Oaks, CA: Sage.

Fitzpatrick, M. A., & Winke, T. (1979). You always hurt the one you love: Strategies and tactics in interpersonal conflict. *Communication Quarterly, 27,* 3–11.

Fleischmann, A. A., Spitzberg, B. H., Andersen, P. A., & Roesch, S. (2005). Tickling the monster: Jealousy induction in relationships. *Journal of Social and Personal Relationships, 22,* 49–73.

Floyd, K. (1995). Gender and closeness among friends and siblings. *Journal of Psychology, 129,* 193–202.

Floyd, K. (2001). Human affection exchange: I. Reproductive probability as a predictor of men's affection with their sons. *Journal of Men's Studies, 10,* 39–50.

Floyd, K. (2002). Human affection exchange: V. Attributes of the highly affectionate. *Communication Quarterly, 50,* 135–152.

Floyd, K. (2006). *Communicating affection: Interpersonal behavior and social context.* Cambridge, UK: Cambridge University Press.

Floyd, K., Hess, J. A., Mizco, L. A., Halone, K. K., Mikkelson, A. C., & Tusing, K. J. (2005). Human affective exchange: VIII. Further evidence of the benefits of expressed affection. *Communication Quarterly, 53,* 285–303.

Floyd, K., Hesse, C., & Haynes, M. T. (2007). Human affection exchange: XV. Metabolic and cardiovascular correlates of trait expressed affection. *Communication Quarterly, 55,* 79–94.

Floyd, K., Mikkelson, A. C., Hesse, C., & Pauley, P. M. (2007). Affectionate writing reduces total cholesterol: Two randomized, controlled trials. *Human Communication Research, 33,* 119–142.

Floyd, K., Mikkelson, A. C., Tafoya, M. A., Farinelli, L., La Valley, A. G., Judd, J., Davis, K. L., Haynes, M. T., & Wilson, J. (2007). Human affection exchange: XIV. Relational affection predicts resting heart rate and free cortisol secretion during acute stress. *Behavioral Medicine, 32,* 151–156.

Floyd, K., & Morman, M. T. (1997). Affectionate communication in non-romantic relationships: Influences of communicator, relational, and contextual factors. *Western Journal of Communication, 61,* 279–298.

Floyd, K., & Morman, M. T. (1998). The measurement of affection communication. *Communication Quarterly, 46,* 144–162.

Floyd, K., & Morman, M. T. (2001). Human affection exchange: III. Discriminative parental solicitude in men's affectionate communication with their biological and nonbiological sons. *Communication Quarterly, 49,* 310–327.

Floyd, K., & Morman, M. T. (2005). Fathers' and son's reports of fathers' affectionate communication: Implications of a naïve theory of affection. *Journal of Social and Personal Relationships, 22,* 99–109.

Floyd, K., & Morr, M. C. (2003). Human affective exchange VII: Affectionate communication in the sibling/spouse/sibling-in-law triad. *Communication Quarterly, 51,* 247–261.

Floyd, K., & Parks, M. R. (1995). Manifesting closeness in the interactions of peers: A look at siblings and friends. *Communication Reports, 8,* 69–76.

Floyd, K., Ramirez, A., & Burgoon, J. K. (2008). Expectancy violations theory. In L. K.Guerrero, J. A. DeVito, & M. L. Hecht (Eds.), *The nonverbal communication reader: Classic and contemporary readings* (3rd ed., pp. 503–510). Prospect Heights, IL: Waveland Press.

Floyd, K., & Ray, G. B. (2003). Human affection exchange: IV. Vocalic predictors of perceived affection in initial interactions. *Western Journal of Communication, 67,* 56–73.

Floyd, K., & Riforgiate, S. (2008). Affectionate communication received from spouses predicts stress hormone levels in healthy adults. *Communication Monographs, 75,* 351–368.

Folkes, V. S. (1982). Communicating the causes of social rejection. *Journal of Experimental Social Psychology, 18,* 235–252.

Folkes, V. S., & Sears, D. O. (1977). Does everybody like a liker? *Journal of Experimental Social Psychology, 13,* 505–519.

Fowler, C., & Afifi, W. A. (in press). Applying the Theory of Motivated Information Management to adult children's discussions of caregiving with aging parents. *Journal of Social and Personal Relationships.*

Fox, G. L. (1981). The family's role in adolescent sexual behavior. In T. Ooms (Ed.), *Teenage pregnancy in a family context* (pp. 73–130). Philadelphia: Temple University Press.

Frank, E., Anderson, C., & Rubinstein, D. (1979). Marital role strain and sexual satisfaction. *Journal of Consulting and Clinical Psychology, 217,* 1096–1103.

Frank, M. G., & Gilovich, T. (1988). The dark side of self- and social perception: Black uniforms and aggression in professional sports. *Journal of Personality and Social Psychology, 54,* 74–85.

Frazier, P. A., & Cook, S. W. (1993). Correlates of distress following heterosexual relationship dissolution. *Journal of Social and Personal Relationships, 10,* 55–67.

Freedman, S. R., & Enright, R. D. (1996). Forgiveness as an intervention goal with incest survivors. *Journal of Consulting and Clinical Psychology, 64,* 983–992.

Friedmann, H. S., Riggio, R. E., & Casella, D. F. (1988). Non-verbal skill, personal charisma, and initial attraction. *Personality and Social Psychology Bulletin, 14,* 203–211.

Frinjs, T., Finkenauer, C., Vermulst, A. A., & Engels, R. C. M. E. (2005). Keeping secrets from parents: Longitudinal associations of secrecy in adolescence. *Journal of Youth and Adolescence, 34,* 137–148.

Gaelick, L., Brodenshausen, G. V., & Wyer, R. S., Jr. (1985). Emotional communication in close relationships. *Journal of Personality and Social Psychology, 49,* 1246–1265.

Gagnon, J. H. (1977). *Human Sexualities.* Glenview, IL: Scott Foresman.

Gahler, M., Hong, Y., & Bernhardt, E. (2009). Parental divorce and union disruption among young adults in Sweden. *Journal of Family Issues, 30,* 688–713.

Gaines, S. O. (1995). Relationships between members of cultural minorities. In J. T. Woods & S. Duck (Eds.), *Understudied relationships: Off the beaten track* (pp. 51–88). Thousand Oaks, CA: Sage.

Gaines, S. O., & Liu, J. H. (2000). Multicultural/multiracial relationships. In C. Hendrick & S. S. Hendrick (Eds.), *Close relationships: A sourcebook* (pp. 97–108). Thousand Oaks, CA: Sage.

Galinsky, A. D., Magee, J. C., Gruenfeld, D. H., & Whitson, J. A. (2008). Power reduces the press of the situation: Implications for creativity, conformity, and dissonance. *Journal of Personality and Social Psychology, 95,* 1450–1466.

Galligan, R. F., & Terry, D. J. (1993). Romantic ideals, fear of negative implications and practice of safe sex. *Journal of Applied Social Psychology, 23,* 1685–1711.

Gangestad, S. W., Garver-Apgar, C. E., Simpson, J. A., & Cousins, A. J. (2007). Changes in women's mate preferences across the ovulatory cycle. *Journal of Personality and Social Psychology, 92,* 151–163.

Gelles, R. J., & Cornell, C. P. (1990). *Intimate violence in families* (2nd ed.). Newbury Park, CA: Sage.

George, J. F., & Robb, A. (2008). Deception and computer-mediated communication in daily life. *Communication Reports, 21,* 92–103.

Gibran, K. (1923/1970). *The prophet.* New York: Knopf.

Gilbert, S. J. (1976). Self disclosure, intimacy, and communication in families. *The Family Coordinator, 25,* 221–230.

Giles, H., & Wiemann, J. M. (1987). Language, social comparison, and power. In C. Berger & S. H. Chafee (Eds.), *Handbook of communication science* (pp. 350–384). Newbury Park, CA: Sage.

Girard, M., & Mullet, E. (1997). Propensity to forgive in adolescents, young adults, older adults, and elderly people. *Journal of Adult Development, 4,* 209–220.

Givens, D. B. (1978). The nonverbal basis of attraction: Flirtation, courtship, and seduction. *Psychiatry, 41,* 346–359.

Givens, D. B. (1983). *Love signals.* New York: Crown.

Glomb, T. M., Richman, W. L., Hulin, C. L., Drasgow, F., Schneider, K. T., & Fitzgerald, L. F. (1997). Ambient sexual harassment: An integrated model of antecedents and consequences. *Organizational Behavioral and Human Decision Processes, 71,* 309–328.

Goffman, E. (1959). *The presentation of self in everyday life.* Garden City, NY: Anchor/Doubleday.

Goffman, E. (1967). *Interaction ritual: Essays on face-to-face behavior.* New York: Pantheon Books.

Goffman, E. (1971). *Relations in public.* New York: Basic Books.

Goldberg, A. E., & Perry-Jenkins, M. (2007). The division of labor and perceptions of parental roles: Lesbian couples across the transition to parenthood. *Human Communication Research, 24,* 297–318.

Golish, T. D., (2000). Changes in closeness between adult children and their parents: A turning point analysis. *Communication Reports, 13,* 79–97.

Golish, T. D. & Caughlin, J. (2002). "I'd rather not talk about it": Adolescents' and young adults' use of topic avoidance in stepfamilies. *Journal of Applied Communication Research, 30,* 78–106.

Goodboy, A. K., & Members of Investigating Communication. (2010). Relational quality indicators and love styles as predictors of negative relational maintenance behaviors in romantic relationships. *Communication Reports, 23.*

Gottman, J. M. (1979). *Marital interaction: Experimental investigations.* New York: Academic Press.

Gottman, J. M. (1993). A theory of marital dissolution and stability. *Journal of Family Psychology, 7,* 57–75.

Gottman, J. M. (1994). *What predicts divorce? The relationship between marital processes and marital outcomes.* Hillsdale, NJ: Lawrence Erlbaum.

Gottman, J. M., & Carrere, S. (1994). Why can't men and women get along? Developmental roots and marital inequities. In D. J. Canary & L. Safford (Eds.), *Communication and relational maintenance* (pp. 203–222). San Diego, CA: Academic Press.

Gottman, J. M., Gottman, J. S., & DeClaire, J. (2006). *10 lessons to transform your marriage.* New York: Three Rivers Press.

Gottman, J. M., & Levenson, R. W. (1988). The social psychophysical of marriage. In P. Noller & M. A. Fitzpatrick (Eds.), *Perspectives on marital interaction* (pp. 182–200). Philadelphia: Multilingual Matters.

Gottman, J. M., & Levenson, R. W. (1992). Marital processes predictive of later dissolution: Behavior, physiology, and health. *Journal of Personality and Social Psychology, 63,* 221–233.

Gottman, J. M., & Levenson, R. W. (2000). The timing of divorce: Predicting when a couple will divorce over a 14-year period. *Journal of Marriage and the Family, 62,* 737–745.

Gottman, J. M., & Levenson, R. W. (2002). A two-factor model for predicting when a couple will divorce: Exploratory analyses using 14-year longitudinal data. *Family Process, 41,* 83–96.

Gouldner, A. W. (1960). The norm of reciprocity: A preliminary statement. *Sociological Review, 25,* 161–178.

Gracyalny, M. L., Jackson, D. C., & Guerrero, L. K. (2008, November). *Associations among victim communication, errant partner communication, and forgiveness following hurtful events in dating relationships.* Paper presented at the annual conference of the National Communication Association, San Diego, CA.

Graham, J. M. (2008). Self-expansion and flow in couples' momentary experiences: An experience sampling study. *Journal of Personality and Social Psychology, 95,* 679–694.

Graham-Kevan, N., & Archer, J. (2003). Patriarchal terrorism and common couple violence: A test of Johnson's predictions in four British samples. *Journal of Interpersonal Violence, 18,* 1247–1270.

Gray, J. (1992). *Men are from Mars, women are from Venus: A practical guide to improving communication and getting what you want in your relationships.* New York: HarperCollins.

Gray-Little, B., & Burks, N. (1983). Power and satisfaction in marriage: A review and critique. *Psychological Bulletin, 93,* 513–538.

Greenstein, T. N. (1990). Marital disruption and the employment of married women. *Journal of Marriage and the Family, 52,* 657–676.

Greitemeyer, T. (2005). Receptivity to sexual offers as a function of sex, socioeconomic status, and intimacy of the offer. *Personal Relationships, 12,* 373–386.

Grice, H. P. (1989). *Studies in the way of words.* Cambridge, MA: Harvard University Press.

Griffit, W. (1970). Environmental effects on interpersonal affective behaviors: Ambient effective temperature and attraction. *Journal of Personality and Social Psychology, 15,* 240–244.

Gross, M. A., & Guerrero, L. K. (2000). Managing conflict appropriately and effectively: An application of the competence model to Rahim's organizational conflict styles. *International Journal of Conflict Management, 11,* 200–226.

Gross, M. A., Guerrero, L. K., & Alberts, J. K. (2004). Perceptions of conflict strategies and communication competence in task-oriented dyads. *Journal of Applied Communication Research, 32,* 249–270.

Grote, N. K., & Frieze, I. H. (1994). The measurement of friendship-based love in intimate relationships. *Personal Relationships, 1,* 275–300.

Grotevant, H. D., & Cooper, C. R. (1985). Patterns of interaction in family relationships and the development of identity exploration in adolescence. *Child Development, 56,* 415–428.

Grotevant, H. D., & Cooper, C. R. (1985). Patterns of interaction in family relationships and the development of identity and role-taking skill in adolescence. *Child Development, 56,* 415–428.

Grusec, J. E., & Kuczynski, L. (1980). Direction of effects in socialization: A comparison of the parent's versus the child's behavior as determinants of disciplinary techniques. *Developmental Psychology, 16,* 1–9.

Guastella, A. J., Mitchell, P. B., & Dadds, M. R. (2008). Oxytocin increases gaze to the eye region of human faces. *Biological Psychiatry, 63,* 3–5.

Gudykunst, W. B. (1988). Culture and the development of interpersonal relationships. In J. A. Anderson (Ed.), *Communication yearbook 12* (pp. 315–354). Newbury Park, CA: Sage.

Gudykunst, W. B. (1989). Uncertainty and anxiety. In Y. Y. Kim & W. B. Gudykunst (Eds.), *Theories in intercultural communication* (pp. 123–156). Newbury Park, CA: Sage.

Gudykunst, W. B., & Nishida, T. (1984). Individual and cultural influences on uncertainty reduction. *Communication Monographs, 51,* 23–36.

Guerrero, L. K. (1996). Attachment-style difference in intimacy and involvement: A test of the four-category model. *Communication Monographs, 63,* 269–292.

Guerrero, L. K. (1997). Nonverbal involvement across interactions with same-sex friends, opposite-sex friends, and romantic partners: Consistency or change? *Journal of Social and Personal Relationship, 14,* 31–59.

Guerrero, L. K. (1998). Attachment-style differences in the experience and expression of romantic jealousy. *Personal Relationships, 5,* 273–291.

Guerrero, L. K. (2000). Intimacy. In D. Levinson, J. Ponzetti, & P. Jorgensen (Eds.), *The encyclopedia of human emotions* (pp. 403–409). New York: Macmillan Reference.

Guerrero, L. K. (2004). Observer ratings of nonverbal involvement and immediacy. In V. Manusov (Ed.), *The sourcebook of nonverbal measures: Going beyond words* (pp. 221–235). Mahwah, NJ: Lawrence Erlbaum.

Guerrero, L. K. (2008). Attachment theory: A communication perspective. In D. O. Braithwaite & L. Baxter (Eds.), *Engaging theory in interpersonal communication* (pp. 295–307). Thousand Oaks, CA: Sage.

Guerrero, L. K., & Afifi, W. A. (1995a). Some things are better left unsaid: Topic avoidance in family relationships. *Communication Quarterly, 43,* 276–296.

Guerrero, L. K., & Afifi, W. A. (1995b). What parents don't know: Topic avoidance in parent-child relationships. In T. J. Socha & G. H. Stamp (Eds.), *Parents, children, and communication: Frontiers of theory and research* (pp. 219–246). Mahwah, NJ: Lawrence Erlbaum.

Guerrero, L. K., & Afifi, W. A. (1998). Communicative responses to jealousy as a function of self-esteem and relationship maintenance goals: A test of Bryson's dual motivation model. *Communication Reports, 11,* 111–122.

Guerrero, L. K., & Afifi, W. A. (1999). Toward a goal-oriented approach for understanding communicative responses to jealousy. *Western Journal of Communication, 63,* 216–248.

Guerrero, L. K., & Andersen, P. A. (1991). The waxing and waning of relational intimacy: Touch as a function of relational stage, gender, and touch avoidance. *Journal of Social and Personal Relationships, 8,* 147–165.

Guerrero, L. K., & Andersen, P. A. (1994). Patterns of matching and initiation: Touch behavior and avoidance across romantic relationship stages. *Journal of Nonverbal Behavior, 18,* 137–153.

Guerrero, L. K., & Andersen, P. A. (1998a). The dark side of jealousy and envy: Desire, delusion, desperation, and destructive communication. In B. H. Spitzberg & W. R. Cupach (Eds.), *The dark side of relationships* (pp. 33–70). Mahwah, NJ: Lawrence Erlbaum.

Guerrero, L. K., & Andersen, P. A. (1998b). The experience and expression of romantic jealousy. In P. A. Andersen & L. K. Guerrero (Eds.), *The handbook of communication and emotion: Research, theory, applications, and contexts* (pp. 155–188). San Diego, CA: Academic Press.

Guerrero, L. K., & Andersen, P. A. (2000). Emotion in close relationships. In C. Hendrick & S. S. Hendrick (Eds.), *Close relationships: A sourcebook* (pp. 171–183). Thousand Oaks, CA: Sage.

Guerrero, L. K., Andersen, P. A., Jorgensen, P. F., Spitzberg, B. H., & Eloy, S. V. (1995). Coping with the green-eyed monster: Conceptualizing and measuring communicative responses to jealousy. *Western Journal of Communication, 59,* 270–304.

Guerrero, L. K., & Bachman, G. F. (2006). Associations among relational maintenance behaviors, attachment-style categories, and attachment dimensions. *Communication Studies, 57,* 341–361.

Guerrero, L. K., & Bachman, G. F. (2008). Communication following relational transgressions in dating relationships: An investment model explanation. *Southern Communication Journal, 73,* 4–23.

Guerrero, L. K., & Bachman, G. F. (2010). Forgiveness and forgiving communication: An expectancy-investment model. *Journal of Social and Personal Relationships, 27,* 801–823.

Guerrero, L. K., & Burgoon, J. K. (1996). Attachment styles and reactions to nonverbal involvement change in romantic dyads: Patterns of reciprocity and compensation. *Human Communication Research, 22,* 335–370.

Guerrero, L. K., & Chavez, A. M. (2005). Relational maintenance in cross-sex friendships characterized by different types of romantic intent: An exploratory study. *Western Journal of Communication, 69,* 341–360.

Guerrero, L. K., & Eloy, S. V. (1992). Jealousy and relational satisfaction across marital types. *Communication Reports, 5,* 23–31.

Guerrero, L. K., Eloy, S. V., & Wabnik, A. I. (1993). Linking maintenance strategies to relationship development and disengagement: A reconceptualization. *Journal of Social and Personal Relationships, 10,* 273–283.

Guerrero, L. K., Farinelli, L., & McEwan, B. (2009). Attachment and relational satisfaction: The mediating effect of emotional communication. *Communication Monographs, 76,* 487–514.

Guerrero, L. K., & Floyd, K. (2006). *Nonverbal communication in close relationships.* Mahwah, NJ: Lawrence Erlbaum.

Guerrero, L. K., Hannawa, A. F., & Gallagher, B. B. (2008, November). *The communicative responses to jealousy scale: Revision and empirical validation.* Paper presented at the annual conference of the National Communication Association, San Diego, CA.

Guerrero, L. K., & Jones, S. M. (2003). Differences in one's own and one's partner's perceptions of social skills as a function of attachment style. *Communication Quarterly, 51,* 277–295.

Guerrero, L. K., & Jones, S. M. (2005). Differences in conversational skills as a function of attachment style: A follow-up study. *Communication Quarterly, 53,* 305–321.

Guerrero, L. K., & La Valley, A. G. (2006). Conflict, emotion, and communication. In J. G. Oetzel & S. Ting-Toomey (Eds.), *The SAGE handbook of conflict communication* (pp. 69–96). Thousand Oaks, CA: Sage.

Guerrero, L. K., La Valley, A. G., & Farinelli, L. (2008). The experience and expression of anger, guilt, and sadness in marriage: An equity theory explanation. *Journal of Social and Personal Relationships, 25,* 699–724.

Guerrero, L. K., & Langan, E. J. (1999, February). *Dominance displays in conversations about relational problems: Differences due to attachment style and sex.* Paper presented at the annual meeting of the Western States Communication Association, Vancouver, BC.

Guerrero, L. K., & Mongeau, P. A. (2008). On becoming "more than friends": The transition from friendship to romantic relationship. In S. Sprecher, J. A. Harvey, & A. Wenzel (Eds.), *The handbook of relationship initiation* (pp. 175–194). Thousand Oaks, CA: Sage.

Guerrero, L. K., & Reiter, R. L. (1998). Expressing emotion: Sex differences in social skills and communicative responses to anger, sadness, and jealousy. In D. J. Canary & K. Dindia (Eds.), *Sex differences and similarities in communication* (pp. 321–350). Mahwah, NJ: Lawrence Erlbaum.

Guerrero, L. K., Spitzberg, B. H., & Yoshimura, S. M. (2004). Sexual and emotional jealousy. In J. Harvey, A. Wenzel, & S. Sprecher (Eds.), *The handbook of sexuality in close relationships* (pp. 311–345). Mahwah, NJ: Lawrence Erlbaum.

Guerrero, L. K., Trost, M. L., & Yoshimura, S. M. (2005). Emotion and communication in the context of romantic jealousy. *Personal Relationships, 12,* 233–252.

Gupta, G. R. (1976). Love, arranged marriage, and the Indian social structure. *Journal of Comparative Family Studies, 7,* 75–85.

Gupta, U., & Singh, P. (1982). An exploratory study of love and liking and type of marriages. *Indian Journal of Applied Psychology, 19,* 92–97.

Gutek, B. A., Morasch, B., & Cohen, A. G. (1983). Interpreting social-sexual behavior in work setting. *Journal of Vocational Behavior, 32,* 30–48.

Haas, A., & Sherman, M. A. (1982). Reported topics of conversation among same sex adults. *Communication Quarterly, 30,* 332–333.

Haas, S. M., & Stafford, L. (1998). An initial examination of maintenance behaviors in gay and lesbian relationships. *Journal of Social and Personal Relationships, 15,* 846–855.

Haas, S. M., & Stafford, L. (2005). Maintenance behaviors in same-sex and marital relationships: A matched sample comparison. *Journal of Family Communication, 5,* 43–60.

Halatsis, P., & Christakis, N. (2009). The challenge of sexual attraction within heterosexuals' cross-sex friendship. *Journal of Social and Personal Relationships, 26,* 919–937.

Hall, E. T. (1968). Proxemics. *Current Anthropology, 9,* 83–109.

Hall, J. A., Coats, E. J., & LeBeau, J. A. (2005). Nonverbal behavior and vertical dimension of social relations: A meta-analysis. *Psychological Bulletin, 131,* 898–924.

Halloran, E. C. (1998). The role of marital power in depression and marital distress. *American Journal of Family Therapy, 26,* 3–14.

Hamadeh, G. N., & Adib, S.M. (1998). Cancer truth disclosure by Lebanese doctors. *Social Science & Medicine, 47,* 1289–1294.

Hamel, J. (2009). Toward a gender-inclusive conception of intimate partner violence research and theory: Part 2—New directions. *International Journal of Men's Health, 8,* 41–59.

Hamida, S. B., Mineka, S., & Bailey, J. M. (1998). Sex differences in perceived controllability of mate value: An evolutionary perspective. *Journal of Personality and Social Psychology, 75,* 953–966.

Hammer, J. C., Fisher, J. D., Fitzgerald, P., & Fisher, W. A. (1996). When two heads aren't better than one: AIDS risk behavior in college-age couples. *Journal of Applied Social Psychology, 26,* 375–397.

Hamilton, W. D. (1964). The genetic evolution of social behavior. *Journal of Theoretical Biology, 7,* 17–18.

Hansen, J. E., & Schuldt, W. J. (1984). Marital self-disclosure and marital satisfaction. *Journal of Marriage and the Family, 46,* 923–926.

Hargrow, A. M. (1997). Speaking our realities: From speculation to truth concerning African American women's experiences of sexual harassment. *Dissertation Abstracts International, 57* (7-B), 4707.

Harry, J. (1984). *Gay couples.* New York: Praeger.

Harry, J., & De Vall, W. B. (1978). *The social organization of gay males.* New York: Praeger.

Hart, C. H., DeWolf, D. M., Wozniak, P., & Burts, D. C. (1992). Maternal and paternal disciplinary styles: Relations with preschoolers' playground behavioral orientations and peer status. *Child Development, 63,* 879–892.

Harter, S., Waters, P. L., Pettitt, L. M., Whitesell, N., Kofkin, J., & Jordan, J. (1997). Autonomy and connectedness as dimensions of relationship styles in men and women. *Journal of Social and Personal Relationships, 14,* 148–164.

Hartill, L. (2001). A brief history of interracial marriage. *Christian Science Monitor, 93,* 15.

Harvey, J. H. (1987). Attributions in close relationships: Recent theoretical developments. *Journal of Social and Clinical Psychology, 5,* 420–434.

Haselton, M. G., & Gangestad, S. W. (2006). Conditional expression of women's desires and men's mate guarding across the ovulatory cycle. *Hormones and Behavior, 49,* 509–518.

Haselton, M. G., Mortezaie, M., Pillsworth, E. G., Bleske-Recheck, A. E., & Frederick, D. A. (2007). Ovulation and human female ornamentation: Near ovulation, women dress to impress. *Hormones and Behavior, 51,* 41–45.

Hatfield, E. (1984). The dangers of intimacy. In V. J. Derlega (Ed.), *Communication, intimacy, and close relationships* (pp. 207–220). New York: Academic Press.

Hatfield, E. (1988). Passionate and companionate love. In R. J. Sternberg & M. L. Barnes (Eds.), *The psychology of love* (pp. 191–217). New Haven, CT: Yale University Press.

Hatfield, E., Greenberger, D., Traupmann, J., & Lambert, P. (1982). Equity and sexual satisfaction in recently married couples. *Journal of Sex Research, 17,* 18–32.

Hatfield, E., & Rapson, R. L. (1987). Passionate love: New directions in research. In W. H. Jones & D. Perlman (Eds.), *Advances in personal relationships* (Vol. 1, pp. 109–139). Greenwich, CT: JAI Press.

Hatfield, E., & Rapson, R. L. (2000). *Rosie.* Pittsburgh, PA: Sterling House.

Hatfield, E., Rapson, R. L., & Aumer-Ryan, K. (2008). Social justice in love relationships: Recent developments. *Social Justice Research, 21,* 413–431.

Hatfield, E., & Sprecher, S. (1986a). Measuring passionate love in intimate relationships. *Journal of Adolescence, 9,* 383–410.

Hatfield, E., & Sprecher, S. (1986b). *Mirror, mirror . . . The importance of looks in everyday life.* Albany, NY: SUNY Press.

Hatfield, E., Greenberger, E., Traupmann, J., & Lambert, P. (1982). Equity and sexual satisfaction in recently married couples. *Journal of Sex Research, 18,* 18–32.

Hays, R. B. (1985). A longitudinal study of friendship development. *Journal of Personality and Social Psychology, 48,* 909–924.

Hazan, C., & Shaver, P. (1987). Conceptualizing romantic love as an attachment process. *Journal of Personality and Social Psychology, 52,* 511–524.

Hazan, C., & Zeifman, D. (1994). Sex and the psychological tether. In K. Bartholomew & D. Perlman (Eds.), *Advances in personal relationships* (Vol. 5, pp. 151–177). London: Kingsley.

Heavey, C. L., Christensen, A., & Malamuth, N. M. (1995). The longitudinal impact of demand and withdrawal during marital conflict. *Journal of Consulting and Clinical Psychology, 63,* 797–801.

Heavey, C. L., Layne, C., & Christensen, A. (1993). Gender and conflict structure in martial interaction: A replication and extension. *Journal of Consulting and Clinical Psychology, 61,* 16–27.

Hebert, S., & Popadiuk, N. (2008). University students' experiences of nonmarital breakups: A grounded theory. *Journal of College Student Development, 29,* 1–14.

Hecht, M. L. (1993). 2002—A research odyssey: Toward the development of a communication theory of identity. *Communication Monographs, 60,* 76–82.

Hecht, M. L., Collier, M. J., & Ribeau, S. (1993). *African American communication: Ethnic identity and cultural interpretations.* Newbury Park, CA: Sage.

Hecht, M. L., Marston, P. J., & Larkey, L. K. (1994). Love ways and relationship quality in heterosexual relationships. *Journal of Social and Personal Relationships, 11,* 25–43.

Hecht, M. L., Warren, J., Jung, J., & Krieger, J. (2004). Communication theory of identity. In W. B. Gudykunst (Ed.), *Theorizing about intercultural communication* (pp. 257–278). Thousand Oaks, CA: Sage.

Heider, F. (1958). *The psychology and interpersonal relations.* New York: Wiley.

Helgeson, V. S., Novak, S. A., Lepore, S. J., & Eton, D. T. (2004). Spouse social control efforts: Relations to heath behavior and well-being among men with prostate cancer. *Journal of Social and Personal Relationships, 21,* 53–68.

Helgeson, V. S., Shaver, P., & Dyer, M. (1987). Prototypes of intimacy and distance in same-sex and opposite-sex relationships. *Journal of Social and Personal Relationships, 4,* 195–233.

Henderson, A. W., Lehavot, K., & Simoni, J. M. (2009). Ecological models of sexual satisfaction among lesbian/bisexual and heterosexual women. *Archives of Sexual Behavior, 38,* 50–65.

Henderson, S., & Gilding, M. (2004). "I've never clicked this much with anyone in my life": Trust and hyperpersonal communication in online friendships. *New Media & Society, 6,* 487–506.

Hendrick, C., & Hendrick, S. S. (1986). A theory and method of love. *Journal of Personality and Social Psychology, 50,* 392–402.

Hendrick, C., & Hendrick, S. S. (1990). A relationship specific version of the love attitude scale. *Journal of Social Behavior and Personality, 5,* 239–254.

Hendrick, S. S., & Hendrick, C. (1987). Love and sex attitudes: A close relationship. In W. H. Jones & D. Perlman (Eds.), *Advances in personal relationships* (Vol. 1, pp. 141–169). Greenwich, CT: JAI Press.

Hendrick, S. S., & Hendrick, C. (1992). *Liking, loving, and relating* (2nd ed.). Pacific Grove, CA: Brooks/Cole.

Hendrick, S. S., & Hendrick, C. (2002). Linking romantic love with sex: Development of the perceptions of love and sex scale. *Journal of Social and Personal Relationships, 19,* 361–378.

Hendrick, S. S., Hendrick, C., & Adler, N. L. (1988). Romantic relationships: Love, satisfaction, and staying together. *Journal of Personality and Social Psychology, 54,* 980–988.

Hendy, H. M., Eggen, D., Gustitus, C., McLeod, K., & Ng, P. (2003). Decision to leave scale. Perceived reasons to stay in or leave violent relationships. *Psychology of Women Quarterly, 27,* 162–173.

Henley, N. M. (1977). *Body politics: Power, sex, and nonverbal communication.* Englewood Cliffs, NJ: Prentice Hall.

Henningsen, D. D., Serewicz, M. C. M., & Carpenter, C. (2009). Predictors of comforting communication in romantic relationships. *International Journal of Communication, 3,* 351–368.

Hensley, W. E. (1994). Height as a basis for interpersonal attraction. *Adolescence, 29,* 469–474.

Herzog, A. (1973). *The B.S. factor: The theory and techniques of faking it in America.* Baltimore: Penguin Books.

Heslin, R., & Boss, D. (1980). Nonverbal intimacy in arrival and departure at an airport. *Personality and Social Psychology Bulletin, 6,* 248–252.

Hess, E. H. (1965). Attitude and pupil size. *Scientific American, 212,* 46–54.

Hess, E. H., & Goodwin, E. (1974). The present state of pupilometers. In M. P. Janisse (Ed.), *Pupillary dynamics and behavior* (pp. 209–246). New York: Plenum Press.

Hesson-McInnis, M. S., & Fitzgerald, L. F. (1997). Sexual harassment: A preliminary test of an integrative model. *Journal of Applied Social Psychology, 27,* 877–901.

Hewes, D. E., Graham, M. L., Doelger, J., & Pavitt, C. (1985). "Second-guessing": Message interpretation in social networks. *Human Communication Research, 11,* 299–334.

Hewitt, J., & Stokes, R. (1975). Disclaimers. *American Sociological Review, 40,* 1–11.

Higgins, R. L., & Berglas, S. (1990). The maintenance and treatment of self-handicapping: From risk-taking to face-saving—and back. In R. L. Higgins (Ed.), *Self-handicapping: The paradox that isn't* (pp. 187–238). New York: Plenum Press.

Hill, C. T., Rubin, Z., & Peplau, L. A. (1976). Breakups before marriage: The end of 103 affairs. *Journal of Social Issues, 32,* 147–168.

Hill, J. P., & Holmbeck, G. (1986). Attachment and autonomy during adolescence. In G. Whitehurst (Ed.), *Annals of child development* (Vol. 3, pp. 145–189). Greenwich, CT: JAI Press.

Himsel, A., & Goldberg, W. A. (2003). Social comparisons and the division of housework among dual-earner couples: Implications for satisfaction and role strain. *Journal of Family Issues, 24,* 843–866.

Hinde, R. A. (1984). Why do the sexes behave differently in close relationships? *Journal of Social and Personal Relationship, 1,* 471–501.

Hogan, T. P., & Brashers, D. E. (2009). The theory of communication and uncertainty management: Implications for the wider realm of information behavior. In T. D. Afifi & W. A. Afifi (Eds.), *Uncertainty, information management, and disclosure decisions: Theories and applications* (pp. 45–66). New York: Routledge.

Hochschild, A. (1997). *The time bind: When work becomes home and home becomes work.* New York: Metropolitan Books.

Hochschild, A., & Machung, A. (1989). *The second shift: Working parents and the revolution at home.* New York: Viking/Penguin.

Hocker, J. L., & Wilmot, W. W. (1998). *Interpersonal conflict* (5th ed.). Dubuque, IA: Brown & Benchmark.

Hocking, J. E., & Leathers, D. G. (1980). Nonverbal indicators of deception: A new theoretical perspective. *Communication Monographs, 47,* 119–131.

Hoffman, M. L. (1970). Power assertion by parents and its impact on the child. *Child Development, 31,* 129–143.

Hoffman, M. L. (1980). Moral development in adolescence. In J. Adelson (Ed.), *Handbook of adolescent psychology* (pp. 295–343). New York: Wiley.

Hogg, M. A., & Abrams, D. (1988). *Social identifications: A social psychology of intergroup relations and group processes.* London: Routledge.

Holmberg, D., & Blair, K. L. (2009). Sexual desire, communication, satisfaction, and preferences of men and women in same-sex versus mixed-sex relationships. *Journal of Sex Research, 46,* 57–66.

Holtgraves, T. (1988). Gambling as self-presentation. *Journal of Gambling Behavior, 4,* 78–91.

Holtgraves, T., & Yang, J. (1990). Politeness as a universal: Cross-cultural perceptions of request strategies and inferences based on their use. *Journal of Personality and Social Psychology, 59,* 719–729.

Holtgraves, T., & Yang, J. (1992). Interpersonal underpinnings of request strategies: General principles and differences due to culture and gender. *Journal of Personality and Social Psychology, 62,* 246–256.

Holtzworth-Munroe, A., & Hutchinson, G. (1993). Attributing negative intent to wife behavior: The attributions of martially violent versus nonviolent men. *Journal of Abnormal Psychology, 102,* 206–211.

Holtzworth-Munroe, A., & Jacobson, N. S. (1985). Causal attributions of married couples: When do they search for causes? What do they conclude when they do? *Journal of Personality and Social Psychology, 48,* 1398–1412.

Holtzworth-Munroe, A., & Smutzler, N. (1996). Comparing the emotional reactions and behavioral intentions of violent and nonviolent husbands to aggressive, distressed, and other wife behaviors. *Violence Victims, 11,* 319–339.

Holtzworth-Munroe, A., Smutzler, N., & Stuart, G. L. (1998). Demand and withdraw communication among couples experiencing husband violence. *Journal of Consulting and Clinical Psychology, 66,* 731–743.

Homans, G. C. (1961). *Social behavior.* New York: Harcourt, Brace & World.

Homans, G. C. (1974). *Social behavior: Its elementary forms* (2nd ed.). New York: Harcourt, Brace & World.

Honeycutt, J. M., & Cantrill, J. G. (2001). *Cognition, communication, and romantic relationships.* Mahwah, NJ: Lawrence Erlbaum.

Honeycutt, J. M., Cantrill, J. G., & Allen, T. (1992). Memory structure of relational decay: A cognitive test of the sequencing of de-escalating actions and stages. *Human Communication Research, 18,* 528–562.

Hoobler, G. D. (1999, June). *Ten years of personal relationships research: Where have we been and where are we going?* Paper presented at the annual meeting of the International Network on Personal Relationships, Louisville, KY.

Hopper, M. L., Knapp, M. L., & Scott, L. (1981). Couples' personal idioms: Exploring intimate talk. *Journal of Communication, 31,* 23–33.

Hosman, L. A., & Tardy, C. H. (1980). Self-disclosure and reciprocity in short- and long-term relationships: An experimental study of evaluational and attributional consequences. *Communication Quarterly, 28,* 20–30.

Howard, J. A., Blumstein, P., & Schwartz, P. (1986). Sex, power, and influence tactics in intimate relationships. *Journal of Personality and Social Psychology, 51,* 102–109.

Howard, J. R., O'Neill, S., & Travers, C. (2006) Factors affecting sexuality in older Australian women: Sexual interest, sexual arousal, relationships and sexual distress in older Australian women, *Climacteric, 9,* 355–367.

Hoyle, R. H., Insko, C. A., & Moniz, A. J. (1992). Self-esteem, evaluative feedback, and preacquaintance attraction: Indirect reactions to success and failure. *Motivation and Emotion, 16,* 79–101.

Hoyt, M. F. (1978). Secrets in psychotherapy: Theoretical and practical considerations. *International Review of Psycho-Analysis, 5,* 231–241.

Hughes, M., Morrison, K., & Asada, J. K. (2005). What's love got to do with it? Exploring the impact of maintenance rules, love attitudes, and network support on friends with benefits relationships. *Western Journal of Communication, 69,* 49–66.

Hunt, M. (1974). *Sexual behavior in the 1970s.* New York: Playboy Press.

Huston, T. L. (1983). Power. In H. H. Kelley, E. Berscheid, A. Christensen, J. H. Harvey, T. L. Huston, G. Levinger, et al. (Eds.), *Close relationships* (pp. 169–219). New York: Freeman.

Huston, T. L. (2009). What's love got to do with it? Why some marriages succeed and others fail. *Personal Relationships, 16,* 301–327.

Huston, T. L., & Levinger, G. (1978). Interpersonal attraction and relationships. *Annual Review of Psychology, 29,* 115–156.

Huston, M., & Schwartz, P. (1995). The relationships of gay men and lesbians. In J. T. Wood & S. Duck (Eds.), *Understudied relationships: Off the beaten track* (pp. 89–121). Thousand Oaks, CA: Sage.

Huston, T. L., Surra, C. A., Fitzgerald, N. M., & Cate, R. M. (1981). From courtship to marriage: Mate selection as an interpersonal process. In S. Duck & R. Gilmour (Eds.), *Personal relationships: Developing personal relationships* (Vol. 2, pp. 53–88). London: Academic Press.

Ickes, W. I., Dugosh, J. W., Simpson, J. A., & Wilson, C. L. (2003). Suspicious minds: The motive to acquire relationship-threatening information. *Personal Relationships, 10,* 131–148.

Imber-Black, E. (1993). Secrets in families and family therapy: An overview. In E. Imber-Black (Ed.), *Secrets in families and family therapy* (pp. 3–28). New York: Norton.

Impett, A., Peplau, L. A., & Gable, S. L. (2005). Approach and avoidance sexual motives: Implications for personal and interpersonal well-being. *Personal Relationships, 12,* 465–482.

Infante, D. A. (1987). Aggressiveness. In J. C. McCroskey & J. A. Daly (Eds.), *Personality and interpersonal communication* (pp. 157–192). Newbury Park, CA: Sage.

Infante, D. A., Chandler, T. A., & Rudd, J. E. (1989). Test of an argumentative skill deficiency model of interpersonal violence. *Communication Monographs, 56,* 163–177.

Infante, D. A., & Rancer, A. S. (1982). A conceptualization and measure of argumentativeness. *Journal of Personality Assessment, 46,* 72–80.

Infante, D. A., Sabourin, T. C., Rudd, J. E., & Shannon, E. A. (1990). Verbal aggression in violent and nonviolent marital disputes. *Communication Quarterly, 38,* 361–371.

Inglis, I. R. (2000). The central role of uncertainty reduction in determining behaviour. *Behaviour, 137,* 1567–1599.

Isnard, C. A., & Zeeman, E. C. (1977). Some models from catastrophe theory in the social sciences. In E. C. Zeeman (Ed.), *Catastrophe theory: Selected papers 1972–1977.* Reading, MA: Addison-Wesley.

Jablonsky, N. G., & Chaplin, G. (2000). The evolution of human skin coloration. *Journal of Human Evolution, 39,* 57–106.

Jackson, L. A., & Ervin, K. S. (1992). Height stereotypes of women and men: The liabilities of shortness for both sexes. *Journal of Social Psychology, 132,* 433–445.

Jackson, R. L., II. (1999). *The negotiation of cultural identity: Perceptions of European Americans and African Americans.* Westport, CT: Praeger.

Jacob, T. (1974). Patterns of family conflict and dominance as a function of child age and social class. *Developmental Psychology, 10,* 1–12.

Jang, S. A. (2008). The effects of attachment style and efficacy of communication on avoidance following a relational partner's deception. *Communication Research Reports, 25,* 300–311.

Jankowiak, W. R., & Fischer, E. F. (1992). A cross-cultural perspective on romantic love. *Ethnology, 31,* 149–155.

Janofsky, A. I. (1971). Affective self-disclosure in telephone versus face-to-face interviews. *Journal of Humanistic Psychology, 11,* 93–103.

Jellison, J. M., & Oliver, D. F. (1983). Attitudinal similarity and attraction: An impression management approach. *Personality and Social Psychology Bulletin, 9,* 111–115.

Jensen-Campbell, L. A., Graziano, W. G., & West, S. G. (1995). Dominance, prosocial orientation, and female preferences: Do nice guys really finish last? *Journal of Personality and Social Psychology, 68,* 427–440.

Johnson, A. J. (2001). Examining the maintenance of friendships: Are there differences between geographically close and long-distance friends? *Communication Quarterly, 49,* 424–435.

Johnson, A. J., Wittenberg, E., Haigh, M., Wigley, S., Becker, J., Brown, K., et al. (2004). The process of relationship development and deterioration: Turning points in friendships that have terminated. *Communication Quarterly, 52,* 54–68.

Johnson, A. J., Wittenberg, E., Villigran, M., Mazur, M., & Villigran, P. (2003). Relational progression as a dialectic: Examining turning points in communication among friends. *Communication Monographs, 70,* 230–249.

Johnson, D. J., & Rusbult, C. E. (1989). Resisting temptation: Devaluation of alternative partners as a means of maintaining commitment in close relationships. *Journal of Personality and Social Psychology, 57,* 967–980.

Johnson, M. L., Afifi, W. A., & Duck, S. (1994). *Social attraction on first dates: Is communication underrated?* Unpublished manuscript.

Johnson, M. P. (1982). Social and cognitive features of the dissolution of commitment to relationships. In S. Duck (Ed.), *Dissolving personal relationships* (pp. 51–73). New York: Academic Press.

Johnson, M. P. (1995). Patriarchal terrorism and common couple violence: Two forms of violence against women. *Journal of Marriage and the Family, 57,* 283–294.

Johnson, M. P., & Ferraro, K. J. (2000). Research on domestic violence in the 1990s: Making distinctions. *Journal of Marriage and the Family, 62,* 948–963.

Johnson, M. P., & Leone, J. M. (2005). The differential effects of intimate terrorism and situational couple violence: Findings from the National Violence Against Women Survey. *Journal of Family Issues, 26,* 322–349.

Joinson, A. N., (2008). "Looking at," "looking up," or "keeping up with" people? Motives and uses of Facebook. *CHI Proceeding,* April 5–10, 2008, Florence, Italy.

Jones, E., & Gallois, C. (1989). Spouses' impressions of rules for communication in public and private marital conflict. *Journal of Marriage and the Family, 51,* 957–967.

Jones, E. E., & Worthman, C. (1973). *Imagination: An attributional approach.* Morristown, NJ: General Learning Press.

Jones, J. T., Pelham, B. W., Carvallo, M., & Mirenberg, M. C. (2004). How do I love thee? Let me count the Js: Implicit egotism and interpersonal attraction. *Journal of Personality and Social Psychology, 87,* 665–683.

Jones, S. M. (2000). *Nonverbal immediacy and verbal comforting in the social process.* Unpublished doctoral dissertation, Arizona State University, Tempe.

Jones, S. M. (2004). Putting the person into person-centered and immediate emotional support: Emotional change and perceived helper competence as outcomes of comforting in helping situations. *Communication Research, 32,* 338–360.

Jones, S. M. (2006). "Why is this happening to me?" The attributional make-up of negative emotions experienced in emotional support encounters. *Communication Research Reports, 23,* 291–298.

Jones, S. M., & Burleson, B. R. (1997). The impact of situational variables on helpers' perceptions of comforting messages: An attributional analysis. *Communication Research, 24,* 530–555.

Jones, S. M., & Burleson, B. R. (2003). Effects of helper and recipient sex on the experience and outcomes of comforting messages: An experimental investigation. *Sex Roles, 48*(1/2), 1–19.

Jones, S. M., & Guerrero, L. K. (2001). The effects of nonverbal immediacy and verbal person-centeredness in the emotional support process. *Human Communication Research, 27,* 567–596.

Jones, S. M., & Wirtz, J. G. (2007). "Sad monkey see, monkey do": Nonverbal matching in emotional support encounters. *Communication Studies, 58,* 71–86.

Jones, T. S. (2000). Emotional communication in conflict: Essence and impact. In W. Eadie & P. Nelson (Eds.), *The language of conflict and resolution* (pp. 81–104). Thousand Oaks, CA: Sage.

Jones, W. H., & Burdette, M. P. (1994). Betrayal in relationships. In A. L. Weber & J. H. Harvey (Eds.), *Perspectives on close relationships* (pp. 243–262). Needham Heights, MA: Allyn & Bacon.

Joseph, N., & Alex, N. (1972). The uniform: A sociological perspective. *American Journal of Sociology, 77,* 719–730.

Joshi, K., & Rai, S. N. (1987). Effect of physical attractiveness upon the inter-personal attraction subjects of different self-esteem. *Perspectives in Psychological Research, 10,* 19–24.

Jourard, S. M. (1959). Self-disclosure and other cathexis. *Journal of Abnormal Social Psychology, 59,* 428–431.

Jourard, S. M. (1964). *The transparent self.* New York: Wiley.

Julien, D., Bouchard, C., Gagnon, M., & Pomperleau, A. (1992). An insider's view of marital sex: A dyadic analysis. *Journal of Sex Research, 29,* 343–360.

Jung, E. & Hecht, M. (2004). Elaborating the communication theory of identity: Identity gaps and communication outcomes. *Communication Quarterly, 52,* 265–283.

Kahneman, D., Slovic, P., & Tvesky, A. (Eds.). (1982). *Judgment under uncertainty: Heuristics and biases.* Cambridge, UK: Cambridge University Press.

Kaiser, S. B. (1997). *The social psychology of clothing: Symbolic appearances in context* (2nd ed.). New York: Fairchild.

Kalbfleisch, P. J., & Herold, A. L. (2006). Sex, power, and communication. In K. Dindia & D. J. Canary (Eds.), *Sex differences and similarities in communication* (2nd ed., pp. 299–313). Mahwah, NJ: Lawrence Erlbaum.

Kalmijn, M., & Poortman, A. R. (2006). His or her divorce? The gendered nature of divorce and its determinants. *European Sociological Review, 22,* 201–214.

Kam, J. A., & Hecht, M. L. (2009). Investigation the role of identity gaps among communicative and relational outcomes within the grandparent-grandchild relationship: The young-adult grandchildren's perspective. *Western Journal of Communication, 73,* 456–480.

Kam, K. Y. (2004). *A cultural model of nonverbal deceptive communication: The independent and interdependent self-construals as predictors of deceptive communication motivations and nonverbal behaviors under deception.* Unpublished doctoral dissertation, University of Arizona, Tucson.

Kan, M. Y. (2008). Does gender trump money? Housework hours of husbands and wives in Britain. Work, *Employment and Society, 22,* 45–66.

Kandel, D. B. (1978). Similarity in real life adolescent friendship pairs. *Journal of Personality and Social Psychology, 36,* 306–312.

Kane, H. S., Jaremka, L. M., Guichard, A. C., Ford, M. B., Collins, N. L., & Feeney, B. C. (2007). Feeling supported and feeling satisfied: How one partner's attachment style predicts the other partner's relationship experience. *Journal of Social and Personal Relationships, 24,* 535–555.

Kanin, E. J., Davidson, K. D., & Scheck, S. R. (1970). A research note on male-female differential in the experience of heterosexual love. *Journal of Sex Research, 6,* 64–72.

Karney, B. R., & Bradbury, T. N. (1995). The longitudinal course of marital quality and stability: A review of theory, method, and research. *Psychological Bulletin, 118,* 3–34.

Karpel, M. (1980). Family secrets. *Family Process, 19,* 295–306.

Katz, J., Street, A., & Arias, I. (1995, November). *Forgive and forget: Women's responses to dating violence.* Paper presented at the annual meeting of the Association for the Advancement of Behavior Therapy, Washington, DC.

Kellerman, J., Lewis, J., & Laird, J. D. (1989). Looking and loving: The effects of mutual gaze on feelings of romantic love. *Journal of Research in Personality, 23,* 145–161.

Kellermann, K. A. (1995). The conversation MOP: A model of patterned and pliable behavior. In D. E. Hewes (Ed.), *The cognitive bases of interpersonal communication* (pp. 181–224). Hillsdale, NJ: Lawrence Erlbaum.

Kellermann, K. A., & Berger, C. R. (1984). Affect and the acquisition of social information: Sit back, relax, and tell me about yourself. In R. N. Bostrom (Ed.), *Communication yearbook 8* (pp. 412–445). Beverly Hills, CA: Sage.

Kellermann, K. A., & Reynolds, R. (1990). When ignorance is bliss: The role of motivation to reduce uncertainty in uncertainty reduction theory. *Human Communication Research, 17,* 5–75.

Kelley, D. (1998). The communication of forgiveness. *Communication Studies, 49,* 255–271.

Kelley, H. H. (1979). *Personal relationships: Their structures and processes.* Hillsdale, NJ: Lawrence Erlbaum.

Kelley, H. H. (1973). The processes of casual attribution. *American Psychologist, 28,* 107–128.

Kelley, H. H. (1986). Personal relationships: Their nature and significance. In R. Gilmour & S. Duck (Eds.), *The emerging field of personal relationships* (pp. 3–19). Hillsdale, NJ: Lawrence Erlbaum.

Kelley, H. H., Berscheid, E., Christensen, A., Harvey, J. H., Huston, T. L., Levinger, G., et al. (1983). Analyzing close relationships. In H. H. Kelley, E. Berscheid, A. Christensen, J. H. Harvey, T. L. Huston, & G. Levinger, (Eds.), *Close relationships* (pp. 20–67). New York: Freeman.

Kelley, K., Pilchowicz, E., & Byrne, D. (1981). Responses of males to female-initiated dates. *Bulletin of the Psychonomic Society, 17,* 195–196.

Kelley, K., & Rolker-Dolinsky, B. (1987). The psycho-sexology of female initiation and dominance. In D. Perlman & S. Duck (Eds.), *Intimate relationships: Development, dynamics and deterioration* (pp. 63–87). Newbury Park, CA: Sage.

Kelly, A. B., Fincham, F. D., & Beach, S. R. H. (2003). Communication skills in couples: A review and discussion of emerging perspectives. In J. O. Greene & B. R. Burleson (Eds.), *Handbook of communication and social skills* (pp. 723–751). Mahwah, NJ: Lawrence Erlbaum.

Kelly, A. E., & McKillop, K. J. (1996). Consequences of revealing personal secrets. *Psychological Bulletin, 120,* 450–465.

Kelsey, C. M. (2007). *Generation MySpace: Helping your teen survive online adolescence.* Boston: Marlowe.

Kennedy, C. W., & Camden, C. (1983). Interruptions and nonverbal gender differences. *Journal of Nonverbal Behavior, 8,* 91–108.

Kennedy, J. H. (1992). Relationship of maternal beliefs and childrearing strategies to social competence in pre-school children. *Child Study Journal, 22,* 39–55.

Kesher, S., Kark, R., Pomerantz-Zorin, L., Koslowsky, M., & Schwarzwald, J. (2006). Gender, status and the use of power strategies. *European Journal of Social Psychology, 36,* 105–117.

Keyton, J. (1996). Sexual harassment: A multidisciplinary synthesis and critique. In B. R. Burleson (Ed.), *Communication yearbook 19* (pp. 92–155). Thousand Oaks, CA: Sage.

Kidwell, J., Fischer, J. L., Dunham, R. M., & Baranowski, M. (1983). Parents and adolescents: Push and pull of change. In H. I. McCubin & C. R. Figley (Eds.), *Stress in the family: Coping with normative transitions* (pp. 74–89). New York: Brunner/Mazel.

Kilmann, R. H., & Thomas, K. W. (1977). Developing a forced-choice measure of conflict-handling behavior: The "MODE" instrument. *Education and Psychological Measurement, 37,* 309–325.

Kim, J., & Gray, K. A. (2008). Leave or stay? Battered women's decision after intimate partner violence. *Journal of Interpersonal Violence, 23,* 1465–1482.

Kim, K. I., Park. H. J., & Suzuki, N. (1990). Reward allocations in the United States, Japan, and Korea: A comparison of individualistic and collectivistic cultures. *Academy of Management Journal, 33,* 188–198.

King, C. E., & Christensen, A. (1983). The relationship events scale: A Guttman scaling of progress in courtship. *Journal of Marriage and the Family, 45,* 671–678.

King, S. W., & Sereno, K. K. (1984). Conversational appropriateness as a conversational imperative. *Quarterly Journal of Speech, 70,* 264–273.

Kisler, T. S., & Christopher, F. S. (2008). Sexual exchanges and relationship satisfaction: Testing the role of sexual satisfaction as a mediator and gender as a moderator. *Journal of Social and Personal Relationships, 25,* 587–602.

Kito, M. (2005). Self-disclosure in romantic relationships and friendships among American and Japanese college students. *The Journal of Social Psychology, 145,* 127–140.

Kitzmann, K. M., & Cohen, R. (2003). Parents' versus children's perceptions of interparental conflict as predictors of children's friendship quality. *Journal of Social and Personal Relationships, 20,* 689–700.

Klein, R. C. A., & Johnson, M. P. (1997). Strategies of couple conflict. In S. Duck (Ed.), *Handbook of personal relationships: Theory, research, and interventions* (2nd ed., pp. 267–486). New York: Wiley.

Kleinke, C. L., Meeker, F. B., & LaFong, C. (1974). Effects of gaze, touch, and use of name on evaluation of "engaged" couples. *Journal of Research in Personality, 7,* 368–373.

Kline, S. L., Horton, B., & Zhang, S. (2008). Communicating love: Comparisons between American and East Asian university students. *International Journal of Intercultural Relations, 32,* 200–214.

Klinetob, N. A., & Smith, D. A. (1996). Demand-withdraw communication in marital interaction: Tests of interspousal contingency and gender role hypotheses. *Journal of Marriage and the Family, 58,* 945–957.

Kluwer, E. S., de Dreu, C. K. W., & Buunk, B. P. (1998). Conflict in intimate vs. non-intimate relationships: When gender role stereotyping overrides biased self-other judgment. *Journal of Social and Personal Relationships, 15,* 637–650.

Knapp, M. L. (1978). *Social intercourse: From greeting to goodbye.* Boston: Allyn & Bacon.

Knapp, M. L. (1983). Dyadic relationship development. In J. Wiemann (Ed.), *Nonverbal interaction* (pp. 179–197). Beverly Hills, CA: Sage.

Knapp, M. L., & Vangelisti, A. L. (2005). *Interpersonal communication and human relationships* (5th ed.). Boston: Allyn & Bacon.

Knee, C. R. (1998). Implicit theories of relationships: Assessment and predictions of romantic relationship initiation, coping, and longevity. *Journal of Personality and Social Psychology, 74,* 360–370.

Knee, C. R., & Bush, A. L. (2008). Relationship beliefs and their role in romantic relationship initiation. In S. Sprecher, A. Wenzel, & J. Harvey (Eds.), *Handbook of relationship initiation* (pp. 471–485). New York: Taylor & Francis.

Knee, C. R., Patrick, H., Vietor, N. A., & Neighbors, C. (2004). Implicit theories of relationships: Moderators of the link between conflict and commitment. *Personality and Social Psychology Bulletin, 30,* 617–628.

Knobloch, L. K. (2005). Evaluating a contextual model of responses to relational uncertainty increasing events: The role of intimacy, appraisals, and emotions. *Human Communication Research, 31,* 60–101.

Knobloch, L. K. (2007a). Perceptions of turmoil within courtship: Associations with intimacy, relational uncertainty, and interference from partners. *Journal of Social and Personal Relationships, 24,* 363–384.

Knobloch, L. K. (2007b). The dark side of relational uncertainty: Obstacle or opportunity. In B. H. Spitzberg & W. R. Cupach (Eds.), *The dark side of interpersonal communication* (2nd ed., pp. 31–60). Mahwah, NJ: Lawrence Erlbaum.

Knobloch, L. K. (2009). Relational uncertainty and interpersonal communication. In S. W. Smith & S. R. Wilson (Eds.), *New directions in interpersonal communication research* (pp. 69–93). Thousand Oaks, CA: Sage.

Knobloch, L. K., & Carpenter-Theune, K. E. (2004). Topic avoidance in developing romantic relationships: Associations with intimacy and relational uncertainty. *Communication Research, 31,* 173–205.

Knobloch, L. K., & Donovan-Kicken, E. (2006). Perceived involvement of network members in courtships: A test of the relational turbulence model. *Personal Relationships, 13,* 281–302.

Knobloch, L. K., & Satterlee, K. L. (2009). Relational uncertainty: Theory and application. In T. D. Afifi & W. A. Afifi (Eds.), *Uncertainty, information management, and disclosure decisions: Theories and applications* (pp. 106–127). New York: Routledge.

Knobloch, L. K., & Solomon, D. H. (1999). Measuring the sources and content of relational uncertainty. *Communication Studies, 50,* 261–278.

Knobloch, L. K., & Solomon, D. H. (2002). Information seeking beyond initial interactions: Negotiating relational uncertainty within close relationships. *Human Communication Research, 28,* 243–257.

Knobloch, L. K., & Solomon, D. H. (2003). Responses to changes in relational uncertainty within dating relationships: Emotions and communication strategies. *Communication Studies, 54,* 282–305.

Knobloch, L. K., & Solomon, D. H. (2004). Interference and facilitation from partners in the development of interdependence with romantic relationships. *Personal Relationships, 11,* 115–130.

Knobloch, L. K., & Solomon, D. H. (2005). Relational uncertainty and relational information processing. *Communication Research, 32,* 349–388.

Knudsen, K., & Waerness, K. (2008). National context and spouses' housework in 34 countries. *European Sociological Review, 24,* 97–113.

Koch, P. B., Mansfield, P. K., Thurau, D., & Carey, M. (2005). Feeling frumpy: The relationships between body image and sexual response changes in midlife women. *Journal of Sex Research, 42,* 215–223.

Koehler, M. H. (2005). *Politics of privacy: The handling of privacy violations experienced by graduate teaching assistants.* Unpublished master's thesis, Arizona State University, Tempe.

Koeppel, L. B., Montagne-Miller, Y., O'Hair, D., & Cody, M. (1993). Friendly? Flirting? Wrong? In P. J. Kalbfleisch (Ed.), *Interpersonal communication: Evolving interpersonal relationships* (pp. 13–32). Hillsdale, NJ: Lawrence Erlbaum.

Koerner, A. F., & Fitzpatrick, M. A. (2002). You never leave your family in a fight: The impact of family of origin on conflict behavior in romantic relationships. *Communication Studies, 53,* 234–251.

Koerner, A. F., & Fitzpatrick, M. A. (2006). Family conflict communication. In J. G. Oetzel & S. Ting-Toomey (Eds.), *The SAGE handbook of conflict communication* (pp. 159–183). Thousand Oaks, CA: Sage.

Kohn, M., Flood, H., Chase, J., & McMahon, P. M. (2000). Prevalence and health consequences of stalking—Louisiana, 1998–1999. *Morbidity and Mortality Weekly Report, 49*(29), 653–655.

Kollock, P., Blumstein, P., & Schwartz, P. (1985). Sex and power in interaction: Conversational privileges and duties. *American Sociological Review, 50,* 34–46.

Korda, M. (1975). *Power: How to get it, how to use it.* New York: Ballantine Books.

Krokoff, L. J., Gottman, J. M., & Roy, A. K. (1988). Blue-collar and white-collar marital interaction and communication orientation. *Journal of Social and Personal Relationships, 5,* 201–221.

Krueger, R. F., & Caspi, A. (1993). Personality, arousal, and pleasure: A test of competing models of interpersonal attraction. *Personality and Individual Differences, 14,* 105–111.

Kruglanski, A. W. (1990). Motivations for judging and knowing: Implications for causal attribution. In E. T. Higgins & R. M. Sorrentino (Eds.), *Handbook of motivation and cognition: Foundation of social behavior* (Vol. 2, pp. 333–368). New York: Guilford Press.

Kruglanski, A. W., Webster, D. M., & Klem, A. (1993). Motivated resistance and openness to persuasion in the presence or absence of prior information. *Journal of Personality and Social Psychology, 65,* 861–876.

Krusiewicz, E. S., & Woods, J. T. (2001). "He was our child from the moment we walked in that room": Entrance stories of adoptive parents. *Journal of Social and Personal Relationships, 18,* 785–803.

Kuchinskas, S. (2009). *The chemistry of love: How the oxytocin response can help you find trust, intimacy, and love.* Oakland, CA: New Harbinger.

Kuczynski, L. (1984). Socialization goals and mother-child interaction: Strategies for long-term and short-term compliance. *Developmental Psychology, 20,* 1061–1073.

Kunce, L. J., & Shaver, P. R. (1994). An attachment-theoretical approach to caregiving in romantic relationships. In K. Bartholomew & D. Perlman (Eds.), *Advances in personal relationships: Vol. 5. Attachment processes in adulthood* (pp. 205–237). Bristol, PA: Kingsley.

Kunkel, A., & Burleson, B. (2003). Relational implications of communication skill evaluations and love styles. *Southern Communication Journal, 68,* 181–197.

Kurdek, L. A. (1989). Relationship quality in gay and lesbian cohabiting couples: A 1-year follow-up study. *Journal of Social and Personal Relationships, 6,* 39–59.

Kurdek, L. A. (1991). The dissolution of gay and lesbian couples. *Journal of Social and Personal Relationships, 8,* 265–278.

Kurdek, L. A. (1993a). The allocation of household labor in gay, lesbian, and heterosexual married couples. *Journal of Social Issues, 49*(3), 127–139.

Kurdek, L. A. (1993b). Predicting marital dissolution: A 5-year prospective longitudinal study of newlywed couples. *Journal of Personality and Social Psychology, 64,* 221–242.

Kurdek, L. A. (2007). The allocation of household labor by partners in gay and lesbian couples. *Journal of Family Issues, 28,* 132–148.

La Valley, A. G., & Guerrero, L. K. (2010, April). *Perceptions of conflict behavior and relational satisfaction in adult parent-child relationships: A dyadic analysis from an attachment perspective.* Paper presented at the annual conference of the Eastern Communication Association, Baltimore.

LaFrance, M., & Mayo, C. (1978). *Moving bodies: Nonverbal communication in social relationships.* Monterey, CA: Brooks/Cole.

Landsford, J. E. (2009). Parental divorce and children's adjustment. *Perspectives on Psychological Science, 4,* 140–152

Laner, M. R., & Ventrone, N. A. (2000). Dating scripts revisited. *Journal of Family Issues, 21,* 488–500.

Langer, E. J. (1989). *Mindfulness.* Reading, MA: Addison-Wesley.

Langlois, J. H., Kalakanis, L., Rubenstein, A. J., Larson, A., Hallam, M., & Smoot, M. (2000). Maxims or myths of beauty? A meta-analytic and theoretical review. *Psychological Bulletin, 126,* 390–423.

Langner, C. A., & Keltner, D. (2008). Social power and emotional experience: Actor and partner effects within dyadic interactions. *Journal of Experimental Social Psychology, 44,* 848–856.

Lannutti, P. J., & Cameron, K. A. (2002). Beyond the breakup: Heterosexual and homosexual post-dissolutional relationships. *Communication Quarterly, 50,* 153–170.

Lannutti, P. J., & Monahan, J. L. (2004). "Not now, maybe later": The influence of relationship type, request persistence and alcohol consumption on women's refusal strategies. *Communication Studies, 55,* 362–378.

Larkin, M. (1998). Easing the way to safer sex. *Lancet, 351,* 964–967.

Lasch, C. (1979). *The culture of narcissism: American life in an age of diminishing expectations.* New York: Warner Books.

Laumann, E. O., Gagnon, J. H., Michael, R. T., & Michaels, S. (1994). *The social organization of sexuality.* Chicago: University of Chicago Press.

Laursen, B., & Collins, W. A. (1994). Interpersonal conflict during adolescence. *Psychological Bulletin, 115,* 197–209.

Lawrence, K., & Byers, E. S. (1995). Sexual satisfaction in long-term heterosexual relationships: The interpersonal exchange model of sexual satisfaction. *Personal Relationships, 2,* 267–285.

Lazarus, R. S. (1985). The trivialization of distress. In J. C. Rose & L. J. Solomon (Eds.), *Primary prevention of psychopathology: Vol. 8. Prevention in health psychology* (pp. 279–298). Hanover, NH: University Press of New England.

Le, B., & Agnew, C. R. (2003). Commitment and its theorized determinants: A meta-analysis of the investment model. *Personal Relationships, 10,* 37–57.

Le Poire, B. A., Hallett, J. S., & Erlandson, K. T. (2000). An initial test of inconsistent nurturing as control theory: How partners of drug abusers assist their partners' sobriety. *Human Communication Research, 26,* 432–457.

Le Poire, B. A., Hallett, J. S., & Giles, H. (1998). Codependence: The paradoxical nature of the functional-afflicted relationship. In B. H. Spitzberg & W. R. Cupach (Eds.), *The dark side of relationships* (pp. 153–176). Mahwah, NJ: Lawrence Erlbaum.

Le Poire, B. A., Shepard, C., & Duggan, A. (1999). Nonverbal involvement, expressiveness, and pleasantness as predicted by parental and partner attachment style. *Communication Monographs, 66,* 293–311.

Lea, M., & Spears, R. (1995). Love at first byte: Building personal relationships over computer networks. In J. T. Wood & S. Duck (Eds.), *Understudied relationships: Off the beaten track* (pp. 197–233). Thousand Oaks, CA: Sage.

Lear, D. (1997). *Sex and sexuality: Risk and relationships in the age of AIDS.* Thousand Oaks, CA: Sage.

Leary, M. R. (1995). *Self-presentation: Impression management and interpersonal behavior.* Madison, WI: Brown & Benchmark.

Leary, M. R., & Kowalski, R. M. (1990). Impression management: A literature review and two-component model. *Psychological Bulletin, 107,* 34–47.

Leary, M. R., Springer, C., Negel, L., Ansell, E., & Evans, K. (1998). The causes, phenomenology, and consequences of hurt feelings. *Journal of Personality and Social Psychology, 74,* 1225–1237.

Leatham, G., & Duck, S. W. (1990). Conversation with friends and the dynamics of social support. In S. W. Duck (Ed., with R. C. Silver), *Personal relationships and social support* (pp. 23–27). London: Sage.

Ledbetter, A. M., & Larson, K. A. (2008). Nonverbal cues in e-mail supportive communication: Associations with sender sex, recipient sex, and support satisfaction. *Information, Communication & Society, 11,* 1089–1110.

Lee, J. A. (1973). *The colors of love: An exploration of the ways of loving.* Don Mills, Ontario, Canada: New Press.

Lee, J. A. (1977). A typology of styles of loving. *Personality and Social Psychology Bulletin, 3,* 173–182.

Lee, J. A. (1988). Love styles. In R. J. Sternberg & M. L. Barnes (Eds.), *The psychology of love* (pp. 38–67). New Haven, CT: Yale University Press.

Lee, J. W., & Guerrero, L. K. (2001). Types of touch in cross-sex relationships by coworkers: Perceptions of relational and emotional messages, inappropriateness and sexual harassment. *Journal of Applied Communication Research, 29,* 197–220.

Lee, T. R., Mancini, J. A., & Maxwell, J. W. (1990). Sibling relations in adulthood: Contact patterns and motivations. *Journal of Marriage and the Family, 52,* 431–440.

Lepore, S. J., & Greenberg, M. A. (2002). Mending broken hearts: Effects of expressive writing on mood, cognitive processing, social adjustment, and health following a relationship breakup. *Psychology and Health, 17,* 547–560.

Leung, K. (1988). Theoretical advances in justice behavior: Some cross-cultural inputs. In M. H. Bond (Ed.), *The cross-cultural challenge to social psychology* (pp. 218–220). Newbury Park, CA: Sage.

Levine, T. R., Aune, K. S., & Park, H. S. (2006). Love styles and communication in relationships: Partner preferences, initiation, and intensification. *Communication Quarterly, 54,* 465–486.

Levine, T. R., & Boster, F. J. (2001). The effects of power and message variables on compliance. *Communication Monographs, 68,* 28–48.

Levine, T. R., & McCornack, S. A. (1992). Linking love and lies: A formal test of the McCornack and Parks model of deception detection. *Journal of Social and Personal Relationships, 9,* 143–154.

Levinger, G., & Senn, D. J. (1967). Disclosure of feelings in marriage. *Merrill-Palmer Quarterly, 13,* 237–249.

Levitt, M. J. (1991). Attachment and close relationships: A life span perspective. In J. L. Gerwitz & W. F. Kurtines (Eds.), *Intersections with attachment* (pp. 183–206). Mahwah, NJ: Lawrence Erlbaum.

Levitt, M. J., Coffman, S., Guacci-Franco, N., & Loveless, S. C. (1994). Attachment relationships and life transitions: An expectancy model. In M. B. Sperling & W. H. Berman (Eds.), *Attachment in adults: Clinical and developmental perspectives* (pp. 232–255). New York: Guilford Press.

Lewandowski, G. W., & Ackerman, R. A. (2006). Something's missing: Need fulfillment and self-expansion as predictors of susceptibility to infidelity. *Journal of Social Psychology, 146,* 389–403.

Lewandowski, G. W., Aron, A., Bassis, S., & Kunak, J. (2006). Losing a self-expanding relationship: Implications for the self-concept. *Personal Relationships, 13,* 317–331.

Lewis, M., & Rosenblum, L. A. (Eds.). (1974). *The effect of the infant on its caregiver.* New York: Wiley.

Lillard, L. L., Brien, M. J., & Waite, L. J. (1995). Premarital cohabitation and subsequent marital dissolution: A matter of self-selection? *Demography, 32,* 437–457.

Lindley, L. L., Barnett, C. L., Brandt, H. M., Hardin, J. M., & Burcin, M. (2008). STDs among sexually active female college students: Does sexual orientation make a difference? *Perspectives on Sexual and Reproductive Health, 40,* 212–217.

Lipsitz, G. (2006). *The possessive investment in whiteness: How white people profit from identity politics.* Philadelphia, PA: Temple University Press.

Livingstone, K. R. (1980). Love as a process of reducing uncertainty. In K. S. Pope (Ed.), *On love and loving* (pp. 133–151). San Francisco: Jossey-Bass.

Lloyd, S. A., & Cate, R. M. (1985). The developmental course of conflict in dissolution of premarital relationships. *Journal of Social and Personal Relationships, 2,* 179–194.

Lloyd, S. A., Cate, R., & Henton, J. (1982). Equity and rewards as predictors of satisfaction in casual and intimate relationships. *Journal of Psychology, 110,* 43–48.

Lucchetti, A. N. (1999). Deception in disclosing one's sexual history: Safe-sex avoidance or ignorance? *Communication Quarterly, 47,* 300–314.

Lykins, A. D., Meana, M., Strauss, G. P. (2008). Sex differences in visual attention to erotic and non-erotic stimuli. *Archives of Sexual Behavior, 37,* 219–228.

MacNeil, S., & Byers, E. S. (2005). Dyadic assessment of sexual self-disclosure and sexual satisfaction in heterosexual dating couples. *Journal of Social and Personal Relationships, 22,* 169–181.

MacNeil, S., & Byers, E. S. (2009). Role of self-disclosure in the sexual satisfaction of long term sexual couples. *Journal of Sex Research, 46,* 3–14.

Magee, J. C. (2009). Seeing power in action: The role of deliberation, implementation, and action in inferences of power. *Journal of Experimental Social Psychology, 45,* 1–14.

Maisel, N. C., & Gable, S. L. (2009). The paradox of received support: The importance of responsiveness. *Psychological Science, 20,* 928–932.

Major, B., & Heslin, R. (1982). Perceptions of cross-sex and same-sex nonreciprocal touch: It is better to give than to receive. *Journal of Nonverbal Behavior, 6,* 148–162.

Mannino, C. A., & Deutsch, F. M. (2007). Changing the divisions of household labor: A negotiated process between partners. *Sex Roles, 56,* 309–324.

Marano, H. E. (1997, November/December). Gottman and Gray: The two Johns. *Psychology Today, 28.*

Marazziti, D., Consoli, G., Silvestri, S., & Dell'Osso, M. C. (2009). Biological correlates of romantic bonding: Facts and hypotheses. *Clinical Neuropsychiatry, 6,* 112–116.

Marks, M. A., & Nelson, E. S. (1993). Sexual harassment on campus: Effects of professor gender on perception of sexually harassing behaviors. *Sex Roles, 28,* 207–217.

Marmo, J., & Bryant, E. M. (2010, November). *The rules of Facebook friendship: A two-stage examination of interaction rules in close, casual, and acquaintance friendship.* Paper presented at the annual meeting of the National Communication Association, San Francisco.

Marshall, L. L. (1994). Physical and psychological abuse. In W. R. Cupach & B. H. Spitzberg (Eds.), *The dark side of interpersonal communication* (pp. 281–311). Hillsdale, NJ: Lawrence Erlbaum.

Marston, P. J., & Hecht, M. L. (1994). Love ways: An elaboration and application to relational maintenance. In D. J. Canary & L. Stafford (Eds.), *Communication and relational maintenance* (pp. 87–202). Orlando, FL: Academic Press.

Marston, P. J., Hecht, M. L., Manke, M., McDaniel, S., & Reeder, H. (1998). The subjective experience of intimacy, passion, and commitment in heterosexual loving relationships. *Personal Relationships, 5,* 15–30.

Marston, P. J., Hecht, M. L., & Robers, T. (1987). True love ways: The subjective experience and communication of romantic love. *Journal of Social and Personal Relationships, 4,* 387–407.

Martin, J. G., & Westie, F. R. (1959). The intolerant personality. *American Sociological Review, 24,* 521–528.

Martin, J. N., Krizek, R. L., Nakayama, T. K., & Bradford, L. (1996). Exploring whiteness: A study of self labels for white Americans. *Communication Quarterly, 44,* 125–144.

Mashek, D., Cannady, L.W., & Tangney, J.P. (2007). Inclusion of community in self-scale: A single-item pictorial study of community connectedness. *Journal of Community Psychology, 35,* 257–275.

Masheter, C. (1997). Former spouses who are friends: Three case studies. *Journal of Social and Personal Relationships, 14,* 207–222.

Mast, M. S. (2002). Dominance as expressed and inferred through speaking time: A meta-analysis. *Human Communication Research, 28,* 420–450.

Mast, M. S. (2005). The world according to men: It is hierarchical and stereotypical. *Sex Roles, 53,* 919–924.

Mast, M. S., Hall, J. A., & Ickes, W. (2006). Inferring power-relevant thoughts and feelings in others: A signal detection analysis. *European Journal of Social Psychology, 36,* 468–478.

Masters, W. H., & Johnson, V. E. (1979). *Homosexuality in perspective.* Boston: Little, Brown.

Matthews, S. (1986). *Friendships through the life course: Oral biographies in old age.* Beverly Hills, CA: Sage.

May, J. L., & Hamilton, P. A. (1980). Effects of musically evoked affect on women's interpersonal attraction toward and perceptual judgments of physical attractiveness of men. *Journal of Social and Clinical Psychology, 6,* 180–190.

Mayback, K. L., & Gold, S. R. (1994). Hyperfemininity and attraction to macho and non-macho men. *Journal of Sex Research, 31,* 91–98.

Mazur, M. A., & Hubbard, A. S. E. (2004). "Is there something I should know?" Topic avoidant responses in parent-adolescent communication. *Communication Reports, 17,* 27–37.

McAdams, D. P. (1985). Motivation and friendship. In S. Duck & D. Perlman (Eds.), *Understanding personal relationships: An interdisciplinary approach* (pp. 85–105). London: Sage.

McAdams, D. P. (1988). Personal needs and personal relationships. In S. Duck (Ed.), *Handbook of personal relationships: Theory, research, and intervention* (pp. 7–22). New York: Wiley.

McCabe, M. P. (1999). The interrelationship between intimacy, relationship functioning, and sexuality among men and women in committed relationships. *Canadian Journal of Human Sexuality, 8,* 31–39.

McCall, K., & Meston, C. (2006). Cues resulting in desire for sexual activity in women. *Journal of Sexual Medicine, 3,* 838–852.

McClanahan, K., Gold, J. A., Lenney, E., Ryckman, R. M., & Kulberg, G. E. (1990). Infatuation and attraction to a dissimilar other: Why is love blind? *Journal of Social Psychology, 130,* 433–445.

McCornack, S. A., (1992). Information manipulation theory. *Communication Monographs, 59,* 1–16.

McCornack, S. A., & Levine, T. R. (1990). When lies are uncovered: Emotional and relational outcomes of discovered deception. *Communication Monographs, 57,* 119–138.

McCornack, S. A., & Parks, M. R. (1986). Deception detection and relationship development: The other side of trust. In M. L. McLaughlin (Ed.), *Communication yearbook 9* (pp. 377–389). Beverly Hills, CA: Sage.

McCroskey, J. C., & McCain, T. A. (1974). The measurement of interpersonal attraction. *Speech Monographs, 41,* 261–266.

McCroskey, J. C., Larson, C. E., & Knapp, M. L. (1971). *An introduction to interpersonal communication.* Englewood Cliffs, NJ: Prentice Hall.

McCullough, M. E., Rachal, K. C., Sandage, S. J., Worthington, E. L., Brown, S. W., & Hight, T. L. (1998). Interpersonal forgiving in close relationships: II. Theoretical elaboration and measurement. *Journal of Personality and Social Psychology, 75,* 1586–1603.

McCullough, M. E., Worthington, E. L., & Rachal, K. C. (1997). Interpersonal forgiving in close relationships. *Journal of Personality and Social Psychology, 73,* 321–336.

McDonald, G. W. (1981). Structural exchange and marital interaction. *Journal of Marriage and the Family, 43,* 825–839.

McEwan, B., & Guerrero, L. K. (2010). Freshmen engagement through communication: Predicting friendship formation strategies and perceived availability of network resources from communication skills. *Communication Studies, 61,* 445–463.

McEwan, B., & Johnson, S. L. (2008). Relational violence: The darkest side of haptic communication. In L. K. Guerrero & M. L. Hecht (Eds.), *The nonverbal communication reader* (3rd ed., pp. 232–241). Long Grove, IL: Waveland Press.

McGinty, K., Knox, D., & Zusman, M. E. (2007). Friends with benefits: Women want "friends," men want "benefits." *College Student Journal, 41,* 1126–1131.

McGoldrick, M., & Carter, E. (1982). The family life cycle. In F. Walsh (Ed.), *Normal family processes* (pp. 167–195). New York: Guilford Press.

McGonagle, K. A., Kessler, R. C., & Gotlib, I. H. (1993). The effects of marital disagreement style, frequency, and outcome on marital disruption. *Journal of Social and Personal Relationships, 10,* 385–404.

McKinnell, J. (2006, May 15). Who not to marry. *Maclean's,* pp. 41–42.

McLaren, R. M., & Solomon, D. H. (2008). Appraisals and distancing responses to hurtful messages. *Communication Research, 35,* 339–367.

Mead, D. E., Vatcher, G. M., Wyne, B. A., & Roberts, S. L. (1990). The comprehensive areas of change questionnaire: Assessing marital couples' presenting complaints. *American Journal of Family Therapy, 18,* 65–79.

Mealy, M., Stephan, W., & Urrutia, I. C. (2007). The acceptability of lies: A comparison of Ecuadorians and Euro-Americans. *International Journal of Intercultural Relationship, 31,* 689–702.

Mearns, J. (1991). Copying with a breakup: Negative mood regulation expectancies and depression following the end of a romantic relationship. *Journal of Personality and Social Psychology, 60,* 327–334.

Mehrabian, A. (1971). *Silent messages.* Belmont, CA: Wadsworth.

Mehrabian, A. (1981). *Silent messages: Implicit communication of emotions and attitudes* (2nd ed.). Belmont, CA: Wadsworth.

Meloy, J. R., & Gothard, S. (1995). Demographic and clinical comparison of obsessional followers and offenders with mental disorders. *American Journal of Psychiatry, 152,* 258–263.

Menzies-Toman, D. A., & Lydon, J. E. (2005). Commitment-motivated benign appraisals of partner transgressions: Do they facilitate accommodation? *Journal of Social and Personal Relationships, 22,* 111–128.

Merolla, A. J., Weber, K. D., Myers, S. A., & Booth-Butterfield, M. (2004). The impact of past dating relationship solidarity on commitment, satisfaction, and investment in current relationships. *Communication Quarterly, 52,* 251–264.

Merton, R. K. (1948). The self-fulfilling prophecy. *Antioch Review, 8,* 193–210.

Messman, S. J., Canary, D. J., & Hause, K. S. (2000). Motives to remain platonic, equity, and the use of maintenance strategies in opposite-sex friendships. *Journal of Social and Personal Relationships, 17,* 67–94.

Meston, C. M., & O'Sullivan, L. F. (2007). Such a tease: Intentional sexual provocation within sexual interactions. *Archives of Sexual Behavior, 35,* 531–542.

Metts, S. (1989). An exploratory investigation of deception in close relationships. *Journal of Social and Personal Relationships, 6,* 159–179.

Metts, S. (1991, February). *The wicked things you say, the wicked things you do: A pilot study of relational transgressions.* Paper presented at the annual meeting of the Western States Communication Association, Phoenix, AZ.

Metts, S. (1992). The language of disengagement: A face-management perspective. In T. L. Orbuch (Ed.), *Close relationships loss: Theoretical approaches* (pp. 111–127). New York: Springer-Verlag.

Metts, S. (1994). Relational transgressions. In W. R. Cupach & B. H. Spitzberg (Eds.), *The dark side of interpersonal communication* (pp. 217–240). Hillsdale, NJ: Lawrence Erlbaum.

Metts, S. (1997). Face and facework: Implications for the study of personal relationships. In S. Duck (Ed.), *Handbook of personal relationships: Theory, research and interventions* (pp. 373–390). Chichester, UK: Wiley.

Metts, S. (2004). First sexual involvement in romantic relationships: An empirical investigation of communicative framing, romantic beliefs, and attachment orientation in the passion turning point. In J. H. Harvey, A. Wenzel, & S. Sprecher (Eds.), *The handbook of sexuality in close relationships* (pp. 135–158). Mahwah, NJ: Lawrence Erlbaum.

Metts, S., & Chronis, H. (1986, May). *An exploratory investigation of relational deception.* Paper presented at the annual meeting of the International Communication Association, Chicago.

Metts, S., & Cupach, W. R. (1986, February). *Disengagement themes in same and opposite sex friendships.* Paper presented at the annual meeting of the Western Speech Communication Association, Tucson, AZ.

Metts, S., Cupach, W. R., & Bejlovich, R. A. (1989). "I love you too much to ever start liking you": Redefining romantic relationships. *Journal of Social and Personal Relationships, 6,* 259–274.

Metts, S., Cupach, W. R., & Imahori, T. T. (1992). Perceptions of compliance-resisting messages in three types of cross-sex relationships. *Western Journal of Communication, 56,* 1–17.

Metts, S., & Grohskopf, E. (2003). Impression management: Goals, strategies, and skills. In J. O. Greene & B. R. Burleson (Eds.), *Handbook of communication and social interaction skills* (pp. 357–402). Mahwah, NJ: Lawrence Erlbaum.

Metts, S., Sprecher, S., & Regan, P. C. (1998). Communication and sexual desire. In P. A. Andersen & L. K. Guerrero (Eds.), *Handbook of communication and emotion: Research, theory, applications, and contexts* (pp. 353–377). San Diego, CA: Academic Press.

Meurling, C. N., Ray, G. E., & LoBello, S. G. (1999). Children's evaluations of classroom friend and classroom best friend relationships. *Child Study Journal, 29,* 79–83.

Meyers, S. A., & Berscheid, E. (1997). The language of love: The difference a preposition makes. *Personality and Social Psychology Bulletin, 23,* 347–362.

Mikulincer, M., & Nachshon, O. (1991). Attachment styles and patterns of self-disclosure. *Journal of Personality and Social Psychology, 61,* 321–331.

Miller, A. J., Worthington, E. L., Jr., & McDaniel, M. A. (2008). Gender and forgiveness: A meta-analytic review and research agenda. *Journal of Social and Clinical Psychology, 27,* 843–876.

Miller, A. L., Notaro, P. C., & Zimmerman, M. A. (2002). Stability and change in internal working models of friendship: Associations with multiple domains of urban adolescent functioning. *Journal of Social and Personal Relationships, 19,* 233–259.

Miller, G. R. (1976). *Explorations in interpersonal communication.* Beverly Hills, CA: Sage.

Miller, G. R., & Boster, F. (1988). Persuasion in personal relationships. In S. Duck (Ed.), *Handbook of personal relationships: Theory, research and interventions* (pp. 275–287). Chichester, UK: Wiley.

Miller, G. R., Boster, F., Roloff, M., & Siebold, D. (1977). Compliance-gaining message strategies: A typology and some findings concerning the effects of situational differences. *Communication Monographs, 44,* 37–51.

Miller, G. R., & Steinberg, M. (1975). *Between people: A new analysis of interpersonal communication.* Chicago: Science Research Associates.

Miller, R. S. (1996). *Embarrassment: Poise and peril in everyday life.* New York: Guilford Press.

Miller, R. S. (1997). Inattentive and contented: Relationship commitment and attention to alternatives. *Journal of Personality and Social Psychology, 73,* 758–766.

Miller, S. (2004, November). Six secret ways to turn her on. *Men's Health,* pp. 138, 140.

Miller, S. M. (1987). Monitoring and blunting: Validation of a questionnaire to assess styles of information-seeking under threat. *Journal of Personality and Social Psychology, 52,* 345–353.

Mills, R. S. L., Nazar, J., & Farrell, H. M. (2002). Child and parent perceptions of hurtful messages. *Journal of Social and Personal Relationships, 19,* 731–754.

Mischel, M. H. (1981). The measurement of uncertainty in illness. *Nursing Research, 30,* 258–263.

Mischel, M. H. (1988). Uncertainty in illness. *Image: Journal of Nursing Scholarship, 20,* 225–232.

Mischel, M. H. (1990). Reconceptualization of the uncertainty in illness theory. *Image: Journal of Nursing Scholarship, 22,* 256–262.

Moller, N. P., Fouladi, R. T., McCarthy, C. J., & Hatch, K. D. (2003). Relationship of attachment and social support to college students' adjustment following relationship breakup. *Journal of Counseling and Development, 81,* 354–369.

Mongeau, P. A., & Carey, C. M. (1996). Who's wooing whom II: An experimental investigation of date-initiation and expectancy violation. *Western Journal of Communication, 60,* 195–213.

Mongeau, P. A., Hale, J. L., & Alles, M. (1994). An experimental investigation of accounts and attributions following sexual infidelity. *Communication Monographs, 61,* 326–344.

Mongeau, P. A., Hale, J. L., Johnson, K. L., & Hillis, J. D. (1993). Who's wooing whom? An investigation of female-initiated dating. In P. J. Kalbfleisch (Ed.), *Interpersonal communication: Evolving interpersonal relationships* (pp. 51–68). Hillsdale, NJ: Lawrence Erlbaum.

Mongeau, P. A., & Henningsen, M. L. M. (2008). Stage theories of relationship development. In L. A. Baxter & D. O. Braithwaite (Eds.), *Engaging theories in interpersonal communication: Multiple perspectives* (pp. 363–376). Thousand Oaks, CA: Sage.

Mongeau, P. A., & Johnson, K. L. (1995). Predicting cross-sex first-date sexual expectations and involvement: Contextual and individual difference factors. *Personal Relationships, 2,* 301–312.

Mongeau, P. A., Ramirez, A., & Vorrell, M. (2003, February). *Friends with benefits: Initial exploration of sexual, non-romantic relationships.* Paper presented at the annual meeting of the Western States Communication Association, Salt Lake City, UT.

Mongeau, P. A., & Schulz, B. E. (1997). What he doesn't know won't hurt him (or me): Verbal responses and attributions following sexual infidelity. *Communication Reports, 10,* 143–152.

Mongeau, P. A., Serewicz, M. C. M., Henningsen, M. L. M., & Davis, K. L. (2006). Sex differences in the transition to a heterosexual romantic relationship. In K. Dindia & D. J. Canary (Eds.), *Sex differences and similarities in communication* (2nd ed., pp. 337–358). Mahwah, NJ: Lawrence Erlbaum.

Mongeau, P. A., Serewicz, M. C. M., & Therrien, L. F. (2004). Goals for cross-sex first dates: The identification, measurement, and influence of contextual factors. *Communication Monographs, 71,* 121–147.

Monroe, S. M., Rohde, P., Seeley, J. R., & Lewinsohn, P. M. (1999). Life events and depression in adolescence: Relationship loss as a prospective risk factor for first onset of major depressive disorder. *Journal of Abnormal Psychology, 108,* 606–614.

Monsour, M. (1992). Meanings of intimacy in cross- and same-sex friendships. *Journal of Social and Personal Relationships, 9,* 277–295.

Montagu, A. (1978). *Touching: The human significance of the skin.* New York: Harper & Row. (Original work published in 1971.)

Montgomery, B. M. (1988). Quality communication in personal relationships. In S. Duck (Ed.), *Handbook of personal relationships* (pp. 343–362). New York: Wiley.

Moore, M. M. (1985). Nonverbal courtship patterns in women: Context and consequences. *Ethology and Sociobiology, 6,* 237–247.

Morf, C. C., & Rhodewalt, F. (2001). Unraveling the paradoxes of narcissism: A dynamic self-regulatory processing model. *Psychological Inquiry, 12,* 177–196.

Morgan, E. M., & Zurbriggin, E. L., (2007). Wanting sex and wanting to wait: Young adults accounts of sexual messages from first significant dating partners. *Feminism and Psychology, 17,* 515–541.

Morman, M. T., & Floyd, K. (1999). Affectionate communication between fathers and young adult sons: Individual- and relational-level correlates. *Communication Studies, 50,* 294–309.

Morr, M. C., & Mongeau, P. A. (2004). First date expectations: The impact of sex of initiator, alcohol consumption, and relationship type. *Communication Research, 31,* 3–35.

Morr Serewicz, M. C., Dickson, F. C., Morrison, J. H. T. A., & Poole, L. L. (2007). Family privacy orientation, relational maintenance, and family satisfaction in young adults' family relationships. *Journal of Family Communication, 7,* 123–142.

Morris, D. (1977). *Manwatching: A field guide to human behavior.* New York: Harry N. Abrams.

Morrison, R. L., Van Hasselt, V. B., & Bellack, A. S. (1987). Assessment of assertion and problem-solving skills in wife abusers and their spouses. *Journal of Family Violence, 2,* 227–256.

Morrison, T. L., Urquiza, A. J., Goodlin-Jones, B. L. (1997). Attachment, perceptions of interaction, and relationship adjustment. *Journal of Social and Personal Relationships, 14,* 627–642.

Morry, M. M. (2005). Relationship satisfaction as a predictor of similarity ratings: A test of the attraction-similarity hypothesis. *Journal of Social and Personal Relationships, 22,* 561–584.

Motley, M. T., & Reeder, H. M. (1995). Unwanted escalation of sexual intimacy: Male and female perceptions of connotations and relational consequences of resistance messages. *Communication Monographs, 62,* 355–382.

Muehlenhard, C. L., & Cook, S. W. (1988). Men's self-reports of unwanted sexual activity. *Journal of Sex Research, 24,* 58–72.

Muehlenhard, C. L., Koralewski, M. A., Andrews, S. L., & Burdick, C. A. (1986). Verbal and nonverbal cues that convey interest in dating: Two studies. *Behavior Therapy, 17,* 404–419.

Muehlenhard, C. L., & Scardino, T. J. (1985). What will he think? Men's impressions of women to initiate dates and achieve academically. *Journal of Counseling Psychology, 32,* 560–569.

Mullen, P. E., & Pathe, M. (1994). Stalking and pathologies of love. *Australian and New Zealand Journal of Psychiatry, 28,* 469–477.

Murnan, S. K., Perot, A., & Byrne, D. (1989). Coping with unwanted sexual activity: Normative responses, situational determinants, and individual differences. *Journal of Sex Research, 26,* 85–106.

Murray, S. L., Holmes, J. G., & Griffin, D. W. (1996). The benefits of positive illusions: Idealization and the construction of satisfaction in close relationships. *Journal of Personality and Social Psychology, 70,* 79–98.

Najib, A., Lorberbaum, J. P., Kose, S., Bohning, D. E., & George, M. S. (2004). Regional brain activity in women grieving a romantic relationship breakup. *American Journal of Psychiatry, 161,* 2245–2256.

Nanus, S. E. (2005, November). How to deal with his ex. *Seventeen,* p. 104.

Neff, K. D., & Suizzo, M. A. (2006). Culture, power, authenticity, and psychological well being within romantic relationships: A comparison of European Americans and Mexican Americans. *Cognitive Development, 21,* 441–457.

Neff, K. D., & Harter, S. (2002). The role of power and authenticity in relationship styles emphasizing autonomy, connectedness, or mutuality among adult couples. *Journal of Social and Personal Relationships, 19,* 835–857.

Nell, K., & Ashton, N. (1996). Gender, self-esteem, and perception of own attractiveness. *Perceptual and Motor Skills, 83,* 1105–1106.

Newcomb, T. M. (1961). *The acquaintance process.* New York: Holt, Rinehart & Winston.

Niehuis, S., & Bartell, D. (2006). The marital disillusionment scale: Development and psychometric properties. *North American Journal of Psychology, 8,* 69–83.

Niehuis, S., & Huston, T. L. (2002, July). *The premarital roots of disillusionment in early marriage.* Paper presented at the International Conference on Personal Relationships, Halifax, Nova Scotia, Canada.

Noar, S. M., Zimmerman, R. S., & Atwood, K. A. (2004). Safer sex and sexually transmitted infections from a relationships perspective. In J. H. Harvey, A. Wenzel, & S. Sprecher (Eds.), *The handbook of sexuality in close relationships* (pp. 519–544). Mahwah, NJ: Lawrence Erlbaum.

Nock, S. L. (1995). A comparison of marriages and cohabiting relationships. *Journal of Family Issues, 16,* 53–76.

O'Connell-Corcoran, K., & Mallinckrodt, B. (2000). Adult attachment, self-efficacy, perspective taking, and conflict resolution. *Journal of Counseling and Development, 78,* 473–483.

O'Hair, D. H., & Cody, M. J. (1994). Deception. In W. R. Cupach & B. H. Spitzberg (Eds.), *The dark side of interpersonal communication* (pp. 181–213). Hillsdale, NJ: Lawrence Erlbaum.

O'Meara, J. D. (1989). Cross-sex friendships: Four basic challenges of an ignored relationship. *Sex Roles, 21,* 525–543.

O'Sullivan, L. F., & Allgeier, E. R. (1994). Disassembling a stereotype: Gender differences in the use of token resistance. *Journal of Applied Social Psychology, 24,* 1035–1055.

O'Sullivan, L. F., & Allgeier, E. R. (1998). Feigning sexual desire: Consenting to unwanted sexual activity in heterosexual dating relationships. *Journal of Sex Research, 35,* 234–243.

O'Sullivan, L. F., & Byers, E. S. (1993). Eroding stereotypes: College women's attempts to influence reluctant male partners. *Journal of Sex Research, 30,* 270–282.

O'Sullivan, L. F., Cheng, M. M., Harris, K. M., & Brooks-Gunn, J. (2007). I wanna hold your hand: The progression of social, romantic, and sexual events in adolescent relationships. *Perspectives on Sexual and Reproductive Health, 39,* 100–107.

O'Sullivan, L. F., & Gaines, M. E. (1998). Decision-making in college student's heterosexual dating relationship: Ambivalence about engaging in sexual activity. *Journal of Social and Personal Relationships, 15,* 347–363.

Oakes, P. (1987). The salience of social categories. In J. C. Turner (Ed.), *Rediscovering the social group* (pp. 117–141). New York: Basil Blackwell.

Olson, L. N. (2002a). Compliance gaining strategies of individuals experiencing "common couple violence." *Qualitative Research Reports in Communication, 3,* 7–14.

Olson, L. N. (2002b). Exploring "common couple violence" in heterosexual romantic relationships. *Western Journal of Communication, 66,* 104–128.

Olson, L. N. (2004). Relational control-motivated aggression: A theoretical based typology of intimate violence. *Journal of Family Communication, 4,* 209–233.

Olson, L. N., & Braithwaite, D. O. (2004). "If you hit me again, I'll hit you back": Conflict management strategies of individuals experiencing aggression during conflicts. *Communication Studies, 55,* 271–285.

Orbe, M. P., & Drummond, D. K. (2009). Negotiations of the complicitous nature of US racial/ethnic categorization: Exploring rhetorical strategies. *Western Journal of Communication, 73,* 437–455.

Ostrow, J. M., & Collins, W. A. (2007). Social dominance in romantic relationships: A prospective longitudinal study of non-verbal process. *Social Development, 16,* 580–581.

Owen, W. F. (1987). The verbal expression of love by women and men as a critical communication event in personal relationships. *Women's Studies in Communication, 10,* 15–24.

Owen, W. F. (1993). Metaphors in accounts of romantic relationship terminations. In P. J. Kalbfleisch (Ed.), *Interpersonal communication: Evolving interpersonal relationships* (pp. 261–268). Hillsdale, NJ: Lawrence Erlbaum.

Paikoff, R. L., & Brooks-Gunn, J. (1991). Do parent-child relationships change during puberty? *Psychological Bulletin, 110,* 47–66.

Palmer, M. T., & Simmons, K. B. (1995). Communicating intentions through nonverbal behaviors: Conscious and nonconscious encoding of liking. *Human Communication Research, 22,* 128–160.

Palomares, N. A. (2009). Women are sort of more tentative than men, aren't they? How men and women use tentative language differently, similarly, and counter-stereotypically as a function of gender salience. *Communication Research, 36,* 538–560.

Papa, M. J., & Canary, D. J. (1995). Communication in organizations: A competence-based approach. In A. M. Nicotera (Ed.), *Conflict and organizations: Communicative processes* (pp. 153–179). Albany, NY: SUNY Press.

Papini, D. R., Sebby, R. A., & Clark, S. (1989). Affective quality of family relations and adolescent identity exploration. *Adolescence, 24,* 457–466.

Parker, B. L., & Drummond-Reeves, S. J. (1993). The death of a dyad: Relational autopsy, analysis and aftermath. *Journal of Divorce and Remarriage, 21,* 95–119.

Parker, R. (1997). The influence of sexual infidelity, verbal intimacy, and gender upon primary appraisal processes in romantic jealousy. *Women's Studies in Communication, 20,* 1–25.

Parks, M. R. (1982). Ideology of interpersonal communication: Off the couch and into the world. In M. Burgoon (Ed.), *Communication yearbook 5* (pp. 79–108). New Brunswick, NJ: Transaction Books.

Parks, M. R., & Adelman, M. B. (1983). Communication networks and the development of romantic relationships: An expansion of uncertainty reduction theory. *Human Communication Research, 10,* 55–79.

Parks, M. R., & Floyd, K. (1996). Meanings for closeness and intimacy in friendship. *Journal of Social and Personal Relationships, 13,* 85–107.

Parsons, J. T., Kelly, B. C., Bimbi, D. S., DiMaria, L., Wainberg, M. L., & Morgenstern, J. (2008). Explanations for the origins of sexual compulsivity among gay and bisexual men. *Archives of Sexual Behavior, 37,* 817–826.

Paulhus, D. L. (1998). Interpersonal and intrapsychic adaptiveness of trait self-enhancement: A mixed blessing. *Journal of Personality and Social Psychology, 74,* 1197–1208.

Pearce, Z., & Halford, W. K. (2008). Do attributions mediate the association of attachment and negative couple communication? *Personal Relationships, 15,* 155–170.

Pendell, S. D. (2002). Affection in interpersonal relationships: Not just a fond or tender feeling. In W. B. Gudykunst (Ed.), *Communication yearbook 26* (pp. 70–115). Mahwah, NJ: Lawrence Erlbaum.

Pennebaker, J. W. (1989). Confession, inhibition, and disease. In L. Berkowitz (Ed.), *Advances in experimental social psychology* (Vol. 22, pp. 211–244). San Diego, CA: Academic Press.

Pennebaker, J. W. (1990). *Opening up: The healing power of confiding in others.* New York: Morrow.

Pennebaker, J. W., Colder, M., & Sharp, L. K. (1990). Accelerating the coping process. *Journal of Personality and Social Psychology, 58,* 528–537.

Peplau, L. A., & Campbell, S. M. (1989). The balance of power in dating and marriage. In J. Freeman (Ed.), *Women: A feminist perspective* (4th ed., pp. 121–137). Mountain View, CA: Mayfield.

Peplau, L. A., & Fingerhut, A. W. (2007). The close relationships of lesbians and gay men. *Annual Review of Psychology, 58,* 405–424.

Peplau, L. A., Fingerhut, A., & Beals, K. P. (2004). Sexuality in the relationships of lesbians and gay men. In J. H. Harvey, A. Wenzel, & S. Sprecher (Eds.), *The handbook of sexuality in close relationships* (pp. 349–369). Mahwah, NJ: Lawrence Erlbaum.

Peplau, L. A., & Spalding, L. R. (2000). The close relationships of lesbians, gay men, and bisexuals. In C. Hendrick & S. S. Hendrick (Eds.), *Close relationships: A sourcebook* (pp. 111–123). Thousand Oaks, CA: Sage.

Perras, M. T., & Lustig, M. W. (1982, February). *The effects of intimacy level and intent to disengage on the selection of relational disengagement strategies.* Paper presented at the annual meeting of the Western Speech Communication Association, Denver, CO.

Perilloux, C., & Buss, D. M. (2008). Breaking up romantic relationships: Costs experienced and coping strategies deployed. *Evolutionary Psychology, 6,* 164–181.

Peterson, C. C. (1990). Husbands' and wives' perceptions of marital fairness across the family life cycle. *International Journal of Aging and Human Development, 31,* 179–188.

Petra, R., & Petra, K. (1993). *The 775 stupidest things ever said.* New York: Doubleday.

Petronio, S. (1991). Communication boundary management: A theoretical model of managing disclosure of private information between marital couples. *Communication Theory, 1,* 311–335.

Petronio, S. (Ed.). (2000). *Balancing the secrets of private disclosures.* Mahwah, NJ: Lawrence Erlbaum.

Petronio, S. (2002). *Boundaries of privacy: Dialectics of disclosure.* Albany, NY: SUNY Press.

Petronio, S., & Harriman, S. (1990, October). *Parental privacy invasion: Tactics and reactions to encroachment.* Paper presented at the annual meeting of the Speech Communication Association, Chicago.

Petronio, S., & Reirseon, J. (2009). Regulating the privacy of confidentiality: Grasping the complexities through communication privacy management theory. In T. D. Afifi &
W. A. Afifi (Eds.), *Uncertainty, information management, and disclosure decisions: Theories and applications* (pp. 365–383). New York: Routledge.

Petronio, S., Sargent, J., Andea, L., Reganis, P., & Cichocki, D. (2004). Family and friends as healthcare advocates: Dilemmas of confidentiality and privacy. *Journal of Social and Personal Relationships, 21,* 33–52.

Pfouts, J. H. (1978). Violent families: Coping responses of abused wives. *Child Welfare, 57,* 101–111.

Philliber, S. (1980). Socialization for childbearing. *Journal of Social Issues, 36,* 20–44.

Phillips, G. M., & Metzger, N. J. (1976). *Intimate communication.* Boston: Allyn & Bacon.

Phillips, M. (2009). *You're invading MySpace! Predicting the use of social networking sites for surveillance in romantic relationships.* Manuscript submitted for publication.

Phillips, M., & Spitzberg, B. H. (in press). Speculating about spying on MySpace and beyond: Social network surveillance and obsessive relational intrusion. In K. B. Wright & L. M. Webb (Eds.), *CMC in personal relationships.* Cresskill, NJ: Hampton Press.

Phillips, M., & Spitzberg, B. H. (February, 2009). *MySpace or yours? Social networking sites' surveillance in romantic relationships.* Paper presented at the annual conference of the Western State Communication Association, Mesa, AZ.

Pierce, C. A. (1996). Body height and romantic attraction: A meta-analytic test of the male-taller norm. *Social Behavior and Personality, 24,* 143–149.

Pierce, T., & Lydon, J. E. (2001). Global and specific relational models in the experience of social interactions. *Journal of Personality and Social Psychology, 80,* 613–631.

Pines, A. (1992). *Romantic jealousy: Understanding and conquering the shadow of love.* New York: St. Martin's Press.

Pines, A. (1998). A prospective study of personality and gender differences in romantic attraction. *Personality and Individual Differences, 25,* 147–157.

Pistole, M. C. (1989). Attachment in adult romantic relationships: Style of conflict resolution and relationship satisfaction. *Journal of Social and Personal Relationships, 6,* 505–510.

Planalp, S., & Honeycutt, J. M. (1985). Events that increase uncertainty in personal relationships. *Human Communication Research, 11,* 593–604.

Polimeni, A., Hardie, E., & Buzwell, S. (2002). Friendship closeness inventory: Development and psychometric evaluation. *Psychological Reports, 91,* 142–152.

Powell, L. A. (2005). Justice judgments as complex psychocultural constructions: An equity-based heuristic for mapping two- and three-dimensional fairness representations in perceptual space. *Journal of Cross-Cultural Psychology, 36,* 48–73.

Prager, K. J. (1995). *The psychology of intimacy.* New York: Guilford Press.

Prager, K. J. (2000). Intimacy in personal relationships. In C. Hendrick & S. S. Hendrick (Eds.), *Close relationships: A sourcebook* (pp. 229–242). Thousand Oaks, CA: Sage.

Prager, K. J., & Buhrmester, D. (1998). Intimacy and need fulfillment in couple relationships. *Journal of Social and Personal Relationships, 15,* 435–469.

Prager, K. J., & Roberts, L. J. (2004). Deep intimate connection: Self and intimacy in couple relationships. In D. J. Mashek & A. P. Aron (Eds.), *Handbook of closeness and intimacy* (pp. 43–60). Mahwah, NJ: Lawrence Erlbaum.

Pruitt, D. G., & Carnevale, P. J. (1993). *Negotiation in social conflict.* Pacific Grove, CA: Brooks/Cole.

Putnam, L. L., & Wilson, C. E. (1982). Communicative strategies in organizational conflicts: Reliability and validity of a measurement scale. In M. Burgoon (Ed.), *Communication yearbook 6* (pp. 629–652). Beverly Hills, CA: Sage.

Rabby, M. K. (2007). Relational maintenance and the influence of commitment in online and offline relationships. *Communication Studies, 58,* 315–337.

Rabby, M. K., & Walther, J. B. (2003). Computer mediated effect on relationship formation and maintenance. In D. J. Canary & M. Dainton (Eds.), *Maintaining relationships through communication: Relational, contextual, and cultural variations* (pp. 141–162). Mahwah, NJ: Lawrence Erlbaum.

Rahim, M. A. (1986). *Managing conflicts in organizations.* New York: Praeger.

Rahim, M. A., & Bonoma, T. V. (1979). Managing organizational conflict: A model for diagnosis and intervention. *Psychological Reports, 44,* 36–48.

Ramirez, A., Jr. (2008). An examination of the tripartite approach to commitment: An actor-partner interdependence analysis of the effect of relational maintenance behavior. *Journal of Social and Personal Relationships, 25,* 943–965.

Rathus, S. A., Nevid, J. S., & Fichner-Rathus, L. (1993). *Human sexuality in a world of diversity.* Boston: Allyn & Bacon.

Rawlins, W. K. (1982). Cross-sex friendship and the communicative management of sex-role expectations. *Communication Quarterly, 30,* 343–352.

Rawlins, W. K. (1983a). Negotiating close friendships: The dialectic of conjunctive freedoms. *Human Communication Research, 9,* 255–266.

Rawlins, W. K. (1983b). Openness as problematic in ongoing friendships: Two conversational dilemmas. *Communication Monographs, 50,* 1–13.

Rawlins, W. K. (1989). A dialectical analysis of the tensions, functions, and strategic challenges of communication in young adult friendships. In J. A. Anderson (Ed.), *Communication yearbook 12* (pp. 157–189). Newbury Park, CA: Sage.

Rawlins, W. K. (1992). *Friendship matters: Communication, dialectics, and the life course.* Hawthorne, NY: Aldine de Gruyter.

Rawlins, W. K. (1994). Being there and growing apart: Sustaining friendships during adulthood. In D. J. Canary & L. Stafford (Eds.), *Communication and relational maintenance* (pp. 275–294). San Diego, CA: Academic Press.

Ray, G. B., & Floyd, K. (2006). Nonverbal expressions of liking and disliking in initial interaction: Encoding and decoding perspectives. *Southern Communication Journal, 71,* 45–64.

Redmond, M. V., & Virchota, D. A. (1994, November). *The effects of varying lengths of initial interaction on attraction and uncertainty reduction.* Paper presented at the annual meeting of the Speech Communication Association, New Orleans, LA.

Reece, M. M., & Whitman, R. N. (1962). Expressive movements, warmth, and verbal reinforcement. *Journal of Abnormal and Social Psychology, 64,* 234–236.

Reeder, H. M. (2000). "I like you . . . as a friend": The role of attraction in cross-sex friendship. *Journal of Social and Personal Relationships, 17,* 329–348.

Reel, B. W., & Thompson, T. L. (1994). A test of the effectiveness of strategies for talking about the effectiveness of condom use. *Journal of Applied Communication Research, 22,* 127–140.

Reese-Weber, S., & Bartle-Haring, S. (1998). Conflict resolution styles in family subsystems and adolescent romantic relationships. *Journal of Youth and Adolescence, 27,* 735–752.

Regan, P. C. (1998a). Of lust and love: Beliefs about the role of sexual desire in romantic relationships. *Personal Relationships, 5,* 139–157.

Regan, P. C. (1998b). What if you can't get what you want? Willingness to compromise ideal mate selection standards as a function of sex, mate value, and relationship context. *Personality and Social Psychology Bulletin, 24,* 1294–1303.

Regan, P. C. (2004). Sex and the attraction process: Lessons learned from science (and Shakespeare) on lust, love, chastity, and fidelity. In J. H. Harvey, A. Wenzel, & S. Sprecher (Eds.), *The handbook of sexuality in close relationships* (pp. 115–133). Mahwah, NJ: Lawrence Erlbaum.

Regan, P. C., & Berscheid, E. (1995). Gender differences in beliefs about the causes of male and female sexual desire. *Personal Relationships, 2,* 345–358.

Regan, P. C., & Berscheid, E. (1999). *Lust: What we know about sexual desire.* Thousand Oaks, CA: Sage.

Regan, P. C., & Dreyer, C. S. (1999). Lust? Love? Status? Young adults' motives for engaging in casual sex. *Journal of Psychology and Human Sexuality, 11,* 1–24.

Reilly, M. E., & Lynch, J. M. (1990). Power-sharing in lesbian partnerships. *Journal of Homosexuality, 19*(1), 1–30.

Reined, C., Byers, E. S., & Pan, S. (1997). Sexual and relational satisfaction in mainland China. *Journal of Sex Research, 34,* 399–410.

Reinisch, J. M., & Beasley, R. (1990). *The Kinsey Institute report on sex: What you must know to be sexually literate.* New York: St. Martin's Press.

Reissman, C., Aron, A., & Bergen, M. R. (1993). Shared activities and marital satisfaction: Causal direction and self-expansion versus boredom. *Journal of Social and Personal Relationships, 10,* 249–254.

Remland, M. S. (1981). Developing leadership skills in nonverbal communication: A situational perspective. *Journal of Business Communication, 18,* 17–29.

Remland, M. S. (1982, November). *Leadership impressions and nonverbal communication in a superior subordinate situation.* Paper presented at the annual meeting of the Speech Communication Association, Louisville, KY.

Reyes, M., Afifi, W., Krawchuk, A., Imperato, N., Shelley, D., & Lee, J. (June, 1999). *Just (don't) talk: Comparing the impact of interaction style on sexual desire and social attraction.* Paper presented at the joint conference of the International Network on Personal Relationships and the International Society for the Study of Personal Relationships, Louisville, KY.

Rhatigan, D. L., & Street, A. E. (2005). The impact of intimate partner violence on decisions to leave dating relationships. *Journal of Interpersonal Violence, 20,* 1580–1597.

Rhodewalt, F., & Eddings, S. K. (2002). Narcissus reflects: Memory distortion in response to ego-relevant feedback among high- and low-narcissistic men. *Journal of Research in Personality, 36,* 97–116.

Ridings, C. M., & Gefen, D. (2004). Virtual community attraction: Why people hang out online. *Computer-Mediated Communication, 10.* Retrieved from http://jcmc.indiana.edu/vol10/issue1/ridings_gefen.html

Ridley, C., & Feldman, C. (2003). Female domestic violence toward male partners: Exploring conflict responses and outcomes. *Journal of Family Violence, 18,* 157–171.

Rindfuss, R., & VandenHeuvel, A. (1990). Cohabitation: A precursor to marriage or an alternative to being single? *Population and Development Review, 16,* 703–726.

Riordan, C. A., & Tedeschi, J. T. (1983). Attraction in aversive environments: Some evidence for classical conditioning and negative reinforcement. *Journal of Personality and Social Psychology, 44,* 683–692.

Rittenour, C. E., Myers, S. A., & Brann, M. (2007). Commitment and emotional closeness in the sibling relationship. *Southern Communication Journal, 72,* 169–183.

Roberson, B. F., & Wright, R. A. (1994). Difficulty as a determinant of interpersonal appeal: A social-motivational application of energization theory. *Basic and Applied Social Psychology, 15,* 373–388.

Roberto, K. A., & Scott, J. P. (1986). Friendships of older men and women: Exchange patterns and satisfaction. *Psychology and Aging, 1,* 103–109.

Robinson, T., & Smith-Lovin, L. (1992). Selective interaction as a strategy for identity maintenance: An affect control model. *Social Psychology Quarterly, 55,* 12–28.

Roese, N. J., Pennington, G. L., Coleman, J., Janicki, M., Norman, P. L., & Kenrick, D. T. (2006). Sex differences in regret: All for love or some for lust? *Personality and Social Psychology Bulletin, 32,* 770–780.

Rogers, E. M. (1995). *Diffusion of innovations* (4th ed.). New York: Free Press.

Rogers, L. A., & Farace, R. V. (1975). Analysis of relational communication in dyads: New measurement procedures. *Human Communication Research, 1,* 222–239.

Rogers, L. A., & Millar, F. E. (1988). Relational communication. In S. Duck (Ed.), *Handbook of personal relationships* (pp. 289–305). New York: Wiley.

Rohlfing, M. E. (1995). "Doesn't anybody stay in one place anymore?" An exploration of the understudied phenomenon of long-distance relationships. In J. T. Wood & S. Duck (Eds.), *Understudied relationships: Off the beaten track* (pp. 173–196). Thousand Oaks, CA: Sage.

Rohrbaugh, J. B. (2006). Domestic violence in same-gender relationships. *Family Court Review, 44,* 287–299.

Roiger, J. F. (1993). Power in friendship and use of influence strategies. In P. J. Kalbfleisch (Ed.), *Interpersonal communication: Evolving interpersonal relationships* (pp. 133–145). Hillsdale, NJ: Lawrence Erlbaum.

Rollie, S., & Duck, S. W. (2006) Divorce and dissolution of romantic relationships: Stage Models and their limitations. In J. H. Harvey & M. Fine (Eds.), *Handbook of divorce and relationship dissolution* (pp. 176–193). Mahwah, NJ: Lawrence Erlbaum.

Roloff, M. E., & Cloven, D. H. (1990). The chilling effect in interpersonal relationships: The reluctance to speak one's mind. In D. D. Cahn (Ed.), *Intimates in conflict: A communication perspective* (pp. 49–76). Hillsdale, NJ: Lawrence Erlbaum.

Roloff, M. E., & Ifert, D. E. (2000). Conflict management through avoidance: Withholding complaints, suppressing arguments, and declaring topics taboo. In S. Petronio (Ed.), *Balancing the secrets of private disclosures* (pp. 151–163). Mahwah, NJ: Lawrence Erlbaum.

Roloff, M. E., & Miller, C. W. (2006). Social cognition approaches to understanding conflict and communication. In J. G. Oetzel & S. Ting-Toomey (Eds.), *The SAGE handbook of conflict communication* (pp. 97–128). Thousand Oaks, CA: Sage.

Roloff, M. E., Soule, K. P., & Carey, C. M. (2001). Reasons for remaining in a relationship and responses to relational transgressions. *Journal of Social and Personal Relationships, 18,* 362–385.

Roscoe, B., Cavanaugh, L. E., & Kennedy, D. R. (1988). Dating infidelity: Behaviors, reasons, and consequences. *Adolescence, 89,* 36–43.

Rose, S. M. (1985). Same- and cross-sex friendships and the psychology of homosociology. *Sex Roles, 12,* 63–74.

Rosen, K. H., & Stith, S. M. (1995). Women terminating abusive relationships: A qualitative study. *Journal of Social and Personal Relationships, 12,* 155–160.

Rosenbluth, P. C., Steil, J. M., & Whitcomb, J. H. (1998). Marital equality: What does it mean? *Journal of Family Issues, 19,* 227–244.

Rosenfeld, L. B. (1979). Self-disclosure avoidance: Why I am afraid to tell you who I am. *Communication Monographs, 46,* 63–74.

Rosenfeld, L. B. (2000). Overview of the ways privacy, secrecy, disclosure are balanced in today's society. In S. Petronio (Ed.), *Balancing secrets of private disclosure* (pp. 3–17). Mahwah, NJ: Lawrence Erlbaum.

Rosenfeld, L. B., & Kendrick, W. L. (1984). Choosing to be open: An empirical investigation of subjective reasons for self-disclosing. *Western Journal of Speech Communication, 48,* 326–343.

Rosenfeld, L. B., & Welsh, S. M. (1985). Differences in self-disclosure in dual-career and single-career marriages. *Communication Monographs, 52,* 253–261.

Rosenthal, D., Gifford, S., & Moore, S. (1998). Safe sex or safe love: Competing discourses. *AIDS Care, 10,* 35–47.

Rosenthal, R., & Jacobson, L. (1968). *Pygmalion in the classroom: Teacher expectation and pupils' intellectual development.* New York: Holt, Rinehart & Winston.

Rosenzweig, J. M., & Lebow, W. C. (1992). Femme on the streets, butch in the sheets? Lesbian sex roles, dyadic adjustment, and sexual satisfaction. *Journal of Homosexuality, 23,* 1–20.

Ross, M., & Sicoly, F. (1979). Egocentric biases in availability and attribution. *Journal of Personality and Social Psychology, 37,* 273–285.

Rowatt, W. C., Cunningham, M. R., & Druen, P. B. (1998). Deception to get a date. *Personality and Social Psychology Bulletin, 24,* 1228–1242.

Rowatt, W. C., Cunningham, M. R., & Druen, P. B. (1999). Lying to get a date: The effects of facial physical attractiveness on the willingness to deceive prospective dating partners. *Journal of Social and Personal Relationships, 16,* 209–233.

Rozema, H. J. (1986). Defensive communications climate as a barrier to sex education in the home. *Family Relations, 35,* 531–537.

Rubin, R. B., & Martin, M. M. (1998). Interpersonal communication motives. In J. C. McCroskey, J. A. Daly, M. M. Martin, & M. J. Beatty (Eds.), *Communication and personality: Trait perspectives* (pp. 287–307). Cresskill, NJ: Hampton Press.

Rubin, Z. (1970). Measurement of romantic love. *Journal of Personality and Social Psychology, 16,* 265–273.

Rubin, Z. (1973). *Loving and liking: An invitation to social psychology.* New York: Holt, Rinehart & Winston.

Rubin, Z. (1974). Lovers and other strangers: The development of intimacy in encounters and relationships. *American Scientist, 62,* 182–190.

Rubovits, P. C., & Maher, M. L. (1973). Pygmalion black and white. *Journal of Personality and Social Psychology, 25,* 210–218.

Ruesch, J. (1951). Communication and human relations: An interdisciplinary approach. In J. Ruesch & G. Bateson (Eds.), *Communication: The social matrix of psychiatry* (pp. 21–49). New York: Norton.

Rusbult, C. E. (1980). Commitment and satisfaction in romantic associations: A test of the investment model. *Journal of Experimental Social Psychology, 16,* 172–186.

Rusbult, C. E. (1983). A longitudinal test of the investment model: The development (and deterioration) of satisfaction and commitment in heterosexual involvements. *Journal of Personality and Social Psychology, 45,* 101–117.

Rusbult, C. E. (1987). Responses to dissatisfaction in close relationships: The exit-voice-loyalty-neglect model. In D. Perlman & S. Duck (Eds.), *Intimacy relationships: Development, dynamics and deterioration* (pp. 209–237). Newbury Park, CA: Sage.

Rusbult, C. E., Arriaga, X. B., & Agnew, C. R. (2001). Interdependence in close relationships. In G. J. O. Fletcher & M. S. Clark (Eds.), *Blackwell handbook of social psychology: Interpersonal processes* (pp. 359–387). Oxford: Blackwell.

Rusbult, C. E., Bissonnette, V. L., Arriaga, X. B., & Cox, C. L. (1998). Accommodation processes during the early years of marriage. In T. N. Bradbury (Ed.), *The developmental course of marital dysfunction* (pp. 74–113). New York: Cambridge University Press.

Rusbult, C. E., & Buunk, B. P. (1993). Commitment processes in close relationships: An interdependence analysis. *Journal of Social and Personal Relationships, 10,* 175–204.

Rusbult, C. E., Drigotas, S. M., & Verette, J. (1994). The investment model: An interdependence analysis of commitment processes and relationship maintenance phenomena. In D. J. Canary & L. Stafford (Eds.), *Communication and relational maintenance* (pp. 115–139). San Diego, CA: Academic Press.

Rusbult, C. E., & Farrell, D. (1983). A longitudinal test of the investment model: The impact on job satisfaction, job commitment, and turnover of variations in rewards, costs, alternatives, and investments. *Journal of Applied Psychology, 68,* 429–438.

Rusbult, C. E., Johnson, D. J., & Morrow, G. D. (1986). Impact of couple patterns of problems solving on distress and nondistress in dating relationships. *Journal of Personality and Social Psychology, 50,* 744–753.

Rusbult, C. E., & Martz, J. (1995). Remaining in an abusive relationship: An investment model analysis of nonvoluntary dependence. *Personality and Social Psychology Bulletin, 21,* 558–571.

Rusbult, C. E., Olsen, N., Davis, J. L., & Hannon, P. (2001). Commitment and relationship maintenance mechanisms. In J. H. Harvey & A. Wenzel (Eds.), *Close romantic relationships: Maintenance and enhancement* (pp. 87–113). Mahwah, NJ: Lawrence Erlbaum.

Rusbult, C. E., Van Lange, P. A. M., Wildschut, T., Yovetich, N. A., & Verette, J. (2000). Perceived superiority in close relationships: Why it exists and persists. *Journal of Personality and Social Psychology, 79,* 521–545.

Rusbult, C. E., Verette, J., Whitney, G. A., Slovik, L. F., & Lipkus, I. (1991). Accommodation processes in close relationships: Theory and preliminary empirical evidence. *Journal of Personality and Social Psychology, 60,* 53–78.

Rusbult, C. E., & Zembrodt, I. M. (1983). Responses to dissatisfaction in romantic involvements: A multidimensional scaling analysis. *Journal of Experimental Social Psychology, 19,* 274–293.

Rusbult, C. E., Zembrodt, I. M., & Gunn, L. K. (1982). Exit, voice, loyalty and neglect: Responses to dissatisfaction in romantic involvements. *Journal of Personality and Social Psychology, 43,* 1230–1242.

Russell, B. (1938). *Power: A new social analysis.* London: Allen and Unwin.

Ryff, C. D., Singer, B. H., Wing, E., & Dienberg Love, G. (2001). Elective affinities and uninvited agonies: Mapping emotion with significant others onto health. In C. Ryff & B. Singer (Eds.), *Emotion, social relationships, and health* (pp. 133–174). New York: Oxford University Press.

Sabatelli, R. M. (1984). The marital comparison level index: A measure for assessing outcomes related to expectations. *Journal of Marriage and the Family, 46,* 651–662.

Sadalla, E. K., Kenrick, D. T., & Vershure, B. (1987). Dominance and heterosexual attraction. *Journal of Personality and Social Psychology, 52,* 730–738.

Saffrey, C., & Ehrenberg, M. (2007). When thinking hurts: Attachment, rumination, and postrelationship adjustment. *Personal Relationships, 14,* 351–368.

Safilios-Rothschild, C. (1970). The study of family power structure: A review 1960–1969. *Journal of Marriage and the Family, 32,* 539–552.

Safron, C. (1979). Troubles that pull couples apart: A *Redbook* report. *Redbook, 83,* 138–141.

Sagrestano, L. M. (1992). Power strategies in interpersonal relationships. *Psychology of Women Quarterly, 16,* 481–495.

Sagrestano, L. M., Heavey, C. L., & Christensen, A. (2006). Individual differences versus social structural approaches to explaining demand-withdraw and social influence behaviors. In K. Dindia & D. J. Canary (Eds.), *Sex differences and similarities in communication* (2nd ed., pp. 379–395). Mahwah, NJ: Lawrence Erlbaum.

Salovey, P., & Rodin, J. (1985, September). The heart of jealousy. *Psychology Today, 19,* 22–25, 28–29.

Salovey, P., & Rodin, J. (1986). Differentiation of social-comparison jealousy and romantic jealousy. *Journal of Personality and Social Psychology, 50,* 1100–1112.

Salovey, P., & Rodin, J. (1989). Envy and jealousy in close relationships. In C. Hendrick (Ed.), *Close relationships* (pp. 221–246). Newbury Park, CA: Sage.

Salt, R. E. (1991). Affectionate touch between fathers and preadolescent sons. *Journal of Marriage and the Family, 53,* 545–554.

Samp, J. A., & Solomon, D. H. (2001). Coping with problematic events in dating relationships: The influence of dependence power on severity appraisals and decisions to communicate. *Western Journal of Communication, 65,* 138–160.

Sanderson, C. A., Rahm, K. B., Beigbeder, S. A, & Metts, S. (2005). The link between the pursuit of intimacy goals and satisfaction in close same-sex friendships: An examination of the underlying processes. *Journal of Social and Personal Relationships, 22,* 75–98.

Scheflen, A. E. (1965). Quasi-courtship behavior in psychotherapy. *Psychiatry, 27,* 245–257.

Scheflen, A. E. (1972). *Body language and the social order: Communication as behavior control.* Englewood Cliffs, NJ: Prentice Hall.

Scheflen, A. E. (1974). *How behavior means.* Garden City, NY: Anchor/Doubleday.

Scherer, K. R. (1972). Judging personality from voice: A cross-cultural approach to an old issue in interpersonal perception. *Journal of Personality, 40,* 191–210.

Scherer, K. R. (1979). Acoustic noncomitants of emotional dimensions: Judging affect from synthesized tone sequences. In S. Weitz (Ed.), *Nonverbal communication: Readings with commentary* (pp. 249–253). New York: Oxford University Press.

Schlenker, B. R. (1980). *Impression management: The self-concept, social identity, and interpersonal relations.* Monterey, CA: Brooks/Cole.

Schlenker, B. R. (1984). Identities, identifications, and relationships. In V. Derlega (Ed.), *Communication, intimacy, and close relationships* (pp. 71–104). San Diego, CA: Academic Press.

Schlenker, B. R. (Ed.). (1985). *The self and social life.* New York: McGraw-Hill.

Schlenker, B. R., Britt, T. W., & Pennington, J. (1996). Impression regulation and management: Highlights of a theory of self-identification. In R. M. Sorrentino &

E. T. Higgins (Eds.), *Handbook of motivation and cognition: The interpersonal context* (Vol. 3, pp. 118–142). New York: Guilford Press.

Schlenker, B. R., Britt, T. W., Pennington, J., Murphy, R., & Doherty, K. J. (1994). The triangle model of responsibility. *Psychological Review, 101,* 632–652.

Schlenker, B. R., & Darby, B. W. (1981). The use of apologies in social predicaments. *Social Psychology Quarterly, 44,* 271–278.

Schlenker, B. R., & Weigold, M. F. (1990). Self-consciousness and self-presentation: Being autonomous versus appearing autonomous. *Journal of Personality and Social Psychology, 59,* 820–828.

Schlenker, B. R., & Weigold, M. F. (1992). Interpersonal processes involving impression regulation and management. *Annual Review of Psychology, 43,* 133–168.

Schmitt, D. P. (2008). Evolutionary approaches to mate choice and relationship initiation. In S. Sprecher, J. Harvey, & A. Wenzel (Eds.), *Handbook of relationship initiation* (pp. 55–74). New York: Taylor & Francis.

Schmookler, T., & Bursic, K. (2007). The value of monogamy e emerging relationships: A gendered perspective. *Journal of Social and Personal Relationships, 24,* 819–835.

Schneider, K. T., Swan, S., & Fitzgerald, L. F. (1997). Job-related and psychological effects of sexual harassment in the workplace: Empirical evidence from two organizations. *Journal of Applied Psychology, 82,* 401–415.

Schoen, R., & Owens, D. (1992). A further look at first marriages and first unions. In S. J. South & S. E. Tolnay (Eds.), *The changing American family: Sociological and demographic perspectives* (pp. 109–117). Boulder, CO: Westview Press.

Schutz, W. C. (1958). *The interpersonal underworld.* Palo Alto, CA: Science and Behavior Books.

Schwartz, P. (1994). *Peer marriage: How love between equals really works.* New York: Macmillan.

Schweinle, W. E., Ickes, W., & Bernstein, I. H. (2002). Empathic inaccuracy in husband to wife aggression: The overattribution bias. *Personal Relationships, 9,* 141–158.

Scobie, E. D., & Scobie, G. E. (1998). Damaging events: The perceived need for forgiveness. *Journal for the Theory of Social Behavior, 28,* 373–401.

Scott, M. D., & Powers, W. G. (1978). *Interpersonal communication: A question of needs.* Boston: Houghton Mifflin.

Segrin, C. (1998). Interpersonal communication problems associated with depression and loneliness. In P. A. Andersen & L. K. Guerrero (Eds.), *Handbook* of communication and emotion: Research, theory, applications, and contexts (pp. 215–242). San Diego, CA: Academic Press.

Segrin, C., Taylor, M. E., & Altman, J. (2005). Social cognitive mediators and relational outcomes associated with parental divorce. *Journal of Social and Personal Relationships, 22,* 361–377.

Seiter, J. S., & Bruschke, J. (2007). Deception and emotion: The effects of motivation, relationship type, and sex on expected feelings of guilt and shame following acts of deception in United States and Chinese samples. *Communication Studies, 58,* 1–16.

Seiter, J. S., Bruschke, J., & Bai, C. (2002). The acceptability of deception as a function of perceivers' culture, deceiver's intention, and deceiver-deceived relationship. *Western Journal of Communication, 66,* 158–180.

Senchak, M., & Leonard, K. E. (1992). Attachment styles and marital adjustment among newlywed couples. *Journal of Social and Personal Relationships, 9,* 51–64.

Shackelford, T. K., & Buss, D. M. (1997). Cues to infidelity. *Personality and Social Psychology Bulletin, 23,* 1034–1045.

Shackelford, T. K., Buss, D. M., & Bennett, K. (2002). Forgiveness or breakups: Sex differences in responses to a partner's responses to a partner's infidelity. *Cognition and Emotion, 16,* 299–307.

Sharabany, R., Gershoni, R., & Hoffman, J. E. (1981). Girlfriend, boyfriend: Age and sex differences in intimate friendship. *Developmental Psychology, 17,* 800–808.

Sharma, V., & Kaur, I. (1996). Interpersonal attraction in relation to the loss-gain hypothesis. *Journal of Social Psychology, 136,* 635–638.

Sharpsteen, D. J. (1991). The organization of jealousy knowledge: Romantic jealousy as a blended emotion. In P. Salovey (Ed.), *The psychology of jealousy and envy* (pp. 31–51). New York: Guilford Press.

Sharpsteen, D. J., & Kirkpatrick, L. A. (1997). Romantic jealousy and adult romantic attachment. *Journal of Personality and Social Psychology, 72,* 627–640.

Shaver, P. R., Collins, N., & Clark, C. L. (1996). Attachment styles and internal working models of self and relationship partners. In G. J. O. Fletcher & J. Fitness (Eds.), *Knowledge structures in close relationships: A social psychological approach* (pp. 25–61). Mahwah, NJ: Lawrence Erlbaum.

Shaver, P. R., Furman, W., & Buhrmester, D. (1995). Aspects of a life transition: Network changes, social skills and loneliness. In S. W. Duck & D. Perlman (Eds.), *Understanding personal relationships research: An interdisciplinary approach* (pp. 193–219). London: Sage.

Shea, B. C., & Pearson, J. (1986). The effects of relationship type, partner intent, and gender on the selection of relationship maintenance strategies. *Communication Monographs, 53,* 352–364.

Shechory, M., & Ziv, R. (2007). Relationships between gender role attitudes, role division, and perceptions of equity among heterosexual, gay, and lesbian couples. *Sex Roles, 56,* 629–638.

Shen, L., & Dillard, J. P. (2005). Psychometric properties of the Hong psychological reactance scale. *Journal of Personality Assessment, 85,* 74–81.

Sheppard, B. M., Hartwick, J., & Warshaw, P. R. (1988). The theory of reasoned action: A meta-analysis of past research with recommendations for modification and future research. *Journal of Consumer Research, 15,* 325–343.

Sheppard, V. J., Nelson, E. S., & Andreoli-Mathie, V. (1995). Dating relationships and infidelity: Attitudes and behaviors. *Journal of Sex and Marital Therapy, 21,* 202–212.

Sherrod, D. (1989). The influence of gender on same-sex friendships. In C. Hendrick & S. S. Hendrick (Ed.), *Close relationships: A sourcebook* (pp. 164–186). Newbury Park, CA: Sage.

Shotland, R. L., & Craig, J. M. (1988). Can men and women differentiate between friendly and sexually interested behavior? *Social Psychology Quarterly, 51,* 66–73.

Shrier, L. A., Shih, M., Hacker, L., & de Moor (2007). A momentary sampling study of the affective experience following coital events in adolescents. *Journal of Adolescent Health, 35,* 357–365.

Shrout, P. E., Herman, C., & Bolger, N. (2006). The costs and benefits of practical and emotional support on adjustment: A daily diary study of couples experiencing acute stress. *Personal Relationships, 13,* 115–134.

Sias, P. M., & Cahill, D. J. (1998). From coworkers to friends: The development of peer friendships in the workplace. *Western Journal of Communication, 62,* 273–299.

Sias, P. M., Smith, G., & Avdeyera, T. (1999, November). *Developmental influences and communication in peer workplace friendships.* Paper presented at the annual meeting of the National Communication Association, Chicago.

Sidelinger, R. J., & Booth-Butterfield, M. (2007). Mate value discrepancy as predictor of forgiveness and jealousy in romantic relationships. *Communication Quarterly, 55,* 207–223.

Siegert, J. R., & Stamp, G. H. (1994). "Our first big fight" as a milestone in the development of close relationships. *Communication Monographs, 61,* 345–360.

Sigall, H., & Landy, D. (1973). Radiating beauty: The effects of having a physically attractive partner on perception. *Journal of Personality and Social Psychology, 28,* 218–224.

Sillars, A. L. (1980). Attributions and communication in roommate conflicts. *Communication Monographs, 47,* 180–200.

Sillars, A. L., Canary, D. J., & Tafoya, M. (2004). Communication, conflict, and the quality of family relationships. In A. L. Vangelisti (Ed.), *Handbook of family interaction* (pp. 413–446). Mahwah, NJ: Lawrence Erlbaum.

Sillars, A. L., Coletti, S. F., Parry, D., & Rogers, M. A. (1982). Coding verbal conflicts: Nonverbal and perceptual correlates of the "avoidance-distributive-integrative" distinction. *Human Communication Research, 9,* 83–95.

Sillars, A., Roberts, L. J., Leonard, K. E., & Dun, T. (2000). Cognition during marital conflict: The relationship of thought and talk. *Journal of Social and Personal Relationships, 17,* 479–502.

Silver, R. L., Boone, C., & Stones, M. H. (1983). Searching for meaning in misfortune: Making sense of incest. *Journal of Social Issues, 39,* 81–102.

Simon, E. P., & Baxter, L. A. (1993). Attachment-style differences in relationship maintenance strategies. *Western Journal of Communication, 57,* 416–430.

Simpson, J. A. (1987). The dissolution of romantic relationships: Factors involved in relational stability and emotional distress. *Journal of Personality and Social Psychology, 53,* 683–692.

Simpson, J. A. (1990). The influence of attachment styles on romantic relationships. *Journal of Personality and Social Psychology, 59,* 971–980.

Simpson, J. A., & Gangestad, S. W. (1991). Individual differences in sociosexuality: Evidence for convergent and discriminant validity. *Journal of Personality and Social Psychology, 60,* 870–883.

Simpson, J. A., Gangestad, S. W., & Lerma, M. (1990). Perception of physical attractiveness: Mechanisms involved in the maintenance of romantic relationships. *Journal of Personality and Social Psychology, 59,* 1192–1201.

Simpson, J. A., & Harris, B. A. (1994). Interpersonal attraction. In A. L. Weber & J. H. Harvey (Eds.), *Perspectives on close relationships* (pp. 45–66). Boston: Allyn & Bacon.

Simpson, J. A., Ickes, W., & Grich, J. (1999). When accuracy hurts: Reactions of anxiously attached dating partners to a relationship-threatening situation. *Journal of Personality and Social Psychology, 76,* 754–769.

Simpson, J. A., & Rholes, W. S. (1994). Stress and secure base relationships in adulthood. In K. Bartholomew & D. Perlman (Eds.), *Attachment processes in adulthood: Advances in personal relationships* (Vol. 5, pp. 181–204). Bristol, PA: Kingsley.

Simpson, J. A., Wilson, C. L., & Winterheld, H. A. (2004). Sociosexuality and romantic relationships. In J. H. Harvey, A. Wenzel, & S. Sprecher (Eds.), *The handbook of sexuality in close relationships* (pp. 87–112). Mahwah, NJ: Lawrence Erlbaum.

Singh, D. (1995). Female judgment of male attractiveness and desirability for relationships: Role of the waist-to-hip ratio and financial status. *Journal of Personality and Social Psychology, 69,* 1089–1101.

Smith, D. A., Vivian, D., & O'Leary, K. D. (1990). Longitudinal prediction of marital discord form premarital expressions of affect. *Journal of Consulting and Clinical Psychology, 59,* 790–798.

Snow, D. A., & Anderson, L. (1987). Identity work among the homeless: The verbal construction and avowal of personal identities. *American Journal of Sociology, 93,* 1336–1371.

Snyder, M., Tanke, E. D., & Berscheid, E. (1977). Social perception and interpersonal behavior: On the self-fulfilling nature of social stereotypes. *Journal of Personality and Social Psychology, 35,* 656–666.

Solomon, D. H., & Knobloch, L. K. (2001). Relationship uncertainty, partner interference, and intimacy within dating relationships. *Journal of Social and Personal Relationships, 18,* 804–820.

Solomon, D. H., & Knobloch, L. K. (2004). A model of relational turbulence: The role of intimacy, relational uncertainty, and interference from partners in appraisal of irritations. *Journal of Social and Personal Relationships, 21,* 795–816.

Solomon, D. H., Knobloch, L. K., & Fitzpatrick, M. A. (2004). Relational power, marital schema, and decisions to withhold complaints: An investigation of the chilling effect of confrontation in marriage. *Communication Studies, 55,* 146–167.

Solomon, D. H., & Samp, J. A. (1998). Power and problem appraisal: Perceptual foundations of the chilling effect in dating relationship. *Journal of Social and Personal Relationships, 15,* 191–209.

Sorensen, R. C. (1973). *Adolescent sexuality in contemporary America.* New York: World Publishing.

Sorrentino, R. M., Holmes, J. G., Hanna, S. E., & Sharp, A. (1995). Uncertainty orientation and trust in close relationships: Individual differences in cognitive styles. *Journal of Personality and Social Psychology, 68,* 314–327.

Sorrentino, R. M., & Short, J. C. (1986). Uncertainty orientation, motivation, and cognition. In R. M. Sorrentino & E. T. Higgins (Eds.), *Handbook of motivation and cognition: Foundations of social behavior* (Vol. 1, pp. 379–403). New York: Guilford Press.

Sorrentino, R. M., Short, J. C., & Raynor, J. O. (1984). Uncertainty orientation: Implications for affective and cognitive views of achievement behavior. *Journal of Personality and Social Psychology, 46,* 189–206.

Speilmann, S. S., McDonald, G., & Wilson, A. E. (2009). On the rebound: Focusing on some new helps anxiously attached individuals let go of ex-partners. *Personality and Social Psychology Bulletin, 35,* 1382–1394.

Sperling, M. B., & Borgaro, S. (1995). Attachment anxiety and reciprocity as moderators of interpersonal attraction. *Psychological Reports, 76,* 323–335.

Spiegel, D. (1992). Effects of psychosocial support on patients with metastatic breast cancer. *Journal of Psychosocial Oncology, 10,* 113–120.

Spitzberg, B. H., & Cupach, W. R. (1988). *Handbook of interpersonal communication competence.* New York: Springer-Verlag.

Spitzberg, B. H., & Cupach, W. R. (Eds.). (1998). *The dark side of close relationships.* Mahwah, NJ: Lawrence Erlbaum.

Sprecher, S. (1986). The relation between emotion and equity in close relationships. *Social Psychological Bulletin, 49,* 309–321.

Sprecher, S. (1987). The effects of self-disclosure given and received on affect for an intimate partner and the stability of the relationship. *Journal of Personal and Social Relationships, 4,* 115–128.

Sprecher, S. (1989). The importance to males and females of physical attractiveness, earning potential, and expressiveness in initial attraction. *Sex Roles, 12,* 449–462.

Sprecher, S. (1998a). Insiders' perspectives on reasons for attraction to a close other. *Social Psychology Quarterly, 61,* 287–300.

Sprecher, S. (1998b). Social exchange theories and sexuality. *Journal of Sex Research, 35,* 32–43.

Sprecher, S. (2001). A comparison of emotional consequences of and changes in equity over time using global and domain-specific measures of equity. *Journal of Social and Personal Relationships, 18,* 477–501.

Sprecher, S., Aron, A., Hatfield, E., Cortese, A., Potapova, E., & Levitskaya, A. (1994). Love: American style, Russian style, and Japanese style. *Personal Relationships, 1,* 349–369.

Sprecher, S., & Cate, R. M. (2004). Sexual satisfaction and sexual expression as predictors of relationship satisfaction and stability. In J. H. Harvey, A. Wenzel, & S. Sprecher (Eds.), *The handbook of sexuality in close relationships* (pp. 235–256). Mahwah, NJ: Lawrence Erlbaum.

Sprecher, S., & Fehr, B. (2005). Compassionate love for close others and humanity. *Journal of Social and Personal Relationships, 22,* 629–651.

Sprecher, S., & Felmlee, D. (1992). The influence of parents and friends on the quality and stability of romantic relationships: A three-wave longitudinal study. *Journal of Marriage and the Family, 54,* 888–900.

Sprecher, S., & Felmlee, D. (1997). The balance of power in romantic heterosexual couples over time from "his" and "her" perspectives. *Sex Roles, 37,* 361–378.

Sprecher, S., & McKinney, K. (1993). *Sexuality.* Newbury Park, CA: Sage.

Sprecher, S., McKinney, K., Walsh, R., & Anderson, C. (1988). A revision of the Reiss premarital sexual permissiveness scale. *Journal of Marriage and the Family, 50,* 821–828.

Sprecher, S., & Regan, P. C. (1996). College virgins: How men and women perceive their sexual status. *Journal of Sex Research, 33,* 3–15.

Sprecher, S., & Regan, P. C. (2000). Sexuality in a relational context. In C. Hendrick & S. S. Hendrick (Eds.), *Close relationships: A sourcebook* (pp. 217–227). Thousand Oaks, CA: Sage.

Sprecher, S., Schmeeckle, M., & Felmlee, D. (2006). The principal of least interest: Inequality in emotional involvement in romantic relationships. *Journal of Family Issues, 27,* 1255–1280.

Sprecher, S., & Toro-Morn, M. (2002). A study of men and women from different sides of earth to determine if men are from Mars and women are from Venus in their beliefs about love and romantic relationships. *Sex Roles, 46,* 131–147.

Stafford, L. (2003). Maintaining romantic relationships: Summary and analysis of one research program. In D. J. Canary & M. Dainton (Eds.), *Maintaining relationships through communication: Relational, contextual, and cultural variations* (pp. 51–77). Mahwah, NJ: Lawrence Erlbaum.

Stafford, L. (2008). Social exchange theories. In L. A. Baxter & D. O. Braithwaite (Eds.), *Engaging theories in interpersonal communication: Multiple perspectives* (pp. 377–390). Thousand Oaks, CA: Sage.

Stafford, L., & Canary, D. J. (1991). Maintenance strategies and romantic relationship type, gender and relational characteristics. *Journal of Social and Personal Relationships, 8,* 217–242.

Stafford, L., & Canary, D. J. (2006). Equity and interdependence as predictors of maintenance strategies. *Journal of Family Communication, 6,* 227–254.

Stafford, L., Kline, S. L., & Rankin, C. T. (2004). Married individuals, cohabiters, and cohabiters who marry: A longitudinal study of relational and individual well-being. *Journal of Social and Personal Relationships, 21,* 231–248.

Stafford, L., & Merolla, A. J. (2007). Idealization, reunions, and stability in long distance dating relationships. *Journal of Social and Personal Relationships, 24,* 37–54.

Stafford, L., & Reske, J. R. (1990). Idealization and communication in long-distance premarital relationships. *Family Relations, 39,* 274–279.

Staines, G., & Libby, P. (1986). Men and women in role relationships. In R. Ashmore & F. Del Bocca (Eds.), *The social psychology of female-male relationships: A critical analysis of central concepts* (pp. 211–257). New York: Academic Press.

Stanger, J. D. (1997). *Television in the home: The 1997 survey of parents and children.* Retrieved from http://www.annenbergpublicpolicycenter.org/Downloads/Media_and_Developing_Child/Media_and_TV_in_the_Home/19970609_Tv_and_home_report.pdf

Stangor, C., & Ruble, D. H. (1989). Strength of expectancies and memory for social information: What we remember depends on how much we know. *Journal of Experimental Social Psychology, 25,* 18–35.

Stark, P. B. (1994). *It's negotiable: The how-to handbook of win/win tactics.* San Diego, CA: Pfieffer.

Steil, J. M. (2000). Contemporary marriage: Still an unequal partnership. In C. Hendrick & S. S. Hendrick (Eds.), *Close relationships: A sourcebook* (pp. 125–136). Thousand Oaks, CA: Sage.

Steil, L. K., Barker, L. L., & Watson, K. W. (1983). *Effective listening: Keys to success.* Reading, MA: Addison-Wesley.

Steinberg, L. D. (1981). Transformations in family relations at puberty. *Developmental Psychology, 17,* 833–840.

Steinberg, L. D. (1987). Impact of puberty on family relations: Effects of pubertal status and pubertal timing. *Developmental Psychology, 23,* 451–460.

Steinberg, L. D., & Silverberg, S. B. (1986). The vicissitudes of autonomy in early adolescence. *Child Development, 57,* 841–851.

Steinbugler, A. C. (2005). Visibility as privilege and danger: Heterosexual and same-sex interracial intimacy in the 21st century. *Sexualities, 8,* 425–443.

Steinmetz, S. K. (1979). Disciplinary techniques and their relationship to aggressiveness, dependency, and conscience. In W. Burr, R. Hill, R. I. Nye, & I. L. Reiss (Eds.), *Contemporary theories about the family* (Vol. 1, pp. 405–438). New York: Free Press.

Stephan, C. W., & Bachman, G. F. (1999). What's sex got to do with it? Attachment, love schemas, and sexuality. *Personal Relationships, 6,* 111–123.

Sternberg, R. J. (1986). A triangular theory of love. *Psychological Review, 93,* 119–135.

Sternberg, R. J. (1987). *The triangle of love: Intimacy, passion, commitment.* New York: Basic Books.

Sternberg, R. J. (1988). Triangulating love. In R. J. Sternberg & M. L. Barnes (Eds.), *The psychology of love* (pp. 119–138). New Haven, CT: Yale University Press.

Steuber, K. R., & Solomon, D. H. (2008). Relational uncertainty, partner interference, and infertility: A qualitative study of discourse within online forums. *Journal of Social and Personal Relationships, 25,* 831–855.

Stier, D. S., & Hall, J. A. (1984). Gender differences in touch: An empirical and theoretical review. *Journal of Personality and Social Psychology, 47,* 440–459.

Stiff, J. B., Dillard, J. P., Somera, L., Kim, H., & Sleight, C. (1988). Empathy, communication, and prosocial behavior. *Communication Monographs, 55,* 198–213.

Stiff, J. B., Kim, H. J., & Ramesh, C. N. (1992). Truth biases and aroused suspicion in relational deception. *Communication Research, 19,* 326–345.

Stiles, W. B. (1987). "I have to talk to somebody": A fever model of disclosure. In V. J. Derlega & J. H. Berg (Eds.), *Self-disclosure: Theory, research, and therapy* (pp. 257–282). New York: Plenum Press.

Stiles, W. B., Shuster, P. L., & Harrigan, J. A. (1992). Disclosure and anxiety: A test of the fever model. *Journal of Personality and Social Psychology, 63,* 980–988.

Straus, M. A., & Gelles, R. J. (1990). How violent are American families? Estimates from the National Family Violence Resurvey and other studies. In M. A. Straus & R. J. Gelles (Eds.), *Physical violence in American families: Risk factors and adaptations to violence in 8,145 families* (pp. 95–112). New Brunswick, NJ: Transaction.

Strong, B., DeVault, C., & Sayad, B. W. (1999). *Human sexuality: Diversity in contemporary America.* Mountain View, CA: Mayfield.

Strong, S. R., Hills, H. J., Kilmartin, C. T., DeVries, H., Lanier, K., Nelson, B. N., et al. (1988). The dynamic relations among interpersonal behaviors: A test of complementarity and anti-complementarity. *Journal of Personality and Social Psychology, 54,* 798–810.

Struckman-Johnson, C. (1988). Forced sex on dates: It happens to men too. *Journal of Sex Research, 24,* 234–241.

Struckman-Johnson, C., & Struckman-Johnson, D. (1991). Men's and women's acceptance of sexually coercive strategies varied by initiator gender and couple intimacy. *Sex Roles, 25,* 661–676.

Struckman-Johnson, C., & Struckman-Johnson, D. (1994). Men pressured and forced into sexual experience. *Archives of Sexual Behavior, 23,* 93–114.

Student Health Services. (1998). *HIV/AIDS facts.* San Diego, CA: San Diego State University.

Sue, S., & Zane, N. (1987). The role of culture and cultural techniques in psychotherapy: A critique and reformulation. *American Psychologist, 42,* 37–45.

Sunnafrank, M. (1986). Predicted outcome value during initial interactions: A reformulation of uncertainty reduction theory. *Human Communication Research, 13,* 3–33.

Sunnafrank, M. (1990). Predicted outcome value and uncertainty reduction theories: A test of competing perspectives. *Human Communication Research, 17,* 76–103.

Sunnafrank, M. (1991). Interpersonal attraction and attitude similarity: A communication-based assessment. In J. A. Anderson (Ed.), *Communication yearbook 14* (pp. 451–483). Newbury Park, CA: Sage.

Sunnafrank, M. (1992). On debunking the attitude similarity myth. *Communication Monographs, 59,* 164–179.

Sunnafrank, M., & Ramirez, A., Jr. (2004). At first sight: Persistent relational effects of get-acquainted conversations. *Journal of Social and Personal Relationships, 21,* 361–379.

Suter, E. A., Bergen, K. M., Daas, K. L., & Durham, W. T. (2006). Lesbian couples' management of public-private dialectical contradictions. *Journal of Social and Personal Relationships, 23,* 349–365.

Swan, S. C. (1997). Explaining the job-related and psychological consequences of sexual harassment in the workplace: A contextual model. *Dissertation Abstractions International, 58*(6-B), 3371.

Swann, W. B. (1983). Self-verification: Bringing social reality into harmony with the self. In J. Suls & G. Greenwald (Eds.), *Psychology perspectives on the self* (Vol. 2, pp. 33–66). Hillsdale, NJ: Lawrence Erlbaum.

Swann, W. B., De LaRonde, C., & Hixon, G. (1994). Authenticity and positive strivings in marriage and courtship. *Journal of Personality and Social Psychology, 6,* 857–869.

Swann, W. B., Griffin, J. J., Predmore, S., & Gaines, B. (1987). The cognitive-affective crossfire: When self-consistency confronts self-enhancement. *Journal of Personality and Social Psychology, 52,* 881–889.

Swann, W. B., & Read, S. J. (1981). Self-verification processes. How we sustain our self-conceptions. *Journal of Experimental Social Psychology, 54,* 268–273.

Swann, W. B., Silvera, D. H., & Proske, C. U. (1995). On "knowing your partner": Dangerous illusions in the age of AIDS? *Personal Relationships, 2,* 173–186.

Tafoya, M. A., & Spitzberg, B. H. (2007). The dark side of infidelity: Its nature, prevalence, and communicative functions. In B. H. Spitzberg & W. R. Cupach (Eds.), *The dark side of interpersonal communication* (pp. 201–242). Mahwah, NJ: Lawrence Erlbaum.

Tagawa, N., & Yashida, T. (2006). The effects of daily communication on romantic relationships. *The Japanese Journal of Social Psychology, 22,* 126–138.

Tannen, D. (1990). *You just don't understand: Women and men in conversation.* New York: Morrow.

Taraban, C. B., Hendrick, S. S., & Hendrick, C. (1998). Loving and liking. In P. A. Andersen & L. K. Guerrero (Eds.), *Handbook of communication and emotion: Research, theory, applications, and contexts* (pp. 331–351). San Diego, CA: Academic Press.

Tardy, C. H. (Ed.). (1988). *A handbook for the study of human communication: Methods for observing, measuring, and assessing communication processes.* Norwood, NJ: Ablex.

Tashiro, T., & Frazier, P. (2003). I'll never be in a relationship like that again: Personal growth following romantic relationship breakups. *Personal Relationships, 10,* 113–138.

Taylor, S. E., Gonzaga, G. C., Klein, L. C., Hu, P., Greendale, G. A., Seeman, T. E., et al. (2006). Relation of oxytocin to psychological stress responses and hypothalamic-pituitary-andrenocortical axis activity in older women. *Psychosomantic Medicine, 68,* 238–245.

Tedeschi, J. T. (1986). Private and public experiences of the self. In R. Baumeister (Ed.), *Public self and private self* (pp. 1–20). New York: Springer-Verlag.

Teitelman, A. M., & Radcliffe, S. J. (2008). Sexual relationship power, intimate partner violence, and condom use among minority urban girls. *Journal of Interpersonal Violence, 23,* 1694–1712.

Tejada-Vera, B., Sutton, P. D. (2009). *Births, marriages, divorces, and deaths: Provisional data for 2008. National vital statistics reports, Vol. 57, No. 19.* Hyattsville, MD: National Center for Health Statistics.

Tesser, A., & Achee, J. (1994). Aggression, love, conformity and other social psychological catastrophes. In R. R. Vallacher & A. Nowak (Eds.), *Dynamical systems in social psychology* (pp. 95–109). San Diego, CA: Academic Press.

Thagaard, T. (1997). Gender, power, and love. *Acta Sociologica, 38,* 357–376.

Theiss, J. A., Knobloch, L. K., Checton, M. G., & Magsamen-Conrad, K. (2009). Relationship characteristics associated with the experience of hurt in romantic relationships: A test of the relational turbulence model. *Human Communication Research, 35,* 588–615.

Theiss, J. A., & Solomon, D. H. (2006). A relational turbulence model of communication about irritations in romantic relationships. *Communication Research, 33,* 391–418.

Thibaut, J. W., & Kelley, J. J. (1959). *The psychology of groups.* New York: Wiley.

Thieme, A., & Rouse, C. (1991, November). *Terminating intimate relationships: An examination of the interactions among disengagement strategies, acceptance, and causal attributions.* Paper presented at the annual meeting of the Speech Communication Association, Atlanta, GA.

Thompson, L., & Walker, A. J. (1989). Gender in families: Women and men in marriage, work, and parenthood. *Journal of Marriage and the Family, 51,* 845–871.

Thorne, B., & Luria, Z. (1986). Sexuality and gender in children's daily worlds. *Social Problems, 33,* 176–190.

Thorton, A., Axinn, W. G., & Teachman, J. D. (1995). The influence of school enrollment and accumulation of cohabitation and marriage in early adulthood. *American Sociological Review, 60,* 207–220.

Tice, D. M., Butler, J. L., Muraven, M. B., & Stillwell, A. M. (1995). When modesty prevails: Differential favorability of self-presentation to friends and strangers. *Journal of Personality and Social Psychology, 69,* 1120–1138.

Timmerman, L. M. (2002). Comparing the production of power in language on the basis of sex. In M. Allen, R. W. Preiss, B. M. Gayke, & N. Burell (Eds.), *Interpersonal communication research: Advances through meta-analysis* (pp. 73–88). Mahwah, NJ: Lawrence Erlbaum.

Tolhuizen, J. H. (1989). Communication strategies for intensifying dating relationships: Identification, use, and structure. *Journal of Social and Personal Relationships, 6,* 413–434.

Tolstedt, B. E., & Stokes, J. P. (1984). Self-disclosure, intimacy and the depenetration process. *Journal of Personality and Social Psychology, 46,* 84–90.

Toma, C. L., Hancock, J. T., & Ellison, N. B. (2008). Separating fact from fiction: An examination of deceptive self-presentation in online dating profiles, *Personality and Social Psychology Bulletin, 34,* 1023–1036.

Tooke, W., & Camire, L. (1991). Patterns of deception in intersexual and intrasexual mating strategies. *Ethology and Sociobiology, 12,* 345–364.

Tornblom, K. Y., & Fredholm, E. M. (1984). Attribution of friendship: The influence of the nature and comparability of resources given and received. *Social Psychology Quarterly, 47,* 50–61.

Tracy, K. (1990). The many faces of facework. In H. Giles & W. P. Robinson (Eds.), *Handbook of language and social psychology* (pp. 209–226). Chichester, UK: Wiley.

Tracy, S. J. (2005a). Fracturing the real-self fake-self dichotomy: Moving toward crystallized organizational identities. *Communication Theory, 15,* 168–195.

Tracy, S. J. (2005b). Locking up emotion: Moving beyond dissonance for understanding emotional labor discomfort. *Communication Monographs, 72,* 261–283.

Tracy, S. J., & Trethewey, A. (2005). Fracturing the real-self fake self dichotomy. Moving toward crystallized organizational identities. *Communication Theory, 15,* 168–195.

Traupmann, J., Hatfield, E., & Wexler, P. (1983). Equity and sexual satisfaction in dating couples. *British Journal of Social Psychology, 22,* 33–40.

Tregenza, T., & Wedell, N. (2002). Polyandrous females avoid the cost of inbreeding. *Nature, 415,* 71–73.

Trost, M. R., & Alberts, J. K. (2006). How men and women communicate attraction: An evolutionary view. In D. J. Canary & K. Dindia (Eds.), *Sex differences and similarities in communication* (2nd ed., pp. 317–336). Mahwah, NJ: Lawrence Erlbaum.

Troy, B. A., Lewis-Smith, J., & Laurenceau, J. (2006). Interracial and intraracial romantic relationships: The search for differences in satisfaction, conflict, and attachment style. *Journal of Social and Personal Relationships, 23,* 65–80.

Tucker, J. S., & Anders, S. L. (1998). Adult attachment style and nonverbal closeness in dating couples. *Journal of Nonverbal Behavior, 22,* 109–124.

Turner, L. H. (1990). The relationship between communication and marital uncertainty: Is "her" marriage different from "his" marriage? *Women's Studies in Communication, 13,* 57–83.

Turner, R. E., Edgley, C., & Olmstead, G. (1975). Information control in conversations: Honesty is not always the best policy. *Kansas Journal of Speech, 11,* 69–89.

Tusing, K. J., & Dillard, J. P. (2000). The sounds of dominance: Vocal precursors of perceived dominance during interpersonal influence. *Human Communication Research, 16,* 148–171.

Tutzauer, F., & Roloff, M. E. (1988). Communication processes leading to integrative agreements: Three paths to joint benefits. *Communication Research, 15,* 360–380.

Twenge, J. M. (2006). *Generation me.* New York: Free Press.

Twenge, J. M., & Campbell, W. K. (2009). The narcissism epidemic: Living in the age of entitlement. New York: Free Press.

Twenge, J. M., Campbell, W. K., & Foster, C. A. (2003). Parenthood and marital satisfaction: A meta-analytic review. *Journal of Marriage and Family, 65,* 574–583.

Ugbah, S., & DeWine, S. (1986, November). *Conflict and relational development: Are the communication strategies the same?* Paper presented at the annual meeting of the Speech Communication Association, Chicago.

Utz, S. (2005). Types of deception and underlying motivation: What people think. *Social Science Computer Review, 23,* 49–56.

Van Horn, K. R., Arnone, A., Nesbitt, K., Desilets, L., Sears, T., Giffin, M., et al. (1997). Physical distance and interpersonal characteristics in college students' romantic relationships. *Personal Relationships, 4,* 15–24.

Van Lange, P. A. M., Rusbult, C. E., Drigotas, S. M., Arriaga, X. B., Witcher, B. S., & Cox, C. L. (1997). Willingness to sacrifice in close relationships. *Journal of Personality and Social Psychology, 72,* 1373–1395.

Van Rosmalen-Noojens, K. A. W. L., Vergeer, C. M., & Lagro-Janssen, A. L. M. (2008). Bed death and other lesbian sexual problems unraveled: A qualitative study of the sexual health of lesbian women involved in a relationship. *Women and Health, 48,* 339–362.

Van Straaten, I., Engles, C. M. E., Finkenauer, C., & Holland, R. W. (2008). Sex differences in short-term mate preferences and behavioral mimicry: A semi-naturalistic experiment. *Archives of Sexual Behavior, 37,* 902–911.

Van Willigen, M., & Drentea, P. (2001). Benefits of equitable relationships: The impact of sense of fairness, household division of labor, and decision making power on perceived social support. *Sex Roles, 44,* 571–597.

Vangelisti, A. L. (1994a). Family secrets: Forms, functions, and correlates. *Journal of Social and Personal Relationships, 11,* 113–135.

Vangelisti, A. L. (1994b). Messages that hurt. In W. R. Cupach & B. H. Spitzberg (Eds.), *The dark side of interpersonal communication* (pp. 53–82). Hillsdale, NJ: Lawrence Erlbaum.

Vangelisti, A. L. (2001). Making sense of hurtful interactions in close relationships: When hurt feelings create distance. In V. Manusov & J. H. Harvey (Eds.), *Attribution, communication behavior, and close relationships: Advances in personal relations* (pp. 38–58). New York: Cambridge University Press.

Vangelisti, A. L. (2002). Interpersonal processes in romantic relationships. In M. L. Knapp & J. A. Daly (Eds.), *Handbook of interpersonal communication* (3rd ed., pp. 643–679). Thousand Oaks, CA: Sage.

Vangelisti, A. L., & Caughlin, J. P. (1997). Revealing family secrets: The influence of topic, function, and relationships. *Journal of Social and Personal Relationships, 14,* 679–706.

Vangelisti, A. L., & Crumley, L. P. (1998). Reactions to messages that hurt: The influence of relational contexts. *Communication Monographs, 65,* 173–196.

Vangelisti, A. L., & Huston, T. L. (1994). Maintaining marital satisfaction and love. In D. J. Canary & L. Stafford (Eds.), *Communication and relational maintenance* (pp. 165–186). San Diego, CA: Academic Press.

Vangelisti, A. L., Knapp, M. L., & Daly, J. A. (1990). Conversational narcissism. *Communication Monographs, 57,* 251–274.

Vangelisti, A. L., & Young, S. L. (2000). When words hurt: The effects of perceived intentionality on interpersonal relationships. *Journal of Social and Personal Relationships, 17,* 393–424.

Vaughn, D. (1986). *Uncoupling: Turning points in intimate relationships.* New York: Oxford University Press.

Vignoles, L., Regalia, C., Manzi, C., Golledge, J., & Scabini, E. (2006). Beyond self-esteem: Influence of multiple motives on identity construction. *Journal of Personality and Social Psychology, 90,* 308–333.

Vohs, K. D., Catanese, K. R., & Baumeister, R. E. (2004). Sex in "his" versus "her" relationship. In J. H. Harvey, A. Wenzel, & S. Sprecher (Eds.), *The handbook of sexuality in close relationships* (pp. 455–474). Mahwah, NJ: Lawrence Erlbaum.

Waldron, V. R., & Kelley, D. L. (2005). Forgiving communication as a response to relational transgressions. *Journal of Social and Personal Relationships, 22,* 723–742.

Waldron, V. R., & Kelley, D. L. (2008). *Communicating forgiveness.* Thousand Oaks, CA: Sage.

Wallace, H., & Silverman, J. (1996). Stalking and post-traumatic stress syndrome. *Police Journal, 69,* 203–206.

Waller, W. W., & Hill, R. (1951). *The family: A dynamic interpretation.* New York: Dryden Press.

Walster, E., Berscheid, E., & Walster, G. W. (1973). Equity and extramarital sexuality. *Archives of Sexual Behavior, 7,* 127–141.

Walster, E., Walster, G. W., & Berscheid, E. (1978). *Equity: Theory and research.* Boston: Allyn & Bacon.

Walster, E., Walster, G. W., Piliavin, J., & Schmidt, L. (1973). "Playing hard-to-get": Understanding an elusive phenomenon. *Journal of Personality and Social Psychology, 26,* 113–121.

Walster, E., Walster, G. W., & Traupmann, J. (1978). Equity and premarital sex. *Journal of Personality, 36,* 82–92.

Ward, L. M. (1995). Talking about sex: Common themes about sexuality in prime-time television programs children and adolescents view most. *Journal of Youth and Adolescence, 5,* 595–615.

Warren, C. (1995). Parent-child communication about sex. In T. Socha & G. H. Stamp (Eds.), *Parents, children, and communication: Frontiers of theory and research* (pp. 173–201). Mahwah, NJ: Lawrence Erlbaum.

Watzlawick, P., Beavin, J. H., & Jackson, D. D. (1967). *Pragmatics of human communication.* New York: Norton.

Webb, L., Delaney, J. J., & Young, L. R. (1989). Age, interpersonal attraction, and social interaction: A review and assessment. *Research on Aging, 11,* 107–123.

Weger, H., Jr., & Emmett, M. C. (2009). Romantic intent, relationship uncertainty, and relationship maintenance in young adults' cross-sex friendships. *Journal of Social and Personal Relationships, 26,* 964–988.

Weger, H., Jr., & Polcar, L. E. (2002). Attachment style and person-centered comforting. *Western Journal of Communication, 66,* 64–103.

Wegner, D. M. (1989). *White bears and other unwanted thoughts.* New York: Viking Press.

Wegner, D. M. (1992). You can't always think what you want: Problems in the suppression of unwanted thoughts. In M. Zanna (Ed.), *Advances in experimental social psychology* (Vol. 25, pp. 193–225). San Diego, CA: Academic Press.

Wegner, D. M., & Erber, R. (1992). The hyperaccessibility of suppressed thoughts. *Journal of Personality and Social Psychology, 63,* 903–912.

Wegner, D. M., Lane, J. D., & Dimitri, S. (1994). The allure of secret relationships. *Journal of Personality and Social Psychology, 66,* 287–300.

Wegner, D. M., Schneider, D. J., Carter, S. R., III, & White, T. L. (1987). Paradoxical effects of thought suppression. *Journal of Personality and Social Psychology, 53,* 5–13.

Weigel, D. J., & Ballard-Reisch, D. S. (1999). The influence of marital duration on the use of relationship maintenance behaviors. *Communication Reports, 12,* 59–70.

Weigel, D. J., & Ballard-Reisch, D. S. (2001). The impact of relational maintenance behaviors on marital satisfaction: A longitudinal analysis. *Journal of Family Communication, 1,* 265–279.

Weigel, D. J., & Ballard-Reisch, D. S. (2002). Investigating the behavioral indicators of relational commitment. *Journal of Social and Personal Relationships, 19,* 403–423.

Weigel, D. J., & Ballard-Reisch, D. S. (2008). Relational maintenance, satisfaction, and commitment in marriages: An actor-partner analysis. *Journal of Family Communication, 8,* 212–229.

Weigel, D. J., Bennett, K. K., & Ballard-Reisch, D. S. (2006). Influence strategies in marriage: Self and partner links between equity, strategy use, and marital satisfaction and commitment. *The Journal of Family Communication, 6,* 77–95.

Weinbach, R. (1989). Sudden death and the secret survivors: Helping those who grieve alone. *Social Work, 34,* 57–60.

Weiner, M., & Mehrabian, A. (1968). *Language within language: Immediacy, a channel in verbal communication.* New York: Appleton-Century-Crofts.

Weis, D. L., & Slosnerick, M. (1981). Attitudes toward sexual and nonsexual extramarital involvement among a sample of college students. *Journal of Marriage and the Family, 43,* 349–358.

Wells, B. E., & Twenge, J. M. (2005). Changes in young people's sexual behavior and attitudes, 1943–1999: A cross-temporal analysis. *Review of General Psychology, 9,* 249–261.

Wellens, A. R. (1987). Heart-rate changes in response to shifts in interpersonal gaze from liked and disliked others. *Perceptual and Motor Skills, 64,* 595–598.

Werking, K. (1997). *We're just good friends: Women and men in nonromantic relationships.* New York: Guilford Press.

Westenhoefer, S., & Mapa, A. (2006, August 15). Five sex tips . . . What can lesbians and gay men teach each other about great sex? *Advocate,* p. 41.

Westerman, C. Y. K., Park, H. W., & Lee, H. E. (2007). A test of equity theory in multidimensional friendships: A comparison of the United States and Korea. *Journal of Communication, 57,* 576–598.

Westhoff, L. A. (1985). *Corporate romance.* New York: Times Books.

Wheeless, L. R., & Grotz, J. (1976). Conceptualization and measurement of reported self-disclosure. *Human Communication Research, 2,* 338–346.

Wheeless, L. R., & Grotz, J. (1977). The measurement of trust and its relationship to self-disclosure. *Human Communication Research, 3,* 250–257.

Wheeless, L. R., Wheeless, V. E., & Baus, R. (1984). Sexual communication, communication satisfaction, and solidarity in the development stages of intimate relationships. *Western Journal of Speech Communication, 48,* 217–230.

White, G. L. (1981). Jealousy and partner's perceived motives for attraction to a rival. *Social Psychology Quarterly, 44,* 24–30.

White, G. L., Fishbein, S., & Rutstein, J. (1981). Passionate love: The misattribution of arousal. *Journal of Personality and Social Psychology, 41,* 56–62.

White, G. L., & Mullen, P. E. (1989). *Jealousy: Theory, research, and clinical strategies.* New York: Guilford Press.

Wiederman, M. W., & Allgeier, E. R. (1993). Gender differences in sexual jealousy: Adaptationist or social learning explanation? *Ethology and Sociobiology, 14,* 115–140.

Wiederman, M. W., & Hurd, C. (1999). Extradyadic involvement during dating. *Journal of Social and Personal Relationships, 16,* 265–274.

Wieselquist, J., Rusbult, C. E., Foster, C. A., & Agnew, C. R. (1999). Commitment, pro-relationship behavior, and trust in close relationships. *Journal of Personality and Social Psychology, 77,* 942–966.

Wiggins, J. D., & Lederer, D. A. (1984). Differential antecedents of infidelity in marriage. *American Mental Health Counseling Association Journal, 6,* 152–161.

Wilkins, R., & Gareis, E. (2006). Emotion expression and the locution "I love you": A cross-cultural study. *International Journal of Intercultural Relations, 30,* 51–75.

Willetts, M. C., Sprecher, S., & Beck, F. D. (2004). Overview of sexual practices and attitudes within relational contexts. In J. H. Harvey, A. Wenzel, & S. Sprecher (Eds.), *The handbook of sexuality in close relationships* (pp. 57–85). Mahwah, NJ: Lawrence Erlbaum.

Williams, A., & Nussbaum, J. F. (2001). *Intergeneration communication across the lifespan.* Mahwah, NJ: Lawrence Erlbaum.

Williams, S., & Andersen, P. A. (1998). Toward an expanded view of interracial romantic relationships. In V. Duncan (Ed.), *Toward achieving malt.* Dubuque, IA: Kendall-Hunt.

Willittis, M., Benzeval, M., & Stansfeld, S. (2004). Partnership history and mental health over time. *Journal of Epidemiology and Community Health, 58,* 53–58.

Wilmot, W. W. (1994). Relationship rejuvenation. In D. J. Canary & L. Stafford (Eds.), *Communication and relational maintenance* (pp. 255–273). San Diego, CA: Academic Press.

Wilmot, W. W. (1995). *Relational communication.* New York: McGraw-Hill.

Wilmot, W. W., Carbaugh, D. A., & Baxter, L. A. (1985). Communicative strategies used to terminate romantic relationships. *Western Journal of Speech Communication, 49,* 204–216.

Wilson, S. E., & Waddoups, S. L. (2002). Good marriages gone bad: Health mismatches as a cause of later life marital dissolution. *Population Research and Policy Review, 21,* 505–523.

Wiseman, J. P. (1986). Friendship: Bonds and binds in a voluntary relationship. *Journal of Social and Personal Relationships, 3,* 191–211.

Wiseman, R. L., & Schenck-Hamlin, W. (1981). A multidimensional scaling validation of an inductively-derived set of compliance gaining strategies. *Communication Monographs, 48,* 251–270.

Witteman, H., & Fitzpatrick, M. A. (1986). Compliance-gaining in marital interaction: Power bases, processes and outcomes. *Communication Monographs, 53,* 130–143.

Wolfinger, N. H. (1999). Trends in the intergenerational transmission of divorce. *Demography, 36,* 415–420.

Wood, J. T. (1994). *Gendered lives: Communications, gender, and culture.* Belmont, CA: Wadsworth.

Wood, J. T. (Ed.). (1996). *Gendered relationships.* Mountain View, CA: Mayfield.

Wood, J. T., & Dindia, K. (1998). What's the difference? A dialogue about the differences and similarities between women and men. In D. J. Canary & K. Dindia (Eds.), *Sex differences and similarities in communication* (pp. 19–39). Mahwah, NJ: Lawrence Erlbaum.

Wood, J. T., & Duck, S. (1995). Off the beaten track: New shores for relationships research. In J. T. Wood & S. Duck (Eds.), *Understudied relationships: Off the beaten track* (pp. 1–21). Thousand Oaks, CA: Sage.

Wood, J., & Inman, C. (1993). In a different mode: Masculine styles of communicating closeness. *Journal of Applied Communication Research, 21,* 279–295.

Wright, D., Parkes, A., Strange, V., Allen, E., & Bonell, C. (2008). The quality of young people's heterosexual relationships: A longitudinal analysis of characteristics shaping the subjective experience. *Perspectives on Sexual and Reproductive Health, 40,* 226–237.

Wright, K. B. (2004). On-line relational maintenance strategies and perceptions of partners within exclusively Internet-based and primarily Internet-based relationships. *Communication Studies, 55,* 239–253.

Wright, P. H. (1982). Men's friendship, women's friendships, and the alleged inferiority of the latter. *Sex Roles, 8,* 1–20.

Wright, R. A., & Contrada, R. J. (1986). Dating selectivity and interpersonal attractiveness: Toward a better understanding of the "elusive phenomenon." *Journal of Social and Personal Relationships, 3,* 131–148.

Wright, R. A., Toi, M., & Brehm, J. W. (1984). Difficulty and interpersonal attraction. *Motivation and Emotion, 8,* 327–341.

Yelsma, P. (1986). Marriage vs. cohabitation: Couples' communication practices and satisfaction. *Journal of Communication, 36,* 94–107.

Yingling, J. (1995). The first relationship: Infant-parent communication. In T. J. Socha & G. H. Stamp (Eds.), *Parents, children, and communication: Frontiers of theory and research* (pp. 23–41). Hillsdale, NJ: Lawrence Erlbaum.

Vogler, C., Lyonette, C., & Wiggins, R. D. (2008). Money, power, and decisions in intimate relationships. *Sociological Review, 56,* 117–143.

Yodanis, C., & Lauer, S. (2007). Money management in marriage: Multilevel and cross-national effects of the breadwinners role. *Journal of Marriage and the Family, 69,* 1307–1325.

Young, S. L. (2004). Factors that influence recipients' appraisals of hurtful communication. *Journal of Social and Personal Relationships, 21,* 291–303.

Young, S. L., & Bippus, A. M. (2001). Does it make a difference if they hurt you in a funny way? *Communication Quarterly, 49,* 35–52.

Young, S. L., Paxman, C. G., Koehring, C. L. E., & Anderson, C. A. (2008). The application of a face work model of disengagement to unrequited love. *Communication Research Reports, 25,* 56–66.

Young, S. M., & Pinsky, D. (2006). Narcissism and celebrity. *Journal of Research in Personality, 40,* 463–471.

Yum, Y., & Canary, D. J. (2009). Cultural differences in equity theory predictions of relational maintenance strategies. *Human Communication Research, 35,* 384–406.

Zeeman, E. C. (1977). Catastrophe theory. *Scientific American, 234,* 65–83.

Zillman, D. (1978). Attribution and misattribution of excitatory reactions. In J. H. Harvey, W. Ickes, & R. F. Kidd (Eds.), *New directions in attribution research* (Vol. 2, pp. 335–368). Hillsdale, NJ: Lawrence Erlbaum.

Zillman, D. (1990). The interplay of cognition and excitation in aggravated conflict. In D. D. Cahn (Ed.), *Intimates in conflict: A communication perspective* (pp. 187–208). Hillsdale, NJ: Lawrence Erlbaum.

Zuckerman, M., DePaulo, B. M., & Rosenthal, R. (1981). Verbal and nonverbal communication of deception. In L. Berkowitz (Ed.), *Advances in experimental social psychology* (Vol. 14, pp. 1–59). New York: Academic Press.

Author Index

Subject Index

ABOUT THE AUTHORS

Laura K. Guerrero (PhD, University of Arizona, 1994) is a professor in the Hugh Downs School of Human Communication at Arizona State University, where she teaches courses in relational communication, nonverbal communication, emotional communication, research methods, and data analysis. Previously, she taught at the Pennsylvania State University and San Diego State University. Her research has examined both the "bright side" of personal relationships, including nonverbal intimacy, forgiveness, relational maintenance, and communication skill; and the "dark side" of personal relationships, including jealousy, hurtful events, conflict, and anger. She has published more than 80 journal articles and chapters related to these topics. Her most recent work focuses on developing and testing a theoretical framework—hurtful events response theory—that explains patterns of communication following hurtful events in close relationships. In addition to *Close Encounters,* her book credits include *Nonverbal Communication in Close Relationships* (coauthored with Kory Floyd), *Nonverbal Communication* (coauthored with Judee Burgoon and Kory Floyd), *The Handbook of Communication and Emotion* (coedited with P. Andersen), and *The Nonverbal Communication Reader* (coedited with Michael Hecht). Her research awards include the Early Career Achievement Award from the International Association for Relationship Research in 2001, the Dickens Research Award from the Western States Communication Association in 1995 and 2001, and the Outstanding Doctoral Dissertation Award from the Interpersonal Communication Division of the International Communication Association in 1995. She serves on editorial boards for several top journals in communication and relationships. During the school year she lives in Phoenix with her husband, Vico, and their daughters, Gabrielle and Kristiana. They live in San Diego during the summer. She enjoys reading, writing fiction (when not writing nonfiction), dancing, and taking long walks in the mountains or on the beach.

Peter A. Andersen (PhD, Florida State University, 1975) is a professor in the School of Communication at San Diego State University, where he teaches courses on topics such as relational communication, nonverbal communication, persuasion, health communication, political communication, quantitative methods, and communication and emotion. He has also taught at the University of Washington; Ohio University; University of Montana; California State University, Fullerton; and California State University, Long Beach. His most recent research focuses on cultural differences in nonverbal communication, risk and crisis communication, skin cancer prevention, tobacco control, social influence, nonverbal intimacy and immediacy, and interpersonal touch. He also developed cognitive valence theory to explain how people react to increases in nonverbal immediacy. He has authored 150 book chapters and journal articles, and has received recognition as one of the 100 most published scholars in the history of the field of communication.

In addition to *Close Encounters,* he is the author of *The Handbook of Communication and Emotion* (1998, edited with Laura Guerrero), *Nonverbal Communication: Forms and Functions* (2008), and *The Complete Idiot's Guide to Understanding Body Language* (2004). He has served as the president of the Western Communication Association, director of research for the Japan-U.S. Telecommunications Research Institute, and editor of the *Western Journal of Communication.* He has also served as a coinvestigator on sun safety, tobacco control, and cancer prevention grants from the National Cancer Institute, and risk communication grants from the U.S. Department of Homeland Security and the county of San Diego. He cherishes the relationships he has with Janis, his wife of 37 years; his daughter Kirsten, who lives with her husband in Long Beach, California; and his mother, Mildred, who lives in Chicago. He is a fast skier, strong swimmer, and a truly slow half-marathon runner.

Walid A. Afifi (PhD, University of Arizona, 1996) is a professor in the Department of Communication at the University of California, Santa Barbara, where he teaches several courses, including interpersonal communication, relational communication, nonverbal communication, and social marketing. He previously held faculty positions at Pennsylvania State University and the University of Delaware. His primary research program revolves around people's experience of uncertainty and their decisions to seek or avoid information in relational contexts. He has applied these interests across several domains, including family discussions about organ donation, college students' search information about their partners' sexual health, people's negotiation of cross-sex friendships, and family members' management of privacy boundaries around sensitive topics. He has also examined people's decisions to avoid disclosure or keep secrets. His most recent research projects approach uncertainty from a more sociological lens, examining uncertainty during or after traumatic community events (e.g., fires, war) and assessing their impact on well-being. He has published more than 50 articles and chapters and coedited the book, *Uncertainty, Information Management, and Disclosure Decisions* with Tammy Afifi. He serves as a member of several editorial boards, has occupied the role of associate editor for both *Personal Relationships* and the *Journal of Social and Personal Relationships,* and has chaired the Interpersonal Communication division of both the International Communication Association and the National Communication Association. He grew up in Beirut, Lebanon, where his sister and her family still reside, and where he recently spent some time as a visiting professor in the Department of Health Behavior and Education at the American University of Beirut. He lives in Goleta (right outside Santa Barbara), California, with his wife Tammy (who studies family communication and is a faculty member in the same department), two daughters (Leila and Rania), and two dogs (Meshi and Maddie). He is an avid sports fan and loves outdoor activities of all kinds.